Cost Accounting

PRINCIPLES AND APPLICATIONS

Fifth Edition

Horace R. Brock, Ph.D., C.P.A.

Distinguished Professor of Accounting
College of Business Administration
University of North Texas
Denton, Texas

Charles E. Palmer, D.C.S., C.P.A.

Chairman of the Board
Strayer College
Washington, D.C.

Linda A. Herrington, M.B.A., C.P.A.

Professor of Accounting
Community College of Allegheny County
Pittsburgh, Pennsylvania

Gregg Division
McGraw-Hill Book Company

New York   Atlanta   Dallas   St. Louis   San Francisco
Auckland   Bogotá   Guatemala   Hamburg   Lisbon   London
Madrid   Mexico   Milan   Montreal   New Delhi   Panama
Paris   San Juan   São Paulo   Singapore   Sydney   Tokyo   Toronto

Sponsoring Editor/*Sharon E. Kaufman*
Editing Supervisor/*Paul Farrell*
Design and Art Supervisor/*Caryl Valerie Spinka*
Production Supervisor/*Al Rihner*

Cover and Text Designer/*Delgado Design, Inc.*
Cover Art/*Marjory Dressler; Burmar Technical Corporation*

Library of Congress Cataloging-in-Publication Data

Brock, Horace R.
    Cost accounting.

    Includes index.
    1. Cost accounting.   I. Palmer, Charles Earl,
date.   II. Herrington, Linda A.   III. Title.
HF5686.C8B679   1989   657'.42   88–8552
ISBN 0–07–008152–2

Cost Accounting: Principles and Applications, Fifth Edition

1 2 3 4 5 6 7 8 9 0 DOCDOC 8 9 5 4 3 2 1 0 9 8

ISBN 0-07-008152-2

The Authors
Dedicate This Book
to the Memory of
BONNIE LIEBERMAN
Editor and Friend

Contents

. . . .

Part 3   *Cost Accounting as a Management Tool*   *395*

Preface

A Total Instructional System

A college accounting instructional system should serve the career objectives of all students who require an understanding of accounting. Its components should satisfy the learning needs of students who are preparing for a wide range of business and professional pursuits. Moreover, instructors should be able to customize their accounting courses by matching instructional components with the abilities of individual students and with the levels of accomplishment that are required for different career objectives. A college accounting instructional system should, therefore, contain performance objectives, reading resources, student application materials, comprehensive projects, student self-checks, and instructor's materials.

In preparing the fifth edition of *Cost Accounting: Principles and Applications,* the authors have created an instructional system that meets all of these criteria.

Textbook

This student resource text is designed for use in postsecondary cost accounting courses. The fifth edition, intended to provide a practical knowledge of cost accounting systems and procedures, will prepare students for many of the career opportunities available in cost accounting. It will also enable them to understand and use cost accounting data in other types of business careers.

The book begins by giving students an overview of the nature and purpose of cost accounting. Then students learn the basic concept that cost flow matches work flow. After that, they are led through the major areas of cost accounting: job order cost accounting, process cost accounting, budgeting, standard costs, direct costing, and nonmanufacturing costs.

Special attention is paid to giving students a grasp of the relationship of one procedure to another and an understanding of the reasons for the procedures. Students quickly learn that a cost accounting system must be adapted to the needs of each business. Then they learn how the system is devised, how the routines work, and what is done with the data that is obtained. Managerial considerations, especially as related to cost control, are indicated at every opportunity in Parts 1 and 2. Part 3 is devoted exclusively to cost accounting as a management tool. Also, the uses of computers in cost accounting are discussed throughout the text.

The comprehensive coverage is organized with special attention to "first things first." Each new segment of instruction is carefully explained and illustrated. Review questions and managerial discussion questions, along with application activities in the form of exercises, problems, and alternate problems, help students to integrate their learning while everything is fresh in their minds. In addition, managerial decision cases require students to synthesize the cost accounting concepts they have learned and to make decisions using cost data and these concepts. The more able students can proceed at their own pace because the text and the accompanying *Study Guide and Working Papers* facilitate self-study. Slower students or those who have been absent will find it easy to review or catch up on their work.

The program is flexible, and the instructor can adjust the course to meet student needs. A very short course in job order cost accounting can be completed by the end of Part 1. Students with more time may cover process cost accounting and terminate their work with Part 2. If time is available for work beyond process costing, instructors may choose from a wide selection of additional topics in Part 3, including Business Project 3, which deals with budgets and standard costs.

Learning Aids

A number of learning aids are available for use with the fifth edition of *Cost Accounting: Principles and Applications*. These materials are designed to enhance the effectiveness of the course for the student.

Study Guide and Working Papers

The traditional workbook has been replaced by the *Study Guide and Working Papers*, which permits each student to study at his or her own pace. Performance objectives tell students what they should know and be able to do after completing each chapter. Reading assignments direct students to the appropriate section in the textbook. Self-checks of reading comprehension help students measure their mastery of each reading assignment. (A self-check key is provided at the end of the *Study Guide and Working Papers*.) All the working papers needed to solve the problems or the alternate problems and the three business projects in the textbook are provided in the *Study Guide and Working Papers*.

Spreadsheet Template Disk

A new feature of the program, this software contains templates for fifteen of the problems from the textbook. The problems are identified in the textbook by a computer symbol. The template disk is to be used in conjunction with *Lotus 1-2-3*. Also included with the software is a user's manual that contains simple step-by-step instructions for completing each problem at the computer and solutions in the form of printouts.

Practice Sets

Two short practice sets are available for use with this textbook: *Robotor Manufacturing, Inc.—A Job Order Practice Set* and *Comptech Manufacturing Corporation—A Standard Costs and Budgeting Practice Set*. These practice sets will enhance the course by allowing students to apply their knowledge of cost accounting to realistic on-the-job situations.

Teaching Aids

A variety of helpful teaching aids are available for use with *Cost Accounting: Principles and Applications*, Fifth Edition.

Solutions Transparencies

New with this edition of *Cost Accounting: Principles and Applications* is a set of transparencies containing solutions for each of the regular problems in the text.

Course Management and Solutions Manual

This teaching aid contains chapter teaching pointers and answers to all the review questions, managerial discussion questions, exercises, and cases found in the textbook. Also included is a facsimile key for the problems, alternate problems, and business projects. Check figures are provided for the problems, alternate problems, and projects, and these may be duplicated for the students.

A new feature of this edition is a separate test for each of the 27 chapters in the textbook. In addition, five comprehensive tests covering the entire text are provided. Both the chapter tests and the comprehensive tests may be duplicated for classroom use.

This manual also contains teaching suggestions, model schedules, large transparency masters of accounting forms, and keys to all the tests.

Special Features of the Text

A number of features to facilitate learning are built into the text.

- *Principles and Procedures Summary.* Each chapter ends with a summary of the basic principles and procedures covered in the chapter. This summary is an excellent reinforcement and review tool.
- *Review Questions.* Each chapter contains questions that check the student's knowledge of the principles and procedures covered in the chapter.
- *Managerial Discussion Questions.* These questions, appearing at the end of each chapter, constantly remind students that cost data serves a meaningful purpose by assisting management in making decisions. The managerial questions are intended to stimulate class discussion and enhance the student's ability to apply the principles learned.
- *Exercises, Problems, and Alternate Problems.* At the end of each chapter, the students are also given exercises and problems correlated with the performance objectives and the concepts and procedures introduced in the chapter. Each problem has a companion, or alternate problem, that involves the same concepts and procedures. Instructors may use different sets of problems for different classes. Or they may work one set of problems in class and assign the alternates for completion by students outside of the classroom. Alternate problems may also be used for remedial work.
- *Managerial Decision Cases.* Students can demonstrate their understanding of cost accounting concepts by responding to the cases that appear in selected chapters.
- *Business Projects.* Three business projects are included in the text. They serve as culminating activities for Chapters 1 to 11 in Part 1, for Chapters 13 to 19 in Part 2, and for Chapters 20 through 23 in Part 3.

■ *Computers in Cost Accounting Vignettes.* Computer technology is playing an increasingly important role in all areas of accounting; therefore, information about the use of computers in cost accounting has been included throughout the text. This information is presented in nontechnical terms and emphasizes the contributions that computers are making to the development of more effective cost accumulation and manufacturing control systems.

. . . .
Acknowledgments

The authors would like to thank the following educators for their thoughtful reviews and careful checking, which provided a solid base for this revision:

Richard C. Bernheim
Montgomery County Community
    College
Blue Bell, Pennsylvania

Jay P. Blazek
Milwaukee Area Technical College
Milwaukee, Wisconsin

Calvin W. Carroll
Sullivan Junior College
Louisville, Kentucky

Steven Fietek
Highline Community College
Midway, Washington

Ann K. Fleming
King's College
Charlotte, North Carolina

Robert Harris
State Technical Institute
Memphis, Tennessee

Bill Huerter
Northeast Iowa Technical
    Institute
Peosta, Iowa

Verna Mae Johnson
The Brown Mackie College
Salina, Kansas

Lillie Lewis
State Technical Institute
Memphis, Tennessee

Mary C. Pretti
State Technical Institute
Memphis, Tennessee

Elaine M. Wright
Platt Career School
Corpus Christi, Texas

Roy Y. Yamida
Leeward Community College
Pearl City, Hawaii

Sherman W. Young, Jr.
Asheville Buncombe Technical College
Asheville, North Carolina

William J. Zahurak
Community College of Allegheny
    County
Pittsburgh, Pennsylvania

Horace R. Brock
Charles E. Palmer
Linda A. Herrington

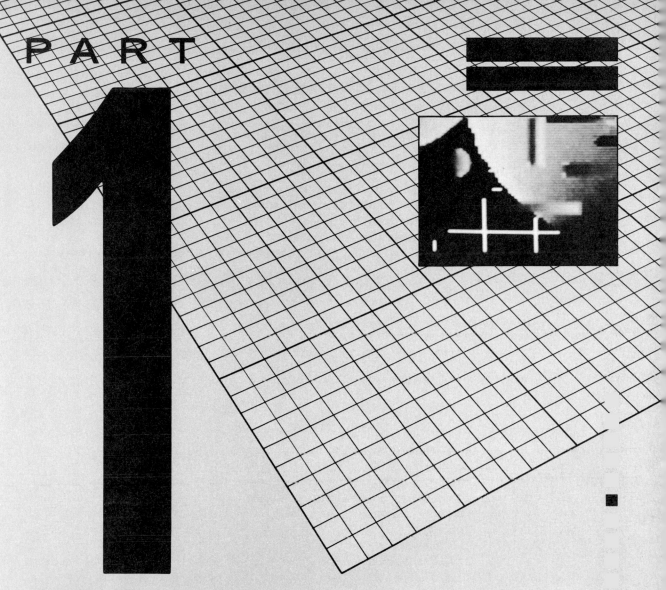

1

Job Order

Cost

Accounting

1

Monitoring Costs

■ ■ ■

Every business is run to make a profit for its owners. *Profit* is the amount of income left after the various costs of operation have been deducted. In general, higher costs mean smaller profits, and lower costs mean larger profits. No wonder the successful manager keeps a close watch on costs: It is necessary for survival. Accounting provides the tools that management needs to monitor costs.

Management's Need for Cost Information

For cost information, management relies heavily on the income statement. The information in this statement helps the company operate on a sound basis. As a business enterprise becomes larger, managers are no longer able to depend solely upon personal observations and involvement in daily operations and must place greater reliance on production reports and cost statements. As a result, the financial statements for the firm become much more elaborate and the costs receive much more detailed treatment.

A wholesale or retail business acquires merchandise to resell to customers. Its income statement shows the details of the cost of goods sold. Computing the cost of goods sold for a merchandising business is a relatively straightforward process. The beginning inventory of merchandise is added to current net purchases to obtain the cost of goods available for sale; then the ending inventory of merchandise is subtracted to obtain the cost of goods sold.

Computing the cost of goods sold for a manufacturing business is much more complex and involves many more cost elements. For a manufacturer, the cost of goods sold in one period does not necessarily equal the cost of goods manufactured. For this reason, the Cost of Goods Sold section of the income statement of a manufacturing business shows the beginning inventory of goods finished in prior periods added to the cost of goods manufactured during the current period to obtain the cost of goods available for sale. The inventory of finished goods on hand at the end of the period is then subtracted from the total available to obtain the cost of goods sold.

A manufacturer must purchase raw materials and then incur many types of costs in converting the raw materials into products to be sold to customers. In a furniture factory, for example, raw materials in the form of lumber must be purchased and then processed by mechanical equipment to achieve the desired dimensions. Workers assemble the individual pieces and paint and finish them to specifications. Overhead expenses such as the consumption of supplies, utilities, building and equipment maintenance, and janitorial services are incurred as part of the process. With so many operations going on, management must maintain a close watch to see that work on the product is done carefully and efficiently and at a reasonable cost. Because of the many elements that comprise the cost of goods manufactured, the income statement of a manufacturing business is supported by a separate report known as a *statement of cost of goods manufactured.*

In a manufacturing business the cost of goods manufactured appears in the Cost of Goods Sold section of the income statement. (The function of cost of goods manufactured is similar to that of merchandise purchases in a merchandising business.) The income statement for the year ended December 31, 19X5, for the Duncan Manufacturing Corporation is shown on page 4. The accompanying statement of cost of goods manufactured is shown on page 7.

. . . .
Manufacturing Costs Classified

Manufacturing is the process of converting *materials* into finished goods by using *labor* and incurring other costs, generally called *manufacturing overhead.* Overhead costs include utilities, supplies, taxes, insurance, and depreciation. One of the functions of a cost accounting system is to classify and record all costs according to category. The three major manufacturing cost classifications—direct materials, direct labor, and manufacturing overhead—are the basis for all modern cost accounting procedures. (See the chart of typical costs on page 5.)

Direct Materials

Direct materials, also called *raw materials,* are those materials used in the manufacturing process that become a significant part of the finished goods. For example, the metal frame and the lumber used in manufacturing a chair and the cloth and buttons used in manufacturing clothing are direct materials.

It is important to note that what is raw material to one manufacturer is considered finished goods by the supplier of that material. For example, to the foundry that makes metal chair frames, these frames are finished goods. They are raw materials, however, to the manufacturer who purchases the frames to make the chairs.

The statement of cost of goods manufactured for the Duncan Manufacturing Corporation (page 7) shows that on January 1, 19X5, the corporation had an inventory of raw materials on hand of $26,000. During the year, net purchases of raw materials amounted to $141,092. The addition of the net purchases amount to the inventory amount makes the total for materials available $167,092. On December 31, 19X5, the raw materials inventory was $25,000. This amount is subtracted from the amount of total materials available to get the cost of raw materials used. Therefore, the cost of raw materials used by the Duncan Manufacturing Corporation for the year ended December 31, 19X5 is $142,092.

DUNCAN MANUFACTURING CORPORATION
Income Statement
Year Ended December 31, 19X5

Revenue			
Sales			$495,138
Less Sales Returns and Allowances			3,782
Net Sales			$491,356
Cost of Goods Sold			
Finished Goods Inventory, Jan. 1		$ 28,700	
Add Cost of Goods Manufactured		**285,192**	
Total Goods Available for Sale		$313,892	
Less Finished Goods Inventory, Dec. 31		27,500	
Cost of Goods Sold			286,392
Gross Profit on Sales			$204,964
Operating Expenses			
Selling Expenses			
Sales Salaries Expense	$26,225		
Payroll Taxes Expense—Sales	1,210		
Delivery Expense	21,240		
Sales Supplies and Expense	31,249		
Advertising Expense	11,710		
Total Selling Expenses		$ 91,634	
Administrative Expenses			
Officers' Salaries Expense	$55,000		
Office Salaries Expense	17,325		
Payroll Taxes Expense—Administrative	2,615		
Office Supplies and Expense	5,310		
Bad Debts Expense	983		
Total Administrative Expenses		81,233	
Total Operating Expenses			172,867
Net Income From Operations			$ 32,097
Add Other Income			
Interest Earned			240
			$ 32,337
Less Other Expense			
Amortization of Organization Costs			100
Net Income Before Income Taxes			$ 32,237
Provision for Income Taxes			8,665
Net Income After Income Taxes			$ 23,572

Direct Labor

The personnel who work directly with the raw materials in converting them to finished goods represent *direct labor*. In a factory that makes chairs, for example, wages of workers who cut and sand lumber and of those who assemble the parts into finished chairs are considered direct labor costs. In the manufacturing of clothing,

CHART OF COSTS FOR A MANUFACTURING COMPANY

Total Costs

Manufacturing Costs

Direct Materials
- Raw Materials
- Semifinished Parts
- Finished Parts for Assembling

Direct Labor
- Factory Payroll

Manufacturing Overhead
- Indirect Labor
- Indirect Materials
- Rent
- Payroll Taxes
- Utilities
- Property Taxes
- Depreciation
- Repairs
- Insurance

Prime Cost

Conversion Cost

Distribution Costs

Delivery
- Freight Out
- Depreciation
- Gasoline and Oil
- Truck Repairs
- Delivery Workers' Salaries
- Warehouse Costs
- Insurance

Sales
- Advertising
- Salespeople's Salaries
- Samples
- Travel
- Depreciation of Equipment
- Rent for Branches
- Telephone
- Sales Supplies
- Property Taxes
- Payroll Taxes
- Insurance

Administration Costs
- Office Salaries
- Executive Salaries
- Office Supplies
- Rent
- Depreciation
- Telephone
- Travel
- Property Taxes
- Payroll Taxes
- Insurance

the earnings of cutters and sewing machine operators are direct labor costs. The statement of cost of goods manufactured for the Duncan Manufacturing Corporation shows a total direct labor cost of $80,870 for 19X5.

Manufacturing Overhead

All costs incurred in the factory that cannot be considered direct materials or direct labor are classified as *manufacturing overhead* (sometimes called *factory overhead, manufacturing expenses,* or *factory burden*). Manufacturing overhead is usually subdivided into three categories: indirect materials, indirect labor, and other manufacturing overhead. The manufacturing overhead items of the Duncan Manufacturing Corporation for 19X5, totaling $61,730, are shown in the statement of cost of goods manufactured on page 7.

Indirect Materials. Materials that are used in small amounts in the manufacturing process or that cannot easily be allocated to specific products are called *indirect materials.* The glue used in manufacturing armchairs and the thread used in sewing a suit are indirect materials. This is because only small amounts of glue and thread are used, even though they clearly become part of the finished goods. Records must be kept to show the exact amount of materials used in completing each specific job or group of products. Keeping detailed records for minor materials, however, would require a great deal more time and cost than the results would justify. It is more practical to group all such materials together without charging them to specific products.

Another type of indirect material, sometimes called *factory supplies* or *operating supplies,* consists of items that are used in the manufacturing process but do not become a part of the finished goods. Examples of these are cleaning supplies used in the factory, oil used for lubricating the factory machinery, and minor repair parts. The Duncan Manufacturing Corporation shows a total of $6,809 for indirect materials for 19X5.

Indirect Labor. The wages of factory personnel who do not work directly on raw materials are called *indirect labor.* For example, the wages and salaries of such factory workers as the storeroom clerks, janitors, superintendent, maintenance crew, and factory foremen are indirect labor costs. The Duncan Manufacturing Corporation's indirect labor cost for 19X5 is $16,763.

Other Manufacturing Overhead. Other manufacturing overhead includes such costs as payroll taxes on factory wages; rent, depreciation, taxes, and insurance on factory buildings and machinery; heat, light, and power; repairs and maintenance of machinery and equipment; and amortization of patents. Many of these relate to the physical plant (building, machinery, and equipment). Other manufacturing overhead is a growing part of the total cost of production because of the increasing use of expensive labor-saving equipment in many manufacturing processes. Sophisticated pieces of equipment such as computers and robots result in more costly maintenance, greater insurance and depreciation charges, and increased utility costs.

DUNCAN MANUFACTURING CORPORATION
Statement of Cost of Goods Manufactured
Year Ended December 31, 19X5

Raw Materials			
Raw Materials Inventory, Jan. 1			$ 26,000
Materials Purchases		$144,092	
Less Purchases Returns and Allowances	$ 380		
Purchases Discount	2,620	3,000	
Net Purchases			141,092
Total Materials Available			$167,092
Less Raw Materials Inventory, Dec. 31			25,000
Raw Materials Used			$142,092
Direct Labor			80,870
Manufacturing Overhead			
Indirect Materials and Supplies		$ 6,809	
Indirect Labor		16,763	
Payroll Taxes Expense—Factory		6,435	
Utilities		8,434	
Repairs and Maintenance		9,392	
Depreciation—Factory Building		750	
Depreciation—Equipment		2,400	
Insurance		4,530	
Property Taxes—Factory Building		6,217	
Total Manufacturing Overhead			61,730
Total Current Manufacturing Costs			$284,692
Add Work in Process Inventory, Jan. 1			10,500
			$295,192
Less Work in Process Inventory, Dec. 31			10,000
Cost of Goods Manufactured			$285,192

Prime and Conversion Costs

In cost accounting, the term for the sum of direct materials and direct labor is *prime cost*. Prime cost reflects the primary sources of costs for units in production. The Duncan Manufacturing Corporation's prime cost for 19X5 is $222,962 ($142,092 + $80,870). The total of direct labor and manufacturing overhead is often called *conversion cost*. Conversion cost indicates the costs required to convert the raw materials into finished products. The Duncan Manufacturing Corporation's conversion cost for 19X5 is $142,600 ($61,730 + $80,870). (See the chart of costs on page 5.)

Inventories for a Manufacturing Concern

A manufacturing business has three distinct inventory accounts: Raw Materials Inventory, Work in Process Inventory, and Finished Goods Inventory. At the end of the fiscal period, the balance of each of the three accounts will appear in the Current Assets section of the balance sheet.

Raw Materials Inventory

The *Raw Materials Inventory account* (sometimes called *Materials and Supplies*) reflects the cost of raw materials and factory supplies that will be used in the manufacturing process. Once direct materials are removed from the storeroom for use in the manufacturing process, their costs are no longer part of the raw materials inventory. Instead, these costs are then classified as part of work in process. In the same way, the costs of factory supplies that have been removed from the storeroom and applied in the manufacturing process are charged to manufacturing overhead. Some manufacturing firms may use a separate Supplies Inventory account if the quantities or value of supplies normally kept on hand are significant enough to justify the additional account.

Work In Process Inventory

The *Work in Process Inventory account* reflects the cost of raw materials, direct labor, and manufacturing overhead of goods on which manufacturing has begun but has not been completed at the end of the fiscal period. The statement of cost of goods manufactured for the Duncan Manufacturing Corporation shows that on January 1, 19X5, the cost of work in process was $10,500. This figure is added to the total manufacturing cost incurred in the current year, $284,692, to determine the total costs to be accounted for, $295,192. Finally, the ending work in process inventory of $10,000 is subtracted to arrive at the cost of goods manufactured of $285,192.

Finished Goods Inventory

The *Finished Goods Inventory account* reflects the costs of goods that have been completed and are ready for sale. This account corresponds to the Merchandise Inventory account of a merchandising business. Any changes in the Finished Goods Inventory account are reflected in the Cost of Goods Sold section of the income statement. As you can see in the Duncan Manufacturing Corporation's income statement for 19X5, shown on page 4, the balance of the Finished Goods Inventory account at the beginning of the fiscal period is added to the cost of goods manufactured to determine total cost of goods available for sale. The balance in the Finished Goods Inventory account on December 31 represents completed goods on hand at the end of the fiscal period. It is subtracted from the total goods available for sale to obtain the cost of goods sold. (See page 4.)

The Purpose of Cost Accounting

Although the income statement and the statement of cost of goods manufactured are valuable in guiding business decisions, they do not supply enough information to achieve the greatest efficiency and profit under competitive conditions. The figures represent *total* costs, which are too broad to permit more than general conclusions.

Alert management, interested in showing a larger profit, will ask itself vital questions that these totals cannot answer. Some of these questions might be as follows:

- Is our plant operating efficiently and economically?
- Which of our costs are out of line, and how can they be controlled?
- Are our sales prices set realistically in relation to costs?
- What is the unit cost of each type of product being manufactured?

The answers to such questions require detailed data based on computations that will pinpoint unit costs of products and processes. This is one of the major functions of cost accounting. Through modern systems of cost accounting, it is possible to know how much it costs to construct, manufacture, or sell goods, or to render various services. The ability to make specific and detailed identification and measurement of cost elements permits management to *reach decisions* and to *evaluate results* with greater intelligence.

Estimating and Bidding

In certain trades, a knowledge of the costs of doing business is needed to estimate a job or to bid for other jobs or contracts. The order generally goes to the lowest bidder. Under competitive pressure, the decisive difference in a bid may be as little as a fraction of a cent per unit. Attempting to bid without detailed cost information can mean losing the job or it can mean winning the job but having to perform the work at a loss. Either result is undesirable.

Planning, Budgets, and Control

The cost accounting system also provides vital information needed to *plan future operations*. Cost data help resolve questions relating to proposed projects or policies, such as the following:

- Should we build a new plant or modernize the old one?
- How far can we go in lowering prices to increase our volume of sales?
- What will be the effect on costs of automating part of our factory operations?

Cost accounting is also used in preparing a company's budget. A *budget* is the overall financial plan for future activities. It is even possible to compute flexible budgets that will tell what the costs for any volume of output should be. Then actual costs can be compared with a realistic budgeted amount.

Standard cost procedures are helpful in evaluating the results of operations. Unit costs are projected on the basis of standard conditions. These standards are often based on the past experience of the firm or on statistics from the industry. Then, as actual costs are incurred, they are compared with these standard costs. The differences between the two sets of cost figures can be noted and investigated while there is still time to take remedial action.

From this brief discussion, it is obvious that cost accounting is one of the most valuable management tools to *control operations*. Knowledge of the costs of making and selling the firm's products or services helps the firm's officers weigh the various courses of action before they make any final commitments. Once operations begin, cost accounting tells them how efficiently the work is being done, where the strong and weak spots are, and how to improve performance.

The cost of making a product is one of the most critical factors in a firm's ability to meet the competition. With cost information to support their decisions, management can issue directives, perform follow-up activities, and obtain the operating results that ensure prosperity and growth for the enterprise.

Types of Cost Systems

One type of accounting system is needed to accumulate costs of goods manufactured where products are produced in jobs or lots of varying quantities and types. A different type of system is used where there is a continuous flow of goods of identical or similar characteristics throughout the manufacturing process. The job order cost system has been developed for the first type of operation, and the process cost system for the second.

Job Order Cost System

The *job order cost system* accumulates costs applicable to each specific job order or lot of similar goods manufactured on a specific order for stock or for a customer. When production on a job begins, the job is assigned a number, and a form called a *job cost sheet* is set up. As direct materials are used, their costs are entered on the job cost sheet. Similarly, direct labor costs incurred on a job are recorded periodically. When the job is completed (or periodically as the job is worked on), manufacturing overhead costs applicable to the job are estimated and entered on the job cost sheet. The job cost sheet, when complete, shows the total cost of the completed job. The cost per unit may then be obtained by dividing the total cost of the job by the number of units completed.

The job order cost system is often used by manufacturers, such as a furniture manufacturer, who produce a variety of products, because such producers need to keep track of each specific order to ensure correct allocation of costs. Also, the actual costs shown on the job cost sheets may be compared with the estimated costs on which the sales prices were based. Any discrepancies or significant variations between estimated costs and actual costs to manufacture are analyzed, and necessary corrective actions are taken to ensure that adequate profit margins are maintained.

Process Cost System

The *process cost system* accumulates costs without attempting to allocate them during the accounting period to specific units of goods being manufactured. At the end of the fiscal period, the average cost per unit is determined by dividing the total number of units produced into the total cost accumulated. Because of this technique, process costing is often referred to as *average costing*. If the process cost system is used, the goods manufactured must be similar in nature so that an average cost will be meaningful. The process cost system is commonly used in such manufacturing operations as cement plants and flour mills, in which the production process is standardized and continuous and the product remains essentially the same from day to day.

In many types of business that use process costing, manufacturing consists of a progressive series of distinct operations or processes. Usually each process is carried out in a different department. A unit cost may be computed for each process or department. This departmental unit cost may be a useful tool in measuring and controlling efficiency. The total cost of production is determined by adding up the departmental costs.

Dual Systems

Some manufacturers use both the job order cost and process cost systems. A dual system is often used when a company makes standard parts or subassemblies continuously and then incorporates them into finished goods built to customer specifications. The cost of the parts is accumulated and determined under a process cost system, and the cost of each customer's order for finished goods is computed under a job order cost system.

The Role of the Cost Accountant

A *cost accountant* is a specialist who analyzes the cost recording and reporting needs of a business and devises a system of records and procedures that will meet these needs. This system will include the necessary forms and other records, recordkeeping procedures, controls, summarizing techniques, and formal reporting methods. In addition, the cost accountant provides up-to-date analyses of the operations of the business to help management make rational and meaningful decisions.

A processor of perishable goods has different needs than an automobile manufacturer. Likewise, a large company with several departments manufacturing many products has different concerns than a small plant making one product. A cost accountant must be able to adapt systems and procedures in order to meet these varying needs.

Data Processing and Cost Accounting

Data processing, also called *information processing,* means handling individual facts to get meaningful information. This information can then be interpreted and used for decision making.

Raw data is a fact or a piece of information. By itself, raw data has little value in decision making. For example, knowing that Homestyle Sofa Makers produced 50 sofas today is not very interesting or meaningful by itself. However, in combination with some other fact, such data about one day's production of sofas can take on meaning.

If the added fact were known that the typical number of sofas produced in a day is 75, Homestyle's management would realize that production is down 25 sofas, or one-third, today. Then management, in conjunction with the cost accountant, can investigate the efficiency of operations to discover ways to get productivity back to the normal level. ■

Principles and Procedures Summary

Management must watch costs closely in order to operate efficiently and achieve maximum profits. Cost information permits more effective control of operations through the pinpointing of unit costs. A statement of cost of goods manufactured is prepared to further explain the cost of goods sold and support the income statement. Specific, up-to-date, and pertinent cost figures also help management in estimating, planning, budgeting, and evaluating.

Manufacturing costs are classified under three major headings: direct materials, direct labor, and manufacturing overhead. The last term includes all costs that cannot be easily and conveniently charged to specific products. Manufacturing overhead is subclassified into indirect materials, indirect labor, and other manufacturing overhead.

There are two major systems for accumulating costs. The job order cost system is used when goods are produced for a specific order or lot. The process cost system is used when similar goods are produced in a continuous flow. When a firm does some manufacturing on a job basis, or a special order basis, and some on a continuous basis, both cost systems may be used.

The cost accountant is an accounting specialist who studies a firm's needs for cost data and devises a cost system that gives management maximum assistance in planning, controlling, and directing operations.

Review Questions

1. What are the three major classifications of manufacturing costs?
2. Define the following:
   a. Direct materials
   b. Direct labor
   c. Manufacturing overhead
3. How do prime costs differ from conversion costs?
4. List four examples of manufacturing overhead costs.
5. What is the difference between direct labor and indirect labor? Give an example of each.
6. What is the difference between direct materials and indirect materials? Give an example of each.
7. List three alternate terms for manufacturing overhead.
8. A retailing business has one inventory account, Merchandise Inventory, listed on its balance sheet. What inventory account(s) appear on the balance sheet of a manufacturing concern?
9. For each of the inventory items listed below, identify on which of the following statement(s) the item will appear: statement of cost of goods manufactured, income statement, or balance sheet.
   a. Raw Materials, beginning inventory balance
   b. Raw Materials, ending inventory balance
   c. Work in Process, beginning inventory balance
   d. Work in Process, ending inventory balance

e. Finished Goods, beginning inventory balance *Income,*

f. Finished Goods, ending inventory balance *Income, Bal*

10. How does the income statement for a retailing business differ from the income statement for a manufacturing business? *Cost of good minu.*

11. In what type of manufacturing operation would the job cost system be used? *Furniture* Where would the process cost system be used? *Flour mills –*

12. What is a budget? *overall plan*

Managerial Discussion Questions

1. How does a cost accounting system help management? Does the statement of cost of goods manufactured provide enough data for decision making? Explain.

2. How are cost accounting records used by management in making contract bids or in estimating the cost of a job?

3. What type of cost systems would you recommend to the management of each of the following types of manufacturing concerns. Why?

   a. Manufacturer of custom-designed mobile homes
   b. Tailor
   c. Company that processes frozen orange juice
   d. Manufacturer of automobiles
   e. Manufacturer of paint

4. What types of manufacturing overhead costs do you think management would closely watch in attempting to control costs? Why?

5. What is the purpose of determining and using standard costs?

6. Explain why an item that is classified as direct materials by one company may be classified as indirect materials by another. Give an example.

7. Classify the following costs of the Best Chocolate Chip Cookies Company as direct materials, direct labor, overhead, selling expenses, or administrative expenses.

   a. Repair of ovens
   b. Salary of president's secretary
   c. Chocolate chips
   d. Freight charges to ship cookies to customers
   e. Flour
   f. Salaries of employees who box cookies
   g. Cookie boxes

Exercises

1. **Calculating manufacturing costs and cost of goods manufactured.** The costs for Simon, Inc., for the year ended June 30, 19X3, are given below.

Direct Materials	$50,370
Direct Labor	73,025
Manufacturing Overhead	26,310
Work in Process Inventory, July 1, 19X2	28,830
Work in Process Inventory, June 30, 19X3	24,500

   a. What are the manufacturing costs for the year? *179335*
   b. What is the cost of goods manufactured for the year? *154835*

2. **Calculating prime costs and conversion costs.** The following costs were incurred by Texas Manufacturers:

Direct Materials	$206,180
Direct Labor	341,220
Manufacturing Overhead	172,382

    a. What were the prime costs for the company?

    b. What were the conversion costs?

3. **Calculating cost of goods sold and gross profit.** The following amounts relate to the Bio-Tech Corporation:

Finished Goods Inventory, April 1, 19X2	$ 58,480
Finished Goods Inventory, April 30, 19X2	52,219
Cost of Goods Manufactured	81,507
Net Sales	127,493

    a. Calculate the cost of goods sold.

    b. Calculate the gross profit on sales.

4. **Calculating cost of goods manufactured, cost of goods sold, and gross profit.** The New Bedford Plumbing Company manufactures water pumps and filters and uses a job cost order accounting system. Cost data for 19X2 are given below.

Raw Materials, January 1, 19X2	$ 348,542
Raw Materials, December 31, 19X2	361,417
Work in Process, January 1, 19X2	283,463
Work in Process, December 31, 19X2	308,182
Finished Goods, January 1, 19X2	221,932
Finished Goods, December 31, 19X2	201,647
Raw Materials Purchases	631,917
Direct Labor	1,082,680
Manufacturing Overhead	714,530
Net Sales	4,608,917

    a. Calculate cost of goods manufactured.

    b. Calculate cost of goods sold.

    c. Calculate gross profit on sales.

5. **Calculating direct materials cost.** The Agricultural Products Company maintains a raw materials inventory account for all materials used in its factory operations. Purchases of both direct and indirect materials are debited to this account. The balance on January 1, 19X4, for the raw materials account was $250,738. Purchases of raw materials for the year were $762,910 and purchase returns totaled $23,853. The ending inventory on December 31, 19X4, was $238,649. Calculate the following:

    a. What was the total of the raw materials available for use?

    b. What was the cost of raw materials used in factory operations?

    c. Materials requisitions show that of the total raw materials used during the year, indirect materials amounted to $63,071. What was the amount of direct materials used during the year?

Problems

PROBLEM 1-1. Preparing a statement of cost of goods manufactured. The data for the year ended June 30, 19X3, that follow relate to the Perez Manufacturing Corporation.

Raw Materials Inventory, July 1, 19X2	$ 60,000
Raw Materials Inventory, June 30, 19X3	52,000
Work in Process Inventory, July 1, 19X2	24,600
Work in Process Inventory, June 30, 19X3	26,000
Materials Purchases	203,600
Direct Labor	118,200
Indirect Labor	11,080
Payroll Taxes Expense—Factory	9,800
Utilities	16,400
Repairs and Maintenance	4,200
Indirect Materials and Supplies	15,480
Depreciation—Factory Equipment	5,100
Insurance	2,460
Rent—Factory Building	57,000

Instructions

Prepare the statement of cost of goods manufactured for the year ended June 30, 19X3.

PROBLEM 1-2. Preparing a statement of cost of goods manufactured and an income statement. The following data pertain to the operations of the Carlson Company, a manufacturer of wooden furniture:

	April 1, 19X2	March 31, 19X3
Inventories:		
Finished Goods	$ 20,000	$ 25,000
Raw Materials	147,000	136,000
Work in Process	118,000	122,000
Raw Material Purchases		284,000
Direct Labor		236,000
Indirect Materials and Supplies		47,000
Indirect Labor		84,000
Other Manufacturing Overhead		157,000
Sales		1,246,000
Selling Expenses		265,000
Administrative Expenses		87,000

Instructions

1. Prepare a statement of cost of goods manufactured for the year ended March 31, 19X3.
2. Prepare an income statement.

PROBLEM 1-3. Preparing a statement of cost of goods manufactured and an income statement. The following data pertain to Chicago Microchips, Inc.:

	Jan. 1, 19X2	Dec. 31, 19X2
Inventories:		
Finished Goods	$43,800	$ 51,700
Raw Materials	12,600	10,650
Work in Process	16,500	15,300
Direct Labor		88,100
Freight In		4,800
Administrative Expenses		31,800
Indirect Labor		18,820
Indirect Materials and Supplies		3,000
Insurance Expense—Factory		1,600
Depreciation—Plant and Equipment		7,400
Raw Materials Purchases		174,210
Payroll Taxes Expense—Factory		3,760
Utilities—Factory		7,600
Property Taxes—Factory		3,820
Raw Materials Purchases Returns and Allowances		3,230
Repairs and Maintenance—Factory		4,220
Sales		502,600
Selling Expenses		88,950
Sales Returns and Allowances		2,530

Instructions

1. Prepare a statement of cost of goods manufactured for the year ended December 31, 19X2. NOTE: Freight In should be added to Raw Materials Purchases to determine the Delivered Cost of Raw Materials Purchases.
2. Prepare an income statement.

Alternate Problems

PROBLEM 1-1A. Preparing a statement of cost of goods manufactured. The data for the year ended July 31, 19X4, given below relate to the Box and Carton Manufacturing Corporation.

Raw Materials Inventory, August 1, 19X3	$ 48,700
Raw Materials Inventory, July 31, 19X4	46,200
Work in Process Inventory, August 1, 19X3	30,900
Work in Process Inventory, July 31, 19X4	33,650
Materials Purchases	180,450
Direct Labor	577,600
Indirect Labor	27,200
Payroll Taxes Expense—Factory	19,930
Utilities	18,060
Repairs and Maintenance	13,800
Indirect Materials and Supplies	26,450
Depreciation—Factory Equipment	9,200
Depreciation—Factory Building	12,680
Insurance	6,430
Property Taxes	15,500

Instructions

Prepare the statement of cost of goods manufactured for the year ended July 31, 19X4.

PROBLEM 1-2A. **Preparing a statement of cost of goods manufactured and an income statement.** The following data pertain to the operations of the Puget Sound Equipment Corporation, a manufacturer of machinery:

	October 1, 19X3	September 30, 19X4
Inventories		
Finished Goods	$210,000	$ 290,000
Raw Materials	345,000	358,000
Work in Process	327,000	318,000
Raw Material Purchases		778,000
Direct Labor		512,000
Indirect Materials and Supplies		88,000
Indirect Labor		144,000
Other Manufacturing Overhead		549,000
Sales		2,500,000
Selling Expenses		500,000
Administrative Expenses		90,000

Instructions

1. Prepare a statement of cost of goods manufactured for the year ended September 30, 19X4.
2. Prepare an income statement.

PROBLEM 1-3A. **Preparing a statement of cost of goods manufactured and an income statement.** The following data pertain to the Federated Manufacturing Company:

	Mar. 1, 19X3	Feb. 28, 19X4
Inventories:		
Finished Goods	$38,400	$ 43,900
Raw Materials	23,825	24,100
Work in Process	16,460	18,280
Direct Labor		73,240
Freight In		14,800
Administrative Expenses		56,890
Indirect Labor		28,500
Indirect Materials and Supplies		14,640
Insurance Expense—Factory		12,760
Depreciation—Plant and Equipment		19,500
Raw Materials Purchases		171,820
Payroll Taxes Expense—Factory		18,700
Utilities—Factory		21,600
Property Taxes—Factory		22,080
Raw Materials Purchases Returns and Allowances		11,400
Repairs and Maintenance—Factory		14,720
Patent Amortization		14,000
Sales		683,450
Selling Expenses		89,340
Sales Returns and Allowances		5,200
Waste Removal		5,800

Instructions

1. Prepare a statement of cost of goods manufactured for the year ended February 28, 19X4. NOTE: Freight In should be added to Raw Materials Purchases to determine the Delivered Cost of Raw Materials Purchases.
2. Prepare an income statement.

CHAPTER

2

■ ■ ■

Job Order Cost Cycle

In the last chapter you learned that total manufacturing cost consists of three elements: direct materials, direct labor, and manufacturing overhead. The flow of these costs through the accounting system parallels the flow of products through the manufacturing operations. In this chapter you will begin to learn how a job order manufacturing firm is organized, how the accounting system is designed, and how accounting records and procedures are established to record, transfer, and summarize these manufacturing costs.

Work Flow

A firm's cost accounting system parallels its flow of operations. The steps in a typical cycle of operations of a firm that makes and sells its own products are outlined below.

1. **Procurement:** Raw materials and supplies needed for manufacturing are ordered, received, and stored. Direct and indirect factory labor and services are obtained.
2. **Production:** Raw materials are transferred from the storeroom to the factory. Labor, tools, machines, power, and other costs are applied to complete the product.
3. **Warehousing:** Finished goods are moved from the factory to the warehouse to be held until they are sold.
4. **Selling:** Customers are found. Merchandise is shipped from the warehouse. Sales to customers are recorded.

The cost accountant's job is to design a system in which all cost elements are recorded as incurred and then charged to production as the work flows through the operating cycle.

Recording Costs as Incurred

As each cost is incurred, it must be recorded in an appropriate general ledger account. Different accounts are needed at different points in the operating cycle. The following information includes typical account numbers:

1. **Procurement:** Accounts must be provided to record the purchase of materials, labor, and overhead. These costs will later be charged to production. Typical general ledger account titles and numbers used for this purpose are Raw Materials 121, Factory Payroll Clearing 500, and Manufacturing Overhead Control 501.
2. **Production:** An account is required to gather procurement costs as they become chargeable to manufacturing operations. This account is Work in Process 122.
3. **Warehousing:** An account must be set up to record the cost of goods that have been completely manufactured. This account is Finished Goods 126.
4. **Selling:** The cost of the completed goods that have been sold must be recorded; an account, Cost of Goods Sold 415, is provided in the general ledger for this purpose. Other general ledger accounts, Accounts Receivable 111 and Sales 401, are used for recording the sale to the customer and the credit to income at selling price.

The illustration below shows the relationship of these accounts to the steps in the operating cycle.

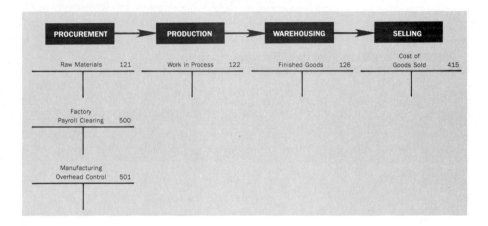

Matching Cost Flow and Work Flow

The provision for special cost accounts sets the stage for the more intricate job of charging costs in accordance with the flow of work. The process can best be understood if analyzed step by step.

1. **Procurement:** Purchases of materials, labor, and overhead are recorded as debits to Raw Materials, Factory Payroll Clearing, and Manufacturing Overhead Control. As these costs are used, or applied, in factory operations, they are credited to these accounts and transferred to production.
2. **Production:** Costs of materials, labor, and overhead transferred into production are debited to Work in Process. As goods are finished and moved from the factory floor, their total cost is removed from the Work in Process account by a credit entry and charged (debited) to Finished Goods.
3. **Warehousing:** The cost of finished goods transferred from Work in Process is recorded as a debit to Finished Goods. The cost of merchandise shipped from the

warehouse to customers is credited to Finished Goods and charged (debited) to Cost of Goods Sold.

4. *Selling:* As indicated above, as finished goods are sold and shipped from the warehouse, their cost is debited to Cost of Goods Sold. At the end of the accounting period, this account is closed by crediting Cost of Goods Sold and debiting Income Summary 399.

The matching of cost and work flow is shown below.

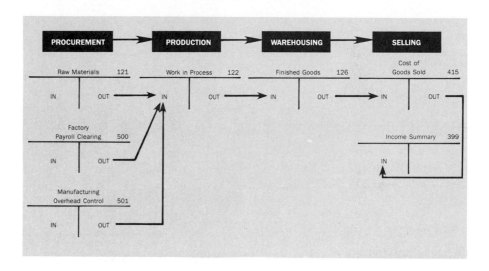

Departmental Cost Centers

Of the four steps in the operating cycle, production is probably the most complicated to account for and to control. Tons of materials and supplies of every description might be used daily by hundreds of workers who complete a wide variety of processes on countless machines. Total costs are not very useful as indicators of efficiency under such conditions. Therefore, when several operations are performed in the factory, it is customary to group similar activities into departments or cost centers. The cost accounting system is then devised to accumulate and report costs separately by department or cost center. Such reporting matches cost flow with work flow down to the smallest functional unit. The person in charge of the department is then held accountable for its efficient performance. Departmentalization thus helps to provide operating control over manufacturing activities and costs.

Factory operations normally include two types of departments: production and service. A *production department,* or *producing department,* engages in work directly related to the product. The finishing department in which the products of a furniture factory are painted is an example of a production department. A *service department* serves or assists production departments. For example, the building services department that maintains a plant so that production can be carried on under the best possible working conditions is a service department.

Recording Cost Flows

We have seen how a cost accounting system is developed by matching the flow of costs with the flow of factory activities. The next step is to examine the cost system of a typical manufacturing corporation in operation.

Space Savers, Inc., manufactures modular and folding desks and tables designed for convenience and saving space. These tables and desks are popular for the home and office because they are sturdy but easy to handle. Most production is to fill specific orders from customers, although some standard models of desks and tables are produced and held in inventory for future sales. The company has annual gross sales in excess of $2,500,000.

Organization

The firm is organized into three major divisions: General Administration, Production, and Sales. (See the organization chart below.) The Production Division, which directs factory operations, consists of five departments: three producing departments and two service departments. The three producing departments are Milling, Assembling, and Finishing. The two service departments are Building Services and General Factory.

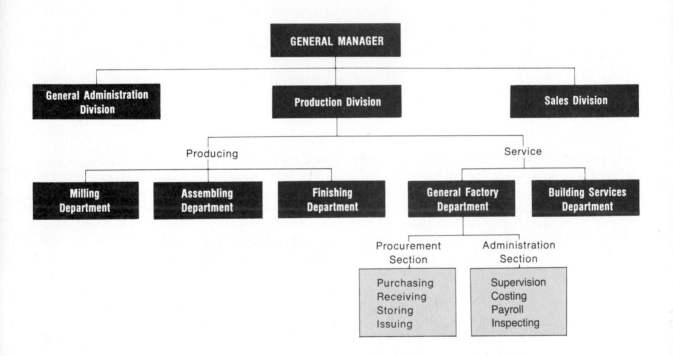

Milling Department. In the Milling Department, rough lumber is trimmed and shaped into finished forms for use in manufacturing tables and desks. The machinery consists of electric and hydraulic saws, routers, sanders, molders, jointers, planers, and drilling, nailing, and milling equipment.

Assembling Department.   Here the individual pieces are put together with screws and glue, and various hardware is attached. When prefabricated parts are purchased to be assembled, work on an order begins in this department. The operations in this department are performed primarily by hand.

Finishing Department.   In this department, the finish is applied to the assembled tables and desks. Sanding, staining, sealing, filling, lacquering, and rubbing operations are performed. The completed goods go from the Finishing Department to the finished goods warehouse for shipment.

Building Services Department.   This department is responsible for maintaining the building and grounds and performing janitorial services. It also maintains the heating, cooling, electrical, and plumbing systems. Heating and cooling costs, building taxes, building insurance, building depreciation, and similar costs are charged to the Building Services Department.

General Factory Department.   This department consists of two sections and performs a variety of activities. The procurement section is responsible for purchasing, receiving, storing, and issuing raw materials and factory supplies. The purchasing agent's staff, the receiving clerk, the storeroom supervisor, and the storeroom clerk make up this section. The administration section includes such personnel as the factory cost clerk, the time clerk, the payroll clerk, inspectors, and the factory superintendent.

Flow of Work

The flow of work at Space Savers, as shown below, follows the flow of operations discussed earlier in this unit. The various operating divisions, departments, and sections are shown as they relate to the basic steps on the flowchart. Since the General Administration Division is not a direct participant in the flow of costs, it is omitted from this illustration.

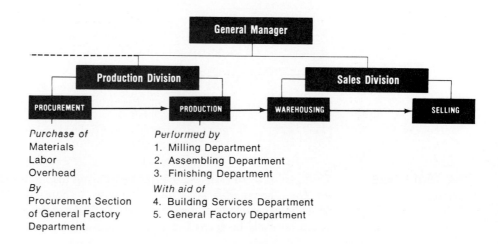

Chart of Accounts

Space Savers, Inc., uses a job order cost system. This system was recommended by Space Savers' accountant after a careful study of their organization and manufacturing procedures. The chart of accounts used is shown on pages 25 and 26.

Most of Space Savers' accounts will be familiar to you from your previous courses. Note, however, the new cost accounts below.

121	Raw Materials
122	Work in Process
126	Finished Goods
415	Cost of Goods Sold
500	Factory Payroll Clearing
501	Manufacturing Overhead Control

Flow of Costs

The following examination of the cost flow of Space Savers, Inc., for October 19X1 will show how the cost flow matches the work flow.

Opening Balances. Space Savers is an established concern, so the cost accounting system has been in use for some time. Assume that on October 1 these balances appear in the following accounts:

121	Raw Materials	$44,114.00
122	Work in Process	33,165.50
126	Finished Goods	24,200.00

These balances are shown in the appropriate general ledger T accounts on the chart below.

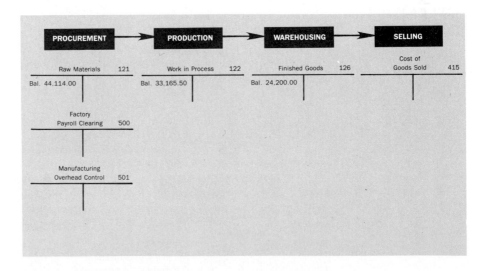

Raw Materials Purchased

Additional raw materials were purchased during the month of October at a cost of $68,760. The purchase is debited to the asset account, Raw Materials. This entry is shown in general journal form on page 25 for illustrative purposes. The transaction would normally be entered in a special journal, such as the voucher register.

19X1		(A)			
Oct. 31	Raw Materials		121	68,760.00	
	Vouchers Payable		201		68,760.00
	Recorded cost of raw materials purchased during the month.				

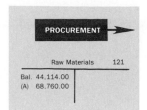

PROCUREMENT

Raw Materials	121
Bal. 44,114.00	
(A) 68,760.00	

Letters will be used to identify the general journal entries in this chapter. For example, the effect of this purchase on the Raw Materials account is indicated in the T account on the left by the entry marked A.

SPACE SAVERS, INC.
Chart of Accounts

Assets

101	Cash
111	Accounts Receivable
112	Allowance for Doubtful Accounts
121	Raw Materials
122	Work in Process
126	Finished Goods
127	Prepaid Insurance
128	Supplies
131	Land
132	Buildings
133	Accumulated Depreciation—Buildings
134	Machinery and Equipment
135	Accumulated Depreciation—Machinery and Equipment
136	Furniture and Fixtures
137	Accumulated Depreciation—Furniture and Fixtures
141	Patents

Liabilities

201	Vouchers Payable
202	Salaries and Wages Payable
211	FICA Taxes Payable
212	Federal Unemployment Taxes Payable
213	State Unemployment Taxes Payable
214	Employee Income Taxes Payable
215	Group Insurance Deductions Payable
216	Property Taxes Payable
217	Income Taxes Payable

Stockholders' Equity

301	Common Stock
302	Retained Earnings
399	Income Summary

```
                        SPACE SAVERS, INC.
                    Chart of Accounts (continued)

Revenue and Expenses
Sales and Cost of Goods Sold
401      Sales
402      Sales Returns and Allowances
415      Cost of Goods Sold

Manufacturing Overhead
500      Factory Payroll Clearing
501      Manufacturing Overhead Control
502      Manufacturing Overhead—Milling Department
503      Manufacturing Overhead—Assembling Department
504      Manufacturing Overhead—Finishing Department
505      Manufacturing Overhead—Building Services Department
506      Manufacturing Overhead—General Factory Department
507      Overapplied or Underapplied Manufacturing Overhead

Operating Expenses
601      Selling Expense Control
611      General Expense Control

Other Expenses and Other Income
701      Interest Expense
702      Sales Discount
711      Interest Earned
712      Purchases Discount
713      Miscellaneous Income
```

Raw Materials Used

During the month, raw materials costing $71,966.11 were used as follows.

Direct Materials, Chargeable to Work in Process	$68,784.76
Indirect Materials, Chargeable to Manufacturing Overhead Control	3,181.35
Total	$71,966.11

The required transfer of raw materials costs is shown in general journal form below.

19X1	(B)			
Oct. 31	Work in Process	122	68,784.76	
	Manufacturing Overhead Control	501	3,181.35	
	Raw Materials	121		71,966.11
	Recorded cost of raw materials used during the month.			

The effect on the various cost accounts is indicated on the flowchart by the entries marked B.

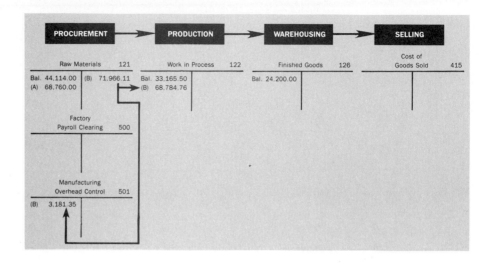

Factory Wages Earned

During the month, wages and salaries totaling $84,728 were earned by the factory employees and charged from the factory payroll register to the Factory Payroll Clearing account, as shown below.

19X1	(C)			
Oct. 31	Factory Payroll Clearing	500	84,728.00	
	Salaries and Wages Payable	202		84,728.00
	Recorded factory payroll for the month.			

The effect on the Factory Payroll Clearing account is indicated by the entry marked C in the T accounts on page 28.

Labor Charged to Operations

An analysis of the records indicates that labor costs of $84,728 should be allocated as follows.

Direct Labor, Chargeable to Work in Process	$58,597.00
Indirect Labor, Chargeable to Manufacturing Overhead Control	26,131.00
Total	$84,728.00

The required transfer of labor costs is shown in general journal form on page 28. The effect on the various cost accounts is indicated by the entries marked D in the T accounts on page 28.

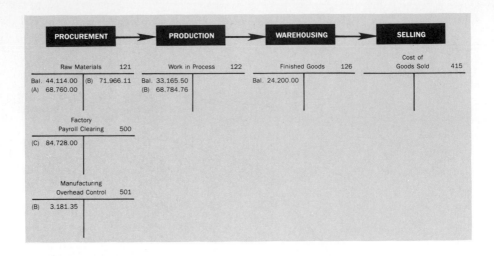

19X1	(D)		
Oct. 31	Work in Process	122	58,597.00
	Manufacturing Overhead Control	501	26,131.00
	Factory Payroll Clearing	500	84,728.00
	Recorded cost of labor used in operations during the month.		

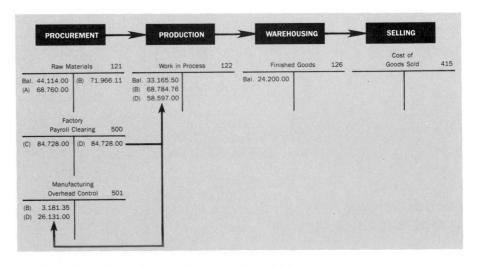

Manufacturing Overhead Costs

In addition to the indirect materials (B) and indirect labor (D), other overhead costs totaling $14,921.39 incurred during the month were charged from various journals. The entry to record these costs is shown on page 29 in general journal form. The effect on the Manufacturing Overhead Control account is shown in the T accounts by the entry marked E in the T accounts on page 29.

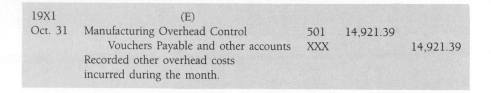

19X1		(E)			
Oct. 31	Manufacturing Overhead Control	501	14,921.39	
	Vouchers Payable and other accounts	XXX		14,921.39
	Recorded other overhead costs			
	incurred during the month.			

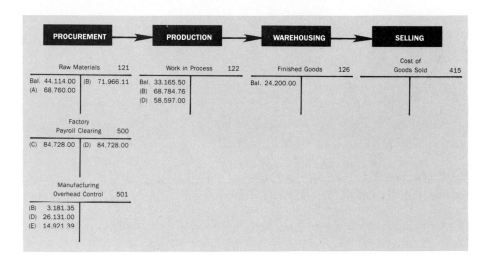

Manufacturing Overhead Applied to Products

It is estimated that overhead costs totaling $42,627.60 are chargeable to jobs worked on during the month of October. An estimate of overhead applicable to each job must be made because it is impossible to determine the exact amount applicable. (The estimation process is explained later.) The required transfer is shown in general journal form.

19X1		(F)			
Oct. 31	Work in Process	122	42,627.60	
	Manufacturing Overhead Control	501		42,627.60
	Recorded overhead applied to jobs			
	during the month.			

The effect of the transfer is shown in the related T accounts on page 30 by the entries marked F. Remember that the credit to Manufacturing Overhead Control 501 is an estimate. There will usually be a small balance in the account. A debit balance means that less overhead was charged, or applied, to production than the total costs incurred. This is called *underapplied overhead*. If the estimated overhead transferred is greater than the actual costs incurred, Manufacturing Overhead Control will have a credit balance. This is called *overapplied overhead*. (The proper handling of underapplied or overapplied overhead will be discussed in later chapters.)

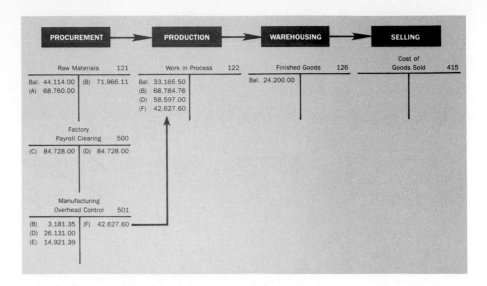

Transfer of Finished Goods

During the month, some jobs were completed and transferred to the finished goods warehouse. These jobs cost $181,342.50. This flow of goods is shown by a debit to Finished Goods 126 and a credit to Work in Process 122. The transfer is shown in the T accounts by the entries marked G.

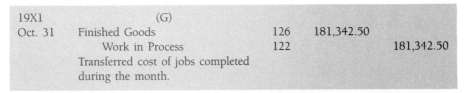

19X1		(G)		
Oct. 31	Finished Goods	126	181,342.50	
	Work in Process	122		181,342.50
	Transferred cost of jobs completed during the month.			

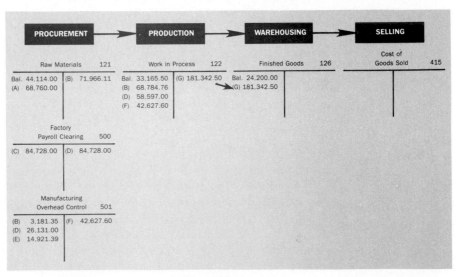

Sale of Finished Goods

During the month, finished goods costing $177,977.90 were sold to various customers. The entry to record this flow is shown in general journal form as follows:

19X1	(H)			
Oct. 31	Cost of Goods Sold	415	177,977.90	
	Finished Goods	126		177,977.90
	Recorded cost of goods sold during the month.			

The transfer is shown in the Finished Goods and Cost of Goods Sold accounts by the entries marked H.

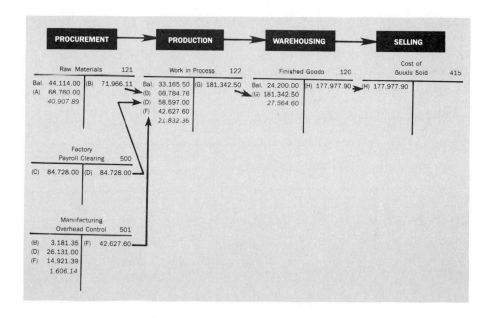

Inspection of Accounts

Examine the postings in the T accounts above to observe the flow of costs.

Entries B, D, and F appear as credits representing the flow of costs out of Raw Materials 121, Factory Payroll Clearing 500, and Manufacturing Overhead Control 501 and as debits representing the flow of costs into Work in Process 122.

Entry G shows the flow of costs out of Work in Process 122 into Finished Goods 126.

Entry H represents a cost flow out of Finished Goods 126 into Cost of Goods Sold 415.

Also note the closing balances in the three inventory accounts.

121	Raw Materials	$40,907.89
122	Work in Process	21,832.36
126	Finished Goods	27,564.60

The handling of the underapplied overhead ($1,606.14 Dr.) will be explained in later chapters.

....

End-of-Period Statements

The cost accounts in the general ledger contain essential figures needed to complete the statement of cost of goods manufactured and the income statement. The statement of cost of goods manufactured is supported by a schedule of manufacturing overhead, which shows details of individual overhead items. As you will learn later, these detailed figures for manufacturing overhead are obtained from subsidiary accounts.

SPACE SAVERS, INC.
Income Statement
Month Ended October 31, 19X1

Revenue		
Sales		$228,176.80
Cost of Goods Sold		
Finished Goods Inventory, Oct. 1	$ 24,200.00	
Add Cost of Goods Manufactured	181,342.50	
Total Goods Available for Sale	$205,542.50	
Deduct Finished Goods Inventory, Oct. 31	27,564.60	
Cost of Goods Sold		177,977.90
Gross Profit on Sales		$ 50,198.90
Operating Expenses		
Selling Expenses	$ 8,784.60	
General Expenses	11,969.20	
Total Operating Expenses		20,753.80
Net Income Before Income Taxes		$ 29,445.10
Provision for Income Taxes		4,845.00
Net Income After Income Taxes		$ 24,600.10

SPACE SAVERS, INC.
Statement of Cost of Goods Manufactured
Month Ended October 31, 19X1

Direct Materials

Raw Materials Inventory, Oct. 1	$ 44,114.00	
Materials Purchases	68,760.00	
Total Materials Available	$112,874.00	
Deduct Raw Materials Inventory, Oct. 31	40,907.89	
Total Materials Used	$ 71,966.11	
Deduct Indirect Materials Used	3,181.35	
Direct Materials Used*		$ 68,784.76
Direct Labor		58,597.00
Manufacturing Overhead Applied		42,627.60
Total Manufacturing Cost		$170,009.36
Add Work in Process Inventory, Oct.1		33,165.50
		$203,174.86
Deduct Work in Process Inventory, Oct. 31		21,832.36
Cost of Goods Manufactured		$181,342.50

*Since indirect materials is classified as part of manufacturing overhead, it is necessary to deduct the amount of indirect materials used from total materials used in order to get the direct materials used.

SPACE SAVERS, INC.
Schedule of Manufacturing Overhead
Month Ended October 31, 19X1

Actual Overhead Costs Incurred

Indirect Materials	$ 3,181.35	
Indirect Labor	26,131.00	
Payroll Taxes Expense	5,037.95	
Depreciation—Buildings	1,520.00	
Depreciation—Equipment	2,640.00	
Repairs and Maintenance	1,534.60	
Utilities	2,488.64	
Insurance	794.05	
Property Taxes	421.00	
Other Taxes	485.15	
Total Actual Overhead Costs Incurred		$44,233.74
Deduct Underapplied Overhead for October		1,606.14
Manufacturing Overhead Applied		$42,627.60

Computers as Data Processing Tools

Computers are valuable tools in handling cost accounting data. A computerized data processing system uses a combination of equipment, or *hardware,* to obtain and process facts and present the resulting information to the user. Computers are especially helpful when computations are complex or repetitious, when the volume of data is very high, or when speed is vital.

For example, Down Under is a skiwear factory and outlet whose primary business comes from mail orders. Since the main ski season is short—between November and March—Down Under must process the sales orders quickly and maintain very accurate inventory records. Two years ago, the accounting staff projected future sales trends and realized that sales and inventory would soon begin to bury the staff in paperwork. This could lead to problems because if deliveries were late or if inventories were low and not replenished in a timely fashion, the firm would lose customers and goodwill.

To ensure goods service, Down Under decided to computerize their sales and inventory processing system in order to keep records up to date and easily accessible. Management along with the cost accountant and other personnel investigated the benefit of going to three different computer systems: mainframe, minicomputer, microcomputer. The typical *mainframe* system was very expensive—$100,000 to millions of dollars—and could take up an entire room. The mainframe systems were really more computer power than Down Under needed. *Minicomputer* systems were more reasonably priced at $50,000 to $100,000 and were considerably smaller than the mainframe systems. They also investigated microcomputers that were small enough to fit on a desk and cost between $2,000 and $10,000 Down Under decided on a minicomputer system for their factory and distribution centers. Over the next three years they plan to computerize all their accounting functions. ■

Principles and Procedures Summary

A cost accounting system parallels the flow of operations. The four steps in the typical operating cycle of a manufacturer are procurement, production, warehousing, and selling.

Procurement is the purchase of materials, labor, and overhead items for use in the factory. Production consists of the actual manufacturing of goods. Warehousing is the movement of finished goods into the warehouse to await sale. Selling includes finding customers and making shipments of merchandise.

The costs involved in the various steps of the operating cycle are recorded in general ledger accounts, such as Raw Materials, Factory Payroll Clearing, Manufacturing Overhead Control, Work in Process, Finished Goods, and Cost of Goods Sold. As work flows from one step to another, costs flow into and out of accounts related to these steps. This is called matching cost flow and work flow.

When manufacturing involves a number of operations, the cost accounting system may accumulate costs by department or cost center. This arrangement pinpoints responsibility for performance.

The cost accountant develops a firm's cost accounting system to fit its organization and flow of work. The chart of accounts makes provision for appropriate cost accounts in the general ledger.

The typical cost flow starts with the beginning balances in the three inventory accounts: Raw Materials, Work in Process, and Finished Goods. Additional raw materials are purchased, and some are used in manufacturing as direct and indirect materials. Factory wages and salaries are earned and allocated as direct and indirect labor charges. Other manufacturing overhead costs are recorded as incurred. At the end of the month, estimated overhead costs are applied to Work in Process. Next, the cost of goods that have been completed is transferred from Work in Process to Finished Goods. When goods are sold, their cost is charged to Cost of Goods Sold.

The statement of cost of goods manufactured and the income statement utilize figures supplied by the special cost accounts in the general ledger.

Review Questions

1. What are the four basic steps in a typical cycle of operations for a manufacturing firm?
2. What general ledger account(s) are used in recording costs during each of the following steps: (a) procurement, (b) production, (c) warehousing, and (d) selling?
3. The cost of materials, labor, and overhead transferred into production are debited to which account?
4. The total cost of finished goods is removed from Work in Process and transferred to which account?
5. Of the four steps in the production cycle, which step is usually the most complicated to account for and to control? Why?
6. How does a production department differ from a service department? Give an example of each type of department.
7. What does a debit balance in the Manufacturing Overhead Control account at the end of an accounting period represent? What does a credit balance represent?   *less/more*
8. What does the ending balance in the Work in Process account represent?
9. Which inventory account or accounts of a manufacturing company appear on the statement of cost of goods manufactured, and which appear on the income statement?
10. What does the beginning balance in the Finished Goods account represent?

Managerial Discussion Questions

1. How does departmentalization aid management in controlling costs?
2. Why is it important that cost accounting systems reflect the flow of costs?
3. Why is good organization important in cost control?
4. Describe how the three inventory accounts assist management in controlling manufacturing operations and production.

Exercises

1. **Analyzing Work in Process.** Work in Process for the Decorative Manufacturing Company is given on page 36.
   a. What are the manufacturing costs for the month?
   b. What is the cost of goods manufactured during the month?
   c. What is the ending inventory balance?

Work in Process				
Jan. 1	Balance	84,390	Jan. 31 Transferred to	
31	Materials	258,714	Finished Goods	705,226
31	Labor	309,167		
31	Mfg. Overhead	140,281		

2. **Analyzing manufacturing overhead.** During May the Manufacturing Overhead Control account for McClear Manufacturers had various debit postings that totaled $86,492 and a credit posting for $89,636. Was the manufacturing overhead for the month overapplied or underapplied? By what amount?

3. **Identifying work flow procedures.** For each procedure identify the steps in the manufacturing cycle in which it occurs: procurement, production, warehousing, or selling.

   a. Materials are requisitioned and transferred to the factory.
   b. An order is sent to a supplier to obtain more raw materials.
   c. A customer's order is received and filled.
   d. The weekly payroll is recorded.
   e. Finished goods are placed in the appropriate storage bins.
   f. New employees are interviewed and hired by the personnel department.
   g. Finished goods are shipped to the customer.
   h. Manufacturing overhead costs are estimated and charged to the product.
   i. A shipment of raw materials arrives and is unpacked.

4. **Analyzing manufacturing transactions.** Eight transactions in the manufacturing process are recorded in the T accounts below. Each transaction is coded by a letter and may be spread over several accounts. Describe what happened in each transaction.

Raw Materials		Work in Process		Vouchers Payable		Factory Payroll Clearing	
(A) 35,000	(B) 28,000	(B) 26,000	(G) 58,500		(A) 35,000	(C) 33,000	(D) 33,000
		(D) 25,000			(E) 3,300		
		(F) 14,200					

Finished Goods		Salaries and Wages Payable		Manufacturing Overhead Control		Cost of Goods Sold	
(G) 58,500	(H) 49,700		(C) 33,000	(B) 2,000	(F) 14,200	(H) 49,700	
				(D) 8,000			
				(E) 3,300			

Problems

PROBLEM 2-1. Recording manufacturing costs. Taylor Corporation manufactures industrial springs and coils that are sold to other companies for assembling into machinery. The following costs were incurred during the month of August 19X7:

1 Raw materials purchased: $182,460
2 Raw materials used: direct materials, $120,290; indirect materials, $24,630
3 Factory wages earned: $92,740
4 Factory wages allocated: direct labor, $77,820; indirect labor, $14,920
5 Voucher recorded for manufacturing overhead costs incurred: $22,800
6 Depreciation on factory building: $30,490
7 Depreciation on factory equipment: $7,480
8 Manufacturing overhead costs applied to jobs worked on: $108,360
9 Finished goods transferred to warehouse: $281,460
10 Finished goods sold and shipped to customers: $198,150 (cost)
11 Finished goods sold and billed to customers $297,225 (selling price)

Instructions

Prepare the general journal entries dated August 31, 19X7.

PROBLEM 2-2. Recording and posting manufacturing costs. United Furniture Inc. manufactures bookshelves. The total manufacturing costs for July 19X5 are as follows:

1 Raw materials purchased: $92,430
2 Raw materials used: direct materials $82,475; indirect materials, $16,175
3 Factory wages earned: $106,620
4 Factory wages allocated: direct labor, $84,060; indirect labor, $22,560
5 Other overhead costs incurred: $30,563 (credit the total to Vouchers Payable 201)
6 Estimated manufacturing overhead costs applied to jobs worked on: $67,248
7 Finished goods transferred to warehouse: $229,348
8 Finished goods sold and shipped to customers: $231, 898
9 Finished goods sold and billed to customers: $336,252 (selling price)

Instructions

1. Prepare the general journal entries to record each of the costs. Date the entries July 31, 19X5.
2. Post the general journal entries to the general ledger accounts. The general ledger accounts 121, 122, and 126 have the following opening balances at July 1, 19X5: Raw Materials 121, $64,820 Dr.; Work in Process 122, $48,370 Dr.; Finished Goods 126, $32,090 Dr. *Save your working papers for use in Problem 2-3.*

PROBLEM 2-3. Preparing financial statements. This problem is a continuation of Problem 2-2.

Instructions

1. Prepare the statement of cost of goods manufactured.
2. Prepare the income statement. Assume selling expenses of $39,174; administrative expenses of $12,800; and estimated federal income taxes of $21,960.

PROBLEM 2-4. Analyzing journal entries. Detroit Custom Automotive, Inc., which uses a job order cost accounting system, recorded the following journal entries during June 19X5:

June 30	Raw Materials	590,360.00	
	Vouchers Payable		590,360.00
30	Work in Process	475,820.00	
	Manufacturing Overhead Control	58,040.00	
	Raw Materials		533,860.00
30	Factory Payroll Clearing	688,713.00	
	Salaries and Wages Payable		688,713.00
30	Work in Process	583,980.00	
	Manufacturing Overhead Control	104,733.00	
	Factory Payroll Clearing		688,713.00
30	Manufacturing Overhead Control	86,190.00	
	Vouchers Payable		86,190.00
30	Work in Process	257,310.00	
	Manufacturing Overhead Control		257,310.00
30	Finished Goods	1,185,200.00	
	Work in Process		1,185,200.00
30	Cost of Goods Sold	1,037,540.00	
	Finished Goods		1,037,540.00
30	Accounts Receivable	1,944,680.00	
	Sales		1,944,680.00

Instructions

Describe each transaction that took place.

PROBLEM 2-1A. Recording manufacturing costs The Alvarez Manufacturing Corporation uses the job order cost system in the manufacturing of its finished product. The costs for the month of April 19X4 follow:

Raw materials purchased on account: $87,920
Raw materials used: direct materials, $67,230; indirect materials, $8,190
Factory wages and salaries earned: $97,780
Factory wages allocated: direct labor, $82,160; indirect labor, $15,620
Voucher recorded for manufacturing overhead costs incurred: $32,660
Depreciation on the factory building: $15,800
Depreciation on factory equipment: $13,000
Manufacturing overhead costs applied to jobs worked on: $84,560
Finished goods transferred to warehouse: $221,500
Finished goods sold and shipped to customers: $192,840
Finished goods sold and billed to customers: $268,200

Instructions

Prepare the general journal entries dated April 30, 19X4.

PROBLEM 2-2A. Recording and posting manufacturing costs. The Stanford Company is a manufacturer of small appliances. The total manufacturing costs for the month of January 19X8, follow:

Raw materials purchased: $202,750
Raw materials used: direct materials, $188,240; indirect materials, $22,650
Factory wages earned: $306,800
Factory wages allocated: direct labor, $241,590 indirect labor, $65,210
Other overhead costs incurred: $88,720 (credit the total to Vouchers Payable 201)
Estimated manufacturing overhead costs applied to jobs worked on: $174,340
Finished goods transferred to warehouse: $581,350
Finished goods sold and shipped to customers: $572,510
Finished goods sold and billed to customers: $908,776 (selling price)

Instructions

1. Prepare the general journal entries to record each of the costs. Date the entries January 31, 19X8.
2. Post the general journal entries to the general ledger accounts. The general ledger accounts 121, 122, and 126 have the following opening balances at January 1, 19X8: Raw Materials 121, $64,820 Dr.; Work in Process 122, $83,920 Dr.; Finished Goods 126, $66,200 Dr. *Save your working papers for use in Problem 2-3A.*

PROBLEM 2-3A. Preparing financial statements. This problem is a continuation of Problem 2-2A.

Instructions

1. Prepare the statement of cost of goods manufactured.
2. Prepare the income statement. Assume selling expenses of $184,922 administrative expenses of $85,200 and estimated federal income taxes of $22,430.

PROBLEM 2-4A. Analyzing journal entries. The Banking Equipment Company, which uses a job order cost system, recorded the following journal entries during March 19X6:

19X6			
Mar. 31	Raw Materials	830,710.00	
	Vouchers Payable		830,710.00
31	Work in Process	682,340.00	
	Manufacturing Overhead Control	64,950.00	
	Raw Materials		747,290.00
31	Factory Payroll Clearing	764,240.00	
	Salaries and Wages Payable		764,240.00
31	Work in Process	691,570.00	
	Manufacturing Overhead Control	72,670.00	
	Factory Payroll Clearing		764,240.00
31	Manufacturing Overhead Control	407,060.00	
	Vouchers Payable		407,060.00
31	Work in Process	558,120.00	
	Manufacturing Overhead Control		558,120.00

Mar. 31	Finished Goods	1,735,290.00	
	Work in Process		1,735,290.00
31	Cost of Goods Sold	1,529,640.00	
	Finished Goods		1,529,640.00
31	Accounts Receivable	2,247,424.00	
	Sales		2,247,424.00

Instructions

Describe each transaction that took place.

Managerial Decisions

CASE 2-1. The Novelty Mug Company was formed recently to manufacture plastic mugs that are custom-decorated with logos designed to customer specifications. The first step in the manufacturing process is molding plastic into the shape of a mug. The second step is applying the logo to the mugs. The final step in the manufacturing process is putting the mugs in an attractive box suitable for gift-giving.

The company has purchased a small building in which to conduct its operations. A portion of the building will contain the factory and have a small staff to handle maintenance and cleaning, factory payroll, and purchasing, receiving, and storing materials. The rest of the building will be occupied by the sales staff and the administrative offices. The president of the company will oversee all operations.

1. Describe the flow of costs for the Novelty Mug Company's manufacturing operations.
2. How does having an organization chart help control operations?
3. Prepare an organization chart for the Novelty Mug Company.

3

Purchasing Materials

■ ■ ■

The last chapter presented the elements of the job order cost cycle and how they relate to each other. The figures that flowed through Space Savers' general ledger cost accounts were provided in summary form. In the rest of the chapters in this section, you will find out where the cost figures originated. You will first study the detailed procedures and records required to account for materials purchased and used. Then you will examine the procedures used to account for labor and manufacturing overhead.

Need for Control of Materials

In most manufacturing businesses, the cost of raw materials is a major part of the total manufacturing cost of each product. Decisions regarding materials and their management are based on product knowledge, good judgment, and accurate, up-to-the-minute data. These are just a few of the problems involved.

- Quality and cost of materials must meet the specifications on which sales prices are based.
- Correct quantities and types of materials must be on hand at the right time for production to move on schedule.
- Materials must be protected from loss or theft.
- Funds must not be tied up in inventory when they could be used more profitably elsewhere.
- Risks of spoilage and obsolescence must be minimized.
- Costs of materials handling and storage must be kept to a minimum.

Specific procedures and methods for controlling materials vary from company to company. Size, organization, and type of goods produced are some of the factors involved. Most modern systems of inventory control include the following features:

- Formal procedures for ordering and paying for materials
- Physical safeguards for receiving, storing, and issuing materials
- Perpetual inventory system to provide a written record of the quantity and value of each type of material received, issued, and on hand

You are already familiar with the size, structure, and operations of Space Savers, Inc. Space Savers' accounting system is designed to achieve maximum internal control. This chapter deals with the procedures for purchasing raw materials. Note that purchases are charged to Raw Materials 121. In order to simplify the discussion on materials, it is assumed that manual records are maintained at Space Savers. In reality, many records used in purchasing, storing, issuing, and controlling inventory are maintained on computers. Computerized records and procedures related to materials are discussed later in this chapter and in Chapters 4 and 5. You will notice that both manual and automated systems require careful attention to internal control.

Materials Purchasing Procedures

The responsibility for purchasing materials is given to the *purchasing agent*. This person must buy materials in correct quantities, at the proper time, and at the most economical cost to the company. At Space Savers, the purchasing agent's staff is part of the procurement section of the General Factory Department. In a larger organization, a whole department might be required to conduct purchasing activities.

The purchasing staff keeps informed of various sources of supply, negotiates purchase contracts, prepares purchase orders, and follows through on delivery. The routine work of the purchasing staff begins upon receipt of a purchase requisition.

Reorder Routine

Let us trace the typical reorder routine step by step. To determine when an item has reached a level where it should be reordered, Space Savers considers these factors:

- The rate at which the material is used.
- The amount of time it takes for the material to be delivered from the supplier. This is known as the *lead time*.
- The minimum level of material that should be on hand to ensure that the company does not run out of the material. This is known as *safety stock*.

For example, the *reorder point* for K-193 folding table-leg sections is 200. Space Savers wants to have at least 100 folding table-leg sections on hand at all times. Since 20 sections are used in production each day and it takes five days to receive an order, the reorder point is calculated as follows.

20 sections (daily usage) × 5 days (lead time)	100
Plus safety stock	100
Reorder point	200

If an order for folding table-leg sections is processed as expected within five days, then the new table-leg sections should arrive at Space Savers as the inventory reaches the safety stock level of 100. Even if the order is delayed, there will still be 100 table-leg sections on hand to meet production requirements.

The standard quantity to be ordered varies from item to item. It should reflect the quantity necessary to get the best price while keeping inventory at an appropriate level to ensure uninterrupted production. To determine this quantity, it is necessary to consider the costs of placing an order as well as the costs of carrying the items in the inventory. The costs of placing an order include:

- Costs of maintaining the purchasing department
- Costs of operating the receiving department
- Clerical costs of processing an order

The costs of carrying items in the inventory include:

- Costs of handling and storing material
- Insurance costs
- Losses due to theft, obsolescence, and spoilage
- Clerical costs of maintaining inventory records

To determine the most advantageous number of units to order, a special formula called the *economic order quantity* (EOQ) has been developed. It is computed as follows:

$$EOQ = \sqrt{\frac{2 \times \text{annual requirements} \times \text{cost of an order}}{\text{cost to carry a single item}}}$$

If Space Savers' cost to order is $1.08, the cost to carry an item in inventory is $.75; and if the firm requires 5,000 table-leg sections during the year, then the EOQ of 120 is calculated as follows:

$$EOQ = \sqrt{\frac{2 \times 5,000 \times 1.08}{.75}}$$

$$= \sqrt{\frac{10,800}{.75}}$$

$$= \sqrt{14,400}$$

$$= 120$$

Purchase Requisition

Once the number of K-193 folding table-leg sections falls below 200, the storeroom supervisor completes a purchase requisition requesting that 120 table-leg sections be ordered. The *purchase requisition* is a properly approved (authorized), written request for materials. An original and one copy of the purchase requisition are made, as shown on page 44. The original is sent to the purchasing unit as a request for the materials. The copy is retained in the storeroom files. Some companies require that three or more copies be completed for various uses.

Purchase Order

When the purchasing staff receives the purchase requisition, a source of supply must be selected. Riverton Manufacturers is the regular supplier of K-193 folding table-leg sections because this firm owns exclusive patent rights. Under other circumstances, several suppliers might be asked to quote prices or make bids. In choosing a supplier, the purchasing agent considers dependability, quality of material, delivery date, and similar factors as well as price.

After the supplier has been chosen, the purchasing agent prepares a purchase

SPACE SAVERS INC.

1180 NORTHERN AVE.
CHICAGO, IL 60785

Purchase Requisition

No. 728

DATE _9/16/X1_
DATE WANTED _9/25/X1_

Ship To

Storeroom

Order From

Riverton Manufacturers
51 Riverton La.
Newark, N.J. 07268

QUANTITY	MATERIAL NO.	DESCRIPTION	PURPOSE
_120_	_K-193_	_Folding table-leg sections, 30"_	_Raw Materials_

CHARGE
▶ ACCT. _121_
▶ JOB _____
▶ DEPT. _____

Requisitioned by _Haw_
Approved by _L.J.J._

1. _Purchasing_
2. _Storeroom_

FORM NO. 1212

order, as shown on the following page. The purchase order represents written authorization to the supplier to ship the specified material. This form contains all necessary details, such as delivery date, method of shipment, unit price, and account number to be charged. The number of copies prepared varies from company to company. At Space Savers, five copies of the purchase order are prepared.

The original is sent to the supplier. Two copies are kept by the purchasing unit in an unfilled order file. One copy is returned to the storeroom as verification. The storeroom clerk compares the purchase order with the requisition and places the purchase order in an on-order file. The final copy tells the receiving clerk when the materials should arrive. This procedure allows time for any preparations that would be needed to receive the shipment, such as designating space for the materials in the storeroom. Space Savers' internal control system requires that all purchase order forms be prenumbered. The purchasing agent must complete a written order for every purchase. At the end of each month, the cost accountant verifies that all numbered forms either have been sent to suppliers, as shown by the copies, or are on hand. This ensures that purchase orders are used only for authorized purposes.

Receiving Report

When the materials are received from the supplier, they go to the receiving clerk. The receiving clerk is responsible for unpacking them, checking quantities and physical condition, and delivering them to the storeroom. Some materials may be of such a technical nature that laboratory tests must be conducted to make sure that they meet all specifications. In this case, the receiving clerk merely counts the items to make sure of the quantities. Laboratory personnel test the materials and send a report on the results to the purchasing unit.

The receiving clerk's copy of the purchase order is a *blind copy*. This means that it does not indicate the quantities ordered. A blind copy ensures an independent check

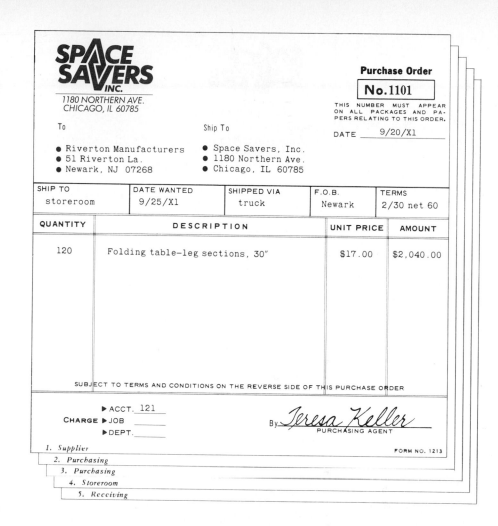

Folding table—leg sections, 30″ ... $17.00 ... $2,040.00 (values within the purchase order image)

of quantities by the receiving clerk. After counting and inspecting the materials, the clerk prepares a receiving report. The *receiving report* shows all details of the shipment, including comments on the condition of materials received.

Note that the receiving clerk has indicated on Receiving Report 207, shown on page 46, that 20 sections were rejected because they were damaged in shipment. All descriptions must agree with the purchase order descriptions to avoid confusion and errors. Some companies merely prepare additional blind copies of the purchase order to serve as the receiving report. This saves the time needed for the receiving clerk to write a description of the material.

Space Savers requires four copies of the receiving report. The original and one copy are sent to the purchasing unit, where they are compared with the purchase order and the supplier's invoice. One copy accompanies the materials to the storeroom for comparison with the purchase order and entry in the storeroom records. The storeroom supervisor signs the final copy to confirm that the materials have reached the storeroom. This copy is then kept in the receiving clerk's permanent file.

SPACE SAVERS INC.

1180 NORTHERN AVE.
CHICAGO, IL 60785

Received From
Riverton Manufacturers
51 Riverton Lane
Newark, N J 07268

Receiving Report
No. 207

DATE RECEIVED *9/25/X1*
PURCHASE ORDER NO. *1101*
INVOICE NO. *15374*

SHIPPED VIA *S.E. Motor Freight*	TRANSPORTATION CHARGES (PREPAID) COLLECT	RECEIVED BY

QUANTITY RECEIVED	QUANTITY ACCEPTED	QUANTITY REJECTED	DESCRIPTION	WEIGHT
120	*100*	*20*	*Folding table-leg sections, 30"*	*600 lb*

INSPECTION RECORD

QUANTITY ACCEPTED	QUANTITY RETURNED	REASON FOR REJECTION
100	*20*	*20 sections bent in shipment*

DATE *9/25/X1* STOREROOM SUPERVISOR *HA W*

1. *Purchasing*
2. *Purchasing*
3. *Storeroom*
4. *Receiving*

FORM NO. 1214

The storeroom clerk records the receipt of raw materials in a subsidiary ledger, the *materials ledger,* by making an entry on the appropriate *materials ledger card.* Materials are also called *stores;* therefore, the materials ledger is also referred to as the *stores ledger.* A separate card, like the one shown on page 47, is kept for each type of material. The card shows receipts, issues, and balance on hand, along with identification, control data, and even cost figures in some systems.

Comparing Documents

When the invoice is received from the supplier, it is sent to the purchasing unit. The invoice will often arrive before the shipment. Many companies prefer this because it allows for verification of the purchase order before the shipment is accepted. The purchasing unit holds the invoice and the purchase order in the *open purchase order file* until the receiving report is available for comparison. The purchasing unit compares the *supplier's invoice (purchase invoice)* with the purchase order and receiving report to make sure of certain points.

MATERIALS LEDGER CARD

Material _Folding table-leg sections, 30"_   Reorder Point _200_
Number _K-193_   Reorder Quantity _120_

DATE	REFERENCE	RECEIVED			ISSUED			BALANCE		
		UNITS	PRICE	AMOUNT	UNITS	PRICE	AMOUNT	UNITS	PRICE	AMOUNT
19X1 Sept. 16	Bal.							175	17 00	2975 00
25	PO1101	100	17 00	1700 00				275	17 00	4675 00

- Goods ordered must have been received in good condition and be those listed on the invoice.
- Terms, unit prices, shipping charges, and other details must agree with order specifications.
- Computations must be correct.

If all documents agree, a member of the staff of the purchasing unit staples together one copy each of the invoice, receiving report, and purchase order and places them in a *completed purchases file* alphabetically by supplier. Next, a disbursement voucher like the one shown on the next page is completed (adjusted to reflect value of damaged items rejected), and a second set of supporting documents is attached to it. (Space Savers normally requests billing in duplicate.) Then the voucher is formally approved and sent to the accounting unit for recording.

Recording the Voucher

When the voucher, invoice, and attached papers reach the accounting unit, the voucher clerk compares quantities, verifies extensions and footings, computes discounts, and checks all other computations. The voucher clerk also checks that all supporting documents are included in the file and that they are properly approved and signed. This double-checking is another part of the internal control system.

After verifying the account distribution against the purchase order, the voucher clerk enters the purchase in the voucher register, as shown on the following page. (Vouchers are often prenumbered for control purposes.) A purchase of direct materials, such as K-193 folding table-leg sections, or indirect materials, such as factory supplies, is entered as a debit in the Raw Materials column and as a credit in the Vouchers Payable column, as shown on page 48.

Note that the summary totals from the October voucher register of Space Savers were the source of Entry A in Chapter 2, debiting Raw Materials.

After the entry is made in the voucher register, the voucher is sent to the treasurer's office. Here it is filed in the unpaid vouchers file according to the last date on which the discount may be taken.

Paying the Voucher

Before the due date, the voucher is removed from the unpaid vouchers file. An employee on the treasurer's staff prepares a check for the net amount of the voucher. The check is then entered in the check register. The employee marks the voucher

DISBURSEMENT VOUCHER

SPACE SAVERS INC.
1180 NORTHERN AVE.
CHICAGO, IL 60785

VOUCHER NO.	10-14
ISSUED DATE	10/2/X1
DISCOUNT DATE	10/24/X1
DUE DATE	11/23/X1

Payee Riverton Manufacturers
51 Riverton Lane
Newark, NJ 07268

INVOICE DATE	TERMS	INVOICE NO.	AMOUNT
9/24/X1	2/30, n/60	15374	$2,040.00
		Less damaged items returned	340.00
			$1,700.00

DISTRIBUTION	
ACCOUNT NUMBER	AMOUNT
121	1,700 00

PRICE O.K.	G.H.
MATERIAL RECEIVED	J.B.
EXTENSIONS O.K.	J.L.N.
GROSS AMOUNT	$1,700.00
DISCOUNT	$ 34.00
NET PAID	$1,666.00
APPROVED FOR PAY.	R.H.
PAID BY CHECK NO. _____ DATE	

FORM NO. 653

"Paid" by using a rubber stamp and enters the check number and date paid on the voucher. The check is mailed to the supplier (Riverton Manufacturers), and the voucher is returned to the voucher clerk. The voucher clerk enters the check number and date of payment in the voucher register.

The voucher, with invoice and supporting documents, is then placed in the *paid vouchers file.*

VOUCHER REGISTER for Month of ____October____ 19 X1

DATE	VOU. NO.	PAYABLE TO	PAID DATE	CHECK NO.	VOUCHERS PAYABLE CR. 201	RAW MATERIALS DR. 121
Oct. 2	10-14	Riverton Manufacturers	10/22	1603	1,700 00	1,700 00
31		Total			156,940 00	68,760 00
					✓	✓

Raw Materials	121	
(Bal.)	44,114.00	
(A)	68,760.00	

Principles of Internal Control

The purchasing procedures used by Space Savers are practical and efficient. They also follow important principles of internal control.

- A request for a purchase must be made by an authorized person.
- A purchase order must be prepared and approved by an authorized person after a purchase requisition has been received.
- All materials received must be carefully checked to see that they correspond to those ordered and are in good condition.
- Payment is made only after proper approval.
- Various steps in the purchasing procedure are delegated to different persons to lessen the risk of fraud or error.
- In order to account for all steps in the purchasing process, all documents are prenumbered.

Special Purchasing Procedures

The normal purchasing procedures can easily be adapted to meet special circumstances.

Bill of Materials

Sometimes several jobs requiring the same materials are started at about the same time. The usual quantities on hand of standard stores items may not be sufficient. To avoid this problem, the production manager may prepare a bill of materials when a new sales order is received. The *bill of materials* lists all materials required on the job and the date they will be needed, as shown on the top of the next page. This record enables the storeroom supervisor to check the quantity of material on hand to make sure that enough is available. To avoid costly delays, the purchasing staff may be asked to buy more materials in advance. The bill of materials used by some companies contains columns for unit costs and total costs. Such a bill may later be used as a materials requisition.

Debit and Credit Memorandums

Occasionally, damaged or defective materials are received. These items are usually returned to the supplier immediately. A note of the return is made on the receiving clerk's copy of the purchase order and on the receiving report. The purchasing agent will then prepare a debit memorandum. The *debit memorandum* is a notice to the vendor of a deduction from the invoice for the cost of the returned materials, as shown on the next page. (Accounting for materials returned after the voucher has been recorded is discussed in Chapter 4.)

There are some cases, too, when not all the materials ordered and shown on the invoice are actually received. If the supplier indicates that the remainder will be sent later, all documents may be held until the balance of the materials is received. If the supplier indicates that the balance will not be shipped within a satisfactory period of time, the materials received may be returned. In most cases, however, the buyer will keep the goods. The purchasing agent will issue a debit memorandum to the vendor for the amount of the goods short.

Sometimes a supplier ships more materials than were ordered. If the materials are

Bill of Materials

Plainview Manufacturing Corp.

Plainview, State 10699

Job _110_
To Be Started _Nov. 10, 19X1_
Date _October 8, 19X1_
For _Goldberg Stores_

WILL REQUIRE THE FOLLOWING MATERIALS:

UNITS	MATERIAL NO.	DESCRIPTION	MATERIALS ISSUED UNIT COST	TOTAL COST
500	K-25	Leg braces		
500	T-16	Klander frames, 24" × 48"		
500	L-22	Mica tops, 30" × 60"		

Materials Received by _____
Date _____

G. Stanopoulos
Department Head

not needed, the purchasing agent normally authorizes their return. Sometimes, however, they are kept for future use. In this case, if the materials have not been included in the vendor's invoice, the purchasing agent prepares a *credit memorandum* for the additional cost. (Many companies will amend the purchase order to include the extra goods shipped instead of issuing a credit memorandum.)

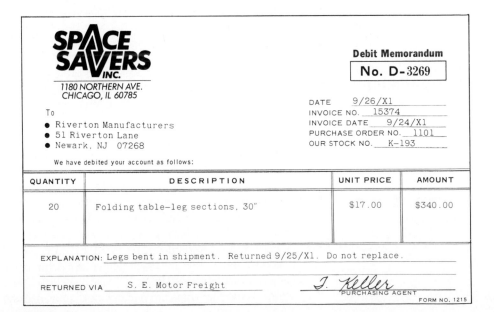

SPACE SAVERS INC.

1180 NORTHERN AVE.
CHICAGO, IL 60785

Debit Memorandum

No. D-3269

To
- Riverton Manufacturers
- 51 Riverton Lane
- Newark, NJ 07268

DATE _9/26/X1_
INVOICE NO. _15374_
INVOICE DATE _9/24/X1_
PURCHASE ORDER NO. _1101_
OUR STOCK NO. _K-193_

We have debited your account as follows:

QUANTITY	DESCRIPTION	UNIT PRICE	AMOUNT
20	Folding table—leg sections, 30"	$17.00	$340.00

EXPLANATION: _Legs bent in shipment. Returned 9/25/X1. Do not replace._

RETURNED VIA _S. E. Motor Freight_

J. Keller
PURCHASING AGENT

FORM NO. 1215

An On-Line Materials Purchases System

Paper Unlimited produces 25 styles of tablets and notebooks. They purchase lined and unlined paper in various colors from ten suppliers. At the factory, the paper is cut to size, gummed at one edge, and attached to cardboard backings or covers. Every June and November production must speed up in preparation for the start of a new school semester. Last year, with so much going on, requisitions and order forms kept getting lost. Salespeople had to wait two weeks for stock reports and sales totals. The management of Paper Unlimited decided to computerize their materials purchasing system to have more up-to-date information available and to better organize the purchasing process.

In computerizing the materials purchasing system, one of the first tasks was to set up computerized files. A computer *file* is a collection of data in a form that the computer can use. Such files are similar to the files previously stored in file cabinets; however, these files are stored on the computer in its memory. *Memory* is internal storage capacity, which varies from machine to machine. Mainframes typically can hold thousands of pages worth of data in memory, whereas microcomputers can hold a few pages to perhaps a hundred pages worth of data. To increase storage capacity, external devices such as magnetic disks or tapes are used.

Paper Unlimited's computer includes memory capacity to hold three files for materials purchases: an inventory file, a supplier file, and an open purchase order file. Upon receipt of a purchase requisition, the purchasing agent will scan the supplier file and choose a supplier. The computer will prepare a purchase order and the purchase order information will be added to the open purchase order file.

When the order arrives, the receiving room clerk will count the items and enter the number into the receiving room terminal (also indicating which, if any, raw materials must be returned). The computer will compare the items ordered (stored in the open purchase order file) with the items received, prepare a receiving report, and update the open purchase order file, the inventory file, and the supplier file.

In addition to faster processing of requisitions, the number of reports in this system is minimized. Information that would have appeared in two weeks in printed reports under the manual system can be accessed, on demand, through the computer terminals for viewing on the screen. ■

Principles and Procedures Summary

Raw materials must be carefully controlled to protect the firm's large investment and to ensure that enough supplies are on hand to meet production schedules.

Purchasing involves the buying of materials in correct quantities, at the proper time, and at the most economical cost to the company. Purchasing procedures are performed by a purchasing unit headed by the purchasing agent. The purchasing cycle actually begins when a purchase requisition is prepared by the storeroom supervisor or the production manager. Next, a purchase order is issued. When the materials are received from the supplier, the payment of the bill is authorized. The purchase is then recorded in the voucher register. Finally, the check in settlement of the bill is issued and recorded in the check register. Many of these steps may be handled by a computer.

All purchasing procedures should reflect certain key principles of internal control. Requests for purchases must be made only by authorized persons. Purchase orders must be properly approved. All materials received must be carefully counted and inspected. Payment should be made only upon proper approval. Purchasing responsibilities should involve a number of persons to lessen risk of fraud or error.

Special recording procedures can be used for handling damaged, lost, or defective materials, and for shortages and overages in shipment.

Review Questions

1. List three factors in determining techniques for controlling materials.
2. How does a purchase requisition differ from a purchase order?
3. What is a receiving report?
4. What is the formula for computing the economic order quantity?
5. What individual costs are considered in determining the total cost to place an order? What individual costs are considered when computing the total cost to carry an item in inventory?
6. Why is a *blind copy* of the purchase order sent to the receiving department?
7. What type of information is shown on a materials ledger card?
8. What procedures should be followed before an entry is made in the voucher register to record the purchase of raw materials?
9. Define *bill of materials*.
10. What document is prepared to inform the supplier of a deduction from an invoice for the cost of goods returned to the supplier?
11. Which departments are responsible for each of the following procedures?
    a. Issuing purchase requisitions
    b. Issuing purchase orders
    c. Recording approved vouchers
    d. Preparing checks to pay vouchers
    e. Counting goods received

Managerial Discussion Questions

1. What are some advantages of maintaining a materials ledger?
2. Under what circumstances would a bill of materials be prepared?
3. Before a disbursement voucher is recorded and approved for payment, copies of the purchases requisition, purchase order, receiving report, and purchase invoices should be compared and double-checked for accuracy. Why?
4. List at least three procedures for purchasing materials that should be followed in order to achieve good internal control. Explain how each helps in achieving internal control.
5. Why is it important for management to have complete and current data on the cost of materials?
6. Prepare a table that shows each step in the purchasing process, who is responsible for each step, and any documents or reports that would be produced during each step. Use the following column headings in the preparation of the table.

   Step in Purchasing Materials
   Person/Department
   Documents/Reports

Exercises

1. **Calculating the amount of a disbursement voucher.** Voucher No. 10-16 was prepared from a purchase invoice for $25,840 and a debit memorandum for $1,100 (for damaged goods returned). What is the gross amount of the voucher?

2. **Calculating the ending balance from a materials ledger card.** Calculate the ending balance of Material No. K-374 (folding-leg sections) based on the following information from the materials ledger card:

	Units	Amount per Unit
Beginning balance	183	$12.50
Issued	159	12.50
Received	225	12.50

3. **Calculating the reorder point.** The Jackson Company uses 8,000 pounds of Material ST400 every day in production. If it takes 12 days for an order to be delivered and if the company always wants to have a three-day supply on hand, what is the point at which it should reorder Material ST400?

4. **Calculating the economic reorder quantity.** The Brent Corporation has determined that the cost to place an order for aluminum couplings is $5 and the cost to carry this item in inventory is $8. If 8,000 couplings are required for production each year, calculate the economic order quantity.

5. **Calculating the net amount of disbursement vouchers.** Calculate the *net* amount of the following disbursement vouchers:

    a. Gross amount of invoice: $25,730; terms: 3/10, n/30; debit memorandum: $1,380.

    b. Gross amount of invoice: $125,703; terms: 4/20, n/60; debit memorandum: $5,460.

Problems

PROBLEM 3-1. Recording raw materials purchases. Western Manufacturers, 231 West Superior Street, Duluth, Minnesota 55802, has an effective system of internal control. During April 19X5, the following transactions took place.

Apr. 4 Purchase Requisition 278 is received in the purchasing department. Purchase Order 644 is issued. The following materials are requisitioned and ordered:

Units	Material No.	Description	Purpose
4,390	603	2′ × 4′ plastic sheeting	Stores
840	622	3′ × 5′ plastic sheeting	Stores
1,890	642	4′ × 6′ plastic sheeting	Stores

14 All materials listed on Purchase Order 644 are received. Receiving Report 703 is completed.

14 All materials listed on Receiving Report 703 go to the storeroom.

19 Debit Memorandum 385 is prepared.

19 Supplier's Invoice 4-539 (shown on the next page) is received. Disbursement Voucher 4-740 is prepared and sent to the accounting department.

Instructions

1. Issue Purchase Order 644 to Quality Products, Inc., 565 Morgan Avenue, Pittsburgh, Pennsylvania 15219. This firm supplies the standard stores that are listed on Purchase Requisition 278. Request delivery to the storeroom on April 28 via motor freight. The terms are 2/10, n/30 f.o.b Duluth. The unit prices are $1.20

QUALITY PRODUCTS, INC.

565 MORGAN AVENUE
PITTSBURGH, PA 15219
(412) 555-8720

SOLD TO   Western Manufacturers
          231 West Superior Street
          Duluth, MN 55802

	INVOICE DATE	INVOICE NUMBER
	4/7/X5	4-539

DATE OF ORDER	CUST. ORDER NO.	TERMS	SHIPPED VIA	F.O.B.
April 4, 19X4	644	2/10, n/30	Industrial Freight Co.	Duluth

QUANTITY	DESCRIPTION	UNIT PRICE	EXTENSION	TOTAL
4,390	603 – 2' × 4' plastic sheeting	$1.20	$5,268.00	
840	622 – 3' × 5' plastic sheeting	1.90	1,596.00	
1,890	642 – 4' × 6' plastic sheeting	2.60	4,914.00	$11,778.00

for each 2' × 4' plastic sheet, $1.90 for each 3' × 5' plastic sheet, and $2.60 for each 4' × 6' plastic sheet. The purchase is charged to Raw Materials 121. Sign your name as the purchasing agent.

2. As the receiving clerk, issue Receiving Report 703. Note that 140 of the 2' × 4' sheets are being returned to the supplier because of imperfections in the sheets. They need not be replaced. The weights are $\frac{1}{10}$ (.10) of a pound each for the 2' × 4' sheets, $\frac{1}{4}$ (.25) of a pound each for the 3' × 5' sheets, and $\frac{1}{2}$ (.50) of a pound each for the 4' × 6' sheets. Record the weights of the goods accepted. The shipment is delivered by the Industrial Freight Company on April 14, 19X5. Charges are prepaid. Sign your name under Received by.

3. Assume that you are the storeroom supervisor. Sign Receiving Report 703 indicating that the materials have been turned over to the storeroom. Post the receipt of the materials to the materials ledger cards. Note the previous balances and the reorder points.

Material No.	BALANCE		Reorder Point
	Units	Amount	
603	2,540	$3,048.00	2,540
622	600	1,140.00	600
642	960	2,496.00	960

4. Assume that you are the purchasing agent. Prepare Debit Memorandum 385 for 140 imperfect sheets returned to the supplier via motor express.

5. As the purchasing agent, compare the supplier's invoice (shown above) with Purchase Order 644 and Receiving Report 703. Prepare Disbursement Voucher 4-740.

6. You represent the accounting department. Complete the first five lines of the

verification block. Lines 1 to 3 require your initials to show that the verification has been completed.

PROBLEM 3-2. Journalizing raw materials purchases. The following are transactions of the Parker Company for the month of November 19X4.

Nov. 4 Purchase Requisition 1185 for 4,800 units of Material 145 is prepared by the storeroom clerk. The material is to be ordered from the Cumberland County Corporation for $21.50 per unit. Terms are 1/10, n/30.

5 Purchase Order 11-48 is completed for materials requisitioned on Requisition 1185.

21 Materials ordered from the Cumberland County Corporation on Purchase Order 11-48 are received. Of the 4,800 units received, 510 are rejected for imperfections and returned at once. Receiving Report 11-11 is prepared. The purchase invoice is included in the carton.

21 A debit memorandum to the Cumberland County Corporation for materials returned is prepared.

21 Materials received today from the Cumberland County Corporation are transferred to the storeroom and entered in the materials ledger.

24 Disbursement Voucher 11-141 to the Cumberland County Corporation is prepared for the amount owed on the firm invoice.

25 A check to the Cumberland County Corporation for the amount due, less discount, is prepared and mailed.

Instructions

Record in general journal form the transactions needing entries.

PROBLEM 3-3. Recording disbursement vouchers. The following vouchers were recorded by the Lincoln Manufacturing Company during the month of November 19X4. For each voucher, determine the amount of the voucher and record it in a voucher register. Foot the columns.

a. Voucher 11-1 payable to the Transcontinental Supply Company. The invoice was for 1,380 units of Material 4-87 at $12.95 each. The receiving report indicates that 1,380 were received. None were defective.

b. Voucher 11-2 payable to the Van Dyke Corporation. The invoice was for 4,398 units of Material 4-113 at $9.63 each and 5,800 units of Material 4-189 at $10.41 each. The receiving report indicates that all materials ordered were received. However, 250 units of Material 4-189 were damaged in transit and were returned to the supplier. A debit memorandum was prepared.

c. Voucher 11-3 payable to First Boise, Ltd. The invoice was for 2,800 units of Material 6-28 at $7.68 each. The receiving report indicates that only 2,200 units were received. A debit memorandum for the shortage was prepared.

d. Voucher 11-4 payable to the Gregory Manufacturing Corporation. The invoice was for the following: 6,500 units of Material 3-87 at $7.90 each; 7,930 units of Material 5-83 at $11.30 each; 5,750 units of Material 4-97 at $8.72 each; and 4,200 units of Material 4-30 at $5.90 each. The receiving report indicates that the units ordered were received except for Material 4-97, which was 900 units short. In addition, 200 units of Material 3-87 were defective and were returned to the supplier. A debit memorandum was prepared.

PROBLEM 3-4. Calculating the economic order quantity and the reorder point. The following information relates to materials purchases for the Fairfield Company:

	Material A	Material B
Annual demand for material	4,000 lb	63,375 lb
Cost to place an order	$10	$10
Cost to carry an item	$2	$3
Safety stock	250 lb	750 lb
Lead time	20 days	10 days
Daily usage	15 lb	250 lb

Instructions

1. Calculate the economic order quantity for each material.
2. Calculate the reorder point for each material.
3. How many days late can an order be before the Fairfield Company will run out of each material?
4. How many times during the year will the Fairfield Company have to place an order?

Alternate Problems

PROBLEM 3-1A. Recording raw materials purchases. Western Manufacturers, 231 West Superior Street, Duluth, Minnesota 55802, has an effective system of internal control. During May 19X4, the following transactions took place.

May   2   Purchase Requisition 589 is received in the purchasing unit. Purchase Order 644 is issued. The materials requisitioned and ordered are as follows:

Units	Material No.	Description	Purpose
4,390	603	2' × 4' plastic sheeting	Stores
840	622	3' × 5' plastic sheeting	Stores
1,890	642	4' × 6' plastic sheeting	Stores

16   All materials listed on Purchase Order 644 are received. Receiving Report 703 is completed.

16   All materials listed on Receiving Report 703 go to the storeroom.

17   Debit Memorandum 385 is prepared.

17   Supplier's Invoice 5-85 (on page 57) is received. Disbursement Voucher 5-740 is prepared and sent to the accounting department.

Instructions

1. Issue Purchase Order 644 to the Portland Supply Company, 1605 SW 4th Avenue, Portland, Oregon 97201. This firm supplies the standard stores that are listed on Purchase Requisition 589. Request delivery to the storeroom on May 16 via motor freight. The terms are 2/15, n/45, f.o.b. Duluth. The unit prices are $1.20 for each 2' × 4' plastic sheet, $1.90 for each 3' × 5' plastic sheet, and $2.60 for each 4' × 6' plastic sheet. The purchase is charged to Raw Materials 121. Sign your name as the purchasing agent.
2. Assume that you are the receiving clerk and issue Receiving Report 703. Note

that 210 of the 2′ × 4′ sheets and 60 of the 4′ × 6′ sheets are being returned to the supplier because they were cracked. The weights are $\frac{1}{20}$ (.05) of a pound each for the 2′ × 4′ sheets, $\frac{1}{10}$ (.10) of a pound each for the 3′ × 5′ sheets, and $\frac{1}{4}$ (.25) of a pound each for the 4′ × 6′ sheets. Record the weights of the goods accepted. The shipment is delivered by the MRL Delivery Corporation on May 16, 19X4. Charges are prepaid. Sign your name in the Received by space.

3. Assume that you are the storeroom supervisor. Sign Receiving Report 703 indicating that the materials have been turned over to the storeroom. Post the receipt of the materials to the materials ledger cards. Note the previous balances and the reorder points.

Material	BALANCE		
No.	Units	Amount	Reorder Point
603	2,540	$3,048.00	2,540
622	600	1,140.00	600
642	960	2,496.00	960

4. Assume that you are the purchasing agent. Prepare Debit Memorandum 385 for the damaged sheets returned to the supplier via motor express.

5. As the purchasing agent, compare the supplier's invoice (shown below) with Purchase Order 644 and Receiving Report 703. Prepare Disbursement Voucher 5-740.

6. You represent the accounting department. Complete the first five lines of the verification block. Lines 1–3 require your initials to show that the verification has been completed.

PORTLAND SUPPLY COMPANY

1605 SW 4TH AVENUE
PORTLAND, OR 97201
(503) 555-1120

SOLD TO Western Manufacturers
231 West Superior Street
Duluth, MN 55802

					INVOICE DATE	INVOICE NUMBER
					5/14/X4	5-85

DATE OF ORDER	CUST. ORDER NO.	TERMS	SHIPPED VIA	F.O.B.
May 2, 19X4	644	2/15, n/45	MRL Delivery Corp.	Duluth

QUANTITY	DESCRIPTION	UNIT PRICE	EXTENSION	TOTAL
4,390	603 – 2′ × 4′ plastic sheeting	$1.20	$5,268.00	
840	622 – 3′ × 5′ plastic sheeting	1.90	1,596.00	
1,890	642 – 4′ × 6′ plastic sheeting	2.60	4,914.00	$11,778.00

PROBLEM 3-2A. Journalizing raw materials purchases. The following are transactions of the Kennedy Manufacturing Company for the month of March 19X5. Record in general journal form those transactions that require entries.

Mar. 3   Purchase Requisition 504 for 1,850 units of Material 72 is prepared by the storeroom clerk. The material is to be ordered from International Associates at a cost of $5.20 per unit. Terms are 2/10, n/30.

      4   Purchase Order 3-41 is completed for the materials specified on Purchase Requisition 504.

   23   Materials ordered on Purchase Order 3-41 are received. Of the 1,850 units received, 20 are rejected because they have imperfections and are immediately returned. Receiving Report 594 is prepared. The purchase invoice is included in the carton.

   23   A debit memorandum to International Associates for materials returned is prepared.

   23   Materials received today from International Associates (except those returned) are transferred to the storeroom and entered in the materials ledger.

   24   Disbursement Voucher 3-62 to International Associates is prepared for the amount owed on the firm's invoice.

   25   A check to International Associates for the amount due, after discount, is prepared and mailed.

PROBLEM 3-3A. Recording disbursement vouchers. The following vouchers were recorded by the Northern Maine Lumber Company during the month of February 19X5. For each voucher, determine the amount of the voucher and record it in the voucher register. Foot the columns.

a. Voucher 2-1 payable to the Everglades Supply Company. The invoice was for 10,600 units of Material A187 at $1.86 each. The receiving report indicates that 10,600 units were received. None were defective.

b. Voucher 2-2 payable to H. Robbins, Inc. The invoice was for 8,600 units of Material C135 at $2.58 each and 5,350 units of Material G658 at $2.05 each. The receiving report indicates that all materials ordered were received. However, 500 units of Material G658 were damaged in transit and were returned to the supplier. A debit memorandum was prepared.

c. Voucher 2-3 payable to the Wood By-Products Corporation. The invoice was for 3,800 units of Material H730 at $4.10 each. The receiving report indicates that only 3,500 units were received. A debit memorandum for the shortage was prepared.

d. Voucher 2-4 payable to the Sioux Falls Metals Company. The invoice was for the following: 4,700 units of Material R870 at $1.86 each; 5,940 units of Material P965 at $3.82 each; 8,125 units of Material J560 at $1.40 each; and 6,450 units of Material L385 at $3.27 each. The receiving report indicates that the units ordered were received except for Material J560, which was 400 units short. In addition, 350 units of R870 were defective and were returned to the supplier. A debit memorandum was prepared.

PROBLEM 3-4A. Calculating the economic order quantity and the reorder point. The following information relates to materials purchases for the B.L. Finley Company:

	Material A	Material B
Annual demand for material	120,000 lb	12,500 lb
Cost to place an order	$30	$20
Cost to carry an item	$20	$8
Safety stock	900 lb	2,800 lb
Lead time	2 days	8 days
Daily usage	300 lb	280 lb

Instructions

1. Calculate the economic order quantity for each material.
2. Calculate the reorder point for each material.
3. How many days late can an order be before the B.L. Finley Company will run out of each material?
4. How many times during the year will the company have to place an order?

Managerial Decisions

CASE 3-1. The All-Pro Paint Company packages enamel paint for automobile touch-up work. The paint is packaged in 1-ounce glass bottles. A small steel bearing is placed in each paint-filled bottle to aid in mixing the paint when the bottle is shaken. The bottles come in boxes of 12 dozen bottles, and the steel bearings come in boxes of 1,000 bearings.

The purchasing department prepares serially numbered purchase orders. The original is sent to the supplier. Two copies are kept by the purchasing department and are filed numerically in an open purchase order file. An exact copy of the purchase order is sent to the receiving clerk. When a delivery of materials is received, the receiving clerk writes "OK" beside the item on the purchase order and returns the copy to the purchasing department.

When the receiving clerk has time, he opens the boxes containing the small bottles and counts them. If a box contains any broken bottles, the receiving clerk calls the supplier and asks for replacements.

Rather than count the steel bearings, the receiving clerk weighs them and converts the weight into number of bearings using a conversion table.

Discuss the adequacies and inadequacies of All-Pro's internal control over its purchasing procedures.

CHAPTER

Storing and Issuing Materials

■ ■ ■

Internal control procedures for purchasing must be matched by similar procedures for storing and issuing materials in order to truly safeguard the investment. These precautionary measures are necessary to avoid damage, waste, theft, and obsolescence. Physical controls begin the moment that the materials are delivered to the storeroom, and continue to be applied during storage and issuance. Written controls begin with the receiving report and recording in the materials ledger, and continue through entries to record issuance and use.

Storage

At Space Savers, Inc., admission to the storeroom area is carefully restricted to the personnel under the immediate supervision of the storeroom supervisor. The storeroom supervisor is responsible for the materials ledger, for the protection of materials in the storeroom, and for identification of the materials. Each type of material is assigned a number, indicating the type of material and its location. Materials are stored in a systematic manner in bins, on racks, or on shelves.

Attached to each bin or rack is a bin tag. The *bin tag* is an informal but carefully maintained record showing the quantities of the material received, issued, and on hand at all times. The bin tag for K-193 table-leg sections is shown at the top of the next page.

Issuance

The use of all materials must be limited to properly authorized purposes.

Materials Requisition

No material may be issued from Space Savers' storeroom without a written form called a materials requisition. The *materials requisition* is prepared in duplicate by the department head or job supervisor. The requisition for the withdrawal of table-leg sections from the storeroom indicates the quantity, material number, description, and job number to which the materials are to be charged. (In the case of indirect materials, the requisition shows the department to which the materials are to be charged.)

BIN TAG

FORM NO. I 4

Material No. _K-193_ Location _Bin K-7_
Reorder Point _200_
Description _Folding table leg sections, 30"_

DATE	QUANTITY RECEIVED	QUANTITY ISSUED	BALANCE
9/1			285
9/4		30	255
9/5		50	205
9/5		10	195
9/16		20	175
9/25	100		275
10/1		55	220
10/6		(5)	225

Upon receipt of the materials requisition, the storeroom supervisor issues the materials and makes the necessary notations on the requisition. One copy is filed as a receipt and the second copy is given to the storeroom clerk. The storeroom clerk enters the unit price and computes and enters the total amount.

Materials Requisition

No. 802

DELIVER TO _Assembling Dept._
► ACCT. _122_
CHARGE ► JOB _101_
► DEPT._____

DATE _10/1/X1_

QUANTITY	MATERIAL NO.	DESCRIPTION	UNIT PRICE	AMOUNT
55	K-193	Folding table-leg sections, 30"	$17 00	$935 00

Entered on Materials Ledger Card	Entered in Materials Requisition Journal	Entered on Job Cost Sheet	Entered on Dept. Overhead Anal. Sheet

Approved By J.E.J.	Delivered By J. R.	Received By J.E.J.

FORM NO. 1217

Materials Ledger

After completing the cost computations on the requisition, the storeroom clerk records the entry in the Issued section of the materials ledger card, computes the new quantity on hand, and records it in the Balance section.

A materials ledger card is kept for each type of material on hand. Each card serves as a perpetual inventory record. The materials ledger is a subsidiary ledger verified against the Raw Materials control account in the general ledger. At the end of the accounting period, the sum of the dollar amount balances on the materials ledger cards should equal the balance of the control account.

MATERIALS LEDGER CARD

Material *Folding table-leg sections, 30"*   Reorder Point __200__

Number *K-193*   Reorder Quantity __120__

DATE	REFERENCE	RECEIVED UNITS	RECEIVED PRICE	RECEIVED AMOUNT	ISSUED UNITS	ISSUED PRICE	ISSUED AMOUNT	BALANCE UNITS	BALANCE PRICE	BALANCE AMOUNT
19X1 Sept. 16	Bal.							175	17 00	2975 00
25	PO1101	100	17 00	1700 00				275	17 00	4675 00
Oct. 1	R802				55	17 00	935 00	220	17 00	3740 00

Materials Requisition Journal

Once the information from the requisition has been recorded on the related materials ledger card, the requisition is forwarded to the cost clerk, who journalizes the transaction in the *materials requisition journal* so that the effect of the issuance will be ultimately reflected in the general ledger cost accounts. The journal below shows how two typical entries might appear in the materials requisition journal.

MATERIALS REQUISITION JOURNAL

for Month of _____ October _____ 19 X1   Page __10__

DATE	REQ. NO.	✔	JOB OR DEPT.	WORK IN PROCESS DR. 122	MFG. OHD. CONTROL DR. 501	RAW MATERIALS CR. 121
Oct. 1	802	✔	101	935 00		935 00
3	808	✔	1		92 50	92 50
31	Total	✔		69,337 26	3,215 35	72,552 61

Special journals, such as a materials requisition journal, are often used in a job order system. Some firms like Space Savers, Inc., find that special journals improve the efficiency of the journalizing process when compared to using only a general journal. These special journals are used to avoid writing the many long and repetitious entries involved in issuing and using materials. Internal control also improves since the recording process can be shared by several employees. Additional special journals will be discussed later in this chapter and in other chapters.

Job Cost Sheet

The cost clerk's next step is to post the information from the requisition to the Materials section of the proper job cost sheet. The illustration below shows that Requisition 802 is charged to Job 101 on October 1.

JOB COST SHEET

Customer _Neeley Furniture Co._
Description _Customer specs on file_
Quantity _100_

Job _101_
Date Started _10/1/X1_
Date Completed _____

MATERIALS			DIRECT LABOR								MANUFACTURING OVERHEAD APPLIED									
				MILLING		ASSEMBLING		FINISHING				MILLING			ASSEMBLING			FINISHING		
DATE	REQ. NO.	AMOUNT	DATE	REF.	HRS.	AMOUNT	HRS.	AMOUNT	HRS.	AMOUNT	DATE	REF.	HRS.	RATE	AMOUNT	HRS.	RATE	AMOUNT	HRS.	RATE	AMOUNT
10/1	R802	93500																			

Departmental Overhead Analysis Sheet

Since indirect materials cannot be charged to a specific job, information is posted from a requisition for such materials to the Indirect Materials section of the departmental overhead analysis sheet. A separate sheet is maintained for each department. The illustration below shows Requisition 808 charged to the Milling Department on October 3. The numbered columns classify the type of overhead involved.

DEPARTMENTAL OVERHEAD ANALYSIS SHEET

Department _Milling_
Month of _October_ 19 _X1_

DATE	REF.	TOTAL	01 INDIRECT MATERIALS	02 INDIRECT LABOR	03 PAYROLL TAXES	04 DEPRECIATION	05 REPAIRS & MAINT.	06 UTILITIES	07 INSURANCE	08 OTHER TAXES	09 OTHER ITEM	AMOUNT
Oct. 3	R808	9250	9250									

....

Principles of Internal Control

Space Savers' procedures for storing and issuing materials reflect important principles of internal control.

- Admittance to the storage area is restricted.
- Materials ledger cards are maintained covering all receipts and issues.
- Each type of material is clearly identified, stored in a particular place, and carefully protected while in storage.
- Materials are issued only upon proper written authorization.
- The accounting system permits a periodic check of the materials ledger against the balance of the Raw Materials control account.
- Several different persons are involved in storage and issuance operations.

Special Issuing Procedures

A complete and well-designed system for the control of materials issuance also includes provision for special situations.

Bill of Materials

In some cases, all the materials for a job will be issued at one time, and the bill of materials (discussed in the previous chapter) serves as a requisition.

Return of Materials to Storeroom

Sometimes materials that have been issued are returned to the storeroom. This may result from requisitioning too much material, withdrawing the wrong materials, or other reasons. All returned materials must be accompanied by a *returned materials report,* which is very similar to the materials requisition. At Space Savers, the returned materials report, shown below, is prepared in duplicate. The report may be filled out either in the department that originally requisitioned the materials or by the storeroom supervisor.

			Returned Materials Report		
			No. 48		
	▸ACCT. *122*				
CREDIT ▸JOB *101*			DATE *10/6/X1*		
	▸DEPT.		DEPT. *Assembling*		

QUANTITY	MATERIAL NO.	DESCRIPTION	UNIT COST	AMOUNT
5	K-193	*Folding table-leg sections, 30"*		

REASON FOR RETURN: *Excess issue*   Authorized By *K.P.*

Entered on Materials Ledger Card	Entered on Job Cost Sheet	Entered on Dept. Overhead Anal.Sheet	Received By *J.R.*

FORM NO. 1218

After the storeroom supervisor checks the returns, the bin tag is adjusted by showing the number of units returned in parentheses in the Quantity Issued column. This is illustrated on page 61. The number of units returned is added to the balance. Then, the returned materials report is given to the storeroom clerk, who follows the steps listed below.

1. Enters the unit and total cost figures on the report. The unit cost figure used is the same as that used when the materials were charged out.
2. Makes an entry in parentheses in the Issued section of the materials ledger card. The new quantity and cost amounts are then entered in the Balance section of the card, as shown below.
3. Sends the returned materials report to the cost clerk.

These steps are illustrated in the following materials ledger card:

MATERIALS LEDGER CARD

Material *Folding table-leg sections, 30"*   Reorder Point _200_
Number *K-193*   Reorder Quantity _120_

DATE	REFERENCE	RECEIVED UNITS	RECEIVED PRICE	RECEIVED AMOUNT	ISSUED UNITS	ISSUED PRICE	ISSUED AMOUNT	BALANCE UNITS	BALANCE PRICE	BALANCE AMOUNT
19X1 Sept 16	Bal.							175	1700	297500
25	PO1101	100	1700	170000				275	1700	467500
Oct. 1	R802				55	1700	93500	220	1700	374000
6	RM48				(5)	1700	(8500)	225	1700	382500

The cost clerk completes two important entries.

1. An entry in parentheses in the Indirect Materials column of the departmental overhead analysis sheet or in the Materials section of the appropriate job cost sheet, as shown below.

JOB COST SHEET

Customer *Neeley Furniture Co.*   Job _101_
Description *Customer specs on file*   Date Started _10/1/X1_
Quantity _100_   Date Completed _____

DATE	REQ. NO.	AMOUNT	DATE	REF.	MILLING HRS.	MILLING AMOUNT	ASSEMBLING HRS.	ASSEMBLING AMOUNT	FINISHING HRS.	FINISHING AMOUNT	DATE	REF.	MILLING HRS.	MILLING RATE	MILLING AMOUNT	ASSEMBLING HRS.	ASSEMBLING RATE	ASSEMBLING AMOUNT	FINISHING HRS.	FINISHING RATE	FINISHING AMOUNT
10/1	R802	93500																			
10/2	R804	280500																			
10/6	RM48	(8500)																			

2. An entry covering the return in the *returned materials journal*, as shown below.

RETURNED MATERIALS JOURNAL
for Month of _____ October _____ 19 X1   Page _10_

DATE	REPT. NO.	✓	JOB OR DEPT.	WORK IN PROCESS CR. 122	MFG. OHD. CONTROL CR. 501	RAW MATERIALS DR. 121
Oct. 6	48	✓	101	85 00		85 00
12	49	✓	3		7 00	7 00
31	Total	✓		552 50	34 00	586 50

The totals of the columns of each journal are posted in summary form to the appropriate general ledger accounts at the end of the month.

For the sake of simplicity, Entry B in Chapter 2 (see page 26) reflected the net effect of the summary postings from the materials requisition journal and the returned materials journal, computed as follows:

	Work in Process	Manufacturing Overhead	Raw Materials
Summary Posting From MRJ	$69,337.26	$3,215.35	$72,552.61
Deduct Summary Posting From RMJ	552.50	34.00	586.50
Net Amount, Entry B	$68,784.76	$3,181.35	$71,966.11

Return of Materials to Supplier

Occasionally, it may be necessary to return materials to the supplier after they are placed in the storeroom. If materials are to be returned, the purchasing unit sends the storeroom supervisor a *return shipping order* authorizing the return and also prepares a debit memorandum. (Returns were also discussed in Chapter 3.) One copy each of the return shipping order and the debit memorandum is kept by the purchasing unit. The shipping unit receives a copy of the return shipping order as authorization to return the merchandise to the supplier. One copy each of the shipping order and the debit memorandum is sent to the accounting unit for its records. The storeroom clerk receives a copy of the debit memorandum. This copy is used in making an entry in parentheses in the materials ledger (in the Received column) showing the return.

If the return is made before the voucher register is closed for the month, the original entry is corrected by making a notation in parentheses for the amount of the return on the same line as the original entry. This is shown below.

At the end of the month, the parenthetical entries are totaled separately. Then these totals are posted as a debit to Vouchers Payable and a credit to Raw Materials.

If the voucher register has been closed for the month in which the purchase was entered, a new voucher is issued and recorded. Vouchers Payable 201 is debited for the original amount and is also credited for the revised amount; the difference is credited to Raw Materials 121.

VOUCHER REGISTER for Month of _____ November _____ 19 XX

DATE	VOU. NO.	PAYABLE TO	PAID DATE	CHECK NO.	VOUCHERS PAYABLE CR. 201	RAW MATERIALS DR. 121
Nov. 3	11-9	King Lumber Co.			(75 00) 1,000 00	(75 00) 1,000 00

Materials Reserved and On Order

In a large business in which many jobs are started and many purchase orders and materials requisitions covering a variety of materials are processed, the materials ledger cards may be expanded to give more information and better control. Three additional columns are often added. These are the On Order, Reserved Quantity, and Free Quantity columns. An expanded materials ledger card with these columns is shown below.

MATERIALS LEDGER CARD

Material _Metal brackets_
Number _R-648_

Reorder Point _250_
Reorder Quantity _200_

DATE	REFERENCE	ON ORDER	RECEIVED			ISSUED			BALANCE			RESERVED QUANTITY	FREE QUANTITY
			UNITS	PRICE	AMOUNT	UNITS	PRICE	AMOUNT	UNITS	PRICE	AMOUNT		
_19XX_ Jan. 1	Bal.								300	1 00	300 00		300
8	PO-608		150	1 00	150 00				450	1 00	450 00		450
12	R-243					200	1 00	200 00	250	1 00	250 00		250
13	PO-625	~~200~~											
16	BM-116								250	1 00	250 00	~~100~~	150
20	PO-625		200	1 00	200 00				450	1 00	450 00		350
25	BM-116					100	1 00	100 00	350	1 00	350 00		350

The On Order column shows the number of units on order and the date of each order. When the order is filled, the storeroom clerk draws a line through the entry. Space Savers does not use an On Order column because the number of different materials in stock is small. The filed copy of the purchase order provides the needed information.

The Reserved Quantity column simply indicates that materials will be needed for a forthcoming job. This column tells the storeroom clerk and storeroom supervisor that additional units of the materials must be ordered before the quantity on hand is down to the normal reorder point. When reserved materials are issued, a line is drawn through the entry in the Reserved Quantity column. The Free Quantity column shows the balance on hand less any reserved quantities. Space Savers does not use the expanded materials ledger card. At Space Savers, a reserved stock tag is clipped to the materials ledger card. This tag shows the amount that will be needed and when the job is to be started if the amount is unusually large.

Computerized Materials Issuance

Steer Inn, Inc., has a chain of fast-food highway franchises specializing in hamburgers. According to the franchise agreements, Steer Inn, Inc., will sell various products to each of the franchises: beef, rolls, catsup, mustard, pickles, and all of the paper products, such as straws, napkins, and paper cups, that must have Steer Inn's logo printed on them. In order to keep product delivery as timely as possible, Steer Inn has a computerized materials issuance system.

Upon receipt of a materials requisition, a returned materials report, or a return shipping order, the storeroom supervisor will enter the material number and the quantity into the computer terminal in the storeroom. This information will be sent to the central computer, which will (1) look up the material number in the inventory file that is stored in memory, (2) find the unit price for that particular material, and (3) compute the total cost by multiplying the unit cost by the quantity. Both the unit price and the total cost will be displayed on the terminal's screen. This information will be used to complete the materials requisition.

The central computer will use the quantity and the material number to update the inventory file for that material and to determine whether more units should be ordered. For example, if the franchise in Buffalo, New York, ordered 100 boxes of napkins, the computer would decrease the balance in the napkin subsidiary ledger file by 100 boxes. If this causes the balance to drop below the reorder point, the computer will automatically order a new batch of napkins from the factory. Steer Inn has found that their computerized system helps facilitate faster delivery to the franchises because orders are processed faster and therefore are on the road sooner. Other benefits of this system are more up-to-date inventory records, simplified processing of purchase orders, and stronger internal control over materials issuance. ■

Principles and Procedures Summary

A firm's procedures for storing and issuing materials must have a variety of internal controls to protect the investment that the firm has in these items.

Materials on hand must be carefully identified, stored, recorded, and preserved by the storeroom supervisor and the storeroom staff. Materials are issued only upon written receipt of a materials requisition. When materials have been issued, entries are recorded on the materials ledger card, the materials requisition journal, and the job cost sheet or departmental overhead analysis sheet.

Special issuing procedures are used when all materials required on a job are issued at one time, when materials are returned to the storeroom or to the supplier, and when the materials are to be reserved for a future job.

A perpetual inventory system operates to record and control both receipts and issues of materials. Entries are made on materials ledger cards as follows:

■ *Materials purchased:* Entry recorded as goods are received. Data taken from receiving report and purchase order.
■ *Materials issued:* Entry recorded as goods are issued. Data taken from materials requisition.
■ *Materials returned to storeroom:* Entry recorded as goods are returned. Data taken from returned materials report.
■ *Materials returned to supplier:* Entry recorded as goods are sent back. Data taken from debit memorandum.

Related entries are made in the Raw Materials account in the general ledger as follows:

- **Materials purchased:** Summary posting at end of period from voucher register's Raw Materials column.
- **Materials issued:** Summary posting at end of period from total of Raw Materials column in materials requisition journal.
- **Materials returned to storeroom:** Summary posting at end of period from total of Raw Materials column in returned materials journal.
- **Materials returned to supplier:** Summary entry at end of period from parenthetical entry total of voucher register's Raw Materials column.

At the end of the period, the balance of the Raw Materials account should equal the total of the dollar amount balances on the materials ledger cards.

Review Questions

1. How does a bin tag differ from a materials ledger card?
2. What is a materials requisition?
3. List the three places where a materials requisition for direct materials must be recorded. List three places where a materials requisition for indirect materials must be recorded.
4. What is a returned materials report? How does a returned materials report differ from a return shipping order?
5. Describe the procedures used in recording materials requisitions and returned materials reports on materials ledger cards.
6. What is the purpose of an On Order column on a materials ledger card? *Back orders*
7. Describe the procedure followed in recording information in the Reserved Quantity column of an expanded materials ledger card.
8. Indicate the sequence in which the following documents would be prepared:
   - 4 **a.** Purchase invoice
   - 1 **b.** Bill of materials
   - 5 **c.** Return shipping order
   - 2 **d.** Purchase requisition
   - 6 **e.** Materials requisition
   - 3 **f.** Purchase order
9. What are the sources for the debit entries in the Raw Materials account in the general ledger? What are the sources for the credit entries?

Managerial Discussion Questions

1. How are materials requisitions used in controlling the materials inventory?
2. What procedures should be used in storing and issuing materials to achieve good internal control?
3. What would be the advantage of using a materials requisition journal?
4. What information can management obtain from the On Order and Reserved Quantity columns of an expanded materials ledger card? Why is this useful?
5. Why is it necessary to maintain departmental overhead analysis sheets for each production and service department?
6. What accounting records and forms would provide information to management that would be useful in analyzing high indirect materials costs in the factory?
7. What are job cost sheets and what types of data do they provide to management?

Exercises

1. **Calculating materials costs.** Calculate the materials cost for Job 304 from the job cost sheet information given below.

Requisitions *3P 9165*		Returned Materials Reports *– 2 Digit*	
476	$798.00	39	$85.00
493	35.97	43	8.50
497	398.00	48	25.80
503	748.35		
514	84.87		

2. **Calculating ending inventory balances.** Compute the ending balance and the cost of the ending inventory of Raw Material 4-89, which has a unit price of $5.75. The materials ledger card shows the following data:

	Units		Units
Beginning balance	8,490	Issuances	1,560
Purchases	4,300		875
	5,100		1,060
			450
			1,480

3. **Journalizing materials requisitions.** During May 19X5, Barclay's Paneling had requisitions totaling $89,620 for direct materials and $9,760 for indirect materials. Prepare the entry in general journal form to record the cost of materials requisitioned for the month.

4. **Journalizing returned materials reports.** During August 19X8, Home Products Inc. had returned $5,350 in direct materials and $460 in indirect materials. Prepare the entry in general journal form to record the cost of the materials returned to the storeroom for the month.

5. **Journalizing a return shipping order.** The McDonald Manufacturing Company returned materials totaling $1,586.20 to its supplier, Martelson Inc. Prepare the entry in general journal form for materials returned.

Problems

PROBLEM 4-1. Recording in the materials ledger. Hideaways Inc. manufactures various sizes of storage boxes. Their 6-inch by 18-inch lid, Material L-487, costs $4.30. The following transactions occurred during the month of May 19X4, for receipts, issuances, and returns of Material L-487. The reorder point for Material L-487 is 900 units, and the reorder quantity is 1,500 units.

May	1	Beginning balance	687
	4	PO308	1,500
	10	R408	225
	15	R490	585
	16	RM48	15
	19	R518	532
	23	PO315	1,500
	27	RS204	20
	29	R691	460
	30	RM65	35

Instructions

Record the purchase orders, materials requisitions, returned shipping order, and returned materials reports in the materials ledger.

PROBLEM 4-2. **Journalizing and posting raw materials transactions.** The raw materials transactions of the Carolinas Corporation for the month of March 19X7 are listed below. First, record the beginning balance in the Raw Materials account. Then record the transactions in the materials requisition journal and the voucher register. Total the columns in the journals and post the totals to the Raw Materials account.

Mar.	1	Beginning inventory of raw materials	$104,160
	4	Disbursement Voucher 3-1 for raw materials purchased from the Wilson Supply Company	22,186
	8	Materials Requisition 416 for direct materials used on Job 20	24,810
	14	Materials Requisition 417 for direct materials used on Job 21	33,914
	17	Disbursement Voucher 3-2 for raw materials purchased from the Avery Corporation	48,260
	21	Materials Requisition 418 for indirect materials used in Finishing Department	15,640
	24	Materials Requisition 419 for direct materials used on Job 21	20,110
	26	Disbursement Voucher 3-3 for raw materials purchased from the Tri-State Company	32,540
	29	Returned Shipping Order 28 for materials returned to the Tri-State Company (voucher register has not been closed)	3,800

PROBLEM 4-3. **Processing source documents.** The Maxwell Corporation manufactures aluminum ladders. The procedures for receiving and issuing materials include the following:

Receiving. A copy of the receiving report accompanies the materials to the storeroom, where it is signed by the storeroom supervisor to show that the materials were received in that area. The storeroom clerk records the receipt of raw materials by posting to the materials ledger cards. The receiving report and the supplier's invoice are checked against the purchase order. A voucher is completed, approved, and entered in the voucher register. Materials returned to the supplier are covered by a return shipping order and a debit memorandum. The debit memorandum is posted to the materials ledger cards and the voucher register.

Issuing. Materials are issued after an approved materials requisition is received in the storeroom. Unit costs are entered and extended on the requisition. The issue is posted to the materials ledger cards and recorded in the materials requisition journal. The requisition is posted to the proper job cost sheet or the departmental overhead analysis sheet. Materials returned to the storeroom are accompanied by a returned materials report. After the returned materials are checked in, they are posted to the materials ledger cards and recorded in the returned materials journal.

The returned materials report is posted to the proper job cost sheet or the departmental overhead analysis sheet.

During December 19X6 the following transactions take place:

Dec. 1 Materials Requisitions 814 is received by the storeroom supervisor, and the materials are issued. The materials requisitioned are for use in the Layout Department on Job 762 for the Singer Supply Company. Job 762 calls for 300 six-foot aluminum ladders. The materials requisitioned are as follows:

> 300 units R-6 side rails, 6'
> 150 units S-12 steps, 4" × 12"
> 300 units S-15 steps, 4" × 15"
> 150 units T-612 tops, 6" × 12"

6 Receiving Report 615 (for Purchase Order 703) is completed by the receiving clerk. Since this report is not shown in this problem, the data to be posted to the materials ledger cards are found on Disbursement Voucher 12-01 shown on page 73, to which you should refer.

6 Disbursement Voucher 12-01 is received.

10 Materials Requisition 815 is received by the storeroom supervisor, and the materials are issued. The materials requisitioned are for use in the Layout Department on Job 763 for the Construction Supplies Company. Job 763 calls for 250 eight-foot aluminum ladders. The materials requisitioned are as follows:

> 250 units R-8 side rails, 8'
> 125 units S-12 steps, 4" × 12"
> 375 units S-15 steps, 4" × 15"
> 125 units T-612 tops, 6" × 12"

Instructions

1. If you are not using the *Study Guide and Working Papers,* open the materials ledger by recording the opening balances on the materials ledger cards. The December balances are as follows:

Material	Reorder Point	Reorder Quantity	BALANCE Units	BALANCE Price	BALANCE Amount
B-10 elbow braces	6,000	13,000	5,485	$ .35	$1,919.75
R-6 side rails, 6'	3,000	8,000	1,970	1.15	2,265.50
R-8 side rails, 8'	1,900	3,850	2,025	1.40	2,835.00
S-12 steps, 4" × 12"	2,500	6,000	1,910	.45	859.50
S-15 steps, 4" × 15"	2,400	4,600	1,700	.60	1,020.00
T-612 tops, 6" × 12"	2,400	5,000	1,440	.75	1,080.00
W-125 washers, $\frac{1}{4}$" flat (box of 100)	300 boxes	940 boxes	675	.80	540.00

2. Prepare the materials requisitions.

3. Process the materials requisitions, receiving report data, and the disbursement voucher data through all the procedures adopted by the Maxwell Corporation. The additional records needed are job cost sheets, a departmental overhead analysis sheet, a voucher register, a materials requisition journal, and a returned materials journal. *Keep all your records for use in Problem 4-4.*

Disbursement Voucher

No. 12-01

PAYEE ▶ Tools-for-You Distributors, Inc.
716 Delaware Avenue
Buffalo, NY 14209

Voucher Date: 12/6/X6
Terms: n/30
Discount Date:
Date Due: 1/6/X7

INVOICE DATE	INVOICE NUMBER	DESCRIPTION		AMOUNT	
11/28/X6	284	6,000 Steps, 4″ x 12″, S-12	@ $.45	$2,700	00
		4,600 Steps, 4″ x 15″, S-15	.60	2,760	00
			Total	$5,460	00

DISTRIBUTION	
ACCT. NO.	AMOUNT
121	$5,460.00

Price O.K. B.A.C.
Material Received
Extensions O.K. J.C.D.
Gross Amount
Discount
Net Paid
Approved for Pay.
Paid By Check No. _____ Date _____

Disbursement Voucher

No. 12-02

PAYEE ▶ Aloha Supplies International
142 Merchant Street
Honolulu, HI 96813

Voucher Date: 12/16/X6
Terms: 3/15, n/45
Discount Date: 12/31/X6
Date Due: 1/30/X7

INVOICE DATE	INVOICE NUMBER	DESCRIPTION		AMOUNT	
12/10/X6	1AX475	5000 Tops, 6″ x 12″, T-612	@ $.75	$3,750	00
			Total	$3,750	00

DISTRIBUTION	
ACCT. NO.	AMOUNT
121	$3,750.00

Price O.K. B.A.C.
Material Received
Extensions O.K. J.C.D.
Gross Amount
Discount
Net Paid
Approved for Pay.
Paid By Check No. _____ Date _____

Disbursement Voucher

No. 12-03

PAYEE ▶ Providence Hardware Corp.
21 Westminster Street
Providence, RI 02903

Voucher Date: 12/20/X6
Terms: 2/10, n/30
Discount Date: 12/30/X6
Date Due: 1/19/X7

INVOICE DATE	INVOICE NUMBER	DESCRIPTION		AMOUNT	
12/18/X6	48-818	13,000 Elbow braces, B-10	@ $.35	$4,550	00
			Total	$4,550	00

DISTRIBUTION

ACCT. NO.	AMOUNT
121	$4,550.00

Price O.K. _B.A.C._
Material Received _____
Extensions O.K. _J.C.D._
Gross Amount _____
Discount _____
Net Paid _____
Approved for Pay. _____
Paid By Check No. _____ Date _____

Disbursement Voucher

No. 12-04

PAYEE ▶ AlumLite Developers, Inc.
2010 Bunker Hill Drive
Baton Rouge, LA 70808

Voucher Date: 12/27/X6
Terms: _____
Discount Date: _____
Date Due: _____

INVOICE DATE	INVOICE NUMBER	DESCRIPTION		AMOUNT	
		To correct Disbursement Voucher 11-24, November 21, 19X6, for excess quantity of materials received, per Return Shipping Order 108, December 20, 19X6, and debit memorandum, December 20, 19X6; copies attached.		$1,125	00
Returned Material		800 Steps, 4″ × 12″, S-12	@ $.45	360	00
			corrected	$ 765	00

DISTRIBUTION

ACCT. NO.	AMOUNT	
201	$1,125.00	Dr.
201	765.00	Cr.
121	360.00	Cr.

Price O.K. _B.A.C._
Material Received _____
Extensions O.K. _J.C.D._
Gross Amount _____
Discount _____
Net Paid _____
Approved for Pay. _____
Paid By Check No. _____ Date _____

PROBLEM 4-4. Processing source documents. This problem is a continuation of Problem 4-3. The following additional transactions take place:

Dec. 16   Receiving Report 616 (for Purchase Order 704) is completed by the receiving clerk. Since this report is not shown, the data to be posted to the materials ledger cards are found on Disbursement Voucher 12-02 shown on page 73, to which you should refer.

16   Disbursement Voucher 12-02 is received.

18   Materials Requisition 816 is received by the storeroom supervisor, and the materials are issued. The materials are for the Assembling Department (Account 502). They consist of 25 boxes of W-125 washers $\frac{1}{4}''$ flat (box of 100).

20   Receiving Report 617 (for Purchase Order 705) is completed by the receiving clerk. Since this report is not shown, the data to be posted to the materials ledger cards are found on Disbursement Voucher 12-03 shown on page 74, to which you should refer.

20   Disbursement Voucher 12-03 is received.

20   Materials Requisition 817 is received by the storeroom supervisor, and the materials are issued. The materials are for the Layout Department on Job 762 and are for the following items:

   300 units R-6 side rails, 6'
   150 units S-12 steps, 4" × 12"
   300 units S-15 steps, 4" × 15"
   150 units T-612 tops, 6" × 12"

21   Returned Materials Report 84 is received by the storeroom supervisor. The accompanying materials are 25 S-15 steps, an excess quantity requisitioned in error on Job 763. The materials are returned to the storeroom.

Instructions

1. Prepare the materials requisitions.
2. Prepare the returned materials report.
3. Process all documents through all the procedures followed by the Maxwell Corporation. Use the records provided in Problem 4-3 as needed. *Keep all your records for use in Problem 4-5.*

PROBLEM 4-5. Processing source documents. This problem is a continuation of Problems 4-3 and 4-4. The following additional transactions take place:

Dec. 22   Materials Requisition 818 is received by the storeroom supervisor, and the materials are issued. The materials are for the Layout Department for use on Job 763 and include the following:

   200 units R-8 side rails, 8'
   100 units S-12 steps, 4" × 12"
   300 units S-15 steps, 4" × 15"
   100 units T-612 tops, 6" × 12"

27   Return Shipping Order 108 (not shown) and the debit memorandum (not shown) dated December 20, 19X6 are received from the purchasing unit. The data to be posted to the materials ledger cards are found on Disbursement Voucher 12-04 shown on page 74, to which you should refer.

27   Disbursement Voucher 12-04 is received.

28   Materials Requisition 819 is received by the storeroom supervisor, and the materials are issued. The materials are for the Layout Department on Job 764 for the O'Dell Company. Job 764 calls for 300 eight-foot aluminum ladders. The materials requisitioned are as follows:

> 300 units R-8 side rails, 8′
> 150 units S-12 steps, 4″ × 12″
> 450 units S-15 steps, 4″ × 15″
> 150 units T-612 tops, 6″ × 12″

Instructions

1. Complete the materials requisitions.
2. Process all documents through all the procedures followed by the Maxwell Corporation. Use the records provided in Problems 4-3 and 4-4.
3. Prove the accuracy of your work by footing and cross-footing all money columns in the voucher register and the materials requisition journal. Double-rule the columns.
4. Post from the voucher register, the materials requisition journal, and the returned materials journal to the Raw Materials account. NOTE: If you are not using the *Study Guide and Working Papers,* open the Raw Materials account by recording the December 1 balance of $10,519.75.
5. Prepare a schedule listing each material in the materials ledger and its ending balance. The total of this schedule should equal the ending balance in the Raw Materials account.

Alternate Problems

PROBLEM 4-1A. Recording in the materials ledger. The Security Container Corporation manufactures six styles of containers that use cork tops. The 7-inch round top, Material X-541, costs $3.80 each. The reorder point for Material X-541 is 2,800 units, and the reorder quantity is 2,500 units. The following transactions occurred during the month of September 19X4, for the receipts, issuances, and returns of Material X-541.

Sept.	1	Beginning balance	2,460
	3	PO8-39	2,500
	6	R812	550
	9	R830	840
	12	RM65	30
	16	R861	1,120
	22	PO8-79	2,500

25	RS0103	50
30	R920	400
30	RM83	10

Instructions

Record the purchase orders, materials requisitions, returned shipping order, and returned materials reports in the materials ledger.

PROBLEM 4-2A. Journalizing and posting raw materials transactions. The raw materials transactions of the Hubbard Corporation for the month of March 19X5 are listed below. First, record the beginning balance in the Raw Materials account. Then record the transactions in the materials requisition journal and the voucher register. Total the columns in the journals and post the totals to the Raw Materials account.

Mar.	1	Beginning inventory of raw materials	$4,680
	5	Disbursement Voucher 3-1 for raw materials purchased from the Riverfront Company	3,805
	9	Materials Requisition 509 for direct materials used on Job 405	1,850
	16	Materials Requisition 510 for direct materials used on Job 406	2,925
	19	Disbursement Voucher 3-2 for raw materials purchased from the New England Supply Company	2,450
	22	Materials Requisition 511 for indirect materials used in Assembling Department	750
	25	Materials Requisition 512 for direct materials used on Job 405	3,180
	27	Disbursement Voucher 3-3 for raw materials purchased from Green & Company	1,470
	28	Returned Shipping Order 30 for materials returned to Green & Company (voucher register has not been closed)	160

PROBLEM 4-3A. Processing source documents. The Maxwell Corporation manufactures aluminum ladders. The procedures for receiving and issuing materials include the following:

Receiving. A copy of the receiving report accompanies the materials to the storeroom, where it is signed by the storeroom supervisor to show that the materials were received in that area. The storeroom clerk records the receipt of raw materials by posting to the materials ledger card. The receiving report and the supplier's invoice are checked against the purchase order. A voucher is completed, approved, and entered in the voucher register. Materials returned to the supplier are covered by a return shipping order and a debit memorandum. The debit memorandum is posted to the materials ledger cards and the voucher register.

Issuing. Materials are issued after an approved materials requisition is received in the storeroom. Unit costs are entered and extended on the requisition. The issue is posted to the materials ledger cards and recorded in the materials requisition journal. The requisition is posted to the proper job cost sheet or the departmental overhead analysis sheet. Materials returned to the storeroom are accompanied by a returned materials report. After the returned materials are checked in, they are posted to the materials ledger cards and recorded in the returned materials journal. The returned materials report is posted to the proper job cost sheet or the departmental overhead analysis sheet.

During December 19X6, the following transactions take place:

Dec. 1 Materials Requisition 814 is received by the storeroom supervisor, and the materials are issued. The materials requisitioned are for use in the Layout Department on Job 762 for the HandiHome Hardware Company. Job 762 calls for 250 six-foot aluminum ladders. The materials requisitioned are as follows:

> 250 units R-6 side rails, 6'
> 125 units S-12 steps, 4" × 12"
> 250 units S-15 steps, 4" × 15"
> 125 units T-612 tops, 6" × 12"

6 Receiving Report 615 (for Purchase Order 703) is completed by the receiving clerk. Since this report is not shown in this problem, the data to be posted to the materials ledger cards are found on Disbursement Voucher 12-01 shown on page 73, to which you should refer.

6 Disbursement Voucher 12-01 is received.

10 Materials Requisition 815 is received by the storeroom supervisor, and the materials are issued. The materials requisitioned are for use in the Layout Department on Job 763 for the Waterbury Supply Company. Job 763 calls for 180 eight-foot aluminum ladders. The materials requisitioned are as follows:

> 180 units R-8 side rails, 8'
> 90 units S-12 steps, 4" × 12"
> 270 units S-15 steps, 4" × 15"
> 90 units T-612 tops, 6" × 12"

Instructions

1. If you are not using the *Study Guide and Working Papers for Cost Accounting,* open the materials ledger by recording the opening balances on the materials ledger cards.

2. Prepare the materials requisitions.

Material	Reorder Point	Reorder Quantity	BALANCE Units	BALANCE Price	BALANCE Amount
B-10 elbow braces	6,000	13,000	5,485	$ .35	$1,919.75
R-6 side rails, 6'	3,000	8,000	1,970	1.15	2,265.50
R-8 side rails, 8'	1,900	3,850	2,025	1.40	2,835.00
S-12 steps, 4" × 12"	2,500	6,000	1,910	.45	859.50
S-15 steps, 4" × 15"	2,400	4,600	1,700	.60	1,020.00
T-612 tops, 6" × 12"	2,400	5,000	1,440	.75	1,080.00
W-125 washers, ¼" flat (box of 100)	300 boxes	940 boxes	675	.80	540.00

3. Process the materials requisitions, receiving report data, and the disbursement voucher data through all the procedures adopted by the Maxwell Corporation.

The additional records needed are job cost sheets, a departmental overhead analysis sheet, a voucher register, a materials requisition journal, and a returned materials journal. *Keep all your records for use in Problem 4-4A.*

PROBLEM 4-4A. Processing source documents. This problem is a continuation of Problem 4-3A. The following additional transactions take place:

Dec. 16 Receiving Report 616 (for Purchase Order 704) is completed by the receiving clerk. Since this report is not shown, the data to be posted to the materials ledger cards are found on Disbursement Voucher 12-02 shown on page 73, to which you should refer.

16 Disbursement Voucher 12-02 is received.

18 Materials Requisition 816 is received by the storeroom supervisor, and the materials are issued. The materials are for the Assembling Department (Account 502). They consist of 40 boxes of W-125 washers, ¼″ flat (box of 100).

20 Receiving Report 617 (for Purchase Order 705) is completed by the receiving clerk. Since this report is not shown, the data to be posted to the materials ledger cards are found on Disbursement Voucher 12-03 shown on page 74, to which you should refer.

20 Disbursement Voucher 12-03 is received.

20 Materials Requisition 817 is received by the storeroom supervisor, and the materials are issued. The materials are for the Layout Department on Job 762 and are for the following items:

     250 units R-6 side rails, 6′
     125 units S-12 steps, 4″ × 12″
     250 units S-15 steps, 4″ × 15″
     125 units T-612 tops, 6″ × 12″

21 Returned Materials Report 84 is received by the storeroom supervisor. The accompanying materials are 25 S-15 steps, excess quantity requisitioned on Job 763. The materials are returned to stock.

Instructions

1. Prepare the materials requisitions.
2. Prepare the returned materials report.
3. Process all documents through all the procedures followed by the Maxwell Corporation. Use the records provided in Problem 4-3A as needed. *Keep all your records for use in Problem 4-5A.*

PROBLEM 4-5A. Processing source documents. This problem is a continuation of Problems 4-3A and 4-4A. The following additional transactions take place:

Dec. 22 Materials Requisition 818 is received by the storeroom supervisor, and the materials are issued. The materials are for the Layout Department for use on Job 763 and include the following:

     100 units R-8 side rails, 8′
      50 units S-12 steps, 4″ × 12″
     150 units S-15 steps, 4″ × 15″
      50 units T-612 tops, 6″ × 12″

27 Return Shipping Order 108 (not shown) and the debit memorandum (not shown)

dated December 20, 19X6 are received from the purchasing unit. The data to be posted to the materials ledger cards are found on Disbursement Voucher 12-04 shown on page 74, to which you should refer.

27 Disbursement Voucher 12-04 is received.

28 Materials Requisition 819 is received by the storeroom supervisor, and the materials are issued. The materials are for the Layout Department on Job 764 for the Massachusetts Company. Job 764 calls for 250 eight-foot aluminum ladders. The materials requisitioned are as follows.

250 units R-8 side rails, 8'
125 units S-12 steps, 4" × 12"
375 units S-15 steps, 4" × 15"
125 units T-612 tops, 6" × 12"

Instructions

1. Prepare the materials requisitions.
2. Process all documents through all the procedures adopted by the Maxwell Corporation. Use the records provided in Problems 4-3A and 4-4A as needed.
3. Prove the accuracy of your work by footing and cross-footing all money columns in the voucher register and the materials requisition journal. Double-rule the columns.
4. Post from the voucher register, the materials requisition journal, and the returned materials journal to the Raw Materials account. NOTE: If you are not using the *Study Guide and Working Papers,* open the Raw Materials account by recording the December 1 balance of $10,519.75.
5. Prepare a schedule listing each material in the materials ledger and its ending balance. The total of this schedule should equal the ending balance in the Raw Materials account.

Managerial Decisions

CASE 4-1. The management of the Sanford Manufacturing Corporation has asked you to review its internal control procedures related to raw materials inventory. You discovered the following problem areas.

Purchase orders. Most purchase orders were prepared as a result of a written purchase requisition. However, some have a notation, "As per phone conversation with MJN," and there is no supporting purchase requisition. In addition, the materials ledger cards do not contain reorder points or quantities. It is not uncommon for the factory to run out of raw materials and to be unable to obtain them from the storeroom. Several jobs have not been completed because the company is waiting for the delivery of the necessary raw materials.

Materials requisitions. Requisitions from last month have yet to be processed on the materials ledger cards and on the job cost sheets. The company does not use returned materials reports; the excess materials are merely returned to the storeroom by the factory personnel. Also, the storeroom does not have limited access. You have observed several factory workers removing raw materials on their own and returning to the factory. They did not prepare requisitions. The factory workers have indicated that often they are "in a hurry and cannot be bothered" with completing requisitions.

Storeroom procedures. The storeroom is not organized according to types of raw materials. During your inspection, you have found that several raw materials have more than one bin location. In addition, the storeroom workers have reported that they have difficulty in locating the raw materials and waste time searching through the storeroom. No special precautions are taken to safeguard some very valuable metals; these metals are located in the same bin area as other low-value metals.

Prepare a report to management in which you recommend procedures to improve the company's internal control over materials. Where appropriate, explain how these procedures will improve the company's cost accounting records.

5

Controlling and Valuing Inventory

■ ■ ■

In the previous two chapters, prices of materials were purposely kept constant to simplify your initial experience with materials ledger card procedures. Prices normally vary from one purchase to the next, and it is often impossible to tell the specific purchase from which an issue is made. In this chapter you will learn how the accountant prices issues of materials. You will also learn how physical inventories of materials are taken and valued and how inventory adjustments are recorded.

Costing: A Complex Problem

The partially completed materials ledger card on page 83 shows unit prices ranging from $10 to $17.50.

How would you price the issue of 150 units? How would you value the 25 units on hand? The valuation directly affects the amount of profit or loss reported for the accounting period. If other factors remain the same, the higher the ending inventory valuation (and therefore the lower the cost of goods sold), the larger the reported profit will be, or the smaller the reported loss. The lower the ending inventory valuation (and therefore the higher the cost of goods sold), the smaller the reported profit, or the larger the reported loss.

Inventory Costing Methods

Since most manufacturers keep perpetual inventory records, unit costs and total costs should be computed each time materials are received or issued. The primary basis of inventory valuation is cost. Because unit prices often vary from one purchase to another, the accountant must make an assumption about the flow of costs. For inventory valuation purposes, it is not necessary that the flow of costs match the physical flow of goods. The accountant will choose the inventory valuation method that best meets the needs of the company. The method selected will determine what unit prices are used to price issues of materials and what cost of goods sold and ending inventory values will be reported.

One assumption the accountant can make is that the first materials purchased

MATERIALS LEDGER CARD

Material *Folding table-leg sections, 28"*
Number *K-205*
Reorder Point _100_
Reorder Quantity _50_

DATE	REFERENCE	RECEIVED UNITS	PRICE	AMOUNT	ISSUED UNITS	PRICE	AMOUNT	BALANCE UNITS	PRICE	AMOUNT
19xx										
Jan. 1	Bal.							25	10.00	250.00
4	PO-1701	50	15.00	750.00				25 / 50	10.00 / 15.00	1000.00
8	PO-1709	50	15.00	750.00				25 / 100	10.00 / 15.00	1750.00
15	PO-1721	50	17.50	875.00				25 / 100 / 50	10.00 / 15.00 / 17.50	2625.00
20	R-216				150	?		25	?	

(the oldest) are the first materials used. The materials on hand are therefore assumed to be the last ones purchased. This is the *first in, first out (FIFO) method* of costing.

Another assumption is that the last materials purchased (the most recent) are the first materials used. Then the materials on hand are assumed to be the first ones purchased. This is the *last in, first out (LIFO) method* of costing.

In order to learn how each of these assumptions would be applied, refer to the following transactions relating to Material T-21, plastic table tops:

Feb. 1 The beginning balance on hand is 150 units, costing $15 each; total cost, $2,250.

6 150 units are purchased on Purchase Order 87 at $15.50 each; total cost, $2,325.

10 180 units are issued for use on Requisition 103.

21 150 units are purchased on Purchase Order 109 for $15.60 each; total cost, $2,340.

23 160 units are issued for use on Requisition 116.

25 10 units are returned to the storeroom as noted on Returned Materials Report 13. These units had been issued on February 10 for use on Requisition 103.

First In, First Out Method

The materials ledger card on page 84 shows the transactions relating to Material T-21 recorded as if the FIFO method were used.

The price to be used for each issue must be individually determined.

■ The issue of 180 units on February 10 includes all the 150 units from the beginning inventory (150 units at $15 each) plus 30 of the units purchased on February 6 (30 units at $15.50 each).

■ The issue of 160 units on February 23 includes the remaining 120 units from the February 6 purchase (120 units at $15.50 each) plus 40 units purchased on February 21 (40 units at $15.60 each).

■ The 10 excess units returned to the storeroom on February 25 are priced at $15.50 because they relate to the issue of February 10 and are assumed to be part of the group of 30 units. The job finally will be charged only with the costs that would have been charged if the correct quantity had been issued on February 10 (150 units at $15 each + 20 units at $15.50 each).

■ Of the 120 units on hand at February 25, all except the 10 units returned are priced at the *most recent* cost, $15.60 per unit.

MATERIALS LEDGER CARD
(FIFO Cost Method)

Material _Plastic table tops_   Reorder Point _150_

Number _T-21_   Reorder Quantity _150_

DATE	REFERENCE	RECEIVED			ISSUED			BALANCE		
		UNITS	PRICE	AMOUNT	UNITS	PRICE	AMOUNT	UNITS	PRICE	AMOUNT
19XX Feb. 1	Bal.							150	15 00	2250 00
6	PO-87	150	15 50	2325 00				150 / 150	15 00 / 15 50	4575 00
10	R-103				150 / 30	15 00 / 15 50	2715 00	120	15 50	1860 00
21	PO-109	150	15 60	2340 00				120 / 150	15 50 / 15 60	4200 00
23	R-116				120 / 40	15 50 / 15 60	2484 00	110	15 60	1716 00
25	RM-13				(10)	15 50	(155 00)	10 / 110	15 50 / 15 60	1871 00

Arguments in favor of the first in, first out method are that it is easy to use; that it reflects the actual physical flow of goods in most cases; and that the inventory shown on the balance sheet reflects current costs and is an approximation of replacement cost.

A strong argument against the first in, first out method is that it does not match current costs against current sales revenue. Under this method, the ending inventory is priced at the most recent costs, leaving the items comprising the cost of goods sold to be priced at the oldest costs. Therefore, when net income is computed, the cost of goods sold that is matched against the current sales does not include the most recent costs. In periods of rising prices, this can lead to distortions in net income because the cost of goods sold is understated. A lower cost of goods sold means less is subtracted from sales, resulting in a higher net income and higher taxes.

Last In, First Out Method

The same transactions for Material T-21 would have different values if the LIFO method were used. (See page 85.)

- The issue of 180 units on February 10 consists of the 150 units purchased on February 6 (150 units at $15.50 each) plus 30 units from the beginning inventory (30 units at $15 each). Note that some accountants prefer to list the issues in reverse order. That is, they would show 30 units at $15 each followed by 150 units at $15.50 each. The sequence used here enables you to compare the FIFO and LIFO methods more easily.

- The issue of 160 units on February 23 consists of the 150 units purchased on February 21 (150 units at $15.60 each) plus 10 units from the beginning inventory (10 units at $15 each).

- The 10 excess units returned to the storeroom on February 25 relate to the issue of February 10 and are assumed to be part of the group of 30 units (the oldest). Thus the job finally will be charged only with the costs that would have been charged if the correct quantity had been issued (150 units at $15.50 each + 20 units at $15 each).

- All the 120 units on hand at February 25 (10+110) are priced at the *earliest* cost, $15 per unit. Note that these units would normally be recorded together as 120 units at $15 each. They are recorded separately here so that you can quickly compare FIFO and LIFO methods.

MATERIALS LEDGER CARD
(LIFO Cost Method)

Material *Plastic table tops* Reorder Point __150__
Number __T-21__ Reorder Quantity __150__

DATE	REFERENCE	RECEIVED			ISSUED			BALANCE		
		UNITS	PRICE	AMOUNT	UNITS	PRICE	AMOUNT	UNITS	PRICE	AMOUNT
19XX Feb. 1	Bal.							150	15.00	2250.00
6	PO-87	150	15.50	2325.00				150 / 150	15.00 / 15.50	4575.00
10	R-103				150 / 30	15.50 / 15.00	2775.00	120	15.00	1800.00
21	PO-109	150	15.60	2340.00				120 / 150	15.00 / 15.60	4140.00
23	R-116				150 / 10	15.60 / 15.00	2490.00	110	15.00	1650.00
25	RM-13				(10)	15.00	(150.00)	110	15.00	1800.00

The major argument in favor of the last in, first out method is that current costs are matched against current revenue, since the costs used are for materials acquired most recently. Therefore, the net income figure is a better measure of current earnings.

LIFO is popular in times of rising prices since inventories under LIFO are lower than under FIFO, resulting in lower profits and, thus, lower taxes. Also the use of LIFO in times of rising prices can improve the cash flow of a company because taxes, which must be paid in cash, will be lower. A company that uses the LIFO method for federal income taxes is also required to use it for financial accounting purposes.

Critics point out that the inventory value under the LIFO method reflects old costs and the inventory value of the balance sheet would be understated during periods of rising prices. In periods of falling prices, inventory costs would be higher, and the related profits and taxes would be higher. Some accountants may oppose the method because it usually represents an unrealistic physical flow of goods. (However, as stated earlier, the physical flow of goods does not have to correspond to the inventory costing method used.)

Moving Average Method

Neither the FIFO nor the LIFO method is entirely satisfactory for valuing inventory under all circumstances. Therefore, the cost accountant may employ the *moving average method* as a compromise. Under this method, the units and cost of each new purchase are added to the balances already on hand when the purchase is received, and a new average cost per unit is computed. At the time materials are issued, they are charged out at this new average cost until another purchase is received or a return is recorded, when a new average cost per unit is calculated. The same transactions show different values if the moving average method is used. (See page 86.)

- The 180 units issued on February 10 are priced at $15.25 per unit (the unit price appearing in the Balance section on the line above).
- The 160 units issued on February 23 are priced at $15.44 per unit ($4,170 ÷ 270).
- The 10 excess units returned to the storeroom on February 25 are priced at $15.25 because

MATERIALS LEDGER CARD
(MOVING AVERAGE COST METHOD)

Material _Plastic table tops_   Reorder Point _150_

Number _T-21_   Reorder Quantity _150_

DATE	REFERENCE	RECEIVED			ISSUED			BALANCE		
		UNITS	PRICE	AMOUNT	UNITS	PRICE	AMOUNT	UNITS	PRICE	AMOUNT
Feb. 1 19xx	Bal.							150	15 00	2250 00
6	PO-87	150	15 50	2325 00				300	15 25	4575 00
10	R-103				180	15 25	2745 00	120	15 25	1830 00
21	PO-109	150	15 60	2340 00				270	15 44	4170 00
23	R-116				160	15 44	2470 40	110	15 44	1699 60*
25	RM-13				(10)	15 25	(152 50)	120	15 43	1852 10

*Adjusted for rounding difference, $1.20.

they are related to the issue of February 10. Again, the job finally will be charged for the same amount as it would have been had the correct quantity been issued in the first place.

■ The 120 units remaining in stock on February 25 are valued at $15.43, the current average price.

One major advantage of the moving average method is that it minimizes the influence of wide fluctuations in the purchase price of materials during the period. The principal drawback is the large number of mathematical computations that have to be made if purchases occur often.

Valuation at Cost or Market, Whichever Is Lower

The methods of inventory valuation that have been discussed so far have been based on cost. Accountants generally believe that the asset valuation used on the balance sheet should be conservative; that is, when there is doubt about the value of an asset, it is better to understate than overstate its value. If the market value of raw materials has declined, the company will probably have trouble selling its products at the usual prices. If the price decline is especially severe, the manufacturer may even have to sell the products at a loss. Consequently, accountants may prefer to value raw materials inventory according to the rule of _cost or market, whichever is lower_. _Market_ should be interpreted as the cost of replacing materials. It is not the selling price. When the market price (replacement cost) of an item has declined below the original cost, the accountant values it at market price instead of at cost. This method reflects the lower current value on the books so that assets are not overstated.

Market price—for the purpose of applying the rule of cost or market, whichever is lower—might be described as the price at which the material could be bought (at the inventory date) through the usual channels and in the usual quantities. In some cases, current market prices are quoted in trade publications. In other cases, a recent purchase may give a price that is reasonably close to current market. In still other circumstances, quotations for use in valuation may be obtained from the firm's regular suppliers. (There are upper and lower limits imposed on the determination of the market price; implementation of these limits is beyond the scope of this text.)

There are several ways of applying the rule of cost or market, whichever is lower.

Lower of Cost or Market by Item. Under one plan, the cost of each item in inventory is determined according to an acceptable valuation method. Current market price is also determined for each material. Then the basis of valuation (the lower figure) is identified for each and is multiplied by the quantity on hand to obtain the value at the lower of cost or market. The lower valuation figure for each item is used to determine the value of the inventory as a whole, as shown below.

Lower of Cost or Market by Item

Description	Quantity	Cost per Unit	Market Price per Unit	Valuation Basis	Lower of Cost or Market
Material A	100	$1.00	$1.10	Cost	$100
Material B	200	1.50	1.20	Market	240
Inventory Valuation					$340

Lower of Total Cost or Total Market. Another method of valuation is to determine the total cost and the total market value of the entire inventory. The lower of these total figures is then used as the inventory valuation, as shown below.

Lower of Total Cost or Total Market

Description	Quantity	Cost per Unit	Market Price per Unit	Total Cost	Total Market
Material A	100	$1.00	$1.10	$100	$110
Material B	200	1.50	1.20	300	240
				$400	$350
Inventory Valuation					$350

If the prices of some materials have risen and others have declined, this procedure gives a less conservative valuation than the by-item procedure. However, those who prefer this method say that only the total inventory figure need be presented conservatively.

Lower of Total Cost or Total Market by Group. A variation on the preceding plan is to classify inventory materials by group or department and to determine the lower of total cost or total market for each classification. The lower figure (cost or market) for each group is added to the lower figure for each of the other groups to obtain the total inventory valuation. Assuming that Materials A and B in the preceding example constitute Group I and that Materials C and D constitute Group II, the basic computations required for the group total method are as follows:

Lower of Total Cost or Total Market by Group

Description	Quantity	Cost per Unit	Market Price per Unit	Total Cost	Total Market
Group I					
Material A	100	$1.00	$1.10	$100	$110
Material B	200	1.50	1.20	300	240
Total Group I				$400	$350*
Group II					
Material C	30	$ .70	$ .60	$ 21	$ 18
Material D	150	.60	.80	90	$120
Total Group II				$111*	$138

*Lower figures for inventory valuation.

Obviously, market ($350) is the lower basis for valuation of the materials in Group I, and cost ($111) is the lower basis for valuation of the materials in Group II. The value of inventory Groups I and II combined would be $461 ($350 + $111). This valuation is between those obtained under the other two methods, as shown below.

Lower of Total Cost or Total Market by Group

Material	Basis	Valuation
Group I (A and B)	Market	$350
Group II (C and D)	Cost	111
Inventory Valuation		$461

Lower of Cost or Market by Item

Material	Basis	Valuation
A	Cost	$100
B	Market	240
C	Market	18
D	Cost	90
Inventory Valuation		$448

Lower of Total Cost or Total Market

Material	Cost	Market
A	$100	$110
B	300	240
C	21	18
D	90	120
Inventory Valuation	$511	$488*

*Lower figure for inventory valuation.

Valuation by the lower of total cost or total market by group produces middle-of-the road figures. It does not reflect individual fluctuations as the lower of cost or market by item method does. But it does not offset market increases against market declines as much as the total cost or total market procedure does. The most commonly used method is the lower of cost or market by item, which produces the most conservative inventory valuation.

Applying the Rule of Cost or Market, Whichever Is Lower

When market value is lower than cost, the inventory would be *written down,* that is, the inventory would be adjusted to show the lower value. This procedure is common except when selling prices are expected to be unaffected by the decline in replacement costs. In such a situation, a write-down of inventory would amount to a fictitious loss. Therefore, cost rather than market would be used. There is also some controversy over when a loss should be recorded. Some accountants feel that the loss should not be reflected on the books until the transactions actually take place. Others prefer that the loss be recorded to prevent overstatement of assets on the balance sheet.

When a company adjusts inventory to show the lower value, two procedures may be used if perpetual inventory records are kept.

1. Each materials ledger card may be adjusted to show the new unit values.
2. A valuation account may be set up to reduce the total value of the inventory to market. The individual materials ledger cards are not changed and continue to reflect cost.

Under the first procedure each materials ledger card is adjusted according to the lower of cost or market value. The cards are then totaled to determine the new valuation. The loss is recorded by a general journal entry debiting an account called Loss on Reduction of Inventory to Market and crediting Raw Materials. After posting this entry, the total of the materials ledger cards will agree with the balance of the Raw Materials account in the general ledger. This method results in an increase to cost of goods sold for the difference between the cost and the market value and does not show the inventory loss as a separate item on the income statement.

A second procedure, which overcomes this objection and identifies the inventory loss as a separate item on the income statement, uses a valuation account that serves a purpose similar to that of Allowance for Uncollectible Accounts. This valuation account is usually called Allowance for Reduction of Inventory to Market. It is adjusted at the end of each fiscal period to value the inventory at the lower of cost or market.

To illustrate how this valuation technique is applied, assume the following data for 19X1 (the first year of operations) and 19X2:

	Dec. 31, 19X1	Dec. 31, 19X2
Inventory at Cost, per Materials Ledger Cards	$180,000	$210,000
Inventory at Market Value	174,000	208,000

On December 31, 19X1, an adjusting entry is made to set up the valuation account for $6,000, the difference between inventory cost and market value.

19X1			
Dec. 31	Loss on Reduction of Inventory to Market	XXX	6,000.00
	Allowance for Reduction of Inventory to Market	XXX	6,000.00
	Recorded loss resulting from decline in market value of inventory.		

In practice, the Loss on Reduction of Inventory to Market account is treated as an adjustment of the cost of goods sold on the income statement, although there is some argument for showing it as an adjustment of either the cost of raw materials used or the manufacturing overhead. Treating the loss as an adjustment of the cost of goods sold is very simple and eliminates the necessity for allocating the loss among the raw materials, work in process, and finished goods inventories. A partial income statement showing the loss as an adjustment of the cost of goods sold is shown here.

MASON METAL FABRICATORS, INC.
Partial Income Statement
Year Ended December 31, 19X1

Revenue		
Sales (Net)		$3,400,000
Cost of Goods Sold		
Finished Goods Inventory, Jan. 1	-0-	
Add Cost of Goods Manufactured (at cost)	$2,940,000	
Total Goods Available for Sale	$2,940,000	
Deduct Finished Goods Inventory, Dec. 31 (at Cost)	180,000	
	$2,760,000	
Add Loss on Reduction of Inventory to Market	6,000	
Cost of Goods Sold		2,766,000
Gross Profit on Sales		$ 634,000

The Allowance for Reduction of Inventory to Market account is shown on the balance sheet as a deduction from inventory.

MASON METAL FABRICATORS, INC.
Partial Balance Sheet
December 31, 19X1

Inventory, at Cost	$180,000	
Deduct Allowance for Reduction of Inventory to Market Value	6,000	
Inventory, at Lower of Cost or Market		$174,000

At the end of later periods, the allowance account will again be adjusted to reflect inventory value at that time. For example, at the end of 19X2, the allowance account of $6,000 should be reduced to $2,000, which is the difference then existing between cost, $210,000, and current market value, $208,000. To reduce the balance of the allowance account from $6,000 to $2,000, you must debit the allowance account for $4,000, the difference between these amounts. This adjustment is shown below in general journal form.

19X2			
Dec. 31	Allow. for Reduction of Inv. to Market	XXX 4,000.00	
	Recovery From Decrease in Allow. for		
	Reduction of Inv. to Market	XXX	4,000.00
	Recorded recovery resulting from adjustment of		
	allowance account.		

The recovery account will be shown on the income statement as a reduction in the cost of goods sold, as shown below.

MASON METAL FABRICATORS, INC.
Partial Income Statement
Year Ended December 31, 19X2

Revenue		
Sales (Net)		$3,900,000
Cost of Goods Sold		
Finished Goods Inventory, Jan 1 (at Cost)	$ 180,000	
Add Cost of Goods Manufactured	3,650,000	
Total Goods Available for Sale	$3,830,000	
Deduct Finished Goods Inventory,	210,000	
Dec. 31 (at Cost)	$3,620,000	
Deduct Recovery From Decrease in Allowance for		
Reduction of Inventory to Market	4,000	
Cost of Goods Sold		3,616,000
Gross Profit on Sales		$ 284,000

The allowance account balance of $2,000 at the end of 19X2 will again be treated as a deduction from the inventory at cost on the balance sheet.

If the cost of the inventory should exceed the market value, the valuation account is no longer needed. An entry would be made to close Allowance for Reduction of Inventory to Market by debiting that account for its current balance and crediting Recovery From Decrease in Allowance for Reduction of Inventory to Market. The inventory would be shown on the balance sheet at cost; inventory is not written up above cost.

This is an incorrect statement

Inventory Management

A primary objective of inventory controls is to achieve maximum profits by keeping the investment in materials inventory at the lowest level consistent with efficient manufacturing operations. Procedures such as holding larger quantities of materials in storage than are needed for normal operations, or purchasing required materials earlier than they are needed for manufacture, tie up working capital unnecessarily. This can cause loss of profits that otherwise could be earned by investment of the capital in other ways or for different purposes.

Cutoff Date

Accuracy in reporting costs of ending materials, work in process, and finished goods inventories is essential to the preparation of reliable financial statements. For ending inventories to be valued as accurately as possible, it is necessary that all costs associated with the items included be recorded. In order to ensure that these costs have been recorded, businesses establish a *cutoff date* for including transactions in a specified period. The cutoff date is usually the last day of the company's fiscal year or the end of an interim period such as a calendar quarter or month.

The accountant examines transactions just before and just after the cutoff date to determine if they are properly classified. All transactions associated with items in the ending inventories are included in the current period. Transactions affecting events after the cutoff date either are not recorded or are entered as deferred items.

Since Space Savers operates on the calendar-year basis, December 31 becomes the annual cutoff date for those transactions that are to be included in the current year. For example, all invoices for materials received on or before December 31 must be entered in the materials ledger and posted to the materials ledger cards. The same principle applies to accounting for labor and overhead transactions.

Periodic Physical Inventory

The perpetual inventory system provides routine internal control over materials. Still, in spite of carefully planned procedures and controls, some differences often occur between the quantity of a material on hand and the quantity shown on the materials ledger card. In order to detect these errors and to correct the records, it is necessary to count the materials on hand periodically and to compare this actual count with the materials ledger cards. A physical inventory can be scheduled in one of two ways.

1. At the end of an accounting period, such as a year, all production is halted and the employees count and tally materials on hand. The plant does not resume operations until the inventory is completed and verified.
2. A less disruptive procedure is the *continuous* or *cycle inventory*. Under this plan, only a few materials are counted each day. A schedule is developed so that all materials will be inventoried at least once each year. Materials that are difficult to measure accurately or that are highly susceptible to theft are inventoried two or more times a year. Some large companies have full-time inventory crews conducting the inventory on a scheduled basis. This avoids overtime work and eliminates errors that occur when untrained people are used.

Inventory-Taking Technique

Space Savers uses a regular end-of-year inventory by actual count, weight, or measurement to check its perpetual inventory system. These are the steps in taking inventory.

1. Serially numbered inventory tags are prepared in advance for each material and for each shelf, stack, or bin in which the material is stored. (See the tag below.)

```
                                         FORM NO. I 5
            INVENTORY TAG
                      No. _35_____

   Material _8" braces_____
   Material No. _2-307_   Location _Bin 3_
   Quantity _400_         Date _12/26/X1_
   Counted by _N.Z._      Verified by _G.H._
   Unit Price _____
   Total Value _____
   Priced by _____ Checked by _____
```

DATE	RECEIVED AFTER COUNT	ISSUED AFTER COUNT	BALANCE
12/27	200		600

2. Tags are attached to the materials to be inventoried.
3. An inventory checker proceeds to count, weigh, or measure each material, recording the count and the date on the inventory tag. This count is often made several days before the official inventory date (the cutoff date). Receipts and issues after the count are recorded on the inventory tag in order to reflect the current balance on hand.
4. Inventory sheets are prepared in advance. The materials to be inventoried are listed on the sheets, usually in the same order as they are physically stored. The material number, description, location, and unit cost are entered. Much of this information is obtained from the materials ledger card.
5. On the inventory date, a checker counts, weighs, or measures each material and records the count on the inventory sheet. This count is completely independent of the first count, which was recorded on the inventory tag.
6. A supervisor or another checker then compares the count (or balance) shown on the inventory tag with the count shown on the inventory sheet. Differences are immediately reconciled so that the inventory sheet contains an actual count, double-checked for accuracy.
7. The inventory sheets are sent to a clerk, who compares the actual counts shown on the sheets with the balances shown on the materials ledger cards. This clerk also verifies the unit costs listed on the inventory sheets. (The inventory tags remain attached to the materials.)

8. Materials are recounted if unusually large differences are noted, and corrections are made.
9. Entries on the inventory sheets are extended, the extensions are totaled, and the complete inventory is summarized, as shown below.

INVENTORY		December 31, 19X1				Page ___9___	

Sheet No. ___1___ Department __Assembling__ Priced By _P.O._
Listed by _F.K._ Location __Factory Bldg. A__ Extended by _J.L._
Checked by _N.Z._

TAG NO.	MATERIAL NO.	DESCRIPTION	QUANTITY	UNIT COST		EXTENDED TOTAL	
35	2–307	8'' Braces	400		40	160	00
36	L–27.	24'' Mica table tops	50	1	50	75	00
37	I–16	Buffer pads	250		61	152	50
		TOTAL				1312	19

10. All inventory computations are independently double-checked.
11. Inventory differences are summarized in an inventory shortage and overage report.
12. The materials ledger cards are corrected to show the actual count and value.
13. The general ledger accounts are adjusted to show the actual inventory valuation.
14. Reasons for inventory differences are looked into. Action is taken to prevent large differences from recurring.

Adjustment of Inventory

Adjusting for an inventory shortage or overage is done in two steps.

1. The individual materials ledger cards must be corrected. A shortage is recorded by an entry in the Issued section of the materials ledger card for the material found to be short. The cost is computed on the regular costing basis (FIFO, LIFO, or moving average) as though the missing materials were being charged out on a requisition on the closing date of the period. An overage is entered in the Received section of the materials ledger card. The cost to be used is the cost of the last issue of that material.
2. A general journal entry is made to adjust the firm's ledger accounts for the net shortage or overage. If the net total inventory shortage at Space Savers, as revealed by the periodic physical inventory, were $835, this adjustment amount would be journalized as a debit to Manufacturing Overhead Control and a credit to Raw Materials. The amount of the shortage is also entered under Indirect Materials on the departmental overhead analysis sheet of the General Factory Department, which is responsible for the control of raw materials.

At Space Savers, the adjusting entry is made on a general journal voucher, as shown on the next page, rather than in the more familiar general journal. Space Savers, like most large businesses, finds that using a separate voucher for each journal entry is more efficient and convenient. Vouchers are numbered for control purposes. The first portion of the number represents the month, and the second portion, the sequence of the entry within the month. General journal vouchers are kept in numeric order in a binder. There is very little difference between the general journal with which you are familiar and the collection of journal vouchers (one entry to a page) used by Space Savers.

JOURNAL VOUCHER	Date Dec. 31,	19 X1	No. 12-37		
ACCOUNT	ACCOUNT NUMBER	✓	DEBIT		CREDIT
Manufacturing Overhead Control	501		835 00		
Raw Materials	121				835 00
EXPLANATION					
Recorded net inventory shortage per schedule.					
PREPARED BY C.J.S.	AUDITED BY JB		APPROVED BY RM		

Computer-Assisted Physical Inventory

When a business has a computerized perpetual inventory system, the computer can assist with the process of taking the physical inventory. The inventory sheets can be prepared by the computer. The materials to be inventoried are listed on individual sheets along with their material numbers, description, and locations. This information comes from the inventory files in the computer's memory.

On the day of the physical inventory, the inventory checkers record the amount of each material on the appropriate inventory sheet. Then the count and material number for each item is entered into the computer. The computer compares the count for each item with the balance carried in the computer's inventory files. Differences are recorded in an error and exception file. This file is specifically set up to store the differences between the physical inventory amounts and the inventory balances recorded in the accounting records. A list of exceptions can be printed for evaluation by the accountant.

Many companies have a policy of examining exceptions only if they exceed a certain level. For example, a company may do a second count and investigate items only if the difference between the physical count and the inventory balance in the computer file is greater than 5 percent. The computer is programmed to produce an exception report listing all items whose differences are greater than 5 percent. Management can use this report to investigate inventory losses.

When the count for all inventory items is complete, the computer can update the inventory records to reflect any changes that have been brought to light by the physical count.

Reasons for Inventory Shortages and Overages

Some differences are almost certain to occur in inventory records under the pressure of large-scale operations. Some reasons for these differences might be the following:

- Failure to complete required paperwork at each step of the flow of materials
- Failure to post receipts
- Failure to post issues
- Incorrect posting of receipts and issues
- Computation errors in day-to-day posting
- Errors in recognizing the correct cutoff dates

Other differences, such as the following, arise from the nature of the material or from storage conditions:

- Spoilage as a result of natural processes or from poor storage conditions.
- Shrinkage due to such natural causes as dehydration.
- Computation errors arising from different units of measurement for receipts and issues. For example, material might be bought by the ton but issued by the pound.

The following differences require special attention:

- Losses due to theft of materials by employees
- Losses arising from theft by outsiders owing to inadequate plant protection
- Losses due to short weight or short measure, often involving collusion between suppliers and receiving and purchasing personnel
- Losses due to unnecessary or deliberate scrapping of materials that are still useful

Since a firm's raw materials represent a large investment, any loss may involve a great deal of money. Accountants must be constantly on guard to see that the business's resources are protected. Knowledge of what conditions to look for is essential if safeguards are to be used effectively.

Computer Simulation and "JIT"–Propelled Inventory Management

The Novodent Corporation is a manufacturer of dental supplies with annual sales of $16 million. The board of directors is satisfied with the sales volume but believes that manufacturing costs can be significantly reduced. Accordingly, the board has hired a new president to run the company. The new president, Frank Wagner, was very successful in streamlining production expenses in two companies at which he worked previously.

Mr. Wagner focused on reducing the cost of inventory by introducing "just in time" (JIT) manufacturing techniques. JIT manufacturing involves restructuring the production process—from receiving new material to shipping the finished product—so that every material arrives at the right place on the assembly line "just in time" to be installed.

Under Mr. Wagner's direction, Novodent ran computer simulations of the current manufacturing process. A computer simulation is a program that copies the behavior of a process and examines it for flaws and bottlenecks by altering different parts of the process or by introducing new volumes of production. Computerized simulations are far less expensive than experimenting by changing the actual assembly line and are faster than if the calculations were done by hand.

The simulation showed that it would be more beneficial to obtain a continuous flow of small quantities of materials from suppliers than to order large quantities at intervals. Inventory costs would be reduced because raw materials inventory on hand could be cut by 27 percent.

Smaller batches of materials would also improve quality control. Currently, finished goods are tested only after a batch is completed. If there are defects in the materials or in the assembly process, they are not discovered until the entire batch is produced. Smaller batches would result in more quality-control checks, and fewer items are lost if a small batch is rejected. The simulation also indicated that Novodent could be more responsive to the market if it were not tied to completion of large batches of goods that customers may not buy if their needs change. ■

Principles and Procedures Summary

The perpetual inventory system provides a complete record of receipts, issues, and balances of materials on hand, item by item. The quantity computations can be made easily enough, but the pricing or valuation process is a difficult one. Prices paid for materials fluctuate from purchase to purchase. Furthermore, it is difficult to relate an issue or a balance on hand to a specific purchase.

The cost accountant resolves the problem of pricing by applying a recognized method of valuation. There are three possible methods of costing. The first in, first out (FIFO) method assumes that the oldest materials are used first. The last in, first out (LIFO) method assumes that the newest materials are used first. In the moving average method, a new average cost is calculated after each receipt of materials. Each method has some advantages and limitations. The accountant will recommend the method that best fits the firm's needs. Valuation of the inventory at the end of the fiscal period may be based on actual cost or according to the rule of cost or market, whichever is lower.

The accuracy of the perpetual inventory must be checked from time to time by an actual physical count. Some firms take inventory periodically; others use the continuous, or cycle, method. Once the count has been fully verified, the inventory sheets are extended, totaled, and double-checked for accuracy. Inventory differences are summarized on an inventory shortage or overage report. In turn, the materials ledger cards are corrected and the general ledger account balances are adjusted. Reasons for differences are determined, and corrective action is taken to prevent recurrence.

A computer can speed up and simplify the process of taking inventory.

Review Questions

1. What is a major advantage of using a perpetual inventory system?
2. Under what method of inventory costing are the materials on hand always considered to be from the last ones purchased?
3. Under what method of inventory costing are the materials on hand always considered to be from the first ones purchased?
4. Which inventory costing method charges current costs against current revenue? What is the benefit of such matching?

5. Under the moving average method, when must a new unit cost be calculated?
6. What are the three ways that the lower of cost or market method can be applied to inventory items? *item, groups, entire inv*
7. In applying the lower of cost or market method to the raw materials inventory, which way results in the lowest possible value for the inventory? Which results in the highest value?
8. Why are general journal vouchers often used in place of recording transactions in a general journal.? *more efficient*
9. How is a loss on the reduction of inventory to market value shown on the income statement? How is a recovery from a decrease in the allowance for the reduction of inventory to market value shown?
10. What is a physical inventory?
11. Inventory shortages may be caused by spoilage, and inventory overages may be caused by duplicate postings prepared by two employees. What are three other causes of shortages and overages?

Managerial Discussion Questions

1. In a period of rising prices, what effect would the use of FIFO have on the net income and the taxes of a company? What effect would LIFO have on the net income and the taxes?
2. Discuss the relationship between the physical flow of goods and the inventory costing method used.
3. Even though a company maintains an effective perpetual inventory system, a periodic physical inventory should be taken. Why?
4. Management is concerned about the rise in inventory shortages. Suggest some security methods and internal control procedures that could be adopted to minimize the inventory shortages.
5. What are the benefits of using continuous or cycle inventory procedures?
6. Why would management want to adopt the lower of cost or market rule?
7. What is the importance to management of adhering to a clearly established inventory cutoff date?
8. How does an inventory exception report aid management in efficient inventory control?

Exercises

1. **Calculating the ending inventory balance and cost using FIFO.** The data given below relate to Material 207, 3-inch wooden handles, used by Colonial Cabinet Makers. Based on this data, determine the ending inventory balance and cost using the FIFO inventory valuation method.

Beginning balance	480 at $4.80 each
Purchase Order 301	600 at $4.90 each
Requisition 469	175
Requisition 493	225
Requisition 504	280
Purchase Order 960	400 at $4.95 each
Requisition 529	310
Returned Material Report 24 (from Requisition 504)	20

2. **Calculating the ending inventory balance and cost using LIFO.** Based on the

data given in Exercise 1, determine the ending inventory balance and cost using the LIFO inventory valuation method.

3. **Calculating the ending inventory balance and cost using the moving average method.** Based on the data given in Exercise 1, determine the ending inventory balance and cost using the moving average inventory valuation method.

4. **Calculating inventory value using the lower of cost or market method.** The data given below relates to the raw materials inventory of the Edgemont Manufacturing Corporation. Determine the value of the inventory if the lower of cost or market method is applied to the individual inventory items.

	Units	Costs	Market
Group I			
Material A	460	$1.40	$1.30
Material B	830	.85	.90
Group II			
Material C	1,290	1.20	1.45
Material D	580	.65	.55

5. **Calculating inventory value by group using the lower of cost or market method.** Based on the data given in Exercise 4, determine the value of the inventory if the lower of cost or market method is applied to the inventory by group.

6. **Calculating inventory value using the lower of cost or market method.** Based on the data given in Exercise 4, determine the value of the inventory if the lower of cost or market method is applied to the inventory as a whole.

7. **Presenting inventory on the balance sheet at the lower of cost or market.** The following information is obtained from the records of the Stratton Corporation:

Inventory (at Cost): $280,680
Allowance for Reduction of Inventory to Market Value: $6,506

Show the balance sheet presentation for these accounts.

8. **Calculating the cost of goods sold.** From the data presented below, determine the cost of goods sold to be shown on the income statement of the Kelley Corporation for the month of September 19X5.

Finished Goods, September 1, 19X5	$ 63,580
Finished Goods, September 30, 19X5	73,420
Cost of Goods Manufactured	195,970
Loss on Reduction of Inventory to Market	4,170

9. **Calculating the cost of goods sold.** From the data presented below, determine the cost of goods sold to be shown on the income statement of the Delta Manufacturing Company for the month of June 19X4.

Finished Goods, June 1, 19X4	$125,620
Finished Goods, June 30, 19X4	113,640
Cost of Goods Manufactured	384,190
Recovery From Decrease in Allowance for Reduction of Inventory to Market	6,370

10. **Journalizing inventory at the lower of cost or market.** The Monroe Company has decided to value its raw materials inventory at the lower of cost or market. The Raw Materials account has an ending balance of $73,970. The market value of the raw materials is $70,130. Record the necessary general journal entry to value the inventory at the lower of cost or market.

11. **Journalizing inventory at the lower of cost or market.** At the end of the current fiscal year, the Raw Materials account for the Sanchez Manufacturing Company has a balance of $286,936. The company has been using the lower of cost or market method for several years. The Allowance for Reduction of Inventory to Market Value account has a balance of $7,490. The market value of the raw materials at the end of the year is $281,520. Record the adjusting entry needed to value the raw materials at the lower of cost or market.

Problems

PROBLEM 5-1. Using different inventory costing methods. The Piedmont Manufacturing Company uses a perpetual inventory system to control materials. Data relating to Material K-5 during January 19X5 are given below.

Jan. 1   Balance, 1,000 units at $12.50 each.
      5   Issued 400 units, Requisition 917.
      9   Received 600 units at $14 each, Purchase Order 16.
     13   Issued 850 units, Requisition 944.
     22   Received 600 units at $14.50 each, Purchase Order 23.
     29   Issued 250 units, Requisition 984.

Instructions

Enter the beginning balance on a materials ledger card for each of the three inventory valuation methods: FIFO, LIFO, and moving average. Record each of the transactions on each of the materials ledger cards. Round unit costs to the nearest cent under the moving average costing method.

PROBLEM 5-2. Using different inventory costing methods. Concepts Furniture, a manufacturer of office equipment, uses a perpetual inventory system to control materials. During July 19X5, the following transactions took place in completing an order for chairs and desks:

July 1   Issued 135 units of Material B-42 on Materials Requisition 711.
      3   Received 650 units of Material B-42 at $.88 and 650 units of Material R-18 at $.76. These goods were ordered on Purchase Order 426.
      4   Issued 135 units of Material R-18 on Materials Requisition 735.
      7   Issued 165 units of Material B-42 and 165 units of Material R-18 on Materials Requisition 749.
     12   Issued 80 units of Material B-42 and 80 units of Material R-18 on Materials Requisition 763.
     21   Issued 304 units of Material B-42 on Materials Requisition 796.
     26   Received 650 units of Material B-42 at $.85 and 650 units of Material R-18 at $.79. These goods were ordered on Purchase Order 471.
     31   Issued 210 units of Material B-42 and 383 units of Material R-18 on Materials Requisition 822.

Instructions

1. The number of units on hand, the unit price, and the total amount on July 1, 19X5 are given below. Record each of the transactions on materials ledger cards. Use the FIFO method of inventory costing.

	Reorder Point	Reorder Quantity	BALANCE Units	BALANCE Price	BALANCE Amount
Material					
B-42 Seats, Plywood	300	650	271	$.95	$257.45
R-18 Tops, Plastic	300	650	83	.70	58.10

2. Record each of the transactions on materials ledger cards. Use the LIFO method of inventory costing.
3. Record each of the transactions on materials ledger cards. Use the moving average method of inventory costing. Compute new unit prices only after each new purchase of materials. Carry your computations to three decimal places.

PROBLEM 5-3. Calculating inventory value at the lower of cost or market. The following data pertain to the raw materials inventory for the Paramount Company on December 31, 19X1:

	Quantity	Cost per Unit	Market Price per Unit
Group I—Frames			
Type 1	250	$ 3.00	$ 3.20
Type 2	400	4.40	4.20
Type 3	370	2.00	2.10
Group II—Assemblies			
Type A	40	170.00	182.00
Type B	20	410.00	400.00
Type C	50	153.00	144.00

Instructions

Determine the amount to be reported as the inventory valuation at cost or market, whichever is lower, under each of the following methods: (1) lower of cost or market for each item, (2) lower of total cost or total market, and (3) lower of total cost or total market by groups.

PROBLEM 5-4. Calculating inventory value at the lower of cost or market and making journal entries. The Worldwide Products Company uses a perpetual inventory system. On April 30, 19X6 its balance sheet included the following items related to the raw materials inventory:

Raw Materials Inventory, at Cost	$478,250
Deduct Allowance for Reduction of Inventory to Market	21,930
Raw Materials Inventory, at Lower of Cost or Market	$456,320

Instructions

1. One year later, on April 30, 19X7, the perpetual inventory account showed a balance of $493,840. The market value of the inventory on that date was determined to be $462,110. Give the entry in general journal form to adjust the allowance account on April 30, 19X7.
2. Assume the same facts as in Instruction 1, except that the market value on April 30, 19X7, was determined to be $480,220. Give the journal entry to adjust the allowance account.
3. Assume the same facts as in Instruction 1, except that the market value on April 30, 19X7, was determined to be $496,910. Give the journal entry to adjust the allowance account.

PROBLEM 5-5. **Calculating inventory at the lower of cost or market and making journal entries.** The following information relates to the raw materials inventory of the Spinelli Manufacturing Corporation on June 30, 19X3: Raw Materials Inventory (at Cost), $648,100; Raw Materials Inventory (Market Value), $619,500.

Instructions

1. Record the general journal entry needed on June 30, 19X3, assuming that the company wants to report the raw materials inventory on its balance sheet using the lower of cost or market valuation method.
2. Record the general journal entry needed the next year on June 30, 19X4, assuming the following: the balance of the Raw Materials inventory account is $592,620; the market value is $581,220; the company uses the lower of cost or market valuation method.
3. At the end of the following year, June 30, 19X5, the balance of the Raw Materials inventory account is $602,260 and the market value is $614,050. Record the necessary general journal entry, assuming that the company still uses the lower of cost or market method of valuing its inventory.
4. Show the balance sheet presentation for the raw materials inventory and related accounts for 19X3, 19X4, and 19X5.

PROBLEM 5-6. **Preparing an income statement.** The fiscal year for the Haskell Corporation ends on January 31, 19X5. Use the data below to prepare an income statement for the current year.

Sales	$749,200
Sales Returns and Allowances	13,760
Finished Goods, February 1, 19X4	74,630
Finished Goods, January 31, 19X5	77,150
Cost of Goods Manufactured	379,280
Selling Expenses	135,260
Administrative Expenses	97,340
Loss on Reduction of Inventory to Market	8,720
Provision for Income Taxes	46,900

Alternate Problems

PROBLEM 5-1A. Using different inventory costing methods. The Shore Drive Manufacturing Company uses a perpetual inventory system to control materials. Data relating to Material M-2 during January 19X5 are given below.

Jan. 1 Balance, 150 units at $4.00 each.
    6 Received 200 units at $4.05 each, Purchase Order 74.
   12 Issued 225 units, Requisition 18.
   14 Received 250 units at $4.10 each, Purchase Order 83.
   17 Issued 200 units, Requisition 23.
   31 Issued 40 units, Requisition 29.

Instructions

Enter the beginning balance on a materials ledger card for each of the three inventory valuation methods: FIFO, LIFO, and moving average. Record each of the transactions on each of the materials ledger cards. Round unit costs to the nearest cent under the moving average costing method.

PROBLEM 5-2A. Using different inventory costing methods. The R. J. Manufacturing Corporation, a manufacturer of office equipment, uses a perpetual inventory system to control materials. During July 19X5, the following transactions took place in completing an order for chairs and desks:

July 1 Issued 110 units of Material B-42 on Materials Requisition 320.
   3 Received 650 units of Material B-42 at $1.02 and 650 units of Material R-18 at $.65. These goods were ordered on Purchase Order 517.
   6 Issued 175 units of Material R-18 on Materials Requisition 347.
   8 Issued 150 units of Material B-42 on Materials Requisition 362.
  12 Issued 80 units of Material R-18 on Materials Requisition 463.
  26 Received 650 units of Material R-18 at $.59. These goods were ordered on Purchase Order 617.
  31 Issued 210 units of Material B-42 and 382 units of Material R-18 on Materials Requisition 822.

Instructions

1. The number of units on hand, the unit price, and the total amount on July 1, 19X5 are given below. Record each of the transactions on materials ledger cards. Use the FIFO method of inventory costing.

	Reorder	Reorder	BALANCE		
Material	Point	Quantity	Units	Price	Amount
B-42 Seats, Plywood	300	650	271	$.95	$275.45
R-18 Tops, Plastic	300	650	83	.70	58.10

2. Record each of the transactions on materials ledger cards. Use the LIFO method of inventory costing.

3. Record each of the transactions on materials ledger cards. Use the moving average method of inventory costing. Compute new unit prices only after each new purchase of materials. Carry your computations to three decimal places.

PROBLEM 5-3A. Calculating inventory at the lower of cost or market. The following data pertain to the raw materials inventory for the Lowell Manufacturing Company on December 31, 19X1:

	Quantity	Cost per Unit	Market Price per Unit
Group I—Base Material			
Type 1	100	$10.00	$11.00
Type 2	200	15.00	13.00
Type 3	120	16.00	15.00
Group II—Conversion Mix			
Type A	120	5.00	4.50
Type B	110	7.50	7.25
Type C	25	6.00	6.30

Instructions

Determine the amount to be reported as the inventory valuation at cost or market, whichever is lower, under each of the following methods: (1) lower of cost or market for each item, (2) lower of total cost or total market, and (3) lower of total cost or total market by groups.

PROBLEM 5-4A. Calculating inventory value at the lower of cost or market and making journal entries. The Barlow Company uses a perpetual inventory system. On August 31, 19X5, its balance sheet included the following items related to the raw materials inventory:

Raw Materials Inventory, at Cost	$122,460
Deduct Allowance for Reduction of Inventory to Market	9,350
Raw Materials Inventory, at Lower of Cost or Market	$113,110

Instructions

1. One year later, on August 31, 19X6, the perpetual inventory account showed a balance of $113,780. The market value of the inventory on that date was determined to be $99,630. Give the entry in general journal form to adjust the allowance account on August 31, 19X6.
2. Assume the same facts as in Instruction 1, except that the market value on August 31, 19X6 was determined to be $108,410. Give the journal entry to adjust the allowance account.
3. Assume the same facts as in Instruction 1, except that the market value on August 31, 19X6 was determined to be $115,160. Give the journal entry to adjust the allowance account.

PROBLEM 5-5A. Calculating inventory value at the lower of cost or market and making journal entries. The following information relates to the raw materials inventory of the Westwood Manufacturing Corporation on September 30, 19X4:

Raw Materials Inventory (at Cost), $584,930
Raw Materials Inventory (Market Value), $596,275

Instructions

1. Record the general journal entry needed on September 30, 19X4, assuming that

the company wants to report the raw materials inventory on its balance sheet using the lower of cost or market valuation method.

2. Record the general journal entry needed the following year on September 30, 19X5, assuming the following: the balance of the Raw Materials inventory account is $514,370; the market value is $496,410; and the company uses the lower of cost or market valuation method.

3. At the end of the following year, September 30, 19X6, the balance of the Raw Materials inventory account is $513,540 and the market value is $510,600. Record the necessary general journal entry, assuming that the company still uses the lower of cost or market method for valuing its inventory.

4. Show the balance sheet presentation for the raw materials inventory and related accounts for 19X4, 19X5, and 19X6.

PROBLEM 5-6A. Preparing an income statement. The fiscal year for the Kenwood Company ends on March 31, 19X6. From the following information, prepare an income statement for the current year.

Sales	$1,385,720
Sales Returns and Allowances	34,643
Finished Goods, April 1, 19X5	94,310
Finished Goods, March 31, 19X6	98,570
Cost of Goods Manufactured	833,270
Selling Expenses	185,417
Administrative Expenses	118,823
Recovery From Decrease in Allowance for Reduction of	
Inventory to Market	18,365
Provision for Income Taxes	98,490

Managerial Decisions

CASE 5-1. The Snyder Supply Company uses the FIFO method in valuing its inventories. At the end of the current fiscal year, management is considering adopting a new method of inventory valuation. The following comparative schedule was prepared showing the inventory costs under the FIFO, LIFO, and moving average methods for the ending inventory on December 31, 19X4.

	FIFO	LIFO	Moving Average
Raw Materials Inventory	$15,890	$13,750	$14,805
Work in Process Inventory	28,750	25,840	26,030
Finished Goods Inventory	16,960	14,280	15,340

Prepare a recommendation to management on which of the three methods the company should use in valuing inventory. Indicate in your recommendation the effect that the inventory value would have on the cost of goods manufactured and on the income statement and the balance sheet.

CASE 5-2. Assume the same facts as above. However, management has indicated to you that the market value of its raw materials has declined by 10 percent. What effect, if any, would this fact have on your recommendation to management?

CHAPTER

6

Timekeeping and Payroll

■ ■ ■

Labor costs are the second major cost element in modern manufacturing operations. These costs must be carefully controlled for good management. A typical system of accounting for labor costs includes keeping records of time worked, computing and recording earnings, and charging costs to production. In this chapter, you will learn about timekeeping, computing, and recording procedures as they relate to the payment of wages. The amounts involved are debited to the Factory Payroll Clearing account. Charging labor costs to production will be covered in the next chapter.

Timekeeping Procedures

The procedure for keeping records of the time worked by each employee is called *timekeeping*. The time records serve as a basis for calculating gross wages. From these amounts, appropriate deductions are computed to determine employees' net pay. These records also serve as the basis to compute the employer's payroll taxes. Space Savers' timekeeping procedures contain the basic payroll elements found in typical manufacturing operations.

Time Cards

Time cards are prepared weekly for each employee by the payroll unit. They are placed in a rack next to an electronic time clock near the plant entrance. When employees enter the factory, they select their time cards and insert them in the clock to record the time of arrival. Employees then replace their cards in the rack. Each time employees enter or leave the plant, they record their time in or out in this way. Some companies station a clerk from the timekeeping unit at the time clock during the periods when most employees are checking in or out. The clerk makes sure that all employees record their time properly and that no one records a time for an employee who is not present. At the end of each day, all time cards are collected from the rack so that the clerks in the timekeeping unit can compute and enter the total hours worked. The time card for the week ending October 5 for Donald Jones, an employee in the Assembling Department, is shown on page 107.

NAME   Donald Jones
NO.   16

WEEK ENDING   OCTOBER 5, 19X1

	REGULAR				EXTRA		
Hrs.	In	Out	In	Out	In	Out	Hrs.
8	≤07₅₅	≤12₀₁	≤12₅₉	≤17₀₀			
8	⊒07₅₇	⊒12₀₀	⊒12₅₈	⊒17₀₃			
8	≥07₅₉	≥12₀₅	≥12₅₉	≥17₀₀			
8	⊤07₅₅	⊤12₀₃	⊤12₅₅	⊤17₀₅			
8	⊢07₅₈	⊢12₀₀	⊢12₅₇	⊢17₀₁	⊢17₃₀	⊢19₃₀	2

Time Tickets

The time card shown indicates the total hours worked by the employee each day, but it does not show the particular jobs worked on, or what type of work was performed. Since labor costs are charged to specific jobs or departments, some record showing the use of time must be prepared. *Time tickets,* sometimes called job time cards, are used for this purpose. (See page 108.)

The time ticket shows the employee's name and number, department worked in, job worked on, operation, starting and stopping time on the job, and time spent on each job. Space Savers computes time on the job to the nearest quarter hour, although some companies keep more exact records. Often, time on the job is measured to the nearest tenth of an hour.

Space Savers requires both direct and indirect workers paid at an hourly wage rate (weekly) to prepare daily time tickets indicating their activities. Workers who earn a fixed monthly salary (paid semimonthly) are not required to prepare time tickets. Their earnings are classified as indirect labor, and each employee of this type works in only one department.

The time ticket used by Space Savers is a card that is perforated into five parts. Four are individual time tickets, and the fifth is used for a summary of the total time worked during the day. Employees fill out a separate part of the time ticket for each different job they work on during a shift. (Workers whose jobs are classified as indirect labor would only enter the department in which they worked.) The time ticket for Donald Jones, shown on the next page, indicates that he is an Assembling

```
Employee No. 16              Date Oct. 1, 19X1
Job No. 101                  Dept. Assembling
Start 08.00        Hours    Rate    Amount
Stop 17.00          8      $8.50   $68.00
Operation attaching hardware

- - - - - - - - - - - - - - - - - - - - - - - - -

Employee No. _____       Date _____
Job No. _____            Dept. _____
Start _____      Hours    Rate    Amount
Stop _____
Operation _____

- - - - - - - - - - - - - - - - - - - - - - - - -

Employee No. _____       Date _____
Job No. _____            Dept. _____
Start _____      Hours    Rate    Amount
Stop _____
Operation _____

- - - - - - - - - - - - - - - - - - - - - - - - -

Employee No. _____       Date _____
Job No. _____            Dept. _____
Start _____      Hours    Rate    Amount
Stop _____
Operation _____

- - - - - - - - - - - - - - - - - - - - - - - - -

Name Donald Jones
Employee No. 16             Date Oct. 1, 19X1
Total Hours 8               Rate $8.50
Total Earnings $68.00       Approved by R.H.
```

Department employee. He worked on Job 101 for eight hours on October 1 at an hourly rate of $8.50.

If workers who normally do direct labor spend time performing indirect functions (such as cleaning or repairing machinery), they also complete a section of the time ticket for this work. The employee completes the time ticket each day, leaving any earnings lines blank.

Although the filling out of time tickets may seem to be a burdensome task, the procedure is really quite simple. Most employees doing direct labor will seldom work on more than one job in a day. Most employees doing indirect labor work in only one department.

Idle Time

It is not always possible to charge every hour spent in the factory to a specific job or department. Some idle, or nonproductive, time is bound to occur, even though a well-managed plant succeeds in keeping it to a minimum. The method of charging idle time varies according to its nature and extent. At Space Savers, the short time spent during the morning and afternoon rest periods is not considered idle time. It is absorbed into whatever job the employee is working on at the time of the break. Sometimes a longer period is involved, such as an hour lost waiting for materials, for assignment to a new job, or for a machine to be repaired. These idle time costs are considered manufacturing overhead. A time ticket is prepared for idle time in exactly the same manner as for time spent on a job. At the end of each week an analysis of idle time is prepared for appropriate action by the production manager or line supervisor.

Daily Analysis of Data

At the end of the day all time tickets are collected by a time clerk, who must complete the following procedures:

1. Compare the hours shown on each employee's time tickets with the total time shown on the employee's time card.
2. Investigate discrepancies between time tickets and time cards.
3. Enter earnings on the time tickets.
4. Enter in the payroll register the number of hours worked during the day by each worker.
5. Separate individual parts of the time tickets to make it easier to sort by job or department.

. . . .

Payroll Procedures

The timekeeping activities described in Steps 4 and 5 above provide the data needed by the payroll unit for computing earnings and completing labor cost records.

Weekly Factory Payroll Register

The record of hours worked each day by hourly wage rate employees is transferred daily from the time tickets to the weekly factory payroll register. After all hours worked by each employee during the week have been entered in the payroll register, regular earnings, overtime premium earnings, and total earnings are computed and extended. Appropriate deductions are made and entered in the proper columns, and the net pay for each employee is determined, as shown on page 110. Some companies, like Space Savers, may also show a distribution of gross earnings into direct and indirect labor.

Overtime Compensation. Firms engaged in interstate commerce are subject to the Fair Labor Standards Act, which regulates wages and working hours of employees. This law requires that employees be paid at one and a half times the regular hourly rate for all time worked in excess of 40 hours in any one work week. For example, an employee with a pay rate of $8 per hour works 44 hours during a week. Four hours are overtime (subject to payment in excess of the regular rate). During these four hours the employee earns his or her regular rate of $8 per hour plus an overtime premium of $4 per hour. Thus the employee's total pay for four hours of

PAYROLL REGISTER   Week Beginning _Oct. 1,_ 19 _XI_   and ending _Oct. 5,_ 19 _XI_   Paid _Oct. 8,_ 19 _XI_

EMPLOYEE NO.	EMPLOYEE	WITH. ALLOW.	MARITAL STATUS	HOURS BY DAYS S	M	T	W	T	F	S	TOTAL	OVERTIME	RATE PER HOUR	EARNINGS REGULAR	OVER. PREM.	TOTAL	TAXABLE EARNINGS FICA	FUTA	DEDUCTIONS FICA	FED. INC. TAX WITH.	OTHER	PAID NET AMOUNT	CK. NO.	DISTRIBUTION DIRECT LABOR	INDIRECT LABOR
16	Jones, Donald	2	M	8	8	8	8	10			42	2	8 50	357 00	8 50	365 50	365 50		25 59	54 83	7 50	277 58	2314	357 00	8 50
33	Newell, Bonnie	2	M	8	8	8	8	8			40		6 25	250 00		250 00	250 00		17 50	37 50	7 50	187 50	2315	250 00	
39	Polara, James	1	S	8	8	8	8	8	4		44	4	5 00	220 00	10 00	230 00	230 00	156 00	16 10	32 20	7 50	174 20	2316	220 00	10 00
51	Stone, Frank	1	S	8	8	8	8	8			40		10 00	400 00		400 00	400 00		28 00	58 00	7 50	306 50	2317	400 00	
72	Lerner, Bruce	3	M	8	8	8	8	8			40		13 00	520 00		520 00	520 00		36 40	67 60	7 50	408 50	2318	520 00	
	Totals for Week										170	12	60	378 40	1739 00	4759 00	3478 00		1033 13	2434 74	22 30	13699 83		13061 00	433 00

overtime is $48 ($12 × 4 hours), of which $32 ($8 × 4 hours) is the regular rate and $16 ($4 × 4 hours) is the overtime premium.

The problem arises as to whether overtime premium should be charged to specific jobs as direct labor or should be charged as manufacturing overhead. When charged as overhead, the overtime premium is spread over all jobs worked on during the year. Space Savers, like most manufacturers, charges all overtime premium to manufacturing overhead. Some companies, however, compute overtime premium on a daily basis and charge it to specific jobs.

Deductions From Employees' Earnings.   A deduction is required by federal law for each employee's share of the tax levied under the Federal Insurance Contributions Act (FICA), popularly called the social security tax. The tax rate and base change often. In this discussion, a FICA tax rate of 7 percent is assumed on a base of $45,000 during the year. The FICA tax base means that after an employee's yearly earnings reach a maximum amount (the base), FICA tax is no longer deducted from his or her wages. For example, an employee whose year-to-date earnings reached $45,000 at the end of October would not have FICA tax deducted from gross wages in November or December. (Accounting for the employer's share of payroll taxes is discussed in Chapter 7.) Another deduction is for the employee's federal income tax withholding. The income tax deduction is usually found by consulting income tax withholding tables. The amount withheld varies with the individual's earnings and marital status and with the number of allowances, or exemptions, claimed.

Certain states require a deduction for state income tax withholding and for taxes to provide unemployment insurance or sickness and disability benefits.

The taxes deducted by the employer from the employee's earnings are remitted at the proper time to the appropriate governmental agencies or depositories designated by law.

A business may also deduct amounts for group life insurance, hospitalization insurance, United States savings bonds, union dues, uniforms, and various other purposes. Employees sign an authorization for such deductions. In most cases, they may change or withdraw the authorization at any time. All amounts deducted must be remitted by the employer to the insurance companies, the federal government, the unions, or other agencies in payment of the obligations for which the money was withheld.

Semimonthly Factory Payroll

A separate semimonthly payroll register is used by Space Savers to record payment of some factory supervisors and managers. These persons earn fixed monthly salaries payable in two installments on the fifteenth and last day of the month. The semimonthly payroll register is similar to the weekly payroll register.

Posting From the Payroll Register

At the end of the payroll period, the total gross earnings and the totals for each of the various liabilities are posted directly from the payroll registers to the general ledger accounts. The effect of this procedure is shown in general journal form for the week ended October 5.

19X1				
Oct. 5	Factory Payroll Clearing	500	17,391.00	
	FICA Taxes Payable	211		1,033.13
	Employee Income Taxes Payable	214		2,434.74
	Group Insurance Deductions Payable	215		223.30
	Salaries and Wages Payable	202		13,699.83
	Recorded weekly factory payroll, Oct. 1–5.			

Space Savers' Factory Payroll Clearing account 500 is shown below with entries posted from the weekly payrolls of October 5, 12, 19, and 26 and from the semi-monthly payrolls of October 15 and 31. The posting reference WP refers to the weekly payroll register; SP refers to the semimonthly payroll register. (Note that the balance ledger form is used.)

				Factory Payroll Clearing			No. 500	
DATE	EXPLANATION	POST. REF.	DEBIT		CREDIT	BALANCE		DR. CR.
19X1								
Oct. 5		WP	17,391	00		17,391	00	Dr.
12		WP	17,282	00		34,673	00	Dr.
15		SP	2,995	00		37,668	00	Dr.
19		WP	16,904	00		54,572	00	Dr.
26		WP	17,113	00		71,685	00	Dr.
31		SP	2,995	00		74,680	00	Dr.

Not shown in the illustration (but explained in detail in the next chapter) are wages of $10,048 earned during the period of October 27 through 31, but not paid in October. When this amount is added to the debit balance of $74,680, the total is $84,728—the same amount shown in Entry C in Chapter 2.

Paying the Payroll

Space Savers uses a special bank account for payroll payments. The payroll clerk initiates a voucher for the net amount of the payroll and forwards it to the voucher clerk, who completes the voucher and records it in the voucher register. The entry is a debit to Salaries and Wages Payable 202 and a credit to Vouchers Payable 201. The voucher then goes to the treasurer, who issues a check on the regular bank account for the amount of the voucher and enters it in the check register. This check is deposited in the special payroll bank account. Finally, a payroll check is made for each employee, drawn on the special payroll bank account.

A few companies still pay employees in cash. When this procedure is used, the voucher is processed in the usual manner. The treasurer issues and cashes a check for the amount of the voucher and turns the money over to the payroll unit. Each employee's net earnings are placed in a separate envelope. A receipt must be signed by the employee for each payment received.

Individual Earnings Records

An employer is required to keep an individual record of each employee's earnings and deductions. This record is the basis for the preparation of various year-end payroll reports, such as Form W-2, the Wage and Tax Statement, which is sent to each employee to aid in the preparation of his or her federal income tax return.

The information for this record is taken from the payroll register at the end of each pay period. The individual earnings record for Donald Jones is shown on the next page. In many companies the payroll register, the individual earnings records, and the paychecks are prepared simultaneously through the use of special forms.

Computerized Payroll

Because of the repetitive nature of the calculations involved with payroll, many companies computerize their payroll records. A company can either have its own computerized payroll system or contract with an outside payroll service bureau to handle this function for it.

If a company decides to have a service bureau process its payroll, it must first supply the bureau with basic personnel data about its employees such as name and address, marital status, number of withholding allowances, and hourly pay rate. Then, each pay period, the company tells the service bureau the number of hours each employee worked. The bureau calculates the payroll and delivers to the company a completed payroll register and payroll checks for all employees. The bureau will also keep an individual earnings record for each employee and prepare all necessary quarterly and yearly payroll tax returns.

Name Jones, Donald
Soc. Sec. No. 160-14-0730
Address 902 Fox Lane, Chicago, IL 60699
Withholding Allow. 2
Employee No. 16
Marital Status M
Date of Birth 10/12/XX

| PERIOD | WEEK ENDED | HOURS WORKED | | RATE PER HOUR | EARNINGS | | | CUMULATIVE TOTAL | DEDUCTIONS | | | NET PAID |
		TOT. HRS.	O.T. HRS.		REGULAR	OVER. PREM.	TOTAL		FICA	FEDERAL INC. TAX WITH.	OTHER	
	Carried Forward							6840 00				
27	7/6	40		8 50	340 00		340 00	7180 00	23 80	51 00	7 50	257 70
28	7/13	40		8 50	340 00		340 00	7520 00	23 80	51 00	7 50	257 70
29	7/20	40		8 50	340 00		340 00	7860 00	23 80	51 00	7 50	257 70
30	7/27	40		8 50	340 00		340 00	8200 00	23 80	51 00	7 50	257 70
	July				1360 00		1360 00		95 20	204 00	30 00	1030 80
31	8/3	40		8 50	340 00		340 00	8540 00	23 80	51 00	7 50	257 70
32	8/10	40		8 50	340 00		340 00	8880 00	23 80	51 00	7 50	257 70
33	8/17	40		8 50	340 00		340 00	9220 00	23 80	51 00	7 50	257 70
34	8/24	41	1	8 50	348 50	4 25	352 75	9572 75	24 69	52 91	7 50	267 65
35	8/31	40		8 50	340 00		340 00	9912 75	23 80	51 00	7 50	257 70
	August				1708 50	4 25	1712 75		119 89	256 91	37 50	1298 45
36	9/7	40		8 50	340 00		340 00	10252 75	23 80	51 00	7 50	257 70
37	9/14	40		8 50	340 00		340 00	10592 75	23 80	51 00	7 50	257 70
38	9/21	40		8 50	340 00		340 00	10932 75	23 80	51 00	7 50	257 70
39	9/28	42	2	8 50	357 00	8 50	365 50	11298 25	25 59	54 83	7 50	277 58
	September				1377 00	8 50	1385 50		96 99	207 83	30 00	1050 68
	3rd Quarter				4445 50	12 75	4458 25		312 08	668 74	97 50	3379 93
40	10/5	42	2	8 50	357 00	8 50	365 50	11663 75	25 59	54 83	7 50	277 58

There are several advantages to this method of processing payroll.

1. For a medium-sized or small company, it may be less expensive and more convenient to pay an outside firm to do the payroll than it is to invest in computer equipment to handle the payroll.
2. Since the employees in the service bureau are in the payroll business, it is easier for them to stay up to date about the frequent changes in tax rates.
3. Confidentiality of payroll is more likely to be maintained when the payroll function is performed outside the company.

Speeding Up Payroll With Computers

Bathtub Rings, Inc., a manufacturer of shower curtain rings, shower curtains, soap dishes, and other items for the bath, has been having trouble getting its payroll out in a timely manner. Product manufacturing is done at the Detroit, Michigan, and Charlotte, North Carolina, factories. Currently, factory employees are paid two weeks after they have earned their wages. First, payroll data must be gathered at the factories and mailed to the home office in Atlanta, Georgia, for processing. After the payroll has been processed, the paychecks must be sorted and mailed back to the factories for distribution. Many workers have voiced dissatisfaction at having to wait two weeks before being paid. In order to keep employee morale high, management wants to remedy the problem.

The solution, as Bathtub Rings sees it, is to put computer terminals in each of the factories. These terminals would have the capacity to send information to and receive information from the central mainframe computer in Atlanta. Each terminal will be equipped with a *badge reader*. This input device reads information, such as an employee identification number, from a badge similar to a plastic charge card. Upon arriving at work, an employee will insert his or her badge in the factory's data collection terminal. The badge reader will read the employee number from the badge, and the terminal will record that employee's arrival time. The employee's exit time will be recorded the same way at the end of the day. On Thursday of each week, the hours worked during the week will be sorted by employee number by the central computer. On Friday morning, after Thursday night processing, paycheck data will be sorted by factory and then by employee number and sent back to the factory terminals. Checks will be printed out on each factory's own printer and distributed.

This solution is appealing for two reasons. With this new system, employees will be paid the day after a week in which they have earned wages. This should boost morale considerably. Another benefit is that the labor information available to management for analysis is much more current. ■

Principles and Procedures Summary

Accounting for labor costs has three phases: keeping track of time worked, computing and recording earnings, and charging costs to production.

The timekeeping process uses time clocks, time cards, and time tickets. Once the record of hours worked is available, the data can be transferred daily to the payroll register. At the end of the pay period, the hours are totaled, and pay and deductions are computed to complete the payroll. The total gross earnings are then debited to the Factory Payroll Clearing account with offsetting credits to various liability accounts.

Many businesses pay their employees by special payroll check. Under this system, a voucher is prepared and a check is issued to cover the net payroll. The check is then deposited in a separate payroll bank account, and payroll checks are drawn against the balance. In other companies, payment may be made to employees in cash. The treasurer cashes a check for the total net payroll and turns the money over to the payroll unit for distribution.

Review Questions

1. Define timekeeping.
2. How do time cards differ from time tickets?
3. What are some causes of idle time? How should long periods of idle time be recorded?
4. What is overtime premium?
5. What are two methods for recording overtime premium?
6. What is the difference between gross pay and net pay?
7. What types of information and payroll calculations are shown in the payroll register?
8. What deductions are employers required by law to make from an employee's gross wages?
9. What accounts are debited and credited in the journal entry to record the payroll? What is the source of the amounts used in this entry?
10. What accounts are debited and credited in the journal entries to record the payment of the payroll?
11. What information is contained in an individual earnings record? Why is it necessary for a company to keep these records?

Managerial Discussion Questions

1. What uses are made of data obtained from time tickets?
2. Why should management analyze idle time?
3. Why should management be concerned with overtime premiums?
4. What types of deductions are required by law? What deductions are optional?
5. Recommend daily procedures to use in accounting for labor cost.

Exercises

The premium is the [handwritten annotation]

1. **Calculating gross earnings.** Determine the amount of gross pay for Rachel Zimmer, who worked 46 hours in a week at a rate of $8.00 an hour. Show the amount of regular earnings and overtime premium if she is paid one and a half times the regular rate for hours worked in excess of 40.
2. **Determining deductions.** Calculate the amount of FICA tax and federal income tax to be withheld from an employee's gross pay of $1,300 if all earnings are taxable, the FICA rate is 7 percent, and the federal income tax rate is 12 percent.
3. **Calculating net pay.** Based on the data that follow, what is the net pay for Peter Monroe for the week ended June 16, 19X4?

Hours/rate	42 hours worked, at $7.00 an hour (overtime at time and a half)
Earnings to date	$10,050
FICA tax	7% on the first $45,000
Federal income tax	12% of earnings

4. **Calculating FICA taxes.** Determine the amounts of FICA tax to be deducted under the assumptions noted on the next page. Use a FICA tax rate of 7 percent on the first $45,000 in wages.

a. An employee earned gross wages of $750 for the week ended and has wages-to-date of $22,500.

b. The same employee, except the wages-to-date total $44,700.

5. **Preparing journal entries.** Charleston Gardening Supplies manufactures pots for plants and small garden tools. The weekly payroll for the factory totaled $20,950. The employees' share of the FICA tax was $1,466, and the federal income taxes withheld were $2,095. Prepare the journal entries to record the weekly payroll for February 1 through 7, to record the voucher to pay the payroll, and to record the payment of the voucher.

Problems

PROBLEM 6-1. Computing gross earnings. From the following data, compute the regular earnings (for regular and overtime hours), overtime premium earnings, and gross earnings of each employee at the Blanchard Corporation for the week ended October 24, 19X5. All employees are paid at the regular hourly rate for the first 40 hours worked during the week. The rate for hours worked in excess of 40 is one and a half times the regular rate. The rate for hours worked on Sunday is twice the regular rate.

Employee	Su	M	Tu	W	Th	F	Sa	Hourly Rate
			Hours Worked					
M. Mariano	—	10	9	8	8	8	—	$4.30
N. Peterson	—	7	8	9	9	8	4	9.10
W. Traski	8	8	8	8	8	9	—	6.80
R. Wilson	—	8	8	8	10	8	4	5.50

PROBLEM 6-2. Preparing a payroll register and the journal entry to record the payroll. The Taylor Manufacturing Company is a manufacturing concern that employs six people on an hourly basis. The following data relate to the week ended November 12, 19X6:

Employee	Su	M	Tu	W	Th	F	Sa	Hourly Rate	Cumulative Total Through November 5, 19X6
			Hours Worked						
A. Aines	—	8	10	8	8	—	4	$18.00	$27,000
C. Barnes	—	8	8	8	10	8	4	23.50	45,960
T. Esposito	—	8	9	8	—	8	—	8.40	11,760
E. Lacombe	—	8	8	9	8	8	—	9.20	14,200
D. Stern	—	8	8	8	9	8	4	12.60	20,160
P. Winger	—	8	8	8	9	8	—	24.90	44,820

Instructions

1. Prepare the payroll register for the week ended November 12, 19X6. For this problem, assume that the FICA tax is 7 percent of the first $45,000 earned by each employee, and the federal income tax withheld is a flat rate of 15 percent of gross earnings. Group insurance is $8.00 per employee. Show total earnings as regular earnings plus overtime premium earnings. Employees are paid one and one-half times the regular rate for hours worked over 40.

2. Prepare in general journal form the entry to record the payroll, using the account titles shown in your textbook.

PROBLEM 6-3. Preparing payroll entries. Data for the payroll of Greater Denver Manufacturers for the week ended August 18, 19X6, are shown below.

Total gross earnings	$81,960
FICA taxes withheld	5,737
Employee income taxes withheld	12,294
Group insurance deductions	2,450

Instructions

Prepare the following entries in general journal form:

1. An entry to record the weekly payroll.
2. An entry to record the issuance of a voucher to pay the net payroll.
3. An entry to record payment of the voucher.

Alternate Problems

PROBLEM 6-1A. Computing gross earnings. From the following data, compute the regular earnings (for regular and overtime hours), overtime premium earnings, and gross earnings of each employee at Delgado, Inc., for the week ended May 7, 19X6. All employees are paid at the regular hourly rate for the first 40 hours worked during the week. The rate for hours worked in excess of 40 is one and a half times the regular rate. The rate for hours worked on Sunday is twice the regular rate.

	Hours Worked							Hourly
Employee	Su	M	Tu	W	Th	F	Sa	Rate
V. James	—	8	10	8	9	10	—	$9.80
F. Michito	4	8	8	8	—	10	—	7.50
H. Neal	—	8	8	10	8	8	4	6.10
W. Werner	—	8	8	8	8	9	4	5.50

PROBLEM 6-2A. Preparing a payroll register and the journal entry to record the payroll. The Atlantic Corporation is a manufacturing concern that employs seven people on an hourly basis. The following data relate to the week ended October 31, 19X6:

	Hours Worked							Hourly	Cumulative Total Through
Employee	Su	M	Tu	W	Th	F	Sa	Rate	October 24, 19X6
C. Costa	—	8	8	9	8	8	—	$14.00	$20,400
A. Davis	—	8	9	8	8	9	4	25.00	46,180
C. Ingles	—	8	10	8	8	9	—	16.50	27,600
D. Lieberman	—	10	8	8	8	8	—	9.30	13,890
H. Norris	—	8	8	8	9	8	4	17.00	27,200
R. Rosanski	—	8	8	8	10	8	—	22.60	44,380
L. Shays	—	8	8	9	9	8	—	8.50	14,860

Instructions

1. Prepare the payroll register for the week ended October 31, 19X6. For this problem, assume that the FICA tax is 7 percent of the first 45,000 earned by each employee, and the federal income tax withheld is a flat rate of 15 percent of gross earnings. Group insurance is $10.00 per employee. Show total earnings as regu-

lar earnings plus overtime premium earnings. Employees are paid one and one-half times the regular rate for hours worked over 40.

2. Prepare in general journal form the entry to record the payroll, using the account titles shown in your textbook.

PROBLEM 6-3A. Preparing payroll entries. Data for the payroll of the Interstate Chemical Corporation for the week ended April 20, 19X6, are shown below.

Total gross earnings	$458,140
FICA taxes withheld	32,069
Employee income taxes withheld	68,721
Group insurance deductions	5,400

Instructions
Prepare the following entries in general journal form:

1. An entry to record the weekly payroll.
2. An entry to record the issuance of a voucher to pay the net payroll.
3. An entry to record payment of the voucher.

Managerial Decisions

CASE 6-1. The Food Movers is a small manufacturer of grocery store shopping carts. The company has 20 employees who normally work a five-day, 40-hour week.

In April, the company experienced an accelerated rate of demand for its product. As a result, all employees worked 8 hours of overtime each Saturday in April in order to eliminate the backlog of orders.

In May, Grand Markets, one of the Food Movers' largest customers, placed a rush order for 50 shopping carts. The carts had to be ready for delivery in one week in order to be available for the opening of one of Grand Markets' new stores. All the employees worked overtime every evening during the second week in May to meet this deadline.

In June, there was a severe thunderstorm causing a two-hour electrical power outage. The employees stayed and worked two hours of overtime to make up for the lost time.

How should overtime be charged in April? In May? In June?

7

Charging Labor Costs Into Production

■ ■ ■

In the last chapter, you learned the various recording phases of accounting for labor costs. This chapter will explain the other half of the operation—how labor costs are charged to production.

Labor Cost Analysis

In Chapter 2, Entry D on the flowchart showed that direct labor costs are charged to Work in Process 122 and indirect labor costs are charged to Manufacturing Overhead Control 501.

Analysis of Time Tickets

Each week an analysis is made of the time tickets that were filled out by the hourly employees. The analysis shows the direct labor costs incurred on each job by each department and the total direct labor costs for each department. It also indicates the indirect labor costs for each department. Postings are made from this summary to the job cost sheets and to the departmental overhead analysis sheets. The analysis of time tickets for the week ended October 5 is shown on page 120.

The analysis indicates that the direct labor used on Job 101 in the Milling Department amounted to 290 hours, at a cost of $1,902. In the Assembling Department, 220 hours of direct labor were expended at a cost of $1,580. In the Finishing Department, 55 hours of direct labor were used on this job, at a cost of $420. These figures are posted directly from the analysis of time tickets to the job cost sheet for Job 101. The posting reference TTA stands for time ticket analysis (see page 121).

The analysis of time tickets for the week also shows that total indirect labor costs of $580 were incurred in the Milling Department. This amount is posted directly from the analysis to the Milling Department overhead analysis sheet shown on page 121.

The overtime premium for each department includes overtime worked by employees classified as direct labor and employees classified as indirect labor. The total of the summary of direct and indirect labor will be the same as the total gross wages shown in the payroll register for that week.

SPACE SAVERS, INC.
Analysis of Time Tickets
Week Ended October 5, 19X1

DIRECT LABOR

JOB	MILLING HOURS	MILLING AMOUNT	ASSEMBLING HOURS	ASSEMBLING AMOUNT	FINISHING HOURS	FINISHING AMOUNT	TOTAL
98					175	$1,252.60	$ 1,252.60
99			35	$ 296.40	120	963.60	1,260.00
100			80	652.00	130	808.00	1,460.00
101	290	$1,902.00	220	1,580.00	55	420.00	3,902.00
102	16	110.00	300	2,688.00	-0-	-0-	2,798.00
103	40	224.00	60	474.00	-0-	-0-	698.00
104	150	968.00	-0-	-0-	-0-	-0-	968.00
105	55	387.00	-0-	-0-	-0-	-0-	387.00
106	-0-	-0-	40	335.40	-0-	-0-	335.40
Total	551	$3,591.00	735	$6,025.80	480	$3,444.20	$13,061.00

INDIRECT LABOR

DEPARTMENT	REGULAR EARNINGS	OVERTIME PREMIUM	TOTAL
Milling	$ 441.60	$138.40	$ 580.00
Assembling	654.00	84.00	738.00
Finishing	564.00	156.00	720.00
Building Services	924.00	-0-	924.00
General Factory	1,368.00	-0-	1,368.00
Total	$3,951.60	$378.40	$4,330.00

SUMMARY

Direct Labor	$13,061.00
Indirect Labor	4,330.00
Total	$17,391.00

Analysis of Semimonthly Payroll

The semimonthly payroll is also analyzed. This payroll represents the wages earned by employees, such as custodial workers and factory office personnel, who are on a fixed monthly salary. Their earnings are classified as indirect labor and are entered in the departmental overhead analysis sheets. The analysis of Space Savers' semimonthly payroll for the period ended October 15 is given on page 121.

JOB COST SHEET

Customer *Neeley Furniture Co.*
Description *Customer specs on file*
Quantity *100*

Job *101*
Date Started *10/1/X1*
Date Completed _____

	MATERIALS		DIRECT LABOR								MANUFACTURING OVERHEAD APPLIED									
					MILLING		ASSEMBLING		FINISHING				MILLING			ASSEMBLING			FINISHING		
DATE	REQ. NO.	AMOUNT	DATE	REF.	HRS.	AMOUNT	HRS.	AMOUNT	HRS.	AMOUNT	DATE	REF.	HRS.	RATE	AMOUNT	HRS.	RATE	AMOUNT	HRS.	RATE	AMOUNT
10/1	R802	93500	10/5	TTA	290	190200	220	158000	55	42000											
10/2	R804	280500																			
10/6	RM48	(8500)																			

DEPARTMENTAL OVERHEAD ANALYSIS SHEET

Department *Milling*
Month of *October* 19 *X1*

DATE	REF.	TOTAL	01 INDIRECT MATERIALS	02 INDIRECT LABOR	03 PAYROLL TAXES	04 DEPRECIATION	05 REPAIRS & MAINT.	06 UTILITIES	07 INSURANCE	08 OTHER TAXES	09 OTHER ITEM	09 OTHER AMOUNT
Oct. 3	R808	10625	10625									
5	TTA	58000		58000								

SPACE SAVERS, INC.
Analysis of Semimonthly Factory Payroll
Period Ended October 15, 19X1

DEPARTMENT	INDIRECT LABOR
Milling	$ -0-
Assembling	-0-
Finishing	-0-
Building Services	640.00
General Factory	2,355.00
Total	$2,995.00

The indirect wages paid in each department are entered in the Indirect Labor column of the appropriate departmental overhead analysis sheet (see page 122).

Analysis of Unpaid Wages

The last day of the weekly pay period usually differs from the last day of the fiscal period. Therefore it is necessary to prepare an analysis of time tickets at the end of the month for those labor costs that have been incurred since the last weekly payroll date but have not yet been paid. In this way, production is charged with all labor

DEPARTMENTAL OVERHEAD ANALYSIS SHEET

Department _Building Services_   Month of _October_   19 XL

DATE	REF.	TOTAL	01 INDIRECT MATERIALS	02 INDIRECT LABOR	03 PAYROLL TAXES	04 DEPRECIATION	05 REPAIRS & MAINT.	06 UTILITIES	07 INSURANCE	08 OTHER TAXES	09 OTHER ITEM	AMOUNT
Oct. 5	TTA	924 00		924 00								
15	SP	640 00		640 00								

DEPARTMENTAL OVERHEAD ANALYSIS SHEET

Department _General Factory_   Month of _October_   19 XL

DATE	REF.	TOTAL	01 INDIRECT MATERIALS	02 INDIRECT LABOR	03 PAYROLL TAXES	04 DEPRECIATION	05 REPAIRS & MAINT.	06 UTILITIES	07 INSURANCE	08 OTHER TAXES	09 OTHER ITEM	AMOUNT
Oct. 5	TTA	1368 00		1368 00								
15	SP	2355 00		2355 00								

costs in the month in which they are incurred. The analysis of time tickets for the period October 27 through 31 is shown on page 123. The direct labor costs are posted to the job cost sheets. The indirect labor costs are posted to the departmental overhead analysis sheets.

. . . .

Transferring Labor Costs to Production

Entries are made during the month to transfer labor costs to job cost sheets and departmental overhead analysis sheets. These transfers are recorded in the general ledger accounts at the end of the month.

Summary of Factory Wages

At the end of the month it is also necessary to prepare a summary of all factory wages earned. This summary consists of the time ticket analyses and the semimonthly payroll analyses that have been prepared and posted to the job cost sheets and departmental overhead analysis sheets during the month. (See page 124.)

The summary of factory wages for October shows total direct labor costs of $58,597 and total indirect labor costs of $26,131. At the end of the month these amounts are transferred to production, as shown on the general journal voucher on page 124.

After the factory labor costs have been posted to production, the Factory Payroll Clearing account appears as shown on page 124.

SPACE SAVERS, INC.
Analysis of Time Tickets
October 27–31, 19X1

DIRECT LABOR

JOB	MILLING HOURS	MILLING AMOUNT	ASSEMBLING HOURS	ASSEMBLING AMOUNT	FINISHING HOURS	FINISHING AMOUNT	TOTAL
108	45	$ 295.00	140	$1,012.00	150	$1,125.00	$2,432.00
109	70	459.00	100	723.00	75	563.00	1,745.00
110	90	590.00	80	578.00	45	337.00	1,505.00
111	85	557.00	75	542.00	-0-	-0-	1,099.00
112	30	198.00	35	255.00	-0-	-0-	453.00
Total	320	$2,099.00	430	$3,110.00	270	$2,025.00	$7,234.00

INDIRECT LABOR

DEPARTMENT	REGULAR EARNINGS	OVERTIME PREMIUM	TOTAL
Milling	$ 487.00	-0-	$ 487.00
Assembling	495.00	-0-	495.00
Finishing	447.00	-0-	447.00
Building Services	507.00	-0-	507.00
General Factory	878.00	-0-	878.00
Total	$2,814.00	-0-	$2,814.00

SUMMARY

Direct Labor	$ 7,234.00
Indirect Labor	2,814.00
Total	$10,048.00

SPACE SAVERS, INC.
Summary of Factory Wages
October 19X1

PAYROLL PERIOD	MILLING DIRECT LABOR	MILLING INDIRECT LABOR	ASSEMBLING DIRECT LABOR	ASSEMBLING INDIRECT LABOR	FINISHING DIRECT LABOR	FINISHING INDIRECT LABOR	BUILDING SERVICES	GENERAL FACTORY	TOTAL
Oct. 1–5	$ 3,591.00	$ 580.00	$ 6,025.80	$ 738.00	$ 3,444.20	$ 720.00	$ 924.00	$ 1,368.00	$17,391.00
6–12	4,234.00	480.00	5,185.00	674.00	3,560.00	708.00	847.00	1,594.00	17,282.00
1–15	-0-	-0-	-0-	-0-	-0-	-0-	640.00	2,355.00	2,995.00
13–19	4,023.00	558.00	5,240.00	744.00	3,380.00	642.00	811.00	1,506.00	16,904.00
20–26	3,850.00	513.00	5,305.00	804.00	3,525.00	719.00	780.00	1,617.00	17,113.00
16–31	-0-	-0-	-0-	-0-	-0-	-0-	640.00	2,355.00	2,995.00
27–31	2,099.00	487.00	3,110.00	495.00	2,025.00	447.00	507.00	878.00	10,048.00
Total	$17,797.00	$2,618.00	$24,865.80	$3,455.00	$15,934.20	$3,236.00	$5,149.00	$11,673.00	$84,728.00

SUMMARY

Direct Labor	$58,597.00
Indirect Labor	26,131.00
Total	$84,728.00

JOURNAL VOUCHER Date *Oct. 31,* 19 *XI* No. *10-48*

ACCOUNT	ACCOUNT NUMBER	✔	DEBIT	CREDIT
Work in Process	122		58597 00	
Manufacturing Overhead Control	501		26131 00	
Factory Payroll Clearing	500	✓		84728 00

Charged labor costs to production for the month.

PREPARED BY *NV*	AUDITED BY *BJ*	APPROVED BY *MP*

Factory Payroll Clearing No. 500

DATE		EXPLANATION	POST. REF.	DEBIT		CREDIT		BALANCE		DR. CR.
19	X1									
Oct.	5		WP	17,391	00			17,391	00	Dr.
	12		WP	17,282	00			34,673	00	Dr.
	15		SP	2,995	00			37,668	00	Dr.
	19		WP	16,904	00			54,572	00	Dr.
	26		WP	17,113	00			71,685	00	Dr.
	31		SP	2,995	00			74,680	00	Dr.
	31		J10-48			84,728	00	10,048	00	Cr.

Balance of Factory Payroll Clearing

The credit to Factory Payroll Clearing ($84,728) consists of October earnings, both paid and unpaid (October 27–31), as follows:

	Paid	Unpaid	Total
Direct Labor Chargeable to Work in Process	$51,363	$ 7,234	$58,597
Indirect Labor Chargeable to Manufacturing Overhead Control	23,317	2,814	26,131
Total Labor Credited to Factory Payroll Clearing	$74,680	$10,048	$84,728

The Factory Payroll Clearing account has been debited for the gross amount of factory wages paid during the month ($74,680). It is credited for the total amount of wages charged to production during the month ($84,728) through the general journal entry. The balance of the Factory Payroll Clearing account after these postings ($10,048 Cr.) represents the amount of factory wages earned and charged to production but unpaid on October 31. This balance, representing unpaid wages at the end of the month, will be shown on the balance sheet as a current liability called Accrued Wages Payable. (Some accountants prefer to make a formal journal entry debiting Factory Payroll Clearing and crediting Salaries and Wages Payable 202 at the end of the month for the amount of unpaid wages.)

When the next payroll is prepared for the week of October 27 through November 2, the total earnings shown in the payroll register ($17,300) is debited to Factory Payroll Clearing, as shown below. Of this amount, $10,048 represents the unpaid wages on October 31 that were charged to production in October. The remaining $7,252 represents wages earned on November 1 and 2 and will be charged to production at the end of November, as shown below.

Factory Payroll Clearing						No. 500	
DATE	EXPLANATION	POST. REF.	DEBIT	CREDIT	BALANCE	DR. CR.
19X1 Nov. 1	Balance	✔			10,048 00	Cr.
2		WP	17,300 00		7,252 00	Dr.

Flow of Costs

Labor costs flow into the Factory Payroll Clearing account as a result of timekeeping and computing procedures. Costs flow out of the account as the direct and indirect labor costs are applied to production. The steps in the complete cycle are given here for review.

1. Record the number of hours worked each day by each employee on a time card.
2. Record the hours and type of work performed each day by each employee on a time ticket.
3. Convert the labor hours into dollar amounts.
4. Record the total earnings, deductions, and net pay of all employees for a payroll period in the payroll register. Post the totals from the payroll register to the general ledger accounts.
5. Post the earnings, deductions, and net pay for each employee to an individual earnings record, which provides cumulative figures for the year.
6. Charge the direct labor costs to the individual job sheets. Enter the indirect labor costs on the departmental overhead analysis sheets by means of postings from analyses of weekly and semimonthly payrolls and analysis of end-of-month unpaid earnings.
7. Prepare a general journal voucher based on the monthly labor summaries. Post the amounts to the Work in Process account, the Manufacturing Overhead Control account, and the Factory Payroll Clearing account.

Special Labor Cost Problems

The labor costs discussed so far were accounted for in the normal routine of preparing time cards, periodic analyses, and payroll summaries. Certain other labor costs require special accounting procedures.

Employer's Payroll Taxes

The employer normally must pay three payroll taxes: FICA tax, federal unemployment tax, and state unemployment tax.

FICA Tax. Under the Federal Insurance Contributions Act (FICA), the employer is currently required to pay a tax equal to the amount levied against the employee. Because of frequent changes in the FICA tax rate and base, an assumed rate of 7 percent on the first $45,000 of wages is used in this text unless noted otherwise.

FUTA Tax. Under the Federal Unemployment Tax Act (FUTA), the federal government levies an unemployment tax. In this text, it is assumed that the rate is 6.2 percent and is based on the first $7,000 of gross earnings paid each employee during the calendar year. However, a credit, not to exceed 5.4 percent, is allowed against the federal tax for taxes levied by states for unemployment insurance. As a result, the net FUTA rate actually paid by most employers is .8 percent (6.2 percent − 5.4 percent = .8 percent). Both the rate and the base are subject to change.

State Unemployment Tax. The typical state unemployment insurance tax (commonly referred to as SUTA) on the employer is 5.4 percent of the first $7,000 of gross earnings paid each employee during the calendar year, although it may be higher or lower. Most states allow credits against the tax due through a merit rating given for a stable employment record. This merit, or experience, rating system may reduce the effective tax rate. In this discussion we will assume that the effective SUTA rate for Space Savers is 5.4 percent. Again, both rate and base are subject to change.

Charging Payroll Taxes. It is customary for the accountant to charge all employer's payroll taxes on factory earnings to manufacturing overhead. Space Savers, Inc., uses a typical four-step procedure, as outlined below, to enter payroll taxes in the accounting records of the firm.

1. The payroll unit prepares a monthly summary of taxable wages by department, as shown on page 127. Taxable wages may differ from total wages (page 124) since some employees have earned wages over the maximum amounts subject to FICA (assume $45,000) and unemployment taxes (assume $7,000).
2. This summary becomes the basis for calculating payroll taxes expense for the period, as shown on page 127.
3. The payroll taxes for each department are posted to the departmental overhead analysis sheets from the summary of factory payroll taxes.
4. A general journal voucher is prepared so that the taxes payable may be recorded in the general ledger accounts, as shown on page 128.

Some companies do not attempt to compute the exact amount of payroll taxes chargeable to each department. Instead, the total monthly payroll taxes expense is

SPACE SAVERS, INC.
Summary of Taxable Factory Wages
October 19X1

WAGES SUBJECT TO FICA TAXES

PAYROLL PERIOD	MILLING	ASSEMBLING	FINISHING	BUILDING SERVICES	GENERAL FACTORY	TOTAL
Oct. 1–5	$ 2,934	$ 4,904	$ 3,846	$ 691	$ 985	$13,360
6–12	3,273	4,064	4,435	611	1,134	13,517
1–15	-0-	-0-	-0-	437	1,681	2,118
13–19	3,078	4,042	2,724	567	1,005	11,416
20–26	2,825	4,014	2,808	528	1,055	11,230
16–31	-0-	-0-	-0-	425	1,587	2,012
27–31	1,860	2,589	1,777	316	505	7,047
Total	$13,970	$19,613	$15,590	$3,575	$7,952	$60,700

WAGES SUBJECT TO FEDERAL AND STATE UNEMPLOYMENT COMPENSATION TAXES

PAYROLL PERIOD	MILLING	ASSEMBLING	FINISHING	BUILDING SERVICES	GENERAL FACTORY	TOTAL
Oct. 1–5	$ 714	$1,201	$ 743	$171	$ 241	$ 3,070
6–12	834	904	678	138	254	2,808
1–15	-0-	-0-	-0-	88	343	431
13–19	704	806	554	100	178	2,342
20–26	665	826	505	76	193	2,265
16–31	-0-	-0-	-0-	70	297	367
27–31	462	503	308	76	93	1,442
Total	$3,379	$4,240	$2,788	$719	$1,599	$12,725

SPACE SAVERS, INC.
Summary of Factory Payroll Taxes
October 19X1

DEPARTMENT	FICA TAX AT 7% (ASSUMED)	UNEMPLOYMENT TAXES STATE AT 5.4%	FEDERAL AT .8%	TOTAL
Milling	$ 977.90	$182.47	$ 27.03	$1,187.40
Assembling	1,372.91	228.96	33.92	1,635.79
Finishing	1,091.30	150.55	22.30	1,264.15
Building Services	250.25	38.83	5.75	294.83
General Factory	556.64	86.35	12.79	655.78
Total	$4,249.00	$687.16	$101.79	$5,037.95

simply allocated to the departments on the basis of the total wages earned in each. Although this procedure is not exact, it will usually result in reasonably accurate cost allocations.

Fringe Benefit Costs

In recent years there has been a tremendous growth in the costs of fringe benefits related to salaries and wages. Fringe benefits include vacation and holiday pay, worker's compensation insurance, pension plans, hospitalization insurance, and group life insurance, to mention only a few. At Space Savers, Inc., such costs are charged to Manufacturing Overhead Control 501. They are entered on the appropriate departmental overhead analysis sheets as they are incurred. For example, if a factory employee is paid while on vacation, the earnings are charged to Manufacturing Overhead Control. They are entered on the overhead analysis sheet of the department in which the employee regularly works. This procedure is the most common one. A few companies, however, do classify the fringe benefits associated with direct labor as part of the direct labor cost rather than as manufacturing overhead.

Computerized Labor Cost Analysis

Uniform Attire, Inc., manufactures uniforms for professional sports teams and large hotel and restaurant chains. The process of making uniforms and shipping them is done in three departments: cutting, sewing, and shipping. Each factory worker is assigned to only one department. Since work is being done for specific clients, the management of Uniform Attire feels that it is very important to keep track of the production costs that relate to each order. The cost accountant and a programmer have designed a system to computerize the gathering and analysis of labor costs by client.

Each of the factory departments is equipped with a computer terminal that is connected to a central computer. The terminals have badge readers (similar to those discussed on page 114), display screens, and printers. When ready to begin a task, an employee inserts his or her badge into the badge reader and keys in a code representing a particular client's batch of work. For example, if Jeremiah Smith is going to begin cutting the uniforms ordered by the Regency Inn, he will insert his badge and key in H1264, the code identifying the client. The computer will note the time the batch was started, the fact that it was started by Jeremiah Smith in the Cutting Department, and that the batch pertains to the Regency Inn order. When Jeremiah Smith finishes working on the batch, he will again insert his badge into the terminal and key in the client code. Now the computer will note the time the batch was finished and will compute the time spent on it by Jeremiah Smith.

Any time during the production of the batch, the cost accountant can request that a partial job cost sheet be printed out on the computer. Such a report is shown below. The data that have been collected will then be used to prepare the payroll, update the general ledger, and prepare a labor analysis sheet.

```
                       JOB COST SHEET
                           LABOR
                        REGENCY INN
                BELL CAPTAIN'S UNIFORMS
                  QUANTITY ORDERED 500

                          CUTTING          SEWING        SHIPPING
  DATE      EMPLOYEE     HRS.  AMOUNT    HRS.  AMOUNT   HRS.  AMOUNT

02/14/X3  JERIMIAH SMITH   8    48.0
02/14/X3  ROBERT MARSHALL                 3   24.00
02/14/X3  LYNN STAHL                      2   16.50
```

Management believes that this is the type of repetitive operation in which the computer will be particularly useful. Not only will production information be available on a more timely basis, but the factory workers will be able to spend more time producing and less time recording their production. The cost accountant believes she will like this computerized system because her staff will have more time to carefully analyze the costs of production to see where operations can become more efficient. ■

Principles and Procedures Summary

After employee earnings are computed through various timekeeping and recording operations, they are analyzed for further cost processing. Data obtained by such analysis are the basis for charging labor costs to specific jobs (direct) or to departments (indirect).

At the end of the month it is necessary to transfer payroll costs to production through a general journal entry. The total costs are credited to the Factory Payroll Clearing account. Direct labor costs are debited to Work in Process. Indirect labor costs are debited to Manufacturing Overhead Control.

Additional labor costs are the various payroll taxes levied upon the employer and the numerous fringe benefits that may be provided for the employees. In most systems of cost accounting, these expenses are debited to Manufacturing Overhead Control.

Review Questions

1. What types of data are found on the weekly analysis of the time tickets?
2. To what subsidiary records are direct labor costs and indirect labor costs posted?
3. What general ledger account is debited for direct labor costs? What account is debited for indirect labor costs?
4. How does an analysis of time tickets differ from a summary of factory wages?
5. At the end of the month, after all postings are made, the Factory Payroll Clearing account has a $6,190 credit balance. What does this credit balance represent, and where is it shown on the financial statements?
6. List the three payroll taxes incurred by employers.
7. What general ledger account is charged with the total employer's payroll taxes liability incurred on the wages of factory employees?
8. What are fringe benefits? How are they typically accounted for? *MOH*

Managerial Discussion Questions

1. What effect would the omission of recording unpaid wages at the end of the month have on the financial statements for a manufacturer? What problems would this omission cause management?
2. Discuss two ways in which a manufacturing firm can allocate payroll taxes to factory departments.
3. What problems might management face in attempting to assign payroll taxes and fringe benefit costs to specific jobs?
4. What uses can management make of the data concerning hours and the amount of direct labor costs recorded on the job cost sheet?
5. At the end of the month, after all postings have been made, the Factory Payroll Clearing account would typically have a credit balance. What would a zero balance indicate? What would a debit balance indicate?

Exercises

1. **Calculating the balance of the Factory Payroll Clearing account.** At the Norway Company, the Factory Payroll Clearing account shows debits totaling $193,640.80 made during the month and a credit of $208,320.80 made at the end of the month.
   a. What is the balance of the Factory Payroll Clearing account? *$14680.*
   b. Is it a debit or credit balance? *CR.*
   c. What does this balance represent? *wages payable*
2. **Distributing wages earned.** Record the general journal entry for Calico Materi-

(handwritten notes at top:)
Work in Process 172460
Mann. O.H. Control 26810   199270
— Wages payable

als Inc. to distribute the following wages earned during the month of October:
direct labor, $172,460; indirect labor, $26,810.

3. **Journalizing the employer's payroll taxes.** For the month of April, the Factory
Products Company incurred the following three payroll taxes:

FICA taxes $3,817.40
FUTA taxes   452.34
SUTA taxes   1,862.70

(handwritten:)
Mann. O.H. Control   6132.44
— FICA Tax payable   3817.40
— FUTA "   "   "   450.34
— SUTA "   "   "   1862.70

Record the general journal entry needed to recognize the payroll taxes liability.

4. **Calculating the employer's payroll taxes.** Calculate the employer's payroll
taxes for Lynn J. Suarez Inc. for the month of June 19X6 from the following data:

Gross wages	$65,300
Taxable wages for FICA	63,190
Taxable wages for FUTA and SUTA	38,920
FICA rate	7%
FUTA rate	.8%
SUTA rate	4.1%

(handwritten:)
FICA $4423.30
FUTA   311.36
SUTA 1595.72

Problems

PROBLEM 7-1. Journalizing payroll and payroll tax entries. The date and instructions given below relate to Salters, Inc., for the month of July 19X5. The beginning credit balance of the Factory Payroll Clearing account on July 1 was $10,860,
representing unpaid wages earned by employees during the last three days of June.

Instructions

1. Set up a Factory Payroll Clearing account and enter the beginning balance.
2. Journalize the summary of weekly and semimonthly payroll paid during the
   month. Use the account titles in your textbook with the data shown here.

Total gross wages	$72,370	Income taxes withheld	$8,684
FICA taxes withheld	5,065	Group insurance deductions	1,440

3. Journalize the charging of labor costs to production. The summary of factory
   wages for the month shows $56,188 for direct labor and $20,796 for indirect
   labor.
4. Journalize the employer's payroll taxes. Assume a federal unemployment tax rate
   of .8 percent and a net state unemployment tax rate of 4.1 percent. The employer's
   FICA taxes were $5,065. The wages subject to unemployment taxes were
   $52,110.
5. Post the journal entries to the Factory Payroll Clearing account.
6. Explain where the balance of the Factory Payroll Clearing account on July 31 is
   shown on the financial statements.

PROBLEM 7-2. Summarizing factory payroll taxes. A summary of taxable factory wages of the Winn Corporation for the month of March 19X6 is shown on page
132. Assume a FICA tax rate of 7 percent, a federal unemployment tax rate of .8
percent, and a net state unemployment tax rate of 4.8 percent.

| Department | Wages Subject to: | |
	FICA Taxes	Federal and State Unemployment Taxes
General Factory	$32,800	$10,130
Building Maintenance	33,260	2,110
Cutting	52,380	18,640
Molding	56,910	23,750
Finishing	64,620	20,970

Instructions

1. Compute the employer's payroll taxes to be charged to each department. Use the data to prepare the summary of factory payroll taxes for March 19X6.
2. Prepare an entry in general journal form to record the taxes. Use the account titles in your textbook.

PROBLEM 7-3. Journalizing payroll entries. Prepare the necessary general journal entries for Sanchez Machines, Inc., a manufacturer of small engines, for the month of April 19X6.

Apr. ✓ 4   The weekly payroll for the hourly factory workers totaled $16,480. Deductions: FICA taxes, $1,909; federal income taxes withheld, $3,070.

✓ 4   Issued a voucher to pay the net payroll.

✓ 4   Recorded payment of the voucher.

11   The weekly payroll for the hourly factory workers totaled $17,920. Deductions: FICA taxes, $1,250; federal income taxes withheld, $2,150.

11   Issued a voucher to pay the net payroll.

11   Recorded payment of the voucher.

18   The weekly payroll for the hourly factory workers totaled $15,190. Deductions: FICA taxes, $1,060; federal income taxes withheld, $1,820.

18   Issued a voucher to pay the net payroll.

18   Recorded payment of the voucher.

25   The weekly payroll for the hourly factory workers totaled $18,460. Deductions: FICA taxes, $1,290; federal income taxes withheld, $2,315.

25   Issued a voucher to pay the net payroll.

25   Recorded payment of the voucher.

30   Recorded distribution of the factory wages earned during the entire month of April. The summary of factory wages showed total direct labor at $61,480 and total indirect labor at $14,720.

30   Recorded employer's payroll tax liability for the month as follows: FICA taxes, $5,509; federal unemployment taxes, $272; and state unemployment compensation taxes, $1,837.

PROBLEM 7-4. Processing payroll records: comprehensive problem. Juvenile Playskills, Inc., manufactures toys. Since the last day of the normal payroll period falls on September 30, there are no accrued wages payable and no analysis of time tickets for a partial pay period. The following reports have been prepared:

JUVENILE PLAYSKILLS, INC.
Analysis of Time Tickets
Week Ended September 30, 19X5

DIRECT LABOR

JOB	MOLDING HOURS	MOLDING AMOUNT	ASSEMBLING HOURS	ASSEMBLING AMOUNT	PAINTING HOURS	PAINTING AMOUNT	TOTAL
479			460	$2,208	272	$1,360	$ 3,568
480			263	1,262	184	920	2,182
481	210	$1,071	216	1,036	133	665	2,772
482	308	1,570	79	379	-0-	-0-	1,949
483	96	490	-0-	-0-	-0-	-0-	490
Total	614	$3,131	1,018	$4,885	589	$2,945	$10,961

INDIRECT LABOR

DEPARTMENT	REGULAR EARNINGS	OVERTIME PREMIUM	TOTAL
Molding	$ 456	$162	$ 618
Assembling	508	98	606
Painting	461	184	645
Building Services	610	-0-	610
General Factory	684	-0-	684
Total	$2,719	$444	$3,163

SUMMARY

Direct Labor	$10,961
Indirect Labor	3,163
Total	$14,124

JUVENILE PLAYSKILLS, INC.
Analysis of Semimonthly Factory Payroll
Period Ended September 30, 19X5

DEPARTMENT	INDIRECT WAGES
Molding	$ -0-
Assembling	-0-
Painting	-0-
Building Services	3,426
General Factory	4,082
Total	$7,508

```
                    JUVENILE PLAYSKILLS, INC.
                   Summary of Factory Payroll Taxes
                        September 19X5
```

		UNEMPLOYMENT TAXES		
	FICA	STATE	FEDERAL	
DEPARTMENT	AT 7%	AT 5.4%	AT .8%	TOTAL
Molding	$1,217.43	$ 349.15	$ 94.10	$1,660.68
Assembling	1,521.22	429.82	115.72	2,066.76
Painting	1,039.83	286.12	77.03	1,402.98
Building Services	382.20	134.16	36.11	552.47
General Factory	792.91	232.10	62.49	1,087.50
Total	$4,953.59	$1,431.35	$385.45	$6,770.39

Instructions

NOTE: If you are using the *Study Guide and Working Papers,* the beginning data from Instructions 1–5 and 8a and 8b have already been recorded for you.

1. Set up the following job cost sheets:

   Job 479, Delta Department Store, 200 units, started Sept. 10
   Job 480, Educational Toys, 300 units, started Sept. 18
   Job 481, Peter Pan Toy Store, 350 units, started Sept. 22
   Job 482, O'Malley's Specialty Store, 200 units, started Sept. 25
   Job 483, Ramirez Toy Shop, 150 units, started Sept. 27

2. Set up the following departmental overhead analysis sheets:

   Molding Department   Building Services Department
   Assembling Department   General Factory Department
   Painting Department

3. **a.** Set up the following general ledger accounts:

   Work in Process 122
   FICA Taxes Payable 211
   Federal Unemployment Taxes Payable 212
   State Unemployment Taxes Payable 213
   Factory Payroll Clearing 500 (Enter the September 1 credit balance of $8,930.)
   Manufacturing Overhead Control 501

   b. Record the following debits in the Factory Payroll Clearing account. Compute the balances.

Date	Post. Ref.	Debits
Sept. 2	WP	$13,740
9	WP	16,190
15	SP	7,320
16	WP	14,950
23	WP	15,130

4. Indirect labor charges for the weeks ended September 2, 9, 16, and 23 are given

below. Post these charges by week to the departmental overhead analysis sheets set up in Instruction 2.

	Molding	Assembling	Painting	Building Services	General Factory
Sept. 2 TTA	$435	$392	$225	$ 386	$ 479
9 TTA	573	415	462	518	833
15 TTA	—	—	—	2,840	4,480
16 TTA	486	512	548	724	1,160
23 TTA	532	583	597	730	1,280

5. The direct labor charges below have been taken from the analysis of time tickets for the week ended September 23. Post the data to the job cost sheets set up in Instruction 1.

	Molding		Assembling		Painting	
Job	Hours	Amount	Hours	Amount	Hours	Amount
479 TTA	125	$ 638	66	$317	16	$ 79
480 TTA	116	592	57	274	12	60
481 TTA	173	882	74	355	—	—
	414	$2,112	197	$946	28	$139

6. **a.** Post the data from the analysis of time tickets for the week ended September 30, 19X5, to the job cost sheets set up in Instruction 1 and the departmental overhead analysis sheets set up in Instruction 2.

b. Post the total amount of this weekly payroll directly as a debit to Factory Payroll Clearing 500 set up in Instruction 3. Omit posting the credit side of the entry.

7. **a.** Post the amounts from the analysis of semimonthly factory payroll for the period ended September 30, 19X5, to the departmental overhead analysis sheets set up in Instruction 2.

b. Post the total amount of this semimonthly payroll directly as a debit to Factory Payroll Clearing 500. Omit posting the credit side of the entry.

8. Prepare the summary of factory wages for the month of September.

a. Enter in the appropriate columns the following departmental direct labor charges for each payroll period:

Payroll Period	Molding	Assembling	Painting
Sept. 1–2	$1,048	$1,253	$ 592
3–9	4,810	3,873	4,706
1–15	-0-	-0-	-0-
10–16	4,672	3,284	3,564
17–23	3,427	4,379	3,602

b. Enter in the appropriate columns the departmental indirect labor charges from the data given in Instruction 4.

c. Enter the departmental direct labor charges from the analysis of time tickets for the week ended September 30.

d. Enter the departmental indirect labor charges from the analysis of time tickets for the week ended September 30.

e. Enter the departmental indirect labor charges from the analysis of semimonthly factory payroll for the period ended September 30, 19X5.

f. Total all columns, crossfoot to prove, and double rule. Prepare the Summary section.

9. a. Prepare a general journal voucher to transfer all direct and indirect labor costs for the month to production. (Voucher 9-33.)

b. Post this journal voucher to the general ledger accounts.

10. Post the amounts from the summary of factory payroll taxes (use the reference SPT) to the departmental overhead analysis sheets set up in Instruction 2.

11. a. Prepare the general journal voucher to record payroll taxes payable. (Voucher 9-34.)

b. Post this journal voucher to the general ledger accounts.

12. Foot all hour and amount columns of the job cost sheets and summarize the data in a schedule showing the totals for each job by department.

13. Foot the amount columns of the departmental overhead analysis sheets and summarize the data in a schedule showing the total for each department by type of cost.

14. Check the extensions of the general ledger account balances, and prepare a schedule showing the name and number of each account, the balance, and whether the balance is a debit or credit.

Alternate Problems

PROBLEM 7-1A. Journalizing payroll and payroll tax entries. The data and instructions given below relate to the Wyoming Corporation for the month of July 19X6. The beginning credit balance of the Factory Payroll Clearing account on July 1 is $12,340, representing unpaid wages earned by employees during the last three days of June.

Instructions

1. Set up a Factory Payroll Clearing account and enter the balance.

2. Journalize the summary of weekly and semimonthly payrolls paid during the month. Use the account titles in your textbook with the data shown here.

Total gross wages	$73,170	Income taxes withheld	$10,243
FICA taxes withheld	4,830	Group insurance deductions	1,553

3. Journalize the charging of labor costs to production. The summary of factory wages for the month shows direct labor costs of $59,206 and indirect labor costs of $11,484.

4. Journalize the employer's payroll taxes. Assume a federal unemployment tax rate of .8 percent and a net state unemployment tax rate of 4.6 percent. The employer's FICA taxes amounted to $4,830. The wages subject to unemployment taxes amounted to $58,110.

5. Post the journal entries to the Factory Payroll Clearing account.

6. Explain where the balance of the Factory Payroll Clearing account on July 31 is shown on the financial statements.

PROBLEM 7-2A. Summarizing factory payroll taxes. A summary of taxable factory wages of Michael Oliver Associates for the month of November 19X6 is shown below. Assume a FICA tax rate of 7 percent, a federal unemployment tax rate of .8 percent, and a net state unemployment tax rate of 5.4 percent.

	Wages Subject to:	
Department	FICA Taxes	Federal and State Unemployment Taxes
Factory Supply	$29,350	$11,640
Factory Administration	26,350	10,290
Cutting	32,780	15,340
Assembling	36,280	16,040
Finishing	34,780	19,260

Instructions

1. Compute the employer's payroll taxes to be charged to each department. Use the data to prepare the summary of factory payroll taxes for November 19X6.
2. Prepare an entry in general journal form to record the taxes. Use the account titles in your textbook.

PROBLEM 7-3A. Journalizing payroll entries. Prepare all the necessary general journal entries for Toronto Manufacturing International, a manufacturer of small engines, for December 19X6.

Dec. 6 The weekly payroll for the hourly factory workers totaled $95,620. Deductions: FICA taxes, $6,693; federal income taxes withheld, $12,386.
   6 Issued a voucher to pay the net payroll.
   6 Recorded payment of the voucher.
   13 The weekly payroll for the hourly factory workers totaled $93,710. Deductions: FICA taxes, $6,560; federal income taxes withheld, $12,182.
   13 Issued a voucher to pay the net payroll.
   13 Recorded payment of the voucher.
   20 The weekly payroll for the hourly factory workers totaled $83,850. Deductions: FICA taxes, $5,870; federal income taxes withheld, $10,062.
   20 Issued a voucher to pay the net payroll.
   20 Recorded payment of the voucher.
   27 The weekly payroll for the hourly factory workers totaled $88,420. Deductions: FICA taxes, $6,189; federal income taxes withheld, $10,610.
   27 Issued a voucher to pay the net payroll.
   27 Recorded payment of the voucher.
   31 Recorded distribution of the factory wages earned during the entire month of December. The summary of factory wages showed total direct labor at $323,102 and total indirect labor at $68,708.
   31 Recorded the employer's payroll tax liability for the month. FICA taxes totaled $25,312; federal unemployment taxes, $1,567; and state unemployment compensation taxes, $10,578.

Managerial Decisions

CASE 7-1. Pounds-a-Way, Inc., is a manufacturer of exercise equipment for home use. Because of the sharp increase in interest in physical fitness, demand for home-exercise equipment is booming, and Pounds-a-Way has received an unprecedented number of orders. The current factory staff, consisting of two supervisors and twelve factory workers, has been unable to meet this increase in demand in its standard 40-hour work week. As a result, Pounds-a-Way has a backlog of unfilled orders.

Thomas Armstrong, president of the company, is anxious to fill these orders as quickly as possible so that the company will benefit from the boom and not lose customers to competitors. He is trying to decide whether to ask the current employees to work 8 hours of overtime on Saturdays until the backlog is satisfied or to hire three additional workers to work a 40-hour week. He asks you, the company's accountant, for your advice.

A study of the records and operating procedures at Pounds-a-Way reveals the following:

- The supervisors each earn $12 an hour, and the twelve factory workers each earn $8 an hour.
- Payroll tax rates are as follows: FICA, 7 percent; FUTA, .8 percent; and SUTA, 5.4 percent. (For simplicity, assume that no employee has reached the yearly maximum for FICA, FUTA, or SUTA.)
- Employees who have worked for the company at least 18 months are covered by a company-paid pension plan. All current employees have been with the company over 2 years. Pounds-a-Way contributes an amount equal to 6 percent of an employee's gross wages to the pension plan.
- The company pays $20 a week for each employee, regardless of length of service, for a hospitalization insurance plan.
- New employees will be hired at $6 an hour.
- To help the supervisors train the new employees, one of the current factory workers would be promoted to assistant supervisor and receive a raise of $2 an hour.

1. To assist Thomas Armstrong in making his decision, prepare a schedule showing the cost of each alternative.
2. What additional information would be useful in making this decision? What nonmonetary factors should be considered?

CHAPTER

8

Departmentalizing Overhead Costs

■ ■ ■

In a job cost system, the costs of direct materials and direct labor are charged to specific jobs. All other costs, including indirect materials and indirect labor, are charged to manufacturing overhead. In this chapter, you will learn how the many other manufacturing costs are classified, recorded, summarized, and distributed. The next two chapters will explain the steps involved in charging overhead costs to production.

Types of Manufacturing Overhead Costs

Manufacturing overhead includes all factory costs other than direct materials and direct labor. Here is a partial listing of the most common costs in a typical factory operation.

Indirect Materials

Shop supplies
Lubricants
Factory office supplies
Small tools
Packaging materials
Items used in small amounts in the manufacturing process

Indirect Labor

Factory line supervisors
Factory clerical workers
Timekeepers
Factory superintendents
Janitors
Receiving clerks
Storeroom supervisors
Storeroom clerks
Purchasing employees
Idle-time costs of direct workers
Overtime premium of direct workers (unless the time is identified with a specific job)

Other Manufacturing Overhead

Employee fringe benefits
Payroll taxes
Workers' compensation insurance
Factory utilities
Rent of factory building, warehouse, and equipment
Depreciation of factory building and equipment
Fire and casualty insurance
Property taxes
Group insurance for factory employees
Repairs and maintenance
Spoiled goods

Control of Manufacturing Overhead Costs

The size of the company, how it is organized, and the types of products manufactured are key factors that have an important bearing upon the method used to account for manufacturing overhead costs. A small company producing only one product or a few products may simply keep a separate general ledger account for each manufacturing overhead cost. If there are many different types of overhead costs, manufacturing overhead analysis sheets would be maintained. These analysis sheets function as a subsidiary ledger that is controlled by the Manufacturing Overhead Control account in the general ledger. This account summarizes the data in the analysis sheets.

Departmentalization of Overhead

In large businesses it is necessary to divide the factory operations into departments. The departments become the centers for effective control of costs. There are two methods of achieving cost departmentalization.

Separate Control Accounts

One method is to maintain a control account for each different manufacturing overhead cost. In a subsidiary ledger, analysis sheets are used to show the amount chargeable to each department.

For example, a control account for indirect labor throughout the factory may be set up such as the one on page 141.

A record of the indirect labor costs charged to each department in the factory is maintained in the subsidiary ledger made up of analysis sheets.

When there are many different types of overhead costs, it is necessary to have a large number of general ledger accounts. This procedure of posting to the control accounts then becomes inefficient.

Single Control Accounts

The second method of achieving cost departmentalization is to set up one control account for all manufacturing overhead costs. (This cuts down on the number of

Indirect Labor — No. 650

DATE	EXPLANATION	POST. REF.	DEPARTMENTAL ANALYSIS					TOTAL
			MILLING	ASSEMBLING	FINISHING	BUILDING SERVICES	GENERAL FACTORY	
19X1 Oct. 5	Time tkt. anal.	TTA	580 00	738 00	720 00	924 00	1368 00	4330 00
12	Time tkt. anal.	TTA	480 00	674 00	708 00	847 00	1594 00	4303 00
15	Semimo. pay.	SP				640 00	2355 00	2995 00
19	Time tkt. anal.	TTA	558 00	744 00	642 00	811 00	1506 00	4261 00
26	Time tkt. anal.	TTA	513 00	804 00	719 00	780 00	1617 00	4433 00
31	Semimo. pay.	SP				640 00	2355 00	2995 00
31	Time tkt. anal.	TTA	487 00	495 00	447 00	507 00	878 00	2814 00
31	Total		2618 00	3455 00	3236 00	5149 00	11673 00	26131 00

accounts in the general ledger.) The subsidiary ledger may organize costs in two ways: by type of cost or by department.

Subsidiary Ledger by Type of Cost. A subsidiary ledger account may be kept for each manufacturing overhead cost. For example, a separate account would be established for indirect materials. This arrangement eliminates many entries in the general ledger and accumulates data by type of cost. It does not, however, accumulate the total factory overhead by departments. Departmental totals are needed at the end of the accounting period. Additional analysis is required to obtain this information.

Subsidiary Ledger by Department. The subsidiary ledger accounts may also take the form of departmental overhead analysis sheets. This is the practice at Space Savers because it offers the most efficient control of costs. Each sheet contains special columns for recording common types of overhead costs such as those listed below.

Indirect materials   Repairs and maintenance
Indirect labor   Utilities
Payroll taxes   Insurance
Depreciation   Other taxes

Each sheet also contains another column for entering infrequent costs. The departmental overhead analysis sheet for the Milling Department for the month of October is shown on page 142.

DEPARTMENTAL OVERHEAD ANALYSIS SHEET

Department _Milling_   Month of _October_   19 XI

DATE	REF.	TOTAL	01 INDIRECT MATERIALS	02 INDIRECT LABOR	03 PAYROLL TAXES	04 DEPRECIATION	05 REPAIRS & MAINT.	06 UTILITIES	07 INSURANCE	08 OTHER TAXES	09 OTHER ITEM	09 OTHER AMOUNT
Oct 3	R808	10625	10625									
5	TTA	58000		58000								
12	TTA	48000		48000								
14	R827	6750	6750									
19	TTA	55800		55800								
(A) 21	10-789	7840					7840					
26	TTA	51300		51300								
27	10-814	1620									permit	1620
27	J10-27	11503									spoilage	11503
31	TTA	48700		48700								
31	R906	29825	29825									
31	SPT	118740			118740							
(C) 31	J10-38	114700				105600			3800	5300		
(B) 31	10-832	62515						62515				
31	J10-44	23400							23400			
TOTAL		649318	47200	261800	118740	105600	7840	62515	27200	5300		13123

....

Recording Overhead Costs

Entries for indirect materials from material requisitions and indirect labor from labor time analyses are recorded on departmental overhead analysis sheets. Other manufacturing overhead costs are posted from disbursement vouchers (purchases from outsiders) and at the end of the month from general journal vouchers (adjusting entries to cover accrued or deferred costs).

Voucher Register Entries

The cost of repairs, utilities, or other overhead items purchased from outsiders is usually obtained from an invoice. A control routine similar to the one relating to the purchase of direct materials (described in Chapter 3) follows:

1. The invoice is compared with the purchase order, and all computations are checked.
2. A voucher is prepared, including a notation of the department to be charged.
3. Upon approval of the voucher, the purchase is entered in the voucher register as a debit to Manufacturing Overhead Control and as a credit to Vouchers Payable (or Accounts Payable).
4. The cost clerk charges the cost to the appropriate departmental overhead analysis sheet.

For example, on October 21 Space Savers received an invoice for $78.40 from Ace Motor Repair Company for repairs to equipment in the Milling Department. The voucher register entry would be as follows:

VOUCHER REGISTER for Month of						October				19 X1	
DATE		VOU. NO.	PAYABLE TO	PAID				VOUCHERS PAYABLE CR. 201		MFG. OHD. CONTROL DR. 501	
				DATE		CHECK NO.					
Oct.	21	10-789	Ace Motor Repair Co.					78	40	78	40

Since only one department is involved in this transaction, the name of the department is noted on the invoice. This information guides the cost clerk to charge the amount to the correct departmental overhead analysis sheet (see Item A on the departmental analysis sheet shown on page 142). If the invoice applies to more than one department, the cost distribution is noted on that form.

Another procedure is to prepare an analysis of the invoice, known as a *distribution memorandum,* indicating how the cost is to be distributed. This analysis is then sent to the cost clerk for entry in the departmental overhead analysis sheets. For example, Space Savers' utility bill for October totals $2,488.64. The invoice is entered in the voucher register as shown:

VOUCHER REGISTER for Month of						October				19 X1	
DATE		VOU. NO.	PAYABLE TO	PAID				VOUCHERS PAYABLE CR. 201		MFG. OHD. CONTROL DR. 501	
				DATE		CHECK NO.					
Oct.	21	10-789	Ace Motor Repair Co.					78	40	78	40
	27	10-832	City Utilities					2,488	64	2,488	64

Then the cost accountant prepares a distribution memorandum for the cost clerk. The distribution memorandum shows how much of the total amount of the voucher is to be allocated to each department. The first three digits of the account number indicate the department to be charged, and the last two digits represent the number of the expense column to be charged. For example, the distribution memorandum on page 144 shows that $625.15 is to be charged to utilities expense (06) on the departmental overhead analysis sheet for the Milling Department on the (see Item B on the departmental overhead analysis sheet shown on page 142).

General Journal Vouchers

Most of the manufacturing overhead costs recorded by end-of-period adjusting entries involve *fixed costs* that do not vary from month to month. For example, depreciation charges, taxes, and property insurance usually remain constant each month. These fixed costs are recorded by adjusting entries. To speed up the journalizing of the adjustments and to facilitate posting to the departmental overhead analysis

REFERENCE _Voucher 10-832_

ITEM _Utilities (06)_

DATE _10/27/X1_

AMOUNT _$2,488.64_

Comments:

DISTRIBUTION	
ACCOUNT NO.	**AMOUNT**
502-06	$625 15
503-06	100 54
504-06	226 96
505-06	1,083 06
506-06	452 93
TOTAL	$2,488 64

By _J. J._
COST ACCOUNTANT

FORM NO. 654

sheets, the cost accountant prepares a schedule of monthly fixed overhead charges, as shown below.

SPACE SAVERS, INC.
Schedule of Monthly Fixed Overhead Charges
Year 19X1

DEPARTMENT	DEPRECIATION OF MACHINERY AND EQUIPMENT	DEPRECIATION OF BUILDINGS	PROPERTY TAXES	PROPERTY INSURANCE	TOTAL
Milling	$1,056.00		$ 53.00	$ 38.00	$1,147.00
Assembling	163.40		12.22	13.30	188.92
Finishing	410.00		23.10	22.00	455.10
Building Services	212.00	$1,520.00	220.00	57.00	2,009.00
General Factory	798.60		112.68	70.70	981.98
Total	$2,640.00	$1,520.00	$421.00	$201.00	$4,782.00

A journal voucher can be quickly prepared from this schedule. See page 145.
The schedule is attached to the journal voucher, and the cost clerk then posts the data to the departmental overhead analysis sheets (see Item C on the departmental overhead analysis sheet shown on page 142).

JOURNAL VOUCHER	Date	Oct. 31,		19 X1		No. 10-38

ACCOUNT	ACCOUNT NUMBER	✓	DEBIT	CREDIT
Manufacturing Overhead Control	501		4782.00	
Accum. Depr. – Buildings	133			1520.00
Accum. Depr. – Machinery and Equipment	135			2640.00
Property Taxes Payable	216			421.00
Prepaid Insurance	127			201.00

EXPLANATION

Recorded monthly adjustments for fixed factory costs.

PREPARED BY	AUDITED BY	APPROVED BY
NV	BJ	MP

Summary Schedule of Departmental Costs

At the end of the month, the cost clerk totals the departmental overhead analysis sheets. The clerk then prepares a schedule showing the total amount of each type of cost incurred in each department. The schedule of departmental overhead costs for the month of October is shown below.

SPACE SAVERS, INC.
Schedule of Departmental Overhead Costs
October 19X1

COST	MILLING	ASSEMBLING	FINISHING	BUILDING SERVICES	GENERAL FACTORY	TOTAL
Indirect Materials	$ 472.00	$ 754.65	$1,224.20	$ 192.30	$ 538.20	$ 3,181.35
Indirect Labor	2,618.00	3,455.00	3,236.00	5,149.00	11,673.00	26,131.00
Payroll Taxes	1,187.40	1,635.79	1,264.15	294.83	655.78	5,037.95
Depreciation	1,056.00	163.40	410.00	1,732.00	798.60	4,160.00
Rep. and Maint.	78.40	92.25	184.00	673.45	506.50	1,534.60
Utilities	625.15	100.54	226.96	1,083.06	452.93	2,488.64
Insurance	272.00	109.55	157.80	98.60	156.10	794.05
Property Taxes	53.00	12.22	23.10	220.00	112.68	421.00
Other Costs	131.23	68.67	137.97	33.76	113.52	485.15
Total	$6,493.18	$6,392.07	$6,864.18	$9,477.00	$15,007.31	$44,233.74

When all charges have been entered for the month, the subsidiary ledger should agree with its related control account. The total amount of overhead shown on the departmental overhead analysis sheets will equal the total charges (debits) in the general ledger account Manufacturing Overhead Control 501.

Allocating Overhead to Jobs

You have seen where all the debit entries in the Manufacturing Overhead Control account come from and how they are entered on departmental overhead analysis sheets. Now the credit side of the control account must be examined. Much more is involved than simply transferring the total manufacturing overhead costs to Work in Process in a quick journal entry. This procedure would produce only a vague total cost of production. The goal of cost accounting is to obtain specific, precise unit cost data. The overhead costs must be associated with products or jobs so that the transfer (the cost flow) will actually parallel the work flow. Distributing overhead costs to departments is the first step in this overall allocation process.

Distributing Service Department Costs

Service departments help producing departments and other service departments to operate efficiently. But service departments do not produce goods themselves. The manufacturing overhead expense charged to service department operations must be redistributed to where goods are produced. (These goods produce the revenue needed to pay for costs.)

Service department costs should be distributed in proportion to the services provided. There are usually as many separate distribution computations as there are service departments.

Order of Allocation

A service department often provides some service to other service departments as well as to producing departments. For example, the Building Service Department of Space Savers provides floor space and heating and cooling services for all other departments. The General Factory Department serves all other departments, including the Building Services Department, by purchasing, receiving, and issuing materials and supplies and by providing recordkeeping and general administrative services. This mutual exchange of services might cause difficulty in apportioning service department costs because the apportionment and reapportionment could be repeated endlessly. For example, unless some workable rule is adopted, the accountant may be faced with the problem of apportioning part of the Building Services Department costs to the General Factory Department and part of the General Factory Department costs to the Building Services Department. Space Savers solves this problem by adopting some generally accepted rules:

1. Distribute first the costs of the service department that serves the greatest number of other departments.
2. Distribute second the costs of the service department that serves the next greatest number of other departments.
3. Follow this procedure until all service department costs are distributed.
4. If no one department serves a larger number of other service departments, apportion the costs of the service department with the largest expenditures first.

5. Once the costs of a service department have been apportioned, no further costs are prorated to it.

A different procedure is followed by some companies, although it is usually unsatisfactory. The costs of each service department are apportioned only to producing departments, and no service department costs are prorated to other service departments. This saves time and work but often results in an inaccurate cost apportionment.

Basis for Allocation

The costs of each service department are redistributed by ratios that express the relationship between the service provided and some functional factor or basis. For example, building service costs may be redistributed according to floor area occupied by other departments. This guideline is logical because the larger the area, the more sweeping, cleaning, heating, cooling, and other services required. On the other hand, since general factory expenses include the costs of factory management, it would be equally logical to allocate these costs in proportion to the amount or value of the labor or labor and materials that are being supervised and controlled. Thus direct labor costs, direct labor hours, and even conversion costs may be used as meaningful bases. (Other bases are described in Chapter 9.)

Allocating Building Services Department Costs.   At Space Savers, the costs of the Building Services Department are apportioned first because it provides service to all other departments. (The General Factory Department primarily serves the producing departments.) This apportionment at the end of the month is made on the basis of the factory floor space occupied by each of the other departments, as indicated below.

Department	Square Feet	Percent
General Factory	16,200	30
Milling	10,800	20
Assembling	15,120	28
Finishing	11,880	22
Total	54,000	100

On this basis, the manufacturing overhead costs of the Building Services Department for October, totaling $9,477 (from the schedule on page 145), will be prorated to the other departments, as follows:

Department	Dollars		Percent		Amount
General Factory	$9,477	×	30	=	$2,843.10
Milling	9,477	×	20	=	1,895.40
Assembling	9,477	×	28	=	2,653.56
Finishing	9,477	×	22	=	2,084.94
Total			100		$9,477.00

Allocating General Factory Department Costs.   The General Factory Department costs are distributed among the producing departments on the basis of total direct labor costs in the producing departments. The direct labor costs for October, taken from the monthly summary of factory wages (shown on page 124), are apportioned as follows:

Department	Direct Labor Cost	Percent
Milling	$17,797.00	30.3719
Assembling	24,865.80	42.4353
Finishing	15,934.20	27.1928
Total	$58,597.00	100.0000

The General Factory Department costs totaling $17,850.41 ($15,007.31 charged directly to the department as shown on page 145, plus $2,843.10 from apportionment of Building Services Department costs) are then prorated according to these percentages of total direct labor costs.

Department	Dollars		Percent		Amount
Milling	$17,850.41	×	30.3719	=	$5,421.51
Assembling	17,850.41	×	42.4353	=	7,574.88
Finishing	17,850.41	×	27.1928	=	4,854.02
Total			100.0000		$17,850.41

The allocations of service department costs are summarized on a worksheet, as shown below.

Space Savers, Inc.
Worksheet for Prorating Service Department Costs
Month Ended October 31, 19X1

ITEM	BASIS OF PRORATION	BUILDING SERVICES	GENERAL FACTORY	MILLING	ASSEMBLING	FINISHING	TOTAL
Bal. of dept. ov. an. sheets		9477 00	15007 31	6493 18	6392 07	6864 18	44233 74
Prorate Bldg. Ser.	floor space	(9477 00)	2843 10	1895 40	2653 56	2084 94	
Prorate Gen. Fact.	dir. labor		(17850 41)	5421 51	7574 88	4854 02	
Total		—0—	—0—	13810 09	16620 51	13803 14	44233 74

After the worksheet is completed, the prorations are entered on the various departmental overhead analysis sheets so that the producing department analysis sheets will reflect all manufacturing overhead. The October analysis sheet for the Milling Department after all service department costs have been apportioned is shown on page 149.

DEPARTMENTAL OVERHEAD ANALYSIS SHEET

Department *Milling* Month of *October* 19 *X1*

DATE	REF.	TOTAL	01 INDIRECT MATERIALS	02 INDIRECT LABOR	03 PAYROLL TAXES	04 DEPRECIATION	05 REPAIRS & MAINT.	06 UTILITIES	07 INSURANCE	08 OTHER TAXES	09 OTHER ITEM	09 OTHER AMOUNT
Oct. 3	R808	10625	10625									
5	TTA	58000		58000								
12	TTA	48000		48000								
14	R827	6750	6750									
19	TTA	55800		55800								
21	10-789	7840					7840					
26	TTA	51300		51300								
27	10-814	1620									permit	1620
27	J10-27	11503									spoilage	11503
31	TTA	48700		48700								
31	R906	29825	29825									
31	SPT	118740			118740							
31	J10-38	114700				105600			3800	5300		
31	10-832	62515						62515				
31	J10-44	23400							23400			
TOTAL	J10-50	649318	47200	261800	118740	105600	7840	62515	27200	5300		13123
31	J10-51	189540	Proration of Building Services Costs									
31	J10-52	542151	Proration of General Factory Costs									
TOTAL		1381009										

Recording Overhead Distribution in the General Ledger

At the end of the month the distribution of overhead costs is entered in the general ledger by a series of general journal entries.

- Manufacturing Overhead Control 501 is closed into five special departmental overhead accounts so that the ledger will reflect the same departmentalized data as summarized in the departmental overhead analysis sheets.
- Distributions of service department costs are journalized in order of allocation.
  1. Building Services Department costs are allocated to the other four departments as shown on page 150.
  2. General Factory Department costs are allocated to the three producing departments as shown on page 151.

After the entries are posted, the Manufacturing Overhead Control account and the departmental overhead accounts appear as shown on pages 151 and 152.

JOURNAL VOUCHER   Date *Oct. 31,*   19 *XL*   No. *10-50*

ACCOUNT	ACCOUNT NUMBER	✓	DEBIT	CREDIT
Mfg. Overhead—Milling Dept.	502	✓	6493 18	
Mfg. Overhead—Assembling Dept.	503	✓	6392 07	
Mfg. Overhead—Finishing Dept.	504	✓	6864 18	
Mfg. Overhead—Building Serv. Dept.	505	✓	9477 00	
Mfg. Overhead—Gen. Factory Dept.	506	✓	15007 31	
Mfg. Overhead Control	501	✓		44233 74

EXPLANATION

Closed out control account and recorded
department costs.

PREPARED BY *NV*   AUDITED BY *BJ*   APPROVED BY *MP*

JOURNAL VOUCHER   Date *Oct. 31,*   19 *XL*   No. *10-51*

ACCOUNT	ACCOUNT NUMBER	✓	DEBIT	CREDIT
Mfg. Overhead—Gen. Factory Dept.	506	✓	2843 10	
Mfg. Overhead—Milling Dept.	502	✓	1895 40	
Mfg. Overhead—Assembling Dept.	503	✓	2653 56	
Mfg. Overhead—Finishing Dept.	504	✓	2084 94	
Mfg. Overhead—Building Services Dept.	505	✓		9477 00

EXPLANATION

Prorated Building Services Department costs to
other departments.

PREPARED BY *NV*   AUDITED BY *BJ*   APPROVED BY *MP*

Note that the total of the balances in Accounts 502, 503, and 504 agrees with the total debits in the Manufacturing Overhead Control account shown on page 151 ($13,810.09 + $16,620.51 + $13,803.14 = $44,233.74).

JOURNAL VOUCHER

Date _Oct. 31,_ _____ 19 _X1_ No. _10-52_

ACCOUNT	ACCOUNT NUMBER	✔	DEBIT	CREDIT
Mfg. Overhead—Milling Dept.	502	✓	5421 51	
Mfg. Overhead—Assembling Dept.	503	✓	7574 88	
Mfg. Overhead—Finishing Dept.	504	✓	4854 02	
Mfg. Overhead—General Factory Dept.	506	✓		17850 41

EXPLANATION

Prorated General Factory Department costs to other departments.

PREPARED BY _NV_   AUDITED BY _BJ_   APPROVED BY _MP_

Manufacturing Overhead Control   No. 501

DATE	EXPLANATION	POST. REF.	DEBIT	CREDIT	BALANCE	DR. CR.
19X1 Oct. 31	Balance	✔			44,233 74	Dr.
31	Close out to other dept. accounts	J10-50		44,233 74	-0-	

Manufacturing Overhead—Milling Department   No. 502

DATE	EXPLANATION	POST. REF.	DEBIT	CREDIT	BALANCE	DR. CR.
19X1 Oct. 31		J10-50	6,493 18		6,493 18	Dr.
31		J10-51	1,895 40		8,388 58	Dr.
31		J10-52	5,421 51		13,810 09	Dr.

Manufacturing Overhead—Assembling Department   No. 503

DATE	EXPLANATION	POST. REF.	DEBIT	CREDIT	BALANCE	DR. CR.
19X1 Oct. 31		J10-50	6,392 07		6,392 07	Dr.
31		J10-51	2,653 56		9,045 63	Dr.
31		J10-52	7,574 88		16,620 51	Dr.

Manufacturing Overhead—Finishing Department   No. 504

DATE		EXPLANATION	POST. REF.	DEBIT		CREDIT		BALANCE		DR. CR.
19X1										
Oct.	31		J10-50	6,864	18			6,864	18	Dr.
	31		J10-51	2,084	94			8,949	12	Dr.
	31		J10-52	4,854	02			13,803	14	Dr.

Manufacturing Overhead—Building Services Department   No. 505

DATE		EXPLANATION	POST. REF.	DEBIT		CREDIT		BALANCE		DR. CR.
19X1										
Oct.	31		J10-50	9,477	00			9,477	00	Dr.
			J10-51			9,477	00	-0-		

Manufacturing Overhead—General Factory Department   No. 506

DATE		EXPLANATION	POST. REF.	DEBIT		CREDIT		BALANCE		DR. CR.
19X1										
Oct.	31		J10-50	15,007	31			15,007	31	Dr.
	31		J10-51	2,843	10			17,850	41	Dr.
	31		J10-52			17,850	41	-0-		

Principles and Procedures Summary

The most effective way to achieve control of costs is by departmentalization. Overhead costs may be departmentalized by one of two methods. A separate control account is used for each cost, and a subsidiary ledger shows the amount chargeable to each department. Or, a single control account is used for all costs, and the subsidiary ledger accounts take the form of an overhead analysis sheet for each department.

Indirect materials and indirect labor costs are recorded from materials requisitions and labor time analyses. Other manufacturing overhead costs appear in the voucher register or general journal vouchers.

After total overhead costs are known, they must be associated with specific departments. The first step in this process is to prepare a general journal entry to close the Manufacturing Overhead Control account (501) and charge each department with its overhead costs as shown on the schedule of departmental overhead costs. Then the service department costs are distributed to the producing departments on a special proration worksheet. The distribution of service department overhead is recorded on the appropriate departmental overhead analysis sheets. This distribution is also recorded by a series of general journal voucher entries that are posted to the manufacturing overhead accounts for the departments in the general ledger.

When these procedures are completed, the service department manufacturing overhead accounts (505 and 506) will be closed. The balance in the manufacturing overhead account of each producing department (502, 503, and 504) should agree with the total on that department's overhead analysis sheet.

Review Questions

1. If a company established a single manufacturing overhead control account, what two forms may be used for the subsidiary ledger accounts?
2. What is a distribution memorandum?
3. In preparing a distribution memorandum, Space Savers, Inc., uses an account distribution code. What two items are included in this code?
4. Do all manufacturing overhead costs require a cash payment? Explain.
5. What are the sources of postings to the departmental overhead analysis sheets?
6. What are typical fixed costs found in a factory?
7. What is a schedule of departmental overhead costs? When is it prepared?
8. What do the debit postings in a Manufacturing Overhead Control account represent?
9. To what departments are service department overhead costs distributed? Why?
10. What is the purpose of a worksheet for prorating service department costs?
11. Why are special departmental overhead accounts established at the end of the month in the general ledger?
12. At the end of the month, the total of the departmental overhead analysis sheets should equal the balance of what account?

Managerial Discussion Questions

1. What is the advantage to management in having manufacturing overhead costs departmentalized?
2. If management is reviewing the overhead costs of a department, which of the costs listed under Other Manufacturing Overhead on page 140 would be most likely to merit close attention? Why?
3. Should management rely on allocated overhead costs from service departments in considering the efficiency of producing departments? Explain.
4. To what extent would the head of a production department be accountable to management for the cost of equipment depreciation? Explain.
5. Why should management have the costs of service departments distributed to producing departments?
6. Describe the two methods of establishing overhead control accounts in the general ledger.

Exercises

1. **Allocating manufacturing overhead costs.** The Katz Manufacturing Company received an invoice for $24,630 for repairs. The allocation is as follows: 60 percent of the repairs were performed in the Cutting Department; 30 percent in the Molding Department; 4 percent in the Stripping Department; and 6 percent in the Finishing Department. Determine the amount of the invoice to be allocated to each department.

2. **Recording manufacturing overhead costs.** For the month of May 19X6, the depreciation expense for the factory building was $15,700; the depreciation expense for the factory machinery and equipment was $13,200; and the cost of insurance expired on the factory was $11,200. Prepare the entry on May 31, 19X6 at the Edison Company to record these manufacturing overhead costs for the month of May 19X6.

3. **Selecting the basis for manufacturing cost allocation.** The Brown Supply Corporation allocates Building Services Department overhead on the basis of the amount of floor space occupied by each producing department in the factory. The Molding Department occupies 4,000 square feet; the Baking Department occupies 6,000 square feet; and the Finishing Department occupies 10,000 square feet. Calculate the amount that should be allocated to each of these producing departments based on the square footage occupied if the Building Services Department incurs $85,400 in overhead costs.

4. **Selecting the basis for manufacturing cost allocation.** The Plaster Corporation allocates the General Factory Department overhead on the basis of direct labor costs incurred by each producing department in the factory. The Mixing Department incurred $7,020 in direct labor costs; the Shaping Department incurred $4,680 in direct labor costs; and the Assembling Department incurred $11,700 in direct labor costs. Determine the amount that should be allocated to each producing department if the General Factory Department incurs overhead costs of $42,500.

5. **Recording the allocation of manufacturing overhead.** The departmental overhead analysis sheets for Knoxville Metal, Inc., for the month of August showed the following overhead amounts:

Cutting Department	$15,840
Pressing Department	18,320
Finishing Department	14,920
Building Services Department	8,530
General Factory Department	6,180

A worksheet was prepared to allocate the overhead of the service departments to the producing departments. The allocations were as follows:

Building Services Department:

To General Factory Department	$1,365
To Cutting Department	1,876
To Pressing Department	3,242
To Finishing Department	2,047

General Factory Department:

To Cutting Department	$2,113
To Pressing Department	2,640
To Finishing Department	2,792

a. Record the general journal entry to close the Manufacturing Overhead Control account.

b. Record the general journal entries to allocate the overhead of the service departments to the producing departments.

Problems

PROBLEM 8-1. Completing departmental overhead analysis sheets. Bismarck Supply manufactures office equipment. The factory is divided into five departments. The Preparing Department, the Assembling Department, and the Finishing Department are producing departments. The Maintenance Department and the General Factory Department are service departments. During September 19X6, the following transactions affecting the Preparing Department take place:

Sept. 4 The weekly analysis of time tickets show direct labor costs of $5,600 and indirect labor costs of $1,060.

5 Indirect materials costing $106 are issued on Materials Requisition 764.

6 Voucher 9-033 for repairs to machinery (total cost $207) is prepared.

8 Voucher 9-071 for allocation of electricity (total cost $310) is prepared.

11 The weekly analysis of time tickets shows direct labor costs of $5,810 and indirect labor costs of $1,120.

12 Indirect materials costing $125 and direct materials costing $720 are issued on Materials Requisition 817.

15 Voucher 9-102 for the water bill (total cost $136) is prepared.

15 The semimonthly payroll records show supervisors' salaries totaling $1,560 (use reference PR9-3).

18 The weekly analysis of time tickets shows direct labor costs of $5,350 and indirect labor costs of $1,230.

19 Indirect materials costing $162 are issued on Materials Requisition 862.

25 The weekly analysis of time tickets shows direct labor costs of $4,110 and indirect labor costs of $982.

26 Indirect materials costing $136 are issued on Materials Requisition 894.

30 The semimonthly payroll records show supervisors' salaries totaling $1,560 (use reference PR9-6).

30 General journal vouchers are prepared as follows: No. 9-7, insurance, $165; No. 9-8, payroll taxes, $1,240; No. 9-9, property taxes, $350; No. 9-12, depreciation, $1,430.

Instructions

1. Enter the overhead expense items given in the transactions on the departmental overhead analysis sheet.
2. Prove the accuracy of your work by footing and crossfooting all money columns.

PROBLEM 8-2. Completing a worksheet for prorating service department costs and making journal entries. Information for prorating service department costs of the J. Johnston Corporation for the month of March 19X6 is given below and on page 156.

Department	Floor Space	Direct Labor Hours
General Factory	1,200 sq. ft.	
Stores	3,000 sq. ft.	
Shaping	12,000 sq. ft.	4,500 — .45
Assembling	6,000 sq. ft.	3,000 — .30
Finishing	9,000 sq. ft.	2,500 — .25

30,000

	Service Departments		Producing Departments			
Overhead Item	General Factory	Stores	Shaping	Assembling	Finishing	Total
Indirect Labor	$5,100	$2,100	$3,300	$2,250	$2,970	$15,720
Payroll Taxes	277	52	152	63	122	666
Indirect Materials	200	250	325	200	260	1,235
Property Taxes	40	85	420	125	170	840
Depreciation	1,020	2,100	2,600	2,100	650	8,470
Power and Light	540	365	340	575	140	1,960
Heat	335	260	345	310	135	1,385
Insurance	34	24	118	273	39	488
Repairs	30	28	242	40	62	402
Totals	$7,576	$5,264	$7,842	$5,936	$4,548	$31,166

Instructions

1. Complete the worksheet for prorating service department costs. The General Factory Department costs are prorated on the basis of floor space occupied. The Stores Department costs are then allocated to the producing departments on the basis of direct labor hours. Round allocated amounts to the nearest whole dollar.
2. Give the general journal entries to close the Manufacturing Overhead Control account into the departmental manufacturing overhead accounts and to prorate the service department costs.

PROBLEM 8-3. Distributing service department costs, making journal entries, and posting to accounts. Data for prorating service department costs for the Seven Oaks Corporation for August 19X6 are given below.

Account Number	Department	Overhead Expenses	Allocation of Maintenance Department	Allocation of General Factory Department
502	Preparing	$ 9,356	26%	32%
503	Assembling	10,417	30%	36%
504	Finishing	8,729	27%	32%
505	Maintenance	3,824		
506	General Factory	5,261	17%	
	Total	$37,587	100%	100%

Instructions

1. Open a departmental overhead analysis sheet for each department using the balances for overhead expenses given above. Open a general ledger account for Manufacturing Overhead Control 501 with a debit balance of $37,587.
2. Prepare the worksheet for prorating service department costs. Use the proration percentages given above. Allocate Maintenance Department costs first; then allocate General Factory Department costs. Round the amounts to the nearest dollar. Post the allocations to the departmental overhead analysis sheets. Total the departmental overhead analysis sheets.

3. Prepare the general journal vouchers to distribute the service departments' costs to the other departments. Begin with journal Voucher 8-37.
   a. Close the Manufacturing Overhead Control account into the special departmental overhead accounts.
   b. Allocate Maintenance Department costs to the other four departments.
   c. Allocate General Factory Department costs to the three producing departments.
4. Post the general journal entries to the general ledger accounts. (NOTE: The balance in each general ledger account should agree with the total on the corresponding departmental overhead analysis sheet.)

Alternate Problems

PROBLEM 8-1A. Completing departmental overhead analysis sheets. Northgate Industrial Supply manufactures tools. The factory is divided into five departments. The Preparing Department, the Assembling Department, and the Finishing Department are producing departments. The Maintenance Department and the General Factory Department are service departments. During October 19X7 the following transactions affecting the Preparing Department take place:

Oct. 4   The weekly analysis of time tickets shows direct labor costs of $2,800 and indirect labor costs of $690.
6   Indirect materials costing $105 are issued on Materials Requisition 472.
6   Voucher 10-28 for repairs to machinery (total cost $275) is prepared.
7   Voucher 10-36 for allocation of electricity (total cost $462) is prepared.
11   The weekly analysis of time tickets shows direct labor costs of $3,200 and indirect labor costs of $710.
14   Indirect materials costing $91 and direct materials costing $860 are issued on Materials Requisition 511.
14   Voucher 10-47 for the water bill (total cost $252) is prepared.
15   The semimonthly payroll records show supervisors' salaries totaling $1,025 (use reference PR10-4).
18   The weekly analysis of time tickets shows direct labor costs of $3,050 and indirect labor costs of $781.
20   Indirect materials costing $127 are issued on Materials Requisition 533.
25   The weekly analysis of time tickets shows direct labor costs of $4,104 and indirect labor costs of $853.
27   Indirect materials costing $180 are issued on Materials Requisition 561.
31   The semimonthly payroll records show supervisors' salaries totaling $1,025 (use reference PR10-7).
31   General journal vouchers are prepared as follows: No. 10-09, insurance, $254; No. 10-10, payroll taxes, $870; No. 10-14, property taxes, $300; No. 10-16, depreciation, $960.

Instructions
1. Enter the overhead expense items given in the transactions on the departmental overhead analysis sheet.
2. Prove the accuracy of your work by footing and crossfooting all money columns.

PROBLEM 8-2A. Completing a worksheet for prorating service department costs and making journal entries. Information for prorating service department costs of the Gettysburg Corporation for July 19X5 is shown on page 158.

Department	Floor Space	Direct Labor Hours
General Factory	1,400 sq. ft.	
Stores	2,400 sq. ft.	
Grinding	5,600 sq. ft.	3,680
Mixing	4,800 sq. ft.	2,300
Finishing	3,200 sq. ft.	3,220

	Service Departments		Producing Departments			
Overhead Item	General Factory	Stores	Grinding	Mixing	Finishing	Total
Indirect Labor	$3,640	$1,720	$1,960	$1,720	$2,440	$11,480
Payroll Taxes	352	183	206	183	256	1,180
Supplies	68	190	63	58	221	600
Property Taxes	1,264	1,967	1,426	1,578	1,727	7,962
Depreciation	1,325	1,400	2,260	1,104	1,156	7,245
Utilities	2,079	1,980	1,485	2,180	2,013	9,737
Insurance	1,000	500	750	750	750	3,750
Repairs	188	106	68	50	238	650
Totals	$9,916	$8,046	$8,218	$7,623	$8,801	$42,604

Instructions

1. Complete the worksheet for prorating service department costs. General Factory Department costs are prorated first to all other departments on the basis of floor space occupied. The Stores Department costs are then allocated to the producing departments on the basis of direct labor hours. Round allocated amounts to the nearest whole dollar.

2. Give the general journal entries to close the Manufacturing Overhead Control account into the departmental manufacturing overhead accounts and to prorate the service department costs.

PROBLEM 8-3A. Distributing service department costs, making journal entries, and posting to accounts. Data for prorating service department costs for Kingstown Inc. for November 19X6 are given below.

Account Number	Department	Overhead Expenses	Allocation of Maintenance Department	Allocation of General Factory Department
502	Preparing	$ 6,544	25%	30%
503	Assembling	7,241	35%	40%
504	Finishing	6,428	25%	30%
505	Maintenance	3,129		
506	General Factory	3,418	15%	
	Total	$26,760	100%	100%

Instructions

1. Open departmental overhead analysis sheets for each department using the balances for overhead expenses given above. Open a general ledger account for Manufacturing Overhead Control 501 with a debit balance of $26,760.

2. Prepare the worksheet for prorating service department costs. Use the proration percentages given on page 158. Allocate Maintenance Department costs first; then allocate General Factory Department costs. Round the amounts to the nearest dollar. Post the allocations to the departmental overhead analysis sheets. Total the departmental analysis sheets.
3. Prepare the general journal vouchers to distribute the service departments' costs to the other departments. Begin with Journal Voucher 11-22.
   a. Close the Manufacturing Overhead Control account into the special department overhead accounts.
   b. Allocate Maintenance Department costs to the other four departments.
   c. Allocate General Factory Department costs to the three producing departments.
4. Post the general journal entries to the general ledger accounts. (NOTE: The balance in each general ledger account should agree with the total on the corresponding departmental overhead analysis sheet.)

Managerial Decisions

CASE 8-1. The Lake Corporation is a furniture manufacturer that is beginning its first month of operations. You have been hired to work in the cost accounting department and to establish procedures for recording factory costs. The factory is organized into three producing departments and two service departments.

Cutting Department. All wood is cut into the appropriate pieces for assembling.

Assembling Department. All pieces of wood are received from the Cutting Department and are assembled into the various pieces of furniture. The wood is either glued or screwed into place.

Finishing Department. The unfinished furniture is transferred to this department, where it is sanded, stained, and polished. From this department it is transferred to Finished Goods.

Building Maintenance Department. The employees in this department are responsible for cleaning each of the producing departments at the end of the day. In addition, they clean the tools used and perform any required repairs and sharpening.

General Factory. This department is responsible for the payroll of all employees. This responsibility includes recording time cards and time tickets. The cost accounting records are also maintained by this department. These include materials ledger cards, job cost sheets, and finished goods and stock ledger cards. Daily materials requisitions are recorded and posted to the appropriate records.

The square feet occupied by each department and the number of employees in each department are given below:

Department	Square Feet Occupied	Number of Employees
Cutting	3,750	20
Assembling	5,000	40
Finishing	3,250	40
Building Maintenance	1,200	10
General Factory	1,000	10

Prepare a report for the corporate controller explaining how you would prorate the costs of the service departments to the producing departments. Include a table indicating the bases of allocation. In addition, show any percentages that would be used. (Carry percents to five places and round to four.) You should also determine the sequence in which the costs of the service departments will be allocated. Give reasons for all of your recommendations.

CHAPTER

9

Setting Overhead Rates

■ ■ ■

After manufacturing overhead costs have been accumulated by departments, they must be allocated to jobs or products. In this chapter, you will learn how the cost accountant selects bases for allocating the departmentalized overhead costs to specific units of production.

Purpose of Overhead Rates

Management cannot wait until the end of the year, or even until the end of the month, to find out how much a particular job costs. Cost data are most useful when they are immediately available. They can then be used to evaluate efficiency, to suggest changes in procedures, and to help in setting profitable selling prices. The cost accountant is usually expected to report the total cost of a job as soon as it is finished. At this time the actual total overhead costs are not available, as they would be at the end of a fiscal period. For example, various bills, such as telephone or utility bills, may not arrive before a job is completed. The accountant must devise a method for rapidly and reliably estimating the overhead costs applicable to the completed job. Since these costs are not yet fully known, predetermined overhead rates are used for estimating overhead costs.

Determining the Overhead Rate

The basic procedure for determining an overhead rate is quite simple. First, a relationship is found between the company's total overhead costs and some second factor or *basis* that relates to the overhead costs of the job in a realistic way. The basis must also be accurately measurable. The basis for allocating overhead might be an amount or quantity, such as direct labor costs, materials costs, or direct labor hours. The ratio between the total overhead costs and the basis, expressed as a percent, is called the *overhead application rate*. For example, assume total overhead costs for the coming year are estimated at $100,000 and direct labor costs are expected to total

$200,000. Direct labor costs are used as the basis for allocating overhead. The ratio of the overhead to the basis is 1:2 ($100,000 : $200,000). The corresponding overhead application rate would be 50 percent of direct labor costs ($100,000 ÷ $200,000).

Once the overhead application rate has been determined, the overhead on each job is estimated by determining the basis amount on the job and applying the rate. For example, with a 50 percent rate, the overhead amount charged to a job with direct labor costs of $3,000 would be $1,500 ($3,000 × .50).

Factors That Affect Rate Setting

Even though the basic process of application is simple, the actual allocation of overhead costs will be strongly affected by several factors. One consideration is the length of the period over which the rate is to be computed. Another is whether a single rate is used for all factory overhead or whether separate rates are used for each producing department. The basis chosen for formulating the rate also affects the allocation.

Length of the Period

Most manufacturers use an annual period as a basis for determining rates. A shorter period for averaging costs is not satisfactory because wide variations can occur from period to period. These variations are due to changes in season, calendar, and volume. For example, heating costs are incurred only in the cold months. However, these costs should be averaged over the entire year.

Similar distortions in unit costs arise because some fixed costs remain constant each month regardless of volume. For example, assume an overhead rate based on direct labor hours. If depreciation for a month is $10,000 and expected direct labor hours that month are 40,000 hours, the overhead rate includes an amount equal to 25 cents per hour of labor for depreciation cost. However, if the expected labor hours are only 20,000 hours in the following month, the rate for that month will include 50 cents per direct labor hour for depreciation. Since volume does normally vary a great deal from month to month, an overhead rate computed each month would be changing constantly. With such a system, identical products manufactured in different months would be assigned widely varying overhead costs.

Fluctuating costs also complicate any attempt to use monthly costs in arriving at overhead rates. For example, repair costs may be extremely high in certain months of the year and low in others. The fact that the repair costs were actually incurred in certain months does not mean that products manufactured during that time should bear all repair costs. These costs are applicable to all goods produced during the year. In fact, many companies close down operations at certain times while repairs are made.

Many accountants argue that neither a monthly period nor a yearly period is long enough to establish overhead rates. They advise the use of a normal cost and a normal volume for computing overhead rates based on a period of time sufficiently long to level out both seasonal and yearly fluctuations in volume and costs. Although the use of a normal overhead rate has much theoretical justification, it is very hard to determine normal volume and normal costs.

Departmental and Factory Rates

A small plant with only one or a few similar departments manufacturing very few types of goods may successfully use a single common rate for the entire factory. However, if several different types of product are manufactured, or if all products do not go through all departments, a single rate is not appropriate. Nor is a single rate suitable if some departments perform largely machine operations and other departments use primarily hand labor. In such a case, a separate rate must be used for each of the producing departments.

Types of Overhead Rate Bases

The primary purpose of using a predetermined overhead rate is to charge a fair share of overhead costs to each job. A number of bases for determining overhead rates may be used in computing factorywide rates and in setting departmental rates. The most common bases are as follows:

- Units of production
- Materials costs
- Machine hours
- Direct labor hours
- Direct labor costs

The cost and production figures used in the calculations are usually derived from budget estimates. To demonstrate the computation procedure for each basis, the following budgeted data are given for a hypothetical producing department:

Manufacturing overhead costs for the year	$48,000
Number of units of production in the year	12,000 units
Direct material costs for the year	$240,000
Machine hours for the year	6,000 hours
Direct labor hours for the year	20,000 hours
Direct labor costs for the year	$100,000

Units of Production Basis

Overhead may be applied on the basis of the number of units manufactured during the period. The estimated manufacturing overhead costs are divided by the estimated total number of units of production to get the overhead cost to be applied to each unit of production.

$$\frac{\text{Estimated Manufacturing Overhead Costs}}{\text{Estimated Units of Production}} = \text{Overhead Cost per Units of Production}$$

Using the figures given above,

$$\frac{\$48,000}{12,000} = \$4 \text{ per unit}$$

Therefore, if a job of 600 units were produced, the overhead applied to the job would be $2,400 (600 × $4).

Unfortunately, the units of production basis has limited application. The rate is meaningful only if the manufacturing process is a simple one and only if one type, or a few very similar types, of goods are produced. For instance, if Product A requires

20 hours to be produced and Product B requires 2 hours, it would be inappropriate to base overhead on units of production. Product A is obviously going to require more overhead.

Materials Costs Basis

Overhead may be applied on the basis of the cost of direct materials used to produce the product. The estimated manufacturing overhead costs are divided by the estimated direct materials costs. This calculation gives the percentage of materials costs to be applied as overhead.

$$\frac{\text{Estimated Manufacturing Overhead Costs}}{\text{Estimated Direct Materials Costs}} = \text{Percentage of Materials Costs}$$

Again, using the figures given on page 163.

$$\frac{\$48,000}{\$240,000} = 20\% \text{ of materials costs}$$

Therefore, if direct materials consumed on a specific job cost $11,000, the overhead applied to that job would be $2,200 ($11,000 × .20).

For materials costs to make a good rate basis, each article manufactured must require approximately the same amount of materials, or materials usage must be distributed uniformly through the manufacturing process. In practice, most overhead costs bear little relationship to materials used, so this basis is seldom appropriate.

Machine Hours Basis

Overhead may be applied as a rate for each machine hour. When work is performed primarily by machines, a large part of the manufacturing overhead costs consists of depreciation, power, repairs, and other costs associated with machinery. Thus, a logical relationship exists between the use of the machinery and the amount of cost incurred. To determine this basis, divide the estimated manufacturing overhead costs by the estimated number of machine hours to get the rate for each machine hour.

$$\frac{\text{Estimated Manufacturing Overhead Costs}}{\text{Estimated Machine Hours}} = \text{Rate per Machine Hour}$$

Using the figures given on page 163.

$$\frac{\$48,000}{6,000} = \$8 \text{ per machine hour}$$

Therefore, if a job requires 200 machine hours, the overhead costs applied would be $1,600 (200 × $8).

In a highly automated factory where machines perform most of the labor and each item goes through a similar sequence of machines, this basis makes sense. However, a machine hours basis is not accurate if different kinds of machines are used for various products. In such a case, variations in original cost, operating costs, machine speed, and labor costs would make this rate inappropriate as an overall formula. A further objection to this method is the additional clerical work required to keep a record of the number of machine hours used on each job.

Direct Labor Hours Basis

Overhead may be applied as a rate for each direct labor hour. This widely used method assumes that overhead costs tend to vary with the number of hours of direct labor used. The estimated manufacturing overhead costs are divided by the estimated number of direct labor hours to obtain an application rate for each hour.

$$\frac{\text{Estimated Manufacturing Overhead Costs}}{\text{Estimated Direct Labor Hours}} = \text{Rate per Direct Labor Hour}$$

Using the figures given on page 163,

$$\frac{\$48,000}{20,000} = \$2.40 \text{ per direct labor hour}$$

Therefore, if a job required 1,125 direct labor hours to be completed, the overhead applied would be $2,700 (1,125 × $2.40).

The direct labor hours basis is usually appropriate if labor operations are a major part of the production process and the wage rates paid different workers vary considerably. As a general rule, there is a correlation between total manufacturing overhead costs and the number of direct labor hours worked. However, the direct labor hours method requires a record of the number of direct labor hours spent on each job, which may necessitate additional recordkeeping. (Total labor costs are part of normal factory records; however, a separate computation of total hours is not typically made.)

Direct Labor Costs Basis

Overhead may be applied as a percentage of the cost of direct labor. This method is the most widely used overhead application basis because it is simple and easy to use. Information concerning direct labor costs of each department and each job is available from the payroll records and the time tickets. Labor costs are normally accumulated by jobs as a routine cost accounting procedure, so that no extra clerical work is involved. The estimated manufacturing overhead costs are divided by the estimated direct labor costs. This calculation results in the percentage of direct labor costs.

$$\frac{\text{Estimated Manufacturing Overhead Costs}}{\text{Estimated Direct Labor Costs}} = \text{Percentage of Direct Labor Costs}$$

Using the figures given on page 163,

$$\frac{\$48,000}{\$100,000} = 48\% \text{ of direct labor costs}$$

Therefore, if direct labor costs incurred on a particular job totaled $3,000, the applied overhead would be $1,440 ($3,000 × .48).

The direct labor costs basis is not generally used in cases where a large proportion of overhead costs relates to the use of machinery. Also, if hourly wage rates vary widely between different workers on the same job or in the same department, the method will result in a larger amount of overhead being charged to those jobs on which higher paid workers are used. Just because an employee is paid more does not necessarily mean that the employee will use more heat, light, power, and so on in producing the product.

Selecting the Overhead Basis

The overhead rate basis selected by a company will depend on many considerations. Factors that affect the choice include the type of goods produced, amount of machinery employed, organization of the firm, type of labor used, wage rates paid, and cost and time involved in collecting the necessary data. Certain guiding principles should be observed in selecting a basis.

- The rate must be easily computed.
- The factor chosen as the basis must be one that can easily be measured for each job.
- There must be some direct relationship between the amount of overhead costs incurred and the factor chosen as a basis.
- The basis should be representative of the overhead costs applicable to each unit.
- Departmental rates should be used if possible. As a result, a number of different bases may be selected to meet the needs of different departments.

Setting Rates

The cost accountant at Space Savers has developed bases for the application of overhead costs after a careful study of all pertinent considerations.

Length of Rate Period

Space Savers bases its predetermined overhead rates on the estimated overhead costs and volume for a one-year period. In December, a budget is prepared for the coming year. This becomes the basis for computing the departmental overhead rates. The budgeted costs of the three producing departments and the two service departments for 19X1 are shown in the table on page 167.

The accountant completes the worksheet to prorate estimated service department costs to the producing departments (see page 167). After the budgeted overhead costs of the service departments are prorated to the producing departments, the overhead rates for the three producing departments are computed.

Extent of Rate Application

Space Savers uses a separate overhead rate for each producing department because the operations in each are so different.

Selection of Rate Basis

In each of the producing departments, the predetermined overhead rate is based on direct labor hours. This method has been selected because of the number of different types of direct workers employed in each of the three departments and because their hourly wage rates vary considerably. Operations performed on each job also vary widely.

SPACE SAVERS, INC.
Overhead Budgets
Year 19X1

COST	MILLING	ASSEMBLING	FINISHING	BUILDING SERVICES	GENERAL FACTORY	TOTAL
Indirect Materials	$ 8,500	$ 11,495	$ 19,570	$ 3,090	$ 8,385	$ 51,040
Indirect Labor	30,000	34,380	33,990	57,475	122,070	277,915
Payroll Taxes	15,000	19,650	14,730	4,380	8,580	62,340
Depreciation	12,875	2,150	5,335	22,545	9,825	52,730
Repairs and Maintenance	2,000	1,370	1,530	7,540	5,850	18,290
Utilities	7,725	1,880	2,885	13,185	4,875	30,550
Insurance	2,975	3,450	2,820	1,890	1,455	12,590
Property Taxes	650	160	300	2,865	1,390	5,365
Other	1,275	740	930	410	2,150	5,505
Total	$ 81,000	$ 75,275	$ 82,090	$113,380	$164,580	$516,325
Estimated Direct Labor Hours	32,000	40,000	28,000			
Estimated Direct Labor Costs	$192,000	$260,000	$188,000			

Space Savers, Inc.
Worksheet for Prorating Budgeted Service Dept. Overhead
Year Ended December 31, 19X1

ITEM	BASIS OF PRORATION	BUILDING SERVICES	GENERAL FACTORY	MILLING	ASSEMBLING	FINISHING	TOTAL
Est. dir. dept. Overhead costs		113380 00	164580 00	81000 00	75275 00	82090 00	516325 00
Prorate Bldg. Ser.	floor space*	(113380 00)	34014 00	22676 00	31746 00	24944 00	
Prorate Gen. Fact.	dir. labor†		(198594 00)	59578 00	81424 00	57592 00	
Total		—0—	—0—	163254 00	188445 00	164626 00	516325 00

*General Factory, 30%; Milling, 20%; Assembling, 28%; Finishing, 22%; (Percentage calculated in Chapter 8.)
†Milling, $192,000 (30%); Assembling, $260,000 (41%); Finishing, $188,000 (29%); Total, $640,000. All amounts are rounded to nearest whole dollar. (See amounts given in table above.)

Computing Departmental Rates

Separate computations are required for each of Space Savers' producing departments. Using the direct labor hours basis, each department's budgeted manufacturing overhead for the year is divided by that department's estimated direct labor hours for the year to determine the application rate.

Milling Department Overhead Rate

Total budgeted overhead of the Milling Department for the year 19X1 is $163,254, including allocated service department costs (see the proration worksheet on page 167). The total direct labor hours for the year are estimated to be 32,000. The departmental rate is computed as follows:

$$\frac{\text{Manufacturing Overhead, } \$163,254}{\text{Direct Labor Hours, } 32,000} = \$5.10 \text{ per Direct Labor Hour}$$

Assembling Department Overhead Rate

The budgeted overhead for the Assembling Department is $188,445, based on an expected 40,000 direct labor hours. The departmental rate is computed as follows:

$$\frac{\text{Manufacturing Overhead, } \$188,445}{\text{Direct Labor Hours, } 40,000} = \$4.71 \text{ per Direct Labor Hour}$$

Finishing Department Overhead Rate

The budgeted overhead for the Finishing Department is $164,626, based on an expected 28,000 direct labor hours. The departmental rate is computed as follows:

$$\frac{\text{Manufacturing Overhead, } \$164,626}{\text{Direct Labor Hours, } 28,000} = \$5.88 \text{ per Direct Labor Hour}$$

Computerized Rate-Setting

Better Business Forms, Inc., is a manufacturer of custom-ordered office stationery, memo pads, telephone message pads, and other office forms. A report on the costs related to each customer's order must be prepared. Management frequently requests these reports at random. Sometimes the staff cannot keep up with the requests, so the reports are not as timely as desired by management.

The head of the cost accounting department has proposed a partial solution to the problem. The computer will be used in determining job overhead costs. Since actual overhead costs are not known until the end of the month, the computer will be used to set standard overhead rates for interim reporting purposes. The computer is being programmed to take the previous year's file of actual departmental overhead costs from memory and develop a budget for the current year based upon various factors. These include changes in volume of production, changes in the economy, and changes in the rates charged by utility companies. A member of the cost accounting staff can "tell" the computer what these factors are by keying that information into the office terminal. Other adjustments to the budget can be made the same way. Standard overhead rates will be determined from this budget.

The computer will also be used to help determine the bases to use in setting overhead rates. A correlation program will compare the change in overhead with the change in units of production, costs of materials, machine hours, direct labor hours, and direct labor costs. The item with the highest correlation will be used as the basis for computing overhead rates. Using correlation analysis on the computer will result in a much more accurate overhead estimation, and future analysis of overhead costs will be much more informative than in the past. ∎

Management needs cost information as soon as a job is finished. Instead of waiting for the end of a fiscal period when the actual cost totals are available, the cost accountant estimates overhead costs for each job.

There are five major types of overhead rate bases used for cost estimating: units of production, materials costs, machine hours, direct labor hours, and direct labor costs. The direct labor costs basis is used by about half the manufacturers in this country. Whatever basis is used, the application rate is determined by dividing the estimated overhead costs by the basis chosen.

An accountant should be guided by the following criteria in choosing a rate basis: The rate should be easily computed. The factor chosen as the basis must be easily measurable. There must be a direct relationship between the amount of overhead costs incurred and the factor chosen as the basis. The basis should be representative of overhead costs applicable to each unit. The rate should meet specific departmental needs. The cost to collect the necessary data should be reasonable.

The figures for the application rate are obtained from budget estimates. For example, if direct labor hours are selected as the rate basis, the estimated number of direct labor hours is divided into the estimated departmental overhead costs (after service department costs have been allocated to producing departments) to determine an overhead application rate for each labor hour.

Review Questions

1. What is the purpose of using predetermined manufacturing overhead rates?
2. List two factors that effect the setting of manufacturing overhead rates.
3. What are the five most common bases used in establishing manufacturing overhead rates?
4. Which of these five bases is used most often? Why?
5. Why is the materials costs basis rarely used?
6. What is the major limitation in using the units of production basis for manufacturing overhead rates?
7. How is the overhead application rate calculated under the machine hours basis?
8. What calculation is used when determining the overhead application rate under the direct labor hours method? The direct labor costs method?
9. In selecting a basis for manufacturing overhead rates, what are four guidelines that should be followed?

Managerial Discussion Questions

1. Why are individual departmental overhead rates often used rather than one single factorywide rate? What are the advantages to management in using departmental rates?
2. What basis should be used in calculating overhead rates in a business where production volume varies greatly from year to year? Why?
3. Under what circumstances would you recommend to management that it use the machine hours basis for setting manufacturing overhead rates?
4. Discuss the difference between the direct labor hours basis and the direct labor costs basis. Under what circumstances should each method be used by management in determining overhead rates?

Exercises

1. **Calculating overhead rates.** For the current year, 19X7, the estimated manufacturing overhead for the Preparing Department is $156,000. The estimated number of units of production is 260,000. The company uses the units of production basis for overhead rates. How much overhead should be applied to (a) Job 240 for 1,780 units and (b) Job 243 for 3,480 units?

2. **Calculating overhead rates.** Job 750 calls for 1,200 units to be produced. The estimate of manufacturing overhead for the year for the Cutting Department is $32,000. The company expects that direct materials will be $400,000 and total machine hours will be 250,000. Job 750 incurred $4,800 in direct materials and used 3,085 machine hours. How much manufacturing overhead should be applied to Job 750 if the company uses (a) the materials costs basis and (b) the machine hours basis?

3. **Calculating overhead rates.** Using the data below, calculate the amount of manufacturing overhead to be applied to Job 817 for 460 units, if (a) the direct labor hours basis is used and (b) the direct labor costs basis is used.

Estimated manufacturing overhead for the year	$350,540
Estimated direct labor hours	412,400 hours
Estimated direct labor costs	$438,175
Job 817: direct labor hours used	1,450 hours
Job 817: direct labor costs incurred	$1,570

4. **Calculating overhead rates.** The Davidoff & Lee Company uses the direct labor costs basis in establishing overhead rates for its producing departments. For the year 19X6, the company estimates the following manufacturing overhead budgets:

Building Services	$48,860
Department 101	75,300
Department 102	83,800
Department 103	78,518

Building Services is a service department that assists the producing departments. Its overhead is allocated to the producing departments on the basis of floor space occupied. The floor space occupied and the estimates for direct labor costs are given below.

	Floor Space	Direct Labor Costs
Department 101	2,660 sq. ft.	$154,000
Department 102	1,900 sq. ft.	148,860
Department 103	3,040 sq. ft.	125,239

Determine the manufacturing overhead rates for each department for the year. Carry your answers to six decimal places, round to five, and then change to percents.

5. **Calculating overhead rates.** Assume the same facts as in Exercise 4, except that the Davidoff & Lee Company uses the direct labor hours basis for overhead rates. Determine the rates for the year if the estimated direct labor hours are as shown on page 171. Round the rates to three decimal places.

	Hours
Department 101	110,000
Department 102	125,000
Department 103	98,000

Problems

PROBLEM 9-1. Calculating departmental overhead rates. A summary of the budget data for the Assembling Department of the Kenosha Company for the year 19X6 is given here.

Manufacturing overhead costs	$936,840
Units of production	450,000 units
Direct materials costs	$738,540
Direct labor costs	$845,920
Direct labor hours	220,000 hours
Machine hours	81,500 hours

Instructions

Determine the manufacturing overhead application rates under each of the following bases. Round percents to three decimal places and rates to the nearest whole cent.

a. Units of production
b. Direct materials costs
c. Machine hours
d. Direct labor hours
e. Direct labor costs

PROBLEM 9-2. Calculating and applying manufacturing overhead. A summary of budget data for the Jones Manufacturing Group for the year 19X6 is given below.

Manufacturing overhead costs	$651,260
Direct materials costs	$326,790
Direct labor costs	$478,200
Direct labor hours	98,250 hours
Machine hours	37,980 hours

Instructions

1. Use each of the following bases to determine the overhead application rate. Round to three decimal places except for percents, which should be carried to six places and rounded to five.
   a. Materials costs
   b. Direct labor costs
   c. Direct labor hours
   d. Machine hours
2. Prepare a schedule showing the amount of overhead that would be applied to Job 78 using each application rate. Assume the following data for the job:

Direct materials costs	$3,618
Direct labor costs	$4,980
Direct labor hours	1,580 hours
Machine hours	465 hours

PROBLEM 9-3. Completing a worksheet for prorating service department costs. Seventh Avenue Designs Inc. is divided into service departments and producing departments. The Warehousing Department, which carries out receiving, storing, and shipping functions, and the Maintenance Department are service departments. The Cutting, Sewing, and Finishing Departments are producing departments. The Maintenance Department serves the other departments in proportion to the area occupied by each department.

Department	Square Feet	
Warehousing	10,500	15
Cutting	17,500	25
Sewing	14,000	20
Finishing	28,000	40

The costs of the Warehousing Department are allocated to the producing departments on the basis of the number of materials requisitions filled.

Department	Number of Materials Requisitions	
Cutting	3,920	28
Sewing	5,880	42
Finishing	4,200	30

Instructions

1. Prepare a worksheet for prorating estimated service department costs for the year 19X5. The totals of the departmental overhead budgets are as follows:

Department	Estimated Direct Departmental Overhead Costs
Maintenance	$29,210
Warehousing	21,390
Cutting	35,870
Sewing	41,552
Finishing	26,760

2. Summarize your computations for the bases and the prorations on three-column analysis paper. (Keep your papers for use in Problem 9-4.)

PROBLEM 9-4. Computing overhead application rates. This problem is a continuation of Problem 9-3. The following data are provided:

Basis	Cutting	Sewing	Finishing
Direct Labor Costs	$85,000	$90,000	$110,000
Direct Labor Hours	24,000 hours	30,000 hours	27,000 hours
Machine Hours	6,600 hours	9,000 hours	8,300 hours

Instructions

Compute three overhead application rates for each of the three producing departments, using the data above. Show your computations in equation form. Carry your answers to three decimal places except for percents. Carry percents to six decimal places, and then round to five.

PROBLEM 9-1A. Calculating departmental overhead rates. A summary of the budget for the Milling Department of the Anaheim Corporation for the year 19X7 is given here.

Manufacturing overhead costs	$372,600
Units of production	155,000 units
Direct materials costs	$436,170
Direct labor costs	$525,760
Direct labor hours	119,000 hours
Machine hours	77,260 hours

Instructions

Determine the manufacturing overhead rates under each of the following bases. Round percents to three decimal places and amounts to the nearest whole cent.

a. Units of production
b. Direct materials costs
c. Machine hours
d. Direct labor hours
e. Direct labor costs

PROBLEM 9-2A. Calculating and applying manufacturing overhead. A summary of budget data for the Cervez Machine Corporation for the year 19X7 is given below.

Manufacturing overhead costs	$196,560
Direct materials costs	$86,400
Direct labor costs	$159,310
Direct labor hours	79,300 hours
Machine hours	16,050 hours

Instructions

1. Use each of the following bases to determine the overhead application rate. Round to three decimal places except for percents, which should be carried to six places and rounded to five.
   a. Materials costs
   b. Direct labor costs
   c. Direct labor hours
   d. Machine hours
2. Prepare a schedule showing the amount of overhead that would be applied to Job 76 using each application rate. Assume the following data for the job:

Direct materials costs	$11,375
Direct labor costs	$12,650
Direct labor hours	840 hours
Machine hours	230 hours

PROBLEM 9-3A. Completing a worksheet for prorating service department costs. The Emerson Garment Company is divided into service departments and producing departments. The Warehousing Department, which carries out receiving, storing, and shipping functions, and the Maintenance Department are service departments. The Cutting, Sewing, and Finishing Departments are producing departments. The Maintenance Department serves the other departments in proportion to the area occupied by each department.

Department	Square Feet
Warehousing	9,300
Cutting	15,500
Sewing	19,840
Finishing	17,360

The costs of the Warehousing Department are allocated to the producing departments on the basis of the number of materials requisitions filled.

Department	Number of Materials Requisitions
Cutting	968
Sewing	1,364
Finishing	2,068

Instructions

1. Prepare a worksheet for prorating estimated service department costs for the year 19X7. The totals of the departmental overhead budgets are as follows:

Department	Estimated Direct Departmental Overhead Costs
Maintenance	$40,540
Warehousing	29,480
Cutting	43,410
Sewing	59,620
Finishing	35,372

2. Summarize your computations for the bases and the prorations on three-column analysis paper. (Keep your papers for use in Problem 9-4A.)

PROBLEM 9-4A. Computing overhead application rates. This problem is a continuation of Problem 9-3A. The following data are provided:

Basis	Cutting	Sewing	Finishing
Direct Labor Costs	$77,400	$82,000	$32,800
Direct Labor Hours	30,000 hours	60,000 hours	70,000 hours
Machine Hours	20,400 hours	7,100 hours	5,900 hours

Instructions

Compute three overhead application rates for each of the three producing departments, using the data above. Show your computations in equation form. Carry your answers to four decimal places except for percent. Carry percents to six decimal places, and then round to five.

Managerial Decisions

CASE 9-1. Outdoor Manufacturers makes hatchets, knives, and other tools for use by campers and hikers. Its employees work in three departments: Machining, Polishing, and Assembling. In the Machining Department, robots are used to handle the metals, and one employee monitors the operations. The employees of the Polishing Department clean and polish the blades. In the Assembly Department, employees inspect each blade for defects and attach wooden handles and the firm's decals.

As the cost accountant you have been asked to determine the overhead application basis most appropriate for each department. In a short written report, present your suggestions on the methods to use and your reasons for choosing each basis.

10

Applying Manufacturing Overhead

■ ■ ■

The overhead application rates that were computed in the last chapter can now be used to allocate manufacturing overhead costs to specific units of production. Allocation is done in two steps. First, estimated manufacturing overhead costs for individual jobs are computed by departments and recorded on the job cost sheets. Then the total overhead accumulated during the month is charged to production by posting from the manufacturing overhead applied journal to the Work in Process account in the general ledger.

Entries on Job Cost Sheets

Space Savers uses the direct labor hours basis for overhead application. The amount of overhead to be charged to each job is calculated by multiplying the number of direct labor hours worked on the job in each department by the predetermined departmental overhead rate. The amount of overhead thus computed is then entered in the Manufacturing Overhead Applied section of the individual job cost sheet. This entry may be made when a job is completed or at the end of the month if the job is still in process. (Some companies apply overhead to jobs each week.)

Applying Overhead to Completed Jobs

At the end of the week in which the job is finished, the labor hours data are taken from the weekly analysis of the time tickets and forwarded to the cost accounting unit. Suppose that the job cost sheet for Job 101, completed October 18, shows the following total direct labor hours after all time tickets have been recorded:

Milling Department	290 hours
Assembling Department	220 hours
Finishing Department	320 hours

If the predetermined departmental overhead rates computed in the last chapter (page 168) are used, the overhead applied to this job for these departments in October is as follows.

Milling Department, 290 hours at $5.10 per hour = $1,479.00
Assembling Department, 220 hours at $4.71 per hour = $1,036.20
Finishing Department, 320 hours at $5.88 per hour = $1,881.60

These amounts are entered in the appropriate columns of the Manufacturing Overhead Applied section of the job cost sheet, as shown below.

Applying Overhead to Jobs in Process

Job cost sheets for jobs still in process are brought up to date at the end of the month by applying overhead based on the direct labor hours recorded during the month. The total number of hours is multiplied by the predetermined overhead application rate for each department. The resulting applied overhead cost is entered in the Manufacturing Overhead Applied section of the job cost sheets.

JOB COST SHEET

Customer **Neeley Furniture Co.**
Description **Customer specs on file**
Quantity **100**

Job **101**
Date Started **10/1/X1**
Date Completed **10/18/X1**

MATERIALS			DIRECT LABOR		MILLING		ASSEMBLING		FINISHING		MANUFACTURING OVERHEAD APPLIED		MILLING			ASSEMBLING			FINISHING		
DATE	REQ. NO.	AMOUNT	DATE	REF.	HRS.	AMOUNT	HRS.	AMOUNT	HRS.	AMOUNT	DATE	REF.	HRS.	RATE	AMOUNT	HRS.	RATE	AMOUNT	HRS.	RATE	AMOUNT
10/1	R802	9 35 00	10/5	TTA	290	1902 00	220	1580 00	55	420 00	10/20	MOA 10	290	5.10	1479 00	220	4.71	1036 20	320	5.88	1881 60
10/2	R804	2805 00	10/12	TTA					95	685 00											
10/6	RM48	(85 00)	10/19	TTA					170	1215 00											
10/8	R809	1598 00																			
10/8	R817	119 00																			
10/16	R843	41 00																			
10/17	R848	27 00																			
10/18	R852	34 00																			
Total							220		320												

SUMMARY		
TOTAL COST	$_____	
UNITS PRODUCED	_____	
MATERIALS	$_____	
LABOR—MILLING		

Entries in the General Ledger

At the end of the month, entries are made in the general ledger accounts to reflect the estimated manufacturing overhead charged to production. In some companies, the information for this entry is obtained by totaling the overhead entries that have been made on the job cost sheets during the month. However, Space Savers simplifies this process by keeping a manufacturing overhead applied journal. Each time an entry for overhead is made on a job cost sheet, the entry is also recorded in the manufacturing overhead applied journal, as shown on page 178.

MANUFACTURING OVERHEAD APPLIED JOURNAL

for Month of _____October_____ 19 X1   Page ___10___

DATE		JOB NO.	WORK IN PROCESS DR. 122		MILLING DEPT. CR. 502			ASSEMBLING DEPT. CR. 503			FINISHING DEPT. CR. 504		
					HOURS	AMOUNT		HOURS	AMOUNT		HOURS	AMOUNT	
Oct.	18	101	4,396	80	290	1,479	00	220	1,036	20	320	1,881	60
	31	Total	42,627	60	2,773	14,142	30	3,370	15,872	70	2,145	12,612	60
						(✔)			(✔)			(✔)	

This journal is totaled, and the totals are posted to the appropriate general ledger accounts at the end of the month.

To illustrate the effect of these postings, they are shown in general journal form here.

19X1				
Oct. 31	Work in Process	122	42,627.60	
	Manufacturing Overhead—Milling Department	502		14,142.30
	Manufacturing Overhead—Assembling Department	503		15,872.70
	Manufacturing Overhead—Finishing Department	504		12,612.60
	Applied departmental manufacturing overhead for the month.			

Posting to Departmental Manufacturing Overhead Accounts

After the totals have been posted to the general ledger from the manufacturing overhead applied journal, the departmental manufacturing overhead accounts involved appear as follows:

Manufacturing Overhead—Milling Department   No. ___502___

DATE		EXPLANATION	POST. REF.	DEBIT		CREDIT		BALANCE		DR. CR.
19	X1									
Oct.	31		J10-50	6,493	18			6,493	18	Dr.
	31		J10-51	1,895	40			8,388	58	Dr.
	31		J10-52	5,421	51			13,810	09	Dr.
	31		MOA10			14,142	30	332	21	Cr.

Manufacturing Overhead—Assembling Department   No. 503

DATE		EXPLANATION	POST. REF.	DEBIT		CREDIT		BALANCE		DR. CR.
19X1										
Oct.	31		J10-50	6,392	07			6,392	07	Dr.
	31		J10-51	2,653	56			9,045	63	Dr.
	31		J10-52	7,574	88			16,620	51	Dr.
	31		MOA10			15,872	70	747	81	Dr.

Manufacturing Overhead—Finishing Department   No. 504

DATE		EXPLANATION	POST. REF.	DEBIT		CREDIT		BALANCE		DR. CR.
19X1										
Oct.	31		J10-50	6,864	18			6,864	18	Dr.
	31		J10-51	2,084	94			8,949	12	Dr.
	31		J10-52	4,854	02			13,803	14	Dr.
	31		MOA10			12,612	60	1,190	54	Dr.

The credit balance in Account 502 represents *overapplied overhead*. This occurs because the overhead applied (the amount credited) is more than the actual overhead costs incurred (the amounts debited) for this department. The situation is reversed in the other two departments, and the overhead applied (the amount credited) is less than the actual overhead costs incurred (the amounts debited). The resulting debit balance represents *underapplied overhead*. The net debit (underapplied) balance in these three accounts is $1,606.14 (a debit balance of $747.81 plus a debit balance of $1,190.54 minus a credit balance of $332.21), which is the same as the debit balance of Manufacturing Overhead Control 501, shown in Chapter 2 (page 31).

Use of Overhead Applied Accounts

Instead of crediting the applied overhead costs directly to the departmental manufacturing overhead accounts, some cost accountants prefer to credit special departmental overhead applied accounts. In this way, the applied overhead costs are kept separate from the actual costs, which appear as debits in the manufacturing overhead accounts. If Space Savers used this method, the postings from the manufacturing overhead applied journal would be recorded in the departmental overhead applied accounts as shown on page 180.

Manufacturing Overhead Applied—Milling Department						No. XXX
DATE	EXPLANATION	POST. REF.	DEBIT	CREDIT	BALANCE	DR. CR.
19X1 Oct. 31		MOA10		14,142 30	14,142 30	Cr.

Manufacturing Overhead Applied—Assembling Department						No. XXX
DATE	EXPLANATION	POST. REF.	DEBIT	CREDIT	BALANCE	DR. CR.
19X1 Oct. 31		MOA10		15,872 70	15,872 70	Cr.

Manufacturing Overhead Applied—Finishing Department						No. XXX
DATE	EXPLANATION	POST. REF.	DEBIT	CREDIT	BALANCE	DR. CR.
19X1 Oct. 31		MOA10		12,612 60	12,612 60	Cr.

The overhead applied accounts are then closed into the departmental manufacturing overhead accounts. The final result of this procedure is exactly the same as though applied overhead costs had been credited directly to the manufacturing overhead accounts.

Overapplied or Under-applied Overhead

The typical cost accounting system includes several provisions for the appropriate treatment of overapplied and underapplied manufacturing overhead.

Monthly Procedure

At Space Savers, the balances of the departmental manufacturing overhead accounts are closed at the end of each month into Overapplied or Underapplied Manufacturing Overhead 507 in the general ledger. The general journal voucher prepared to close the three departmental overhead accounts at the end of October is shown on page 181.

The Overapplied or Underapplied Manufacturing Overhead account is not closed monthly. Instead, it reflects the cumulative overapplied or underapplied overhead to date, as shown on page 181.

JOURNAL VOUCHER	Date _Oct. 31,_		19 _X1_	No. _10-54_	
ACCOUNT	ACCOUNT NUMBER	✔	DEBIT	CREDIT	
Overapplied or Underapplied Mfg. Overhead	507		1606 14		
Mfg. Overhead—Milling Dept.	502		332 21		
Mfg. Overhead—Assembling Dept.	503			747 81	
Mfg. Overhead—Finishing Dept.	504			1190 54	

EXPLANATION

Closed out departmental manufacturing overhead accounts at end of the month.

PREPARED BY _GAR_	AUDITED BY _KC_	APPROVED BY _SH_

The debit balance of $1,588.40 represents the excess of cumulative actual overhead costs over cumulative applied overhead costs for the months of January through September. The debit of $1,606.14 posted to Account 507 on October 31 (to close the departmental manufacturing overhead accounts for October) increases the cumulative underapplied manufacturing overhead to $3,194.54 for the first ten months of the year, as shown below.

Overapplied or Underapplied Manufacturing Overhead					No.	507
DATE	EXPLANATION	POST. REF.	DEBIT	CREDIT	BALANCE	DR. CR.
19 X1 Oct. 1	Balance	✔			1,588 40	Dr.
31		J10-54	1,606 14		3,194 54	Dr.

Balance Sheet Presentation

The actual overhead incurred will seldom equal the overhead applied during any one month, but the two overhead amounts should be almost equal at the end of the year (assuming that accurate estimates were made). Amounts of overapplied overhead during some months of the year are expected to be offset by underapplied overhead during other months. Thus during the year, the cumulative amounts of overapplied or underapplied manufacturing overhead are considered amounts related to future months of the year. Any debit balance in Account 507 represents underapplied manufacturing overhead. This amount is considered a deferred charge and is shown under Prepaid Expenses on the interim balance sheet. Any credit balance during the year, representing overapplied manufacturing overhead, is shown on the interim balance sheet as a deferred credit. At the end of the year, any balance of underapplied or overapplied manufacturing overhead is closed into Cost of Goods Sold. Thus the balance will not appear on the end-of-year balance sheet.

Income Statement Presentation

As previously pointed out, the cumulative underapplied manufacturing overhead does not appear on income statements prepared during the year. The amount is carried forward as a deferred charge or deferred credit on the interim balance sheets. The Cost of Goods Sold section of the monthly income statement (see page 200) includes the Cost of Goods Manufactured during the current period. In turn, the statement of cost of goods manufactured (see page 200) shows direct materials used, direct labor, and manufacturing overhead applied.

End-of-Year Procedures

At the end of the year, Overapplied or Underapplied Manufacturing Overhead 507 must be closed. Any balance at the end of the year represents a discrepancy between overhead costs applied to goods worked on during the year and the actual overhead costs that were incurred in producing these goods.

From the viewpoint of accounting theory, the overapplied or underapplied overhead should be allocated proportionately to all goods that have been worked on during the year. Some of the goods are still in process, some are in finished goods, and some have already been sold. Thus the overapplied or underapplied balance should logically be allocated or subdivided among Work in Process, Finished Goods, and Cost of Goods Sold. However, this procedure is so difficult and time-consuming that the theoretical benefits obtained usually do not warrant the amount of work involved. In addition, most of the goods worked on during the year have probably been transferred to finished goods and sold to customers, so that most of the overapplied or underapplied overhead would be closed into Cost of Goods Sold. For these reasons, it is customary to close any balance of Overapplied or Underapplied Manufacturing Overhead at the end of the year into Cost of Goods Sold.

The following entry is required to close any balance of overapplied manufacturing overhead at the end of the year:

19X1				
Dec. 31	Overapplied or Underapplied Manufacturing			
	Overhead	507	XXX.XX	
	Cost of Goods Sold	415		XXX.XX
	Closed overapplied manufacturing overhead at end of year.			

When there is a balance of underapplied manufacturing overhead at the end of the year, the entry shown on page 183 is required to close the account.

The overapplied or underapplied overhead is included in the Cost of Goods Sold section of the yearly income statement. It is shown below as an adjustment of Cost of Goods Sold. (Some accountants prefer to show it as an adjustment of Cost of Goods Manufactured.) If overhead has been underapplied, less overhead was charged to production than was actually incurred. Therefore, Cost of Goods Sold is understated, and the amount of the understated overhead is added to Cost of Goods Sold on the income statement. If overhead has been overapplied, the opposite is true and more overhead was charged to production than was incurred. Therefore, Cost of Goods Sold is overstated, and the amount of overstated overhead is subtracted from Cost of Goods Sold.

SPACE SAVERS, INC.
Income Statement
Year Ended December 31, 19X1

Revenue		
Sales		$1,280,000
Cost of Goods Sold		
Finished Goods Inventory, Jan. 1	$ 15,000	
Add Cost of Goods Manufactured	1,010,000	
Total Goods Available for Sale	$1,025,000	
Less Finished Goods Inventory,		
Dec. 31	12,800	
Cost of Goods Sold		$1,012,200
Add Underapplied Overhead for Year		1,020
Cost of Goods Sold (Adjusted)		1,013,220
Gross Profit on Sales		$ 266,780

Analysis of Overapplied or Underapplied Overhead

Management wants to know why overhead costs applied differ from the actual overhead costs incurred during the fiscal period. An analysis of the underapplied or overapplied overhead is more meaningful when used in the context of a flexible budgeting and standard cost system, such as the one discussed in Part 3. A brief summary of the basic ideas involved, however, will help show how the difference between actual costs and applied costs might be examined and explained.

The actual and applied overhead for the Milling Department and the Finishing Department of Space Savers, Inc., for the month of October 19X1 are repeated below.

	Actual Costs	Applied Costs	Underapplied or (Overapplied)
Milling Department	$13,810.09	$14,142.30	$ (332.21)
Finishing Department	13,803.14	12,612.60	1,190.54

In Chapter 9 you learned that the Milling Department and Finishing Department overhead rates were determined as follows:

$$\text{Overhead Rate, Milling Dept.} = \frac{\text{Budgeted Overhead for Year, \$163,254}}{\text{Budgeted Direct Labor Hours, 32,000 hours}}$$
$$= \$5.10 \text{ per hour}$$

$$\text{Overhead Rate, Finishing Dept.} = \frac{\text{Budgeted Overhead for Year, \$164,626}}{\text{Budgeted Direct Labor Hours, 28,000 hours}}$$
$$= \$5.88 \text{ per hour}$$

Milling Department Overapplied Overhead. An examination of the budgeted overhead of the Milling Department for the year shows that $99,226 of the budgeted costs are *fixed*. That is, they do not vary substantially (in total) regardless of fluctuations in the number of labor hours worked during the year. The remaining budgeted costs of $64,028 are *variable*. These costs tend to vary in proportion to the number of direct labor hours worked during the year. (Procedures for separating fixed and variable costs are discussed in Chapter 20.) Thus, out of the total overhead application rate of $5.10 per hour, $3.10 per hour is for estimated fixed costs, as shown below. The balance, $2 per hour, is for estimated variable costs.

$$\frac{\$99,226}{32,000 \text{ hours}} = \$3.10 \text{ per hour}$$

If the actual direct labor hours worked in the department in a given month are equal to the number of direct labor hours budgeted (2,666.7 hours, or 32,000 hours per year divided by 12 months), the amount of fixed overhead charged to work in process for the month should be exactly equal to the actual fixed costs of $8,268.83 incurred in the month ($99,226 divided by 12 months). However, if fewer than 2,666.7 hours are worked during the month, the fixed costs applied will be less than the actual fixed overhead costs, which will remain unchanged at $8,268.83. Thus, the fixed overhead costs will be *underapplied*. On the other hand, if there are more than 2,666.7 hours of direct labor during the month, the fixed overhead costs applied will exceed $8,268.83. In this case, the fixed overhead will be *overapplied*. There will be underapplied fixed overhead of $3.10 for each hour less than 2,666.7 hours of direct labor used during the month. For each hour of direct labor over 2,666.7 employed during the month, fixed overhead will be overapplied by $3.10.

This overapplication or underapplication of fixed overhead results from the fact that the number of labor hours actually worked during the month deviates from the estimated number of labor hours used in determining the overhead rate. This deviation is known as a *volume variance*. The remainder of the underapplied or overapplied overhead represents the amount by which actual expenditures exceed the amount that should have been spent for overhead based on the number of hours worked. This amount is often called a *spending variance*.

The $332.21 of overapplied overhead in the Milling Department for October can be analyzed as follows:

Volume Variance:
Fixed overhead applied ($3.10 × 2,773)	$ 8,596.30	
Fixed overhead budgeted	8,268.83	
Volume Variance (favorable)		$327.47

Spending Variance:
Actual overhead for month		$13,810.09	
Budgeted overhead for hours worked:			
Fixed	$8,268.83		
Variable (2,773 × $2)	5,546.00		
Total budgeted		13,814.83	
Spending Variance (favorable)			4.74
Total Variance (favorable)			$332.21

These variances are called favorable because the actual overhead costs were less than the costs applied to production.

Finishing Department Underapplied Overhead.

The $1,190.54 of underapplied overhead in the Finishing Department for October can be analyzed in the same way as done for the Milling Department.

A $164,626 yearly overhead budget was used in setting the Finishing Department overhead rate for the year. Fixed costs accounted for $100,422 of the total yearly overhead budget ($8,368.50 per month). The balance of $64,204 budgeted for the year represented variable costs. Thus, the $5.88 per labor hour overhead rate includes $3.59 per hour of fixed costs ($100,422 divided by 28,000 hours) and $2.29 per hour of variable costs ($64,204 divided by 28,000 hours). An unfavorable volume variance of $667.97 and an unfavorable spending variance of $522.57 can be computed.

Volume Variance:
Fixed overhead applied ($3.59 × 2,145)	$ 7,700.55	
Fixed overhead budgeted	8,368.50	
Volume Variance (unfavorable)		$ 667.95

Spending Variance:
Actual overhead for month		$13,803.14	
Budgeted overhead for hours worked:			
Fixed	$8,368.50		
Variable (2,145 × $2.29)	4,912.05		
Total budgeted		13,280.55	
Spending Variance (unfavorable)			522.59
Total Variance (unfavorable)			$1,190.54

These variances are called unfavorable because the actual costs were more than the costs applied to production. The concept of variance analysis will be examined more closely in Chapters 22 and 23.

Computerizing Departmental Overhead Costs

Any good computer application takes time and the efforts of many people. The cost accountant at Uniform Attire Company wanted a program to handle departmental overhead costs. She had to give the systems analyst a detailed description of how she expected the application to work. This information included the following items:

1. The accounts to which the overhead costs are charged.
2. Any significance to the account numbers; for example, related categories of items such as expenses.
3. Which overhead costs are fixed, which will change each period, and which must be computed.
4. For any costs that must be computed, a description of the formula to be used.
5. A description of how service department costs are distributed.
6. Types and formats of reports to be generated.
7. How often data will be updated and entered into the system.
8. How often reports are needed.

Writing the program is just the start for all involved. It must be carefully tested, corrected (debugged), and tested again. Then personnel who will use the program must be trained so that the program can be successfully implemented for the company. ■

Principles and Procedures Summary

The major steps in the process of charging manufacturing overhead costs to production are outlined here for review.

1. Service department costs are distributed to producing departments on the basis of the service provided (Chapter 8).
2. An appropriate rate basis is selected for use in cost allocation (Chapter 9). A different basis may be used to allocate the costs of each department.
3. Departmental application rates are computed (Chapter 9).
4. Application rates are used to charge manufacturing overhead costs to jobs completed or in process (Chapter 10).
5. The amount of overhead applied to each job is entered in the manufacturing overhead applied journal. The totals of this journal are posted to the appropriate departmental overhead accounts and to the Work in Process account at the end of each month.
6. The balances of the departmental overhead accounts are closed monthly into an Overapplied or Underapplied Manufacturing Overhead account. This account re-

mains open during the year and is shown on the interim balance sheets as a deferred charge or deferred credit.

7. At the end of the year, any balance of Overapplied or Underapplied Manufacturing Overhead is closed into Cost of Goods Sold and is included in the Cost of Goods Sold section of the income statement.

Overapplied or underapplied manufacturing overhead is analyzed to determine what part, if any, is due to variations between the volume of activity planned and the volume of activity actually achieved and what part, if any, resulted from a lack of control over the manufacturing costs incurred.

Review Questions

1. When are manufacturing overhead costs recorded on the job cost sheet?
2. The job cost sheets are subsidiary records for what control account in the general ledger? *W.I.P.*
3. Explain the procedure for using a manufacturing overhead applied journal. What is an advantage of using this journal?
4. What does a debit posting to a departmental manufacturing overhead account represent? What does the credit posting at the end of the month represent?
5. After all the postings are recorded at the end of the month, the Manufacturing Overhead—Milling Department account has a debit balance. What does this balance represent?
6. What does a credit balance in a departmental manufacturing overhead account represent? *overapplied*
7. Is the Overapplied or Underapplied Manufacturing Overhead account closed at the end of the month? Explain. *end of year*
8. How is the account Overapplied or Underapplied Manufacturing Overhead presented on interim monthly financial statements?
9. To what account is the Overapplied or Underapplied Manufacturing Overhead account closed? When?
10. What does a favorable variance represent? What does an unfavorable variance represent?

Managerial Discussion Questions

1. How does management benefit from having manufacturing overhead applied to jobs as the work is being done?
2. Assume that at the end of the month the manufacturing overhead was not applied to the job cost sheets for the jobs being worked on but not completed. What effect would this omission have on the financial statement prepared at the end of the month?
3. What suggestions would you make to management to correct a volume variance and a spending variance?
4. Describe the presentation of overapplied or underapplied overhead on the income statement at the end of the year.

Exercises

1. **Applying manufacturing overhead costs.** Job 417 was completed on June 10, 19X7. The job cost sheet indicates that 135 direct labor hours were spent on Job 417 in the Cutting Department and 186 hours were spent on it in the Finishing Department. If the manufacturing overhead rates are $1.38 per direct labor hour

for the Cutting Department and $1.90 per direct labor hour for the Finishing Department, how much manufacturing overhead should be added to the job cost sheet for Job 417?

2. **Journalizing applied manufacturing overhead costs.** For the month of September 19X6, the following manufacturing overhead costs were applied on the job cost sheets for the Manitoba Supply Corporation:

Shearing Department	$23,960.82
Molding Department	19,860.37
Finishing Department	24,210.48

Prepare the general journal entry to record the manufacturing overhead costs applied for the month.

3. **Journalizing overapplied or underapplied overhead.** At the end of May, after posting has been done, the following account balances appear in the general ledger of the Chin Industrial Supply Company:

Manufacturing Overhead—Department 102	$1,251.82 Dr.
Manufacturing Overhead—Department 103	1,520.80 Cr.
Manufacturing Overhead—Department 104	784.29 Cr.
Manufacturing Overhead—Department 105	834.37 Dr.

Prepare the general journal entry to close the overhead accounts and to record the overapplied or underapplied overhead for the month.

4. **Closing Overapplied or Underapplied Manufacturing Overhead.** Prepare the necessary general journal entry to close the Overapplied or Underapplied Manufacturing Overhead account under each of the following assumptions:
   a. The Overapplied or Underapplied Manufacturing Overhead account has a debit balance of $1,830.46.
   b. The Overapplied or Underapplied Manufacturing Overhead account has a credit balance of $1,057.28.

5. **Calculating the Cost of Goods Sold.** Determine the amount of Cost of Goods Sold (Adjusted) to be shown on the income statement of the Gregory Company from the following data:

Finished Goods, July 1, 19X6	$152,820
Finished Goods, June 30, 19X7	168,290
Cost of Goods Manufactured	376,340
Overapplied or Underapplied Manufacturing Overhead	1,630 Dr. Balance

Problems

PROBLEM 10-1. Completing a job cost sheet. The partially completed job cost sheet prepared at the Ortega Manufacturing Company for Job 4-09 is given on page 189. (This sheet is reproduced in the *Study Guide and Working Papers*. If you are using the workbook, do all of the following activities there.)

Instructions

1. Compute and enter the departmental direct labor costs on the job cost sheet for Job 4-09. The labor rates are as follows: Cutting Department, $4.60 per hour; Sewing Department, $5.25 per hour; and Finishing Department, $4.30 per hour.
2. The Ortega Manufacturing Company applies overhead to work in process on the

JOB COST SHEET

Customer *Watson Stores, Inc.*
Description *Style 2357, mixed colors*
Quantity *300 dozen*

Job *4-09*
Date Started *4/12/X6*
Date Completed *4/24/X6*

MATERIALS			DIRECT LABOR		CUTTING		SEWING		FINISHING		MANUFACTURING OVERHEAD APPLIED		CUTTING			SEWING			FINISHING		
DATE	REQ. NO.	AMOUNT	DATE	REF.	HRS.	AMOUNT	HRS.	AMOUNT	HRS.	AMOUNT	DATE	REF.	HRS.	RATE	AMOUNT	HRS.	RATE	AMOUNT	HRS.	RATE	AMOUNT
4/12	R385	150 00	4/14	TTA	120																
4/12	R391	125 00	4/21	TTA	55		95														
4/16	R404	175 00	4/28	TTA			64		113												
4/17	R408	42 05																			
4/17	R415	36 10																			
4/19	R422	14 87																			
4/21	R425	22 18																			
4/21	R428	19 87																			
4/23	R432	54 37																			
4/24	R435	9 98																			

basis of direct labor hours. Use the overhead application rates given below to determine the manufacturing overhead to be applied to each department. Record the applied overhead on the job cost sheet for Job 4-09.

Cutting Department	$5.15 per direct labor hour
Sewing Department	3.48 per direct labor hour
Finishing Department	7.75 per direct labor hour

3. Total all columns and draw a double rule. Complete the Summary and Total Cost sections of the job cost sheet for Job 4-09.

PROBLEM 10-2. Recording applied manufacturing overhead. The Corwin Manufacturing Company completed five jobs during April 19X6. The company applies overhead to work in process on the basis of direct labor hours and has calculated the following overhead application rates:

Cutting Department	$2.17 per direct labor hour
Sewing Department	1.62 per direct labor hour
Finishing Department	1.63 per direct labor hour

The manufacturing overhead account balances in the ledger are as follows:

Manufacturing Overhead—Cutting Department	$1,580.11 Dr.
Manufacturing Overhead—Sewing Department	1,430.66 Dr.
Manufacturing Overhead—Finishing Department	872.11 Dr.
Overapplied or Underapplied Manufacturing Overhead	306.82 Cr.

Instructions

1. **a.** Compute the manufacturing overhead to be applied to each department for each of the jobs completed in April. Use the following data:

Date	Job No.	Cutting	Sewing	Finishing
Apr. 5	4-01	201 hours	248 hours	192 hours
10	4-02	175 hours	159 hours	113 hours
16	4-03	86 hours	150 hours	86 hours
21	4-04	96 hours	160 hours	54 hours
29	4-05	135 hours	125 hours	115 hours

   b. Record the jobs in the manufacturing overhead applied journal.

   c. Prove the accuracy of your work by footing and crossfooting all columns of the manufacturing overhead applied journal. Enter the totals and draw a double rule.

2. Post the totals of the manufacturing overhead applied journal to the departmental manufacturing overhead accounts in the general ledger and extend the balance of each account.

3. **a.** Prepare the general journal voucher to close the departmental manufacturing overhead accounts into the Overapplied or Underapplied Manufacturing Overhead account. Number the voucher 4-22.

   b. Post General Journal Voucher 4-22 to the general ledger accounts and extend the balance of each account.

PROBLEM 10-3. Computing overhead and analyzing volume and spending variances. Selected data for Brown & Brown Inc. for the year 19X7 follows:

	Budgeted for Year	Actual for Year
Direct Labor Hours	60,000	62,400
Manufacturing Overhead		
Fixed	$ 42,000	$ 42,000
Variable	168,000	171,100
Total Overhead	$210,000	$213,100

Overhead is applied on the basis of direct labor hours.

Instructions

1. Compute the overhead application rate.
2. Compute the applied overhead for the year.
3. Compute the total overapplied or underapplied overhead for the year.
4. Analyze the total overapplied or underapplied overhead into a volume variance and a spending variance.

PROBLEM 10-4. Analyzing underapplied or overapplied overhead. The New Britain Company uses the direct labor hours method for applying overhead. The overhead application rate for 19X8 is $8.60 per hour, based on expected fixed costs of $348,000 and expected variable costs of $684,000 with a total volume of 120,000 hours.

During the year, the company actually operated for 115,800 hours, incurring fixed overhead of $348,000 and variable overhead of $637,880.

Instructions

1. Compute the total underapplied or overapplied overhead for the year.
2. Analyze the total overapplied or underapplied overhead into a volume variance and a spending variance.

PROBLEM 10-5. Preparing an income statement. For the fiscal year 19X8, the Phoenix Manufacturing Corporation accumulated the following data:

Sales	$960,540
Sales Returns and Allowances	43,780
Finished Goods, January 1, 19X8	98,730
Finished Goods, December 31, 19X8	94,520
Cost of Goods Manufactured	641,193
Overapplied or Underapplied Overhead	3,531 Cr. Balance
Selling Expenses	65,496
Administrative Expenses	82,526
Provision for Income Taxes	58,652

Instructions

Prepare an income statement for the Phoenix Manufacturing Corporation for the year ended December 31, 19X8.

Alternate Problems

PROBLEM 10-1A. Completing a job cost sheet. The partially completed job cost sheet prepared at the Ortega Manufacturing Company for Job 4-09 is given below. (This sheet is reproduced in the *Study Guide and Working Papers*. If you are using the workbook, do all of the following activities there.)

JOB COST SHEET

Customer *Watson Stores, Inc.*
Description *Style 2357, mixed colors*
Quantity *300 dozen*

Job *4-09*
Date Started *4/12/X6*
Date Completed *4/24/X6*

MATERIALS			DIRECT LABOR							MANUFACTURING OVERHEAD APPLIED										
					CUTTING		SEWING		FINISHING				CUTTING			SEWING			FINISHING	
DATE	REQ. NO.	AMOUNT	DATE	REF.	HRS.	AMOUNT	HRS.	AMOUNT	HRS.	AMOUNT	DATE	REF.	HRS.	RATE	AMOUNT	HRS.	RATE	AMOUNT	HRS.	RATE	AMOUNT
4/12	R385	150 00	4/14	TTA	120																
4/12	R391	125 00	4/21	TTA	55		95														
4/16	R404	175 00	4/28	TTA			64		113												
4/17	R408	42 05																			
4/17	R415	36 10																			
4/19	R422	14 87																			
4/21	R425	22 18																			
4/21	R428	19 87																			
4/23	R432	54 37																			
4/24	R435	9 98																			

Instructions

1. Compute and enter the departmental direct labor costs on the job cost sheet for Job 4-09. The labor rates are as follows: Cutting Department, $4.60 per hour; Sewing Department, $5.25 per hour; and Finishing Department, $4.30 per hour.

2. The Ortega Manufacturing Company applies overhead to work in process on the basis of direct labor hours. Use the overhead application rates given below to determine the manufacturing overhead to be applied to each department. Record the applied overhead on the job cost sheet for Job 4-09.

Cutting Department $8.25 per direct labor hour
Sewing Department   6.42 per direct labor hour
Finishing Department   9.20 per direct labor hour

3. Total all columns and draw a double rule. Complete the Summary and Total Cost sections of the job cost sheet for Job 4-09.

PROBLEM 10-2A. Recording applied manufacturing overhead. The Vandermeer Manufacturing Company completed five jobs during April 19X6. The company applies overhead to work in process on the basis of direct labor hours and has calculated the following overhead application rates:

Cutting Department $2.17 per direct labor hour
Sewing Department   1.62 per direct labor hour
Finishing Department   1.63 per direct labor hour

The manufacturing overhead account balances in the ledger are as follows:

Manufacturing Overhead—Cutting Department $1,580.11 Dr.
Manufacturing Overhead—Sewing Department   1,430.66 Dr.
Manufacturing Overhead—Finishing Department   872.11 Dr.
Overapplied or Underapplied Manufacturing Overhead   306.82 Cr.

Instructions

1. a. Compute the manufacturing overhead to be applied to each department for each of the jobs completed in April. Use the following data:

Date	Job No.	Cutting	Sewing	Finishing
Apr. 9	4-01	450 hours	136 hours	102 hours
14	4-02	75 hours	130 hours	80 hours
18	4-03	100 hours	155 hours	55 hours
23	4-04	125 hours	110 hours	95 hours
29	4-05	135 hours	125 hours	115 hours

   b. Record the jobs in the manufacturing overhead applied journal.

   c. Prove the accuracy of your work by footing and crossfooting all columns of the manufacturing overhead applied journal. Enter the totals and draw a double rule.

2. Post the totals of the manufacturing overhead applied journal to the departmental manufacturing overhead accounts in the general ledger and extend the balance of each account.

3. a. Prepare the general journal voucher to close the departmental manufacturing overhead accounts into the Overapplied or Underapplied Manufacturing Overhead account. Number the voucher 4-17.

b. Post General Journal Voucher 4-17 to the general ledger accounts and extend the balance of each account.

PROBLEM 10-3A. Computing overhead and analyzing volume and spending variances. Selected data for the Yee Manufacturing Company for the year 19X6 follow:

	Budgeted for Year	Actual for Year
Direct Labor Hours	260,000	248,300
Manufacturing Overhead		
Fixed	$ 585,000	$ 578,400
Variable	1,092,000	1,039,940
Total Overhead	$1,677,000	$1,618,340

Overhead was applied on the basis of direct labor hours.

Instructions

1. Compute the overhead application rate.
2. Compute the applied overhead for the year.
3. Compute the total overapplied or underapplied overhead for the year.
4. Analyze the total overapplied or underapplied overhead into a volume variance and a spending variance.

PROBLEM 10-4A. Analyzing underapplied or overapplied overhead. Pappas Manufacturers uses the direct labor hours method for applying manufacturing overhead. The overhead application rate for 19X7 is $5.49 per hour, based on anticipated fixed costs of $272,250 and anticipated variable costs of $633,600 with an expected volume of 165,000 labor hours.

Instructions

1. Compute the total underapplied or overapplied overhead for the year.
2. Analyze the total overapplied or underapplied overhead into a volume variance and a spending variance.

PROBLEM 10-5A. Preparing an income statement. For the fiscal year 19X7, the Nagata Machinery Corporation accumulated the following data:

Sales	$824,384
Sales Returns and Allowances	32,714
Finished Goods, July 1, 19X6	82,844
Finished Goods, June 30, 19X7	85,834
Cost of Goods Manufactured	448,721
Overapplied or Underapplied Overhead	4,190 Dr. Balance
Selling Expenses	94,348
Administrative Expenses	72,200
Provision for Income Taxes	80,650

Instructions

Prepare an income statement for the Nagata Machinery Corporation for the year ended June 30, 19X7.

Completing the Cost Cycle

■ ■ ■

When jobs have been completed, the finished goods are moved from the factory to the warehouse. Since the flow of costs must follow the flow of the goods, the cost of completed jobs is transferred from the Work in Process account to the Finished Goods account in the general ledger. Later, when finished goods are sold, their cost is transferred to the Cost of Goods Sold account. In this chapter, you will learn how warehousing and selling operations are controlled through cost records and reports.

Recording Completion of Jobs

After completion of a job, the final entries covering materials, labor, and overhead are recorded on the job cost sheet (page 195). Then the following steps are performed:

1. All columns on the job cost sheet are totaled, and the amounts are entered in the Summary section.
2. The total cost is computed and entered.
3. The unit cost is determined and recorded.

Completed Jobs Journal

The job cost sheet is removed from the job cost ledger after the final calculations have been made. An entry to record the completion of the job is made in a special journal called a *completed jobs journal* (page 195).

At the end of the month, the total of the completed jobs journal is debited to Finished Goods and credited to Work in Process. The effect is shown below.

19X1				
Oct. 31	Finished Goods	126	181,342.50	
	Work in Process	122		181,342.50
	Transferred cost of jobs completed during the month.			

When the transfer is posted, the balance of the Work in Process account, $21,832.36 (page 196), is the same as shown in the T account in Chapter 2.

COMPLETED JOBS JOURNAL
for Month of _____ October _____ 19 X1 _____ Page ___10___

DATE		JOB NO.	MANUFACTURED FOR	FINISHED GOODS DR. 126 WORK IN PROCESS CR. 122 ✓	AMOUNT
Oct.	3	98	Martin Wholesale Furniture Company	✓	26,573 82
	9	99	Yorktown Board of Control	✓	48,628 05
	15	100	Stock (End Tables 327)	✓	11,743 20
	18	101	Neeley Furniture Company	✓	15,672 80
	31		Total		181,342 50

JOB COST SHEET

Customer _Neeley Furniture Co._
Description _Customer specs on file_
Quantity _100_

Job ___101___
Date Started _10/1/X1_
Date Completed _10/18/X1_

MATERIALS DATE	REQ. NO.	AMOUNT	DIRECT LABOR DATE	REF.	MILLING HRS.	AMOUNT	ASSEMBLING HRS.	AMOUNT	FINISHING HRS.	AMOUNT	M.O. APPLIED DATE	REF.	MILLING HRS.	RATE	AMOUNT	ASSEMBLING HRS.	RATE	AMOUNT	FINISHING HRS.	RATE	AMOUNT
10/1	R802	935 00	10/5	TTA	290	1902 00	220	1580 00	55	420 00	10/20	MOA 10	290	5.10	1479 00	220	4.71	1036 20	320	5.88	1881 60
10/2	R804	2805 00	10/12	TTA					95	685 00											
10/6	RM48	(85 00)	10/19	TTA					170	1215 00											
10/8	R809	1598 00																			
10/8	R817	119 00																			
10/16	R843	41 00																			
10/17	R848	27 00																			
10/18	R852	34 00																			
Total		5474 00			290	1902 00	220	1580 00	320	2320 00			290		1479 00	220		1036 20	320		1881 60

TOTAL COST $15,672.80
UNITS PRODUCED ___100___
COST PER UNIT $156.73
COMMENTS:

Contract Price $18,200.00

SUMMARY

MATERIALS	$5,474.00
LABOR—MILLING	1,902.00
LABOR—ASSEMBLING	1,580.00
LABOR—FINISHING	2,320.00
OVERHEAD—MILLING	1,479.00
OVERHEAD—ASSEMBLING	1,036.20
OVERHEAD—FINISHING	1,881.60
TOTAL	$15,672.80

| | | Work in Process | | | | No. ___122___ | | |
DATE		EXPLANATION	POST. REF.	DEBIT	CREDIT	BALANCE	DR. CR.
19X1 Oct.	1	Balance	↙			33,165 50	Dr.
	31	Direct Materials Issued	MR10	69,337 26		102,502 76	Dr.
	31	Direct Labor	J10-48	58,597 00		161,099 76	Dr.
	31	Dir. Mat. Ret. to Storeroom	RM10		552 50	160,547 26	Dr.
	31	Manufacturing Overhead Applied	MOA10	42,627 60		203,174 86	Dr.
	31	Cost of Goods Completed	CJ10		181,342 50	21,832 36	Dr.

Proving the Job Cost Ledger

The balance of Work in Process 122 must equal the total of all costs charged to goods still in process at the end of the month. The cost accountant prepares a proof in the form of a schedule of work in process listing the uncompleted jobs and the costs that have been charged against them.

	SPACE SAVERS, INC. Schedule of Work in Process October 31, 19X1			
JOB	MATERIALS	LABOR	OVERHEAD	TOTAL
109	$3,709.08	$2,558.00	$2,220.06	$ 8,487.14
110	3,336.13	2,060.25	1,820.09	7,216.47
111	1,675.66	1,182.62	1,047.71	3,905.99
112	1,254.74	521.72	446.30	2,222.76
Total	$9,975.61	$6,322.59	$5,534.16	$21,832.36

Finished Goods Ledger

In the journal entry illustrated on page 194, finished goods costing $181,342.50 were transferred from Work in Process 122 to Finished Goods 126. Some of these goods were manufactured to customers' specifications (custom orders), and other goods were manufactured to be held for future sale (goods for stock). The treatment of custom orders will be discussed later in this chapter.

The completion of goods for stock is recorded in a *finished goods ledger* as well as in the completed jobs journal. This subsidiary ledger (Finished Goods 126 is the control account in the general ledger) consists of a stock ledger card for each type of product that the firm manufactures for stock. The design of the stock ledger card is very similar to the design of the materials ledger card discussed in Chapter 3. In fact, many companies use the same form for both ledgers.

The completion of 400 end tables (Stock 327) at Space Savers is recorded as shown on page 197.

STOCK LEDGER CARD

Material *End tables*　　　　　　　　　Number 327

DATE	REFERENCE	RECEIVED			SOLD			BALANCE		
		UNITS	PRICE	AMOUNT	UNITS	PRICE	AMOUNT	UNITS	PRICE	AMOUNT
19 X1 Oct. 1	Bal.							200	2810	562000
6	S-611				140	2810	393400	60	2810	168600
15	J-100	400	29358	1174320				60 } 400 }	2810 29358	1342920

Recording Sales of Finished Goods

Operations flow from warehousing to selling. As goods are sold, they are shipped from the warehouse to the customers. The costs being recorded must be transferred from Finished Goods to Cost of Goods Sold to parallel this flow.

Sales From Stock

When finished goods that have been manufactured for stock are sold to a customer, the warehouse clerk receives a copy of the sales invoice. This invoice tells the clerk that goods have been sold and that an entry should be made in the finished goods ledger to show the sale of the goods and to record the new balance of goods on hand. Assume that on October 20, Space Savers sells 100 end tables (Stock 327) at $38 each. The sale would be recorded on the stock ledger card as follows. (Note that the FIFO method of inventory valuation is used.)

STOCK LEDGER CARD

Material *End tables*　　　　　　　　　Number 327

DATE	REFERENCE	RECEIVED			SOLD			BALANCE		
		UNITS	PRICE	AMOUNT	UNITS	PRICE	AMOUNT	UNITS	PRICE	AMOUNT
19 X1 Oct. 1	Bal.							200	2810	562000
6	S-611				140	2810	393400	60	2810	168600
15	J-100	400	29358	1174320				60 } 400 }	2810 29358	1342920
20	S-621				60 } 40 }	2810 29358	286032	360	29358	1056888

As the entry on the stock ledger card is made, the cost of goods sold ($1,686.00 + $1,174.32 = $2,860.32) is entered on the Accounting Department's copy of the invoice. The information on the invoice copy then serves as the basis for an entry in a specially designed sales journal (page 198), in which both sales price (100 × $38 = $3,800) and cost of goods sold are recorded. (In some companies, cost data are entered on the shipping documents rather than on the invoice copy.)

SALES JOURNAL for Month of ____October____ 19 X1 Page ___10___

DATE		INVOICE NUMBER	CUSTOMER'S NAME	TERMS	✔	ACCOUNTS REC. DR. 111 SALES CR. 401		COST OF GOODS SOLD DR. 415 FINISHED GOODS CR. 126	
Oct.	3	610	Martin Wholesale Furniture Company	n/30	✔	32,340	00	26,573	82
	6	611	Kible Supply	n/30	✔	5,670	60	4,362	00
	9	612	Yorktown Bd. of Control	n/30	✔	61,785	10	48,628	05
	20	621	The Furniture Mart	n/30	✔	3,800	00	2,860	32

Sales of Custom Orders

When a firm completes a job that has been manufactured to fill a customer's specifications, it ships the goods at once, and records an entry in the sales journal. The following sales journal shows a sale that Space Savers made to the Neeley Furniture Company on October 18 for goods produced on Job 101.

SALES JOURNAL for Month of ____October____ 19 X1 Page ___10___

DATE		INVOICE NUMBER	CUSTOMER'S NAME	TERMS	✔	ACCOUNTS REC. DR. 111 SALES CR. 401		COST OF GOODS SOLD DR. 415 FINISHED GOODS CR. 126	
Oct.	3	610	Martin Wholesale Furniture Company	n/30	✔	32,340	00	26,573	82
	6	611	Kible Supply	n/30	✔	5,670	60	4,362	00
	9	612	Yorktown Bd. of Control	n/30	✔	61,785	10	48,628	05
	20	621	The Furniture Mart	n/30	✔	3,800	00	2,860	32
	18	622	Neeley Furniture Company	n/30	✔	18,200	00	15,672	80
	31		Total			228,176	80	177,977	90

Since the special order goods never actually enter the warehouse stock, they are not picked up in the finished goods ledger.

At the end of the month, the column totals of the sales journal are posted to the general ledger accounts. The effects of these postings are shown below in general journal form.

19X1					
Oct. 31	Accounts Receivable	111	228,176.80	
	Sales	401		228,176.80
	Recorded sales for month.			
31	Cost of Goods Sold	415	177,977.90	
	Finished Goods	126		177,977.90
	Recorded cost of goods sold during October.			

Proving the Finished Goods Account

The firm's inventory of finished goods is a valuable asset that requires close watching. Therefore, at the end of each month, the cost accountant will prove the finished goods ledger to the control account, Finished Goods, in the general ledger.

DATE		EXPLANATION	POST. REF.	DEBIT	CREDIT	BALANCE	DR. CR.
19X1							
Oct.	1	Balance	✔			24,200 00	Dr.
	31	Cost of Goods Completed	CJ10	181,342 50		205,542 50	Dr.
	31	Cost of Goods Sold	S10		177,977 90	27,564 60	Dr.

Finished Goods   No. 126

The finished goods ledger is subsidiary to the Finished Goods account in the general ledger. Thus, at the end of the period, the total of the individual balances of the stock ledger cards should always agree with the balance of the control account. A schedule of finished goods is prepared from the subsidiary ledger at that time to prove it to the control account.

SPACE SAVERS, INC.
Schedule of Finished Goods
October 31, 19X1

STOCK	STOCK NO.	UNITS	AMOUNT
Coffee Tables	312	100	$ 2,806.00
Step Tables	325	50	2,140.00
Casual Tables	326	108	2,290.70
End Tables	327	360	10,568.88
Total			$27,564.60

Periodic inventories of finished goods must be taken. The procedures are much like those for taking inventory of raw materials, discussed on pages 92 to 94. Shortages of finished goods are usually charged to Cost of Goods Sold 415.

. . . .

Manufacturing Costs on Financial Statements

The manufacturing costs for a fiscal period are reported in the form of a summary total in the Cost of Goods Sold section of the income statement as shown on page 200.

```
                    SPACE SAVERS, INC.
                     Income Statement
                 Month Ended October 31, 19X1

Revenue
  Sales                                                    $228,176.80
Cost of Goods Sold
  Finished Goods Inventory, Oct. 1           $ 24,200.00
  Add Cost of Goods Manufactured              181,342.50
  Total Goods Available for Sale             $205,542.50
  Deduct Finished Goods Inventory, Oct. 31     27,564.60
  Cost of Goods Sold                                        177,977.90
Gross Profit on Sales                                     $ 50,198.90
Operating Expenses
  Selling Expenses                           $  8,784.60
  General Expenses                             11,969.20
  Total Operating Expenses                                  20,753.80
Net Income Before Income Taxes                            $ 29,445.10
  Provision for Income Taxes                                 4,845.00
Net Income After Income Taxes                             $ 24,600.10
```

The details supporting the Cost of Goods Manufactured ($181,342.50) are shown in the statement of cost of goods manufactured.

```
                    SPACE SAVERS, INC.
          Statement of Cost of Goods Manufactured
                 Month Ended October 31, 19X1

Direct Materials
  Raw Materials Inventory, Oct. 1            $ 44,114.00
  Materials Purchases                          68,760.00
  Total Materials Available                  $112,874.00
  Deduct Raw Materials Inventory, Oct. 31      40,907.89
  Total Materials Used                       $ 71,966.11
  Deduct Indirect Materials used                3,181.35
Direct Materials Used                                     $ 68,784.76
Direct Labor                                                58,597.00
Manufacturing Overhead Applied                              42,627.60
Total Manufacturing Cost                                  $170,009.36
Add Work in Process Inventory, Oct. 1                       33,165.50
                                                          $203,174.86
Deduct Work in Process Inventory, Oct. 31                   21,832.36
Cost of Goods Manufactured                                $181,342.50
```

Only manufacturing overhead applied is shown on the statement of cost of goods manufactured. A supplementary schedule, the schedule of manufacturing overhead, is prepared, giving the details of the actual overhead costs incurred and the underapplied or overapplied overhead for the period. (Some accountants prefer to show all the details of manufacturing overhead directly on the statement of cost of goods manufactured.)

SPACE SAVERS, INC.
Schedule of Manufacturing Overhead
Month Ended October 31, 19X1

Actual Overhead Costs Incurred		
Indirect Materials	$ 3,181.35	
Indirect Labor	26,131.00	
Payroll Taxes	5,037.95	
Depreciation—Buildings	1,520.00	
Depreciation—Equipment	2,640.00	
Repairs and Maintenance	1,534.60	
Utilities	2,488.64	
Insurance	794.05	
Property Taxes	421.00	
Other Overhead Costs	485.15	
Total Actual Overhead Costs Incurred		$44,233.74
Deduct Underapplied Overhead for October		1,606.14
Manufacturing Overhead Applied		$42,627.60

The statements shown above and on page 201 are the same as the statements illustrated in Chapter 2. You have now learned how every figure on the statement of cost of goods manufactured is developed.

Computerized Cost Accumulation

City Bread, Inc., is located in Houston, Texas. Although years ago it was a family-owned bakery supplying bread only to the neighborhood, it now supplies bread to the cities of Austin, San Antonio, Dallas, and Fort Worth. City Bread currently has five lines of bakery products: bread, dinner rolls, hamburger and hot dog buns, sweet rolls, and doughnuts. Each line passes through three production stages: mixing, baking, and packaging. Sweet rolls and doughnuts also pass through a glazing stage before packaging.

City Bread has computerized its product costing and inventory systems. As materials, labor, and manufacturing overhead are added to the production process of a particular product, job costs are accumulated in its work-in-process file. Materials codes are keyed into the terminal at the mixing station as materials are added to the product. Labor time is accumulated as workers in each of the production stages insert their badges into badge-reading terminals. (For a more in-depth description of how this works, see the discussion of Uniform Attire's system on pages 128 and 129.) The computer calculates overhead costs by multiplying standard overhead rates by labor hours.

When a product, such as dinner rolls, is completed for the day, the costs related to dinner rolls are transferred by the computer from the dinner rolls work-in-process cost file to the finished goods inventory master file. As the rolls physically move from the bakery into the warehouse, the factory supervisor enters into a terminal the number of packages of dinner rolls (1,000) that are complete and ready to be moved. This signals the computer to reduce the dinner rolls work-in-process file by 1,000 and increase the dinner rolls finished goods file by 1,000.

The cost of any of the five products manufactured by City Bread is available to management at any time through the computer terminal. If costs appear to be too high at any stage of production, management can make changes in the production process. The cost accountant can now spend time analyzing costs for each product line. These costs may suggest that the prices of certain product lines be raised or lowered. Management believes that timely information such as this may give the firm a pricing edge over its competition. ■

Principles and Procedures Summary

When the factory completes a job, all costs are totaled, and the overall cost of the job is transferred from Work in Process to Finished Goods. If the goods are manufactured for stock, the cost of the completed goods is also recorded in the finished goods ledger.

The sale of merchandise from stock is recorded as a deduction on the stock ledger card involved. The cost of the goods sold is noted on a copy of the sales invoice so that it can be recorded along with the sales price in the sales journal. At the end of the month, a summary posting from the sales journal transfers the total cost of the goods sold during the month as a debit to Cost of Goods Sold and a credit to Finished Goods. Another summary posting transfers the total sales for the month as a debit to Accounts Receivable and a credit to Sales.

The finished goods ledger is proved to its control account, Finished Goods, at the end of each month. The accountant prepares a schedule of finished goods, the total of which should agree with the balance of the control account in the general ledger.

The cost of goods manufactured appears on the financial statements of the firm in two ways. In the Cost of Goods Sold section of the income statement, these costs are represented by a summary total. In the statement of cost of goods manufactured, all facts are supplied in detail.

Accounting for the completion and sale of goods are the last two phases of the typical job order cost accounting cycle.

Review Questions

1. What general ledger account is charged for the cost of jobs completed? Is the entry a debit or a credit to this account?
2. What information does a completed jobs journal provide? What is the source for entries in this journal? Describe a typical entry.

3. Work in Process is a control account in the general ledger. The balances in what subsidiary records must equal the balance of this account?
4. Why is a schedule of work in process prepared?
5. What is the control account for the finished goods ledger?
6. Why should a physical inventory of finished goods be taken?
7. How are shortages of finished goods accounted for?
8. When finished goods are sold, what two amounts must be recorded in the sales journal? Describe a typical entry.
9. Are special order goods entered in the finished goods ledger? Explain.
10. Which inventory accounts appear on the statement of cost of goods manufactured? On the income statement? On the balance sheet?

Managerial Discussion Questions

1. What are the benefits of using special journals such as the completed jobs journal?
2. When a job is completed, management should review the job cost sheet. Which cost items would management look at most closely? Why?
3. What are the limitations on the usefulness to management of the statement of cost of goods manufactured? Why?
4. What are the advantages of maintaining a perpetual inventory record for finished goods?
5. If the monthly schedule of manufacturing overhead shows that overhead was overapplied or underapplied, what additional information about this item would management want to have?

Exercises

1. **Totaling job costs.** The Kelly Manufacturing Company finished Job 643 for 250 engines on July 30, 19X7. The following costs were recorded on the job cost sheet:

Materials	$23,650
Labor—Milling	18,480
Labor—Assembling	19,250
Labor—Finishing	12,670
Overhead—Milling	9,830
Overhead—Assembling	10,175
Overhead—Finishing	8,020

Complete the following calculations. (You may want to review Chapter 2 on prime and conversion costs.)
a. What are the prime costs for this job?
b. What are the conversion costs?
c. Determine the total cost for this job and the unit cost for each engine.

2. **Journalizing the cost of completed jobs.** At the end of June, the total of the completed jobs journal was $263,870. Prepare the entry in general journal form to record the cost of the completed jobs.

3. **Analyzing Work in Process account postings.** The Work in Process account for the Andover Supply Corporation is shown on page 204. All journal entries for the month of November have been posted. Describe each of the six postings.

4. **Recording cost of goods sold and sales.** For the month of March 19X8, the Rivera Corporation sold goods that cost $738,240 to produce. The corporation

	Work in Process					No. 122	
DATE	EXPLANATION	POST. REF.	DEBIT	CREDIT	BALANCE	DR. CR.	

DATE	EXPLANATION	POST. REF.	DEBIT	CREDIT	BALANCE	DR. CR.
19X8						
Nov. 1 (a)		✔			35,790 65	Dr.
30 (b)		MR11	65,830 20		101,620 85	Dr.
30 (c)		J11-38	82,438 56		184,059 41	Dr.
30 (d)		RM11		1,463 90	182,595 51	Dr.
30 (e)		MOA11	58,741 82		241,337 33	Dr.
30 (f)		CJ11		202,812 38	38,524 95	Dr.

billed its customers $1,108,360 for these goods. Prepare the entries in general journal form to record the cost of goods sold and the sales for the month.

5. **Calculating gross profit.** The sales journal for the New Orleans Machine Company is shown below.

SALES JOURNAL for Month of May 19 X7 Page 5						
DATE	INVOICE NUMBER	CUSTOMER'S NAME	TERMS	✔	ACCOUNTS REC. DR. 111 SALES CR. 401	COST OF GOODS SOLD DR. 415 FINISHED GOODS CR. 126
May 4	501	Washington Supply Co.	n/30	✔	23,400 00	15,212 80
8	502	Page & Orlez Co.	n/30	✔	36,250 00	23,562 68
10	503	Riverton Wholesale Co.	n/30	✔	25,850 00	16,921 53
15	504	Flatlands Machine Corp.	n/30	✔	43,150 00	48,390 15
22	505	Rosenberg Supply Co.	n/30	✔	34,200 00	22,237 83
29	506	Davis Industrial Supply	n/30	✔	18,400 00	7,692 71
31		Total			181,250 00	134,017 70
					(111) (401)	(415) (216)

a. Calculate the amount of gross profit (or loss) for each job and the total gross profit for the month.

b. What was the gross profit percentage for the total sales for the month?

Problems

PROBLEM 11-1. Journalizing manufacturing cost transactions. The Danish Designs Company is a manufacturer of custom-designed furniture. During the month of July 19X8, the firm had the following transactions and incurred the following costs:

a. Raw materials were purchased on credit for $14,960.

b. Direct materials costing $9,530 and indirect materials costing $1,760 were used during the month.

c. Factory wages paid during the month totaled $13,560. The deductions were: FICA taxes, $950; federal income taxes, $1,760, and group insurance premiums, $260.

d. Direct labor costs were $12,680 and indirect labor costs were $2,190 as shown on the summary of factory wages for the month.

e. Vouchers for various types of manufacturing overhead costs totaled $2,820 and were recorded in the voucher register.

f. Depreciation for the month was $2,700 on the factory building and $930 on the factory equipment and tools.

g. Expired factory insurance for the month totaled $510.

h. Accrued property taxes on the factory for the month were $965.

i. Employer's payroll taxes were: FICA, $950; federal unemployment taxes, $108; and state unemployment taxes, $480.

j. Manufacturing overhead applied to the job cost sheets during the month totaled $14,260.

k. Jobs completed and transferred to finished goods cost $35,730.

l. Cost of goods sold during the month was $29,965. The sales were made on credit for $41,950. (Prepare two separate entries.)

Instructions

Prepare the general journal entries to record the above transactions. Date the entries July 31.

PROBLEM 11-2. Journalizing and posting transactions. The Nadal Company manufactures a single product. On June 1, 19X7, the company's inventory accounts showed the following balances:

Raw Materials	$32,750
Work in Process	22,900
Finished Goods	39,500

Transactions that occurred during the month of June are summarized below.

a. Raw materials were purchased on credit for $38,400.

b. Direct materials costing $35,071 and indirect materials costing $6,189 were used during the month.

c. Factory wages earned during June totaled $54,625. (Credit Salaries and Wages Payable 202; payroll taxes should be ignored.)

d. Direct labor costs for the month amounted to $43,700, and indirect labor costs amounted to $10,925.

Additional factory costs incurred are as follows:

e. Employer's payroll taxes, $5,720 (credit Taxes Payable 212).

f. Machinery repairs, $1,430 (credit Vouchers Payable 201).

g. Depreciation for the month on the factory building, $490; on the factory equipment, $2,030.

h. Factory insurance expired, $220.

i. Property taxes accrued, $710.

j. Manufacturing overhead chargeable to Work in Process is estimated at $27,091.

k. Jobs completed and transferred to finished goods cost $104,157.

l. Cost of goods sold during the month, $107,822. Price of goods sold (on credit) during the month $140,160. (Prepare two entries.)

Instructions

1. Open accounts for Raw Materials 121, Work in Process 122, Finished Goods 126, Sales 401, Cost of Goods Sold 415, Factory Payroll Clearing 500, and Manufacturing Overhead Control 501.
2. Enter the beginning balances in the three inventory accounts.
3. Record the above transactions in general journal form. Date the entries June 30.
4. Post to the accounts provided. (No accounts have been opened for some asset and liability items.)
5. Prepare a schedule of manufacturing overhead costs showing the underapplied or overapplied overhead and the overhead applied to production, and prepare a statement of cost of goods manufactured.
6. Prepare an income statement for the month, assuming that selling expenses totaled $11,800 and that general and administrative expenses totaled $4,720.

PROBLEM 11-3. Completing a job cost sheet. Snyder Manufacturers uses a job order cost system. The data below applies to Job 6-6B, which is for 150 Model MT-4 tables ordered by the Grady Furniture Store. The job was started on June 10, 19X7.

Materials

June 10, Requisition 314, $1,500
June 15, Requisition 331, $520
June 20, Requisition 360, $160
June 22, Returned Materials Report 18, $32 (materials returned to storeroom)

Labor

Week ended June 14:
    Milling Department, 120 hours, $630
    Assembling Department, 55 hours, $325
Week ended June 21:
    Milling Department, 30 hours, $157.50
    Assembling Department, 110 hours, $561
Week ended June 28:
    Assembling Department, 12 hours, $63
    Finishing Department, 45 hours, $229.50

The job was completed on June 26, and overhead was applied as follows:

Milling Department	$4.05 per direct labor hour
Assembling Department	4.30 per direct labor hour
Finishing Department	6.80 per direct labor hour

Instructions

Complete a job cost sheet for this job.

PROBLEM 11-4. Recording finished jobs and sales. The Durand Company is a manufacturer of warm-up suits. It manufactures standard gray men's, women's, and children's models for stock. In addition, the Durand Company accepts custom orders from colleges and universities to produce warm-up suits in the school's colors.

On March 1, 19X6, the company's inventory accounts showed the following balances:

Work in Process $6,215 ✓
Finished Goods 4,375 ✓

On March 1, 19X6, the finished goods ledger included three stock ledger cards, with the following information:

Number	Stock Item	Balance
100	Men's Warm-Up Suits	100 at $20 each
101	Women's Warm-Up Suits	125 at $15 each
102	Children's Warm-Up Suits	50 at $10 each

Transactions relating to completion and sales of warm-up suits for the month of March were as follows:

Mar. 4 Completed Job 20 for 60 men's warm-up suits at a cost of $20 each and transferred the goods to the warehouse.

7 Completed Job 21 for 50 women's warm-up suits at a cost of $15 each and transferred the goods to the warehouse.

11 Completed Job 22 for 24 blue and white warm-up suits for Granville College and shipped the goods to the customer. Issued Invoice 109. The cost to manufacture was $18 each and the price was $27 each.

14 Sold 30 women's warm-up suits to the Lindberg Department Store at a price of $23 each. Issued Invoice 110. 4/5

17 Sold 75 men's warm-up suits to the Western Sporting Goods Store for $30 each. Issued Invoice 111.

19 Completed Job 23 for 45 children's warm-up suits at a cost of $10 each and transferred the goods to the warehouse.

25 Completed Job 24 for (15) red and gold women's warm-up suits for Northern Utah University and shipped the goods to the customer. Issued Invoice 112. The cost to manufacture was $16 each and the price was $24 each.

27 Completed Job 25 for 120 men's warm-up suits at a cost of $20 each and transferred the goods to the warehouse.

29 Sold 100 men's warm-up suits at a price of $30 each to the Timberline Pro Shop. Issued Invoice 113.

Instructions

1. Open general ledger accounts for the following: Accounts Receivable 111, Work in Process 122, Finished Goods 126, Sales 401, and Cost of Goods Sold 415. Enter the March 1, 19X6, balances in the inventory accounts.

2. Open stock ledger cards in the finished goods ledger as follows: Men's Warm-up Suits, Number 100; Women's Warm-up Suits, Number 101; and Children's Warm-up Suits, Number 102. Enter the March 1, 19X6, balances.

3. Record the March transactions in the completed jobs journal and the sales journal. Use page number 12.

4. Post the jobs manufactured for stock to the finished goods ledger.

5. Post the summary totals of the completed jobs journal and the sales journals to the general ledger accounts.

6. Prepare a schedule of finished goods. This schedule should agree with what account in the general ledger?

PROBLEM 11-5. Analyzing manufacturing cost transactions. NOTE: The transaction listing for this problem is provided only in the *Study Guide and Working Papers*.

This problem illustrates the flow of work in job order cost accounting and the flow of costs through the accompanying general ledger accounts. Selected transactions for Space Savers are given in the first column of the forms in the *Study Guide and Working Papers*.

Instructions

Analyze each transaction given in the *Study Guide and Working Papers*. Insert a check mark in the appropriate debit or credit column of the general ledger accounts affected. Transaction 1 has been completed as an example.

Alternate Problems

PROBLEM 11-1A. Journalizing manufacturing cost transactions. The Petersen Company is a manufacturer of kitchen cabinets. During the month of January 19X7, the firm had the following transactions and incurred the following costs:

a. Raw materials were purchased on credit for $33,720.
b. Direct materials costing $24,050 and indirect materials costing $8,470 were used during the month.
c. Factory wages paid during the month totaled $52,140. The deductions were: FICA taxes $3,650; federal income taxes, $7,820; and group insurance premiums, $520.
d. Direct labor costs were $44,060 and indirect labor costs were $10,865 as shown on the summary of factory wages for the month.
e. Vouchers for various types of manufacturing overhead costs totaled $30,290 and were recorded in the voucher register.
f. Depreciation for the month was $1,820 on the factory building and $395 on the factory equipment and tools.
g. Expired factory insurance for the month totaled $2,090.
h. Accrued property taxes on the factory for the month were $4,270.
i. Employer's payroll taxes were: FICA, $3,650; federal unemployment taxes, $420; and state unemployment taxes, $2,300.
j. Manufacturing overhead applied to the job cost sheets during the month totaled $63,155.
k. Jobs completed and transferred to finished goods cost $123,265.
l. Cost of goods sold during the month was $110,500. The sales were made on credit for $135,915. (Prepare two separate entries.)

Instructions

Prepare the general journal entries to record the above transactions. Date the entries January 31.

PROBLEM 11-2A. Journalizing and posting transactions. The Haynes Corporation manufactures a single product. On October 1, 19X8, the company's inventory accounts showed the following balances:

Raw materials	$52,300
Work in Process	50,500
Finished Goods	73,000

Transactions that occurred during the month of October are summarized below.

a. Raw materials were purchased on credit for $100,380.
b. Direct materials costing $88,120 and indirect materials costing $9,380 were used during the month.
c. Factory wages earned during October totaled $67,200. (Credit Salaries and Wages Payable 202; payroll taxes should be ignored.)
d. Direct labor costs for the month amounted to $49,000 and indirect labor costs amounted to $18,200.

Additional factory costs incurred are as follows:

e. Employer's payroll taxes, $4,610 (credit Taxes Payable 212).
f. Machinery repairs, $1,720 (credit Vouchers Payable 202).
g. Depreciation for the month on the factory building, $3,080; on the factory equipment, $5,600.
h. Factory insurance expired, $590.
i. Property taxes accrued, $2,378.
j. Manufacturing overhead chargeable to work in process is estimated to be $47,115.
k. Jobs completed and transferred to finished goods cost $186,755.
l. Cost of goods sold during the month, $197,015. Price of goods sold (on credit) during the month, $262,555. (Prepare two entries.)

Instructions

1. Open accounts for Raw Materials 121, Work in Process 122, Finished Goods 126, Sales 401, Cost of Goods Sold 415, Factory Payroll Clearing 500, and Manufacturing Overhead Control 501.
2. Enter the beginning balances in the three inventory accounts.
3. Record the transactions in general journal form. Date the entries October 31.
4. Post to the accounts provided. (No accounts are provided for some items.)
5. Prepare a schedule of manufacturing overhead costs showing the underapplied or overapplied overhead and the overhead applied to production, and prepare a statement of cost of goods manufactured.
6. Prepare an income statement for the month, assuming that selling expenses totaled $30,880 and general and administrative expenses totaled $13,600.

PROBLEM 11-3A. Completing a job cost sheet. The Landis & Lakely Company uses a job order cost system. The data below applies to Job 11-24, which is for 600 Model F-108 chairs ordered by the Hogarth Furniture Store. The job was started on November 14, 19X6.

Materials

November 14, Requisition 811, $4,016
November 19, Requisition 825, $1,055
November 24, Requisition 840, $179
November 27, Returned Materials Report 64, $60 (materials returned to storeroom)

Week ended November 14:
    Milling Department, 130 hours, $728
Week ended November 21:
    Milling Department, 95 hours, $532
    Assembling Department, 40 hours, $232
Week ended November 28:
    Assembling Department, 55 hours, $319
    Finishing Department, 90 hours, $540

The job was completed on November 27, and overhead was applied as follows:

Milling Department	$4.85 per direct labor hour
Assembling Department	3.60 per direct labor hour
Finishing Department	6.40 per direct labor hour

Instructions
Complete a job cost sheet for this job.

Job Order Cost Accounting

You have learned how to account for the basic elements of manufacturing costs. This project combines these various techniques and principles in a practical application connected with Space Savers' November transactions. You will be required to perform the duties not only of the cost accountant but also of the storeroom clerk, voucher clerk, and other personnel.

Cost Accounting System

Space Savers' cost accounting system includes a number of journals, ledgers, and cost accounting forms. All forms required are found in the *Study Guide and Working Papers*. Entries have been made on these forms where indicated. If you are not using the *Study Guide and Working Papers,* you will have to record on appropriate forms all the data shown on pages 219 to 225 of this text.

Journals

Seven journals are used for making original entries.

Voucher Register	VR
Materials Requisition Journal	MR
Returned Materials Journal	RM
Manufacturing Overhead Applied Journal	MOA
Completed Jobs Journal	CJ
Sales Journal	S
General Journal (vouchers)	J

Summary entries for November 1 through 25 have been recorded in these journals.

General Ledger

The firm's chart of accounts includes the following accounts relating to the flow of manufacturing costs. The balances as of November 1, 19X1 are given.

121	Raw Materials,	$40,907.89
122	Work in Process,	$21,832.36
126	Finished Goods,	$27,564.60
401	Sales,	$-0-
415	Cost of Goods Sold,	$-0-

500　Factory Payroll Clearing, $10,048 Cr. (See text page 221.)
501　Manufacturing Overhead Control, $-0-
502　Manufacturing Overhead—Milling Department, $-0-
503　Manufacturing Overhead—Assembling Department, $-0-
504　Manufacturing Overhead—Finishing Department, $-0-
505　Manufacturing Overhead—Building Services Department, $-0-
506　Manufacturing Overhead—General Factory Department, $-0-
507　Overapplied or Underapplied Manufacturing Overhead, $3,194.54 Dr.

The November 1 balances and the postings occurring between November 1 and November 25 have been recorded in the general ledger accounts.

Subsidiary Ledgers

Four subsidiary cost ledgers are used, and the necessary forms are provided in the *Study Guide and Working Papers*. Space Savers uses the FIFO method of costing all inventories.

Materials Ledger. In order to simplify the work in this project, the materials ledger, which actually contains several dozen cards, has been condensed to four cards showing the activities up to the close of business on November 25. (See page 221.) You will make detailed entries for Materials K-196 (chrome legs), L-27 (24-inch mica tops), and I-16 (buffer pads). All other materials are summarized in total on the fourth materials ledger card, and no entries are required on it.

Job Cost Ledger. The job cost ledger currently consists of four job cost sheets. Job 112 was begun in October; Jobs 118, 119, and 120 were started in November. Various entries have been posted through November 25.

Departmental Overhead Analysis Sheets. Overhead analysis sheets are provided for each of the five departments in the organization: Milling, Assembling, Finishing, Building Services, and General Factory.

The first entry on each sheet summarizes the postings of November 1 through November 25.

Finished Goods Ledger. The finished goods ledger consists of three stock ledger cards showing all postings through November 25. (See pages 224 and 225.) You will make entries involving two types of finished goods. Stock 18 desks and Stock 327 end tables, as required during the remainder of the month. All other types of finished goods are summarized on the third card, and no entries are required on it.

Transactions

Record the following daily transactions in the proper journals. Post to the subsidiary ledgers daily.

November 26
Materials Issued. Requisition 613 for 30 units of Material L-27 for Job 112. Requisition 614 for 100 units of Material K-196 for Job 118.

When you record a requisition for direct materials, you will perform the duties of both the storeroom clerk and the cost clerk. (See Chapter 4.) The following recording steps are required:
1. Compute the cost and enter the requisition on the materials ledger card.
2. Record the appropriate entries in the materials requisition journal.
3. Post to the job cost sheet.

November 27

Materials Received. 400 units at $15.95 each of Material K-196, obtained on Purchase Order 1194, from the Town Supply Company, Voucher 11-72.

When you record receipts of materials, you will perform the work normally assigned to the storeroom clerk and the voucher clerk. (See Chapter 4.) The following recording steps are required:
1. Record the receipt on the materials ledger card.
2. Enter the voucher in the voucher register.

Materials Issued. Requisition 615 for 18 units of Material L-27 for Job 120.

November 28

Materials Issued. Requisition 616 for 150 units of Material K-196 for Job 119. Requisition 617 for 100 units of Material I-16 for the Assembling Department.

Remember that issues of indirect materials require a different recording procedure. (See Chapter 4.)
1. Enter the issue on the materials ledger card.
2. Record the issue in the materials requisition journal.
3. Post to the departmental overhead analysis sheet.

Sale of Finished Goods. Sold 55 desks (Stock 18) to the Retail Outlets Company for $160.50 each on Invoice 716; terms 2/10, n/30.

For sales, the following recording steps are required. (See Chapter 11.)
1. Enter the issue on the finished goods stock ledger card.
2. Record the sale in the sales journal.

November 29

Materials Issued. Requisition 618 for 450 units of Material L-27 for Job 119. Requisition 619 for 100 units of Material I-16 for the Finishing Department.

Materials Received. 1,000 units at $2.25 each of Material L-27, obtained on Purchase Order 1195, from the Mica Supply Company, Voucher 11-73.

Services Received. Repairs to equipment in the Milling Department performed by the Sure Repair Service for $90, Voucher 11-74.

For transactions of this type, the following recording steps are required (see Chapter 8):
1. Enter the voucher in the voucher register.
2. Post to the departmental overhead analysis sheet.

Sale of Finished Goods. Sold 100 tables (Stock 327) to Statewide Discount Markets for $32 each on Invoice 717; terms 2/10, n/30.

November 30

Materials Issued. Requisition 620 for 300 units of Material L-27 for Job 118. Requisition 621 for 200 units of Material I-16 for the Finishing Department.

Materials Returned to Storeroom. 20 units of Material L-27, originally issued on November 26, Requisition 613, for Job 112. Returned Materials Report 70 has been prepared.

> Complete the entries normally made by the storeroom clerk and the cost clerk. (See Chapter 4.) The following recording steps are required:
> 1. Determine the cost and make the entry (in parentheses) in the Issued section of the materials ledger card.
> 2. Post to the job cost sheet.
> 3. Record the return in the returned materials journal.

Sale of Finished Goods. Sold 50 tables (Stock 327) to the Fair Furniture Company for $32 each on Invoice 718; terms 2/10, n/30.

Services Received. Utilities for factory operations in November, payable to City Utilities, Voucher 11-75. The cost of $2,062 should be allocated as follows to the departments:

Milling	$502
Assembling	90
Finishing	190
Building Services	903
General Factory	377

Interim Procedures

Complete the necessary recording and posting relating to the weekly and semi-monthly payrolls.

Weekly Payroll Register

The weekly factory payroll register for November 24 through 30 shows the following:

Gross earnings	$16,489.25
FICA taxes withheld	1,154.25
Income taxes withheld	2,507.63
Group insurance withheld	207.50

Record the payroll using a general journal voucher (11-1), since the factory payroll register is not provided. Then post the gross earnings to the Factory Payroll Clearing account. Other items are not posted because no accounts are provided for them.

Analysis of Time Tickets

An analysis of the time tickets for the week ended November 30 is shown below. The following recording steps are required:

1. Post direct labor to the job cost sheets.
2. Post indirect labor to the departmental overhead analysis sheets.

SPACE SAVERS, INC.
Analysis of Time Tickets
Week Ended November 30, 19X1

DIRECT LABOR

JOB	MILLING HOURS	MILLING AMOUNT	ASSEMBLING HOURS	ASSEMBLING AMOUNT	FINISHING HOURS	FINISHING AMOUNT	TOTAL
112			185	$1,110	110	$ 715.00	$ 1,825.00
118	113	$ 706.25	133	798	148	962.00	2,466.25
119	235	1,468.75	356	2,136	240	1,560.00	5,164.75
120	285	1,781.25	165	990	-0-	-0-	2,771.25
	633	$3,956.25	839	$5,034	498	$3,237.00	$12,227.25

INDIRECT LABOR

DEPARTMENT	REGULAR EARNINGS	OVERTIME PREMIUM	TOTAL
Milling	$ 606	$29	$ 635
Assembling	771	-0-	771
Finishing	635	26	661
Building Services	910	-0-	910
General Factory	1,285	-0-	1,285
Total	$4,207	$55	$4,262

Semimonthly Payroll Register

The semimonthly payroll register for November 16 through 30 shows the following:

Gross earnings	$3,024.00
FICA taxes withheld	211.68
Income taxes withheld	453.60
Group insurance withheld	60.50

Enter as you did the weekly payroll, using a general journal voucher (11-2).

Analysis of Semimonthly Payroll

An analysis of the semimonthly payroll for November 16 through 30 shows the following charges to be posted to the respective departmental overhead analysis sheets:

Building Services	$ 870
General Factory	2,154
	$3,024

End-of-Month Procedures

The end-of-month procedures for Space Savers will be completed in the order in which you studied the cost accounting elements: materials, labor, and manufacturing overhead.

Materials

Total the following journals and post to the appropriate general ledger accounts:

1. Voucher register
2. Materials requisition journal
3. Returned materials journal

Labor

A summary of factory wages for the month must be completed before labor costs can be charged to production.

1. Enter the weekly payroll figures for the week ended November 30 and the semi-monthly payroll for the period ended November 30 in the partially completed monthly summary provided. (See page 225.)
2. Total the summary and compute the total direct labor and indirect labor.
3. Prepare a general journal voucher (11-3) to transfer the cost of labor used during the month from Factory Payroll Clearing 500 to Work in Process 122 (direct labor) and to Manufacturing Overhead Control 501 (indirect labor).
4. Post to the general ledger accounts supplied.

Next, the employer's payroll taxes for the month must be entered in the accounting records. The summary of taxable factory wages for November follows. (NOTE: SUTA is used for state unemployment insurance tax.)

<table>
<tr><th colspan="3">SPACE SAVERS, INC.
Summary of Taxable Factory Wages
November 19X1</th></tr>
<tr><th></th><th colspan="2">WAGES SUBJECT TO:</th></tr>
<tr><th>DEPARTMENT</th><th>FICA TAX</th><th>FUTA AND SUTA TAXES</th></tr>
<tr><td>Milling</td><td>$19,907.25</td><td>$2,785</td></tr>
<tr><td>Assembling</td><td>26,049.00</td><td>3,105</td></tr>
<tr><td>Finishing</td><td>17,901.00</td><td>1,384</td></tr>
<tr><td>Building Services</td><td>5,852.00</td><td>250</td></tr>
<tr><td>General Factory</td><td>10,148.00</td><td>845</td></tr>
<tr><td></td><td>$79,857.25</td><td>$8,369</td></tr>
</table>

1. Prepare a summary of payroll taxes for November similar to the one shown on page 127 of the textbook. Use the following rates: FICA, 7 percent; FUTA, .8 percent; and SUTA, 5.4 percent.
2. Post from the schedule to the departmental overhead analysis sheets.
3. Prepare a general journal voucher (11-4) to record the payroll taxes.
4. Post to the general ledger account Manufacturing Overhead Control 501.

Manufacturing Overhead

Overhead costs include both fixed and variable elements. Fixed overhead cost adjustments for November are identical to those for October. Therefore, use the schedule on text page 144 as a basis for the following steps:

1. Prepare a general journal voucher (11-5) to record the fixed overhead costs.
2. Post to the Manufacturing Overhead Control account.
3. Post to the departmental overhead analysis sheets.

Workers' compensation insurance is estimated as follows for the departments:

Milling $220
Assembling   230
Finishing   174
Building Services   58
General Factory   101

To enter these costs, perform the following steps:

1. Prepare a general journal voucher (11-6) to record workers' compensation insurance. Credit Worker's Compensation Insurance Payable 218.
2. Post to the Manufacturing Overhead Control account.
3. Post to the departmental overhead analysis sheets.

Applying Overhead to Completed Goods

Overhead costs are ordinarily applied to finished goods as soon as possible after the factory operations are completed. Jobs 118 and 119 were completed on November 30. Perform the following procedures for each job:

1. Compute and enter the applied overhead on the job cost sheets. The following overhead rates are to be used:

Milling $5.10 per direct labor hour
Assembling   4.71 per direct labor hour
Finishing   5.88 per direct labor hour

2. Record the amount of overhead applied in the manufacturing overhead applied journal.
3. Total all columns of the job cost sheets and complete the summary block on the job cost sheets.

Applying Overhead to Work in Process

Jobs 112 and 120 are incomplete at the end of November. Use the following procedures to apply overhead to these jobs:

1. Compute and enter the overhead to be applied for the month on the job cost sheets. Use the overhead rates given above for Jobs 118 and 119.
2. Record the amount of overhead applied in the manufacturing overhead applied journal.
3. Foot the columns of the job cost sheets.

Summary of Manufacturing Overhead Costs

Manufacturing overhead costs are drawn together by completing a monthly summary, as follows:

1. Total the departmental overhead analysis sheets.
2. Prepare a schedule of departmental overhead costs similar to the one shown on page 145 of this textbook.
3. Prepare a general journal voucher (11-7) to close Manufacturing Overhead Control 501 into the departmental manufacturing overhead accounts.
4. Post to the general ledger accounts involved.

Allocating Service Department Costs

The allocation of the cost of service departments to the producing departments is made easier by the preparation of a worksheet similar to the one shown on page 148 of the textbook. Building Services Department costs are to be allocated on the basis of floor space occupied (see page 147). General Factory Department costs are to be allocated on the basis of the direct labor costs shown by the factory wage summary for November that you have already prepared.

1. Complete the allocation worksheet.
2. Prepare general journal vouchers (11-8 and 11-9) to apportion the service department costs to the producing departments.
3. Post to the general ledger accounts.

Overapplied and Underapplied Overhead

Since the month's activities are completed, total the manufacturing overhead applied journal to prepare the way for the following steps:

1. Post the totals to the Work in Process account and to the appropriate departmental overhead accounts in the general ledger.
2. Close the balances of the departmental overhead accounts into Overapplied or Underapplied Manufacturing Overhead 507 by doing the following:
   a. Prepare a general journal voucher (11-10).
   b. Post the entry to the general ledger accounts involved. (The balance of Account 507 is continued from month to month.)

Completion of Jobs

Jobs 118 and 119 were completed during the period, and all costs have been totaled and summarized on the job cost sheets. Therefore, the following steps are to be performed:

1. Record completion of the two jobs in the completed jobs journal.
2. Total the completed jobs journal and post.
3. Since Job 118 was for stock, record the receipt of 100 desks (Stock 18) on the finished goods stock ledger card.

Sale of Finished Goods

Job 119 was manufactured for the Newport Wholesale Furniture Company and is shipped immediately upon completion, on November 30. The sale, amounting to $28,300, is covered by Invoice 719; the terms are 2/10, n/30.

1. Enter the sale in the sales journal.
2. Since this is the final sale of the month, total the sales journal.
3. Post to the accounts supplied.

Schedules

Schedules are prepared to prove the balances of the subsidiary ledgers to their control accounts in the general ledger before any financial statements are prepared.

1. Prepare a schedule of raw materials. Compare the total with the balance of Raw Materials 121.
2. Prepare a schedule of work in process. Compare the total with the balance of Work in Process 122.
3. Prepare a schedule of finished goods. Compare the total with the balance of Finished Goods 126.

Statements

The final cost data are now ready for inclusion in the monthly financial statements. Assume selling expenses of $8,463.40 and general expenses of $7,290.65, estimate federal income tax at 15 percent of net income for the period, and complete the following statements:

1. Schedule of manufacturing overhead for November
2. Statement of cost of goods manufactured for November
3. Income statement covering November operations

VOUCHER REGISTER for Month of _November_   19 _X1_   Page _11_

DATE	VOU. NO.	PAYABLE TO	PAID DATE	CHECK NO.	VOUCHERS PAYABLE CR. 201	RAW MATERIALS DR. 121	MFG. OHD. CONTROL DR. 501	OTHER DEBITS ✓	AMOUNT
Nov. 1-25	11-1 to 11-71	Various			79247 34	49349 02	1798 32		28100 00

MATERIALS REQUISITION JOURNAL
for Month of _November_   19 _X1_   Page _11_

DATE	REQ. NO.	✓	JOB OR DEPT.	WORK IN PROCESS DR. 122	MFG. OHD. CONTROL DR. 501	RAW MATERIALS CR. 121
Nov. 1-25	540-612		Var.	44399 00	3105 18	47504 18

RETURNED MATERIALS JOURNAL
for Month of _November_   19 _X1_   Page _11_

DATE	REPT. NO.	✓	JOB OR DEPT.	WORK IN PROCESS CR. 122	MFG. OHD. CONTROL CR. 501	RAW MATERIALS DR. 121
Nov. 1-25	61-69		Var.	298 70	31 90	330 60

MANUFACTURING OVERHEAD APPLIED JOURNAL
for Month of _November_ 19 X1   Page _11_

DATE	JOB NO.	WORK IN PROCESS DR. 122	MILLING DEPT. CR. 502		ASSEMBLING DEPT. CR. 503		FINISHING DEPT. CR. 504	
			HOURS	AMOUNT	HOURS	AMOUNT	HOURS	AMOUNT
Nov. 9	111	2309 22			122	574 62	295	1734 60
9	109	2944 65	139	708 90	225	1059 75	200	1176 00
16	110	6805 50	310	1581 00	510	2402 10	480	2822 40
16	116	2779 80	123	627 30	70	329 70	310	1822 80
16	114	4862 25	290	1479 00	375	1766 25	275	1617 00
23	117	5829 90	370	1887 00	550	2590 50	230	1352 40
23	113	2961 75	245	1249 50	195	918 45	135	793 80
23	115	2304 60	220	1122 00	120	565 20	105	617 40

COMPLETED JOBS JOURNAL
for Month of _November_ 19 X1   Page _11_

DATE	JOB NO.	MANUFACTURED FOR	FINISHED GOODS DR. 126 WORK IN PROCESS CR. 122 ✔	AMOUNT
Nov. 9	111	Stock 22 (Other Finished Goods)	✓	6916 40
9	109	Klarno School District		18494 20
16	110	Executives Office Furn. Co.		19941 85
16	116	Stock 18	✓	5321 50
16	114	Central Church Furniture Co.		31633 37
23	117	Mayfair Furniture Co.		15374 34
23	113	Stock 57 (Other Finished Goods)	✓	11249 55
23	115	Stock 337 (Other Finished Goods)	✓	12598 31

SALES JOURNAL for Month of _November_ 19 X1   Page _11_

DATE	INVOICE NUMBER	CUSTOMER'S NAME	TERMS	✔	ACCOUNTS REC. DR. 111 SALES CR. 401	COST OF GOODS SOLD DR. 415 FINISHED GOODS CR. 126
Nov. 1-25	695-715	Various	✓	✓	153348 63	117443 82

Factory Payroll Clearing   No. 500

DATE	EXPLANATION	POST. REF.	DEBIT	CREDIT	BALANCE	DR. CR.
19X1 Nov. 1	Balance	✓			1004800	Cr.
2		WP	1659000		654200	Dr.
9		WP	1593700		2247900	Dr.
15		SP	302400		2550300	Dr.
16		WP	1738400		4288700	Dr.
23		WP	1745700		6034400	Dr.

MATERIALS LEDGER CARDS

Material Legs, chrome   Reorder Point 225
Number K-196   Reorder Quantity 400

DATE	REFERENCE	RECEIVED UNITS	PRICE	AMOUNT	ISSUED UNITS	PRICE	AMOUNT	BALANCE UNITS	PRICE	AMOUNT
19X1 Nov. 25	Bal.							225	1450	326250

Material Tops, mica, 24"   Reorder Point 550
Number L-27   Reorder Quantity 1,000

DATE	REFERENCE	RECEIVED UNITS	PRICE	AMOUNT	ISSUED UNITS	PRICE	AMOUNT	BALANCE UNITS	PRICE	AMOUNT
19X1 Nov. 25	Bal.							580	218	126440

Material Pads, buffer   Reorder Point 500
Number I-16   Reorder Quantity 500

DATE	REFERENCE	RECEIVED UNITS	PRICE	AMOUNT	ISSUED UNITS	PRICE	AMOUNT	BALANCE UNITS	PRICE	AMOUNT
19X1 Nov. 25	Bal.							1,000	88	88000

Material All other materials   Reorder Point _____
Number _____   Reorder Quantity _____

DATE	REFERENCE	RECEIVED UNITS	PRICE	AMOUNT	ISSUED UNITS	PRICE	AMOUNT	BALANCE UNITS	PRICE	AMOUNT
19X1 Nov. 25	Bal.									367643

JOB COST SHEET

Customer *National Furniture Outlet*
Description *Customer's specs on file*
Quantity *300*

Job *112*
Date Started *10/16/X1*
Date Completed _____

\multicolumn{3}{c}{MATERIALS}			\multicolumn{8}{c}{DIRECT LABOR}								\multicolumn{11}{c}{MANUFACTURING OVERHEAD APPLIED}										
DATE	REQ. NO.	AMOUNT	DATE	REF.	MILLING HRS.	AMOUNT	ASSEMBLING HRS.	AMOUNT	FINISHING HRS.	AMOUNT	DATE	REF.	MILLING HRS.	RATE	AMOUNT	ASSEMBLING HRS.	RATE	AMOUNT	FINISHING HRS.	RATE	AMOUNT
11/1	Bal.	125474	11/1	TTA		52172					11/1	Bal			44630						
11/2	R540	76850	11/2	TTA	35	21875															
11/8	R551	69600	11/9	TTA	110	68750	33	19800													
11/21	R589	2900	11/16	TTA	35	21875	65	39000													
			11/23	TTA			100	60000	65	42250											

JOB COST SHEET

Customer *Stock*
Description *Desks #18*
Quantity *100*

Job *118*
Date Started *11/12/X1*
Date Completed _____

\multicolumn{3}{c}{MATERIALS}			\multicolumn{8}{c}{DIRECT LABOR}								\multicolumn{11}{c}{MANUFACTURING OVERHEAD APPLIED}										
DATE	REQ. NO.	AMOUNT	DATE	REF.	MILLING HRS.	AMOUNT	ASSEMBLING HRS.	AMOUNT	FINISHING HRS.	AMOUNT	DATE	REF.	MILLING HRS.	RATE	AMOUNT	ASSEMBLING HRS.	RATE	AMOUNT	FINISHING HRS.	RATE	AMOUNT
11/12	R566	261000	11/16	TTA	71	44375															
11/13	R568	20300	11/23	TTA	71	44375	67	40200													
11/18	R574	23200																			
11/23	R606	5800																			

JOB COST SHEET

Customer *Newport Whol. Furniture Co.*
Description *Customer's specs on file*
Quantity *150*

Job *119*
Date Started *11/19/X1*
Date Completed _____

\multicolumn{3}{c}{MATERIALS}			\multicolumn{8}{c}{DIRECT LABOR}								\multicolumn{11}{c}{MANUFACTURING OVERHEAD APPLIED}										
DATE	REQ. NO.	AMOUNT	DATE	REF.	MILLING HRS.	AMOUNT	ASSEMBLING HRS.	AMOUNT	FINISHING HRS.	AMOUNT	DATE	REF.	MILLING HRS.	RATE	AMOUNT	ASSEMBLING HRS.	RATE	AMOUNT	FINISHING HRS.	RATE	AMOUNT
11/19	R581	275000	11/23	TTA	60	37500	18	10800													
11/20	R588	28450																			
11/22	R601	2740																			
11/23	R609	17580																			

JOB COST SHEET

Customer _Conrad Office Supply_
Description _Customer's specs on file_
Quantity _120_

Job _120_
Date Started _11/21/X1_
Date Completed _____

MATERIALS			DIRECT LABOR									MANUFACTURING OVERHEAD APPLIED											
					MILLING		ASSEMBLING		FINISHING				MILLING			ASSEMBLING			FINISHING				
DATE	REQ. NO.	AMOUNT	DATE	REF.	HRS.	AMOUNT	HRS.	AMOUNT	HRS.	AMOUNT	DATE	REF.	HRS.	RATE	AMOUNT	HRS.	RATE	AMOUNT	HRS.	RATE	AMOUNT		
11/21	R591	287040	11/23	TTA	25	15625																	
11/22	R598	5520																					

DEPARTMENTAL OVERHEAD ANALYSIS SHEET

Department _Milling (1)_ Month of _November_ 19 _X1_

DATE	REF.	TOTAL	01 INDIRECT MATERIALS	02 INDIRECT LABOR	03 PAYROLL TAXES	04 DEPRECIATION	05 REPAIRS & MAINT.	06 UTILITIES	07 INSURANCE	08 OTHER TAXES	09 OTHER ITEM	AMOUNT
Nov. 1-25	Var.	295656	60269	205400			22572				Various	7415

DEPARTMENTAL OVERHEAD ANALYSIS SHEET

Department _Assembling (2)_ Month of _November_ 19 _X1_

DATE	REF.	TOTAL	01 INDIRECT MATERIALS	02 INDIRECT LABOR	03 PAYROLL TAXES	04 DEPRECIATION	05 REPAIRS & MAINT.	06 UTILITIES	07 INSURANCE	08 OTHER TAXES	09 OTHER ITEM	AMOUNT
Nov. 1-25	Var.	320816	70266 (1120)	237300			2930				Various	11440

DEPARTMENTAL OVERHEAD ANALYSIS SHEET

Department _Finishing (3)_ Month of _November_ 19 _X1_

DATE	REF.	TOTAL	01 INDIRECT MATERIALS	02 INDIRECT LABOR	03 PAYROLL TAXES	04 DEPRECIATION	05 REPAIRS & MAINT.	06 UTILITIES	07 INSURANCE	08 OTHER TAXES	09 OTHER ITEM	AMOUNT
Nov. 1-25	Var.	399215	99480 (1385)	269000			22615				Various	9505

DEPARTMENTAL OVERHEAD ANALYSIS SHEET

Department _Building Services (4)_   Month of _November_ 19 X1

DATE	REF.	TOTAL	01 INDIRECT MATERIALS	02 INDIRECT LABOR	03 PAYROLL TAXES	04 DEPRECIATION	05 REPAIRS & MAINT.	06 UTILITIES	07 INSURANCE	08 OTHER TAXES	09 OTHER ITEM	09 OTHER AMOUNT
Nov. 1-25	Var.	483523	32018 (685) 407200				38350				Various	6640

DEPARTMENTAL OVERHEAD ANALYSIS SHEET

Department _General Factory (5)_   Month of _November_ 19 X1

DATE	REF.	TOTAL	01 INDIRECT MATERIALS	02 INDIRECT LABOR	03 PAYROLL TAXES	04 DEPRECIATION	05 REPAIRS & MAINT.	06 UTILITIES	07 INSURANCE	08 OTHER TAXES	09 OTHER ITEM	09 OTHER AMOUNT
Nov. 1-25	Var.	777750	48485	670900			43525				Various	14840

FINISHED GOODS LEDGER

Material _Desks_
Number _18_

DATE	REFERENCE	RECEIVED UNITS	RECEIVED PRICE	RECEIVED AMOUNT	SOLD UNITS	SOLD PRICE	SOLD AMOUNT	BALANCE UNITS	BALANCE PRICE	BALANCE AMOUNT
19X1 Nov. 1	Bal.							30	107 30	321900
9	S702				20	107 30	214600	10	107 30	107300
16	J113	50	106 43	532150				10 / 50	107 30 / 106 43	639450

Material _End tables_
Number _327_

DATE	REFERENCE	RECEIVED UNITS	RECEIVED PRICE	RECEIVED AMOUNT	ISSUED UNITS	ISSUED PRICE	ISSUED AMOUNT	BALANCE UNITS	BALANCE PRICE	BALANCE AMOUNT
19X1 Nov. 1	Bal.							360	23 64	851040

Material _All other finished goods_
Number _Various_

DATE	REFERENCE	RECEIVED UNITS	RECEIVED PRICE	RECEIVED AMOUNT	SOLD UNITS	SOLD PRICE	SOLD AMOUNT	BALANCE UNITS	BALANCE PRICE	BALANCE AMOUNT
19X1 Nov. 25	Bal.									1674540

Space Savers, Inc.
Summary of Factory Wages
November 19X1

PAYROLL PERIOD	MILLING		ASSEMBLING		FINISHING		BUILDING SERVICES	GENERAL FACTORY	TOTAL
	DIRECT LABOR	INDIRECT LABOR	DIRECT LABOR	INDIRECT LABOR	DIRECT LABOR	INDIRECT LABOR			
Nov. 1-2	161700	21500	201600	27300	125800	69500	44000	51500	702900
3-9	369500	58500	504000	65000	315000	64500	86700	130500	1593700
1-15	—0—	—0—	—0—	—0—	—0—	—0—	87000	215400	302400
10-16	402000	62500	546000	72500	356500	67000	94500	137400	1738400
17-23	393000	62900	535500	72500	334000	68000	95000	136100	1697000

12

Scrap, Spoiled Goods, and Defective Goods

■ ■ ■

In the manufacturing activities discussed so far, it has been assumed that the materials issued were completely used up in the production of finished goods. However, in almost every factory certain losses of materials occur as an inevitable part of normal operations. Materials lost may take the form of scrap, spoiled goods, or defective goods.

A cost accounting system must provide for recording these losses, so that the unit cost figures will be as accurate as possible. The accounting technique varies according to the type of loss involved.

Accounting for Scrap

Scrap is the residue of manufacturing processes. In a radio assembly plant, it might include bits and pieces of wire and solder. In a metal toy factory, it would include blanks and countless fragments produced by punch-press operations. In a sawmill, it would be sawdust, bark, and discarded end pieces. Other scrap materials are paper, wood, or metal shavings; cloth remnants and clippings; and chemical sediments.

Scrap material has value. It is normally stored in a shed, hopper car, or pile until a marketable quantity is collected. Then it is sold to scrap dealers, other industries, or individuals. The cost accountant considers how much the scrap is worth, how fast it accumulates, and other factors in selecting a procedure for recording it.

Low-Value Scrap

If the value of the scrap is low and if it is sold at irregular intervals, customarily no entry is made in the accounts until the scrap is sold.

Credit to Miscellaneous Income. At the time of sale, the simplest recording procedure is to debit Cash or Accounts Receivable and to credit Miscellaneous Income. A sale for cash is recorded in the cash receipts journal. A sale on credit is entered on a general journal voucher, as shown on page 227.

JOURNAL VOUCHER	Date Oct. 9,		19 XX	No. 10-10	
ACCOUNT	ACCOUNT NUMBER	✓	DEBIT	CREDIT	
Accounts Receivable	111		60 00		
Miscellaneous Income	713			60 00	
EXPLANATION					
Sold scrap materials.					
PREPARED BY ang	AUDITED BY KLM		APPROVED BY PON		

Because of the difficulty of identifying scrap with a specific job or department, this is the procedure used by most manufacturers. Some firms, however, prefer to apply the proceeds from the sale of scrap to the cost of producing the product. There are two methods that may be used to accomplish this.

Credit to a Specific Job. Sometimes it is possible to determine the specific job from which the scrap accumulated. If so, and if the job requires a long time to complete, the proceeds from the sale are subtracted from the cost of the materials that have been charged to that job. The debit is to Cash or Accounts Receivable as before, but the credit is to Work in Process, as shown in general journal form below.

19XX				
Oct. 9	Accounts Receivable	111	60.00	
	Work in Process	122		60.00
	Sold scrap materials arising from Job 141.			

The credit amount is also recorded in the Materials column of the job cost sheet as an entry in parentheses to indicate that the cost reduction is an offset against previous charges, as shown on page 228.

Credit to Manufacturing Overhead. If the scrap cannot be identified with a specific job, the proceeds from the sale may be used to reduce product costs by crediting Manufacturing Overhead Control, as shown in general journal form below.

19XX				
Oct. 9	Accounts Receivable	111	60.00	
	Manufacturing Overhead Control	501		60.00
	Sold scrap materials arising from the Milling Department.			

JOB COST SHEET

Customer **Stock**
Description **Conference Table #479**
Quantity _____

Job **141**
Date Started **9/6/XX**
Date Completed _____

| MATERIALS | | | DIRECT LABOR | | MILLING | | ASSEMBLING | | FINISHING | | MANUFACTURING OVERHEAD APPLIED | | MILLING | | ASSEMBLING | | FINISHING | |
DATE	REQ. NO.	AMOUNT	DATE	REF.	HRS.	AMOUNT	HRS.	AMOUNT	HRS.	AMOUNT	DATE	REF.	HRS.	RATE	AMOUNT	HRS.	RATE	AMOUNT	HRS.	RATE	AMOUNT
9/6	R906	2700.00	9/12	TTA	200	1300.00															
9/8	R911	1350.00	9/18	TTA	100	675.00	65	462.00													
9/15	R920	162.00	9/24	TTA					75	518.00											
9/20	R924	108.00	10/6	TTA					75	542.00											
10/1	R935	270.00	10/13	TTA					30	205.00											
10/9	J10-10	(60.00)																			

The credit to Manufacturing Overhead Control is also recorded on the departmental overhead analysis sheet as an entry in parentheses, as shown below.

DEPARTMENTAL OVERHEAD ANALYSIS SHEET

Department **Milling**
Month of **October** 19 **XX**

DATE	REF.	TOTAL	01 INDIRECT MATERIALS	02 INDIRECT LABOR	06 ʼILITIES	07 INSURANCE	08 OTHER TAXES	09 OTHER ITEM	AMOUNT
Oct. 4	R943	121.00	121.00						
6	TTA	265.00		265.00					
7	R948	27.00	27.00						
9	J10-10	(60.00)						Scrap	(60.00)

This procedure assumes that the scrap can be associated with a specific producing department. If this cannot be done, a common practice is to credit the proceeds from the sale as a reduction of the costs of a service department.

High-Value Scrap

The valuable scrap material (such as precious metal shavings) that results from certain industrial processes requires special care in control and storage. For this reason, a *scrap report* is prepared when scrap is moved from the factory floor to storage, as shown on page 229.

The storeroom supervisor, who controls the scrap in storage, prepares a scrap inventory ledger card for each type of scrap. This card resembles a materials ledger card, as shown on page 229.

Fluctuating Value. When the market price for a scrap material changes often, the value of the scrap inventory is uncertain. The scrap inventory ledger card therefore

OLD DUTCH IRONWORKS
Plainview, Texas 79016

Date 11/5/XX   Department *Cutting*

No. 80248

Item No.	Description	Quantity	Unit Value	Total Value
	metal cuttings	*500 lbs.*		

Delivered by *X. N.*   Storeroom Clerk _____

FORM NO. S17

SCRAP INVENTORY LEDGER CARD

Material *Metal Cuttings*

DATE	REFERENCE	RECEIVED			ISSUED			BALANCE		
		UNITS	PRICE	AMOUNT	UNITS	PRICE	AMOUNT	UNITS	PRICE	AMOUNT
19XX Nov. 5	SR 80248	500 lbs.								

shows only the quantity. When the scrap is sold, the proceeds are debited to Cash or Accounts Receivable and credited to Miscellaneous Income, Work in Process, or Manufacturing Overhead Control. If the dollar amount is large, it should be identified with product costs whenever possible. Most accountants would therefore not use the Miscellaneous Income account. If Work in Process is credited, the amount must also be recorded on the job sheet. If Manufacturing Overhead Control is used, an entry must be made on the departmental overhead analysis sheet.

Stable Value.   When the market price for scrap material remains at a fairly constant level, the scrap report and the scrap inventory ledger card may show the market value as well as the quantity. Also, a new general ledger account, called *Scrap Inventory,* is opened. As soon as the scrap materials are moved from the factory floor, this account is debited for the estimated market value. The credit is to Work in Process, Manufacturing Overhead Control, or, rarely, Miscellaneous Income.

19XX			
Nov. 25	Scrap Inventory	118	250.00
	Work in Process	122	250.00
	Transferred 500 pounds of metal cuttings from factory to storeroom.		

Entries must be made on the job cost sheet if Work in Process is used or on the departmental overhead analysis sheet if Manufacturing Overhead Control is used.

When the scrap is sold, an entry is made debiting Accounts Receivable or Cash and crediting Scrap Inventory.

19XX				
Nov. 28	Accounts Receivable	111	250.00	
	Scrap Inventory	118		250.00
	Sold scrap at recorded value.			

Sale at Different Value. Sometimes scrap is sold for more or for less than the value at which it is recorded. Any difference between the sales price and the recorded value is treated as an adjustment to the account that was originally credited (Work in Process, Manufacturing Overhead Control, or Miscellaneous Income). For example, if the scrap in the illustration above were sold for only $225, the entry to record the sale would be as follows:

19XX				
Nov. 28	Accounts Receivable	111	225.00	
	Work in Process	122	25.00	
	Scrap Inventory	118		250.00
	Sold scrap at less than recorded value.			

Accounting for Spoiled Goods

Goods that have been damaged through imperfect machining or processing, so that they do not measure up to quality standards or specifications, are called *spoiled goods*. Spoiling occurs in batches or in isolated instances, whereas scrap is inevitable and recurs constantly in specific manufacturing processes. In some cases, spoiled goods may be sold as *seconds*. For example, textile and shoe manufacturers often produce goods with slight defects that are sold as seconds at substantial discounts. In other instances, spoiled goods must be discarded as waste.

The basic problem in accounting for spoiled goods is how the loss due to spoilage should be charged. The loss may be charged to manufacturing overhead and thus spread over all jobs worked on during the period. Or the loss may be charged to the particular job from which the spoiled goods were recovered.

If spoilage occurs often and is a regular part of the manufacturing process, it is not logical to charge the loss to a specific job merely because that job happened to be the one on which the spoilage occurred. On the other hand, if the spoilage is caused by unusual standards, specifications, or processes required for a particular job, that one job should bear the spoilage loss.

Loss Charged to Manufacturing Overhead

Most manufacturers charge routine, recurring spoilage to Manufacturing Overhead Control. Space Savers uses this procedure. To see how it works, assume that Job 161 calls for the production of 250 unpainted end tables (Model T). These tables were put into production in the Milling Department, and the costs accumulated to date are as follows:

	Total	Per Unit
Materials	$4,191.20	$16.7648
Labor		
Milling Department	499.20	1.9968
Assembling Department	361.00	1.6640
Finishing Department	55.00	
Manufacturing Overhead		
Milling Department	493.00	1.9720
Assembling Department	345.20	1.6024
Finishing Department	55.40	
Total	$6,000.00	$24.0000

Suppose that an inspector discovers that the lumber used in ten of the tables was improperly cured. These tables are spoiled goods that may be sold as seconds. If a dealer in unpainted furniture buys the tables for $10 each (a loss of $14 per table), the following steps are required:

1. A *spoiled goods report* is completed listing the quantity and the dollar value, as shown.

SPACE SAVERS INC.

1180 NORTHERN AVE.
CHICAGO, IL 60785

SPOILED GOODS REPORT

JOB _161_

DEPARTMENT _Milling_

REPORT NO. _16_

DATE _11/27/X2_

QUANTITY	DESCRIPTION	EST. UNIT VALUE	TOTAL EST. VALUE
10	Model T end tables	10 00	100 00

EXPLANATION: _lumber warped, improperly cured._

Department Foreman _K. T._   Received by _____

FORM NO. S16

2. A general journal entry is prepared, as shown on page 232, to do the following:
   a. Record the estimated sales value of the spoiled goods as a debit to a Spoiled Goods Inventory account (10 × $10 = $100).
   b. Record the loss as a debit to Manufacturing Overhead Control (10 × $14 = $140).
   c. Transfer the total cost of the spoiled goods from Work in Process by a credit entry (10 × $24 = $240).

```
19XX
Nov. 27    Spoiled Goods Inventory                    119    100.00
           Manufacturing Overhead Control             501    140.00
               Work in Process                        122              240.00
           Recorded estimated market value of spoiled
           goods (Job 161) and charged loss to
           Manufacturing Overhead—Milling Department.
```

3. The loss of $140 is recorded on the overhead analysis sheet for the Milling Department, as shown below.

DEPARTMENTAL OVERHEAD ANALYSIS SHEET
Department _Milling_

DATE	REF.	TOTAL	01 INDIRECT MATERIALS	02 INDIRECT LABOR	P	05 REPAIRS & MAINT.	I	09 OTHER ITEM	AMOUNT
Nov 3	R1014	18575	18575						
5	TTA	87600		87600					
12	TTA	91000		91000					
14	R1019	9000	9000						
19	TTA	57500		57500					
21	VR12	24450				24450			
26	TTA	41460		41460					
27	J11-27	14000						Sp. Goods	14000

4. The credit to Work in Process is recorded on the job cost sheet for Job 161 by entries in parentheses. The credits in the individual cost element columns are computed at 4 percent of previous charges because the quantity of spoiled goods represents 4 percent of the order (10 ÷ 250 = .04). For example, a credit entry of $14.44 (4 percent of the $361.00 accumulated total) is entered in the Assembling Amount column in the Direct Labor section, as shown on page 233.

After the above credit is posted, the summary block of the job cost sheet for Job 161 is completed. The cost of the remaining 240 tables amounts to $5,760, which is $24 per table ($5,760 ÷ 240 = $24). Note that $24 per table is the same as the cost would have been if there had been no spoiled goods and 250 good tables had been produced, as shown on page 233.

Loss Absorbed in the Cost of a Specific Job

If the loss on spoiled goods is to be left as part of the total cost of a specific job, a simple entry is made removing the estimated value of the spoiled goods from Work in Process. If Space Savers had used this procedure, the spoilage on Job 161 would have been recorded as shown on page 233.

JOB COST SHEET

Customer _Stock_
Description _Model T End Tables_
Quantity _250_

Job ___161___
Date Started _11/5/xx_
Date Completed _11/27/xx_

	MATERIALS			DIRECT LABOR									MANUFACTURING OVERHEAD APPLIED								
					MILLING		ASSEMBLING		FINISHING					MILLING			ASSEMBLING			FINISHING	
DATE	REQ. NO.	AMOUNT	DATE	REF.	HRS.	AMOUNT	HRS.	AMOUNT	HRS.	AMOUNT	DATE	REF.	HRS.	RATE	AMOUNT	HRS.	RATE	AMOUNT	HRS.	RATE	AMOUNT
11/5	R691	3950 00	11/5	TTA	75	499 20	56	361 00	8	55 00	11/27	MOA 11	75	6.573	493 00	56	6.163	345 20	8	6.925	55 40
11/7	R712	191 20	11/27	SGR 16		(19 97)		(14 44)		(2 20)					(19 72)			(13 81)			(2 21)
11/12	R778	50 00																			
11/27	SGR 16	(167 65)																			
Total		4023 55				479 23		346 56		52 80					473 28			331 39			53 19

TOTAL COST $ _5,760.00_
UNITS PRODUCED _240_
COST PER UNIT $ _24.00_
COMMENTS:

10 tables spoiled (4% of original order)

SUMMARY

MATERIALS	$4,023.55
LABOR—MILLING	479.23
LABOR—ASSEMBLING	346.56
LABOR—FINISHING	52.80
OVERHEAD—MILLING	473.28
OVERHEAD—ASSEMBLING	331.39
OVERHEAD—FINISHING	53.19
TOTAL	$5,760.00

19XX				
Nov. 27	Spoiled Goods Inventory	119	100.00	
	Work in Process	122		100.00
	Removed estimated market value of spoiled goods			
	(Job 161) from Work in Process.			

The exact form of the entry on the job cost sheet depends upon whether the value of the spoiled goods is considered a reduction of materials costs, labor costs, overhead costs, or all three.

Reduction of Cost Elements. If the cost accountant prefers to record the $100 as a reduction involving each of the cost elements, the estimated value of the spoiled goods must be apportioned. The apportionment is usually done on the basis of the relative amount of cost incurred on the job to date. In the example, the division of the value of the spoiled goods would be made as shown on page 234.

Allocation of Estimated Market Value of Spoiled Goods to Individual Cost Elements

MATERIALS

$$\frac{\text{Materials Cost, \$4,191.20}}{\text{Total Cost, \$6,000.00}} \times \text{Spoiled Goods Value, \$100.00} \quad = \quad \$69.85$$

LABOR—MILLING DEPARTMENT

$$\frac{\text{Dept. Labor Cost, \$499.20}}{\text{Total Cost, \$6,000.00}} \times \text{Spoiled Goods Value, \$100.00} \quad = \quad 8.32$$

LABOR—ASSEMBLING DEPARTMENT

$$\frac{\text{Dept. Labor Cost, \$361.00}}{\text{Total Cost, \$6,000.00}} \times \text{Spoiled Goods Value, \$100.00} \quad = \quad 6.02$$

LABOR—FINISHING DEPARTMENT

$$\frac{\text{Dept. Labor Cost, \$55.00}}{\text{Total Cost, \$6,000.00}} \times \text{Spoiled Goods Value, \$100.00} \quad = \quad .92$$

OVERHEAD—MILLING DEPARTMENT

$$\frac{\text{Dept. Overhead Cost, \$493.00}}{\text{Total Cost, \$6,000.00}} \times \text{Spoiled Goods Value, \$100.00} = \quad 8.22$$

OVERHEAD—ASSEMBLING DEPARTMENT

$$\frac{\text{Dept. Overhead Cost, \$345.20}}{\text{Total Cost, \$6,000.00}} \times \text{Spoiled Goods Value, \$100.00} = \quad 5.75$$

OVERHEAD—FINISHING DEPARTMENT

$$\frac{\text{Dept. Overhead Cost, \$55.40}}{\text{Total Cost, \$6,000.00}} \times \text{Spoiled Goods Value, \$100.00} \quad = \quad .92$$

Total Estimated Market Value $\underline{\underline{\$100.00}}$

Based on these computations, entries in parentheses would be made on the job cost sheet, as shown on page 235.

Reduction of Total Cost. A simpler solution is to show one entry in parentheses for the total value of the spoiled goods ($100) on the job cost sheet and to deduct this amount from the total cost of the job. If this is done, it is not necessary to analyze the value of the spoiled goods by department. No special entries are needed in the individual columns of the job cost sheet for each of the various cost elements.

When the $100 is entered as a reduction on the job cost sheet for Job 161, the cost of the remaining tables is $5,900 ($6,000 − $100), or $24.5833 each. Thus,

JOB COST SHEET

Customer: **Stock**
Description: **Model T End Tables**
Quantity: **250**

Job: **161**
Date Started: **11/5/xx**
Date Completed: **11/27/xx**

MATERIALS			DIRECT LABOR		MILLING		ASSEMBLING		FINISHING		MANUFACTURING OVERHEAD APPLIED		MILLING			ASSEMBLING			FINISHING		
DATE	REQ. NO.	AMOUNT	DATE	REF.	HRS.	AMOUNT	HRS.	AMOUNT	HRS.	AMOUNT	DATE	REF.	HRS.	RATE	AMOUNT	HRS.	RATE	AMOUNT	HRS.	RATE	AMOUNT
11/5	R691	3950 00	11/5	TTA	75	499 20	56	361 00	8	55 00	11/27	MOA 11	75	6.573	493 00	56	6.163	345 20	8	6.925	55 40
11/7	R712	191 20	11/27	SGR 16		(8 32)		(6 02)		(92)	11/27	SGR 16			(8 22)			(5 75)			(92)
11/12	R778	50 00																			
11/27	SGR 16	(69 85)																			
Total		4121 35				490 88		354 98		54 08					484 78			339 45			54 48

TOTAL COST $**5,900.00**
UNITS PRODUCED **240**
COST PER UNIT $**24.5833**
COMMENTS:

10 tables spoiled (4% of original order)

SUMMARY

MATERIALS	$4,121.35
LABOR—MILLING	490.88
LABOR—ASSEMBLING	354.98
LABOR—FINISHING	54.08
OVERHEAD—MILLING	484.78
OVERHEAD—ASSEMBLING	339.45
OVERHEAD—FINISHING	54.48
TOTAL	$5,900.00

SUMMARY

MATERIALS	$4,191.20
LABOR—MILLING	499.20
LABOR—ASSEMBLING	361.00
LABOR—FINISHING	55.00
OVERHEAD—MILLING	493.00
OVERHEAD—ASSEMBLING	345.20
OVERHEAD—FINISHING	55.40
TOTAL	$6,000.00
Less Spoiled Goods	(100.00)
Net Cost	$5,900.00

under this method, each of the 240 tables has absorbed $.5833 of the loss on the spoiled goods ($24.5833 − $24 = $.5833, and $.5833 × 240 = $140 loss).

It is obvious that if the product has been processed through several departments, complex computations are required to record the value of the spoiled goods as a reduction involving each of the cost elements. Therefore, most companies use the simpler procedure of reducing the total cost.

Accounting for Defective Goods

Units of production that fail to meet production standards but that can be brought up to standard by putting in more materials, labor, and overhead are generally referred to as *defective goods*. The additional costs required to bring these goods up to standard are known as *rework costs*.

Accounting for rework costs may be handled in two ways.

1. The additional manufacturing costs are charged to Manufacturing Overhead Control, and are thus spread over all jobs.
2. The additional costs are charged to the particular job of which they are a part.

Rework Costs Charged to Manufacturing Overhead

If defective goods appear often in a firm's normal operations, the rework costs are usually treated as an addition to manufacturing overhead. The defects may result from mass-production techniques and have no special connection with a specific job or production order. The rework costs applied to goods that became defective through an accident or negligence are also charged to manufacturing overhead. Space Savers, Inc., uses this method of charging the rework costs of defective goods as manufacturing overhead.

To illustrate the procedure, assume that a specific job of 200 tables is being completed for stock. A quick-dry varnish is applied incorrectly to the tables by a new employee in the Finishing Department. As a result, the varnish on four tables is blotched and must be removed and reapplied. The additional costs of reworking the tables consist of materials, $5; labor, $16; and manufacturing overhead applied, $18.78. These costs are charged to the manufacturing overhead of the Finishing Department.

Accounting for the rework costs is simplified at Space Savers by treating the rework operation as a separate job. Materials, labor, and overhead are charged in the regular manner to the rework job. Cost details are recorded on a new job cost sheet.

When the units have been reprocessed, an entry is made to transfer the rework costs to manufacturing overhead as follows:

19XX				
Nov. 29	Manufacturing Overhead Control	501	39.78	
	Work in Process	122		39.78
	Transferred cost of reworked defective units (Job 153) to Manufacturing Overhead.			

An appropriate entry to record the $39.78 is made in the Other column of the departmental overhead analysis sheet of the Finishing Department.

Treating the rework operation as a separate job permits entries for materials, labor, and overhead to be made in the regular way. It also allows the total cost of a rework operation to be accumulated and reported. Management can then see the cost and take corrective action.

Rework Costs Charged to a Specific Job

If the rework costs are charged to the job of which the defective units are a part, no special accounting procedures are necessary. The additional materials, labor, and overhead are recorded in the normal manner and are entered on the job cost sheet for that job. The final unit costs will reflect both regular and reprocessing costs. Unit costs may vary a great deal from job to job when this method is used.

Principles and Procedures Summary

Modern mass-production methods of factory operation often result in some losses of materials as scrap, spoiled goods, and defective goods. The procedure of accounting for these losses varies with the type of loss, value, frequency, and other factors.

Scrap is material residue from manufacturing operations. If the scrap is of low value and does not occur often, no record is made until it is sold. Then the simplest recording procedure is to credit the proceeds to Miscellaneous Income. These scrap losses may also be credited to Work in Process or Manufacturing Overhead (with entries in related subsidiary ledgers). The difficulty of identifying the loss with a job or department makes this procedure impractical when a small dollar value is involved.

High-value scrap is recorded on a scrap report and moved to a storage area. The storeroom supervisor enters the amount of scrap on a scrap inventory ledger card. If the scrap has a stable and easily measurable value, the scrap inventory records will show dollar value as well as quantity. If not, the records will list quantity only until the scrap is sold. The proceeds from high-value scrap are normally used to reduce Work in Process or Manufacturing Overhead Control.

Spoiled goods appear less often than scrap. They may be sold as seconds or treated as scrap. The losses involved may be charged to manufacturing overhead or to a particular job. The first method spreads the cost over all jobs completed during the period. The second method is justified when the spoilage is directly related to special processes or exacting specifications required for a particular job.

Defective goods also represent a loss to a firm. However, these items can be reprocessed into salable merchandise. The costs of the reprocessing, known as rework costs, may be charged to manufacturing overhead or added to existing charges against a specific job. Again, the deciding factor is the nature of the defect. If it is a recurring result of typical production processes, the loss is charged to manufacturing overhead. If it is unusual and identifiable with a specific job, it should be added to the cost of that job.

Review Questions

1. What are the three categories of lost materials?
2. What is scrap? Give three examples.
3. What are two factors that should be considered by the cost accountant in selecting a procedure for recording scrap?
4. When scrap has a low value, what account is credited for the proceeds of its sale?

5. If scrap can be identified with a special job, what account is credited for the proceeds of its sale?
6. If scrap can be identified with a specific department, what account is credited for the proceeds of its sale?
7. What is a scrap report and when is it used?
8. Scrap may have a high value that changes often. If this is the case, when is the transfer from the factory to the storeroom recorded? What information is given?
9. Scrap may have a high value that is relatively stable. If this is the case, when is the transfer of the scrap from the factory to the storeroom recorded? What information is given?
10. Are gains and losses recorded on the sale of scrap? Explain.
11. What are spoiled goods?
12. What are seconds?
13. What are two ways of accounting for the loss due to spoiled goods?
14. When spoilage is routine and recurring, what account should be charged for the loss?
15. Define defective goods. What are rework costs?
16. List two ways of accounting for rework costs.

Managerial Discussion Questions

1. When would management want the cost of spoiled goods to be considered as a part of the cost of the specific job on which the spoilage occurred?
2. At the Sampson Company, the cost of spoiled goods averages about 4 percent of the total manufacturing costs. Management learns that the cost of spoiled goods at the Mulligan Supply Company, a competitor that produces a similar product, averages less than 1 percent of the total manufacturing costs. Comment on the managerial implications of this. What factors could cause such a difference?
3. The management of the Cedar Rapids Manufacturing Corporation learns that the cost allocated to spoiled goods on Job 833 totals $3,860. They are also told that the goods could be sold for $3,450 if additional costs of $950 are incurred. What would be your recommendation to management regarding these goods?
4. Why should management keep a close watch on any changes in the ratio of costs of spoiled goods to total manufacturing costs?
5. When would management want to maintain a perpetual inventory for scrap?

Exercises

1. **Recording a sale of scrap.** On June 15, 19X7, the Wagner Manufacturing Company sold scrap with a low value. The scrap was sold on credit for $650 and the company records such proceeds as Miscellaneous Income. Prepare the general journal entry to record this sale.
2. **Recording a sale of scrap.** The partially completed job cost sheet for Job 351 is shown on page 239. On April 19, 19X8, scrap material was recovered from this job and sold on credit for $475.
   a. Prepare the general journal entry to record the sale of this scrap.
   b. How should the sale of scrap be recorded on the job cost sheet?
   c. What is the total materials cost for Job 351?
3. **Recording a sale of scrap.** The Nash Manufacturing Company sold scrap for $2,380 on credit. The scrap was sold on May 31, 19X8, and had accumulated

JOB COST SHEET

Customer *Kelley Furniture Store*
Description *Table, Model #384 – Walnut*
Quantity *100*

Job *351*
Date Started *4/1/X8*
Date Completed _____

MATERIALS			DIRECT LABOR		MILLING		ASSEMBLING		FINISHING		MANUFACTURING OVERHEAD APPLIED		MILLING			ASSEMBLING			FINISHING.		
DATE	REQ. NO.	AMOUNT	DATE	REF.	HRS.	AMOUNT	HRS.	AMOUNT	HRS.	AMOUNT	DATE	REF.	HRS.	RATE	AMOUNT	HRS.	RATE	AMOUNT	HRS.	RATE	AMOUNT
4/1	R840	800.00	4/4	TTA	85	446.25															
4/2	R871	2145.00	4/11	TTA	110	575.50	38	247.00													
4/6	RM-58	(53.00)	4/17	TTA			125	812.50													
4/12	R892	1827.00																			
4/17	R910	2815.00																			
4/18	RM-61	(82.50)																			
4/19	R953	1135.00																			
		(475)																			

during the month in the Assembling Department, which is to receive credit for the proceeds.

   a. Prepare the general journal entry to record the sale of this scrap.

   b. How should the sale of the scrap be recorded on the departmental overhead analysis sheet?

4. **Accounting for spoiled goods.** Job 451 was completed on June 25, 19X7. The job was for 300 chairs ordered by the Davenport Company. The job cost sheet shows the following costs incurred:

Materials	$6,390
Labor—Milling	2,460
Labor—Assembling	1,875
Labor—Finishing	1,950
Overhead—Milling	2,091
Overhead—Assembling	1,594
Overhead—Finishing	1,658

Upon inspection, 24 chairs were found to be spoiled and could be sold as seconds for $45 each.

   a. Prepare the general journal entry to establish the spoiled goods inventory, assuming that the loss is charged to Manufacturing Overhead.

   b. Determine the amount of the credits to be recorded in the individual cost element columns of the job cost sheet for Job 451.

5. **Accounting for spoiled goods.** Assume the same facts as in Exercise 4 except that the loss is to be absorbed in the cost of Job 451.

   a. Prepare the general journal entry to establish the spoiled goods inventory.

   b. Determine the amount of the credits to be recorded in the individual cost element columns of the job cost sheet for Job 451.

6. **Accounting for defective goods.** In completing Job 650, 15 units were found to be defective and required rework costs of $1,130.76. The rework costs were recorded on a new job cost sheet. What general journal entry is needed to transfer the rework costs to manufacturing overhead?

Problems

PROBLEM 12-1. Recording a sale of scrap. The Eastern Nevada Supply Company applies the proceeds from the sale of scrap against the cost of production. On April 10, 19X8, scrap was sold on credit for $3,120.

Instructions
Prepare a general journal entry to record the sale of the scrap in each of the following cases. Use the account names in your textbook.

1. The firm credits the income from the sale of scrap to Job 717, from which it was derived.
2. The firm credits the income from the sale of scrap to the Manufacturing Overhead Control account for the Fabricating Department, where the scrap originated.

PROBLEM 12-2. Recording scrap inventory. Melendez Manufacturers maintains a Scrap Inventory account for metal scrap recovered from operations in the Molding Department. On February 15, 19X6, 1,500 pounds of scrap with an estimated market value of $975 are transferred from the factory to the storeroom.

Instructions
Use the account names found in your textbook to do the following:

1. Prepare the general journal entry to record the storage of the metal scrap. Credit Work in Process.
2. Prepare the general entry to record the sale of 300 pounds of scrap at $.58 a pound on credit.
3. Prepare the general journal entry to record the sale of 500 pounds of scrap at $.72 a pound on credit.

PROBLEM 12-3. Recording spoiled and defective goods. The Fairbanks Machine Company produced 4,000 units on Job 218 at a unit cost of $55 each. On September 8, 19X7, it is found that 60 units have defects and have an estimated sales value of only $34 each.

Instructions
Use the account names found in your textbook to do the following:

1. a. Assume that the units are spoiled. Prepare the general journal entry to record the estimated market value of the rejected units. Assume that the spoilage costs are to be charged to Manufacturing Overhead Control.
   b. Compute the unit cost of the remaining finished units.
2. a. Prepare the general journal entry to record the estimated market value of the rejected units. Assume that the spoilage costs are to be absorbed in the cost of the specific job.
   b. Compute the unit cost of the remaining finished units.

3. Assume that the units are defective instead of spoiled. Prepare the general journal entry to record the total rework costs of $585. Also assume that Job 229 is assigned to the necessary rework. The rework is completed on September 8, and the rework costs are to be charged to Manufacturing Overhead Control.

PROBLEM 12-4. Recording a sale of scrap. Carey Business Supply manufactures various types of paper forms for use in business. Scrap paper is accumulated and periodically sold. The value of this scrap is quite small. Therefore, the company merely collects the material from the factory floor and stores it until it is sold, at which time an entry is made.

Job 439, for a large quantity of carbon-back forms, was in production during the month of May 19X7. Scrap materials from this job were collected and sold on June 6, 19X7, for $267 in cash.

Instructions

Give the general journal entry to record the sale in each of the following cases. Also indicate which subsidiary records would be affected.

1. Sales proceeds to be treated as income.
2. Sales proceeds to be treated as a recovery from the specific job.
3. Sales proceeds to be treated as a reduction of manufacturing overhead.

PROBLEM 12-5. Recording spoiled goods. During the month of November 19X6, the following events involving losses from spoilage took place at the Lombardo Tool Company.

On November 8 the control mechanism on an automatic machine became defective while Job 384 for 200 units was in production. As a result, nine units for which materials had cost $198 were spoiled. Estimated sales value as seconds is $55 each. Total costs accumulated to date on the order are: materials, $6,600; direct labor, $10,800; and manufacturing overhead, $5,400.

Instructions

1. Give the general journal entry to have the loss on the nine spoiled units absorbed by Job 384.
2. Compute the allocation of the estimated market value of the nine spoiled items to the individual cost elements on Job 384.
3. The spoiled items were later sold on November 29 for $400 cash. Give the general journal entry to record this sale.

Alternate Problems

PROBLEM 12-1A. Recording a sale of scrap. The Gibson Manufacturing Company applies the proceeds from the sale of scrap against the cost of production. On October 15, 19X8, scrap was sold on credit for $782.

Instructions

Prepare a general journal entry to record the sale of the scrap in each of the following cases. Use the account names in your textbook.

1. The firm credits the income from the sale of scrap to Job 484, from which it was derived.

2. The firm credits the income from the sale of scrap to the Manufacturing Over-head Control account for the Fabricating Department, where the scrap originated.

PROBLEM 12-2A. Recording scrap inventory. The Richter Supply Corporation maintains a Scrap Inventory account for metal scrap recovered from operations in the Cutting Department. On December 12, 19X4, 5,300 pounds of scrap with an estimated market value of $2,385 are transferred from the factory to the storeroom.

Instructions

Use the same account names found in your textbook to do the following:

1. Prepare the general entry to record the storage of the metal scrap. Credit Work in Process.
2. Prepare the general journal entry to record the cash sale of 1,900 pounds of scrap at recorded value.
3. Prepare the general journal entry to record the sale of 2,100 pounds of scrap at $.52 a pound on credit.
4. Prepare the general journal entry to record the sale on credit of 1,300 pounds of scrap at $.39 a pound.

PROBLEM 12-3A. Recording spoiled and defective goods. The Newton Corporation produced 500 units of Job 451 at a unit cost of $15 each. On January 4, 19X8, inspection shows that 17 units have defects and have an estimated sales value of only $6 each.

Instructions

Use the account names found in your textbook to do the following:

1. a. Assume that the units are spoiled. Prepare the general journal entry to record the estimated market value of the rejected units as a debit to Spoiled Goods Inventory. Assume that the spoilage costs are to be charged to Manufacturing Overhead Control.
   b. Compute the unit cost of the remaining finished units.
2. a. Prepare the general journal entry to record the estimated market value of the rejected units. Assume that the spoilage costs are to be absorbed in the cost of the specific job.
   b. Compute the unit cost of the remaining finished units.
3. Assume that the units are defective instead of spoiled. Prepare the general journal entry to record the total rework costs of $35. Also assume that Job 470 is assigned to the necessary rework. The rework is completed on January 4, and the rework costs are to be charged to Manufacturing Overhead Control.

PROBLEM 12-4A. Recording a sale of scrap. The Flores Motor Corporation manufactures various types of electric motors on special order. Scrap metal is accumulated and periodically sold. The value of this scrap is quite small. Therefore, the company merely collects the material from the factory floor and stores it until it is sold, at which time an entry is made.

Job 748 was in production during the month of July 19X8. Scrap materials from this job were collected and sold on August 10 for $714 in cash.

Instructions

Give the general journal entry to record the sale for cash in each of the following cases. Also indicate which subsidiary records would be affected.

1. Sales proceeds to be treated as income.
2. Sales proceeds to be treated as a recovery from the specific job.
3. Sales proceeds to be treated as a reduction of manufacturing overhead.

PROBLEM 12-5A. Recording spoiled goods. During the month of March 19X7, the following events involving losses from spoilage took place at the Woodridge Corporation. On March 14, a heating mechanism on a cooking machine became defective while Job 743 for 70 units was in production. As a result, four units for which materials had cost $24 were spoiled. Estimated sales value as seconds is $56 each. Total costs accumulated to date on the order are: materials, $420; direct labor, $735; and manufacturing overhead, $315.

Instructions

1. Give the general journal entry to have the loss on the four spoiled units absorbed by Job 743.
2. Compute the allocation of the estimated market value of the four spoiled items to the individual cost elements on Job 743.
3. The spoiled items were sold for $75 on credit on March 28. Give the general journal entry to record the sale.

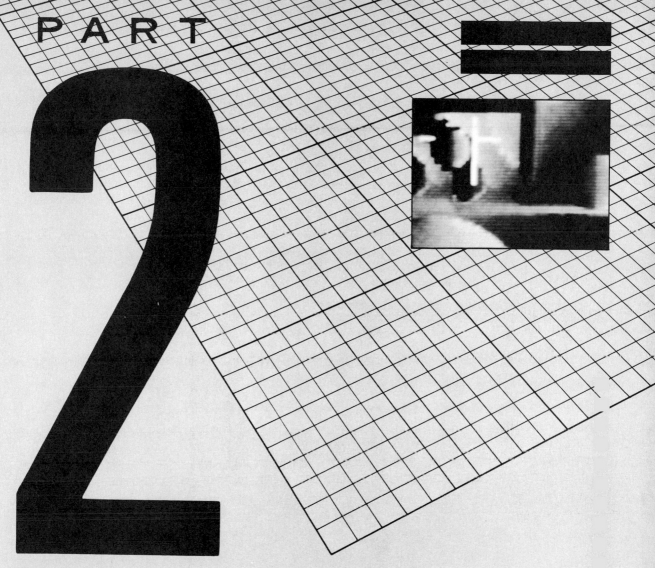

PART

2

Process

Cost

Accounting

CHAPTER

13

Process Cost System

In Chapter 2 you learned that a firm's cost accounting system parallels its flow of operations. In later chapters you studied Space Savers' flow of operations. This flow consisted of procurement, production, warehousing, and selling for each separate job or special order. The cost accountant chose a job order cost accounting system to meet Space Savers' needs. Other firms' needs are best met with a process cost system.

Choosing a Cost System

A job order cost system is expensive to operate even in a modest-sized business because of the work involved in analyzing each cost and recording it on a job cost sheet. For example, all materials used and all direct labor hours must be recorded by job number. As a result, a job order cost system should be used only when costs must be identified with specific jobs. A process cost system requires much less effort and expense in accumulating costs than a job order cost system.

The process cost system is used in accounting for costs in mass-production operations such as flour milling, gasoline refining, cement production, and the manufacture of insulating materials for houses. Typically, in such operations, all goods are produced for stock, one unit of production is identical with the other, goods move down the production line in a continuous stream, and all factory procedures are standardized. The identification of any specific unit of production or specific unit cost is not feasible because costs cannot be readily identified with any single unit of product or group of units. Identification is not necessary because all units manufactured are identical and are not "made to order" for a specific customer. Under these conditions, an average cost per unit is adequate for most control purposes. The *average cost per unit* is obtained by dividing total costs by total production.

The Flow of Process Costs

Many procedures and records used in the process cost system are similar to those in job order cost accounting. Here is an overview of the process cost system.

Procurement

Three familiar general ledger accounts are used: Raw Materials 121; Factory Payroll Clearing 500, and Manufacturing Overhead Control 501.

Materials. Purchases of materials are first recorded in the voucher register and are charged to the Raw Materials account. The raw materials inventory is controlled through the materials ledger. Issues are made by an authorized requisition or a bill of materials, and requisitions are recorded in a materials requisition journal. It is often unnecessary to distinguish between the direct and indirect materials used in a given process because both types of materials apply proportionately to all units manufactured during the period. Also, some firms using process costing do not keep perpetual inventory records for raw materials, especially if only a single product is manufactured. Instead, a monthly inventory is taken, and the cost of materials used is computed and recorded at that time.

Labor. The same time card and payroll summary procedures are used as in the job order cost system. Since there are no individual jobs, a daily time ticket for each worker is used to accumulate the data required for charging labor costs to departments. The charging is done in a weekly or monthly payroll analysis by processes or departments. As with materials costs, many accountants do not distinguish between direct and indirect labor costs incurred in producing departments. They prefer to charge both directly to the Work in Process accounts for the departments.

Overhead. Other manufacturing costs are recorded as usual through the payroll register, the voucher register, and general journal vouchers. Details are posted to departmental overhead analysis sheets in the same way as under job order costing. At the end of the month, overhead costs are allocated to producing departments or processes, as explained later.

Production

Costs are charged to Work in Process by one of several arrangements, according to the complexity of the firm's operations.

- A single Work in Process account may be used by a company that has only one producing department or continuously produces a single product, such as ice, salt, cement, a single style of chair, or a single type of sheet metal.
- Departmental Work in Process accounts are preferable if production flows through several cost centers or departments. Separate cost figures for each process might also be desirable. This is the most commonly used procedure and is the one illustrated on page 248.
- A separate Work in Process account for each of the three cost elements allows more accurate costing if the business produces multiple products. Costs can later be analyzed for identification with each production run.
- A Work in Process account for each product is commonly used if a number of products are processed in the same department.

You are already familiar with the use of a single Work in Process account. Now let us examine the procedures involved in the second plan—departmental Work in Process accounts. A firm with three departments would have the following accounts:

123	Work in Process—Department 1
124	Work in Process—Department 2
125	Work in Process—Department 3

Costs are charged against production as follows:

1. The costs of materials issued during the month are charged to Work in Process and to Manufacturing Overhead through postings from the materials requisition journal.

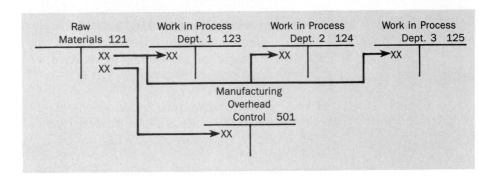

2. Labor charges are obtained from monthly summaries of payroll by processes.

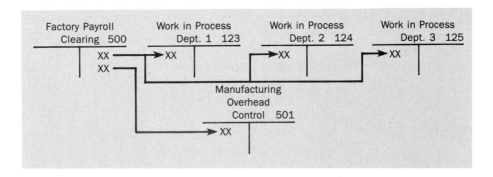

3. Manufacturing overhead costs that have been accumulated and classified in departmental overhead analysis sheets during the period (usually a month) are allocated to producing departments or processes. They may be allocated either directly, by predetermined rate, or by some combination plan.

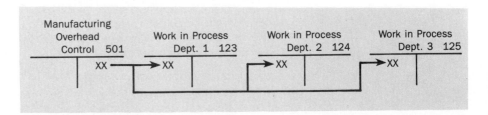

4. Output data from each department are summarized in periodic production reports. Then the average costs are computed and presented in cost of production reports.
5. Costs are transferred from one process to the other as the product flows toward completion.

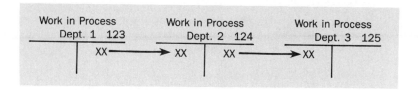

Warehousing

When the goods are finished and transferred to the warehouse to await sale, their cost is debited to Finished Goods 126. The corresponding credit is posted to the Work in Process account of the last department in the producing sequence.

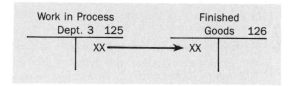

Selling

The cost of products sold is debited to Cost of Goods Sold 415 and credited to Finished Goods 126. In turn, Sales 401 is credited for the selling price, and Cash or Accounts Receivable is debited.

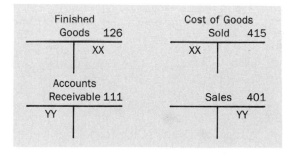

Operations Reorganized at Space Savers

You already have a general idea of the nature and purpose of process cost accounting and of the basic recording procedures involved. Now it is time to learn how a typical system works in detail.

After several years of successful experience in the manufacturing of tables and desks to order and for stock, the management of Space Savers, Inc., has decided to change its marketing policy. Instead of supplying a variety of products, the firm has decided to concentrate on the manufacture and sale of only one product, the Model 298 desk. A large furniture wholesaler has contracted to purchase several thousand of these desks every year and to take periodic deliveries. Other trade buyers have also expressed strong interest in placing quantity orders on the same terms.

Space Savers' decision was made after careful consideration of the profit margins obtained from its special order business and from the sale of its line of stock items. The new plans appear to be more promising for the following reasons:

1. Concentration on one consistently profitable product lowers the cost and increases the profit margin because of specialization of labor and a reduction in the variety of equipment and workers needed.
2. Sales contracts permit scheduling production more evenly throughout the year.
3. Stable production means more uninterrupted employment for workers.
4. Regular workers become more and more skilled at their jobs, resulting in superior workmanship, possibly even at a lower cost.
5. Selling a single product to a limited number of outlets reduces marketing and administrative costs to a minimum.
6. The streamlining of operations combined with the full use of equipment in the most profitable direction is expected to produce greater net gains.

This change in policy requires a change from the job order cost accounting system to the process cost accounting system. Production no longer centers around individual jobs. Average costs are adequate in the new continuous flow of operations because every item produced is identical and requires the same amount of materials, labor, and overhead. While the cost accountant works out the new procedures in detail, the following steps are taken to prepare for a smooth changeover on January 1, 19X5:

1. During December 19X4, all jobs previously begun are completed and removed from the factory.
2. All stocks of raw materials not required for the manufacture of the Model 298 desk are liquidated.
3. Equipment in the factory is modified to meet the new requirements for continuous production.
4. Sales and administrative staffs are reduced or reassigned.
5. The job cost ledger is discontinued.

Process Cost System at Space Savers

On January 1, 19X5, the process system of cost accounting is instituted at Space Savers. Many of the changes are minor. Some of the accounting procedures even become simpler.

Procurement

The cost records relating to the procurement functions remain unchanged. The same three general ledger accounts are used.

121 Raw Materials
500 Factory Payroll Clearing
501 Manufacturing Overhead Control

Purchases of materials are recorded in the purchases journal, and a materials ledger is maintained. Weekly and semimonthly payroll registers are prepared as before.

Production

The single general ledger account Work in Process 122 and its related subsidiary job cost ledger are eliminated. Since production will flow through all three producing departments, a separate Work in Process account is opened for each:

123   Work in Process—Milling Department
124   Work in Process—Assembling Department
125   Work in Process—Finishing Department

The use of three Work in Process accounts permits the pinpointing of responsibility for production costs to the individual department managers.

Costs are charged into production as materials and services are used in factory operations. The materials requisition journal, monthly payroll summary, voucher register, and general journal vouchers are used to do this. All materials issued are recorded in the materials requisition journal. The materials requisition journal contains a column for accumulating the costs of the direct materials requisitioned by each producing department, which are charged to the Work in Process account for each department, and for accumulating the costs of the indirect materials, which are charged to Manufacturing Overhead Control. A payroll summary provides the basis for charging salaries and wages to the departments.

During the month, overhead costs are accumulated in Manufacturing Overhead Control 501 and on the departmental overhead analysis sheets in exactly the same manner as under the job order cost system. These postings come from the materials requisition journal, the payroll summary, the voucher register, and general journal vouchers. At the end of the month, service department overhead costs are allocated to producing departments on a worksheet, as shown on page 254. Then Manufacturing Overhead Control 501 is closed directly into the three departmental Work in Process accounts by an entry on a general journal voucher.

Warehousing

Cost procedures related to warehousing are almost the same as those in job order costing. One difference is that the cost of goods completed is transferred from Work in Process—Finishing Department to Finished Goods Inventory by an entry on a general journal voucher rather than an entry in the completed jobs journal. (The Finishing Department is the last producing department.) One summary entry is made at the end of the month to record the cost of all goods completed during the month.

Selling

All recording steps for sales are similar to those used when goods are sold from stock under the job order cost system.

. . . .

January Transactions

Before making a detailed study of Space Savers' procedures, let us review the data on the use of materials, labor, and overhead during January.

Materials

Requisitions for direct and indirect materials have been recorded in the materials requisition journal. The requisitions for indirect materials are also posted to the related departmental overhead analysis sheets. At the end of the month, the journal totals are posted in summary form in order to charge the costs of those materials to factory operations. The materials requisition journal below shows that the total cost of materials issued in January was $44,329.80.

MATERIALS REQUISITION JOURNAL

for Month of _____ January _____ 19 X5 _____ Page ___1___

DATE	REQ. NO.	✔	WORK IN PROCESS MILLING DEPT. DR. 123	WORK IN PROCESS ASSEMBLING DEPT. DR. 124	WORK IN PROCESS FINISHING DEPT. DR. 125	MFG. OVERHEAD CONTROL DR. 501	RAW MATERIALS CR. 121
Jan. 2	1	✔	1,854 40				1,854 00
2	2	✔				90 00	90 00
3	3	✔		926 36			926 36
31	Total	✔	27,000 00	10,560 00	3,160 00	3,609 80	44,329 80
			✔	✔	✔	✔	✔

Labor

Total charges posted from the payroll registers to the Factory Payroll Clearing account for gross salaries and wages are $66,732. A summary of time tickets for the month shows that actual direct labor earnings for the month total $56,412 and actual indirect labor earnings total $18,720. The direct labor costs are debited to the related departmental Work in Process accounts. The indirect labor costs are debited to Manufacturing Overhead Control 501. Factory Payroll Clearing is credited for the total actual earnings of $75,132. A journal voucher is used to make the necessary entry, as shown below.

JOURNAL VOUCHER Date _Jan. 31,_ _____ 19 X5 No. _1-40_

ACCOUNT	ACCOUNT NUMBER	✔	DEBIT	CREDIT
Work in Process—Milling Dept.	123	✓	19240 00	
Work in Process—Assembling Dept.	124	✓	20740 00	
Work in Process—Finishing Dept.	125	✓	16432 00	
Manufacturing Overhead Control	501	✓	18720 00	
Factory Payroll Clearing	500	✓		75132 00

EXPLANATION

Charged labor cost to production for the month.

PREPARED BY _MEL_   AUDITED BY _BH_   APPROVED BY _SZ_

The balance of $8,400 in the Factory Payroll Clearing account represents unpaid wages at the end of the month. The amounts chargeable to each department are obtained from the regular monthly summary of wages prepared by the payroll unit.

			Factory Payroll Clearing			No.	500
DATE	EXPLANATION	POST. REF.	DEBIT	CREDIT	BALANCE		DR. CR.
19X5							
Jan. 5		WP	16,480 00		16,480	00	Dr.
12		WP	16,332 00		32,812	00	Dr.
15		SP	2,560 00		35,372	00	Dr.
19		WP	14,400 00		49,772	00	Dr.
26		WP	14,400 00		64,172	00	Dr.
31		SP	2,560 00		66,732	00	Dr.
31		J1-40		75,132 00	8,400	00	Cr.

Overhead

Total manufacturing overhead costs incurred during January are $37,878.

			Manufacturing Overhead Control			No.	501
DATE	EXPLANATION	POST. REF.	DEBIT	CREDIT	BALANCE		DR. CR.
19X5							
Jan. 31	Indirect materials	MR1	3,609 80		3,609	80	Dr.
31	Indirect labor	J1-40	18,720 00		22,329	80	Dr.
31	Other overhead	J1-51	5,896 00		28,225	80	Dr.
31	Other costs	VR1	9,652 20		37,878	00	Dr.

The departmental analysis sheets show the following departmental figures:

Building Services	$ 9,200.00
General Factory	11,343.00
Milling	9,470.00
Assembling	2,779.00
Finishing	5,086.00

Charging these costs to production is a two-step process. First, a worksheet (page 254), similar to the one used in job order cost accounting, is prepared to allocate service department costs to the three producing departments.

Second, the figures from the worksheet allocation are entered in a general journal voucher (page 254) to close Manufacturing Overhead Control 501 into the three departmental Work in Process accounts. (No overhead application rate is used in this procedure because overhead costs are expected to be incurred evenly throughout the year, production is expected to occur evenly throughout the year, and all costs are to be absorbed by the units produced.)

Space Savers, Inc.
Worksheet for Prorating Service Dept. Costs
Month Ended January 31, 19X5

ITEM	BASIS OF PRORATION	BUILDING SERVICES	GENERAL FACTORY	MILLING	ASSEMBLING	FINISHING	TOTAL
Bal. of dept. ov. an. sheets		9200 00	11343 00	9470 00	2779 00	5086 00	37878 00
Prorate Bldg. Ser.	floor space*	(9200 00)	2760 00	1840 00	2576 00	2024 00	
Prorate Gen. Fact.	dir. labor†		(14103 00)	4810 00	5185 00	4108 00	
Total		–0–	–0–	16120 00	10540 00	11218 00	37878 00

*General Factory, 30%; Milling, 20%; Assembling, 28%; Finishing, 22%.
†Milling, $19,240 (34.1062%); Assembling, $20,740 (36.7652%); Finishing, $16,432
(29.1286%); Total, $56,412.

JOURNAL VOUCHER Date _Jan. 31,_ 19 _X5_ No. _1-52_

ACCOUNT	ACCOUNT NUMBER	✔	DEBIT	CREDIT
Work in Process—Milling Dept.	123	✓	16120 00	
Work in Process—Assembling Dept.	124	✓	10540 00	
Work in Process—Finishing Dept.	125	✓	11218 00	
Manufacturing Overhead Control	501	✓		37878 00

EXPLANATION

Closed out control account and recorded
department costs.

PREPARED BY JAN	AUDITED BY JB	APPROVED BY RM

At this point all three elements of manufacturing costs—materials, labor, and overhead—have been charged to work in process. These charges are shown in the departmental Work in Process accounts on page 255.

The charges are made more easily and directly under the process cost system because many time-consuming details, such as those relating to job cost sheets and time tickets, are no longer required.

Work in Process—Milling Department   No. ___123___

DATE		EXPLANATION	POST. REF.	DEBIT		CREDIT		BALANCE		DR. CR.
19	X5									
Jan.	31	Materials	MR1	27,000	00			27,000	00	Dr.
	31	Labor	J1-40	19,240	00			46,240	00	Dr.
	31	Overhead	J1-52	16,120	00			62,360	00	Dr.

Work in Process—Assembling Department   No. ___124___

DATE		EXPLANATION	POST. REF.	DEBIT		CREDIT		BALANCE		DR. CR.
19	X5									
Jan.	31	Materials	MR1	10,560	00			10,560	00	Dr.
	31	Labor	J1-40	20,740	00			31,300	00	Dr.
	31	Overhead	J1-52	10,540	00			41,840	00	Dr.

Work in Process—Finishing Department   No. ___125___

DATE		EXPLANATION	POST. REF.	DEBIT		CREDIT		BALANCE		DR. CR.
19	X5									
Jan.	31	Materials	MR1	3,160	00			3,160	00	Dr.
	31	Labor	J1-40	16,432	00			19,592	00	Dr.
	31	Overhead	J1-52	11,218	00			30,810	00	Dr.

Principles and Procedures Summary

The process cost system is well suited to accounting for the costs of typical mass-production operations. An average unit cost, adequate for most control purposes, is obtained with a minimum of recordkeeping.

Process cost accounting uses many of the same procedures that are used in job order cost accounting. Purchases and issues of materials are recorded the same way, except that job cost sheets are not used. Payroll procedures are also very similar, but they are even simpler because the number of time tickets is reduced. Manufacturing overhead is recorded in the general ledger control account and departmental overhead analysis sheets as before.

When a factory operation involves more than one process, the single Work in Process account used in job order cost accounting may be replaced by separate accounts for each process, each cost element, or each product. If, for example, multiple Work in Process accounts are kept, costs are transferred from one process to the other as goods move through operations. Production data is obtained from production reports. Then average unit costs can be computed by dividing total costs by total production.

Cost procedures for warehousing and selling are unchanged. Goods flow out of the last factory process into stock. From that point the accounting work is the same as the sale of goods from stock in the job order cost system.

Review Questions

1. In what journal are requisitions for direct materials recorded? Indirect materials?
2. When is the process cost system desirable?
3. Why is it possible under the process cost system to charge indirect labor in a production department directly to work in process instead of having to charge those costs to manufacturing overhead?
4. Why is the job order cost ledger eliminated under the process cost system?
5. Why is the process cost system referred to as a method used for determining average cost?
6. Under job order costing, the daily time ticket for each worker whose wages are classified as direct labor shows the job worked on. What does the time ticket for such workers show if the process cost system is used?
7. A Work in Process account may be used for each producing department. What other arrangements for Work in Process accounts might be used?
8. Postings from the payroll registers of the Shaw Company to its Factory Payroll Clearing account totaled $97,000 for the month of April. However, a summary of the time tickets for April showed that actual labor earnings for the month totaled $102,500, which was credited to Factory Payroll Clearing at the end of April. What does the $5,500 difference in those two figures represent?
9. Is it always necessary to use an overhead application rate under the process cost system? Explain.
10. Why is a completed jobs journal not used in a process cost accounting system?

Managerial Discussion Questions

1. Under what conditions might management decide that a process cost system is appropriate?
2. The Brooks Company is trying to decide whether to manufacture a variety of products to customer specifications or to manufacture a single, uniform product. What are the advantages of each alternative?
3. Assume that you are a cost accountant. The management of the firm where you work has asked how the accounts differ under process and job order cost accounting. How would you answer this question?
4. Your employer manufactures iron products. Most of the products are made to meet customer specifications on special orders. Management has asked you about using process costing. How would you answer?
5. Process cost accounting is sometimes described as a procedure for computing the average cost of products manufactured. Suppose that the management of a firm that employs you wishes to know if this system is satisfactory as a tool for controlling costs. What is your reply to management?

Exercises

1. **Making a journal entry for labor costs charged to departments.** A summary of the factory wages at Harris Manufacturers for the month of June shows the following costs. Give the entry in general journal form to charge these costs to the departments.

Milling Department	$21,000
Assembly Department	28,000
Finishing Department	17,000
Manufacturing Overhead	19,000

2. **Preparing a worksheet to prorate service department costs.** Harris Manufacturers produce wooden cabinets. The balances of the departmental overhead analysis sheets for June show the following costs:

Department	Cost	Percent of Floor Space
Building Services	$10,000	
General Factory	12,000	30
Milling	14,000	25
Assembly	3,000	28
Finishing	5,000	17

   Prepare a worksheet for prorating service department costs, similar to that on page 254 of the text. The overhead cost of the Building Services Department is allocated on the basis of the percent of space occupied. The overhead cost of the General Factory Department is allocated on the basis of direct labor costs as shown in Exercise 1.

3. **Making a journal entry to charge overhead costs to producing departments.** Based on the worksheet in Exercise 2, give the general journal entry to close Manufacturing Overhead Control into the three departmental Work in Process accounts.

4. **Making a journal entry for cost of goods completed.** The last department in the production process is the Finishing Department. At the end of June, the cost of goods completed during the month was determined to be $114,000. Give the general journal entry to record the cost of goods completed during the month.

5. **Making journal entries for sales and cost of goods sold.** During the month of June total sales were $233,000. The cost of those goods was $151,000. Give the general journal entries to record the sales and the cost of goods sold.

6. **Allocating service department costs.** The Lewis Group, Inc., allocates the costs of its Building Services Department to the producing departments on the basis of square feet of floor space occupied. The Grinding Department occupies 3,000 square feet; the Mixing Department occupies 1,500 square feet; and the Finishing Department occupies 2,000 square feet. The costs of the Building Services Department for March 19X4 totaled $6,820. How much is allocated to each producing department?

7. **Making journal entries for sales and cost of goods sold.** During March 19X4, the Phoenix Manufacturing Company had total sales of $1,200,000. The goods were sold at a gross profit rate of 15 percent on sales. Give the journal entries to record the sales and the cost of goods sold.

8. **Making a journal entry to charge labor costs to departments.** The William Manning & Sons Corporation uses a process cost system. During its first month of manufacturing operations, it had total labor costs of $30,000 applicable to the producing departments. These costs were charged to the Factory Payroll Clearing account. An analysis shows that $17,000 was applicable to the Shaping Department, $4,500 to the Tooling Department, and $8,500 to the Polishing Department. Give the journal entry to charge labor costs to production.

9. **Allocating and journalizing service department costs.** For the month of July 19X4, the Stern Manufacturing Company had the following direct labor costs. The overhead costs of $2,400 incurred by the Building Services Department are allocated to the three other departments on the basis of floor space occupied. The overhead costs of $6,200 incurred by the General Factory Department plus the allocated costs of the Building Services Department are allocated on the basis of direct labor costs.

Department	Floor Space	Direct Labor Costs
General Factory	2,000 square feet	
Milling	7,000 square feet	$12,000
Finishing	5,000 square feet	30,000

a. What amount of the costs of the Building Services Department should be allocated to each of the other departments?

b. Give the journal entry to close the Manufacturing Overhead—General Factory Department account.

10. **Making a journal entry for materials requisitions.** Rockwell Associates uses the process cost system. Details of three materials requisitions issued during January 19X4 are shown below. Give the journal entry to record the issue of these materials.

■ Requisition 105 for direct materials for use in the Milling Department (122), a producing department, $780.

■ Requisition 110 for indirect materials used in the Milling Department, $38.

■ Requisition 162 for cleaning materials used in the Building Services Department, a service department, $24.

Problems

PROBLEM 13-1. Analyzing, recording, and posting process cost transactions. The Clifford Manufacturing Company uses the process cost system. General ledger accounts and balances as of July 1, 19X5, are listed below.

111	Accounts Receivable	$160,000
121	Raw Materials	240,000
123	Work in Process—Forming Department	-0-
124	Work in Process—Finishing Department	-0-
126	Finished Goods	360,000
201	Vouchers Payable	760,000
202	Salaries and Wages Payable	-0-
204	Other Accounts	-0-
401	Sales	-0-

415	Cost of Goods Sold	$-0-
500	Factory Payroll Clearing	-0-
501	Manufacturing Overhead Control	-0-

Instructions

1. Enter the July 1, 19X5, balances in the general ledger accounts.
2. The transactions for July 19X5 are listed below. Record the July transactions in general journal form. Date all entries July 31. Start with journal page 7.
3. Post the July transactions to the accounts listed.

1. Purchased raw materials for $218,000 on credit.
2. Issued raw materials from the storeroom as follows:

To Forming Department	$204,000
To Finishing Department	14,000
To Service Departments	18,000

3. Recorded labor costs of $264,000 at the payroll dates.
4. Charged labor costs to production as follows:

To Forming Department	$ 52,000
To Finishing Department	174,000
To Service Departments	36,000

5. Incurred $32,000 in miscellaneous manufacturing overhead costs, such as repairs, power, lighting, and taxes. (Credit Other Accounts.)
6. Allocated manufacturing overhead costs to the producing departments as follows:

| To Forming Department | $26,000 |
| To Finishing Department | 44,000 |

7. Transferred goods costing $282,000 from the Forming Department to the Finishing Department.
8. Transferred goods costing $413,000 from the Finishing Department to Finished Goods Inventory.
9. Sold goods for $655,000 on credit in July.
10. Incurred costs of $454,000 on merchandise sold in July.

PROBLEM 13-2. Preparing journal vouchers and posting; prorating service department costs. The management of Wood Systems, Inc., producers of wooden desks, has decided that the process cost accounting system is best for its purposes. During August 19X4, the following data appear in the firm's records. Page 8 of the voucher register shows a debit of $16,471.54 to Raw Materials 121 and a debit of $1,770.60 to Manufacturing Overhead Control 501. Page 8 of the materials requisition journal shows issues of raw materials as follows:

Distribution	Amount
Shaping Department	$ 6,200
Painting Department	4,750
Finishing Department	906
Manufacturing Overhead Control	1,620
Raw Materials	13,476

The weekly payroll register shows labor costs as follows:

Date	Amount
Aug. 4	$2,375
11	2,638
20	2,874
25	2,518

The monthly payroll register shows salaries of $3,895. The monthly summary of labor costs shows the distribution of the charges as follows:

Distribution	Amount
Shaping Department	$4,805
Painting Department	3,251
Finishing Department	4,620
Manufacturing Overhead Control	1,476

The schedule of monthly fixed overhead charges contains the following figures:

Overhead	Amount
Insurance	$118
Taxes	847
Depreciation	486

Instructions

1. Post the debit entries from the voucher register to the appropriate general ledger accounts.
2. Post the distribution of raw materials from the materials requisition journal to the appropriate general ledger accounts.
3. Post the debit entries for each week from the weekly payroll register to the appropriate general ledger account.
4. Post the debit entry from the monthly payroll register to the appropriate general ledger account.
5. Prepare the general journal voucher to charge labor costs to production. Number the voucher 8-11. Post to the general ledger accounts.
6. Post the debit entries from the schedule of monthly fixed overhead charges to the appropriate general ledger account.
7. Complete the worksheet for prorating the costs of the General Factory Department to the producing departments. Prorate on the basis of 34 percent to Shaping, 25 percent to Painting, and 41 percent to Finishing. The departmental totals are as follows:

General Factory Department	$1,810.00
Shaping Department	1,012.00
Painting Department	1,561.00
Finishing Department	1,934.60

8. Prepare the general journal voucher to apportion manufacturing overhead to the producing departments. Number the voucher 8-12. Post to the general ledger accounts.

Alternate Problems

PROBLEM 13-1A. Analyzing, recording, and posting process cost transactions. The Montrose Manufacturing Company uses the process cost system. General ledger accounts and balances as of May 1, 19X7, are listed below.

111	Accounts Receivable	$ 80,000
121	Raw Materials	100,000
123	Work in Process—Forming Department	-0-
124	Work in Process—Finishing Department	-0-
126	Finished Goods	180,000
201	Vouchers Payable	360,000
202	Salaries and Wages Payable	-0-
204	Other Accounts	-0-
401	Sales	-0-
415	Cost of Goods Sold	-0-
300	Factory Payroll Clearing	-0-
501	Manufacturing Overhead Control	-0-

Instructions

1. Enter the May 1, 19X7, balances in the general ledger accounts.
2. The transactions for May 19X7 are listed below. Record the May transactions in general journal form. Date all entries May 31. Start with journal page 5.
3. Post the May transactions to the accounts listed.

1. Purchased raw materials for $114,000 on credit.
2. Issued raw materials from the storeroom as follows:

To Forming Department	$102,000
To Finishing Department	26,000
To Service Departments	39,000

3. Recorded labor costs of $123,000 at the payroll dates.
4. Charged labor costs to production as follows:

To Forming Department	$31,000
To Finishing Department	56,000
To Service Departments	15,000

5. Incurred $16,000 in miscellaneous manufacturing overhead costs, such as power, lighting, taxes, and repairs. (Credit Other Accounts.)
6. Allocated manufacturing overhead costs to the producing departments as follows:

To Forming Department	$18,000
To Finishing Department	23,500

7. Transferred goods costing $149,000 from the Forming Department to the Finishing Department.
8. Transferred goods costing $254,500 from the Finishing Department to Finished Goods Inventory.
9. Sold goods for $327,000 on credit in May.
10. Incurred costs of $224,000 on merchandise sold in May.

PROBLEM 13-2A. **Preparing journal vouchers and posting; prorating service department costs.** The management of Western Furniture, Inc., producers of wooden chairs, has decided that the process cost accounting system is best for its purposes. During May 19X6 the following data appear in the firm's records. Page 5 of the voucher register shows a debit of $9,302.75 to Raw Materials 121 and a debit of $1,177.61 to Manufacturing Overhead Control 501. Page 5 of the materials requisition journal shows issues of raw materials as follows:

Distribution	Amount
Shaping Department	$3,625.56
Painting Department	2,814.00
Finishing Department	809.88
Manufacturing Overhead Control	734.99
Raw Materials	7,984.43

The weekly payroll register shows labor costs as follows:

Date	Amount
May 4	$1,920.30
14	1,878.54
18	1,952.42
27	1,937.16

The monthly payroll register shows salaries of $2,529. The monthly summary of labor costs shows the distribution of the charges as follows:

Distribution	Amount
Shaping Department	$2,764.32
Painting Department	3,813.96
Finishing Department	3,982.17
Manufacturing Overhead Control	1,528.14

The schedule of monthly fixed overhead charges contains the following figures:

Overhead	Amount
Insurance	$ 85.00
Taxes	821.72
Depreciation	432.00

Instructions

1. Post the debit entries from the voucher register to the appropriate general ledger accounts.
2. Post the distribution of raw materials from the materials requisition journal to the appropriate general ledger accounts.
3. Post the debit entries for each week from the weekly payroll register to the appropriate general ledger account.
4. Post the debit entry from the monthly payroll register to the appropriate general ledger account.
5. Prepare a general journal voucher to charge labor costs to production. Number the voucher 5-11. Post to the general ledger accounts.

6. Post the debit entries from the schedule of monthly fixed overhead charges to the appropriate general ledger account.

7. Complete the worksheet for prorating the costs of the General Factory Department to the producing departments. Prorate on the basis of 45 percent to Shaping, 35 percent to Painting, and 20 percent to Finishing. The departmental totals are as follows:

General Factory Department	$ 672.00
Shaping Department	981.44
Painting Department	1,605.52
Finishing Department	1,520.50

8. Prepare the general journal voucher to apportion manufacturing overhead to the producing departments. Number the voucher 5-12. Post to the general ledger accounts.

CHAPTER

14

■ ■ ■

Production Data and Cost Flow

The systematic accumulation of costs by processes or departments is the first phase in determining unit costs. The second phase is to find the total production for each process during the period. Once the production data are available, an average unit cost for the process may be established by dividing the total output into the total cost.

Production Reports

Departmental supervisors are responsible for achieving the production goals assigned to their departments. They direct and control the performance of the workers so that the desired output is achieved on schedule and according to specifications. Production records are an inevitable and necessary part of this managerial activity. The departmental supervisor uses these production records to prepare periodic production reports for cost purposes.

The supervisor of each producing department at Space Savers is required to submit a monthly production report. This report includes the following data, as illustrated on page 265:

1. Number of units started in production
2. Number of units completed and transferred out of the department
3. Number of units remaining in process
4. Stage of completion of the ending work in process

The last section of the report is an estimate of the stage of completion of the work still in process at the end of the month. Production efforts and the related costs are expended during the month on incomplete as well as on fully processed goods. This fact must be recognized in the reports and statements. The supervisor draws on past experience to supply figures that estimate the stage of completion of the ending work in process.

```
                    MILLING DEPARTMENT
                  Monthly Production Report
                       January 19X5

    Quantity
        Started in Production—Current Month          1,080
        Transferred Out to Next Department             880
        Work in Process—Ending                         200

    Stage of Completion of Ending Work in Process
        Materials                                   complete
        Labor                                           80%
        Overhead                                        80%
```

Equivalent Production Units

The cost accountant uses the supervisor's stage-of-completion estimate to equate the incomplete and completed goods in terms of a common denominator. This common denominator is *equivalent units of production* for each cost element. Units of incomplete goods are converted to equivalent production units by multiplying the number of units by the percentage of completion. Thus 200 units that are estimated to be 80 percent completed are equivalent to 160 completed units (200 × .80 = 160).

From the monthly production report of the Milling Department, shown above, the equivalent production for each cost element (materials, labor, and overhead) is computed as shown below.

```
                    MILLING DEPARTMENT
              Equivalent Production Computations
                  Month of January 19X5

    Materials
        Transferred Out to Next Department             880
        Work in Process—Ending (200 desks × 100%)      200
        Equivalent Production for Materials          1,080

    Labor and Manufacturing Overhead
        Transferred Out to Next Department             880
        Work in Process—Ending (200 desks × 80%)       160
        Equivalent Production for Labor and Overhead 1,040
```

Materials

The equivalent production for materials is the sum of the number of units completed and transferred to the next department and the number of units remaining in process (880 + 200). This is because the supervisor's estimate of completion shows that all materials needed to process these units in the Milling Department have been issued.

Labor and Overhead

The equivalent production for labor and manufacturing overhead involves two factors. The first factor is the 880 units transferred to the next department, which are 100 percent complete in terms of labor and manufacturing overhead. The second factor is the 200 desks still in process, which are estimated to be 80 percent complete as to both labor and manufacturing overhead (200 × .80 = 160). The resulting equivalent production is 1,040 desks (880 + 160). This figure means that enough labor and overhead have been expended on a total of 1,080 desks (some only partially finished) to have fully completed 1,040 desks, if the costs had been expended entirely on the smaller number of units.

· ·

Cost of Production Report

The cost data accumulated in the Work in Process accounts (see Chapter 13) and the equivalent production data now available make it possible to establish, at the end of the accounting period, an average unit cost for the goods in production during the period.

The cost of production report of Space Savers' Milling Department is shown on page 267 as an example. The report contains two sections: the Quantity Schedule and the Cost Schedule.

Quantity Schedule

The Quantity Schedule section is divided into two parts. The first half, (a) Quantity to Be Accounted For, shows the number and source of the units handled during the month. Since January 19X5 is the first month of Space Savers' process cost operation, production of all units was started during the current month. The second half, (b) Quantity Accounted For, shows what happened to the units reported in the first half of the Quantity Schedule. In this instance, 880 units were completely processed and transferred out to the next department, and 200 units remained on hand at the end of the month. The two parts of the Quantity Schedule complete a reconciliation of physical units *to be* accounted for with physical units that *are* accounted for.

Cost Schedule

The first half of the Cost Schedule, (c) Costs to Be Accounted For, shows the total cost and the unit cost of each element.

- The total costs come from the general ledger account Work in Process—Milling Department 123, shown on page 267.
- The unit cost is computed by dividing the total cost of the element by the related equivalent production units shown on the departmental equivalent production report (page 265). In the case of materials, all units are considered to be 100 percent complete. The total materials cost of $27,000 is divided by 1,080 units to give a unit cost of $25 for materials in the milling process.
- In the case of labor and overhead, the total cost for each element (from the general ledger) is divided by the 1,040 equivalent production units (from the equivalent production report) to give the unit costs, $18.50 and $15.50, for these elements in the milling process.
- After the unit costs for each of the three elements are computed, they are added to determine the cumulative total cost per equivalent unit, $59. The cumulative total cost for all

MILLING DEPARTMENT
Cost of Production Report
Month of January 19X5

QUANTITY SCHEDULE	UNITS
(a) Quantity to Be Accounted For:	
Started in Production—Current Month	1,080
Total to Be Accounted For	1,080
(b) Quantity Accounted For:	
Transferred Out to Next Department	880
Work in Process—Ending	200
Total Accounted For	1,080

COST SCHEDULE	TOTAL COST	E.P. UNITS	UNIT COST
(c) Costs to Be Accounted For:			
Costs in Current Department			
Materials	$27,000.00 ÷	1,080 =	$25.00
Labor	19,240.00 ÷	1,040 =	18.50
Overhead	16,120.00 ÷	1,040 =	15.50
Total Costs to Be Accounted For	$62,360.00		$59.00
(d) Costs Accounted For:			
(1) Transferred Out to Next Department	$51,920.00 =	880 × $59.00	
(2) Work in Process—Ending			
Materials	$ 5,000.00 =	200 × $25.00	
Labor	2,960.00 =	160 × $18.50	
Overhead	2,480.00 =	160 × $15.50	
Total Work in Process	$10,440.00		
Total Costs Accounted For	$62,360.00		

units, $62,360, agrees with the balance of the general ledger account Work in Process—Milling Department 123, as shown below.

Work in Process—Milling Department   No. ___123___

DATE		EXPLANATION	POST. REF.	DEBIT		CREDIT		BALANCE		DR. CR.
19 X5										
Jan.	31	Materials	MR1	27,000	00			27,000	00	Dr.
	31	Labor	J1-40	19,240	00			46,240	00	Dr.
	31	Overhead	J1-52	16,120	00			62,360	00	Dr.

■ The unit costs for each element and the total unit cost are then used in the second half of the Cost Schedule.

The second half of the Cost Schedule—(d) Costs Accounted For—relates costs to the production operations of the period.

- The total cost of the units completely processed and transferred out to the next department is calculated in Part 1 of Section (d), Transferred Out to Next Department. This is done by multiplying the cumulative unit cost from the previous half of the Cost Schedule ($59) by the number of units transferred out (880, from the Quantity Schedule). The result is $51,920.
- Part 2 of Section (d) shows the cost of the work remaining in process. The unit costs for each element, computed in Section (c), are multiplied by the equivalent units of that element in the work in process. The total cost of the materials in the work in process is computed by multiplying the materials element unit cost of $25 by 200 units (100 percent completed as shown as the second item on the equivalent production report on page 265) for a total of $5,000. The labor cost is computed by multiplying the labor element unit cost of $18.50 by the 160 equivalent production units in process (shown on the equivalent production report). When all three elements have been costed in this manner, the total cost of the work in process is found to be $10,440.

The Cost Schedule is designed to reconcile total cost figures. The total costs incurred in the production process must agree with the total costs related to the units that were fully or partially completed during the month. If small errors occur as a result of rounding off numbers, the cost of goods transferred out as shown in Part 1 of Section (d) of the Cost Schedule is adjusted to absorb the rounding error. Technically, a portion of the rounding error should be allocated to work in process. However, this would require a great deal of effort and would not have a meaningful result. Since most of the costs apply to work transferred out of the department, it is customary to adjust this cost element for the amount of the rounding error.

Flow of Units and Costs

From the Milling Department, the product moves into the Assembling Department and then to the Finishing Department. Equivalent units are computed and a cost of production report is prepared for each department.

Assembling Department

The second department in Space Savers' production sequence is the Assembling Department. The 880 units transferred out of the Milling Department become the input for the Assembling Department's operations during the month. These units appear in the Assembling Department's monthly production report, as shown on page 269.

Equivalent Production Units. Not all units in the Assembling Department are completely processed before January 31. Equivalent units of production must, therefore, be computed from the production data supplied by the supervisor. The equivalent production computations are shown on page 269.

```
                    ASSEMBLING DEPARTMENT
                    Monthly Production Report
                         January 19X5

Quantity
      Transferred In From Prior Department              880
      Transferred Out to Next Department                820
      Work in Process—Ending                             60

Stage of Completion of Ending Work in Process
      Materials                                      complete
      Labor                                             50%
      Overhead                                          50%
```

```
                    ASSEMBLING DEPARTMENT
                Equivalent Production Computations
                    Month of January 19X5

Materials
      Transferred Out to Next Department                820
      Work in Process—Ending (60 desks × 100%)           60
          Equivalent Production for Materials           880

Labor and Manufacturing Overhead
      Transferred Out to Next Department                820
      Work in Process—Ending (60 desks × 50%)            30
          Equivalent Production for Labor and Overhead  850
```

Cost of Production Report. The costs accumulated in the account Work in Process—Assembling Department 124 and the equivalent production unit data provide the information needed to complete the cost of production report for the second department, as shown below.

	Work in Process—Assembling Department		No. 124				
DATE	EXPLANATION	POST. REF.	DEBIT	CREDIT	BALANCE	DR. CR.
19X5						
Jan. 31	Materials	MR1	10,560 00		10,560 00	Dr.
31	Labor	J1-40	20,740 00		31,300 00	Dr.
31	Overhead	J1-52	10,540 00		41,840 00	Dr.

The first half of the Quantity Schedule, (a) Quantity to Be Accounted For, reflects the receipt of 880 units from the Milling Department. The second half, (b) Quantity

Accounted For, shows what was done with them. Of the 880 units, 820 were fully processed and transferred out to the Finishing Department. The remaining 60 desks are still in process at the end of the month.

This time the first half of the Cost Schedule, (c) Costs to Be Accounted For, includes the total costs in the prior department as well as costs by elements incurred in the current department. The figures on the Costs in Prior Department line are the same as those in Part 1 of Section (d) in the cost of production report of the Milling Department, shown on page 267. The total costs incurred in the current department are taken from Work in Process—Assembling Department 124, as shown on page 269.

ASSEMBLING DEPARTMENT
Cost of Production Report
Month of January 19X5

QUANTITY SCHEDULE	UNITS
(a) Quantity to Be Accounted For:	
Transferred In From Prior Department	880
Total to Be Accounted For	880
(b) Quantity Accounted For:	
Transferred Out to Next Department	820
Work in Process—Ending	60
Total Accounted For	880

COST SCHEDULE	TOTAL COST	E.P. UNITS	UNIT COST
(c) Costs to Be Accounted For:			
Costs in Prior Department	$51,920.00 =	880	× $ 59.00
Costs in Current Department			
Materials	$10,560.00 ÷	880	= $ 12.00
Labor	20,740.00 ÷	850	= 24.40
Overhead	10,540.00 ÷	850	= 12.40
Total Costs in Current Dept.	$41,840.00		$ 48.80
Total Costs to Be Accounted For	$93,760.00		$107.80
(d) Costs Accounted For:			
(1) Transferred Out to Next			
Department	$88,396.00 =	820	× $107.80
(2) Work in Process—Ending			
Costs in Prior Department	$ 3,540.00 =	60	× $ 59.00
Costs in Current Department			
Materials	720.00 =	60	× $ 12.00
Labor	732.00 =	30	× $ 24.40
Overhead	372.00 =	30	× $ 12.40
Total Work in Process	$ 5,364.00		
Total Costs Accounted For	$93,760.00		

Other current department cost data are obtained as follows:

- The unit cost of each element in the current department is computed by dividing the equivalent production units into the total cost of that element. In the case of materials, all units are again considered to be 100 percent complete. Thus $10,560 divided by 880 gives a unit cost of $12 for materials in the Assembling Department. In the case of labor and overhead, the total cost of each element is divided by the 850 equivalent production units (from the equivalent production report) to give the unit costs for these elements in the assembling process.

- The costs in the current department are added to the prior department costs (both total and unit) to obtain new cumulative total costs to be accounted for. The cost of production report shows that total costs incurred to date amount to $93,760 and that the average unit cost is $107.80.

- The unit cost for each element and the total unit cost are used to complete the first half of the Cost Schedule.

Costs are accounted for in the second half of the Cost Schedule—Section (d)—as follows:

- The value of the goods transferred out to the Finishing Department (Part 1) is determined by multiplying the unit cost of $107.80 by the 820 units involved ($107.80 × 820 = $88,396). This total cost figure will ultimately flow into Work in Process—Finishing Department 125 in the general ledger.

- The value of the work in process is again costed (in Part 2) by multiplying the unit costs of the various elements by the number of equivalent units of each element.

- Note that work in process costs must now include the $59 unit cost that originated in the Milling Department.

When all costs have been computed and added, the value of the work remaining in process amounts to $5,364. Also note that the total costs to be accounted for have been reconciled with the total costs accounted for ($93,760).

Finishing Department

The third department in Space Savers' production sequence is the Finishing Department. The 820 units transferred out of the Assembling Department become the basis of the Finishing Department's operations during the month, as shown below.

FINISHING DEPARTMENT Monthly Production Report January 19X5	
Quantity	
Transferred In From Prior Department	820
Transferred Out to Finished Goods	780
Work in Process—Ending	40
Stage of Completion of Ending Work in Process	
Materials	25%
Labor	25%
Overhead	25%

Equivalent Production Units. At the end of the month, the equivalent production units must be calculated because not all units are fully completed during the month. Again, the data come from the monthly equivalent production computations.

FINISHING DEPARTMENT
Equivalent Production Computations
Month of January 19X5

Materials, Labor, and Manufacturing Overhead
Transferred Out to Finished Goods   780
Work in Process—Ending (40 desks × 25%)   10
Equivalent Production for Materials, Labor, and Overhead   790

Cost of Production Report. The costs accumulated in Work in Process—Finishing Department 125 are used with the equivalent production unit data to prepare the cost of production report. This report is shown on page 273.

The entire quantity to be accounted for (820 units) was received from the Assembling Department. A total of 780 units were then fully processed and transferred to Finished Goods, leaving 40 desks in process.

The costs to be accounted for are determined in the usual way.

■ The figures on the line Costs in Prior Department are the same as in Part 1 of Section (d) in the cost of production report of the Assembling Department shown on page 270. The total costs incurred in the current department are obtained from the Work in Process—Finishing Department 125 account.

	Work in Process—Finishing Department			No. 125			
DATE	EXPLANATION	POST. REF.	DEBIT	CREDIT	BALANCE		DR. CR.
19 X5							
Jan. 31	Materials	MR1	3,160 00		3,160 00		Dr.
31	Labor	J1-40	16,432 00		19,592 00		Dr.
31	Overhead	J1-52	11,218 00		30,810 00		Dr.

Other current department cost data are obtained as follows:

■ The unit cost of each element is computed by dividing the equivalent production units into the total cost.
■ Prior department costs are added to current department costs (both total and unit) to obtain total and unit cumulative costs ($119,206 total; $146.80 per unit).
■ The element cost and the processed unit cost are used in completing Section (d) of the report.

```
                    FINISHING DEPARTMENT
                   Cost of Production Report
                   Month of January 19X5

        QUANTITY SCHEDULE                         UNITS
(a) Quantity to Be Accounted For:
        Transferred In From Prior Department        820
            Total to Be Accounted For               820

(b) Quantity Accounted For:
        Transferred Out to Finished Goods           780
        Work in Process—Ending                       40
            Total Accounted For                      820
```

COST SCHEDULE	TOTAL COST	E.P. UNITS	UNIT COST
(c) Costs to Be Accounted For:			
Costs in Prior Department	$ 88,396.00 =	820	× $107.80
Costs in Current Department			
Materials	$ 3,160.00 ÷	790	= $ 4.00
Labor	16,432.00 ÷	790	= 20.80
Overhead	11,218.00 ÷	790	= 14.20
Total Costs in Current Department	$ 30,810.00		$ 39.00
Total Costs to Be Accounted For	$119,206.00		$146.80
(d) Costs Accounted For:			
(1) Transferred Out to Finished Goods	$114,504.00 =	780	× $146.80
(2) Work in Process—Ending			
Costs in Prior Department	$ 4,312.00 =	40	× $107.80
Costs in Current Department			
Materials	40.00 =	10	× $ 4.00
Labor	208.00 =	10	× $ 20.80
Overhead	142.00 =	10	× $ 14.20
Total Work in Process	$ 4,702.00		
Total Costs Accounted For	$119,206.00		

Costs are accounted for in Section (d) as follows:

■ The first costs accounted for are those relating to the 780 completed units transferred to Finished Goods. The value of the new finished goods is computed by multiplying the unit cost of $146.80 by the 780 units involved.
■ The value of the work remaining in process is again computed by using previously determined prior department unit costs and the unit cost for each element in the current department. When all amounts are totaled, the value of the work in process is found to be $4,702.

Recording Departmental Transfers

The departmental cost of production reports supply the figures that the cost accountant needs to record the flow of costs in the accounting records. Part *1* of Section (d) in the Cost Schedule portion of each cost of production report shows the cost of desks transferred to the next department.

Each transfer is formally recorded in the accounting records by a general journal voucher entry. The entry to transfer the $51,920 cost of the 880 units from the Milling Department to the Assembling Department is shown below.

JOURNAL VOUCHER	Date *Jan. 31,* 19 *X5*		No. *1-53*		
ACCOUNT	**ACCOUNT NUMBER**	✔	**DEBIT**	**CREDIT**	
Work in Process—Assembling Dept.	*124*		51920 00		
Work in Process— Milling Dept.	*123*			51920 00	
EXPLANATION					
Recorded transfer of goods from Milling Department to Assembling Department.					
PREPARED BY *MEL*	AUDITED BY *BH*		APPROVED BY *SZ*		

The entry to record the transfer of 820 units costing $88,396 from the Assembling Department to the Finishing Department is as follows:

JOURNAL VOUCHER	Date *Jan. 31,* 19 *X1*		No. *1-54*		
ACCOUNT	**ACCOUNT NUMBER**	✔	**DEBIT**	**CREDIT**	
Work in Process—Finishing Dept.	*125*		88396 00		
Work in Process— Assembling Dept.	*124*			88396 00	
EXPLANATION					
Recorded transfer of goods from Assembling Department to Finishing Department.					
PREPARED BY *MEL*	AUDITED BY *BH*		APPROVED BY *SZ*		

The entry for the third transfer, of 780 units with a cost of $114,504, from the Finishing Department to Finished Goods is handled in the same way:

JOURNAL VOUCHER	Date Jan. 31,	19 X5	No. 1-55		
ACCOUNT	ACCOUNT NUMBER	✓	DEBIT	CREDIT	
Finished Goods	126		114504 00		
Work in Process—					
Finishing Dept.	125			114504 00	
		EXPLANATION			
Recorded completion of goods and transfer to Finished Goods Inventory.					
PREPARED BY MEL	AUDITED BY BH		APPROVED BY SZ		

Proof of Work in Process

After the transfer entries are posted, the balance remaining in the Work in Process accounts (shown below and on page 276) is the same as the value of the total work in process computed in Part 2 of Section (d) of each departmental cost of production report.

Work in Process—Milling Department — No. 123

DATE	EXPLANATION	POST. REF.	DEBIT	CREDIT	BALANCE	DR. CR.
19 X5						
Jan. 31	Materials	MR1	27,000 00		27,000 00	Dr.
31	Labor	J1-40	19,240 00		46,240 00	Dr.
31	Overhead	J1-52	16,120 00		62,360 00	Dr.
31	Transferred to Assembling Dept.	J1-53		51,920 00	10,440 00	Dr.

Work in Process—Assembling Department — No. 124

DATE	EXPLANATION	POST. REF.	DEBIT	CREDIT	BALANCE	DR. CR.
19 X5						
Jan. 31	Materials	MR1	10,560 00		10,560 00	Dr.
31	Labor	J1-40	20,740 00		31,300 00	Dr.
31	Overhead	J1-52	10,540 00		41,840 00	Dr.
31	Transferred from Milling Dept.	J1-53	51,920 00		93,760 00	Dr.
31	Transferred to Finishing Dept.	J1-54		88,396 00	5,364 00	Dr.

	Work in Process—Finishing Department				No. 125	

DATE	EXPLANATION	POST. REF.	DEBIT	CREDIT	BALANCE	DR. CR.
19X5						
Jan. 31	Materials	MR1	3,160 00		3,160 00	Dr.
31	Labor	J1-40	16,432 00		19,592 00	Dr.
31	Overhead	J1-52	11,218 00		30,810 00	Dr.
31	Transferred from Assembling Dept.	J1-54	88,396 00		119,206 00	Dr.
31	Transferred to Finished Goods	J1-55		114,504 00	4,702 00	Dr.

Computerized Process Control

Thai, Lane, Cho Pharmaceuticals (TLC) is a manufacturer of over-the-counter and prescription drugs. The production of chemicals for the drugs is a continuous activity. A mistake in the production process or a slight deviation from the formula for a particular chemical could damage the drugs, causing batches of drugs to be wasted. Because the production process allows only slight room for error and because errors can be so expensive, TLC uses a process control system in their production.

A process control system monitors production, checking key variables such as air temperature, humidity, chemical temperature, and chemical flow to detect deviations from allowable levels. If a deviation is detected, corrective action is taken immediately either by the system or by an operator. This prevents the production of a substandard product.

The monitor in a process control system is a computer. Two other components of process control are sensors and an actuator. Sensors gather information about the key variables of the production process. The computer compares this information with the predetermined limits for each of these variables and determines whether any corrective action is necessary. If corrective action is needed the computer instructs the actuator to make the adjustments. The corrections are then monitored and the process reevaluated by the computer.

Frequent process control ensures a quality product and minimizes variances between actual and expected production costs that are caused by inefficiency and errors. However, frequent process control also means high computing costs. Therefore, the number of times the process is sampled must be balanced against the cost of sampling and the time required.

In addition to analyzing production costs, the cost accountant must also monitor the costs of the system itself. However, this extra bit of work is more than offset by the benefits of the system to the cost accountant. TLC uses a program package with their process control system that provides the cost accountant with comparative data for cost control purposes. The information will be timely enough for management to act in a manner that will allow the company to remain competitive in the market place. ■

Principles and Procedures Summary

Once costs are accumulated in Work in Process accounts, production data must be assembled for use in computing unit costs. The supervisor's monthly production report provides information about quantities started, quantities transferred in and out, and quantities in process. This report also estimates the stage of completion of the work still in process at the end of the month. The cost accountant then computes equivalent units of production to show the amount of production done on both completed and partially processed units in each department. The next step is to use the cost figures from the general ledger accounts and the equivalent production unit figures to complete a cost of production report for each process.

The cost of production report has two main schedules. The first presents quantity data, and the second gives cost data. Each of these schedules is arranged in parts. The first half of the Quantity Schedule assembles unit data. The second half explains what happened to the units that were handled in the department. In the first half of the Cost Schedule, total costs are assembled, and element and processed unit costs are computed. The second half accounts for the costs. Some costs are transferred with processed units to the next department. Other costs remain as part of the cost of work in process.

The value of the goods transferred from one department to the next, determined in the Cost Schedule, is recorded by means of a general journal entry and posted to the general ledger. When all transfers have been recorded, the balance in each Work in Process account should equal the value of work in process shown in the cost of production report.

Review Questions

1. What information is contained in the monthly production report? What is the purpose of this report? Who prepares it? Who receives it?
2. What is meant by the term *equivalent units of production?*
3. What are the two major schedules in a cost of production report? Describe them briefly.
4. What information is included in the Quantity Schedule of a cost of production report? What is the source of this information?
5. What is the relationship between a departmental Work in Process account and the department's cost of production report?
6. On a journal voucher, which account is debited and which is credited to record the cost of work transferred from the Milling Department to the Assembling Department? Why?
7. Explain what is meant by "Costs in Prior Departments." What happens to these costs as the product moves through production?
8. What is the source of information for recording the flow of costs? What entry is made to record the flow of costs from one department to another?
9. After the transfer entries are posted, the balances in the Work in Process accounts should agree with what figures?

Managerial Discussion Questions

1. How does process cost accounting assist in measuring the efficiency of departmental supervisors?
2. What data is provided to management by the monthly production report for each department?
3. Why is it necessary for the departmental supervisor to estimate the stage of completion of work in process?
4. What is the cost of production report? What information does it contain for management?
5. Is it likely that work in process will be at the same stage of completion for each of the cost elements? Explain.
6. Why should management compare the equivalent costs per unit for one month with those for prior months?

Exercises

Assume in all the exercises that the company uses the average cost method for costing work in process.

1. **Computing units started in production.** Sorrento Products makes spaghetti that it markets to restaurants and schools. During the month, the Cooking Department completed 5,000 units of the product. The ending work in process inventory was 700 units, and there was no beginning inventory. How many units were started in production during the month? 5700

2. **Computing equivalent production.** A department had no beginning work in process inventory. During the month, 3,250 units were transferred in from the prior department. Of this amount, 3,000 were completed by the end of the month and transferred to finished goods. The ending work in process inventory was complete as to materials and one-half complete as to labor and overhead.
   a. What is the equivalent production for materials? 3250
   b. What is the equivalent production for labor and overhead? 3125

3. **Computing equivalent production for materials and cost per unit.** The cost of materials put into production in a department during the month totaled $124,800. By the end of the month, these materials had been used for 62,400 units, of which 58,000 were completed and transferred out and 4,400 were in process. All materials were added to the units in process.
   a. What is the equivalent production for materials? 62400
   b. What is the cost per equivalent unit for materials? $2.00 per unit

4. **Computing equivalent production for labor, cost per unit, and ending work in process.** During the month, 82,000 units were started into production, of which 79,000 units were completed and transferred out during the month. It is estimated that the units in process have had one-third of the labor added. Total labor costs for the month were $20,000.
   a. What is the cost per equivalent unit of labor? $.25
   b. What is the labor cost applicable to the ending work in process? $250

5. **Computing equivalent production for labor, cost per unit, and ending work in process.** The following data are given for the Baking Department of the Hatfield Company in January 19X3:

Beginning inventory, -0-
Units transferred in during month, 8,000
Units transferred to next department during month, 7,500
Ending work in process, 500 units (one-quarter completed as to labor)
Labor costs incurred for month, $20,968.75

   a. What is the equivalent production for labor during the month?
   b. What is the labor cost per equivalent unit?
   c. What is the labor cost in the ending inventory of work in process?

6. **Computing equivalent production for overhead, cost per unit, and ending work in process.** The following data are given for the Grinding Department of the Jacobs Tool and Die Company in May 19X5:

   Beginning inventory, -0-
   Units placed in production during month, 21,000
   Units transferred to next department during month, 20,000
   Ending work in process, 1,000 units (25 percent complete as to overhead)
   Overhead costs incurred for month, $27,135

   a. What is the equivalent production for overhead during the month?
   b. What is the overhead cost per equivalent unit?
   c. What is the overhead cost in the ending inventory of work in process?

7. **Computing equivalent production for materials, cost per unit, and ending work in process.** The following data are given for the Assembly Department of the Mercury Company in November 19X4:

   Beginning inventory, -0-
   Units transferred in during month, 30,000
   Units transferred out to next department during month, 24,000
   Ending work in process, 6,000 (75 percent complete as to materials)
   Material costs incurred for the month, $3,028,125

   a. What is the equivalent production for materials during the month?
   b. What is the materials cost per equivalent unit?
   c. What is the materials cost in the ending inventory of work in process?

8. **Computing equivalent production for labor, cost per unit, and costs transferred out.** Assume the same facts as in Exercise 4 above, except that half the labor has been added to the ending work in process (instead of one-third of the labor having been added).
   a. What is the cost per equivalent unit of labor?
   b. What is the labor cost applicable to the 79,000 units transferred out of the department?

9. **Computing equivalent production for overhead, cost per unit, costs transferred out, and ending work in process.** During the month, 6,800 units of product were started into production in a department, of which 6,500 were completed. Of the 6,500 completed units, 250 are still on hand and have not been physically transferred to the next department. The 300 units still in pro-

cess are estimated to be one-third complete as to labor and overhead. Overhead for the month was $46,000.

a. What is total overhead cost applicable to the 6,300 units transferred to the next department?

b. What is the overhead cost applicable to the 250 units completed and still on hand?

c. What is the overhead cost applicable to the uncompleted units on hand?

10. **Making journal entries to record the transfer of costs.** The following data are given for the two production departments, the Mixing and Finishing Departments, of the Deluxe Paint Company for the month of May 19X8. Materials, labor, and overhead charged to production are as follows:

	Materials	Labor	Overhead
Mixing Department	$79,000	$4,000	$21,000
Finishing Department	14,000	3,000	12,500

The costs of work transferred were as follows:

From Mixing Department to Finishing Department	$ 90,000
From Finishing Department to Finished Goods	109,000

Give the journal entries to charge the costs to production and to record the transfer of work from the Mixing Department to the Finishing Department and from the Finishing Department to Finished Goods.

Problems

PROBLEM 14-1. Computing equivalent production. The Chesapeake Bay Corporation, which has four producing departments, uses the process cost accounting system. Production data for the first month's operations are given below.

	Dept. A	Dept. B	Dept. C	Dept. D
Quantity				
Started in Production	72,000			
Transferred In From Prior Department		64,000	57,500	50,400
Transferred Out to Next Department	64,000	57,500	50,400	
Transferred Out to Finished Goods				47,600
Work in Process—Ending	8,000	6,500	7,100	2,800
Stage of Completion of Ending Work in Process				
Materials	100%	100%	90%	80%
Labor	20%	40%	60%	80%
Overhead	20%	40%	60%	80%

Instructions

Compute the equivalent units of production for materials, labor, and overhead for each department for the first month.

PROBLEM 14-2. Computing equivalent production; preparing a cost of production report for one department; making journal entries. The Elias Company manufactures one product, involving three processing departments. During the month of April 19X7, the company's first month of production, 144,000 units were placed in production in the first department with the following costs being added: · materials, $146,880; labor, $82,350; and overhead, $48,300. On April 30, 15,000 units were in process in this department with all materials having been added and 60 percent of the labor and overhead added.

Instructions

1. Prepare a schedule of equivalent production for the first department for April.
2. Prepare a cost of production report for the first department for April.
3. Give the entries in general journal form to charge the costs to production and to record the transfer of units to the second department.

PROBLEM 14-3. Computing equivalent production; preparing a cost of production report for three departments; making journal entries. The departmental supervisors of James Manufacturing, Inc., have submitted the monthly production reports for September 19X3. These reports have been summarized and the result is shown below.

	Shaping Department	Painting Department	Finishing Department
Quantity			
Started in Production—Current Month	1,800	-0-	-0-
Transferred In From Prior Department	-0-	1,600	1,400
Transferred Out to Next Department	1,600	1,400	-0-
Transferred Out to Finished Goods	-0-	-0-	1,275
Work in Process—Ending	200	200	125
Stage of Completion of Ending Work in Process			
Materials	complete	complete	$66\frac{2}{3}$%
Labor	50%	75%	$66\frac{2}{3}$%
Overhead	50%	75%	$66\frac{2}{3}$%

The materials requisition journal shows issues of raw materials as follows:

Distribution	Amount
Shaping Department	$8,400
Painting Department	4,200
Finishing Department	1,600

The monthly payroll register shows the following totals:

Distribution	Amount
Shaping Department	$4,625
Painting Department	3,650
Finishing Department	2,580

The schedule of monthly overhead charges from the worksheet for prorating the costs of the General Factory Department to the producing departments shows the following figures:

Distribution	Amount
Shaping Department	$2,300
Painting Department	1,825
Finishing Department	1,250

Instructions

1. Prepare the equivalent production computations for each department.
2. Prepare the cost of production report for each department. Round off to three decimal places when calculating unit costs.
3. **a.** Prepare the general journal voucher to record the transfer of goods from the Shaping Department to the Painting Department. Number the voucher 9-13.
   b. Prepare the general journal voucher to record the transfer of goods from the Painting Department to the Finishing Department. Number the voucher 9-14.
   c. Prepare the general journal voucher to record the completion of goods and the transfer to Finished Goods. Number the voucher 9-15.

Alternate Problems

PROBLEM 14-1A. Computing equivalent production. The Oakland Manufacturing Company, which has four producing departments, uses the process cost accounting system. Production data for the first month's operations are given below.

	Dept. 1	Dept. 2	Dept. 3	Dept. 4
Quantity				
Started in Production	18,000			
Transferred In From Prior Department		15,000	14,000	12,600
Transferred Out to Next Department	15,000	14,000	12,600	
Transferred Out to Finished Goods				9,000
Work in Process—Ending	3,000	1,000	1,400	3,600
Stage of Completion of Ending Work in Process				
Materials	100%	100%	90%	80%
Labor	20%	40%	30%	80%
Overhead	20%	40%	40%	80%

Instructions

Compute the equivalent units of production for materials, labor, and overhead for each department for the first month.

PROBLEM 14-2A. Computing equivalent production; preparing a cost of production report for one department; making journal entries. The Douglas Processing Company began operations on June 1, 19X6. During the month of June, 4,860 units of its product were started in production in the first department, the Mixing Department. Of these, all but 1,000 were completed during the month and transferred out to the second department, the Cooking Department. All materials had been added to the 1,000 units, but only 75 percent of the labor and overhead had been added. The costs incurred during the month were: materials, $121,500; labor, $88,560; and manufacturing overhead, $72,540.

Instructions

1. Prepare a schedule of equivalent production for the Mixing Department for June.
2. Prepare a cost of production report for the Mixing Department for June.
3. Give the entries in general journal form to charge the costs to production and to record the transfer of units to the Cooking Department.

PROBLEM 14-3A. Computing equivalent production; preparing a cost of production report for three departments; making journal entries. The departmental supervisors of Creative Toys International have submitted the monthly production reports for July 19X8. These reports have been summarized, and the result is shown below.

	Shaping Department	Painting Department	Finishing Department
Quantity			
Started in Production—			
Current Month	1,580	-0-	-0-
Transferred In From Prior Department	-0-	1,500	1,385
Transferred Out to Next Department	1,500	1,385	-0-
Transferred Out to Finished Goods	-0-	-0-	1,360
Work in Process—Ending	80	115	25
Stage of Completion of Ending			
Work in Process			
Materials	complete	complete	25%
Labor	60%	85%	25%
Overhead	60%	85%	25%

The materials requisition journal shows issues of raw materials as follows:

Distribution	Amount
Shaping Department	$1,580
Painting Department	3,000
Finishing Department	6,830

The monthly payroll register shows the following totals:

Distribution	Amount
Shaping Department	$3,096
Painting Department	2,966
Finishing Department	1,366

The schedule of monthly overhead charges from the worksheet for prorating the costs of the General Factory Department to the producing departments shows the following figures:

Distribution	Amount
Shaping Department	$6,192
Painting Department	1,483
Finishing Department	683

Instructions

1. Prepare the equivalent production computations for each department.
2. Prepare the cost of production report for each department.
3. a. Prepare the general journal voucher to record the transfer of goods from the Shaping Department to the Painting Department. Number the voucher 7-13.
   b. Prepare the general journal voucher to record the transfer of goods from the Painting Department to the Finishing Department. Number the voucher 7-14.
   c. Prepare the general journal voucher to record the completion of goods and the transfer to Finished Goods. Number the voucher 7-15.

Managerial Decisions

CASE 14-1. The Kiln Burning Department of the Delaware Chemical Company typically has little work in process at the end of the month. The controller of the company has studied the cost and production records of the department for the past several years and has expressed concern over the overhead and labor cost behavior in the department. The costs per unit of these elements have increased substantially in the summer months, although materials costs per unit have remained fairly constant in each month. For example, the data below show the costs per equivalent unit during the last 12 months. A similar pattern was found in other years.

Cost per Unit

	Materials	Labor	Overhead
January	$15.01	$ 9.00	$3.00
February	14.98	8.87	3.20
March	15.03	9.06	3.15
April	15.05	9.03	3.18
May	15.04	9.07	3.26
June	15.06	11.11	3.43
July	15.05	13.52	4.01
August	15.07	15.04	6.92
September	15.04	9.44	3.41
October	15.08	9.28	3.33
November	15.09	9.37	3.37
December	15.07	9.45	3.34

1. List some other factors that might logically explain this cost behavior.
2. Assume that the controller has investigated the situation and has found the following:
   a. Production workers take their vacations in the summer, especially in July or August. Their vacation pay is treated as direct labor.
   b. During vacation periods, the kilns and tanks are cleaned and repaired and all costs of these activities are charged to the Kiln Department's overhead.

   The controller expresses her belief that these huge variations in unit cost are misleading and asks you, as cost accountant, to suggest accounting procedures that will yield "more logical" results. Write a brief report responding to the controller's request.

CHAPTER

15

Average Costing of Work in Process

■ ■ ■

In the course of normal operations, the producing departments in continuous process industries carry forward inventories of work in process from one month to the next. For example, Space Savers' general ledger shows Work in Process balances on February 1, 19X5. The accountant must be sure to include these balances when determining the total costs and the unit costs to be accounted for in February.

Accounting for Beginning Work in Process

Space Savers' cost accountant considered two generally recognized methods of handling the cost of the beginning work in process inventory: the first in, first out method and the average cost method.

First In, First Out Costing

Under the *first in, first out (FIFO) method,* the partially processed units carried over from the previous month are costed separately from the units started in the current month.

■ The costs of the beginning inventory and the additional costs incurred to complete these units are added to obtain the total and unit costs for the carried-over units of production.
■ The costs of the units started during the month are assembled separately to obtain a second set of total and unit costs for the new production.
■ Transfers are costed on the assumption that the oldest units (first in) will move out first (first out).

This method is explained in detail in Chapter 17.

Average Costing

The *average cost method* combines rather than separates the costs of carried-over and new production.

- The cost of each element (materials, labor, and overhead) applicable to the beginning work in process inventory is added to the cost incurred for that element in the current month.
- A single cumulative total and unit cost is obtained.
- One unit cost figure is used for costing transfers.

Space Savers' ending work in process inventory will usually be small in relation to total monthly production and will vary only slightly from month to month. As a result, there will be little difference between the unit costs computed under the FIFO method and the average cost method. Therefore, the cost accountant decides to adopt the simpler average cost method of accounting for beginning inventories and costs added during the month.

You will learn how this method works step by step as the February costs are calculated. Departments will be studied in the sequence in which materials are processed.

Milling Department

The cost data and production data for the Milling Department are assembled from the sources described in Chapters 13 and 14. These sources include the materials requisition journal, the summary of time tickets, the departmental overhead analyses, and the monthly production reports.

Cost Data

The Work in Process—Milling Department 123 account shows a balance of $54,950.64 on February 28.

	Work in Process—Milling Department					No. 123	
DATE	EXPLANATION	POST. REF.	DEBIT	CREDIT	BALANCE		DR. CR.
19 X5							
Feb. 1	Balance	✔			10,440	00	Dr.
28	Materials	MR2	19,920 00		30,360	00	Dr.
28	Labor	J2-50	13,243 96		43,603	96	Dr.
28	Overhead	J2-52	11,346 68		54,950	64	Dr.

The balance of this account is broken down into cost elements in two simple steps.

1. Analyze the beginning work in process, as given below, by referring to the work in process data in Part 2 of Section (d) of the cost of production report for January (shown on page 267).

Beginning Work in Process
Materials	$ 5,000
Labor	2,960
Overhead	2,480
Balance of Account, Jan. 31	$10,440

2. Determine the cost incurred for each element in the current month by referring to the general ledger postings in the Work in Process account.

Current Month
Materials	$19,920.00
Labor	13,243.96
Overhead	11,346.68
Total Current Month's Costs	$44,510.64

Production Data

The supervisor's production report for the month of February is shown below.

MILLING DEPARTMENT
Monthly Production Report
February 19X5

Quantity

Work in Process—Beginning	200
Started in Production—Current Month	800
Transferred Out to Next Department	820
Work in Process—Ending	180

Stage of Completion of Ending Work in Process

Materials	complete
Labor	30%
Overhead	30%

Equivalent Production Data

The cost accountant computes the equivalent production for the Milling Department in February in the same manner as in January. The 820 units transferred to the Assembling Department are obviously 100 percent complete as to materials, labor, and overhead. The remaining 180 units are also 100 percent complete as to materials according to the supervisor's report. However, these desks are regarded by the supervisor as only 30 percent complete in terms of labor and overhead. Thus, the equivalent production for February is computed as 1,000 units for materials and 874 units for labor and overhead (180 × .30 = 54; 54 + 820 = 874), as shown on page 288.

Cost of Production Report

The cost of production report for February is now completed, as shown on page 289. There are several new details that should receive special attention.

Quantity Schedule. The first half of the Quantity Schedule—(a) Quantity to Be Accounted For—now starts with Work in Process—Beginning. The total of 200 units is taken from the supervisor's monthly production report for February. The number of units started into production also comes from the supervisor's report. No figure is shown as Transferred In From Prior Department because milling is the first manufacturing operation.

```
                    MILLING DEPARTMENT
                Equivalent Production Computations
                    Month of February 19X5

    Materials

        Transferred Out to Next Department                 820
        Work in Process—Ending (180 desks × 100%)          180
            Equivalent Production for Materials          1,000

    Labor and Manufacturing Overhead

        Transferred Out to Next Department                 820
        Work in Process—Ending (180 desks × 30%)            54
            Equivalent Production for Labor and Overhead    874
```

The second half of the Quantity Schedule—(b) Quantity Accounted For—is completed in the same way as it was for January.

Cost Schedule. In the first half of the Cost Schedule—(c) Costs to Be Accounted For—there are no figures under Costs in Prior Department because milling is the first operation. Under Costs in Current Department, the cost of each element in the beginning work in process is added to the additional cost of that element incurred during the month, as explained below.

- The materials cost of the beginning work in process, $5,000, is added to the cost of materials issued during February, $19,920. The total cost of materials, $24,920, is then divided by the equivalent production for materials, 1,000 units. The resulting average unit cost is $24.92.
- The labor cost of the beginning work in process, $2,960, is added to the labor costs incurred in February, $13,243.96, for a total of $16,203.96. Dividing this figure by the equivalent production for labor of 874 units (as computed above) yields an average equivalent unit cost for labor of $18.54.
- The overhead cost of the beginning work in process, $2,480, is added to the overhead cost incurred in February, $11,346.68, for a total of $13,826.68 and an average equivalent unit cost for overhead of $15.82.

The rest of the Cost Schedule for February is prepared as before.

. . . .

Assembling Department

The costs for the Assembling Department for February are found by using procedures very similar to those described for the Milling Department. However, certain details are different because assembling is the second process in the manufacturing sequence, and costs from the prior department must be considered.

MILLING DEPARTMENT
Cost of Production Report
Month of February 19X5

QUANTITY SCHEDULE	UNITS
(a) Quantity to Be Accounted For:	
Work in Process—Beginning	200
Started in Production—Current Month	800
Transferred In From Prior Department	-0-
Total to Be Accounted For	1,000
(b) Quantity Accounted For:	
Transferred Out to Next Department	820
Transferred Out to Finished Goods	-0-
Work in Process—Ending	180
Total Accounted For	1,000

COST SCHEDULE	TOTAL COST	E.P. UNITS	UNIT COST
(c) Costs to Be Accounted For:			
Costs in Prior Department			
Work in Process—Beginning	-0-		
Transferred In—Current Month	-0-		
Total Prior Department Costs	-0-		
Costs in Current Department			
Materials—Beginning Work in Process	$ 5,000.00		
Added in Current Month	19,920.00		
Total Materials	$24,920.00 ÷	1,000 =	$24.92
Labor—Beginning Work in Process	$ 2,960.00		
Added in Current Month	13,243.96		
Total Labor	$16,203.96 ÷	874 −	18.54
Overhead—Beginning Work in Process	$ 2,480.00		
Added in Current Month	11,346.68		
Total Overhead	$13,826.68 ÷	874 =	15.82
Total Costs in Current Department	$54,950.64		$59.28
Total Costs to Be Accounted For	$54,950.64		59.28
(d) Costs Accounted For:			
Transferred Out to Next Department	$48,609.60 =	820 × $59.28	
Transferred Out to Finished Goods	-0-		
Total Transferred Out	$48,609.60		
Work in Process—Ending			
Costs in Prior Department	-0-		
Costs in Current Department			
Materials	$ 4,485.60 =	180 × $24.92	
Labor	1,001.16 =	54 × $18.54	
Overhead	854.28 =	54 × $15.82	
Total Work in Process	$ 6,341.04		
Total Costs Accounted For	$54,950.64		

Cost Data

The account below shows a balance of $46,360.40 on February 28.

	Work in Process—Assembling Department					No.	124

DATE	EXPLANATION	POST. REF.	DEBIT	CREDIT	BALANCE	DR. CR.
19 X5						
Feb. 1	Balance	✔			5,364 00	Dr.
28	Materials	MR2	9,910 40		15,274 40	Dr.
28	Labor	J2-50	20,322 00		35,596 40	Dr.
28	Overhead	J2-52	10,764 00		46,360 40	Dr.

The balance of this account is made up of cost elements obtained from the following sources:

1. The work in process data in Part (2) of Section (d) of the Cost Schedule portion of the cost of production report for January (shown on page 270). This data shows the costs of the prior department (the Milling Department) as well as the costs of the Assembling Department for the January 31 ending work in process inventory. These costs, shown below, become the beginning work in process costs.

    Beginning Work in Process
    Costs in Prior Department $3,540
    Costs in Current Department
        Materials   720
        Labor   732
        Overhead   372
    Balance of Account, Jan. 31 $5,364

2. The general ledger postings in the Work in Process account during the current month. These postings total $40,996.40 for February, as shown below.

    Current Month
        Materials $ 9,910.40
        Labor   20,322.00
        Overhead   10,764.00
    Total Current Month's Costs $40,996.40

Production Data

The supervisor of the Assembling Department completes the following report:

ASSEMBLING DEPARTMENT
Monthly Production Report
February 19X5

Quantity

Work in Process—Beginning	60
Transferred In From Prior Department	820
Transferred Out to Next Department	840
Work in Process—Ending	40

Stage of Completion of Ending Work in Process

Materials	complete
Labor	75%
Overhead	75%

Equivalent Production Data

The equivalent production report prepared by the accountant is shown below.

ASSEMBLING DEPARTMENT
Equivalent Production Computations
Month of February 19X5

Materials

Transferred Out to Next Department	840
Work in Process—Ending (40 desks × 100%)	40
Equivalent Production for Materials	880

Labor and Manufacturing Overhead

Transferred Out to Next Department	840
Work in Process—Ending (40 desks × 75%)	30
Equivalent Production for Labor and Overhead	870

Cost of Production Report

The February cost of production report, shown on page 293, is patterned after the one used in January for the Assembling Department. Note that unit cost computations have been carried to four decimal places (rounded to three) because the number of equivalent production units is not evenly divisible into the total cost. The extra decimal places permit a greater degree of accuracy, which is important when large quantities and values are involved. Some companies carry unit costs to four or more decimal places when large numbers of units are involved. This is because large dollar amounts result when small unit costs are applied to a large number of units.

Quantity Schedule. The first half of the Quantity Schedule—(a) Quantity to Be Accounted For—now shows that 60 units are involved in the beginning work in process. This figure comes from the monthly production report and can be verified by referring to the January cost of production report.

Cost Schedule. In the first half of the Cost Schedule—(c) Costs to Be Accounted For—note the following:

- The Costs in Prior Department section includes the cost of the beginning work in process of $3,540. This figure is picked up from the ending work in process on the January cost of production report (60 × $59). This cost is added to the $48,609.60 transferred in from the Milling Department in the current month, resulting in total prior department costs of $52,149.60. This total is divided by the 880 equivalent units involved to obtain a prior department average unit cost of $59.261.

    This average unit cost is different from the $59.28 transferred into the Assembling Department from the Milling Department during the month of February. The reason is that the $59.26 figure is an average of the cost of 60 units at $59 in the beginning work in process from January and the 820 units at $59.28 transferred in from the Milling Department in February.

- The Costs in Current Department section shows that each cost element relating to the beginning work in process (obtained from the January cost of production report) is added to the cost incurred for that element during February (from the general ledger). This addition produces a total for each cost element. The total is divided by the equivalent production units for the cost element to determine the unit cost.

The rest of the cost of production report, including the cost of the ending work in process, is computed as before.

. . . .

Finishing Department

The costs for the Finishing Department are found by the same procedures as those described for the Assembling Department.

Cost Data

The Work in Process—Finishing Department 125 account shows a balance of $37,547.00 on February 28.

Work in Process—Finishing Department						No. 125	
DATE	EXPLANATION	POST. REF.	DEBIT	CREDIT	BALANCE		DR. CR.
19X5 Feb. 1	Balance	✔			4,702 00		Dr.
28	Materials	MR2	3,360 00		8,062 00		Dr.
28	Labor	J2-50	17,302 00		25,364 00		Dr.
28	Overhead	J2-52	12,183 00		37,547 00		Dr.

ASSEMBLING DEPARTMENT
Cost of Production Report
Month of February 19X5

QUANTITY SCHEDULE	UNITS
(a) Quantity to Be Accounted For:	
Work in Process—Beginning	60
Started in Production—Current Month	-0-
Transferred In From Prior Department	820
Total to Be Accounted For	880
(b) Quantity Accounted For:	
Transferred Out to Next Department	840
Transferred Out to Finished Goods	-0-
Work in Process—Ending	40
Total Accounted For	880

COST SCHEDULE	TOTAL COST		E.P. UNITS		UNIT COST
(c) Costs to Be Accounted For:					
Costs in Prior Department					
Work in Process—Beginning	$ 3,540.00				
Transferred In—Current Month	48,609.60				
Total Prior Department Costs	$52,149.60	÷	880	=	$ 59.261
Costs in Current Department					
Materials—Beginning Work in Process	$ 720.00				
Added in Current Month	9,910.40				
Total Materials	$10,630.40	÷	880	=	$ 12.080
Labor—Beginning Work in Process	$ 732.00				
Added in Current Month	20,322.00				
Total Labor	$21,054.00	÷	870	=	24.200
Overhead—Beginning Work in Process	$ 372.00				
Added in Current Month	10,764.00				
Total Overhead	$11,136.00	÷	870	=	12.800
Total Costs in Current Department	$42,820.40				$ 49.080
Total Costs to Be Accounted For	$94,970.00				$108.341
(d) Costs Accounted For:					
Transferred Out to Next Department	$91,006.36*	=	840	×	$108.341
Transferred Out to Finished Goods	-0-				
Total Transferred Out	$91,006.36				
Work in Process—Ending					
Costs in Prior Department	$2,370.44	—	40	×	$ 59.261
Costs in Current Department					
Materials	483.20	=	40	×	$ 12.080
Labor	726.00	=	30	×	$ 24.200
Overhead	384.00	=	30	×	$ 12.800
Total Work in Process	$ 3,963.64				
Total Costs Accounted For	$94,970.00				

*Adjusted for rounding difference, $.08. Customarily, any difference resulting from rounding off figures is considered an adjustment of the cost of goods transferred out of the department.

Reference to prior reports and analysis of ledger entries shows that this balance is made up of the following:

Beginning Work in Process	
Costs in Prior Department	$ 4,312.00
Costs in Current Department	
Materials	40.00
Labor	208.00
Overhead	142.00
Balance of Account, Jan. 31	$ 4,702.00
Current Month	
Materials	$ 3,360.00
Labor	17,302.00
Overhead	12,183.00
Total Current Month's Costs	$32,845.00

Production Data

The supervisor of the Finishing Department completes the monthly production report.

FINISHING DEPARTMENT
Monthly Production Report
February 19X5

Quantity

Work in Process—Beginning	40
Transferred In From Prior Department	840
Transferred Out to Finished Goods	820
Work in Process—Ending	60

Stage of Completion of Ending Work in Process

Materials	50%
Labor	50%
Overhead	50%

Equivalent Production Data

The equivalent production report for February prepared by the accountant is shown below.

FINISHING DEPARTMENT
Equivalent Production Computations
Month of February 19X5

Materials, Labor, and Manufacturing Overhead

Transferred Out to Finished Goods	820
Work in Process—Ending (60 desks × 50%)	30
Equivalent Production for Materials, Labor, and Overhead	850

Cost of Production Report

The Finishing Department's cost of production report can now be completed in the usual manner. This report is shown below.

FINISHING DEPARTMENT
Cost of Production Report
Month of February 19X5

QUANTITY SCHEDULE	UNITS
(a) Quantity to Be Accounted For:	
Work in Process—Beginning	40
Started in Production—Current Month	-0-
Transferred In From Prior Department	840
Total to Be Accounted For	880
(b) Quantity Accounted For:	
Transferred Out to Next Department	-0-
Transferred Out to Finished Goods	820
Work in Process—Ending	60
Total Accounted For	880

COST SCHEDULE	TOTAL COST	E.P. UNITS	UNIT COST
(c) Costs to Be Accounted For:			
Costs in Prior Department			
Work in Process—Beginning	$ 4,312.00		
Transferred In—Current Month	91,006.36		
Total Prior Department Costs	$ 95,318.36 ÷	880 =	$108.316
Costs in Current Department			
Materials—Beginning Work in Process	$ 40.00		
Added in Current Month	3,360.00		
Total Materials	$ 3,400.00 ÷	850 =	$ 4.000
Labor—Beginning Work in Process	$ 208.00		
Added in Current Month	17,302.00		
Total Labor	$ 17,510.00 ÷	850 =	20.600
Overhead—Beginning Work in Process	$ 142.00		
Added in Current Month	12,183.00		
Total Overhead	$ 12,325.00 ÷	850 =	14.500
Total Costs in Current Department	$ 33,235.00		$ 39.100
Total Costs to Be Accounted For	$128,553.36		$147.416
(d) Costs Accounted For:			
Transferred Out to Next Department	-0-		
Transferred Out to Finished Goods	$120,881.40* =	820 ×	$147.416
Total Transferred Out	$120,881.40		
Work in Process—Ending			
Costs in Prior Department	$ 6,498.96 =	60 ×	$108.316
Costs in Current Department			
Materials	120.00 =	30 ×	$ 4.000
Labor	618.00 =	30 ×	$ 20.600
Overhead	435.00 =	30 ×	$ 14.500
Total Work in Process	$ 7,671.96		
Total Costs Accounted For	$128,553.36		

*Adjusted for rounding difference, $.28.

Combined Cost of Production Report

Most accountants prefer to use one combined report of departmental production costs, as shown below, rather than a separate report for each department. The single report is simpler to prepare, permits quicker cross-checking, and makes it possible to trace transfers from department to department more easily. The equivalent production unit figures are normally omitted from the combined report to save space.

Combined Cost of Production Report
Month of February 19X5

	Milling Department UNITS	Assembling Department UNITS	Finishing Department UNITS
QUANTITY SCHEDULE			
(a) Quantity to Be Accounted For:			
Work in Process—Beginning	200	60	40
Started in Production—Current Month	800	-0-	-0-
Transferred In From Prior Department	-0-	820	840
Total to Be Accounted For	1,000	880	880
(b) Quantity Accounted For:			
Transferred Out to Next Department	820	840	-0-
Transferred Out to Finished Goods	-0-	-0-	820
Work in Process—Ending	180	40	60
Total Accounted For	1,000	880	880

	Milling TOTAL COST	Milling UNIT COST	Assembling TOTAL COST	Assembling UNIT COST	Finishing TOTAL COST	Finishing UNIT COST
COST SCHEDULE						
(c) Costs to Be Accounted For:						
Costs in Prior Department						
Work in Process—Beginning	-0-		$ 3,540.00		$ 4,312.00	
Transferred In—Current Month	-0-		48,609.60		91,006.36	
Total Prior Department Costs	-0-		$52,149.60	$ 59.261	$ 95,318.36	$108.316
Costs in Current Department						
Materials—Beg. Work in Process	$ 5,000.00		$ 720.00		$ 40.00	
Added in Current Month	19,920.00		9,910.40		3,360.00	
Total Materials	$24,920.00	$24.920	$10,630.40	$ 12.080	$ 3,400.00	$ 4.000
Labor—Beginning Work in Process	$ 2,960.00		$ 732.00		$ 208.00	
Added in Current Month	13,243.96		20,322.00		17,302.00	
Total Labor	$16,203.96	18.540	$21,054.00	24.200	$ 17,510.00	20.600
Overhead—Beg. Work in Process	$ 2,480.00		$ 372.00		$ 142.00	
Added in Current Month	11,346.68		10,764.00		12,183.00	
Total Overhead	$13,826.68	15.820	$11,136.00	12.800	$ 12,325.00	14.500
Total Costs in Current Dept.	$54,950.64	$59.280	$42,820.40	$ 49.080	$ 33,235.00	$ 39.100
Total Costs to Be Accounted For	$54,950.64	$59.280	$94,790.00	$108.341	$128,553.36	$147.416
(d) Costs Accounted For:						
Transferred Out to Next Department	**$48,609.60**	$59.280	**$91,006.36**	$108.341	-0-	
Transferred Out to Finished Goods	-0-		-0-		**$120,881.40**	$147.416
Total Transferred Out	$48,609.60		$91,006.36		$120,881.40	
Work in Process—Ending						
Costs in Prior Department	-0-		$ 2,370.44	$ 59.261	$ 6,498.96	$108.316
Costs in Current Department						
Materials	$ 4,485.60	$24.920	483.20	$ 12.080	120.00	$ 4.000
Labor	1,001.16	$18.540	726.00	$ 24.200	618.00	$ 20.600
Overhead	854.28	$15.820	384.00	$ 12.800	435.00	$ 14.500
Total Work in Process	$ 6,341.04		$ 3,963.64		$ 7,671.96	
Total Costs Accounted For	$54,950.64		$94,970.00		$128,553.36	

Recording Departmental Transfers

Section (d) in the Cost Schedule of the combined report shows that the following transfers must be recorded at the end of February: Milling to Assembling, $48,609.60; Assembling to Finishing, $91,006.36; Finishing to Finished Goods, $120,881.40.

The general journal voucher entries needed to complete the transfers are shown here and on page 298.

JOURNAL VOUCHER	Date Feb. 28,	19 X5	No. 2-53		
ACCOUNT	ACCOUNT NUMBER	✓	DEBIT	CREDIT	
Work in Process—Assembling Dept.	124		4860960		
Work in Process— Milling Dept.	123			4860960	
EXPLANATION					
Recorded cost of work transferred from Milling Department to Assembling Department for the month.					
PREPARED BY JAN	AUDITED BY JB		APPROVED BY RM		

JOURNAL VOUCHER	Date Feb. 28,	19 X5	No. 2-54		
ACCOUNT	ACCOUNT NUMBER	✓	DEBIT	CREDIT	
Work in Process—Finishing Dept.	125		9100636		
Work in Process— Assembling Dept.	124			9100636	
EXPLANATION					
Recorded cost of work transferred from Assembling Department to Finishing Department for the month.					
PREPARED BY JAN	AUDITED BY JB		APPROVED BY RM		

JOURNAL VOUCHER Date *Feb. 28,* 19 X5 No. *2-55*

ACCOUNT	ACCOUNT NUMBER	✔	DEBIT	CREDIT
Finished Goods	126		120881 40	
Work in Process —				
Finishing Dept.	125			120881 40

EXPLANATION
Recorded cost of work transferred from Finishing Department to Finished Goods for the month.

PREPARED BY *JAN*	AUDITED BY *JB*	APPROVED BY *RM*

After the transfer entries are posted, the departmental Work in Process accounts for January and February appear below and on page 299.

Work in Process—Milling Department   No. 123

DATE		EXPLANATION	POST. REF.	DEBIT		CREDIT		BALANCE		DR. CR.
19	X5									
Jan.	31	Materials	MR1	27,000	00			27,000	00	Dr.
	31	Labor	J1-40	19,240	00			46,240	00	Dr.
	31	Overhead	J1-52	16,120	00			62,360	00	Dr.
	31	Tr. to Assem. Dept.	J1-53			51,920	00	10,440	00	Dr.
Feb.	28	Materials	MR2	19,920	00			30,360	00	Dr.
	28	Labor	J2-50	13,243	96			43,603	96	Dr.
	28	Overhead	J2-52	11,346	68			54,950	64	Dr.
	28	Tr. to Assem. Dept.	J2-53			48,609	60	6,341	04	Dr.

Work in Process—Assembling Department   No. 124

DATE		EXPLANATION	POST. REF.	DEBIT		CREDIT		BALANCE		DR. CR.
19	X5									
Jan.	31	Materials	MR1	10,560	00			10,560	00	Dr.
	31	Labor	J1-40	20,740	00			31,300	00	Dr.
	31	Overhead	J1-52	10,540	00			41,840	00	Dr.
	31	Tr. from Mill. Dept.	J1-53	51,920	00			93,760	00	Dr.
	31	Tr. to Fin. Dept.	J1-54			88,396	00	5,364	00	Dr.
Feb.	28	Materials	MR2	9,910	40			15,274	40	Dr.
	28	Labor	J2-50	20,322	00			35,596	40	Dr.
	28	Overhead	J2-52	10,764	00			46,360	40	Dr.
	28	Tr. from Mill. Dept.	J2-53	48,609	60			94,970	00	Dr.
	28	Tr. to Fin. Dept.	J2-54			91,006	36	3,963	64	Dr.

		Work in Process—Finishing Department				No.	125	

DATE		EXPLANATION	POST. REF.	DEBIT		CREDIT		BALANCE		DR. CR.
19X5										
Jan.	31	Materials	MR1	3,160	00			3,160	00	Dr.
	31	Labor	J1-40	16,432	00			19,592	00	Dr.
	31	Overhead	J1-52	11,218	00			30,810	00	Dr.
	31	Tr. from Assem. Dept.	J1-54	88,396	00			119,206	00	Dr.
	31	Tr. to Fin. Goods	J1-55			114,504	00	4,702	00	Dr.
Feb.	28	Materials	MR2	3,360	00			8,062	00	Dr.
	28	Labor	J2-50	17,302	00			25,364	00	Dr.
	28	Overhead	J2-52	12,183	00			37,547	00	Dr.
	28	Tr. from Assem. Dept.	J2-54	91,006	36			128,553	36	Dr.
	28	Tr. to Fin. Goods	J2-55			120,881	40	7,671	96	Dr.

Proof of Work in Process

Each ledger account balance should agree with the ending work in process cost shown on the corresponding departmental cost of production report for the period.

Accounting for Sales and Cost of Goods Sold

Under the process cost system, goods manufactured are usually produced for stock. These goods are stored in the warehouse until orders are received. When goods are transferred from the factory to the warehouse, the receipt of the new stock is recorded on finished goods stock ledger cards. At the end of the period, after unit costs have been computed and transfer entries posted, the finished goods stock ledger should be in balance with the amount of its control account in the general ledger, Finished Goods 126.

Sales are recorded exactly as in the job order cost system. The sales journal provides space for recording both cost and selling price. At the end of the period the usual summary postings are completed. Cost of Goods Sold 415 is debited and Finished Goods 126 is credited. Accounts Receivable 111 (or Cash 101) is debited and Sales 401 is credited.

Principles and Procedures Summary

The cost of the work in process inventory carried over from one period to the next must be included in determining unit costs in the new month. Under the first in, first out (FIFO) method, the partially processed products carried over are costed separately from the units started in the current month. Under the average cost method, all costs are combined and an average unit cost is found.

Cost procedures in the second and later months of a process cost system follow a familiar pattern. Cost data is assembled and the production report is prepared. The equivalent units are computed, and the cost of production report is completed. Finally, the transfers are journalized and posted.

Quantities and related costs of beginning work in process appear on the cost of production report. The accountant may want to prepare a combined cost report instead of a separate report for each department. Under a process cost system, sales and the cost of goods sold are accounted for in the same way as when stock items are sold under the job order cost system.

Review Questions

1. What are the main characteristics of the average cost method of handling beginning work in process inventories?
2. How are equivalent units computed if there are beginning work in process inventories and the average cost method is used? How are the beginning work in process units treated in equivalent production computations?
3. Describe the journal entry used to record the transfer of a product from one producing department to another.
4. Describe the journal entry used to record the transfer of finished goods from the last producing department to the warehouse.
5. A department's beginning inventory of work in process was 1,000 units that were 25 percent complete. During the month, 9,000 units were transferred into the department; 8,600 were completed and transferred out, and the 1,400 on hand were 60 percent complete. What is the equivalent production for the month?
6. What is meant by a *transfer entry*?
7. **a.** What does the opening balance in the first producing department's Work in Process account represent?
   b. What is the source for work in process costs in the second department?
8. Under average costing, why is the amount of each cost element in the beginning work in process inventory combined with the amount of that cost element added during the current period?
9. What is a combined report of departmental production costs? Why is it used?
10. With which general ledger account should the finished goods ledger be in balance?
11. From what source does the accountant obtain the figures for the Beginning Inventory of Work in Process?
12. Why does the magnitude of the number of units involved in production affect the number of decimal places to which unit costs are carried?
13. How does the cost of production report for the second department in the production process differ from that of the first department?

Managerial Discussion Questions

1. Look at the cost of production report of the Milling Department on page 289. What figure would mean most to management in measuring the efficiency of labor during the month of February? What figure would probably be the best measure of the performance of the supervisor of the Milling Department?

2. What benefits are there to management from using a combined cost of production report instead of a separate statement for each department?

3. The president of your company has observed that you spend a great deal of time computing equivalent production units and costs per equivalent unit. He suggests that it would be much more efficient for you to ignore the beginning and ending work in process inventories. What is your response? Under what conditions might the president's suggestion be a logical one?

Exercises

NOTE: Assume in all the exercises that the company uses the average cost method for costing work in process.

1. **Computing equivalent production, cost per unit, and beginning and ending work in process.** Andover Cleaning Supplies produces a disinfectant used in hospitals. The beginning work in process inventory in the Mixing Department is 1,000 units, whose total cost includes $1,500 of prior department costs. During the month, 15,000 units with prior department costs of $29,400 were transferred into the department. During the month, 13,500 units were transferred out to the next department and 2,500 units were in the ending work in process inventory.
   a. Determine the equivalent units of production for prior department costs.
   b. Compute the cost per equivalent unit for prior department costs.
   c. Calculate the prior department costs in the ending work in process inventory of the Mixing Department.

2. **Computing equivalent production for materials, cost per unit, units transferred out, and beginning and ending work in process.** Assume the same facts as in Exercise 1. In addition, the materials cost in the beginning work in process inventory was $4,000. Materials costing $94,580 were added during the period. It was estimated that 80 percent of the materials were added in the preceding month to the beginning work in process. The ending work in process was 60 percent complete as to materials.
   a. Determine the equivalent units of production for materials.
   b. Compute the cost per equivalent unit for materials.
   c. Compute the materials cost in the units transferred out during the month.
   d. Compute the materials cost in the ending work in process inventory for the Mixing Department.

3. **Computing equivalent production for labor, cost per unit, units transferred out, and beginning and ending work in process.** The beginning work in process inventory in the Assembling Department of the Hauser Company on August 1, 19X7, was 600 units, to which 60 percent of labor had been applied at a cost of $720. During August, 8,000 units were transferred into the department and 6,800 units were transferred out. Labor costs of $15,360 were incurred during the month. The 1,800 units in the ending work in process for the Assembling Department were estimated to be 50 percent complete as to labor.
   a. Determine the equivalent units of production for labor.
   b. Compute the cost per equivalent unit for labor.
   c. Compute the labor cost in the units transferred out during the month.
   d. Compute the labor cost in the ending work in process inventory for the Assembling Department.

4. **Computing equivalent production for overhead, cost per unit, units transferred out, and beginning and ending work in process.** The beginning work in process inventory in the Mixing Department of Frank Hanson & Sons, Inc., on March 1, 19X3, was 12,000 units, to which 50 percent of overhead had been applied at a cost of $6,000. During March, 48,000 units were transferred into the department and 50,000 units were transferred out. Overhead costs of $49,550 were incurred during the month. The 10,000 units in process were estimated to be 80 percent complete as to overhead.
   a. Determine the equivalent units of production for overhead.
   b. Compute the cost per equivalent unit for overhead.
   c. Compute the overhead cost in the units transferred out during the month.
   d. Compute the overhead cost in the ending work in process inventory for the Mixing Department.

5. **Computing equivalent production for materials, cost per unit, units transferred out, and beginning and ending work in process.** The beginning work in process inventory in the Curing Department of Light Fixtures, Inc., on March 1, 19X5, was 1,000 units, to which 100 percent of materials had been added at a cost of $2,500. During March, 6,000 units were transferred into the department and 6,700 units were transferred out. Materials costs of $15,860 were incurred during the month. The 300 units in the ending work in process were 60 percent complete as to materials.
   a. Determine the equivalent units of production for materials.
   b. Compute the cost per equivalent unit for materials.
   c. Compute the materials cost in the units transferred out during the month.
   d. Compute the materials cost in the ending work in process inventory for the Curing Department.

6. **Making a journal entry to transfer costs.** Total costs incurred in the Planing Department of the Diaz Corporation during October 19X6 were $74,510. Of this amount, $2,600 is determined to be applicable to the ending work in process and the balance is applicable to work transferred to the Sanding Department. Give the journal entry to record the transfer of units between the departments.

Problems

NOTE: Assume in all the problems that each company uses the average cost method for costing work in process.

PROBLEM 15-1. Preparing a cost of production report; comparing unit costs. The Heller Company produces a single product, involving three processing departments. All materials are added at the beginning of production. On May 1, 19X2, there were 20,000 liters of the product in process in the first department. During the month of May, 195,000 liters were placed into production and 170,000 liters were transferred out to the next department. The ending work in process inventory is one-half completed. The beginning inventory costs were: materials, $80,000; labor, $36,000; and overhead, $18,000. During May, additional costs were: materials, $725,000; labor, $332,600; and overhead, $164,400.

Instructions

1. Prepare a cost of production report for the first department for the month of May.
2. In the month of April 19X2, the costs per equivalent unit in the first department were as follows: materials, $3.81; labor, $1.86; and overhead, $.90. If you were part of management at the Heller Company, what steps would you take after comparing the costs per equivalent unit for May and April? Suggest possible reasons for the differences.

PROBLEM 15-2. **Making journal entries to record and transfer costs.** Using the data from the cost of production report prepared in Problem 15-1, give the entries in general journal form to charge costs to production and to record the transfer of units to the second department. Date the entries May 31. For the Work in Process accounts, use account numbers 123 and 124.

PROBLEM 15-3. **Preparing a cost of production report.** The Columbus Chemical Company produces a single product. All materials are added at the beginning of production. On November 1, 19X6, 2,000 liters of the product were in process in the first department. During the month of November, 24,000 liters were put into production. On November 30, 4,000 liters were still in process. The ending inventory is estimated to be complete as to materials and 75 percent complete as to labor and overhead. Cost data for the month of November are shown below.

	Materials	Labor	Overhead
Beginning Work in Process Inventory	$ 16,200	$ 1,850	$ 3,700
Added During November	201,000	23,916	47,800

Instructions

Prepare a cost of production report for the month of November.

PROBLEM 15-4. **Computing equivalent production; preparing a cost of production report for two departments.** Texas Industries uses a process cost accounting system. All materials in the first department (Forming) are added at the start of production. Raw materials put into production in the second department (Finishing) are added in proportion to labor and manufacturing overhead. Data for the month of August 19X8 are given below and on page 304.

	Forming Department	Finishing Department
Costs		
Beginning Work in Process		
Costs in Prior Department	-0-	$26,178
Costs in Current Department		
Materials	$ 6,180	980
Labor	2,610	730
Manufacturing Overhead	1,710	580
Current Department Costs—August		
Materials	92,520	10,135
Labor	76,650	8,090
Manufacturing Overhead	62,190	6,770

	Forming Department	Finishing Department
Quantities		
Beginning Work in Process	1,500	2,400
Started in Production	21,000	-0-
Transferred In From Prior Department	-0-	21,500
Transferred Out to Next Department	21,500	-0-
Transferred Out to Finished Goods	-0-	21,000
Ending Work in Process	1,000	2,900
Stage of Completion of Work in Process		
Beginning		
Material	complete	75%
Labor and Manufacturing Overhead	40%	75%
Ending		
Material	complete	70%
Labor and Manufacturing Overhead	50%	70%

Instructions

1. Complete the equivalent production computations for each department.
2. Prepare separate cost of production reports for the two departments.

PROBLEM 15-5. Making journal entries to record and transfer costs. Using the data from the cost of production report completed in Problem 15-4, prepare entries in general journal form to record the costs charged to each department, the costs transferred between departments, and the costs transferred out to finished goods. Date the entries August 31. Use the accounts Work in Process—Forming 123 and Work in Process—Finishing 124. Combine the amounts and accounts in entries whenever possible.

PROBLEM 15-6. Computing equivalent production; preparing a combined cost of production report; making journal entries to transfer costs. The Miller Company has three producing departments: the Cutting Department, the Assembling Department, and the Painting Department. The departmental Work in Process accounts are completed for June 19X6 as shown below and on page 305.

	Work in Process—Cutting Department				No. 134		
DATE	EXPLANATION	POST. REF.	DEBIT	CREDIT	BALANCE		DR. CR.
19X6							
June 1	Balance	✓			2,824	47	Dr.
30	Materials	MR4	10,206 27		13,030	74	Dr.
30	Labor	J4-9	4,161 62		17,192	36	Dr.
30	Overhead	J4-10	9,345 64		26,538	00	Dr.

Work in Process—Assembling Department   No. _____135_____

DATE		EXPLANATION	POST. REF.	DEBIT		CREDIT	BALANCE		DR. CR.
19 X6									
June	1	Balance	✔				5,981	95	Dr.
	30	Materials	MR4	720	10		6,702	05	Dr.
	30	Labor	J4-9	6,331	17		13,033	22	Dr.
	30	Overhead	J4-10	1,152	34		14,185	56	Dr.

Work in Process—Painting Department   No. _____136_____

DATE		EXPLANATION	POST. REF.	DEBIT		CREDIT	BALANCE		DR. CR.
19 X6									
June	1	Balance	✔				1,142	47	Dr.
	30	Materials	MR4	1,526	20		2,668	67	Dr.
	30	Labor	J4-9	3,159	82		5,828	49	Dr.
	30	Overhead	J4-10	3,653	47		9,481	96	Dr.

The departmental supervisors have submitted their cost of production reports for May 19X6. A summary of the results for the work in process sections is shown below.

Data for Work in Process on May 31	Cutting Department	Assembling Department	Painting Department
Prior Department Costs	-0-	$4,334.56	$1,016.41
Materials	$1,632.48	838.40	22.10
Labor	385.63	331.33	48.18
Overhead	806.36	477.66	55.78
Totals of Work in Process on June 1	$2,824.47	$5,981.95	$1,142.47

The monthly departmental production reports for June 19X6 have been submitted and summarized. The results are shown below.

	Cutting Department	Assembling Department	Painting Department
Quantity			
Work in Process—Beginning	430	630	56
Started in Production—Current Month	1,915	-0-	-0-
Transferred In From Prior Department	-0-	1,975	1,955
Transferred Out to Next Department	1,975	1,955	-0-
Transferred Out to Finished Goods	-0-	-0-	1,970
Work in Process—Ending	370	650	41

	Cutting Department	Assembling Department	Painting Department
Stage of Completion of Ending Work in Process			
Materials	100%	25%	30%
Labor	50%	25%	60%
Overhead	50%	25%	60%

Instructions

1. Prepare the equivalent production computations for the Cutting Department for June 19X6.
2. Prepare the equivalent production computations for the Assembling Department and the Painting Department for June 19X6.
3. Prepare the combined cost of production report for June 19X6. Carry the unit costs to four decimal places.
4. a. Prepare the general journal voucher (Number 6-11) to record the transfer of goods from the Cutting Department to the Assembling Department.
   b. Prepare the general journal voucher (Number 6-12) to record the transfer of goods from the Assembling Department to the Painting Department.
   c. Prepare the general journal voucher (Number 6-13) to record the completion of goods and their transfer to Finished Goods 126.

Alternate Problems

NOTE: Assume in all the problems that each company uses the average cost method for costing work in process.

PROBLEM 15-1A. Preparing a cost of production report; comparing unit costs. April 19X3 is the first month of operations for the Denmead Processing Company. In the Mixing Department (the second department), 3,960 units were transferred in from the Grinding Department during April. These units were transferred in at a total cost of $233,640 ($59 each). Additional costs incurred in the Mixing Department during April were: materials, $47,520; labor, $93,330; and overhead, $43,474. Of the 3,960 units, 3,690 were completed and transferred out to finished goods. The remaining 270 were still in process on April 30. All materials had been added, but only 25 percent of the labor and 25 percent of the overhead had been added.

Instructions

1. Prepare a cost of production report for the Mixing Department for the month of April.
2. In the month of May, the costs per equivalent unit in the Mixing Department were as follows: materials, $12.01; labor, $21.16; and overhead, $11.60. If you were a part of the management at the Denmead Processing Company, what steps would you take after comparing the costs per equivalent unit for April and May? Suggest possible reasons for the differences.

PROBLEM 15-2A. **Making journal entries to record and transfer costs.** Using the data from the cost of production report prepared in Problem 15-1A, give the entries in general journal form to charge costs to production and to record the transfer of units to finished goods. Date the entries April 30. (Use Work in Process—Mixing Department 123.)

PROBLEM 15-3A. **Preparing a cost of production report.** The Kilbride Corporation produces a single product. All materials are added at the beginning of production. On January 1, 19X7, 8,000 pounds of the product were in process in the first department. During the month of January, 75,000 pounds were put into production. On January 31, 12,000 pounds were still in process. The ending inventory is estimated to be complete as to materials and two-thirds complete as to labor and overhead. Cost data for the month of January are shown below.

	Materials	Labor	Overhead
Beginning Work in Process Inventory	$ 32,000	$ 14,400	$ 7,200
Added During January	288,000	133,040	68,800

Instructions

Prepare a cost of production report for the month of January.

PROBLEM 15-4A. **Computing equivalent production; preparing a cost of production report for two departments.** The Amalfi Company uses a process cost accounting system. All materials in the first department (Grinding) are added at the start of production. Raw materials put into production in the second department (Finishing) are added in proportion to labor and manufacturing overhead. Data for the month of February 19X8 are given below.

	Grinding Dept.	Finishing Dept.
Costs		
Beginning Work in Process		
Costs in Prior Department	-0-	$3,046
Costs in Current Department		
Materials	$ 1,500	312
Labor	430	263
Manufacturing Overhead	730	291
Current Department Costs—February		
Materials	19,020	7,848
Labor	17,860	5,884
Manufacturing Overhead	16,270	4,908
Quantities		
Beginning Work in Process	150	125
Started in Production	1,250	-0-
Transferred In From Prior Department	-0-	1,225
Transferred Out to Next Department	1,225	-0-
Transferred Out to Finished Goods	-0-	1,200
Ending Work in Process	175	150

Stage of Completion of Work in Process	Grinding Dept.	Finishing Dept.
Beginning		
Materials	complete	$66\frac{2}{3}\%$
Labor and Manufacturing Overhead	25%	$66\frac{2}{3}\%$
Ending		
Materials	complete	50%
Labor and Manufacturing Overhead	60%	50%

Instructions

1. Complete equivalent production computations for each department.
2. Prepare separate cost of production reports for the two departments.

PROBLEM 15-5A. Making journal entries to record and transfer costs. Using the data from the cost of production report completed in Problem 15-4A, prepare entries in general journal form to record the costs charged to each department, the costs transferred between departments, and the costs transferred out to finished goods. Date all entries February 29. (Use the accounts Work in Process—Grinding 123 and Work in Process—Finishing 124.) Combine the amounts and accounts in entries whenever possible.

CHAPTER

16

Units Lost or Increased in Production

■ ■ ■

The mass-production techniques and high-speed machinery used in continuous process operations occasionally fail to function properly. Similarly, production workers sometimes make mistakes. Both situations can result in the loss of units in production. Losses may also be due to spoilage, shrinkage, evaporation, condensation, leakage, damage, or other factors in the manufacturing operations. Other manufacturing techniques may produce an increase in the number of units in production by expansion, blending, and other processes. These losses or increases must be considered so that the final unit cost will relate to the actual output for the period.

Accounting for Lost Units

Units are lost in Space Savers' factory when products in process are spoiled or damaged so badly that they must be discarded as worthless. Costs for lost units are absorbed by the remaining good units produced in the month because lost units are considered a routine part of production at Space Savers. The accounting procedure used to record this absorption depends on whether the department in which the loss occurs is first in the producing sequence or later.

Units Lost in First Department

When the lost units occur in the first department, no special calculations are required. The costs incurred for materials, labor, and overhead are merely spread over the equivalent units of production for each element. Let us assume that in March 19X5 the supervisor of the Milling Department at Space Savers reports that 20 desks are damaged and are a complete loss. The cost and production data for the department for March are assembled in the usual order.

Cost Data. The Work in Process—Milling Department 123 account in the general ledger (page 310) shows a balance of $63,564.40 on March 31.

	Work in Process—Milling Department				No. 123	
DATE	EXPLANATION	POST. REF.	DEBIT	CREDIT	BALANCE	DR. CR.
19X5 Mar. 1	Balance	✔			6,341 04	Dr.
31	Materials	MR3	23,564 40		29,905 44	Dr.
31	Labor	J3-50	18,156 84		48,062 28	Dr.
31	Overhead	J3-51	15,502 12		63,564 40	Dr.

This balance consists of the following costs:

Beginning Work in Process
Materials	$ 4,485.60	
Labor	1,001.16	
Overhead	854.28	
Balance of Account, Feb. 28		$ 6,341.04

Current Month
Materials	$23,564.40	
Labor	18,156.84	
Overhead	15,502.12	
Total Current Month's Costs		$57,223.36
Balance of Account, Mar. 31		$63,564.40

Production Data. The 20 units lost in production are reported on the last line of the Quantity section of the monthly production report.

MILLING DEPARTMENT
Monthly Production Report
March 19X5

Quantity
Work in Process—Beginning	180
Started in Production—Current Month	940
Transferred Out to Next Department	960
Work in Process—Ending	140
Lost in Production	20

Stage of Completion of Ending Work in Process
Materials	complete
Labor	50%
Overhead	50%

Equivalent Production Data. In computing equivalent production, the cost accountant ignores the lost units because all costs must be absorbed by the good units. Only the good units (those transferred out to the next department and those in the ending work in process) are considered.

```
                    MILLING DEPARTMENT
                 Equivalent Production Computations
                      Month of March 19X5

    Materials
        Transferred Out to Next Department                    960
        Work in Process—Ending (140 desks × 100%)             140
           Equivalent Production for Materials              1,100

    Labor and Manufacturing Overhead
        Transferred Out to Next Department                    960
        Work in Process—Ending (140 desks × 50%)               70
           Equivalent Production for Labor and Overhead     1,030
```

Cost of Production Report. The March cost of production report, shown on page 312, is very similar to the department's February report. However, note the details given in connection with lost units.

- In the Quantity Schedule, all units are included under Quantity to Be Accounted For. The lost units are reported separately under Quantity Accounted For.
- In the Cost Schedule, the cost of each element in the beginning work in process inventory is combined as usual with the cost incurred during the month. However, note that all costs are absorbed by the good units in determining average unit costs. This is done by dividing the total cost of each element by the equivalent production units. Remember that the lost units were ignored when the equivalent units were computed. The term *equivalent units* actually means *equivalent good units*.

Units Lost in Subsequent Departments

When units of a product are lost in departments that work on the product after the first department, the accounting procedures are more complex. The good units must absorb not only all the costs incurred in the department in which the loss occurs, but also the costs incurred in prior departments. Since prior departmental costs have already been identified with the total number of units transferred out of the preceding department and into the current department, there must be a recalculation of the unit cost from prior departments. This recalculation of prior department unit costs may be made by merely dividing the total prior departmental costs by the good units. In this case, no separate disclosure is made of the amount of change in the cost per unit resulting from the loss. This procedure is illustrated for Space Savers' Assembling Department for March. In that month the Assembling Department lost 25 units through breakage. These units cannot be repaired and have no salvage value. Here is how the firm's records are adjusted to obtain accurate unit costs.

Cost Data. The Work in Process—Assembling Department 124 account (page 313) shows a balance of $49,409.44 on March 31.

MILLING DEPARTMENT
Cost of Production Report
Month of March 19X5

QUANTITY SCHEDULE	UNITS
(a) Quantity to Be Accounted For:	
Work in Process—Beginning	180
Started in Production—Current Month	940
Transferred In From Prior Department	-0-
Total to Be Accounted For	1,120
(b) Quantity Accounted For:	
Transferred Out to Next Department	960
Transferred Out to Finished Goods	-0-
Work in Process—Ending	140
Lost in Production	20
Total Accounted For	1,120

COST SCHEDULE	TOTAL COST	E.P. UNITS	UNIT COST
(c) Costs to Be Accounted For:			
Costs in Prior Department			
Work in Process—Beginning	-0-		
Transferred In—Current Month	-0-		
Total Prior Department Costs	-0-		
Costs in Current Department			
Materials—Beginning Work in Process	$ 4,485.60		
Added in Current Month	23,564.40		
Total Materials	$28,050.00 ÷	1,100 =	$25.500
Labor—Beginning Work in Process	$ 1,001.16		
Added in Current Month	18,156.84		
Total Labor	$19,158.00 ÷	1,030 =	18.600
Overhead—Beginning Work in Process	$ 854.28		
Added in Current Month	15,502.12		
Total Overhead	$16,356.40 ÷	1,030 =	15.880
Total Costs in Current Dept.	$63,564.40		$59.980
Total Costs to Be Accounted For	$63,564.40		$59.980
(d) Costs Accounted For:			
Transferred Out to Next Department	$57,580.80 =	960 ×	$59.980
Transferred Out to Finished Goods	-0-		
Total Transferred Out	$57,580.80		
Work in Process—Ending			
Materials	$ 3,570.00 =	140 ×	$25.500
Labor	1,302.00 =	70 ×	$18.600
Overhead	1,111.60 =	70 ×	$15.880
Total Work in Process	$ 5,983.60		
Total Costs Accounted For	$63,564.40		

DATE		EXPLANATION	POST. REF.	DEBIT		CREDIT		BALANCE		DR. CR.

Work in Process—Assembling Department   No.   124

DATE		EXPLANATION	POST. REF.	DEBIT	CREDIT	BALANCE	DR. CR.
19X5 Mar.	1	Balance	✔			3,963 64	Dr.
	31	Materials	MR3	11,411 80		15,375 44	Dr.
	31	Labor	J3-50	22,576 00		37,951 44	Dr.
	31	Overhead	J3-51	11,458 00		49,409 44	Dr.

This balance consists of the following costs:

Beginning Work in Process
    Costs in Prior Department $ 2,370.44
    Costs in Current Department
        Materials   483.20
        Labor   726.00
        Overhead   384.00
        Balance of Account, Feb. 28 $ 3,963.64

Current Month
    Materials $11,411.80
    Labor   22,576.00
    Overhead   11,458.00
    Total Current Month's Costs $45,445.80
    Balance of Account, Mar. 31 $49,409.44

Production Data. The departmental production report shows the 25 units lost during the period.

ASSEMBLING DEPARTMENT
Monthly Production Report
March 19X5

Quantity
    Work in Process—Beginning   40
    Transferred In From Prior Department   960
    Transferred Out to Next Department   925
    Work in Process—Ending   50
    Lost in Production   25
Stage of Completion of Ending Work in Process
    Materials   complete
    Labor   60%
    Overhead   60%

Equivalent Production Data. In determining equivalent production, the lost units are again ignored. As before, the result reflects good units only, as shown on page 314 in the equivalent production computations.

```
┌─────────────────────────────────────────────────────────────┐
│                   ASSEMBLING DEPARTMENT                       │
│              Equivalent Production Computations               │
│                   Month of March 19X5                        │
│                                                              │
│   Materials                                                  │
│      Transferred Out to Next Department              925     │
│      Work in Process—Ending (50 desks × 100%)         50     │
│      Equivalent Production for Materials             975     │
│                                                              │
│   Labor and Overhead                                         │
│      Transferred Out to Next Department              925     │
│      Work in Process—Ending (50 desks × 60%)          30     │
│      Equivalent Production for Labor and Overhead    955     │
└─────────────────────────────────────────────────────────────┘
```

Cost of Production Report. The Quantity Schedule of the cost of production report is prepared in the same way as the corresponding section of the Milling Department's report. However, several details in the Cost Schedule for the Assembling Department require careful attention because now all costs must be absorbed only by the remaining good units.

■ The total of prior department costs, $59,951.24, is divided by the 975 total equivalent (good) units for an average prior department unit cost of $61.488, as shown on the cost of production report on page 315.
■ The total of each cost element under Costs in Current Department is divided by its equivalent production of good units to obtain the average unit cost shown on the cost of production report.

Some accountants believe that the Costs in Prior Department section should be made more informative. That is, in dealing with lost units they prefer to show the following:

1. What the unit cost would have been if there had been no lost units.
2. The adjusted unit cost, which is the same as the unit cost obtained by using equivalent *good* units. This is the figure shown in the illustration on page 315.
3. The lost unit cost, which is the difference between what the cost would have been and the adjusted unit cost.

The partial cost of production report illustrated on page 316 shows a more expanded presentation of prior department costs. Note the following items:

■ The Total Prior Department Costs are first divided by 1,000 units. This is a gross amount consisting of 40 units from Work in Process—Beginning on March 1 and 960 units Transferred In From Prior Department.
■ The 25 lost units are noted on the Adjustment for Lost Units line in the Equivalent Units column so that they may be subtracted.
■ The Adjusted Prior Department Costs line shows the same total cost ($59,951.24) divided by the 975 equivalent good units only.

ASSEMBLING DEPARTMENT
Cost of Production Report
Month of March 19X5

QUANTITY SCHEDULE	UNITS
(a) Quantity to Be Accounted For:	
Work in Process—Beginning	40
Started in Production—Current Month	-0-
Transferred In From Prior Department	960
Total to Be Accounted For	1,000
(b) Quantity Accounted For:	
Transferred Out to Next Department	925
Transferred Out to Finished Goods	-0-
Work in Process—Ending	50
Lost in Production	25
Total Accounted For	1,000

COST SCHEDULE	TOTAL COST	E.P. UNIT	UNIT COST
(c) Costs to Be Accounted For:			
Costs in Prior Department			
Work in Process—Beginning	$ 2,370.44		
Transferred In—Current Month	57,580.80		
Total Prior Department Costs	$ 59,951.24 ÷	975 =	$ 61.488
Costs in Current Department			
Materials—Beginning Work in Process	$ 483.20		
Added in Current Month	11,411.80		
Total Materials	$ 11,895.00 ÷	975 =	$ 12.200
Labor—Beginning Work in Process	$ 726.00		
Added in Current Month	22,576.00		
Total Labor	$ 23,302.00 ÷	955 =	24.400
Overhead—Beginning Work in Process	384.00		
Added in Current Month	11,458.00		
Total Overhead	$ 11,842.00 ÷	955 =	12.400
Total Costs in Current Department	$ 47,039.00		$ 49.000
Total Costs to Be Accounted For	$106,990.24		$110.488
(d) Costs Accounted For:			
Transferred Out to Next Department	$102,201.84* =	925 ×	$110.488
Transferred Out to Finished Goods	-0-		
Total Transferred Out	$102,201.84		
Work in Process—Ending			
Costs in Prior Department	$ 3,074.40 =	50 ×	$ 61.488
Costs in Current Department			
Materials	610.00 =	50 ×	$ 12.200
Labor	732.00 =	30 ×	$ 24.400
Overhead	372.00 =	30 ×	$ 12.400
Total Work in Process	$ 4,788.40		
Total Costs Accounted For	$106,990.24		

*Adjusted for rounding, $.44.

- The difference between the unit costs ($61.488 − $59.951 = $1.537), called lost unit cost, is then entered on the Adjustment for Lost Units in the Unit Cost column to complete the record.

COST SCHEDULE	TOTAL COST	E.P. UNITS	UNIT COST
(c) Costs to Be Accounted For:			
Costs in Prior Department			
Work in Process—Beginning	$ 2,370.44		
Transferred In—Current Month	57,580.80		
Total Prior Department Costs	$59,951.24 ÷	1,000 =	$59.951
Adjustment for Lost Units		25	1.537
Adjusted Prior Department Costs	$59,951.24 ÷	975 =	$61.488

Abnormal Loss of Units

If units of product are spoiled or ruined because of unusual or *abnormal* conditions that are not a typical, recurring part of the manufacturing process, it is customary to assign to such goods their usual share of costs as though the spoiled units were good units. Then the cost assigned to them is removed from work in process and charged to a special loss account by an entry similar to the following:

Loss From Abnormally Spoiled Units	1,000.00	
Work in Process—Department 2		1,000.00
Charged the cost of abnormal spoilage to the loss account.		

Fortunately, abnormal spoilage is by definition not common.

Accounting for Unit Increases

Because of the nature of Space Savers' operation, it is not possible for the firm to have unit increases in production. Units may be spoiled, but a desk can never be more than the single unit that it started out to be. However, in certain industries, the addition of materials in later departments and the further processing of the product result in an increase in the number of physical units. For example, if 100 pounds of flour are sifted and mixed with water, yeast, sugar, and fats, and are then baked, the resulting loaves of bread will weigh much more than 100 pounds. The accounting problem involved is the reverse of that caused by lost units. The solution is to spread the total costs among the larger number of units to produce a lower average unit cost.

Units Increased in Production

In order to study how increases in units of production are accounted for, let us trace the costs pertaining to the second department, the Mixing Department, of the Southern Soap Company for January 19X6. The department receives barrels of dry detergent from the first department, the Cooking Department. Fragrance and water are added to the detergent, and when properly mixed, the resulting increased quantity of product is transferred to the Finishing Department.

Cost Data. The Work in Process—Mixing Department 124 account shows a balance of $505,536 on January 31, 19X6, including costs transferred in during January from the Cooking Department.

DATE		EXPLANATION	POST. REF.	DEBIT		CREDIT		BALANCE		DR. CR.
19X6										
Jan.	1	Balance	✔					15,488	00	Dr.
	31	Materials	MR1	45,156	00			60,644	00	Dr.
	31	Labor	J1-60	36,303	60			96,947	60	Dr.
	31	Overhead	J1-62	48,588	40			145,536	00	Dr.
	31	Transferred In	J1-70	360,000	00			505,536	00	Dr.

Work in Process—Mixing Department   No. 124

The balance of this account consists of the following costs:

Beginning Work in Process (1,000 units)
Costs in Prior Department	$12,620.00	
Costs in Current Department		
Materials	1,468.00	
Labor	600.00	
Overhead	800.00	
Balance of Account, Dec. 31		$ 15,488.00
Current Month		
Materials	$45,156.00	
Labor	36,303.60	
Overhead	48,588.40	
Total Current Month's Costs		130,048.00
Transferred In From Cooking Department		360,000.00
Balance of Account, Jan. 31		$505,536.00

Production Data. The supervisor's production report for the month, given on page 318, shows an increase of 10,000 units (barrels) of product.

Equivalent Production Data. In the accountant's schedule of equivalent production (page 318), note that the number of units indicated as transferred to the next department, 29,800, includes the increase of 10,000 units in this process. Thus, equivalent units mean *expanded* equivalent units in this system. (It is assumed that all materials have been added to the beginning inventory of work in process.)

```
MIXING DEPARTMENT
Monthly Production Report
January 19X6

Quantity
    Work in Process—Beginning                                1,000
    Transferred In From Prior Department                    20,000
    Transferred Out to Next Department                      29,800
    Work in Process—Ending                                   1,200
    Increase in Production                                  10,000
Stage of Completion of Ending Work in Process
    Materials                                             complete
    Labor                                                    66⅔%
    Overhead                                                 66⅔%
```

```
MIXING DEPARTMENT
Equivalent Production Computations
Month of January 19X6

Prior Department Costs
    Transferred Out to Next Department                      29,800
    Work in Process—Ending                                   1,200
        Equivalent Production for Prior Department          31,000

Materials
    Transferred Out to Next Department                      29,800
    Work in Process—Ending (1,200 barrels × 100%)            1,200
        Equivalent Production for Materials                 31,000

Labor and Overhead
    Transferred Out to Next Department                      29,800
    Work in Process—Ending (1,200 barrels × 66⅔%)             800
        Equivalent Production for Labor and Overhead        30,600
```

Cost of Production Report. There are several fine points to be noted in the treatment of increased units on the cost of production report shown on page 319.

Quantity Schedule. The increase in units is reported under Quantity to Be Accounted For because the units to be accounted for must equal the units accounted for.

Cost Schedule. The actual spreading of the costs among the larger number of units is shown under Costs to Be Accounted For since all costs must be absorbed by all the units produced.

MIXING DEPARTMENT
Cost of Production Report
Month of January 19X6

QUANTITY SCHEDULE	UNITS
(a) Quantity to Be Accounted For:	
Work in Process—Beginning	1,000
Transferred In From Prior Department	20,000
Increase in Production	10,000
Total to Be Accounted For	31,000
(b) Quantity Accounted For:	
Transferred Out to Next Department	29,800
Work in Process—Ending	1,200
Total Accounted For	31,000

COST SCHEDULE	TOTAL COST	E.P. UNITS	UNIT COST
(c) Costs to Be Accounted For:			
Costs in Prior Department			
Work in Process—Beginning	$ 12,620.00		
Transferred In—Current Month	360,000.00		
Total Prior Department Costs	$372,620.00 ÷	31,000 =	$12.020
Costs in Current Department			
Materials—Beginning Work in Process	$ 1,468.00		
Added in Current Month	45,156.00		
Total Materials	$ 46,624.00 ÷	31,000 =	$ 1.504
Labor—Beginning Work in Process	$ 600.00		
Added in Current Month	36,303.60		
Total Labor	$ 36,903.60 ÷	30,600 =	1.206
Overhead—Beginning Work in Process	$ 800.00		
Added in Current Month	48,588.40		
Total Overhead	$ 49,388.40 ÷	30,600 =	1.614
Total Costs in Current Department	$132,916.00		$ 4.324
Total Costs to Be Accounted For	$505,536.00		$16.344
(d) Costs Accounted For:			
Transferred Out to Next Department	$487,051.20 =	29,800 ×	$16.344
Work in Process—Ending			
Costs in Prior Department	$ 14,424.00 =	1,200 ×	$12.020
Costs in Current Department			
Materials	1,804.80 =	1,200 ×	$ 1.504
Labor	964.80 =	800 ×	$ 1.206
Overhead	1,291.20 =	800 ×	$ 1.614
Total Work in Process	$ 18,484.80		
Total Costs Accounted For	$505,536.00		

Internal Control in a Computerized Information System

One of the major functions of the cost accountant is to provide management with the detailed costs of manufacturing a product or delivering a service. Since these costs are used by management to make decisions, information about costs can be thought of as one of management's major resources. The accuracy and timeliness of cost information are vital to the decision-making process. Therefore the system used to generate cost information must be carefully controlled.

In a computerized system many of the internal control procedures will be the concern and responsibility of the information systems department of the firm. However, the cost accountant should be sure that the following controls are implemented with respect to the input and output of accounting data and information.

1. Input data should be prepared outside of the data processing department.
2. Responsibility for approving transactions should be assigned to someone outside of the data processing department. For example, the computer may automatically generate a purchase order when inventory reaches a certain level. Before that order is mailed, it should be approved by the purchasing agent.
3. Transactions that are to be processed together should be sent to the data processing department in batches along with a transaction count. This will keep transactions from being processed more than once and provides assurance that all transactions have been processed.
4. Terminal users should have a password code that will be keyed in before transactions can be processed. Not only will the code allow only authorized personnel to use the terminal, but it will also limit the type of transactions that the user may record on the computer.
5. Only approved changes should be made to master files (those files that contain information such as sales prices, customer and vendor listings, pay rates).
6. The cost accountant should arrange to review all transactions that are rejected by the computer. This will prevent transactions from being lost.
7. Output should be reviewed by the cost accountant for reasonableness. For example, a shipment scheduled from New York to Australia by truck would not be reasonable.

Controls will not catch all errors or fraud in a system. However, a lack of controls is an open invitation to problems. ■

- The Total Prior Department Costs figure, $372,620, is divided by the 31,000 expanded equivalent units to obtain an average unit cost of $12.02.
- The total for each cost element in the Costs in Current Department section is divided by its expanded equivalent units to determine an average unit cost.

Accountants who prefer more detail in the Costs in Prior Department section may show units and unit costs for beginning work in process and work transferred in. (The latter figures are the same as those shown as Transferred Out to Next Department in the cost of production report of the Cooking Department.) The partial cost of production report shown below includes an adjustment for the increase of 10,000 units, which leads to Total Prior Department Costs of $372,620. This amount is divided by 31,000 units in order to calculate an average unit cost of $12.02, as shown previously.

COST SCHEDULE	TOTAL COST	E.P. UNITS	UNIT COST
(c) Costs to Be Accounted For:			
Costs in Prior Department			
Work in Process—Beginning	$ 12,620.00 ÷	1,000 =	$12.620
Transferred In—Current Month	$360,000.00 ÷	20,000 =	$18.000
Adjustment for Increase in Units		10,000	$ 6.000
Adjusted Cost Transferred—Current Month	$360,000.00 ÷	30,000 =	$12.000
Total Prior Department Costs	$372,620.00 ÷	31,000 =	$12.020

Completion of the balance of the report is the same as in other similar illustrations. Adjustments for increases and lost units may be shown on a single combined report as well as presented in the separate departmental reports illustrated.

In some instances, defective units that occur under the process system may be reworked and completed as good units. Normally, this does not require additional accounting entries. Any additional costs that are incurred are treated in the usual manner as Costs to Be Accounted For in the current department.

Defective units are often spoiled (or "lost") and cannot be processed, but the salvaged material may be sold as scrap. In this event, it is customary to treat the salvaged material as a by-product. A by-product is one that has little value compared to other products being manufactured in the process. Accounting for by-products is discussed in Chapter 18.

Principles and Procedures Summary

Losses or increases in units of production reported by supervisors must be taken into account when average unit costs are determined.

Losses in units are absorbed by the remaining good units in production during the month, resulting in a higher average unit cost. Lost units are ignored in computing equivalent units. The lost units are reported in the Quantity Accounted For section of the Quantity Schedule of the cost of production report. They may also be noted on the line for Adjustment for Lost Units under Costs in Prior Department if the accountant prefers to make a detailed presentation in the Cost Schedule section. The average unit cost in the prior department is finally determined by dividing the adjusted prior department costs by the equivalent good units. The average cost of other elements is obtained in a similar way.

Increases in units of production result in lower average unit costs because total charges are spread among a greater number of units. Increases are included in the calculation of equivalent units. They are also reported in the Quantity Schedule section of the cost of production report. The increase directly affects Costs in Prior Department. The average unit cost is determined by using the number of expanded units as a divisor. The amount of detail regarding the unit increase that is shown on the report depends upon the accountant's preference. Detailed presentations supply more information and permit easier cross-checking.

Review Questions

1. How are units lost in production?
2. Are lost units considered in computing equivalent units? Explain.
3. How are costs of lost units treated in the first department? How are they treated in later departments?
4. Equivalent units of production actually refers to equivalent *good* units. Explain.
5. How can units increase in production?
6. A separate calculation is not shown for changes in unit costs resulting from increases in units. Why?
7. What is the effect of spoiled goods on prior department costs per unit? How does this differ from their effect on the cost per unit in the current department?
8. Are costs of reprocessing spoiled units accounted for separately? Explain.
9. How would the presentation of the cost of units lost in the first department differ from the presentation of the cost of units lost in later departments?

Managerial Discussion Questions

1. Why should management be very interested in units lost in production?
2. How would you explain to management why some spoilage could be considered normal while other spoilage is abnormal?
3. Would you recommend that the cost of production report show a separate adjustment resulting from lost units? Why?
4. How do units lost in production affect the unit cost of the beginning work in process inventory?
5. Assume that during one month your company had abnormally high spoilage. You have recommended that the applicable costs be removed from the current month and allocated other several months. Why?
6. Over a period of several months the adjustment for lost units has steadily decreased in one department. Is this favorable or unfavorable? What factors could account for this?

Exercises

1. **Computing equivalent production for labor when there are lost units.** The following data pertain to labor used in the Packing Department of the Emerson Company during July 19X5. Calculate the equivalent units of production for labor for the month.

Beginning work in process, 200 units, ½ complete
Started in production, 4,000 units
Transferred out to next department, 3,800 units
Ending work in process, 100 units, ½ complete
Lost in production, 300 units

The handwritten margin notes (next to exercise 2):
1950
85770
85770
87720 = $22.78
(A) 87720
(B) ÷ 3850 = 11.39
(C) 22.78 × 50 = 1139

2. **Computing cost per unit for labor and ending work in process when there are lost units.** Assume the same data as in Exercise 1. In addition, assume that the labor costs in the beginning work in process inventory were $1,950 and that the labor costs incurred during the month were $85,770.

  a. Compute the total labor costs.

  b. Determine the cost per equivalent unit for labor.

  c. Calculate the labor costs in the ending work in process inventory.

3. **Computing equivalent production for overhead when there are lost units.** The following data pertains to overhead for the Assembly Department of Richardson Transistors for August 19X7. Calculate the equivalent units of production for overhead for the month.

The handwritten margin notes (next to exercise 3):
11600 (1.0)
+ 2080 (.60)
12848

Beginning work in process, 1,000 units, 75 percent complete
Started in production, 12,800 units
Transferred out to next department, 11,600 units
Ending work in process, 2,080 units, 60 percent complete
Lost in production, 120 units

4. **Computing cost per unit for overhead and ending work in process when there are lost units.** Assume the same data as in Exercise 3. In addition, assume that the overhead costs in the beginning work in process inventory were $1,500 and that the overhead costs incurred during the month were $32,700.

  a. Compute the total labor costs.

  b. Determine the cost per equivalent unit for overhead.

  c. Calculate the overhead costs in the ending work in process inventory.

The handwritten margin notes (next to exercise 4):
1500
32700
(A) $34200
(B) ÷ 12848 = $2.66
(C) $2.66 × 2080 (.6) =
= $3319.68

5. **Computing costs in a prior department when there are lost units.** On January 1, 19X4, beginning work in process inventory for the Machining Department of the Allen Company was 6,000 units with prior department costs of $18,000. During the month, 30,000 units were transferred into the Machining Department with prior department costs of $90,000. A total of 34,600 units were transferred to the next department, and 1,200 units were in the ending work in process inventory. Prepare the Quantity Schedule section of the cost of production report.

6. **Computing costs in a prior department when there are lost units.** On March 1, 19X5, the beginning work in process inventory for the Framing Department of the Reed Company was 100 units. The prior department costs for these units were $1,000. During the month, 2,400 units with prior department costs of $26,375 were transferred into the Framing Department, and 2,300 units were completed and transferred to the next department. The ending work in process inventory was 150 units, and 50 units were lost in production. Show how the Costs in Prior Departments section of Costs to Be Accounted For would appear in the cost of production report for March, assuming that there is a separate adjustment for lost units.

7. **Computing costs in a prior department when there are lost units.** On November 1, 19X8, the beginning work in process inventory for the Heating Department of the Gordon Company was 14,000 units with prior department costs of $22,800. During November, 65,000 units with prior department costs of

$129,000 were transferred into the Heating Department, and 70,000 units were transferred out to the next department. The ending work in process inventory was 8,400 units.

a. Show how the Costs in Prior Departments section of Costs to Be Accounted For would appear in the cost of production report for November, assuming that a separate adjustment for lost units is shown.

b. What is the amount of prior department costs in the ending work in process inventory?

8. **Computing equivalent production when there are increased units.** On October 1, 19X2, the beginning work in process inventory for the Mixing Department of Natural Care Products, a cosmetic producer, was 1,000 units with prior department costs of $1,000. During the month, 22,000 units were transferred into the Mixing Department with prior department costs of $33,220. Because of the addition of water to the solution, the number of units was increased. A total of 32,000 units were transferred to the next department, and 2,000 units were in the ending work in process inventory.

a. Compute the equivalent production for prior department costs.

b. What is the amount of prior department costs in the ending work in process inventory?

Problems

PROBLEM 16-1. Preparing a cost of production report when there are lost units. The Hernandez Company uses a process cost system. On October 1, 19X6, the company had 800 units in production in the Cooking Department, the second of three producing departments. All materials had been added to this beginning inventory, but labor and overhead were only 75 percent complete. Costs applicable to the beginning work in process inventory follow:

Costs in Prior Department	$15,182.00
Materials	2,416.00
Labor	3,360.00
Overhead	1,920.00

During the month of October, an additional 19,200 units were transferred into the Cooking Department with prior department costs of $143,952. Additional costs were incurred in the Cooking Department as follows:

Materials	$57,059.00
Labor	11,268.00
Overhead	57,920.00

A total of 18,500 units were transferred out to the third department during the month, 1,000 units were still in production at the end of the month, and 500 units were lost in production. All materials had been added to the ending work in process inventory, but labor and overhead were only 70 percent complete.

Instructions

1. Prepare the equivalent production computations for the Cooking Department for October 19X6.

2. Prepare the cost of production report for the Cooking Department for October 19X6, assuming that the average cost method of handling work in process inventory is used. Show a separate adjustment for lost units.

PROBLEM 16-2. Preparing a cost of production report when there are lost units. The South Boston Company makes parts for textile machinery. The first producing department is the Machine Shop. The average cost method is used to price the beginning work in process inventory. The cost of lost units is absorbed by the remaining good units. The Work in Process—Machine Shop account is shown below.

	Work in Process—Machine Shop				No. 123		
DATE	EXPLANATION	POST. REF.	DEBIT	CREDIT	BALANCE	DR. CR.
19X5 Dec. 1	Balance	✓			4,034 52	Dr.
31	Materials	MR10	49,451 84		53,495 36	Dr.
31	Labor	J10-26	10,546 16		64,041 52	Dr.
31	Overhead	J10-27	31,638 48		95,680 00	Dr.

The balance of this account on December 1, 19X5, consists of the following costs:

Materials	$2,148.16
Labor	473.84
Overhead	1,421.52
Total	$4,043.52

The monthly production report for December is as follows:

MACHINE SHOP
Monthly Production Report
December 19X5

Quantity	
Work in Process—Beginning	300
Started in Production—Current Month	2,400
Transferred Out to Next Department	2,200
Work in Process—Ending	400
Lost in Production	100
Stage of Completion of Ending Work in Process	
Materials	100%
Labor	60%
Overhead	60%

Instructions

1. Prepare the equivalent production computations for the Machine Shop for December 19X5.
2. Prepare the cost of production report for the Machine Shop for December 19X5. (Do not show a separate entry for lost units.)

PROBLEM 16-3. Preparing a cost of production report when there are lost units. The second producing department of the South Boston Company is the Cleaning Room. The average cost method is used to price its beginning work in process inventory. The cost of lost units is absorbed by the remaining good units. The Work in Process—Cleaning Room account is shown below.

	Work in Process—Cleaning Room				No. 124		
DATE	EXPLANATION	POST. REF.	DEBIT	CREDIT	BALANCE	DR. CR.	
19X5							
Dec. 1	Balance	✔			13,655 00	Dr.	
31	Materials	MR10	10,212 50		23,867 50	Dr.	
31	Labor	J10-26	28,000 00		51,867 50	Dr.	
31	Overhead	J10-27	13,440 00		65,307 50	Dr.	
31	From Machine Shop	J10-28	89,100 00		154,407 50	Dr.	

The balance of this account on December 1, 19X5, consists of the following costs:

Costs in Prior Department	$10,020.00
Costs in Current Department	
Materials	1,785.00
Labor	1,250.00
Overhead	600.00
Total	$13,655.00

The monthly production report for December is as follows:

CLEANING ROOM
Monthly Production Report
December 19X5

Quantity	
Work in Process—Beginning	250
Transferred In From Prior Department	2,200
Transferred Out to Next Department	2,300
Work in Process—Ending	100
Lost in Production	50
Stage of Completion of Ending Work in Process	
Materials	100%
Labor	60%
Overhead	60%

Instructions

1. Prepare the equivalent production computations for the Cleaning Room for December 19X5.
2. Prepare the cost of production report for the Cleaning Room for December 19X5. (Do not show a separate entry for lost units.)

PROBLEM 16-4. Preparing a cost of production report when there are increased units. The DeCarlo Company uses a process cost accounting system and the average cost method. The data given below relate to the Baking Department for August 19X3. Because material is added in this department, the number of units is increased during production.

Costs
Beginning Work in Process	
Costs in Prior Department	$12,000
Costs in Current Department	
Materials	2,600
Labor	1,700
Overhead	800
Current Department Costs—August	
Materials	82,775
Labor	49,500
Overhead	22,300
Transferred In From Prior Department—Current Month	64,150

Quantities
Beginning Work in Process	100
Transferred In From Prior Department	1,900
Transferred Out to Next Department	1,800
Ending Work in Process	350

Stage of Completion of Work in Process
Beginning Materials, Labor, and Overhead	60%
Ending Materials, Labor, and Overhead	50%

Instructions

1. Compute the equivalent units of production for each element.
2. Prepare the cost of production report for the department. (It is not necessary to show separately an adjustment for increased units.)

Alternate Problems

PROBLEM 16-1A. Preparing a cost of production report when there are lost units. The Chang Company uses a process cost system. On March 1, 19X1, the company had 500 units in production in the Assembly Department (the second department). All materials had been added to these units, but production was only one-half complete. Costs applicable to the beginning work in process inventory follow:

Costs in Prior Department	$10,400
Materials	7,000
Labor	3,000
Overhead	6,000

During the month of March, an additional 10,250 units were transferred into the Assembly Department with prior department costs of $196,400. Additional costs were incurred in the Assembly Department as follows:

Materials	$152,800
Labor	117,048
Overhead	223,821

A total of 9,600 units were transferred out to finished goods. The ending work in process inventory consisted of 400 units, to which all materials had been added, but only 75 percent of the processing had been completed. The other units were lost at the start of production in this department.

Instructions

1. Prepare the equivalent production computations for the Assembly Department for March 19X1.
2. Prepare the cost of production report for the Assembly Department for March 19X1, assuming that the company uses the average cost method to account for beginning work in process inventories. Show a separate adjustment for lost units.

PROBLEM 16-2A. Preparing a cost of production report when there are lost units. The Northwestern Company makes small appliances. The first producing department is the Framing Department. The average cost method is used to price the beginning work in process inventory. The cost of lost units is absorbed by the remaining good units. The Work in Process—Framing Department account is shown below.

	Work in Process—Framing Department				No. 123	
DATE	EXPLANATION	POST. REF.	DEBIT	CREDIT	BALANCE	DR. CR.
19X5						
Mar. 1	Balance	✔			7,934 22	Dr.
31	Materials	MR10	98,903 68		106,837 90	Dr.
31	Labor	J10-26	21,092 32		127,930 22	Dr.
31	Overhead	J10-27	63,276 96		191,207 18	Dr.

The balance of this account on March 1, 19X5, consists of the following costs:

Materials	$4,296.32
Labor	794.86
Overhead	2,843.04
Total	$7,934.22

The monthly production report for March is given on page 329.

```
                      FRAMING DEPARTMENT
                    Monthly Production Report
                         March 19X5

      Quantity
          Work in Process—Beginning                      200
          Started in Production—Current Month          4,900
          Transferred Out to Next Department           4,440
          Work in Process—Ending                         460
          Lost in Production                             200
      Stage of Completion of Ending Work in Process
          Materials                                     100%
          Labor                                          50%
          Overhead                                       50%
```

Instructions

1. Prepare the equivalent production computations for the Framing Department for March 19X5.
2. Prepare the cost of production report for the Framing Department for March 19X5. Carry the unit costs to three decimal places. (Do not show a separate entry for lost units.)

PROBLEM 16-3A. **Preparing a cost of production report when there are lost units.** The second producing department of the Northwestern Company is the Finishing Department. The average cost method is used to price its beginning work in process inventory. The cost of lost units is absorbed by the remaining good units. The Work in Process—Finishing Department account is shown below.

DATE		EXPLANATION	POST. REF.	DEBIT		CREDIT	BALANCE		DR. CR.
19X5									
Mar.	1	Balance	✓				26,997	00	Dr.
	31	Materials	MR10	20,425	00		47,422	00	Dr.
	31	Labor	J10-26	56,000	00		103,422	00	Dr.
	31	Overhead	J10-27	28,000	00		131,422	00	Dr.
	31	From Framing	J10-28	174,572	04		305,994	04	Dr.

Work in Process—Finishing Department No. 124

The balance of this account on March 1, 19X5, consists of the following costs:

Costs in Prior Department	$20,040.00
Costs in Current Department	
Materials	3,257.00
Labor	2,500.00
Overhead	1,200.00
Total	$26,997.00

The monthly production report for March is shown below.

```
┌─────────────────────────────────────────────────────────────┐
│                    FINISHING DEPARTMENT                      │
│                  Monthly Production Report                   │
│                        March 19X5                            │
│                                                              │
│   Quantity                                                   │
│       Work in Process—Beginning                    500       │
│       Transferred In From Prior Department       4,440       │
│       Transferred Out to Finished Goods          4,600       │
│       Work in Process—Ending                       150       │
│       Lost in Production                           190       │
│   Stage of Completion of Ending Work in Process              │
│       Materials                                    80%       │
│       Labor                                      33⅓%        │
│       Overhead                                   33⅓%        │
└─────────────────────────────────────────────────────────────┘
```

Instructions

1. Prepare the equivalent production computations for the Finishing Department for March 19X5.
2. Prepare the cost of production report for the Finishing Department for March 19X5. Carry the unit costs to three decimal places. (Do not show a separate entry for lost units.)

PROBLEM 16-4A. Preparing a cost of production report when there are increased units. The Great Lakes Company uses a process cost accounting system and the average cost method. The data given below and on page 331 relate to the Treating Department for July 19X7. Because material is added in this department, the number of units is increased during production.

Costs
   Beginning Work in Process
      Costs in Prior Department $ 12,184
      Costs in Current Department
         Materials   1,248
         Labor   944
         Overhead   768
   Current Department Costs—July
      Materials   31,392
      Labor   23,536
      Overhead   19,632
   Transferred In From Prior Department—Current Month   316,660

Quantities
   Beginning Work in Process   150
   Transferred In From Prior Department   1,225
   Transferred Out to Next Department   1,475
   Ending Work in Process   100

Stage of Completion of Work in Process

Beginning	
Materials	66%
Labor and Overhead	70%
Ending	
Materials	80%
Labor and Overhead	75%

Instructions

1. Compute the equivalent units of production for each element.
2. Prepare the cost of production report for the department. (It is not necessary to show separately an adjustment for increased units.)

Managerial Decisions

CASE 16-1. On the average, 6,000 decorative enameled trays are transferred into the Finishing Department of the Home Products Corporation with prior department costs of $112,000. Of these trays, on the average, 5,500 units are transferred out of the department to Finished Goods and 500 are lost in production with no salvage value. The work in process inventory remains constant. Monthly departmental costs include: labor—$33,000 and overhead—$16,500.

The department is presently operating at full capacity. A study has shown that all the spoilage is due to defects in materials added in the prior department. The defects cannot be detected until the work is completed in the Finishing Department. A better quality of materials can be purchased for an additional $2 per unit of goods in the prior department. It is estimated that this would reduce the spoiled units in the Finishing Department from an average of 500 to an average of 200 each month.

1. Compute the unit cost of each tray based on the materials presently used.
2. Compute the unit cost of each tray if the more expensive materials are used.
3. Should the more expensive materials be purchased? Explain.

CHAPTER

17

First In, First Out Costing of Work in Process

■ ■ ■

In Chapter 15 we examined the average cost method of accounting for the costs of the beginning work in process inventory. In this chapter we will examine the first in, first out (FIFO) cost method, using the data for accounting for post units from Chapter 16.

Average Cost Method and FIFO Cost Method

Under the average cost method, no distinction is made between the cost per unit of products that were both started and completed during the current period and those that were completed this period but on which work was begun in a prior period. Each element of cost in the beginning work in process inventory is combined with the amount of cost of that element added in the current period. The total cost is assigned to the equivalent units of production for the period. As a result, the unit cost for each element is an average of that element's cost in the beginning inventory and the cost added in the current period.

Under first in, first out (FIFO) costing, however, the costs of the beginning work in process inventory are assigned only to the units that were included in that inventory. Costs of units that are started and finished in the current period are computed separately. Thus units transferred out are identified as having come in part from the beginning work in process inventory and in part from units that were started or transferred into the department during the current period.

Choosing a Costing Method

In Chapter 15 you learned that Space Savers' cost accountant chose the average cost method of accounting for beginning inventories for the following reasons:

- The ending work in process inventory was small in relation to the total monthly production.
- The rate of production was stable, so the work in process inventory was fairly constant.
- The average cost method is simple to use.

Some accountants, however, prefer to use the FIFO method of accounting for costs of beginning inventories. They cite the following advantages:

- The unit costs are more accurate because they more directly relate to specific units of product.
- The unit costs reflect current conditions more clearly because the cost of completed units from the work in process inventory at the beginning of the period and the cost of units started during the period are computed separately.
- Major changes in costs can easily be monitored for control purposes.

Choosing the method that will best fit the firm's accounting system is not difficult as long as the accountant knows how both methods work and understands fully the advantages and disadvantages of each. With the same data that were used to illustrate accounting for lost units by means of average costing in Chapter 16, we can examine the procedures and results of the FIFO method. Then we can compare the results with those of the average cost method. Remember that under the FIFO method, the cost incurred in completing the beginning work in process inventory is computed separately from the cost of the units started into production during the month.

Milling Department

The activities of the Milling Department of Space Savers, the first department, for March 19X5 were first discussed on pages 309 and 310. This is the third month of operations and the first period in which there are lost units.

Cost Data

The Work in Process—Milling Department 123 account on March 31 is illustrated below.

	Work in Process—Milling Department				No. 123	
DATE	EXPLANATION	POST. REF.	DEBIT	CREDIT	BALANCE	DR. CR.
19X5						
Mar. 1	Balance	✔			6,341 04	Dr.
31	Materials	MR3	23,564 40		29,905 44	Dr.
31	Labor	J3-50	18,156 84		48,064 28	Dr.
31	Overhead	J3-51	15,502 12		63,564 40	Dr.

The balance of $63,564.40 includes the following costs:

Beginning Work in Process		
Materials	$4,485.60	
Labor	1,001.16	
Overhead	854.28	
Balance of Account, Feb. 28		$6,341.04

Current Month
Materials	$23,564.40	
Labor	18,156.84	
Overhead	15,502.12	
Total Current Month's Costs		$57,223.36
Balance of Account, Mar. 31		$63,564.40

Production Data

The production data of the Milling Department for March appears on the monthly production report illustrated below. The Transferred Out to Next Department section shows units from the beginning work in process inventory and units started and completed in the current month. The latter is determined by subtracting the ending inventory and the units lost in production from the units started in production during the month (940 − 140 − 20 = 780). In this example, it is assumed that all losses are incurred early in the production process. The losses involve goods started in production during the current month.

MILLING DEPARTMENT
Monthly Production Report
March 19X5

Quantity

Work in Process—Beginning			180
Started in Production—Current Month			940
Transferred Out to Next Department			
From Work in Process—Beginning		180	
Started and Completed in Current Month		780	960
Work in Process—Ending			140
Lost in Production			20

Stage of Completion of Work in Process

	Beginning	**Ending**
Materials	complete	complete
Labor	30%	50%
Overhead	30%	50%

Equivalent Production Data

The FIFO method of costing tries to separate the costs of new units from the costs of units in the beginning inventory. Equivalent production units that will be used to determine unit costs must be separated in the same way. The equivalent production is therefore computed so that the final figure relates only to the current month's work.

Observe the following on the equivalent production computations for March 19X5 shown on page 335.

■ The first two lines in each section are the same as they are when the average cost method is used.

- With the FIFO method, the Total Units Accounted For (1,100 for materials and 1,030 for labor and overhead) are the ones used as the total equivalent production figures under the average cost method.
- The fourth line in each section shows the beginning inventory for the month expressed in equivalent units. It is subtracted from the total units accounted for to give the equivalent production for the month under the FIFO method.

MILLING DEPARTMENT
Equivalent Production Computations
Month of March 19X5

Materials

Transferred Out to Next Department	960
Work in Process—Ending (140 desks × 100%)	140
Total Units Accounted For	1,100
Deduct Units of Work in Prior Month (180 desks × 100%)	180
Equivalent Production for Materials (FIFO)	920

Labor and Manufacturing Overhead

Transferred Out to Next Department	960
Work in Process—Ending (140 desks × 50%)	70
Total Units Accounted For	1,030
Deduct Units of Work in Prior Month (180 desks × 30%)	54
Equivalent Production for Labor and Overhead (FIFO)	976

Cost of Production Report

Under the FIFO method, the cost of production report retains the two-schedule organization. The Quantity Schedule is very similar to the one used with the average cost method. The Cost Schedule, however, is different. Refer to the report on page 336.

Quantity Schedule. The second part—(b) Quantity Accounted For—of the Quantity Schedule has been modified to show the source of the units transferred out. Specifically, on the Transferred Out to Next Department line, units transferred out are now identified as beginning inventory or new production. The rest of the Quantity Schedule is the same as when the average cost method is used (see Chapter 16).

Cost Schedule. The changes in the Cost Schedule are extensive. They are outlined below.

Section (c)—Costs to Be Accounted for:

- The beginning inventory appears under Costs to Be Accounted For in one total amount, $6,341.04 (see the balance of the general ledger account on March 1). The cost elements of this work in process are not shown in detail because the entire amount will apply to the completed units that came out of the beginning inventory.

MILLING DEPARTMENT
Cost of Production Report (FIFO)
Month of March 19X5

QUANTITY SCHEDULE		UNITS
(a) Quantity to Be Accounted For:		
Work in Process—Beginning		180
Started in Production—Current Month		940
Total to Be Accounted For		1,120
(b) Quantity Accounted For:		
Transferred Out to Next Department		
From Beginning Work in Process	180	
Started and Completed in Current Month	780	960
Work in Process—Ending		140
Lost in Production		20
Total Accounted For		1,120

COST SCHEDULE	TOTAL COST	E.P. UNITS	UNIT COST
(c) Costs to Be Accounted For:			
Beginning Inventory of Work in Process	$ 6,341.04		
Costs Charged in Current Month			
Transferred In From Prior Department	-0-		
Costs Added in Current Department			
Materials	$23,564.40	÷ 920 =	$25.613
Labor	18,156.84	÷ 976 =	18.603
Overhead	15,502.12	÷ 976 =	15.883
Total Added in Current Department	$57,223.36		$60.099
Total Costs Charged in Current Month	$57,223.36		$60.099
Total Costs to Be Accounted For	$63,564.40		
(d) Costs Accounted For:			
Transferred Out to Next Department			
From Beginning Work in Process			
Beginning Inventory	$ 6,341.04		
Materials Added in Current Month	-0-		
Labor Added in Current Month	2,343.98	= 126 ×	$18.603
Overhead Added in Current Month	2,001.26	= 126 ×	$15.883
Total Cost of Goods From Beginning Work in Process	$10,686.28	÷ 180 =	$59.368
Goods Started and Completed in Current Month	46,878.28*	= 780 ×	$60.099
Total Cost of Goods Transferred Out	$57,564.56	÷ 960 =	$59.963
Work in Process—Ending			
Costs in Current Department			
Materials	$ 3,585.82	= . 140 ×	$25.613
Labor	1,302.21	= 70 ×	$18.603
Overhead	1,111.81	= 70 ×	$15.883
Total Work in Process	$ 5,999.84		
Total Costs Accounted For	$63,564.40		

*Adjusted for rounding, $1.06.

- The title of the subsection Costs Charged in Current Month reflects continued emphasis on current production and related costs.
- There is no figure for Transferred In From Prior Department since Milling is the first department.
- The total cost figures appearing under Costs Added in Current Department come from the general ledger account and represent the current month's costs only. Each cost element is divided by the equivalent production units, as computed on page 335, for that element to obtain a unit cost for the month. The total unit cost, $60.099, is the sum of the costs of the elements added in March and does not contain any costs relating to the beginning work in process inventory on March 1.
- The amount labeled Total Costs Charged in Current Month includes costs from the prior department (none in this case) and costs of the current department.
- The amount labeled Total Costs to Be Accounted For is the sum of Beginning Inventory of Work in Process and Total Costs Charged in Current Month.

Section (d)—Costs Accounted For:

- In (d) Costs Accounted For, the Transferred Out to Next Department subsection is presented in detail in order to separate costs relating to the beginning inventory from those connected with goods started and finished in the current month.
- The costs associated with the beginning inventory are assembled, starting with the total cost in the beginning inventory.
- No materials were added in the current month because all units were 100 percent complete as to materials at the start of the month.
- The cost of the labor added during the month is computed by multiplying the equivalent units of production for labor by the related unit cost of current production (as calculated in the previous section). The percent of completion required is 70 percent (100 percent minus the 30 percent stage of completion at the beginning of the month).

$$\text{Units} \times \text{Percent of Completion Required} \times \text{Unit Cost} = \text{Labor Added}$$
$$180 \times 70\% \times \$18.603 = \$2,343.98$$

- A similar computation is made to determine the amount of overhead added to the beginning work in process inventory during March.

$$\text{Units} \times \text{Percent of Completion Required} \times \text{Unit Cost} = \text{Overhead Added}$$
$$180 \times 70\% \times \$15.883 = \$2,001.26$$

- The Total Cost of Goods From Beginning Work in Process (prior period costs plus current period costs added) amounts to $10,686.28. This total divided by the 180 equivalent units added gives a unit cost of $59.368. Thus the FIFO method yields a separate unit cost figure for the units in the beginning inventory.
- The FIFO method is applied to determine the number of equivalent units of new production that were transferred out. In March, a total of 960 units were transferred out. The beginning inventory contained 180 units. Since the units in the beginning inventory were the *first in,* they are *first* to be transferred *out.* The difference between the total units transferred out and the beginning inventory represents the number of units of production started and finished in March that were also transferred out (960 − 180 = 780). The 780 units are then multiplied by the total unit cost figure applicable to new production, $60.099. This yields the total cost of goods started and finished in the current period, $46,877.22. (However, a rounding adjustment of $1.06 increases this amount to $46,878.28 in the report.)

- The Total Cost of Goods Transferred Out is divided by the total number of units transferred out to obtain an average unit cost of $59.963. The total cost of $57,564.56 is used in the end-of-month transfer entry. The same total and the related unit cost of $59.963 are recorded on the cost of production report of the next department as Transferred In From Prior Department in the Costs to Be Accounted For Section of the Cost Schedule.
- One might normally expect to find each segment of the month's production (beginning inventory and units started and completed in the current month) costed out separately. However, any attempt to trace these segments through the production process would result in confusion and extra recordkeeping not justified by the small additional degree of accuracy achieved.
- The presentation of data regarding the ending work in process inventory under the FIFO method is essentially the same as that used with the average cost method. The value of each cost element is determined by multiplying the equivalent production units by the current unit costs for each element. Thus the total of $3,585.82 for materials was computed by multiplying 140 equivalent units by $25.613, the current unit cost for materials. The unit cost of labor ($18.603) and the unit cost of overhead ($15.883) are also multiplied by the equivalent units of production (70).
- The amount labeled Total Costs Accounted For consists of the total costs transferred out to the next department plus the total value of the ending work in process inventory.

Comparison of Results

An accountant who has completed a detailed comparison of the average cost (see page 312) and FIFO methods for the Milling Department at Space Savers would note the following:

1. With the FIFO method, the desired separation of costs has been achieved. The unit cost of the completed units from the beginning inventory, $59.368, is different from the unit cost of new production started and finished in the current period, $60.099.
2. The distinction between unit costs under the FIFO method requires about 50 percent more calculations to pinpoint a difference of about $.73 (1.2 percent) between Total Cost of Goods From Beginning Work in Process and Goods Started and Completed in Current Month ($60.099 − $59.368 = $.731).
3. The difference of $.017 between the $59.98 unit cost of goods transferred out computed under the average cost method (page 312) and the average unit cost of $59.963 computed under the FIFO method is insignificant.
4. Once the Total Cost of Goods Transferred Out is computed, the FIFO method reverts to an average cost to make accounting easier in the next department.

Assembling Department

It is now time to find how the FIFO method is applied as goods move from department to department.

Cost Data

As shown on page 313, the Work in Process—Assembling Department account has a balance of $49,409.44 on March 31. This balance includes the following costs:

Work in Process
Costs in Prior Department $2,370.44
Costs in Current Department
    Materials   483.20
    Labor   726.00
    Overhead   384.00
    Balance of Account, Feb. 28 $3,963.64

Current Month
    Materials $11,411.80
    Labor   22,576.00
    Overhead   11,458.00
    Total Current Month's Cost $45,445.80
      Balance of Account, Mar. 31 $49,409.44

Production Data

Again, the monthly production report is the same as the one submitted under the average cost method, except that the units transferred out to the next department are analyzed. This analysis shows units from the beginning work in process inventory and units started and completed in the current month.

ASSEMBLING DEPARTMENT
Monthly Production Report
March 19X5

Quantity

Work in Process—Beginning			10
Transferred In From Prior Department			960
Transferred Out to Next Department			
From Work in Process—Beginning		40	
Started and Completed in Current Month		885	925
Work in Process—Ending			50
Lost in Production			25
Stage of Completion of Work in Process			

	Beginning	Ending
Materials	complete	complete
Labor	75%	60%
Overhead	75%	60%

Equivalent Production Data

The FIFO method of computing equivalent production, described in connection with the Milling Department, is applied to the Assembling Department. The final figure for each element represents work performed in the current month. (See page 340.)

```
                    ASSEMBLING DEPARTMENT
                  Equivalent Production Computations
                       Month of March 19X5

    Materials
       Transferred Out to Next Department                         925
       Work in Process—Ending (50 desks × 100%)                    50
          Total Units Accounted For                               975
          Deduct Units of Work in Prior Month (40 desks × 100%)    40
             Equivalent Production for Materials (FIFO)           935

    Labor and Manufacturing Overhead
       Transferred Out to Next Department                         925
       Work in Process—Ending (50 desks × 60%)                     30
          Total Units Accounted For                               955
          Deduct Units of Work in Prior Month (40 desks × 75%)     30
             Equivalent Production for Labor and Overhead (FIFO)  925
```

Cost of Production Report

The Quantity Schedule of the cost of production report follows the pattern previously used for the Milling Department, with the normal exception that the item called Transferred In From Prior Department is used for Started in Production. Additional items are needed in the Cost Schedule since the costs in the prior department must be accounted for in all later departments. Note the following on the report shown on page 341:

Section (c)—Costs to Be Accounted For:

■ Beginning Inventory of Work in Process is shown separately, as in the report for the Milling Department.
■ Under Costs Charged in Current Month, the cost figures labeled Transferred In From Prior Department are new items on the report. Note that these figures are the same as the ones that appear on the Total Cost of Goods Transferred Out line of the Milling Department's report. Remember that the unit cost of $59.963 is an average.
■ The 25 lost units (from the monthly production report) are entered on the line labeled Adjustment for Lost Units. The lost units are deducted from the 960 units transferred in. (It is assumed that the loss occurred at the beginning of production in the department so that the lost units are from those transferred in during the current month.)
■ The Adjusted Prior Department Unit Cost is obtained by dividing the 935 units remaining into the total cost ($57,564.56 ÷ 935 = $61.566). The difference of $1.603 between $61.566 and $59.963 is the lost unit cost, which is shown on the Adjustment for Lost Units line.
■ The same procedure as that described for the Milling Department is used in completing the Costs Added in Current Department section. The cost for each element, as shown in the general ledger, is divided by the related equivalent production units to obtain the unit costs.

ASSEMBLING DEPARTMENT
Cost of Production Report
Month of March 19X5

QUANTITY SCHEDULE		UNITS
(a) Quantity to Be Accounted For:		
Work in Process—Beginning		40
Transferred In From Prior Department		960
Total to Be Accounted For		1,000
(b) Quantity Accounted For:		
Transferred Out to Next Department		
From Beginning Work in Process	40	
Started and Completed—Current Month	885	925
Work in Process—Ending		50
Lost in Production		25
Total Accounted For		1,000

COST SCHEDULE	TOTAL COST	E.P. UNITS	UNIT COST
(c) Costs to Be Accounted For:			
Beginning Inventory of Work in Process	$ 3,963.64		
Costs Charged in Current Month			
Transferred In From Prior Department	$ 57,564.56 =	960 ×	$ 59.963
Adjustment for Lost Units		25	1.603
Adjusted Prior Department Costs	$ 57,564.56 ÷	935 =	$ 61.566
Costs Added in Current Department			
Materials	$ 11,411.80 ÷	935 =	$ 12.205
Labor	22,576.00 ÷	925 =	24.406
Overhead	11,458.00 ÷	925 =	12.387
Total Added in Current Department	$ 45,445.80		$ 48.998
Total Costs Charged in Current Month	$103,010.36		$110.564
Total Costs to Be Accounted For	$106,974.00		
(d) Costs Accounted For:			
Transferred Out to Next Department			
From Beginning Work in Process (40 units)			
Beginning Inventory	$ 3,963.64		
Materials Added in Current Month	-0-		
Labor Added in Current Month	244.06 =	10 ×	$ 24.406
Overhead Added in Current Month	123.87 =	10 ×	$ 12.387
Total Cost of Goods From Beginning			
Work in Process	$ 4,331.57 ÷	40 =	$108.289
Goods Started & Completed in Current Month	97,850.09* =	885 ×	$110.564
Total Cost of Goods Transferred Out	$102,181.66 ÷	925 =	$110.467
Work in Process—Ending			
Costs in Prior Department	$ 3,078.30 =	50 ×	$ 61.566
Costs in Current Department			
Materials	610.25 =	50 ×	$ 12.205
Labor	732.18 =	30 ×	$ 24.406
Overhead	371.61 =	30 ×	$ 12.387
Total Work in Process	$ 4,792.34		
Total Costs Accounted For	$106,974.00		

*Adjusted for rounding, $.95.

- The amount labeled Total Costs Charged in Current Month is the sum of the Adjusted Prior Department Costs and the Total Added in Current Department.
- The amount labeled Total Costs to Be Accounted For is the sum of the Beginning Inventory of Work in Process and the Total Costs Charged in Current Month.

Section (d)—Costs Accounted For:

- The computation techniques for the costs that appear in the Transferred Out to Next Department Subsection are the same as before. Note that the total cost and unit cost figures for the beginning inventory are separate from the costs for the new production. The total and unit costs shown on the Total Cost of Goods Transferred Out line will be used in the transfer of costs to the Finishing Department. Remember that the unit cost of $110.467 is an average cost ($102,181.66 ÷ 925).
- The only new item under Work in Process—Ending is Costs in Prior Department. The unit cost of $61.566 is taken from Adjusted Prior Department Costs in the first part of the Cost Schedule. It is multiplied by the 50 units of work in process to obtain the total of $3,078.30. All other computations follow the familiar pattern.

Determining Space Savers' Costing Method

An accountant who completed a detailed comparison of the FIFO method and the average cost method (see page 315) for the Assembling Department at Space Savers would note the following:

1. Use of the FIFO method for the second department has again made extra data and computations necessary on the report.
2. The separate unit cost of completed units from the beginning work in process inventory and those started during the current period reflect a difference of $2.28 ($110.564 − $108.289 = $2.275), or about 2 percent of the value involved.
3. The average cost used for transfer to the next department under the FIFO method is $110.467, compared with $110.488 computed under the average cost method—a difference of slightly more than 2 cents.

These points, along with those mentioned on page 338, convinced Space Savers' accountant to choose the average cost method of accounting for beginning inventories. Space Savers' production is stable and its inventory is fairly constant. The value of its inventory is low relative to production. These factors make the slightly greater accuracy provided by the FIFO method of minimal importance. The average cost method, because it is simple and convenient, is far more useful for Space Savers.

Using Unit Costs for Control Purposes

The unit cost figures shown on the monthly cost of production reports provide useful information to management on how well costs are being controlled. By comparing monthly unit costs, meaningful changes can be detected and promptly investigated. For example, the unit cost of materials in the Assembling Department for March 19X5 is shown in the cost of production report on page 342 as $12.205. If the corresponding cost in April were $12.85, this significant increase would promptly be looked into.

Data Communications

In addition to communicating with humans, computers can communicate with other computers. For example, the processing of data may be performed in all the branch offices of a company, with results then sent to the home office mainframe computer for consolidation. The data are transmitted over ordinary telephone lines. In a large manufacturing company that has many factories in widely scattered locations, this technique may be used to bring cost accounting data into the home office quickly so that management will have current information available for decision making.

Data transmission via the telephone generally works as follows. The sending computer telephones the receiving computer. When the receiving computer answers, it sends out a signal indicating that it is able to communicate. The sending computer responds with its own signal, and then transmits communication *protocols*—information on how fast it sends data and how the data are to be verified for accuracy. The receiver adjusts itself according to the protocols. When it gives the sender a go-ahead signal, data transmission begins. A device called a *modem* (*modulator-demodulator*) links the sending computer to a telephone line and transforms (or modulates) data from the computer into a form suitable for transmission. The receiving computer also has a modem that transforms (or demodulates) the data signals into a form that can be read and stored by the receiving computer.

Computers within the same building may communicate by being directly linked to each other by cable. A common setup is a local area network (LAN) of microcomputers. LANs are becoming common in small businesses in which all data processing occurs in the same building and in firms that already have one or more microcomputers and find that it is less expensive to network than to upgrade to a more expensive minicomputer. ■

Principles and Procedures Summary

The first in, first out (FIFO) method of costing beginning work in process inventory is preferred by some accountants over the average cost method under certain circumstances.

The FIFO method uses the same cost and production data as required in average costing. However, equivalent production is computed so that the final figure relates only to work performed in the current month.

The presentation of data on the cost of production report under the FIFO method is quite different from the presentation under the average cost method. The differences occur primarily in the Cost Schedule, where costs of beginning inventory are separated from costs of current production. Although separate total and unit costs are obtained for both segments of the month's production, an average unit cost is actually used to make the transfer to the next department simpler.

At Space Savers, Inc., the slightly more accurate results under the FIFO method are not important enough to justify the extra work involved. In another business, the situation might be different.

1. Briefly describe the FIFO method of determining unit costs.
2. What are some of the advantages of the FIFO method over the average cost method for determining the cost of the work in process inventories?
3. How does the computation of equivalent units of production under the FIFO method differ from the computation under the average cost method?
4. Why is the cost of the beginning work in process inventory separated from costs of current production under the FIFO method?
5. Is the average cost method or the FIFO method of accounting for work in process more difficult? Explain.
6. When the FIFO method is used, how would a firm compute the unit cost of goods transferred out to the next department?
7. Are the differences between the average cost method and the FIFO method likely to be greater when the work in process inventory is large or when it is small compared to the total costs to be accounted for? Explain.
8. When the FIFO method is used, how does the monthly production report differ from the monthly production report prepared under the average cost method?
9. Will the number of equivalent units of production be larger or smaller if the FIFO method is used rather than the average cost method?

1. Results obtained from accounting for work in process can differ depending on the costing method used. Explain briefly how the results obtained using the FIFO method would differ from the results obtained using the average cost method.
2. Explain why equivalent unit computations for work in process are so important under the FIFO method.
3. The management of a company uses cost data in setting the price of its products. In a period of rapid inflation, would the unit cost figures resulting from FIFO be preferable to those under average costing? Explain.
4. The president of the company where you are employed as cost accountant has suggested that you switch from the average cost method to the FIFO method. The work in process inventory is small and relatively stable. Give arguments that you might use against the change.
5. Management is interested in detecting and measuring changes in unit labor and overhead costs as quickly as they occur. Would the average cost method or the FIFO method be more suitable for this purpose? Explain.

NOTE: Assume in all the exercises that the FIFO method of costing the work in process inventory is used.

1. **Computing equivalent production for labor.** The following information is given for the final producing department of the Watson Company. Compute the equivalent production for labor.

   Beginning work in process inventory, 180 units, 40 percent complete as to labor
   Transferred in during month, 1,020 units
   Transferred out during month, 1,000 units
   Ending work in process, 200 units, 80 percent complete as to labor

2. **Computing cost per unit for labor.** Assume the same facts as in Exercise 1. In addition, the labor cost in the beginning work in process inventory was $3,600. Labor costs incurred during the month were $96,332. Compute the cost per equivalent unit for labor.

3. **Computing labor costs transferred out.** Using the data in Exercises 1 and 2, calculate the labor costs in the units transferred out of the department during the month.

4. **Making an adjustment for rounding.** Costs to be accounted for in a department total $684,520. Costs accounted for include the cost of the ending work in process, $63,200, and the cost of the completed units from the beginning work in process, $108,000. The unit cost for the prior department costs and from the department costs added in the current period have been computed as $2.5667. A total of 200,000 units started and completed this month were transferred out to the next department. What is the adjustment due to rounding error, and where will the adjustment be shown in the cost of production reports?

5. **Making an adjustment for lost units.** The Forming Department had prior department costs of $18,000 in its beginning work in process inventory (100 units) for the current month. During the current month, 1,000 units were transferred into the Forming department with total prior department costs of $18,740, and 25 units were lost in production. It is assumed that the lost units came from units transferred into the Forming department this month. Show how the adjustment for lost units would appear in the cost of production report for the month.

6. **Computing equivalent production for materials when there are lost units.** The following information is given for the Toning Department of the Burlington Company for the current month. Compute the equivalent production for materials for the month.

Beginning work in process inventory, 1,000 units, 100 percent complete as to materials
Transferred in during month, 4,000 units
Transferred out to next department during month, 4,400 units.
Ending work in process inventory, 500 units, complete as to materials
Units lost in production, 100 units

7. **Computing cost per unit for materials.** Assume the same facts as in Exercise 6. In addition, the cost of materials in the beginning work in process inventory was $10,000. Materials added during the current month cost $45,600. Compute the cost per equivalent unit for materials.

8. **Computing materials costs transferred out.** Using the data in Exercises 6 and 7, calculate the materials costs in the units transferred out of the department during the month.

9. **Computing equivalent production for overhead.** The information on page 346 is given for the final producing department of the Santa Fe Company, a furniture manufacturer, for the month of May 19X5. Compute the equivalent production for overhead.

Beginning work in process inventory, 2,400 units, 66⅔ percent complete as to overhead

Transferred in during month, 9,600 units

Transferred out during month, 8,000 units

Ending work in process inventory, 4,000 units, 75 percent complete as to overhead

10. **Computing cost per unit for overhead.** Assume the same facts as in Exercise 9. In addition, the overhead cost in the beginning work in process inventory was $1,900. Overhead costs incurred for the month were $33,200. Compute the cost per equivalent unit for overhead.

$ 3.53

11. **Computing overhead costs transferred out.** Using the data in Exercises 9 and 10, calculate the overhead costs in the units transferred out of the department during the month.

24492

Problems

PROBLEM 17-1 Preparing a cost of production report for two departments and making journal entries. All-Star Industries uses a process cost accounting system. All materials in the first department (Cutting) are placed in production at the start of the manufacturing process. Materials put into production in the second department (Mixing) are added in proportion to labor and overhead. Data for the month of March 19X5 follow. Assume that the company uses the FIFO method of costing.

	Cutting Department	Mixing Department
Costs		
Beginning Work in Process		
Costs in Prior Department	-0-	$21,678
Costs in Current Department		
Materials	$ 6,840	908
Labor	2,106	370
Overhead	1,170	850
Current Department Costs—March		
Materials	95,220	13,150
Labor	75,660	8,900
Overhead	61,290	7,670
Quantities		
Beginning Work in Process	1,500	2,400
Started in Production	21,000	-0-
Transferred In From Prior Department	-0-	20,700
Transferred Out to Next Department	20,700	-0-
Transferred Out to Finished Goods	-0-	21,000
Ending Work in Process	1,800	2,100
Stage of Completion of Work in Process		
Beginning		
Materials	complete	50%
Labor and Overhead	30%	50%
Ending		
Materials	complete	75%
Labor and Overhead	40%	75%

Instructions

1. Complete the equivalent production computations for each department.
2. Prepare a cost of production report for each of the two departments. Carry the unit costs to three decimal places.
3. Prepare entries in general journal form to record the costs charged to each department, the costs transferred between departments, and the costs transferred out to finished goods. Date all entries March 31, 19X5.

PROBLEM 17-2 **Preparing a cost of production report when there are lost units.** The Brooks Company uses a process cost accounting system. On November 1, 19X3, the firm had 900 units in production in the Forming Department, the second of three producing departments. All materials had been added to this beginning inventory, but labor and overhead were only 60 percent complete. Costs applicable to the beginning work in process inventory follow:

Costs in prior department	$18,152
Materials	4,261
Labor	6,330
Overhead	2,910

During the month of November, an additional 12,500 units were transferred into the department with total prior department costs of $194,352. Also during November, additional costs were incurred in the department as follows:

Materials	$59,570
Labor	18,126
Overhead	52,790

A total of 12,900 units were transferred out to the third department during the month, 400 units were still in production at the end of the month, and 100 units were lost in production. All materials had been added to the ending work in process inventory, but labor and overhead were only 80 percent complete. Assume that the company uses the FIFO method of costing.

Instructions

1. Complete the equivalent production computations.
2. Prepare a cost of production report for the Forming Department. Assume that the loss of units occurs at the beginning of production in the department and that all lost units came from the work transferred into the department during the month of November 19X3.

PROBLEM 17-3. **Making journal entries to record and transfer costs.** Using your solution to Problem 17-2, give entries in general journal form to record the costs charged to production in the Forming Department and to record the cost of work transferred from the Forming Department to the Finishing Department. Date the entries November 30, 19X3.

PROBLEM 17-4. **Preparing a cost of production report for two departments.** The Montez Manufacturing Company has three producing departments: the Casting Department, the Assembling Department, and the Painting Department, The FIFO method of pricing the beginning work in process inventory is used. Two departmental Work in Process accounts with data for July 19X5 are given below. The monthly departmental production reports for July 19X5 have been submitted. The reports have been summarized, and the result is shown below and on page 349. The departmental supervisors have submitted their cost of production reports for June 19X5. These reports have also been summarized, and the result for the work in process sections is shown on page 349.

Work in Process—Casting Department   No.   134

DATE	EXPLANATION	POST. REF.	DEBIT		CREDIT		BALANCE		DR. CR.
19X5									
Jul. 1	Balance	✔					2,977	20	Dr.
31	Materials	MR8	10,206	27			13,183	47	Dr.
31	Labor	J8-9	4,161	62			17,345	09	Dr.
31	Overhead	J8-10	9,345	64			26,690	73	Dr.

Work in Process—Assembling Department   No.   135

DATE	EXPLANATION	POST. REF.	DEBIT		CREDIT		BALANCE		DR. CR.
19X5									
Jul. 1	Balance	✔					3,880	15	Dr.
31	Materials	MR8	720	10			4,600	25	Dr.
31	Labor	J8-9	6,331	17			10,931	42	Dr.
31	Overhead	J8-10	1,152	34			12,083	76	Dr.

Summary of Monthly Production Reports

	Casting Department		Assembling Department	
Quantities				
Work in Process—Beginning		680		720
Started in Production—Current Month		3,830		
Transferred In From Prior Department				3,950
Transferred Out to Next Department				
From Work in Process—Beginning		680		720
Started and Completed in Current Month	3,270	3,950	3,190	3,910
Work in Process—Ending		560		760
Stage of Completion of Ending Work in Process				
Materials		100%		25%
Labor		60%		25%
Overhead		60%		25%

Stage of Completion of Beginning Work
in Process

Materials	100%	50%
Labor	30%	20%
Overhead	30%	20%

Summary of Cost of Production Reports

Data for Work in Process on June 30	Casting Department	Assembling Department
Prior Department Costs	-0-	$3,443.65
Materials	$1,632.48	38.40
Labor	538.36	331.33
Overhead	806.36	66.77
Totals of Work in Process at July 1	$2,977.20	$3,880.15

Instructions

1. Prepare the equivalent production computations and the cost of production report for the Casting Department for July 19X5.
2. Prepare the equivalent production computations and the cost of production report for the Assembling Department for July 19X5.

Alternate Problems

PROBLEM 17-1A. Preparing a cost of production report for two departments and making journal entries. The Wallace Company uses a process cost accounting system. All materials in the first department (Shaping) are placed in production at the start of the manufacturing process. Materials put into production in the second department (Finishing) are added in proportion to labor and overhead. Data for the month of April 19X9 are given below and on page 350. Assume that the company uses the FIFO method of costing.

	Shaping Department	Finishing Department
Costs		
Beginning Work in Process		
Costs in Prior Department	-0-	$3,064
Costs in Current Department		
Materials	$1,500	213
Labor	340	362
Overhead	370	192
Current Department Costs—April		
Materials	19,200	7,488
Labor	17,680	5,488
Overhead	16,720	4,980

Quantities

Beginning Work in Process	100	75
Started in Production	1,250	-0-
Transferred In From Prior Department	-0-	1,225
Transferred Out to Next Department	1,225	-0-
Transferred Out to Finished Goods	-0-	1,200
Ending Work in Process	125	100

Stage of Completion of Work in Process

Beginning		
Materials	complete	60%
Labor and Overhead	35%	60%
Ending		
Materials	complete	80%
Labor and Overhead	50%	80%

Instructions

1. Complete the equivalent production computations for each department.
2. Prepare a cost of production report for each of the two departments.
3. Prepare entries in general journal form to record the costs charged to each department, the costs transferred between departments, and the costs transferred out to finished goods. Date the entries April 30, 19X9.

PROBLEM 17-2A. **Preparing a cost of production report when there are lost units.** The Lakeside Company uses a process cost accounting system. On May 1, 19X8, the company had 600 units in production in the Assembly Department (the second department). All materials had been added to these units, but processing was only 60 percent complete. Costs applicable to the beginning work in process inventory follow:

Costs in prior department	$14,000
Materials	4,000
Labor	3,000
Overhead	5,000

During the month of May an additional 10,500 units were transferred into the department with prior department costs of $185,000. Also during May, additional costs were incurred in the department as follows:

Materials	$158,200
Labor	117,800
Overhead	232,200

A total of 9,800 units were transferred out to finished goods. The ending work in process inventory consisted of 1,000 units, to which all materials had been added, but only 80 percent of the production had been completed. The other units were lost at the start of the manufacturing process in this department. Assume that the company uses the FIFO method of costing.

Instructions

1. Complete the equivalent production computations.
2. Prepare a cost of production report for the Assembly Department. Assume that the loss of units occurs at the beginning of production in the department and that all lost units came from the work transferred into the department during the month of May 19X8.

PROBLEM 17-3A. Making journal entries to record and transfer costs. Using your solution to Problem 17-2A, prepare entries in general journal form to record the costs charged to production in the Assembly Department and to record the cost of work transferred from the Assembly Department to the Finishing Department. Date the entries May 31, 19X8.

CHAPTER

18

By-Products

■ ■ ■

Although Space Savers, Inc., makes only one product, many factories produce several different products simultaneously from a single process. In fact, there has been a constant growth in multiple-product processing as a result of the tremendous technological advances in recent years. Chapters 18 and 19 will examine accounting procedures for multiple products.

Multiple-Product Processing

In some cases of multiple-product processing, only one product is of major importance. The other products are incidental to production. For example, bone meal and tallow are produced incidentally in meat-packing operations. In other cases, several products of comparable value or importance emerge from a single process. For example, gasoline, jet fuel, and lubricants all result from petroleum refining.

The accountant classifies multiple products according to their relative importance. The principal product is called the *main product*. Incidental products of lesser value are usually called *by-products*. Products of nearly equal value are usually called *joint products,* or *co-products*.

At some point in the sequence of manufacturing operations, multiple products are separated from one another. In accounting for these products, the basic question is how much of the production costs incurred before separation should be allocated to each product. Costs incurred up to the point of separation are often called *common costs,* or *joint costs*. In this unit you will learn how to account for manufacturing costs when by-products result from the processing of a main product. In the next unit you will learn how to allocate common production costs between joint products.

Methods of By-Product Costing

A by-product may be sold as a completed commodity at the time of its separation from the main product, or it may require further processing after separation to prepare it for sale. There are two popular methods of costing by-products that require no further processing. In the first, the proceeds from the sale of the by-product are considered as other income, and all manufacturing costs are applied to the main product. In the second, the estimated selling price (or proceeds from the sale) of the by-product is considered to be a reduction in the cost of the main product and is credited to the Work in Process account.

There are also two basic methods for costing by-products that require further processing after separation from the main product. The difference between these two methods pertains to the allocation of common costs. In one method, the by-product is charged only with the additional manufacturing costs incurred after separation. It is assumed that no part of the common costs applies to the by-product. In the other method, part of the common costs is assigned to the by-product, and the by-product is also charged with any additional costs incurred after separation.

Data for a seed processing company will be used to illustrate each of these methods of by-product costing.

The Reliable Seed Company

The Reliable Seed Company purchases seed grains from growers. The seeds are cleaned, treated, bagged, and stored for resale to wholesalers and retailers. There are three departments in the operation: Cleaning, Treating, and Warehousing.

The operations and costs of the Cleaning Department will be used to illustrate the comparison of the various methods of accounting for by-products. In this department, the grain is weighed and then passed through a series of blowers and screens that separate the seeds into standard sizes. Small seeds, husks, and foreign matter that are sifted out are called *screenings*. These screenings are removed in the cleaning process and are stored in bins. They are used in preparing mixed feed for livestock.

Cost Data

The general ledger accounts show the following costs incurred during the current month:

Materials (Grain)	$81,774
Labor	16,992
Overhead	14,868

Production Data

The supervisor of the Cleaning Department supplies the monthly production report shown below. For the sake of simplicity, it is assumed that there is no beginning or ending inventory involved. (The abbreviation *cwt.* shown on this report stands for hundredweight, a unit of measure commonly equivalent to 100 pounds.)

CLEANING DEPARTMENT
Monthly Production Report
May 19X1

Materials Placed in Production	5,900 cwt.
Grain Seed Transferred to Treating Department	5,310 cwt.
Screenings Removed	590 cwt.
Beginning and Ending Inventories of Work in Process	none

Equivalent Production Data	The computation of equivalent production is simplified by the absence of an ending work in process inventory.

CLEANING DEPARTMENT
Equivalent Production Computations
Month of May 19X1

Transferred to Treating Department	5,310
Work in Process—Ending	-0-
Equivalent Production	5,310

. . . .

By-Products Not Processed Further

The screenings described earlier are sold by the Reliable Seed Company without any additional processing. The method of accounting for this by-product was chosen by the accountant after consideration of the values and other circumstances involved. As previously discussed, there are two methods that can be used. The proceeds may be treated as other income, or the estimated selling price may be treated as a reduction in the cost of the main product.

Proceeds as Other Income

If the proceeds from the sale of a by-product are small, they are considered as other income. The accounting treatment is identical to that for scrap sales under the job order cost system. No entry is made until the by-product is sold. At that time Accounts Receivable or Cash is debited and Miscellaneous Income is credited for the amount of the sale. For example, if the 590 cwt. of screenings are sold for $3.40 per cwt. (590 × $3.40 = $2,006), the entry, in general journal form, would be as shown below.

19X1				
May 28	Accounts Receivable (or Cash)	111	2,006.00	
	Miscellaneous Income	713		2,006.00
	Recorded sale of by-product.			

Analysis of the Method. If this procedure is followed, no cost is assigned or allocated to the by-product. In addition, the sale of the by-product has no effect on the cost of the main product.

This sale is not included on the departmental cost of production report that is shown on page 355.

This procedure is simple and practical and requires no computations of the cost of the by-product. However, it does not give a true measure of the cost of manufacturing the main product.

```
                    CLEANING DEPARTMENT
                   Cost of Production Report
                     Month of May 19X1

          QUANTITY SCHEDULE                    CWT.
(a) Quantity to Be Accounted For:
      Started in Production—
        Current Month                          5,900
                                               ─────

(b) Quantity Accounted For:
      Seed Grain Transferred Out to
        Next Dept.                             5,310
      Screenings Removed                         590
        Total Accounted For                    5,900
                                               ─────

                                    TOTAL    E.P.      UNIT
          COST SCHEDULE              COST    UNITS     COST
(c) Costs to Be Accounted For:
      Costs in Current Month
        Materials              $ 81,774 ÷ 5,310 = $15.40
        Labor                    16,992 ÷ 5,310 =   3.20
        Overhead                 14,868 ÷ 5,310 =   2.80
      Total Costs to Be Accounted For  $113,634      $21.40
                                       ────────      ──────

(d) Costs Accounted For:
      Seed Grain Transferred Out
        to Next Dept.           $113,634 = 5,310 × $21.40
      Total Costs Accounted For  $113,634
                                 ────────
```

Estimated Sales Value as Cost Reduction

If the estimated sales value of the by-product is treated as a reduction in the cost of the main product, the following entry would be made to record the removal of the by-product at the point of separation:

```
19X1
May 28    Inventory of By-Product            119    2,006.00
             Work in Process—Cleaning Dept.  126                2,006.00
          Recorded by-product at estimated
          sales value and removed this assigned
          cost from the main product.
```

Analysis of the Method. If this procedure is followed, the cost assigned to the by-product is equal to its estimated sales value. The value of the by-product reduces the cost of the main product. This value appears on the cost of production report under Costs Accounted For. It is treated as a reduction in the cost of goods transferred out of the department during the current month. For example, as a result of the reduction in the total cost of goods transferred to the Treating Department, the unit cost is reduced from $21.40 ($113.634 ÷ 5,310) to $21.022 ($111,628 ÷ 5,310). The adjustment of $.378 appears on the Deduct Value of the By-Product Removed line.

CLEANING DEPARTMENT
Cost of Production Report
Month of May 19X1

QUANTITY SCHEDULE	CWT.
(a) Quantity to Be Accounted For:	
Started in Production—Current Month	5,900
(b) Quantity Accounted For:	
Seed Grain Transferred Out to Next Dept.	5,310
Screenings Removed	590
Total Accounted For	5,900

COST SCHEDULE	TOTAL COST	E.P. UNITS	UNIT COST
(c) Costs to Be Accounted For:			
Costs in Current Month			
Materials	$ 81,774	÷ 5,310 =	$15.40
Labor	16,992	÷ 5,310 =	3.20
Overhead	14,868	÷ 5,310 =	2.80
Total Costs to Be Accounted For	$113,634		$21.40
(d) Costs Accounted For:			
Production Completed in Current Month	$113,634	= 5,310 ×	$21.400
Deduct Value of By-Product Removed	2,006		.378
Adjusted Cost of Seed Grain Transferred Out			
to Next Dept.	$111,628	÷ 5,310 =	$21.022
Cost Assigned to By-Product	2,006		
Total Costs Accounted For	$113,634		

When the by-product is later sold, the Inventory of By-Product account is credited for the recorded estimated value. Any difference between the sales price and the recorded value is shown as Gain or Loss on Sale of By-Product and is treated as Other Income or Other Expense on the income statement.

For example, if the screenings recorded previously at $2,006 were sold for $1,960, the entry in general journal form would be as follows:

19X1				
May 31	Cash	101	1,960.00	
	Gain or Loss on Sale of By-Product	XXX	46.00	
	Inventory of By-Product	119		2,006.00
	Recorded sale of by-product at a loss.			

This method is simple and does show the net cost of manufacturing the main product. However, the value of the by-product may be difficult to estimate if market prices tend to vary widely.

By-Products Processed Further

In many cases, the manufacturer may find it more profitable to process the by-product further rather than to sell it in the form in which it exists when it is separated from the main product. In some cases, additional processing may be necessary to make the by-product marketable at all.

Assume that the Reliable Seed Company further processes the screenings instead of selling them at the point of separation. The 590 cwt. of screenings are mixed with an equal weight of feed material and milled into a finished feed product. The additional processing costs for the 1,180 cwt. of finished feed product in the month of May are as follows:

Materials	$2,478
Labor	240
Overhead	260
	$2,978

Assignment of Additional Costs Only

If only the additional processing costs after separation are assigned to the by-product, they are debited to a special Work in Process account for the by-product, as shown below.

19X1					
May 28	Work in Process—By-Product	128	2,978.00	
	Raw Materials	121		2,478.00
	Factory Payroll Clearing	500		240.00
	Manufacturing Overhead Control	501		260.00
	Recorded additional costs of			
	processing by-product.			

Analysis of the Method. One feature of this procedure is that only the additional costs after separation are charged to the by-product. Another feature is that the value of the by-product has no effect on the costs incurred in the Cleaning Department before separation. This value does not appear on the Cleaning Department's cost of production report shown on page 358.

This method is widely used because it is simple and practical. However, it is subject to criticism because it understates the total cost of the by-product and overstates the total cost of the main product.

Common Costs and Additional Costs Assigned

Many accountants prefer to charge to the by-product not only the costs incurred after separation but also part of the common costs. One popular method used to allocate common costs to the by-product is the *reversal cost method* (sometimes

```
                      CLEANING DEPARTMENT
                     Cost of Production Report
                       Month of May 19X1

           QUANTITY SCHEDULE                      CWT.
(a) Quantity to Be Accounted For:
      Started in Production—
        Current Month                             5,900

(b) Quantity Accounted For:
      Seed Grain Transferred Out to
        Next Dept.                                5,310
      Screenings Removed                            590
        Total Accounted For                       5,900


                                          TOTAL    E.P.    UNIT
              COST SCHEDULE               COST     UNITS   COST
(c) Costs to Be Accounted For:
      Costs in Current Month
        Materials                      $ 81,774 ÷ 5,310 = $15.40
        Labor                            16,992 ÷ 5,310 =   3.20
        Overhead                         14,868 ÷ 5,310 =   2.80
      Total Costs to Be Accounted For   $113,634          $21.40

(d) Costs Accounted For:
      Seed Grain Transferred Out to
        Next Dept.                      $113,634 = 5,310 × $21.40
      Total Costs Accounted For         $113,634
```

called the *normal net profit method*). The amount to be allocated is computed so that the by-product will yield the normal percentage of profit on sales that the company makes, on the average. To see how this method works, assume the following data:

- The feed by-product can be sold for $5.60 per cwt.
- The selling and administrative expenses will total 10 percent of the sales value.
- The normal net profit of the business is 5 percent of sales.

The estimated cost of the by-product is obtained by working back from the estimated sales value, as shown in the computation below.

Estimated Sales Price of Finished By-Product		
(1,180 cwt. at $5.60 each cwt.)		$6,608.00
Estimated Selling and Administrative Expenses (10 percent)	$660.80	
Estimated Normal Net Profit (5 percent)	330.40	991.20
Total Estimated Manufacturing Cost		$5,616.80
Estimated Manufacturing Cost After Separation		2,978.00
Estimated Manufacturing Cost Before Separation		$2,638.80

Estimated selling and administrative expenses and estimated normal profit are deducted from the total estimated sales price to obtain the total estimated manufacturing cost of $5,616.80. From this figure, the costs after separation are subtracted to leave the estimated costs before separation.

Once the cost figures are determined, two general journal voucher entries are required to make the appropriate charges to the Work in Process account of the by-product. The first entry transfers estimated costs incurred before separation.

JOURNAL VOUCHER	Date May 31,	19 X1	No. 5-75		
ACCOUNT	ACCOUNT NUMBER	✓	DEBIT	CREDIT	
Work in Process—By-Product	128		2638 80		
Work in Process—					
Cleaning Dept.	126			2638 80	
EXPLANATION					
Charged cost before separation applicable to by-product.					
PREPARED BY JAN	AUDITED BY JB		APPROVED BY RM		

The second entry charges the additional costs after separation to the by-product in the usual manner.

JOURNAL VOUCHER	Date May 31,	19 X1	No. 5-76		
ACCOUNT	ACCOUNT NUMBER	✓	DEBIT	CREDIT	
Work in Process—By-Product	128		2978 00		
Raw Materials	121			2478 00	
Factory Payroll Clearing	500			240 00	
Manufacturing Overhead					
Control	501			260 00	
EXPLANATION					
Charged additional manufacturing costs after separation applicable to by-product.					
PREPARED BY JAN	AUDITED BY JB		APPROVED BY RM		

After the transfer entries are posted, the Work in Process accounts appear as shown on below.

DATE		EXPLANATION	POST. REF.	DEBIT		CREDIT		BALANCE		DR. CR.

Work in Process—Cleaning Department   No. 126

DATE		EXPLANATION	POST. REF.	DEBIT		CREDIT		BALANCE		DR. CR.
19X1										
May	31	Materials	MR5	81,774	00			81,774	00	Dr.
	31	Labor	J5-70	16,992	00			98,766	00	Dr.
	31	Overhead	J5-71	14,868	00			113,634	00	Dr.
	31	Before Separation Cost	J5-75			2,638	80	110,995	20	Dr.

Work in Process—By-Product   No. 128

DATE		EXPLANATION	POST. REF.	DEBIT		CREDIT		BALANCE		DR. CR.
19X1										
May	31	Before Separation Cost	J5-75	2,638	80			2,638	80	Dr.
	31	After Separation Cost	J5-76	2,978	00			5,616	80	Dr.

Analysis of the Method. If this procedure is followed, both common costs and costs incurred after separation are assigned to the by-product. The transfer of the common costs affects the cost of the main product processed in the Cleaning Department. Thus, the cost assigned to the by-product before separation appears on the departmental cost of production report. It is shown on the report as a reduction in the cost of the main product.

This method is complicated and often difficult to apply. Theoretically, all costs to sell the by-products should be used in the computation. However, it is almost impossible to determine the normal selling costs that are applicable. Thus, most companies merely consider the incremental selling costs related specifically to the by-product. Other firms consider both the incremental costs and the normal selling expenses, which are assumed to be the same percentage of the by-product's selling price as the normal overall percentage of total selling expenses to total sales. The computations are made from so many estimates that the results may not be sufficiently reliable. Therefore, if the amount of a by-product is small, it may not be worthwhile to use this method because of the time and effort required.

Market Value at Point of Separation Assigned as Cost of By-Product

Some accountants prefer to remove the present market value of the by-product at the point of separation even though the by-product is to be processed further. If this procedure had been followed in the Cleaning Department of the Reliable Seed Company, the market value of the by-product at the point of separation (590 cwt. at $3.40 each = $2,006) would be credited to Work in Process—Cleaning Department and debited to Work in Process—By-Product. The additional processing costs of the by-product, $2,978, would also be charged to the Work in Process—By-Product account.

In other cases, by-products are treated in the same manner as joint products. That is, they are accounted for by one of the methods discussed in the next chapter. This, however, is not customary.

Computing Net Profit

Many firms enjoy sizable profits from the sale of their by-products. However, profits are not assured, particularly when further processing is involved, without alert supervision and control. The cost accountant can prepare reports of estimated net profit on by-products to assist management in the appraisal of its by-product policies and operations. The net profit shown on the report will vary according to the method of costing used.

If only the *additional costs* are assigned to the by-product, the cost of the by-product is understated. Therefore, since the cost is understated, the resulting profit of $2,969.20 on the by-product, as shown in the computation below, is overstated.

Sales (1,180 cwt. at $5.60 each)		$6,608.00
Manufacturing Costs After Separation		
Materials	$2,478.00	
Labor	240.00	
Overhead	260.00	2,978.00
Gross Profit on Sale of By-Product		$3,630.00
Estimated Selling and Administrative Expenses		660.80
Estimated Net Profit on By-Product		$2,969.20

Under the *reversal cost method,* costs assigned to the by-product include common costs as well as costs after separation. The profit computed ($330.40) is much lower than that shown under the previous method.

Sales (1,180 cwt. at $5.60 each)			$6,608.00
Cost of Sales			
Common Costs		$2,638.80	
Costs Added After Separation			
Materials	$2,478.00		
Labor	240.00		
Overhead	260.00	2,978.00	
Total Cost of Sales			5,616.80
Gross Profit on Sale of By-Product			$ 991.20
Estimated Selling and Administrative Expenses			660.80
Estimated Net Profit on By-Product			$ 330.40

If the common costs assigned to the by-product are equal to its *present market value at the point of separation,* the profit will be $963.20. The computation of the profit on the by-product with this method is as shown on page 362.

Sales (1,180 cwt. at $5.60 each)			$6,608.00
Cost of Sales			
Common Costs		$2,006.00	
Costs Added After Separation			
Materials	$2,478.00		
Labor	240.00		
Overhead	260.00	2,978.00	
Total Cost of Sales			4,984.00
Gross Profit on Sale of By-Product			$1,624.00
Estimated Selling and Administrative Expenses			660.80
Estimated Net Profit on By-Product			$ 963.20

The profit obtained by this method may be interpreted as an increase in the firm's profit resulting from the decision to process the by-product further rather than to sell it in the form it was in at the point of separation.

Electronic Data Interchange

North Country Fashions manufactures casual clothing and makes most of its sales to a few large retail chains. One of its most important customers is MegaMart, a discount clothing chain, with hundreds of stores in shopping malls throughout the country. MegaMart's board of directors has been concerned about sales lost through shortages of merchandise. When individual stores run out of popular items at the peak of the season, orders cannot be placed quickly enough—and thus cannot be filled by suppliers quickly enough—to meet the customer demand. MegaMart's president called on the chain's major supplier, North Country Fashions, to work with MegaMart to come up with a solution. The goal: to ensure timely shipments of merchandise.

North Country was already using electronic data interchange (EDI) with some of its large customers, and it suggested that MegaMart join its EDI system. EDI has been called an electronic "pipeline" because it links suppliers and customers via computers. This means that purchase orders are sent from a customer to a supplier instantaneously. The side benefits of EDI are that fewer clerical and data-entry employees are needed, lower inventory levels can be maintained, and lost and misplaced purchase orders are no longer a problem.

The initial installation cost at MegaMart was high. The firm needed special programs for its computers and had to change the formats of its purchase orders and other forms. But because of the anticipated gain in sales, MegaMart bought and installed the EDI programs.

The result of using EDI? North Country receives orders from MegaMart much more quickly and can therefore give MegaMart the merchandise it needs on time. MegaMart's sales have increased because its stores are now better stocked to meet seasonal demand, and this means more business for North Country. ■

Principles and Procedures Summary

Many manufacturing processes yield multiple products. When one product is small in value compared to the others, it is called a *by-product*. The major question in accounting for by-products is whether any part of the costs incurred prior to separation (called common costs) should be allocated to the by-product.

By-products that require no further processing may be costed by crediting the proceeds of their sale to other income or by using the proceeds or the estimated sales value to reduce the cost of the main product.

Three methods are used for costing by-products that require further processing. In the first method, only additional costs are charged to the by-product. In the second method, both common and after-separation costs are charged to the by-product. The third method assigns the market value at the point of separation as the cost of the by-product.

Each method has advantages and limitations. Statements of estimated profits from by-products are directly affected by the costing method used.

Review Questions

1. What is a by-product?
2. What are common costs?
3. How does a by-product differ from a joint product?
4. If a company treats the sales proceeds from by-products as other income, how does a sale of a by-product affect the cost of goods manufactured for the main product?
5. If a company treats the value of a by-product as a reduction in the cost of goods manufactured, how does this reduction appear on the cost of production report?
6. A company records the estimated market value of a by-product as a reduction in cost. During the month, a quantity of the by-product with an estimated market value (inventory value) of $1,800 was sold for $2,000. How is the sale recorded?
7. If a by-product is to be processed further after separation, in what ways might the value of the by-product be determined?
8. Explain in detail the reversal cost method of allocating common costs to by-products.
9. In general terms, explain how a decision is made on whether to further process a by-product or to sell it without additional processing.
10. Assume that a by-product is accumulated for several months before it is sold.
    a. Explain why an accountant would make an entry crediting Work in Process for the by-product's estimated value at the time of its removal from factory operation.
    b. Explain why an accountant would make an entry only when the by-product is sold.
11. What are the disadvantages of the reversal cost method?

1. Why would management be concerned over the methods used in accounting for by-products?
2. Under what circumstances would it be desirable to keep a perpetual inventory of by-products?
3. Why might management be interested in using the method in which only additional costs incurred after separation are assigned to by-products?
4. A company's income statement shows a net profit of $1,500 on the sale of by-products. Comment on the usefulness of this information to the company's management.
5. Why might management be interested in using the reversal cost method to cost by-products.?
6. Management has asked you if the existence of a by-product affects the cost of the main product. Give an appropriate answer.
7. What factors should management consider when deciding how to dispose of by-products?

Exercises

1. **Making a journal entry for a sale of a by-product that is treated as other income.** The Carrara Company uses marble and other types of stone in the manufacture of its products. Shavings are gathered and sold to a landscape company as filler material. During the month of November 19X3, shavings were sold for $183. Give the general journal entry to record the sale if the company treats the proceeds from the sale of the by-product as other income.
2. **Making a journal entry for a by-product that is treated as a reduction in the main product cost.** The manufacturing process in the Cutting Department of the Baum Company results in a by-product. The company accumulates the by-product and periodically sells it. During the month of June 19X6, a quantity of the by-product with an estimated sales value of $900 was recovered. The company treats the by-product as a reduction in the cost of production completed during the current month. The total cost of the 20,000 units completed during the month was $48,000 before considering the by-product.
   a. Give the general journal entry to record the removal of the by-product from factory operations and its storage in inventory.
   b. Calculate the revised cost per unit of the goods transferred out of the department during the month.
3. **Computing the value of a by-product by the reversal cost method.** In the Shaping Department of Spira Company, a by-product is removed. The material is further processed and then sold. The company uses the reversal cost method to account for the by-product. Data for December 19X7 follow. Compute the value to be assigned to the by-product and removed from Work in Process at the point of separation.

   Amount of by-product removed, 7,800 pounds
   Estimated sales price of by-product, $1 per pound
   Estimated manufacturing cost after separation, $.30 per pound
   Estimated selling and administrative expenses, 20 percent of sales price
   Estimated normal net profit, 6 percent of sales price

4. **Making a by-product processing decision based on a difference in income.** A company is attempting to decide whether to sell a by-product without additional processing or to process it further. Refer to the data below. Calculate the difference in income between additional processing and no further processing. Should the company sell the by-product without further processing?

> Estimated units of by-product per month, 1,500 units
> Estimated selling price without further processing, $3.50 per unit
> Estimated selling price with further processing, $4.25 per unit
> Estimated labor costs to process further, $1,000 per month
> Estimated additional material costs to process further, $.30 per unit
> Estimated additional overhead costs to process further, $.20 per unit

5. **Making a journal entry to transfer a by-product to inventory.** Each week the Willis Company accumulates the by-product arising from its manufacturing process and transfers it to a storage area. The by-product is recorded at its estimated value at the time of removal, and the value is credited to Work in Process. On May 7, 19X8, a quantity of the by-product with an estimated value of $150 was removed from factory operations. Give the entry in general journal form to record the transfer from factory operations to inventory.

6. **Making journal entries to record the cost and the sale of a by-product.** The Juniper Company assigns to its by-products only the additional cost needed to process them. Give all journal entries related to the by-product that are called for by the data given below.
   a. During July 19X5, by-product with an estimated value of $350 was removed from factory operations.
   b. The by-product was further processed at a cost of $100 for materials, $200 for labor, and $100 for overhead.
   c. The finished by-product was transferred to inventory.
   d. The by-product was sold for $600.

7. **Making journal entries for the proceeds from by-product sales according to two methods.** The Harmon Company produces seed. Screenings are sold to a garden outlet to be used in mulch products. During the month of May 19X4, screenings with an estimated value of $1,250 were removed from factory operations and stored in a warehouse. In June, the materials were sold for $1,180. Give the general journal entries to record these facts if the following procedures are used:
   a. The company treats proceeds from the sale as miscellaneous income at the time of sale.
   b. The company treats the estimated value of its by-products as a reduction in the cost of the main product at the time of removal.

8. **Computing the value assigned to a by-product by the reversal cost method.** In the Packaging Department of the Valenti Company, scrap materials (a by-product) are removed, further processed, and sold. The company uses the reversal cost method to account for the by-product. Data for April 19X2 follow on page 366. Compute the value to be assigned to the by-product and removed from Work in Process at the point of separation.

Amount of by-product removed, 4,300 kilograms
Estimated sales price of by-product after further processing, 70 cents per kilogram
Estimated processing cost after separation, 12 cents per kilogram
Estimated selling expenses, 10 pecent of sales price
Estimated normal profit margin, 10 percent of sales price

Problems

PROBLEM 18-1. Making journal entries for a sale of a by-product when different accounting methods are used. The Houston Chemical Company manufactures a commercial chemical. In the Filtering Department, the product is allowed to stand for several hours so that certain impurities will settle to the bottom. The purified chemical is then transferred out to the next department, and the impurities are removed to be sold as a by-product.

Instructions

1. On January 1, 19X4, 2,800 barrels of the by-product recovered in the month of December 19X3 were in storage awaiting sale. These 2,800 barrels were sold on January 8, 19X6 for $3 per barrel. Assume that no entry is made for the by-product until it is sold. Give the entries in general journal form to record the sale for cash of the 2,800 barrels under these procedures.
   a. The proceeds of the sale are treated as miscellaneous income. (Date the entry January 31, 19X4.)
   b. The proceeds of the sale are treated as a reduction in the cost of the main product. (NOTE: Credit Work in Process—Filtering Department 122 instead of Miscellaneous Income.)
2. During the month of January 19X4, 2,680 additional barrels of the by-product were recovered. These were sold on February 4. Instead of using the procedures in Instruction 1, assume that the estimated sales value of the by-product is treated as a reduction in the cost of the main product when it is removed. Give the entries in general journal form to record the following:
   a. Removal of the 2,680 barrels during January, assuming an estimated value of $3 per barrel. (Date the entry January 31, 19X4).
   b. Sale on credit of the 2,680 barrels on February 4 at $2.94 per barrel.

PROBLEM 18-2. Computing the cost of a by-product by the reversal cost method; preparing a cost of production report. Departmental production data is given for the Melting Department of the Hartford Products Company for the month of April 19X3.

	Cost
Work in Process—Beginning	-0-
Costs in Current Month	
Transferred In From Prior Department	$120,000
Costs Added in Current Department	
Materials	-0-
Labor	10,000
Manufacturing Overhead	14,000

	Units
Work in Process—Beginning	-0-
Transferred In From Prior Department	12,000 cwt.
Transferred Out to Next Department	10,000 cwt.
Amount of By-Product	2,000 cwt.
Work in Process—Ending	-0-

In the Melting Department, a by-product is recovered that reduces the quantity of the main product transferred out. This by-product is transferred to another department, where it is further processed into a chemical called Lenzoid. For each hundred pound unit (cwt.) of the by-product recovered from the main product, .5 cwt. of additional material costing $2 per cwt. must be added. Each hundredweight of Lenzoid requires additional labor of $.12 and manufacturing overhead of $.18. (Note that for each hundredweight of the by-product recovered, 1.5 cwt. of Lenzoid will be produced.) Lenzoid has a sales value of $2.70 per hundredweight. The normal net profit margin of the company is 6 percent on sales. Estimated selling and administrative expenses are $.14 per hundredweight of Lenzoid.

Instructions

1. Compute the cost to be assigned to the 2,000 cwt. of by-product before separation, using the reversal cost method.
2. Prepare a cost of production report for the Melting Department for the month of April 19X3, based on the above data.

PROBLEM 18-3. Making journal entries to record the cost and the sale of a by-product. The Blue Ridge Flour Company has three producing departments: the Grinding Department, the Mixing Department, and the Packaging Department. Five percent of the wheat put into production in the Grinding Department becomes a by-product that has an estimated sales value of $2.30 per cwt. The estimated sales value of the by-product is treated as a reduction in the cost of the main product. During February 19X6, 500,000 pounds of wheat are put into production. There are no beginning and ending inventories. During February 19X6, the following costs are incurred in the Grinding Department:

Cost	Amount	Posting Reference
Materials	$77,330.00	MR2
Labor	9,795.00	J2-10
Overhead	7,125.00	J2-11

Instructions

1. Enter the materials, labor, and overhead costs in the Work in Process—Grinding Department account. Open the Inventory of By-Product account.
2. Prepare the general journal voucher to record the removal of the by-product from the Grinding Department. Number the voucher 2-12. Post the voucher to the general ledger accounts opened.
3. Prepare the general journal voucher to record the sale of half the by-product inventory for $247.50 cash. Number the voucher 2-13. Use the same account names and numbers that are used in the text. Post the voucher to the Inventory of By-Product account.

PROBLEM 18-4. Making journal entries for sales of a by-product when different accounting methods are used. The Abernathy Milling Company manufactures a single product—flour. In the Screening Department, husks and other impurities are removed and become a by-product.

Instructions
1. On March 1, 19X8, 21,000 pounds of the by-product recovered in the month of February were in storage waiting to be sold. These 21,000 pounds were sold on April 3 for $.07 per pound. Assume that no entry is made for the by-product until it is sold. Give the entry in general journal form to record the sale of 21,000 pounds for cash, using the following procedures:
   a. The proceeds of the sale are treated as miscellaneous income.
   b. The proceeds of the sale are treated as a reduction in the cost of the main product. (NOTE: Credit Work in Process—Screening Department 122)
2. During the month of March, an additional 19,500 pounds of the by-product were recovered. These were sold on May 1. Instead of following the procedures in Instruction 1, assume that the estimated sales value of the by-product is treated as a reduction in the cost of the main product when it is removed. Give the entries in general journal form to record the following:
   a. Recovery of the 19,500 pounds in March, assuming an estimated value of $.07 per pound. (Date the entry March 31, 19X8.)
   b. Sale on credit of the 19,500 pounds on May 1 at $.075 per pound.

Alternate Problems

PROBLEM 18-1A. Making journal entries for a sale of a by-product when different accounting methods are used. The Wilkinson Company manufactures a single product in powdered form. In the Cooking Department, certain impurities are removed and become a by-product.

Instructions
1. On July 1, 19X7, 13,800 kilograms of the by-product recovered in the month of June were in storage awaiting sale. These 13,800 kilograms were sold on July 5 for $.28 per kilogram. Assume that no entry is made for the by-product until it is sold. Give the entry in general journal form to record the sale for cash of 13,800 kilograms under the following procedures:
   a. The proceeds of the sale are treated as miscellaneous income. (Date the entry July 31, 19X7.)
   b. The proceeds of the sale are treated as a reduction in the cost of the main product. (Credit Work in Process—Cooking Department 122 instead of Miscellaneous Income.)
2. During the month of July, an additional 21,700 kilograms of the by-product were recovered. These were sold on August 6. Instead of the procedures in Instruction 1, assume that the estimated sales value of the by-product is treated as a reduction in the cost of the main product when it is removed. Give the entries in general journal form to record the following:
   a. Recovery of the 21,700 kilograms during July, assuming an estimated value of $.28 per kilogram. (Date the entry July 31, 19X7.)
   b. Sale on credit of the 21,700 kilograms on August 6 at $.30 per kilogram.

PROBLEM 18-2A. Computing the cost of a by-product by the reversal cost method; preparing a cost of production report. Production data is given for the Screening Department of the O'Shea Products Company for June 19X9:

	Cost
Work in Process—Beginning	-0-
Costs in Current Month	
Transferred In From Prior Department	$136,000
Costs Added in Current Department	
Materials	-0-
Labor	11,900
Manufacturing Overhead	17,500

	Units
Work in Process—Beginning	-0-
Transferred In From Prior Department	2,000 metric tons
Transferred Out to Finished Goods	1,750 metric tons
Amount of By-Product Recovered	250 metric tons
Work in Process—Ending	-0-

In the Screening Department, a by-product is recovered and is further processed to form a chemical called Milron. For each metric ton of by-product recovered, it is necessary to add an additional metric ton of filler to form Milron. The filler costs $5 per metric ton. Each metric ton of Milron requires additional labor costs of $1 and manufacturing overhead of $1.50. (Note that for each metric ton of by-product recovered, 2 metric tons of Milron will be produced.) Milron has an established selling price of $12 per metric ton. The normal net profit margin of the company is 8 percent of sales. The estimated selling and administrative expenses are $1 per metric ton of Milron.

Instructions

1. Compute the cost to be assigned to the 250 metric tons of by-product before separation, using the reversal cost method.
2. Prepare a cost of production report for the Screening Department for the month of June 19X9, based on the above data.

PROBLEM 18-3A. Making journal entries to record the cost and the sale of a by-product. The Republic Company has three producing departments: the Grinding Department, the Mixing Department, and the Packaging Department. Five percent of the raw materials put into production in the Grinding Department become a by-product that has an estimated sales value of $.06 per kilogram. The estimated sales value of the by-product is treated as a reduction in the cost of the main product. During November 19X3, 500,000 kilograms are put into production. There are no beginning and ending inventories. During November 19X3, the following costs are incurred in the Grinding Department:

Cost	Amount	Post Reference
Materials	$80,560.40	MR1
Labor	11,232.32	J1-10
Overhead	7,847.40	J1-11

Instructions

1. Enter the materials, labor, and overhead costs in the Work in Process—Grinding Department account. Open the Inventory of By-Product account.
2. Prepare the general journal voucher to record the removal of the by-product from the Grinding Department. Number the voucher 11-12. Post the voucher to the general ledger accounts opened.
3. Prepare the general journal voucher to record the sale of half the by-product inventory for $776.45 cash. Number the voucher 11-13. Use the same account names and numbers that are used in the text. Post the voucher to the Inventory of By-Product account.

PROBLEM 18-4A. **Making journal entries for sales of a by-product when different accounting methods are used.** The Roanoke Corporation manufactures a single product from a plastic material. In the Trimming Department, plastic shavings are created by the manufacturing process and become a by-product.

Instructions

1. On August 1, 19X4, 7,450 pounds of the plastic by-product recovered in July were in storage. These 7,450 pounds were sold on August 4 for $.30 per pound. Assuming that no entry is made for the by-product until it is sold, give the entry in general journal form to record the sale for cash of the 7,450 pounds under the following procedures:
   a. The amount received from the sale is recorded as miscellaneous income.
   b. The amount received from the sale is treated as a reduction in the cost of the main product. (NOTE: Credit Work in Process—Trimming Department 123.)
2. During the month of August 19X4, an additional 10,520 pounds of the plastic by-product were recovered. This amount was sold on September 2, 19X4. Instead of following the procedures given in Instruction 1, assume that the estimated sales value of the by-product is treated as a reduction in the cost of the main product when it is removed. Give the entries in general journal form to record the following:
   a. Recovery of the 10,520 pounds during August, assuming an estimated value of $.30 per pounds. (Date the entry August 31, 19X4.)
   b. Sale for cash of the 10,520 pounds on September 2 at $.28 per pound.

Managerial Decisions

CASE 18-1. The Lazar Company has two producing departments: the Shaving Department and the Polishing Department. In the Shaving Department, shavings are collected and sold as a by-product. Management follows the policy of assigning the market value at the point of separation as the cost of the by-product. Without further processing, the by-product could be sold for $7.50 per kilogram, but selling and administrative expenses of $.17 per kilogram would be incurred. After further processing, the by-product could be sold for $11.70 per kilogram, but selling and administrative expenses of $.23 per kilogram would be incurred. The necessary processing costs for 3,010 kilograms are estimated as shown on page 371.

Materials $2,244
Labor   4,860
Overhead   2,520

1. Prepare a schedule showing the estimated net profit or loss from the sale of 3,010 kilograms of the by-product without further processing.
2. Prepare a schedule showing the estimated net profit or loss from the sale of 3,010 kilograms of the by-product after further processing. Remember to take the common costs of the by-product into consideration as well as the expenses of further processing.
3. Should the by-product be processed further? Explain.

CHAPTER

19

Joint Products

■ ■ ■

Joint products arise whenever two or more products result from a single manufacturing process. Each joint product is considered to be of equal importance. Since all joint products from a process are significant, the costing procedures they require are different from those used to account for by-products.

Processing Joint Products

Sometimes joint products emerging from the manufacturing process can be sold without further processing. For example, in an oil refinery, the refining process will yield both gasoline and residual fuel oil. In other cases, one or more of the products emerging from the joint process may require additional processing to make them salable. An oil well, for instance, may produce crude oil, which must be refined into products such as gasoline and jet fuel. It may also produce natural gas, which can be marketed without additional processing.

Bases for Allocating Common Costs

When a firm produces joint products, there is no main product to bear the common costs. Each joint product must carry its share of the costs of production. The cost accountant must therefore devise a system for allocating common costs to the various joint products.

Four common bases are used to assign joint costs to individual products.

- A *common physical unit of measure,* such as gallons, pounds, or feet.
- The *relative sales value* of products, set to yield a uniform rate of gross profit.
- The *adjusted sales value,* reflecting additional processing costs.
- *Assigned weights,* based on technical studies. For example, production managers may conclude based on their experience or on technical studies that a unit of one product emerging from a process is more difficult to handle, has greater spoilage, and requires higher selling costs than a unit of the second product from the same process. Based on these studies or

on experience, each equivalent unit of the first product may be assigned twice as much cost as the second product.

Each of these methods is discussed and illustrated with data relating to the operations of a chemical manufacturing firm, the Delta Chemical Company.

The Delta Chemical Company

The Delta Chemical Company manufactures two joint products for industrial use: Release, a liquid solvent, and Buff, a cleaning compound. These two products are joint products because the manufacturing process automatically results in both being produced, and both have a relatively high value.

The raw chemicals are processed through a single department and are then removed to tanks to await sale. The average cost method is used to account for the beginning work in process inventories.

Cost Data

The Work in Process account in Delta's general ledger shows the following cost information:

Beginning Work in Process	
Materials	$ 4,800
Labor	508
Overhead	752
Balance of Account, May 31	$ 6,060
Current Month	
Materials	$49,200
Labor	12,232
Overhead	17,868
Total Current Month's Costs	$79,300

Production Data

The production report for June, shown on page 374, contains the usual information. However, note that the quantity of each product manufactured is shown under Transferred Out to Finished Goods.

Equivalent Production Data

Since all costs have been incurred to process all the products, the total cost must now be allocated to the individual products. Equivalent units of production for joint products are computed in the same way as for a single product. Using the average cost method, the cost accountant at Delta prepares the equivalent production computations in order to assign the total cost to individual products for June. These computations are shown on page 374.

Cost of Production Report

Delta's cost of production report for June is shown on page 375. This report is similar to the ones discussed in Chapter 15 for the average cost system.

```
┌────────────────────────────────────────────────────────────────┐
│                  DELTA CHEMICAL COMPANY                         │
│                 Monthly Production Report                       │
│                        June 19X1                               │
│                                                                │
│  Quantity                                                      │
│     Work in Process—Beginning                  16,000 gallons  │
│     Started in Production—Current Month       184,000 gallons  │
│     Transferred Out to Finished Goods                          │
│        Release Solvent                        128,000 gallons  │
│        Buff Cleaning Compound                  62,000 gallons  │
│     Work in Process—Ending                     10,000 gallons  │
│  Stage of Completion of Ending Work in Process                 │
│     Materials                                       complete   │
│     Labor                                              60%     │
│     Overhead                                           60%     │
└────────────────────────────────────────────────────────────────┘
```

```
┌────────────────────────────────────────────────────────────────┐
│                  DELTA CHEMICAL COMPANY                         │
│              Equivalent Production Computations                │
│                   Month of June 19X1                           │
│                                                                │
│  Materials                                                     │
│     Transferred Out to Finished Goods         190,000 gallons  │
│     Work in Process—Ending                     10,000 gallons  │
│        Equivalent Production for Materials    200,000 gallons  │
│                                                                │
│  Labor and Manufacturing Overhead                              │
│     Transferred Out to Finished Goods         190,000 gallons  │
│     Work in Process—Ending (10,000 gal. × 60%)  6,000 gallons  │
│        Equivalent Production for Labor and Overhead 196,000 gallons │
└────────────────────────────────────────────────────────────────┘
```

Quantity Schedule. The quantity of each product transferred out to finished goods is shown in Section (b), Quantity Accounted For.

Cost Schedule. In Section (c), Costs to Be Accounted For, the costs are computed as though a single product were being produced. All the costs incurred must be carried by the two products. Average equivalent production unit costs for materials, labor, and overhead are calculated. Both total and unit costs are then added to arrive at the total costs to be accounted for of $85,360 and an average unit cost of $.430.

Next, in Section (d), Costs Accounted For, a total of 190,000 gallons of product is transferred out at a total cost of $81,700. It is at this point that the basic accounting problem arises. How much of the $81,700 total cost of goods produced applies to the 128,000 gallons of Release solvent produced, and how much applies to the

DELTA CHEMICAL COMPANY
Cost of Production Report
Month of June 19X1

QUANTITY SCHEDULE	GALLONS
(a) Quantity to Be Accounted For:	
Work in Process—Beginning	16,000
Started in Production—Current Month	184,000
Total to Be Accounted For	200,000
(b) Quantity Accounted For:	
Transferred Out to Finished Goods	
Release Solvent	128,000
Buff Cleaning Compound	62,000
Total to Finished Goods	190,000
Work in Process—Ending	10,000
Total Accounted For	200,000

COST SCHEDULE	TOTAL COST	E.P. UNITS	UNIT COST
(c) Costs to Be Accounted For:			
Materials—Beginning Work in Process	$ 4,800		
Added in Current Month	49,200		
Total Materials	$54,000 ÷	200,000	= $.270
Labor—Beginning Work in Process	$ 508		
Added in Current Month	12,232		
Total Labor	$12,740 ÷	196,000	= .065
Overhead—Beginning Work in Process	$ 752		
Added in Current Month	17,868		
Total Overhead	$18,620 ÷	196,000	= .095
Total Costs to Be Accounted For	$85,360		$.430
(d) Costs Accounted For:			
Transferred Out to Finished Goods	$81,700 =	190,000	× $.430
Release Solvent	$55,040 =	128,000	× $.430
Buff Cleaning Compound	26,660 =	62,000	× $.430
Total Transferred Out	$81,700		
Work in Process—Ending			
Materials	$ 2,700 =	10,000	× $.270
Labor	390 =	6,000	× $.065
Overhead	570 =	6,000	× $.095
Total Work in Process	$ 3,660		
Total Costs Accounted For	$85,360		

62,000 gallons of Buff cleaning compound produced? Allocation may be done in several ways: by physical units, by relative sales value, by adjusted sales value, or by assigned weights.

Allocation by Physical Unit

Production in the Delta Chemical Company is measured in gallons. The cost of production report shows common costs allocated on the basis of a physical unit (the gallon) under Transferred to Finished Goods. The necessary computations appear below.

Total Cost of Product Transferred Out as Computed in the Cost of Production Report	$ 81,700
Total Number of Gallons Produced	190,000

$$\text{Cost per Gallon} = \frac{\$81,700}{190,000} = \$.43 \text{ per gallon}$$

Cost Applicable to Release, 128,000 gallons at $.43 each	$ 55,040
Cost Applicable to Buff, 62,000 gallons at $.43 each	26,660
Total Cost Allocated	$ 81,700

Analysis of Method

Note the following features of this method:

- The physical unit (the gallon) is easy to use because the product can be measured in gallons.
- The cost is easily distributed between the two products.
- The cost of each product is shown in the monthly cost of production report.
- Unit costs for both products are identical because they were computed by dividing the total cost by the total units.
- No consideration is given to relative sales values, special processing or handling required, the content of the product, or other special characteristics.
- Not all costs are directly related to physical quantities.

Allocation by Relative Sales Value

The relative sales value method of allocating joint costs is used very often. It is based on the theory that the product with the higher selling price should bear a proportionately higher share of the common costs. Under this procedure, costs are set for each product, so that they will yield a uniform rate of gross profit.

Procedure to Allocate the Costs

The cost accountant for Delta would use a four-step procedure to allocate the costs by this method.

Step 1. Compute the total sales value of the joint products by multiplying the number of units by the unit sales price. For illustrative purposes, assume a sales price per gallon of 60 cents for Release and 80 cents for Buff.

Product	No. of Units	Sales Value per Unit	Total Sales Value
Release	128,000	$.60	$ 76,800
Buff	62,000	.80	49,600
Total Sales Value			$126,400

Step 2. Calculate the percentage of total sales value that each product represents by dividing each product's total sales value by the total sales value of all products.

$$\frac{\text{Sales Value of Release}}{\text{Sales Value of All Products}} = \frac{\$76,800}{\$126,400} = 60.76\%$$

$$\frac{\text{Sales Value of Buff}}{\text{Sales Value of All Products}} = \frac{\$49,600}{\$126,400} = \frac{39.24\%}{100.00\%}$$

Step 3. Allocate a portion of the cost to each product by multiplying the total cost assigned to finished products ($81,700) by the percentage computed in Step 2.

Allocated to Release	60.76% × $81,700 = $49,640.92
Allocated to Buff	39.24% × $81,700 = 32,059.08
Total Cost Allocated	$81,700.00

Step 4. Determine the unit cost for each product by dividing the total cost of the product by the number of units produced. (Because of the large number of units and low unit cost, calculations have been carried to five decimal places and rounded to four places.)

$$\frac{\text{Total Cost of Release}}{\text{Gallons Produced}} = \frac{\$49,640.92}{128,000} = \$.3878 \text{ per gallon}$$

$$\frac{\text{Total Cost of Buff}}{\text{Gallons Produced}} = \frac{\$32,059.08}{62,000} = \$.5171 \text{ per gallon}$$

Eventually, the amounts to be allocated are listed in Costs Accounted For, Section (d) of the firm's cost of production report (shown below). Note that the total transferred out ($81,700) is the same as under the physical unit basis, but the total and average unit costs for each product are different. The average unit cost for a gallon of Release is $.3878, and the average unit cost for a gallon of Buff is $.5171.

(d) Costs Accounted For:	
Transferred Out to Finished Goods	
Release Solvent	$49,640.92 ÷ 128,000 = $.3878
Buff Cleaning Compound	32,059.08 ÷ 62,000 = $.5171
Total Transferred Out	$81,700.00
Work in Process—Ending	
Materials	$ 2,700.00 = 10,000 × $.270
Labor	390.00 = 6,000 × $.065
Overhead	570.00 = 6,000 × $.095
Total Work in Process	$ 3,660.00
Total Costs Accounted For	$85,360.00

Analysis of Method

Note the following features of this method:

- The computations are slightly more involved than those required by the physical unit basis.
- Costs are allocated in proportion to what products are worth.
- Both the total and unit costs are easily allocated to products.
- The costs are shown on the monthly cost of production report.
- There is an implication that selling price determines cost, whereas cost may not be directly related to sales value.
- It is assumed that all products should yield the same rate of gross profit.
- Changing prices may produce wide differences in costs from month to month.

Allocation by Adjusted Sales Value

If the joint products must be processed further before sale, the relative sales value method of allocation does not measure the true value of the products at the point of their separation. The additional processing costs must be deducted from the sales value before making the cost allocation. Similarly, if the costs of selling the products vary widely because of advertising, transportation costs, or different methods of distribution, it may be desirable to deduct the estimated selling costs from the sales prices in order to arrive at adjusted relative sales values.

To see how this procedure works, assume that the sales price of Release solvent remains at $.60 per gallon but that Buff cleaning compound must be processed further after its separation to make it marketable. The additional costs of processing the 62,000 gallons of Buff during June are labor, $2,015, and overhead, $2,635.

The allocation of the $81,700 of joint costs between the two products would be computed in the same four steps used to allocate costs by relative sales value. In Step 1, however, the cost of any additional processing needed for completion is deducted from the sales value to find the adjusted sales value. The adjusted sales value is then used in later computation steps.

Step 1: Adjusted Sales Value

Product	No. of Units	Sales Value per Unit	Sales Value	Additional Completion Cost	Adjusted Sales Value
Release	128,000	$.60	$76,800	-0-	$ 76,800
Buff	62,000	.80	49,600	$4,650	44,950
Total Sales Value					$121,750

Step 2: Percent of Total Value

$$\frac{\text{Sales Value of Release}}{\text{Sales Value of All Products}} = \frac{\$76,800.00}{\$121,750.00} = 63.08\%$$

$$\frac{\text{Sales Value of Buff}}{\text{Sales Value of All Products}} = \frac{\$44,950.00}{\$121,750.00} = \frac{36.92\%}{100.00\%}$$

Step 3: Allocation of Cost

Allocated to Release	63.08% × $81,700	=	$51,536.36
Allocated to Buff	36.92% × $81,700	=	30,163.64
			$81,700.00

Step 4: Cost per Unit

$$\frac{\text{Total Cost of Release}}{\text{Gallons Produced}} = \frac{\$51,536.36}{128,000} = \$.4026 \text{ per gallon}$$

$$\frac{\text{Total Cost of Buff}}{\text{Gallons Produced}} = \frac{\$30,163.64}{62,000} = \$.4865 \text{ per gallon}$$

The new allocation of costs is shown in Costs Accounted For, Section (d) of the following cost of production report. (The remainder of the cost of production report is identical with the illustration on page 375.) Again, the total and average unit costs for each product are different.

(d) Costs Accounted For:

Transferred Out of Department	$81,700.00 = 190,000 × $.430	
Release Solvent—to Finished		
Goods	$51,536.36 ÷ 128,000 = $.4026	
Buff Cleaning Compound—to Next		
Department	$30,163.64 ÷ 62,000 × $.4865	
Total Transferred Out	$81,700.00	
Work in Process—Ending		
Materials	$ 2,700.00 = 10,000 × $.270	
Labor	390.00 = 6,000 × $.065	
Overhead	570.00 = 6,000 × $.095	
Total Work in Process	$ 3,660.00	
Total Costs Accounted For	$85,360.00	

Analysis of Method

Note the following features of the method:

- The computations are very similar to those made when the relative sales value method is used.
- The costs may present a truer picture of the values at the point of separation of the products.
- The procedures involved are simple and relatively easy to apply.
- The cost allocations are still derived from the market price, which may have little or no relationship to the actual cost.

Computerized Costing of Joint Products

Break Fast, Inc., is a manufacturer of a popular brand of frozen donuts and sweet rolls. These are all made from one basic recipe with differences added after the initial mixing, kneading, and rising joint processes. At any point in time some units are only partially complete. Therefore, when it is time for the cost accountant to prepare reports for management, equivalent units of production must be computed for each type of donut or sweet roll so that joint costs can be allocated to different products by adjusted sales value.

Break Fast uses a computer system to collect data about the production process. The amounts of materials are keyed into the system through terminals as they enter production. Labor data enters the system when workers insert their badges into the terminals to record their time on each job. Overhead is computed by an overhead-rate computer program. Joint costs are recorded separately from costs incurred after the point of separation. Then the number of donuts and sweet rolls transferred to finished goods is entered into the factory terminal as they are moved to the freezer.

When it is time to generate reports, the cost accountant obtains the factory supervisor's best estimate of the percentage of completion of any unfinished products. The computer is used to determine the equivalent units of production for the current reporting period. The sales value per unit is already stored in the computer and need not be keyed in unless there is a change. The computer then uses the computed equivalent units to generate a cost of production report and then to allocate the joint costs to completed products. ■

Allocation by Assigned Weights

Each time a method of costing has been analyzed, it has become increasingly evident that there is no single completely accurate and satisfactory basis for allocating joint costs. For this reason, many cost accountants develop their own formulas for apportionment. They consider many factors involved in the manufacturing and marketing processes, such as volume and weight, technical processing, selling costs, and selling prices. They use this survey data to prepare an allocation formula expressed in terms of assigned weights (a percentage, or points) to show how to divide joint costs. This allocation technique is sometimes called the *survey method*.

For example, it may be decided that each gallon of Release should be assigned a weight of 3 points, and each gallon of Buff a weight of 4 points. Thus the joint costs for June would be allocated between the two products in the ratio of 384,000 to 248,000, as shown below.

Product	Gallons Produced	Weight Assigned	Weighted Production
Release	128,000	3	384,000
Buff	62,000	4	248,000
Total Weighted Production			632,000

Analysis of Method

Note the following features of this method:

- It may often yield more logical costs than any single allocation basis.
- The determination of weights is complicated, especially when many products are involved.
- Weight assignment is, in the long run, still another arbitrary process.

Limitations of Joint Costing

It is obviously impossible to allocate common costs precisely to each joint product. At best, the cost accountant may determine what appears to be a reasonable cost for each product. In view of the arbitrary manner in which costs must be allocated, the resulting figures should be used with extreme caution. For example, it would be completely unrealistic in most cases to use these allocated costs as a basis for setting selling prices of individual products or for making other managerial decisions. The total costs and the total selling prices of all products are the important factors. Joint costing, when used in industry, can probably best be described as a means of estimating a cost figure for valuation of finished goods inventories.

Principles and Procedures Summary

Joint products are multiple products of one process and have equal or nearly equal value or importance to the manufacturer. The cost accountant must devise a system for allocating common costs to these joint products on some equitable basis. One of four methods is generally used.

Common costs can easily be assigned to products on the basis of the physical units involved. For example, if the products are measured in pounds, feet, or gallons, the costs can be allocated in proportion to the physical quantity of each.

Joint costs may also be allocated on the basis of relative sales value. The common costs are divided among the products in the proportion that their sales values bear to the total sales value of all products. This basis may be adjusted if any products require further processing beyond the point of separation (adjusted sales value basis).

Another method for allocating common costs is on the basis of assigned weights. A comprehensive survey is made of many factors that have a bearing on the costs of various products. Relative weights are determined for the products to allocate the costs as accurately as possible.

Joint costing is not an exact procedure. Each method produces different costs, and none is completely accurate. The limitations of these methods should be kept in mind when using the figures obtained.

Review Questions

1. Why does joint production occur?
2. How do joint products differ from by-products?
3. How does the monthly production report differ when a manufacturing process produces joint products rather than a single product?

4. Is the method used to compute the equivalent units of production for joint products the same as the method used for a single product? Explain.
5. How does the relative sales value method of allocating common costs to joint products differ from the adjusted sales value method?
6. What is the assigned weights method for allocating common costs?
7. If one of the joint products requires further processing and the other one does not, would the relative sales value method be an appropriate allocation method? Explain.
8. When is it appropriate to use a physical unit to allocate common costs?

Managerial Discussion Questions

1. Why is it important for management to know the costs of individual products that are jointly produced?
2. It is not always possible to use physical units as a basis for allocating common costs. Why?
3. What cautions should be given about using the data produced by joint costing methods?
4. Assume that you are a cost accountant and the management of the firm where you are employed asks about the advantages of allocating costs by assigned weights rather than by physical units. What explanation would you give?
5. Management wishes to set the price of joint products on the basis of the costs of the products. Comment on this proposal.
6. Why is the relative sales value method for allocating joint costs often preferred by management?
7. What factors should management consider when deciding whether to further process a joint product or to sell it at the point of separation?

Exercises

1. **Allocating common costs to joint products by physical units.** As a result of the manufacturing process, the Blending Department of the Cooper Company produces two joint chemical products. During March 19X3, the total manufacturing costs of the goods transferred out of the department were $29,960. A total of 6,000 pounds of Salzine, with a sales value of $7 per pound, and 7,000 pounds of Ethalide, with a sales value of $9 per pound, were produced. Determine the cost per pound of each product if physical units are used as the basis for allocating common costs.
2. **Allocating common costs to joint products by relative sales value.** Assume the same data as in Exercise 1. Determine the cost per pound of each product if relative sales value is used as the basis for allocating common costs.
3. **Allocating common costs to joint products by adjusted sales value.** The total manufacturing costs applicable to two joint cleaning products transferred out of a department in July 19X4 were $30,000. As a result of the manufacturing process, 5,000 units of Magic Glow (a finished product) were produced. The sales value of Magic Glow was $6 per unit. In addition, 6,000 units of Lemonite were produced. Lemonite must be further processed at an estimated cost of $2 per unit before it can be sold for $7 per unit. Using the adjusted sales value method, compute the total common costs to be assigned to each product in July 19X4.

4. **Allocating common costs to joint products by assigned weights.** The total costs of two joint products transferred out of the final producing department of the Steinberg Company during June 19X6 were $160,000. As a result of the manufacturing process, 20,000 units of Marnate and 6,000 units of Selatate were produced. Based on the difficulty of handling the products, additional sales efforts necessary, and other factors, the cost accountant has decided to use the survey method to allocate costs. Each unit of Selatate has been assigned a weight of 2, and each unit of Marnate has been assigned a weight of 3. Determine the total cost to be assigned to each product for the month.

5. **Allocating common costs to joint products by three different methods.** The following information relates to the costs and production for the Mixing Department of Househelper Products Inc. for the month of March:

Product	Units Produced
Lineup	2,000 pounds, sales price of $15 per pound with no additional manufacturing costs after separation
Fade-away	3,000 pounds, sales price of $25 per pound with additional manufacturing costs of $5 per pound after separation

The total manufacturing costs applicable to Lineup and Fade-away in this department were $65,000. Compute the amount of common costs to be allocated to each pound of each product using the following bases:

a. Physical units
b. Relative sales price
c. Adjusted relative sales price

6. **Allocating common costs to joint products by assigned weights.** The Walton Company produces oil and gas from the same wells. During October 19X2, the total operating costs of a lease were $68,000. Production was 6,000 barrels of oil and 20,000 cubic feet of gas. Each barrel of oil has about 5 times the energy content of a thousand cubic feet (an mcf.) of gas. What total cost should be allocated to the oil produced and to the gas produced if assigned weights are to be used as the basis of the allocation?

7. **Allocating common costs to joint products by relative sales value.** Assume the same facts as in Exercise 6. In addition, assume that the oil sold for $30 per barrel and the gas sold for $3 per mcf. What total cost should be allocated to the oil produced and to the gas produced if relative sales value is to be used as the basis of allocation?

Problems

PROBLEM 19-1. Allocating common costs to joint products by two methods—relative sales value and relative BTUs. The West Texas Petroleum Company owns a lease on a well that produces both crude oil and natural gas. During the year 19X6, the well produced 6,000 barrels of oil, which were sold at $16 per barrel, and 100,000 mcf. (thousand cubic feet) of natural gas, which were sold at $1.80 per mcf. Total costs of producing the oil and the gas were $14,300. Two proposals have been made for allocating the common costs of production between gas and oil.

■ On the basis of relative sales value.
■ On the basis of heat content, measured in British thermal units (BTUs). Each barrel of oil contains about 6 times as many BTUs as each mcf. of natural gas.

Instructions

1. Compute the total cost and the cost per unit to be allocated to gas and to oil under each of the proposed methods. Round off the unit costs to four decimal places.
2. Briefly compare the effects on costs of the two bases. What factors should a cost accountant consider in choosing a basis?

PROBLEM 19-2. Allocating common costs to joint products by three methods—physical units, relative sales value, and net realizable sales value. Santana Chemical Company uses a manufacturing process that produces two major products, Fluinol and Volumol. In the first department, the raw materials are mixed and treated. In the second department, some additional raw materials are added, the mix is further processed, and the two products are then separated. Cost and production data for the second department for the month of October 19X8 are given.

	Quantity	Cost
Materials Transferred In From Prior Department	120,000 bbl	$360,000
Materials Added in This Department	30,000 bbl	45,000
Labor Added in This Department		12,000
Manufacturing Overhead Added in This Department		18,000
Finished Products Transferred Out		
Fluinol	80,000 bbl	
Volumol	50,000 bbl	
Units Lost in Production (evaporation)	20,000 bbl	

There was no beginning or ending work in process inventory. Fluinol has a sales price of $7 per barrel, and Volumol has a sales price of $6 per barrel. It is estimated that selling and administrative expenses are $2.40 per barrel for Fluinol and $.80 per barrel for Volumol.

Instructions

1. Prepare schedules showing the allocation of each element of manufacturing cost to each barrel of Fluinol and each barrel of Volumol, using the assumptions listed below. (Round off the unit costs to four decimal places.)
   a. Costs are allocated on a per-barrel basis to the joint products.
   b. Costs are allocated to the two products on the basis of relative sales value.
   c. Costs are allocated to each product on the basis of net realizable sales value (the sales price less applicable selling and administrative expenses).
2. Prepare condensed income statements showing the profit that would be reported on each product under each of the three allocation methods.

PROBLEM 19-3. Allocating common costs to joint products by two methods—relative sales value and adjusted relative sales value. The Wayne Company has a single manufacturing process that results in two products. Salgon, a salt, has a sales price of $18 per kilogram, while Lorex, a liquid, has a sales price of $54 per liter. During May 19X7, total manufacturing costs in the final department were $708,000. Production for the month was 20,000 kilograms of Salgon and 15,000 liters of Lorex. Additional costs to process Lorex are estimated to be $5 per liter.

Instructions

1. Compute the cost to be allocated to each unit of each product for May 19X7, under the following assumptions:
   a. The relative sales value method is used to allocate costs.
   b. The adjusted relative sales value method is used to allocate costs.
2. Briefly compare the effects of the two methods of allocating costs.

PROBLEM 19-4. **Allocating common costs to joint products by two methods— physical units and relative sales value, and computing the profit or loss per quart.** The manufacturing process in the Cooking Department of the Decorative Paint Company produces two products. Each gallon of raw material placed in production in the department results in 3 quarts of Long Life Coating and 1 quart of Super Glo. Long Life Coating has a sales price of $4 per quart and Super Glo has a sales price of $2.25 per quart. Data for July 19X3 are given below. There was no beginning or ending work in process inventory.

Total raw materials placed in production in the department	40,000 gallons
Manufacturing costs incurred in the department	
Materials	$350,000
Labor and overhead	85,000

Instructions

1. Compute the cost allocated to each quart of Long Life Coating and the cost allocated to each quart of Super Glo if costs are allocated on the basis of physical units (quarts).
2. Compute the cost allocated to each quart of Long Life Coating and to each quart of Super Glo if common costs are allocated on the basis of relative sales value.
3. Compute the gross profit or loss on Long Life Coating and on Super Glo based on the computations in Instructions 1 and 2.
4. Which of the cost allocation methods used above is preferable? Explain.

Alternate Problems

PROBLEM 19-1A. **Allocating common costs to joint products by two methods—relative sales value and relative BTUs.** The Lone Star Petroleum Company owns a lease on a well that produces both crude oil and natural gas. During the year 19X5, the well produced 2,800 barrels of oil, which were sold at $16 per barrel, and 80,000 mcf. (thousand cubic feet) of natural gas, which were sold at $1.50 per mcf. Total costs of producing the oil and the gas were $12,000. Two proposals have been made for allocating the costs of production between the gas and the oil.

■ On the basis of relative sales value.
■ On the basis of heat content, measured in British thermal units (BTUs). Each barrel of oil contains about 6 times as many BTUs as each mcf of natural gas.

Instructions

1. Compute the total cost and the cost per unit to be allocated to gas and to oil under each of the proposed methods. Round off the unit costs to four decimal places.
2. Briefly compare the effects on costs of the two bases. What factors should a cost accountant consider in choosing a basis?

PROBLEM 19-2A. Allocating common costs to joint products by three methods—physical units, relative sales value, and net realizable sales value. The Shreveport Chemical Company uses a manufacturing process that produces two major products, Eroxin and Surinex. In the first department, the raw materials are mixed and treated. In the second department, some additional raw materials are added, the mix is further processed, and the two products are then separated. Cost and production data for the second department for the month of June 19X2 are as follows:

	Quantity	Cost
Materials Transferred In From Prior Department	125,000 kg	$32,000
Materials Added in This Department	30,000 kg	3,000
Labor Added in This Department		1,800
Manufacturing Overhead Added in This Department		1,200
Finished Products Transferred Out		
Surinex	100,000 kg	
Eroxin	50,000 kg	
Units Lost in Production (evaporation)	5,000 kg	

There was no beginning or ending work in process inventory. Surinex has a sales price of $.36 per kilogram, and Eroxin has a sales price of $.32 per kilogram. Estimated selling and administrative expenses: Surinex, $.09 per kilogram, and Eroxin, $.02 per kilogram.

Instructions

1. Prepare schedules showing the allocation of each element of manufacturing cost to each kilogram of Surinex and each kilogram of Eroxin, using the following assumptions. (Round off the unit costs to four decimal places.)
   a. Costs are allocated on a per-kilogram basis to the joint products.
   b. Costs are allocated to the two products on the basis of relative sales value.
   c. Costs are allocated to each product on the basis of net realizable sales value (the sales price less applicable selling and administrative expenses).
2. Prepare condensed income statements showing the profit that would be reported on each product under each of the three allocation methods.

PROBLEM 19-3A. Allocating common costs to joint products by two methods—relative sales value and adjusted relative sales value. The Black Rock Corporation has a single manufacturing process that results in two products. Monex, a powder, has a sales price of $4 per pound. Tegor, a liquid, has a sales price of $10 per gallon.

During January 19X4, total manufacturing costs in the final department were $98,000. Production for the month consisted of 30,000 pounds of Monex and 12,000 gallons of Tegor. Because of its volatile nature, Tegor must be carefully packed. The costs of packing and selling Tegor are $3.50 per gallon. The costs of packing and selling Monex are $.50 per pound.

Instructions

1. Compute the cost to be allocated to each unit of each product for January 19X1.
   a. The relative sales value method is used to allocate costs.

b. The adjusted relative sales value method is used to allocate costs.

2. Briefly compare the effects of the two methods of allocating costs.

PROBLEM 19-4A. Allocating common costs to joint products by two methods—physical units and relative sales value, and computing the profit or loss per pound. Two products result from production activities in the Straining Department of the Hanson Company. Each pound of raw material put into production in the department results in $\frac{1}{4}$ pound of Mela and $\frac{3}{4}$ pound of Bano. Mela is sold for $.60 per pound, and Bano is sold for $1.25 per pound. Data for April 19X3 are given below. There was no beginning or ending work in process inventory.

Total raw materials placed in production in the department	104,000 pounds
Manufacturing costs incurred in the department	
Raw materials	$83,200
Labor and overhead	10,400

Instructions

1. Compute the cost allocated to each pound of Mela and to each pound of Bano if common costs are allocated on the basis of physical units (pounds).

2. Compute the cost allocated to each pound of Mela and each pound of Bano if common costs are allocated on the basis of relative sales value.

3. Compute the gross profit or loss on Mela and on Bano based on the computations in Instructions 1 and 2.

4. Which of the cost allocation methods used above is preferable? Explain.

Managerial Decisions

CASE 19-1. The following data relate to the manufacturing process of Hilton Laboratories, which produces two joint products:

Joint Costs

Materials	$120,000
Labor	80,000
Overhead	60,000

Production

Kelton	6,000 pounds. Sales price, $42 per pound; additional costs to package and sell, $7 per pound.
Yelon	4,000 pounds. Sales price, $40 per pound; additional costs to package and sell, $4 per pound.

The production manager has proposed that management consider a small change in the manufacturing process. By cooking the material slightly longer, the ratio of production for the two products can be changed to 50 percent each. However, as a result of the increased cooking time, there would be a shrinkage of 3 percent in volume, and additional labor costs of $1,400 per month would be incurred. There would be no change in the sales or the selling cost per unit.

Prepare an analysis of the current profitability and the future profitability if the proposed manufacturing change were to be made. What course of action would you recommend that management take?

CASE 19-2. The Vista Chemical Company manufactures several chemical compounds. The manufacturing process in the Cooking Department can be varied to produce different proportions of its two joint products, Bilide and Carlide, at no additional cost. Carlide must be further processed at a cost of $.30 per pound of finished product after separation. Total capacity of the Cooking Department is 10,000 pounds per month. The company can sell up to 8,000 pounds of Bilide each month at $10 per pound. It can also sell up to 4,000 pounds of Carlide for $11.50 per pound. However, because of the manufacturing process used for Carlide after separation, it takes 1.25 pounds of the product at the point of separation to manufacture 1 pound of Carlide. For example, if the company decides to manufacture 4,000 pounds of Carlide, it will require an output of 5,000 pounds of the joint product from the Cooking Department. Common costs for 10,000 pounds of departmental output are shown below.

Materials	$40,000
Labor	9,000
Overhead	15,000

1. If the company decides to continue producing both Carlide and Bilide, what will be the gross profit, assuming that the physical units method of allocation is used and the maximum amount of Carlide is produced?
2. If the company decides to produce only Bilide, what will be the gross profit, assuming that the physical units method of allocation is used?
3. Based on gross profit alone, which alternative should the company select?
4. What factors other than gross profit should be considered in deciding whether to continue producing Carlide?

BUSINESS PROJECT

2

Process Cost Accounting

In this project you will apply the techniques and principles of process cost accounting to record and summarize the flow of costs at the City Beverage Company during the month of January 19X1.

The City Beverage Company

The City Beverage Company manufactures three main products, sold to restaurants and supermarkets, and one by-product. The continuous production operation starts in the Mixing Department, where raw fruits are crushed and blended. Some of the mixture is transferred from the Mixing Department to the Fruit Fizz Department, and the remainder is transferred to the Quick Mix Department. In the Fruit Fizz Department, additional raw materials are added, and the mixture is further processed. Two finished products, Fruit Fizz and Fruit Punch, are obtained. These are transferred to the refrigerated storeroom. The mix transferred from the Mixing Department to the Quick Mix Department also receives further processing, including dehydration, in which Quick Mix is produced. A by-product of the fruit pulp, FP-Mix, is also derived from the operations and is sold as a flavoring.

The manufacturing flow is summarized by the diagram on page 390.

Cost Accounting System

The firm's process cost accounting system includes the usual journals and ledgers. All forms required are found in the *Study Guide and Working Papers*. If you are not using the *Study Guide and Working Papers*, you will have to record all such data on blank forms.

Journals

Special journals have been omitted from this project for the sake of simplicity. Cost data is supplied for each department as required.

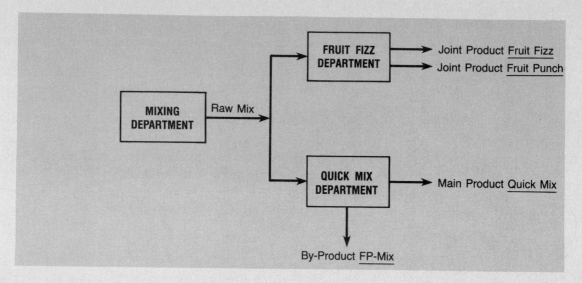

General Ledger

The City Beverage Company's chart of accounts includes the following accounts related to the flow of manufacturing costs. The January 1 balance for each account is given.

121	Raw Materials	-0-	Dr.
123	Work in Process—Mixing Department	$ 3,400.00	Dr.
124	Work in Process—Fruit Fizz Department	14,560.00	Dr.
125	Work in Process—Quick Mix Department	5,600.00	Dr.
126	Finished Goods	35,800.00	Dr.
127	Inventory of By-Product	248.00	Dr.
500	Factory Payroll Clearing	-0-	
501	Manufacturing Overhead Control	-0-	

General ledger account forms are provided in the *Study Guide and Working Papers*. The January 1 balances have been entered. Accounts 121, 500, and 501 are not shown. You may omit posting to these accounts.

Subsidiary Ledgers

Three subsidiary cost ledgers are used in the normal operations of the firm's cost accounting system.

Materials Ledger

Departmental Overhead Analysis Sheets

Finished Goods Ledger

The first two ledgers are not required for the solution of this project. The finished goods ledger provided in the *Study Guide and Working Papers* contains separate accounts for Fruit Fizz, Fruit Punch, and Quick Mix. The January 1 balances, shown on page 391, have been entered.

| | Balance | | |
Product	Units	Price	Amount
Fruit Fizz	3,000	$4.96	$14,880.00
Fruit Punch	2,700	4.00	10,800.00
Quick Mix	4,000	2.53	10,120.00

. . . .

Cost Data

The cost data accumulated for each department are given in summary form.

Mixing Department

Prior period and current costs for the Mixing Department are as follows:

Beginning Work in Process
Materials	$1,000
Labor	1,280
Overhead	1,120
Balance of Accounts, Jan. 1	$3,400

Current Month
Materials	$ 34,200
Labor	50,200
Overhead	69,080
Total Current Month's Costs	$153,480

Fruit Fizz Department

The beginning inventory of the Fruit Fizz Department includes costs in the prior department, as shown.

Beginning Work in Process
Costs in Prior Department	$ 8,200
Costs in Current Department	
Materials	600
Labor	2,160
Overhead	3,600
Balance of Accounts, Jan. 1	$14,560

Current Month
Materials	$ 13,800
Labor	38,640
Overhead	63,600
Total Current Month's Costs	$116,040

Quick Mix Department

The Quick Mix Department's cost data also include prior elements.

Beginning Work in Process
Costs in Prior Department	$3,400	
Costs in Current Department		
Materials	800	
Labor	600	
Overhead	800	
Balance of Accounts, Jan. 1	$5,600	

Current Month
Materials	$ 7,700
Labor	10,200
Overhead	12,920
Total Current Month's Costs	$30,820

Production Data

Data regarding the factory operations during January are reported by the department supervisors. The monthly departmental production reports are shown below and on page 393.

MIXING DEPARTMENT
Monthly Production Report
January 19X1

Work in Process—Beginning	2,000 units
(All materials have been added; 25% of labor and overhead have been added.)	
Started in Production—Current Month	80,000 units
Completed and Transferred Out	
To Fruit Fizz Department	48,000 units
To Quick Mix Department	28,000 units
Work in Process—Ending	4,000 units
(All materials have been added; 50% of labor and overhead have been added.)	
Lost in Production	2,000 units

Costing Procedures to Be Completed

In this project you will complete the following typical steps in the firm's cost accounting cycle:

1. Charge the costs of materials used, direct labor, and manufacturing overhead to the producing departments.
2. Compute the equivalent production for each department.
3. Prepare a cost of production report for each department (Carry the unit costs to four decimal places and round to three.)

```
┌─────────────────────────────────────────────────────────────────┐
│                   FRUIT FIZZ DEPARTMENT                         │
│                  Monthly Production Report                      │
│                       January 19X1                             │
│                                                                 │
│   Work in Process—Beginning                      4,000 units    │
│       (All materials have been added; 75% of                    │
│       labor and overhead have been added.)                      │
│   Transferred In From Mixing Department         48,000 units    │
│   Finished Goods Transferred Out                                │
│       Fruit Fizz                                28,000 units    │
│       Fruit Punch                               18,000 units    │
│   Work in Process—Ending                         4,000 units    │
│       (50% of materials have been added; 50% of                 │
│       labor and overhead have been added.)                      │
│   Lost in Production                             2,000 units    │
└─────────────────────────────────────────────────────────────────┘
```

```
┌─────────────────────────────────────────────────────────────────┐
│                   QUICK MIX DEPARTMENT                         │
│                  Monthly Production Report                      │
│                       January 19X1                             │
│                                                                 │
│   Work in Process—Beginning                      2,000 units    │
│       (All materials have been added; 50% of                    │
│       labor and overhead have been added.)                      │
│   Transferred In From Mixing Department         28,000 units    │
│   Increase in Number of Units Due to Added Materials  7,000 units│
│   Main Product Completed and Transferred Out    34,000 units  -2000│
│   Work in Process—Ending                         3,000 units    │
│       (All materials have been added; 33⅓% of                   │
│       labor and overhead have been added.)                      │
│   FP-Mix By-Product Recovered                    2,000 pounds   │
└─────────────────────────────────────────────────────────────────┘
```

4. Transfer the costs from one process to another.
5. Transfer the value of any finished products to the Finished Goods account.
6. Transfer the value of any by-product to the Inventory of By-Product account. Observe the specific instructions that follow as you proceed.

Charging Costs to Production

Each current cost element is to be charged to production by a general journal voucher entry. (The amounts are included in the cost data for each department.)

1. Record the entries on the general journal vouchers. Use the following voucher numbers: 1-1 for materials used, 1-2 for direct labor, and 1-3 for manufacturing overhead.

2. Post each entry to the general ledger accounts provided. (Be sure that you have entered the January 1, 19X1, balances given on page 390 before posting to the accounts.)

Departmental Procedures

Perform the departmental costing procedures as outlined below.

Mixing Department. Complete the following steps to summarize and record the cost flow of this first department:

1. Compute the equivalent production using the average cost method for handling inventories.
2. Prepare a cost of production report.
3. Prepare a general journal voucher (1-4) to transfer costs out of the Mixing Department to the Fruit Fizz Department and to the Quick Mix Department. Then post this entry to the ledger accounts.

Fruit Fizz Department. Complete the costing procedures outlined, giving careful attention to special directions.

1. Compute the equivalent production data using the average cost method.
2. Prepare a cost of production report. Show an adjustment for lost units on the report. Allocate joint production costs between the two finished products on the basis of the relative sales value of the products. Fruit Fizz sells for $9 per unit, and Fruit Punch sells for $7 per unit. Show in a footnote to the report how you computed the joint cost allocation.
3. Prepare a general journal voucher (1-5) to transfer costs out of the Work in Process—Fruit Fizz Department account and into the Finished Goods account. Then post this entry to the general ledger accounts and to the two finished goods subsidiary ledger accounts affected. (Be sure that you have entered the January 1, 19X1, balances given on pages 390 and 391 before posting to the accounts.)

Quick Mix Department. Complete the required cost procedures, including the recording of the by-product, as indicated.

1. Compute the equivalent units of production. Since the ending inventories are sometimes quite high, the company uses the first in, first out (FIFO) method of costing production in this department.
2. Prepare a cost of production report. Show an adjustment for the increase in units under Costs in Prior Department on the report, assuming that all materials are added in this department at the beginning of the departmental processing. Use the reversal cost method for assigning common costs to the by-product, FP-Mix. This by-product material is collected and stored in bins. Periodically it is sent to a subcontractor who processes it for $.34 per pound and returns it to the City Beverage Company for resale. The City Beverage Company sells the FP-Mix for $1.20 per pound after it has been treated. The company's normal gross margin on sales is 45 percent of the sales price. Because the total amount is small, the portion of the common costs assigned to the by-product is shown as a reduction in the costs of units started and completed in the current month.
3. Prepare general journal vouchers to record the completion of the main product (1-6) and the recovery of the by-product (1-7). Post the entries to the appropriate general and subsidiary ledger accounts.

3

Cost Accounting

As a Management

Tool

20

The Analysis of Cost Behavior

■ ■ ■

In Parts 1 and 2 of this book you have seen how cost accounting is used to accumulate data about the costs of constructing, manufacturing, and selling goods or services. Cost accounting is also used in other ways. It helps management to plan future operations and to control and evaluate results. In Part 3 we will examine the use of cost accounting as a management tool.

Cost Behavior

One of the most basic concepts of cost accounting is *cost behavior,* sometimes called *variability.* Cost behavior is the manner in which costs change as the volume (units of output, direct labor hours, or some other factor) changes. An understanding of cost behavior is essential to anyone who wishes to use accounting as a tool for planning, controlling, and evaluating operations. In general, costs can be classified as either *fixed, variable,* or *semivariable.* A fourth category—*stair-step,* or *semifixed, costs*—is also used by some accountants. Each of these classifications will now be discussed.

Variable Costs

Variable costs are those costs that vary in direct proportion to changes in volume or level of activity. Direct materials, direct labor, and, in some instances, indirect materials are examples of variable costs. Direct materials and direct labor vary with the number of units produced. Indirect materials may vary with the number of units produced or the number of direct labor hours worked. If the direct materials cost for manufacturing one unit is $100, the direct materials cost for producing ten units is generally expected to be $1,000. If the indirect materials cost is $.80 per direct labor hour and 27,000 hours are budgeted for the period, the total estimated indirect materials cost is $21,600 (27,000 hours × $.80 for each direct labor hour). If 33,000 direct labor hours are worked, the total indirect materials cost should be $26,400 (33,000 hours × $.80 per hour).

Assuming that the cost of indirect materials is a purely variable cost, its behavior can be plotted on a graph showing the relationship between volume expressed in terms of direct labor hours and indirect materials cost. A graph reflecting the costs discussed in the preceding paragraph ($.80 for each direct labor hour) is shown below. Remember that while the *total* of the variable cost changes in direct proportion to volume, such as level of activity, the cost per unit of measurement is constant. The following graph illustrates the behavior of variable costs:

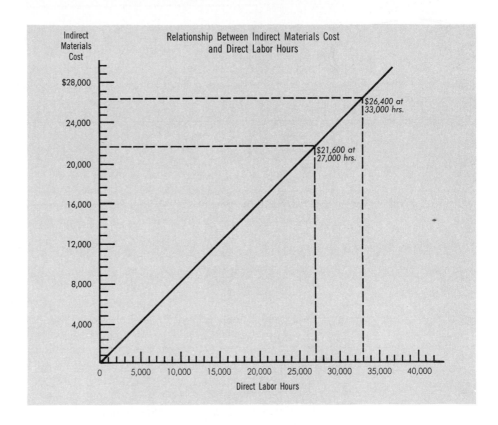

Fixed Costs

Fixed costs are costs that do not change in total amount as changes in volume of output or activity occur. The salary of the plant manager, for example, is the same in a given period regardless of changes in the level of production.

Depreciation of machinery and equipment is another fixed cost. If depreciation is $36,000 per year, it is irrelevant whether the level of activity is 27,000 direct labor hours or 33,000 direct labor hours. The depreciation is still $36,000 per year. Obviously, however, the fixed cost *per unit* decreases as volume increases. If depreciation is $36,000 per year and 24,000 hours of direct labor are worked, the cost is $1.50 per hour. On the other hand, if depreciation is $36,000 and 30,000 direct labor hours are worked, the depreciation is $1.20 per hour.

The relationship between total cost and volume expressed in terms of direct labor hours and depreciation of machinery and equipment is shown in the following graph:

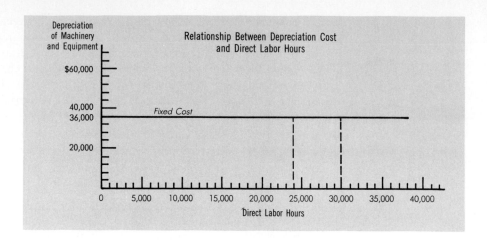

Semivariable Costs

It is obviously an easy task to estimate purely variable costs and purely fixed costs that are expected to occur at any given level of output. However, not all costs are purely fixed or purely variable. Some costs are semivariable.

Semivariable costs are those costs that vary in some degree with volume but not in direct proportion to it. These semivariable costs consist of a basic fixed element that is immune to changes in activity or volume and a variable element that reflects changes in activity or volume.

The cost of utilities is usually semivariable since it is necessary to have light, heat, and cooling in a factory whether goods are being produced or not. The portion of utilities cost that is needed to provide this basic service is the fixed element. Power is also required to operate machinery used in production, and the total amount varies with hours of operation. This portion of the cost is the variable element.

If the utilities cost for a department is estimated to be $1,200 a year (fixed) plus $.40 per direct labor hour (variable), total costs at 27,000 hours are estimated to be $12,000 (27,000 hours × $.40 + $1,200). A graph illustrating the relationship between utilities cost and direct labor hours is shown on the top of page 399. This graph has two solid lines. The solid horizontal line represents fixed costs ($1,200), and the solid diagonal line represents total costs. Broken lines are used to indicate the total utilities cost at various levels of activity; for example, $14,400 at 33,000 hours.

Other examples of semivariable costs are indirect labor, maintenance, and payroll taxes.

Stair-Step Costs

Stair-step costs are costs that are basically fixed within a narrow range but show abrupt and distinct increases when there are periodic volume increases. This type of cost behavior is characteristic of many supervisory salary costs and inspection labor costs. For example, only one inspector (with an annual salary of $24,000) may be required if production is not more than 5,000 direct labor hours. A second inspector (also earning $24,000 per year) must be added if production exceeds 5,000 direct

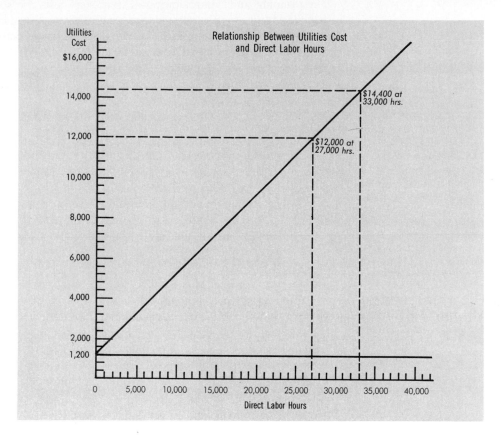

Relationship Between Utilities Cost and Direct Labor Hours

$14,400 at 33,000 hrs.

$12,000 at 27,000 hrs.

labor hours but is less than 10,000 direct labor hours. In a similar fashion, an additional inspector earning $24,000 annually is needed for each additional 5,000 direct labor hours. The behavior of a stair-step cost appears in the graph below.

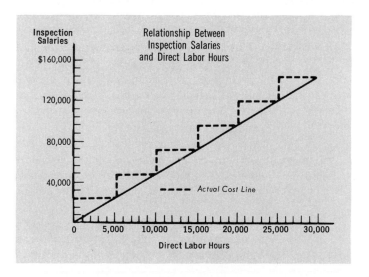

Relationship Between Inspection Salaries and Direct Labor Hours

Actual Cost Line

For planning and control purposes, stair-step costs are sometimes treated as variable costs and are often referred to as *semifixed costs*. A diagonal line representing the budget allowance is fitted to the bottom of the stair-step pattern. In this way, the budget allowance never exceeds the amount that actually should be spent at any volume of activity. The diagonal line in the graph above depicts a cost with a variable rate of $4.80 per direct labor hour ($24,000 ÷ 5,000 direct labor hours).

Methods of Analyzing Cost Behavior

Knowledge of cost behavior is a fundamental part of product costing, controlling costs, and decision making. As we have already seen, some costs are purely fixed, some are purely variable, and others are semivariable. How are the fixed and variable elements of a cost determined? There are two basic approaches to determining cost behavior. One is the analysis, based on engineering studies, of what cost behavior should be. The other is the analysis of accounting and statistical records to project what cost behavior will be in the future, based on what it has been in the past.

The Engineering Analysis of Costs

The engineering approach is commonly used in analyzing direct materials and direct labor costs. Detailed engineering specifications are normally available to show precisely what materials are required in manufacturing a product. With known prices for materials, it is possible to determine with a high degree of accuracy how much the cost of materials should be.

Engineering specifications and time and motion studies may also be used to determine accurately the amount of time that should be required for each step in the production process. With known wage rates, labor costs per unit of production can be budgeted with confidence.

Analysis of Past Cost Behavior

Because of the rather general nature of most overhead costs, it is usually difficult to use the engineering approach to determine what such costs should be. Instead, an analysis of past cost data is normally the starting point for making projections into the future.

There are many techniques for analyzing past cost-volume relationships. Some of these are highly technical, involving complex mathematical formulas. These statistical techniques require the development of precise formulas to express cost behavior. Only one of these, the *method of least squares,* is examined in this chapter. (The other statistical techniques are beyond the scope of this book.) Computer software programs for complex statistical techniques are widely available and are often used by accountants in analyzing cost behavior.

Other techniques for analyzing cost-volume relationships are less exact and are designed to give only a close approximation of the cost behavior, which is sufficient for preparing a budget. Three widely used nontechnical approximation methods are the *scattergraph method,* the *high-low points method,* and the *direct estimate method.*

An overview of cost behavior analysis techniques follows. For the purpose of this discussion, we will examine the record of the utilities cost and the direct labor hours in the Forming Department of the Industrial Tray Company for the period of September 19X0 to August 19X1. The accountant has accumulated the figures to use in analyzing cost behavior. These data are shown in the following table:

Month	Direct Labor Hours	Utilities Cost
September	2,140	$ 956
October	2,680	1,172
November	3,004	1,304
December	1,890	856
January	2,360	1,044
February	1,940	876
March	2,880	1,252
April	2,520	1,108
May	3,080	1,332
June	2,850	1,240
July	2,960	1,284
August	3,160	1,364

Scattergraph Method. In the *scattergraph method,* production and cost data for representative prior months (usually the 12 months or 24 months before the date of the computation) are plotted as points on a graph. (Many spreadsheet and database software packages for the microcomputer provide graphing capabilities.) If the points seem to form a clear pattern showing a high degree of correlation between volume and costs, a line is drawn to fit the trend of the points. For example, the utilities cost and the direct labor cost in the Forming Department of the Industrial Tray Company for the 12-month period from September 19X0 through August 19X1 are plotted in the graph on page 402. Since it is clear that the points fall into a pattern, a line is drawn to fit the trend of the points, as shown.

The plotted line intersects the vertical axis at $100. This represents the fixed portion of the monthly utilities cost that is not dependent on the level of activity. The variable element is computed from the cost of a month for which the plotted line lies directly on the cost line. For example, the total utilities cost for the month of May was $1,332, and 3,080 direct labor hours were used. The fixed amount ($100) is deducted from the total utilities cost for the month to compute the total variable utilities cost for the month. The total variable cost of $1,232 is then divided by the number of direct labor hours (3,080) to obtain the cost per direct labor hour of $.40.

Total Utilities Cost	$1,332
Deduct Fixed Portion	100
Total Variable Cost	$1,232

$$\frac{\text{Total Variable Cost}}{\text{Total Direct Labor Hours}} = \text{Variable Rate per Direct Labor hour}$$

$$\frac{\$1,232}{3,080 \text{ hr}} = \$.40 \text{ per Direct Labor Hour}$$

The same computations applied to the months of September and November will yield the same rounded rate. Thus the semivariable cost rate for utilities amounts to $100 per month (or $1,200 per year) plus $.40 per direct labor hour.

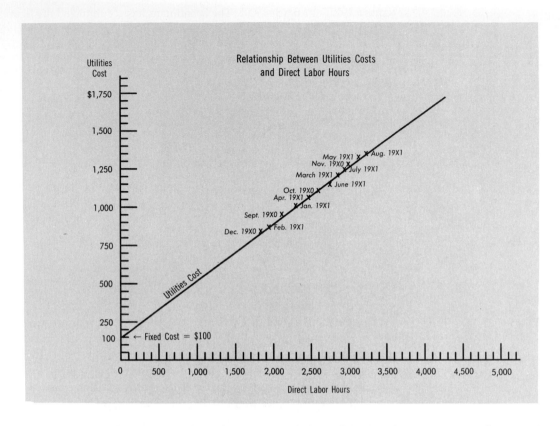

The scattergraph method is particularly useful when data are available for several prior periods and when the trend of the points is clearly evident. If the points on a scattergraph do not fit a reasonably clear pattern, it will be difficult to draw a line to fit the trend. Thus the scattergraph method may be inappropriate.

High-Low Points Method. In the *high-low points method*, the cost and production data for the months of highest and lowest volume of production are determined. The differences are then computed. On the previous graph, August and December are the high and low months. The difference between these months is computed as follows:

Month	Direct Labor Hours	Utilities Cost
August (High)	3,160	$1,364
December (Low)	1,890	856
Differences	1,270	$ 508

The difference in the utilities cost divided by the difference in direct labor hours will yield the variable rate per hour.

$$\frac{\text{Difference in Cost}}{\text{Difference in Hours}} = \text{Variable Rate per Direct Labor Hour}$$

$$\frac{\$508}{1,270 \text{ hr}} = \$.40 \text{ per Direct Labor Hour}$$

The fixed cost is then computed by deducting the known variable cost from the total cost in a certain month. In August, for example, the fixed cost amounts to $100, as shown below.

Total Cost	$1,364	
Deduct Total Variable Cost	1,264	(3,160 Hours × $.40 per Hour)
Total Fixed Cost	$ 100	

The major advantage of the high-low points method is its simplicity. There is always a danger in using only the data for the high month and the low month, however, because the behavior of costs for other months may be inconsistent with these two months. Sometimes accountants make a similar computation using the second highest and second lowest months and compare the results of this computation with those obtained using the high and low months. If the two sets of results are about the same, the high-low points computations will be used. If the two calculations are very different, a more technical approach may be necessary.

The Method of Least Squares. When there are erratic relationships between the volume of activity and a cost item, it may be difficult to draw a line to fit the points on a scattergraph. In such circumstances the high-low points method may also give incorrect results. Thus it may be desirable or necessary to use a more precise and complex statistical method. One relatively simple statistical technique that is often used for determining the fixed and variable components of a cost is the *method of least squares*. This is also sometimes referred to as *simple regression analysis*. This method determines mathematically a *line of best fit* through a set of plotted points in much the same way that a line is fitted to a set of points in a scattergraph. However, using the least squares method does not require that the points actually be plotted. Instead, a mathematical formula is developed for the line, and fixed and variable elements are computed from the formula.

When a line is drawn through a set of points at its best location, the sum of the deviations of the points from the line is at a minimum. Under the least squares method, the line is computed so that the sum of the *squares* of the deviations is at a minimum. (There are mathematical reasons why the squares of the deviations are used rather than the actual deviations. Those reasons are not important to the student of accounting.)

The least squares method is demonstrated below, using the data given on page 401 for the utilities cost in the Forming Department of the Industrial Tray Company for the months of September 19X0 through August 19X1. The steps in the process are as described below and as illustrated in the table on page 404.

1. Compute the average monthly direct labor hours. To do this, add the direct labor hours for each month and divide the total by 12 months. The figures are entered in Column B in the table below (31,464 ÷ 12 = 2,622 hours per month).
2. Compute the average monthly utilities cost. To do this, determine the total utilities cost for all months and then divide the total by 12. The figures are shown in Column D ($13,788 ÷ 12 = $1,149 per month).

LEAST SQUARES METHOD OF
DETERMINING VARIABLE AND FIXED COSTS

A	B	C	D	E	F	G
		DEVIATION FROM AVERAGE		DEVIATION FROM AVERAGE	DIRECT LABOR HOURS DEVI-ATION SQUARED	COLUMN C TIMES
MONTH	DIRECT LABOR HOURS	DIRECT LABOR HOURS	UTILITIES COST	UTILITIES COST	(COLUMN C SQUARED)	COLUMN E
September	2,140	(482)	$ 956	$(193)	232,324	$ 93,026
October	2,680	58	1,172	23	3,364	1,334
November	3,004	382	1,304	155	145,924	59,210
December	1,890	(732)	856	(293)	535,824	214,476
January	2,360	(262)	1,044	(105)	68,644	27,510
February	1,940	(682)	876	(273)	465,124	186,186
March	2,880	258	1,252	103	66,564	26,574
April	2,520	(102)	1,108	(41)	10,404	4,182
May	3,080	458	1,332	183	209,764	83,814
June	2,850	228	1,240	91	51,984	20,748
July	2,960	338	1,284	135	114,244	45,630
August	3,160	538	1,364	215	289,444	115,670
Totals	31,464		$13,788		2,193,608	878,360
Average	2,622		$ 1,149			

$$\text{Variable Costs} = \frac{\$878,360}{2,193,608 \text{ hours}} = \$.400417941 \text{ per hour}$$

3. Compute the difference between (a) the actual labor hours each month and (b) the average monthly labor hours computed in Step 1. The difference for each month is entered in Column C.
4. Compute the difference between (a) the actual utilities cost for each month and (b) the average monthly utilities cost computed in Step 2. The difference for each month is entered in Column E.
5. The difference between monthly direct labor hours and average monthly labor hours computed in Step 3 is squared. Each square is entered in Column F. These squares are then added and the total (2,193,608) is entered.
6. The difference between each month's labor hours and the average monthly labor hours (previously entered in Column C) is multiplied by the difference between that month's utilities cost and the average monthly utilities cost (previously entered in Column E). The products are entered in Column G. The products are then added, and the total (878,360) is entered.
7. The total of Column G (878,360) is divided by the total of Column F (2,193,608). The quotient (.400417941) represents the variable rate per hour for utilities cost.
8. The fixed utilities cost per month can now be computed.
   a. The average utility cost per month is $1,149.
   b. The variable portion of the average utilities cost is $1,049.90. This is the average direct

Computer Programs Solve Cost Problems

Software houses specialize in writing computer programs that will be sold to other companies. Since many firms have similar information requirements, programs can be written to serve many organizations. Software packages have been developed for payroll and inventory control. The major advantage of purchasing "canned" programs is the savings in development costs and time.

An example of such a software package would be a production scheduling program. The goal of such a package is a production schedule that will tie up the minimum number of dollars in inventories while requiring the least amount of direct labor capable of maintaining these levels of inventories. If several products demand inventory investment, the programs will determine the funding for each product necessary to maximize total return. The costs of having too little inventory (lost sales, idle production, higher purchase costs) are balanced against the costs of having too much inventory (storage costs, obsolescence, interest expense). The proposed solutions will fall within any constraints entered into the package by the company's cost accountant (for example, production capacities or workforce limitations).

This type of canned program can be individualized for any company. The cost accountant would enter a minimum amount of information to generate the scheduling reports. The information needed includes the following.

1. Current inventory
2. Sales forecast
3. Product cost and margins
4. Current level of labor
5. Current levels of production

When this information is entered, the program will then generate the production schedules that will minimize costs while meeting the sales forecast. ■

labor hours (2,622) multiplied by the variable rate of $.400417941 per hour, computed in Step 7.

c. The difference between the total average utilities cost ($1,149) and the variable portion of the average utilities cost ($1,049.90) represents the fixed portion ($99.10) of the cost.

Direct Estimate Method. A direct estimate is used when data on past performance are unavailable, when historical cost records are unreliable or incomplete, or when operating changes make existing data no longer applicable. Responsible operating managers then use whatever data are available, plus their knowledge of plans and methods and their experience, to reach a conclusion as to what costs should be.

Selecting the Method of Analysis

The scattergraph method is appropriate when there are several points to be observed and when the plotted points representing costs clearly fall into a pattern. However, if there are only a few volume levels for which costs are known, it may be difficult to fit a line to the points. In this case, the high-low points method may be preferable.

When many factors are involved or costs do not clearly fit a pattern on the scattergraph, the direct estimation procedure may be the most logical approach to determining cost behavior. In more complex cases, the method of least squares or even more sophisticated statistical methods using computer programs may be necessary to satisfactorily separate the fixed and variable costs.

It is important to note the limitations of the nontechnical methods for analyzing cost behavior discussed in this chapter. Unless the cost-volume relationship shows a high degree of correlation, it will be impossible to fit a cost line to the points on the scattergraph. Likewise, the high and low points will not be representative of the cost-volume relationship. The direct estimate method, as its name implies, is fundamentally imprecise. However, the nontechnical methods usually yield results that are meaningful at a practical level.

Principles and Procedures Summary

In previous chapters attention has been concentrated on product costing and inventory valuation. Also important is cost behavior. Costs are classified as fixed, variable, or semivariable depending on the manner in which they change as volume changes.

Various techniques are used to analyze costs and classify them into their fixed and variable elements. These techniques vary in both precision and difficulty. The specific cost being analyzed and the use to be made of the results should be considered in selecting the technique to be used. Nontechnical methods such as the scattergraph method, the high-low points method, and the direct estimate method give close approximations that are often sufficient for budgeting purposes. Sophisticated statistical techniques that often involve the use of computer programs are necessary where precise analysis of cost behavior is required. One relatively simple statistical technique that is often used is the method of least squares.

Review Questions

1. What happens to variable costs per unit as the level of activity changes?
2. Explain how total variable costs change as the level of activity changes.
3. How do fixed costs per unit change as the level of activity changes?
4. Explain how total fixed costs change as the level of activity changes.
5. What are semivariable costs? Give several examples.
6. Are materials and labor costs fixed costs or variable costs?
7. Explain stair-step costs and give an example.
8. For planning and control purposes, how are stair-step costs generally treated? Why are they treated in this manner?
9. What is meant by the engineering analysis of costs? What costs are commonly analyzed by this method? Why are these costs particularly adaptable to engineering analysis?
10. Explain the high-low points method of estimating the fixed and variable portions of semivariable costs.
11. Describe the scattergraph method of analyzing costs.
12. Explain the approach that the method of least squares takes to analyzing semivariable costs.

13. What is the greatest disadvantage to using the method of least squares?
14. What is the direct estimate method of analyzing cost behavior? When is it used?
15. In a factory using high technology, do you think that a greater portion or a lesser portion of its manufacturing costs would be considered as fixed costs in comparison to a factory in which most of the work is done by hand? Explain.
16. Which of the following costs do you think is more likely to be a variable cost? A fixed cost? A semivariable cost?
    a. Factory payroll taxes
    b. A royalty paid by a manufacturing company to a patent owner for using the patent to make a product
    c. Rent on the factory building

Managerial Discussion Questions

1. Explain why a distinction between fixed costs and variable costs is important to management when a factory is operating at less than full capacity.
2. The president of a corporation claims that depreciation is a variable cost because the depreciation cost per unit of output decreases as the volume of output increases. Comment on this.
3. How would a distinction between fixed and variable costs help management in forecasting cash needs for the business?
4. The president of the March Company has expressed concern to the corporation's controller over the fact that the controller has been using the scattergraph method for estimating fixed and variable costs. The president feels that the method is not reliable enough. What is your reply?
5. You, as cost accountant for your company, have suggested that the firm install a budgeting system. You explain to management that you wish to separate each factory overhead item into its fixed and variable components. The factory manager argues that this is not possible. To back up his position, he gives you the following example: If production is increased by 1,000 direct labor hours, inspection costs will remain constant, but for every 3,000 additional hours above that level, inspection costs will increase by $5,000 per month. How will you treat this cost in your analysis?
6. You have been asked by the controller of your company to analyze manufacturing costs for the past year in order to arrive at the variable and fixed components. In what circumstances would you choose each of the following activity bases as the unit of activity?
    a. Machine hours
    b. Direct labor hours
    c. Direct materials costs
    d. Direct labor costs
7. Explain why an understanding of past cost behavior is important in the budgeting process.
8. For several years the Meyer Company's cost accountant has analyzed the company's semivariable manufacturing costs by breaking them into fixed and variable components. During the past year, the company's production declined by more than 25 percent but the variable portions of some costs decreased by only 10 to 15 percent. Management has asked, "What is wrong?" What are the most likely reasons for this behavior?

Exercises

1. **Determining cost behavior for depreciation.** The depreciation cost for the Scott Company is $40,000 per month.
   a. What should the depreciation cost per direct labor hour be if 2,000 hours are worked? *$20, per hour*
   b. What should the depreciation cost per direct labor hour be if 2,500 hours are worked? *$16 per hour*
   c. Is depreciation a fixed cost or a variable cost? Explain.

2. **Determining cost behavior with the high-low points method.** The monthly supervisory costs of the Able Company's factory for each month of 19X1 have been analyzed. The month in which the greatest number of direct labor hours were worked was March, with 10,000 hours. The supervisory costs for that month totaled $80,000. In July, the month of fewest direct labor hours, 6,800 hours were worked, and supervisory costs were $64,000. Use the high-low points method to do the following:
   a. Compute the variable cost per direct labor hour using the high-low points method.
   b. Compute the fixed cost per month.

3. **Determining cost behavior for direct supervision.** The Neptune Company's accountant has accumulated cost figures at various activity levels. The following data shows the activity levels and the direct supervision costs for six months:

Direct Labor Hours	Direct Supervision Costs
14,620	$82,000
15,108	94,000
11,200	60,000
10,000	60,000
13,360	82,000
15,980	94,000

   a. What term can be used to describe this cost behavior?
   b. Explain this cost behavior.

4. **Determining variable costs for indirect materials.** At the Shelby Company, indirect materials are purely variable costs, varying in proportion to direct labor hours worked at the rate of $.80 per direct labor hour.
   a. Compute the total indirect materials cost for each of the following four levels of activity:
      (1) 16,212 direct labor hours *12969.60*
      (2) 18,714 direct labor hours *14971.20*
      (3) 20,000 direct labor hours *16000.00*
      (4) 28,714 direct labor hours *22971.20*
   b. What is the effect of increases in direct labor hours on the total cost of indirect materials?

5. **Determining fixed costs for supervision.** At the Shelby Company, factory supervision is a fixed cost of $10,000 per month.
   a. Compute the supervision cost per direct labor hour at each of the following monthly activity levels:
      (1) 10,000 hours
      (2) 11,000 hours

(3) 12,500 hours

(4) 14,285 hours

    b. What is the effect of increases in direct labor hours on the fixed cost per unit?

6. **Determining fixed, variable, and semivariable costs.** Indicate whether each of the following costs is likely to be fixed, variable, or semivariable, based on physical units of output:

    a. Direct materials

    b. Direct labor

    c. Depreciation

    d. Salaries of factory supervisors

    e. Insurance on factory building

    f. Heat, light, and power

    g. Indirect materials

    h. Indirect labor

    i. Payroll taxes

    j. Warehouse rental

DATA FOR EXERCISES 7–10

The Reed Company's records show the following data for the four quarters of 19X2:

Quarter	Direct Labor Hours	Indirect Labor	Utilities
First	10,200	$13,040	$1,520
Second	14,600	13,920	1,960
Third	12,800	13,560	1,780
Fourth	13,000	13,600	1,800

7. **Using the high-low points method.** Compute the fixed and variable elements of the indirect labor cost, using the high-low points method.

8. **Computing fixed and variable costs for utilities.** Compute the fixed and variable elements of the utilities cost, using the high-low points method.

9. **Computing indirect labor costs for different levels of activity.** What would be the expected indirect labor costs for each of the following levels of activity?

    a. 11,600 direct labor hours

    b. 13,320 direct labor hours

10. **Computing utilities cost at different levels of activity.** What would be the total fixed costs and the total variable costs for utilities if 12,900 direct labor hours were worked?

Problems

PROBLEM 20-1. Using the scattergraph and high-low points methods. The cost accountant of the Ramirez Corporation has compiled the following information about the direct labor hours and the indirect labor costs for each month of 19X0:

Month	Direct Labor Hours	Indirect Labor Costs
January	32,000	$18,800
February	28,500	17,400
March	29,400	17,700

April	24,080	15,632
May	30,350	18,050
June	30,100	18,040
July	34,600	19,840
August	35,900	20,360
September	37,800	21,120
October	35,350	20,140
November	33,600	19,375
December	32,400	18,960

Instructions

1. Plot these data on a scattergraph. Fit the points with a line and estimate the fixed costs from the graph.
2. Compute the monthly fixed costs and the variable costs per hour, using the high-low points method.

PROBLEM 20-2. Using the high-low points method. The Endicott Company's direct labor hours and indirect materials costs for the year ended March 31, 19X5 were as follows:

Month	Direct Labor Hours	Indirect Materials Costs
April	25,700	$ 8,120
May	28,950	8,780
June	32,800	10,520
July	37,450	11,540
August	38,600	11,720
September	41,900	12,740
October	42,875	13,200
November	42,000	13,112
December	38,100	12,040
January	36,785	11,580
February	35,420	11,360
March	30,180	9,640
Total	430,760	$134,352

Instructions

Compute the variable rate per direct labor hour using the high-low points method. Show your computations. Carry the answer to four decimal places and round to three.

PROBLEM 20-3. Using the high-low points method. Direct labor hours and indirect labor costs for each quarter of 19X1 for the Rosedale Company are shown below.

	Direct Labor Hours	Indirect Labor Costs
First Quarter	60,000	$208,000
Second Quarter	68,000	224,000
Third Quarter	57,000	202,000
Fourth Quarter	64,000	216,000

Instructions

Using the high-low points method, compute the variable rate per direct labor hour and the fixed cost per quarter. Show your computations.

PROBLEM 20-4. Using the high-low points method for indirect labor costs at different levels of activity. The following data involve the direct labor hours worked and indirect labor costs for the Mixing Department of the Glenwood Company for each quarter of 19X1.

	Direct Labor Hours	Indirect Labor Costs
First Quarter	10,400	$23,460
Second Quarter	12,100	25,100
Third Quarter	9,200	22,200
Fourth Quarter	10,700	23,780

Instructions

1. Using the high-low points method, compute the variable rate per direct labor hour and the fixed cost per month for indirect labor. Show your computations.
2. In the first quarter of 19X2, 12,800 direct labor hours were worked in the Mixing Department. Compute the expected indirect labor costs for the quarter.
3. In the first quarter of 19X2, the indirect labor costs in the Mixing Department were $27,100. Does this show that indirect labor costs were well controlled? Explain.

PROBLEM 20-5. Using the high-low points method and the method of least squares. The direct labor hours and payroll taxes and fringe benefits of the Cleary Company for six months during 19X1 are shown below.

Month	Direct Labor Hours	Payroll Taxes and Fringe Benefits
January	4,800	$6,960
February	3,900	5,900
March	4,600	6,680
April	5,100	7,400
May	4,900	6,040
June	4,320	6,370

Instructions

1. Using the high-low points method, compute the variable rate per direct labor hour and the fixed cost per month for payroll taxes and fringe benefits.
2. Using the method of least squares, compute the variable rate per direct labor hour and the fixed cost per month for payroll taxes and fringe benefits. (Round the variable costs to the nearest tenth of a cent per hour and the fixed costs to the nearest whole dollar per month.)

Alternate Problems

PROBLEM 20-1A. Using the scattergraph and high-low points methods. The cost accountant of the Gale Corporation has compiled the following information about the direct labor hours and the indirect labor costs for each month of 19X2:

Month	Direct Labor Hours	Indirect Labor Costs
January	4,600	$6,220
February	4,200	5,940
March	3,600	5,520
April	3,950	5,765
May	4,070	5,910
June	4,480	6,120
July	4,950	6,465
August	4,840	6,300
September	4,720	6,304
October	4,680	6,276
November	5,020	6,514
December	4,800	6,360

Instructions

1. Plot these data on a scattergraph. Fit the points with a line and estimate the fixed costs from the graph.
2. Compute the monthly fixed costs and the variable costs per hour, using the high-low points method.

PROBLEM 20-2A. Using the high-low points method. The Hallman Company recorded the following data about direct labor hours and indirect materials costs for the year ended May 31, 19X5:

Month	Direct Labor Hours	Indirect Materials Costs
June	16,000	$ 9,400
July	14,250	8,700
August	14,700	8,850
September	12,040	7,816
October	15,175	9,025
November	15,050	9,020
December	17,300	9,920
January	17,950	10,180
February	18,900	10,560
March	17,675	10,070
April	16,800	9,688
May	16,200	9,480
Total	192,040	$112,709

Instructions

Compute the variable rate per direct labor hour, using the high-low points method. Show your computations.

PROBLEM 20-3A. Using the high-low points method. Direct labor hours and indirect labor costs for each quarter of 19X2 for the Daley Company are shown on page 413.

	Direct Labor Hours	Indirect Labor Costs
First Quarter	36,000	$146,000
Second Quarter	30,800	127,800
Third Quarter	42,000	167,000
Fourth Quarter	38,400	154,400

Instructions

Using the high-low points method, compute the variable rate per direct labor hour and the fixed cost per quarter. Show your computations.

PROBLEM 20-4A. **Using the high-low points method for supplies cost at different levels of activity.** The following data involve the direct labor hours worked and the cost of supplies for eight months of 19X1 in the Joining Department of the Empire Company.

	Direct Labor Hours	Cost
January	1,200	$1,480
February	1,080	1,432
March	1,290	1,516
April	1,400	1,562
May	1,450	1,580
June	1,300	1,521
July	1,100	1,440
August	1,020	1,402

Instructions

1. Using the high-low points method, compute the variable rate per direct labor hour and the fixed cost per month. Show your computations.
2. In the month of January 19X2, 1,370 direct labor hours were worked in the Empire Company's Joining Department. Compute the expected cost of supplies for the month.
3. In January 19X2 the cost of supplies in the Joining Department was $1,550. Does this indicate that the cost of supplies was well controlled? Explain.

PROBLEM 20-5A. **Using the high-low points method and the method of least squares.** The direct labor hours and payroll taxes and fringe benefits of the Moreland Company for six months during 19X0 are shown below.

Month	Direct Labor Hours	Payroll Taxes and Fringe Benefits
July	6,500	$ 9,150
August	8,100	10,910
September	8,600	11,475
October	8,820	11,702
November	7,340	10,085
December	6,550	9,240

Instructions

1. Using the high-low points method, compute the variable rate per direct labor hour and the fixed cost per month for payroll taxes and fringe benefits. (Round the variable costs to the nearest tenth of a cent per hour and the fixed costs to the nearest whole dollar per month.)
2. Using the method of least squares, compute the variable rate per direct labor hour and the fixed cost per month for payroll taxes and fringe benefits. (Round the variable costs to the nearest tenth of a cent per hour and the fixed costs to the nearest whole dollar per month.)

Managerial Decisions

CASE 20-1. The Alameda Manufacturing Company uses a budgeting system in its manufacturing operations. The company's management wishes to apply some of these budgetary techniques to its other operations and has chosen the Billing Department as the first department for which a budgetary control system will be applied. This department prepares and mails statements to customers on a monthly basis. Each bill shows details such as beginning balance, purchases, returns, and payments. The first step is to determine the fixed and variable costs in the department.

1. Suggest two activity bases that might be used in measuring variability.
2. Assume that the activity base to be used is the number of billings per month. An analysis of data for the past six months shows the following:

Month	Number of Billings	Total Cost
January	4,200	$8,531
February	4,100	8,455
March	3,600	8,160
April	4,750	8,842
May	5,380	9,228
June	5,200	9,118

Management has asked you to determine the variable cost for each bill sent and the estimated monthly fixed costs of the department. Prepare the analysis.

3. Based on an analysis of billings in the past year, it is anticipated that activity in July will be high, at an estimated 5,460 billings, but that in August billings will drop to 4,250. What is the estimated total billing cost in each of these two months?

CASE 20-2. The Swenson Company is developing a budgeting program for its manufacturing operations. In analyzing indirect labor costs, figures for each month in the past year, 19X1, have been assembled.

Month	Direct Labor Hours	Indirect Labor Costs
January	2,800	$4,300
February	2,300	4,260
March	2,900	4,180
April	3,100	4,420

Month	Direct Labor Hours	Indirect Labor Costs
May	3,600	4,680
June	3,400	5,060
July	3,000	4,720
August	2,700	4,300
September	2,820	4,110
October	2,825	4,135
November	2,900	4,116
December	2,300	4,360

1. What does this pattern of cost behavior suggest about the control of indirect labor costs in the factory?
2. Using the high-low points method, compute the fixed element and the variable element of indirect labor costs.
3. Is the high-low points method satisfactory for budgeting indirect labor in this example? Explain.

CHAPTER

21

Budgeting

■ ■ ■

The cost data provided by a job order or process cost accounting system help management make decisions and improve the efficiency of operations. However, these decisions and improvements can be made only after the cost data are available at the completion of the specific job or operation. Although past experience is a helpful guide in planning, management needs a more formal and reliable method of anticipating future conditions and evaluating performance. A *budget* provides the means for planning and controlling future activities.

Budgetary Control

A *budget* is a business's financial plan. It is also the foundation of a firm's financial control system. Once financial goals are established, the budget is used to check and control operations. Actual results are compared with budgeted goals. Variations between actual results and planned results are investigated and analyzed. Action is taken to correct these variations while operations continue.

The budgetary control system covers all phases of business activity: sales, production, administration, and finance. In a large company, many individuals participate in developing the budget. The responsibility for coordinating the budget is delegated to a budget committee under the supervision of a budget director, who usually reports to the controller. In a small company, the accountant serves as budget director. The budget director suggests procedures for budget preparation and gives assistance and information to those responsible for preparing preliminary budgets for their departments. The budget director also reviews the departmental budgets to make certain that they are compatible and will achieve the common goals. The budget director then assembles the final departmental budgets and prepares the master budget.

A typical *master budget* consists of individual budgets for sales, production, manufacturing costs, operating expenses, cash receipts and payments, and capital assets, and a set of projected financial statements for the budgetary period. The master budget is often called the *operating budget* because it provides the basic plan for operations during the period.

The operating budget is a tool that makes planning and control easier. Planning involves identifying objectives and determining the steps for achieving these objectives. Control refers to the means by which management is assured that all parts of the company function properly and that the objectives identified in the planning stage are attained.

The development of the master budget of the Industrial Tray Company will be discussed in detail in this chapter. The firm manufactures metal trays covered with a special hard noncorrosive plastic. These trays are used by chemical companies to hold raw materials while the materials are being processed.

The Sales Budget

The sales budget presents the sales department's objectives for the budgetary period. The sales budget is the key to the overall company budget because the anticipated sales volume determines the amount of goods produced; the labor, equipment, and capital required; and the nature and amount of various selling, administrative, and financial expenses. Sales estimates are based on past performance and on the forecast of business conditions for the coming period. The accounting department, sales management, and salespeople all have a role in developing the sales budget.

Analysis of Past Performance

As sales are made, sales data are accumulated by products, territories, customers, and other categories. These data are studied in detail or summarized for planning purposes. The following territorial sales summary of the Industrial Tray Company is for the year 19X1:

INDUSTRIAL TRAY COMPANY
Analysis of Sales
Year Ended December 31, 19X1

(Figures show number of trays sold)

	INDUSTRIAL CHEMICAL MANUFACTURING	HOUSEHOLD CHEMICAL MANUFACTURING	OIL REFINERIES	OTHERS	TOTAL SALES
Mountain Territory					
Denver District	6,200	2,800	200	1,500	10,700
Albuquerque District	3,200	5,700	700	800	10,400
Tulsa District	1,600	3,200	-0-	1,100	5,900
Total	11,000	11,700	900	3,400	27,000
Central Territory					
Houston District	8,700	1,300	6,200	900	17,100
New Orleans District	4,300	600	4,800	300	10,000
Jackson District	1,600	800	1,000	500	3,900
Total	14,600	2,700	12,000	1,700	31,000
Total	25,600	14,400	12,900	5,100	58,000

The sales manager's staff analyzes all available data about past performance to evaluate the sales force's efforts and to set new plans and goals. The new plans may call for introducing new products and services and entering new markets. The new goals usually include increases in sales revenue.

Forecast of Business Conditions

General economic conditions and specific factors relating to a firm and its industry must also be considered in determining sales prospects. Every company knows that certain economic indexes are major indicators of its sales prospects. For example, one firm may find that its sales vary with changes in the volume of automobile production. The sales of another firm may have a high correlation with the national income. Many large companies hire professional economists to make economic analyses and forecasts for them.

Other factors may also affect sales prospects. For example, a manufacturer of home building products would be very interested in the local marriage rate, the birth rate, the availability of rental housing, the movement of new families to the suburbs, and interest rates. Another important factor in sales forecasting is the nature of the individual product. New uses for the product bring about wider sales possibilities. Changing habits, competitive items, and substitutes may lessen sales prospects. Certainly, a manufacturer of glass bottles for the soft drink industry would be vitally affected by the general acceptance of canned soft drinks. Similarly, sales of automobiles will be greatly affected by the supply and price of gasoline.

The sales managers of the Industrial Tray Company have considered the economic and other factors relevant to their future prospects in arriving at the sales budget for 19X2 (Schedule A), shown on page 419.

The Production Budget

After the sales budget has been determined, a production budget can be prepared to meet the requirements of the sales budget. The actual number of units to be completed is computed from the following data: the units to be sold, the desired size of the ending inventory, and the units in the beginning inventory.

The sales budget of the Industrial Tray Company, shown in Schedule A, projects sales of 62,000 trays in 19X2. Assume that an ending inventory of 12,000 is expected on December 31, 19X2, and that the beginning inventory on January 1, 19X2, is 14,000. This means that 60,000 trays must be produced during the year to meet the sales objective. The other 2,000 trays are made available by a planned reduction in the inventory. The production budget (Schedule B), which is shown on page 420, is computed by adding the estimated sales to the desired ending inventory and subtracting the beginning stock on hand.

The task of producing 60,000 trays in 19X2 requires the scheduling of productive capacity in accordance with circumstances and company policies. The production could be distributed evenly throughout the year at the rate of 5,000 trays a month, or the operations might be concentrated into a few months of intensive effort. A level rate of production usually results in a more stable and experienced work force and fuller use of plant capacity. There is less need for overtime opera-

| | INDUSTRIAL TRAY COMPANY
Sales Budget
Year Ending December 31, 19X2 | | | | Schedule A |

(Figures show number of trays to be sold)

	INDUSTRIAL CHEMICAL MANUFACTURING	HOUSEHOLD CHEMICAL MANUFACTURING	OIL REFINERIES	OTHER	TOTAL SALES
Mountain Territory					
Denver District	6,200	2,700	400	1,900	11,200
Albuquerque District	3,400	5,800	700	900	10,800
Tulsa District	1,800	3,200	100	1,400	6,500
Total	11,400	11,700	1,200	4,200	28,500
Central Territory					
Houston District	9,000	1,600	6,200	1,000	17,800
New Orleans District	4,800	800	4,800	400	10,800
Jackson District	1,800	800	1,400	900	4,900
Total	15,600	3,200	12,400	2,300	33,500
Total in Units	27,000	14,900	13,600	6,500	62,000
Total in Dollars at $64 per tray	$1,728,000	$953,600	$870,400	$416,000	$3,968,000

tions, and a smaller investment in plant and equipment is required. The accumulation of inventories, especially in seasonal industries, may cause storage and warehousing problems. Interest rates, insurance, and other costs of carrying and storing inventories will increase. The additional funds tied up in the inventories may be sizable and costly. The inventories may even deteriorate or become obsolete.

Most companies seek a balance between completely stable production and highly seasonal production. This involves balancing the storage, financing, warehousing, and handling costs associated with stable output against idle facility costs, labor supply problems, overtime pay, and similar factors associated with a highly seasonal production. The Industrial Tray Company follows a policy of level production throughout the year since its sales are not seasonal.

Manufacturing Costs Budget

Once the estimated production is determined, the cost of materials, labor, and manufacturing overhead at that production level must be computed. These costs are presented in the *manufacturing costs budget,* also called the *cost of goods manufactured budget.*

Unfortunately, manufacturing costs cannot be budgeted for only one production level, since actual production may differ from the originally planned production. Changes in anticipated (budgeted) sales volume during the year are generally re-

	NUMBER OF TRAYS
Budgeted Sales for Year	62,000
Budgeted Ending Inventory of Finished Goods, Dec. 31	12,000
Total Budgeted Requirements	74,000
Deduct Finished Goods Inventory, Jan. 1	14,000
Budgeted Production	60,000*

*Work in process inventories expected to remain constant.

flected in changes in levels of production. A *flexible budget* permits computation of costs for any attained volume of activity or output. For control purposes, the actual costs incurred at the level of production reached can be compared with the budgeted or estimated costs at that level. These data can be used to judge performance and fix responsibility for differences between actual and budgeted costs.

The flexible budget takes both fixed and variable manufacturing costs into account. The analysis of costs by breaking them into their fixed and variable components, discussed in the previous chapter, is a vital part of budgeting for both planning and control purposes. Each variable manufacturing cost element is budgeted as an amount per unit of product, per direct labor hour, or other activity indicator. Each fixed cost element is budgeted at a single amount per period. Since budgets are, at best, skilled estimates, budgeted amounts are rounded off to the nearest dollar. Many companies round off budgeted figures to the nearest hundred or even to the nearest thousand dollars, depending on the company's size.

The preparation of a manufacturing costs budget is made easier by the use of standards. A *standard* is the amount of material, labor, or other cost element that is normally used under efficient operating conditions. The standards for materials and labor are presented in a schedule of direct costs (Schedule C), as shown on page 421.

The Materials Budget

The materials budget is developed to indicate the materials to be purchased and the materials usage for the period. The materials budget for the Industrial Tray Company (Schedule D) is shown on page 422.

Since materials are variable costs, the quantity required for production is computed by multiplying the budgeted production (Schedule B: 60,000 trays) by the quantity of materials required for each completed unit (Schedule C: 6 feet per tray for SM-2). The cost of materials used in production is the quantity required extended at the cost per unit. For material SM-2, this amount is $720,000 (Schedule D-2: 360,000 feet at $2).

Note that you can quickly compute the total cost of materials required for the period. Multiplying the quantity of trays to be produced (Schedule B) by the cost of

```
                    INDUSTRIAL TRAY COMPANY              Schedule C
                      Schedule of Direct Costs
                     Year Ending December 31, 19X2

                           DIRECT MATERIALS

                                            COST              COST
   MATERIAL          QUANTITY             PER UNIT          PER TRAY
   SM-2               6 feet          $ 2.00 per foot        $12.00
   LF-6               4 sets             .40 per set           1.60
   MS-1              12 sets             .10 per set           1.20
   PV-2              1/25 gal         16.00 per gal             .64
        Total Materials Cost per Tray                        $15.44

                            DIRECT LABOR

                      HOURS               RATE              COSTS
   DEPARTMENT        PER UNIT           PER HOUR           PER TRAY
   Forming              .5               $12.00            $ 6.00
   Finishing            .7                14.00              9.80
        Total Labor Cost per Tray                          $15.80
```

the direct materials for each tray (Schedule C) gives a total of $926,400 this budget year (60,000 trays at $15.44 per tray).

The materials purchase requirements in units are determined by adjusting the production requirements according to anticipated changes in raw materials inventories. The resulting unit figure is extended at the estimated price per unit. For example, an increase in inventories of 2,000 feet of material SM-2 results in purchase requirements for 362,000 feet. At $2 per foot, estimated purchases of SM-2 total $724,000 for the year.

A schedule of monthly production is essential for efficient purchasing. Factors affecting the schedule include storage problems, quantity discounts, time required to receive materials from suppliers, and costs of carrying inventory. A balance between different types of materials must be carefully maintained so that the proper amount of each type will be available as needed. The materials budget is, of course, extremely important in determining future cash requirements.

Direct Labor Budget

The direct labor budget (Schedule E), shown on page 422, is an estimate of the total direct labor hours and direct labor cost required to complete the expected production during the budgetary period. The direct labor hours are estimated by multiplying the total hours in each department required to produce one tray (Schedule C) by the total number of trays to be produced (Schedule B). The result is multiplied by the dollar rate per hour (Schedule C) to obtain the total direct labor cost.

As with materials, the total direct labor cost for the period may be computed easily by multiplying the scheduled production (Schedule B) by the direct labor cost per tray (Schedule C) for a total of $948,000 (60,000 trays at $15.80 per tray).

It is usually possible to estimate with a fair degree of accuracy the number of

INDUSTRIAL TRAY COMPANY   Schedule D
Materials Budget
Year Ending December 31, 19X2

SCHEDULE 1: MATERIALS PURCHASES BUDGET

	Material Number			
	SM-2 (IN FEET)	LF-6 (IN SETS)	MS-1 (IN SETS)	PV-2 (IN GAL)
Quantity Required per Tray	6	4	12	$\frac{1}{25}$
Total Quantity Required for 60,000 Trays (Schedule B)	360,000	240,000	720,000	2,400
Budgeted Ending Inventory of Raw Materials, Dec. 31	22,000	16,000	40,000	400
Total Budgeted Requirements	382,000	256,000	760,000	2,800
Beginning Inventory of Raw Materials, Jan. 1	20,000	16,000	50,000	150
Total Budgeted Purchases	362,000	240,000	710,000	2,650
Price per Unit (Schedule C)	$ 2.00	$ .40	$ .10	$ 16
Cost of Purchases	$724,000	$ 96,000	$ 71,000	$ 42,400
Total				$933,400

SCHEDULE 2: MATERIALS USAGE BUDGET

Total Quantity Required	360,000	240,000	720,000	2,400
Price per Unit (Schedule C)	$ 2	$ .40	$ .10	$ 16
Budgeted Cost of Materials Required	$720,000	$ 96,000	$ 72,000	$ 38,400
Total				$926,400

direct labor hours required to manufacture a product. The estimate is customarily based on data from past experience or on established labor standards. A level production rate will obviously simplify the job of estimating the number of direct hours because no major allowances need be made for training inexperienced extra workers during peak periods or for carrying an oversized work force during lean periods.

INDUSTRIAL TRAY COMPANY   Schedule E
Direct Labor Budget
Year Ending December 31, 19X2

DEPARTMENT	SCHEDULED PRODUCTION (SCHEDULE B)	HOURS PER UNIT (SCHEDULE C)	TOTAL ESTIMATED HOURS	RATE PER HOUR (SCHEDULE C)	TOTAL COST
Forming	60,000	.5	30,000	$12.00	$360,000
Finishing	60,000	.7	42,000	14.00	588,000
Total					$948,000

The Manufacturing Overhead Budget

The manufacturing overhead cost is usually more difficult to budget than either direct materials or direct labor. Both labor and materials are variable costs and tend to vary directly with the volume of output. Manufacturing overhead costs are less consistent. Some of these costs, such as indirect materials, are variable. These tend to vary in direct proportion to the volume of production. (Volume of production for this purpose usually refers to the number of direct labor hours.) Other manufacturing overhead costs, such as depreciation and supervisors' salaries, are fixed. These tend to remain constant during the period regardless of the level of activity. Still other overhead costs, such as utilities and payroll taxes, are semivariable. These vary to some degree with changes in volume or level of activity but not in direct proportion.

The manufacturing overhead budget for the company is developed by preparing a flexible budget for each department. Usually the flexible budget shows expected costs at volumes ranging from 80 to 120 percent of expected volume at intervals of 5 percent, such as 80, 85, 90, 95 percent, and so on. This range is used because rarely does a company operate at less than 80 percent or more than 120 percent of its normal capacity. Using 5 percent intervals makes it easy to quickly compare actual results with the budget at very near the actual level of output.

The simplified budget for the Forming Department (Schedule F), shown on page 423, includes costs at 90, 100, and 110 percent of capacity (normal expected production). Schedule E showed that normal expected production amounts to 30,000 direct labor hours in the Forming Department.

Note that all overhead costs have been classified as fixed or variable. They also have been identified as controllable or noncontrollable at the departmental level. This is consistent with the use of the flexible budget as a tool for cost control. The line supervisor or department head has some degree of control over the costs classified as controllable but almost none over noncontrollable costs. This classification of costs will make it easier to compare budgeted and actual performance in order to evaluate managerial efficiency.

In this example, the fixed and variable cost estimates have, for the sake of simplicity, been assumed to be the same as those calculated in Chapter 20 for the period of September 1, 19X0, through August 31, 19X1. In practice, these amounts would be adjusted for inflation and other cost changes when the budget is prepared.

The variable cost items are those that vary directly in total with the number of direct labor hours worked. For example, the costs of indirect materials in the Forming Department are budgeted at $.80 per direct labor hour. Based on the expected production in that department for 19X2, the total indirect materials costs for the department are budgeted at $24,000 ($.80 per hour × 30,000 hours).

The fixed cost items are those that remain constant regardless of the volume of production. For example, depreciation of the machinery and equipment in the Forming Department is budgeted at $36,000 for the year. This total amount remains constant even if the actual volume is something other than 30,000 direct labor hours.

Some cost items are shown in both the Variable Costs and Fixed Costs sections of the budget because they are partly fixed and partly variable. These are the semivariable costs. For example, the utilities costs of the Forming Department are shown in the Variable Costs section as being $.40 per hour. Based on the expected volume of

30,000 direct labor hours, the total variable utilities costs in the department are expected to be $12,000. At the same time, certain basic utilities costs will be incurred even if there is no production. These fixed utilities costs in the Forming Department are shown as $1,200 per year. Thus the total budgeted utilities costs in the Forming Department are $13,200 ($12,000 variable plus $1,200 fixed).

	VARIABLE COST ELEMENT PER HOUR	FIXED COST ELEMENT	90%OF CAPACITY (27,000 HOURS)	100%OF CAPACITY (30,000 HOURS)	110%OF CAPACITY (33,000 HOURS)
INDUSTRIAL TRAY COMPANY Forming Department Yearly Flexible Overhead Budget Year Ending December 31, 19X2					Schedule F
				Total Budgeted Costs at	
Controllable Costs					
Indirect Materials	$ .80		$ 21,600	$ 24,000	$ 26,400
Indirect Labor	1.60	$36,000	79,200	84,000	88,800
Payroll Taxes and Fringe Benefits	1.36	3,600	40,320	44,400	48,480
Utilities	.40	1,200	12,000	13,200	14,400
Repairs and Maintenance	.12	3,600	6,840	7,200	7,560
Total Controllable Costs	$4.28	$44,400	$159,960	$172,800	$185,640
Noncontrollable Costs					
Depreciation—Machinery and Equipment	-0-	$36,000	$ 36,000	$ 36,000	$ 36,000
Depreciation—Buildings	-0-	-0-	-0-	-0-	-0-
Property Taxes	-0-	4,800	4,800	4,800	4,800
Property Insurance	-0-	480	480	480	480
Total Noncontrollable Costs	-0-	$41,280	$ 41,280	$ 41,280	$ 41,280
Total Budgeted Costs	$4.28	$85,680	$201,240	$214,080	$226,920

The data from the flexible budgets prepared for each department (such as Schedule F) are used to put together the departmental manufacturing overhead budget (Schedule G). The departmental manufacturing overhead budget (Schedule G) for the Industrial Tray Company shows data for the two producing departments as well as for the service department. This combined schedule provides a handy resource for comparing the cost data in the three departments and the breakdown of variable and fixed elements. (See page 425.)

The cost per unit manufactured is shown at the bottom of the manufacturing costs budget. The materials and labor costs per tray are from Schedule C. The manufacturing overhead cost per unit is calculated by dividing the total manufacturing overhead cost by the number of trays produced.

INDUSTRIAL TRAY COMPANY
Departmental Manufacturing Overhead Budget
Year Ending December 31, 19X2

	Forming Department*		Finishing Department†		Factory Services Department‡		TOTAL COST
	PER HOUR	TOTAL	PER HOUR	TOTAL	PER HOUR	TOTAL	
Variable Costs							
Indirect Materials	$ .80	$ 24,000	$ .48	$ 20,160	$ .60	$ 43,200	$ 87,360
Indirect Labor	1.60	48,000	2.00	84,000	.80	57,600	189,600
Payroll Taxes and Fringe Benefits	1.36	40,800	1.48	62,160	.08	5,760	108,720
Utilities	.40	12,000	.24	10,080	.16	11,520	33,600
Repairs and Maintenance	.12	3,600	.04	1,680	.12	8,640	13,920
Total Variable Costs	$4.28	$128,400	$4.24	$178,080	$1.76	$126,720	$433,200
Fixed Costs							
Depreciation—Machinery and Equipment		$ 36,000		$ 5,040		$ 11,520	$ 52,560
Depreciation—Buildings		-0-		-0-		17,280	17,280
Property Taxes		4,800		840		4,320	9,960
Property Insurance		480		168		1,440	2,088
Indirect Labor and Supervision		36,000		33,600		86,400	156,000
Payroll Taxes and Fringe Benefits		3,600		3,360		8,640	15,600
Utilities		1,200		672		2,880	4,752
Repairs and Maintenance		3,600		840		4,320	8,760
Total Fixed Costs		$ 85,680		$ 44,520		$136,800	$267,000
Total Manufacturing Overhead		$214,080		$222,600		$263,520	$700,200

*Based on 30,000 direct labor hours
†Based on 42,000 direct labor hours
‡Based on total of 72,000 direct labor hours in two producing departments

Combining the Manufacturing Budgets

The manufacturing costs budget (Schedule H), shown on page 426, is prepared from the budgets of the three manufacturing cost elements. In this example, the work in process inventories have been omitted because based on past experience they are expected to remain unchanged. This is a commonly made assumption in preparing manufacturing budgets since work in process inventories are usually only a small part of the total costs to be accounted for and any change in them is not important.

Operating Expenses Budget

Detailed budgets are normally prepared for the selling and administrative expenses anticipated as a result of the estimated sales and production operations. Since we are mainly interested in production costs at this time, only a summary of budgeted operating expenses is shown in Schedule I, on page 426.

```
INDUSTRIAL TRAY COMPANY                Schedule H
                Manufacturing Costs Budget
                Year Ending December 31, 19X2

Materials Used (Schedule D-2)                            $  926,400
Direct Labor (Schedule E)                                   948,000
Total Manufacturing Overhead Costs (Schedule G)             700,200
Cost of Goods Manufactured (To Exhibit 1)                $2,574,600

Cost per Unit Manufactured
   Materials (Schedule C)                                $     15.44
   Direct Labor (Schedule C)                                   15.80
   Manufacturing Overhead Costs
      ($700,200 ÷ 60,000 trays)                                11.67
      Total Manufacturing Cost per Tray
      ($2,574,600 ÷ 60,000 trays)                        $     42.91
```

```
INDUSTRIAL TRAY COMPANY                 Schedule I
                Operating Expenses Budget
                Year Ending December 31, 19X2

Operating Expenses
   Selling Expenses
      Sales Salaries and Commissions        $450,000
      Payroll Taxes and Fringe Benefits       50,000
      Delivery Expense                        80,000
      Advertising Expense                     30,000
      Travel Expense                          40,000
         Total Selling Expenses                         $650,000

   Administrative and General Expenses

      Officers' Salaries                    $120,000
      Office Salaries                         80,000
      Payroll Taxes and Fringe Benefits       30,000
      Office Supplies and Postage Expense     14,000
      Bad Debts Expense                       14,000
      Miscellaneous Expenses                  20,000
         Total Administrative and General Expenses       278,000
   Total Operating Expenses (To Exhibit 1)              $928,000
```

. . . .

Budgeted Income Statement

Data from the supporting budgets (Schedules A, H, and I) are combined to prepare a budgeted income statement for the Industrial Tray Company for 19X2 (Exhibit 1). The finished goods inventories are priced at the cost per unit manufactured (Schedule H). The January 1 inventory is $600,740. This represents 14,000 trays (Schedule B) at $42.91 per tray. The December 31 inventory equals 12,000 trays (Schedule B) at $42.91 per tray.

INDUSTRIAL TRAY COMPANY		Exhibit 1

INDUSTRIAL TRAY COMPANY
Budgeted Income Statement
Year Ending December 31, 19X2

Revenue		
Sales (Schedule A)		$3,968,000
Cost of Goods Sold		
Finished Goods Inventory, Jan. 1	$ 600,740	
Add Cost of Goods Manufactured (Schedule H)	2,574,600	
Total Goods Available for Sale	$3,175,340	
Deduct Finished Goods Inventory, Dec. 31	514,920	
Cost of Goods Sold		2,660,420
Gross Profit on Sales		$1,307,580
Operating Expenses (Schedule I)		928,000
Net Income Before Income Taxes		$ 379,580
Provision for Income Taxes		120,000
Net Income After Income Taxes		$ 259,580

Other Budget Schedules

The budget director then proceeds to complete and assemble the other schedules in the master budget, including the schedule of budgeted cash receipts and payments, the budget of asset acquisitions and retirements, and the budgeted balance sheet for December 31, 19X2. Since these items are not immediately related to product cost accounting, they will not be discussed here.

Using the Flexible Budget as a Management Tool

Budgets are commonly used as a control device. Actual results are compared with budgeted amounts, and any important variations are investigated. The use of a flexible budget makes it possible to estimate what the overhead costs should be for any volume actually attained so that the comparison between actual costs and budgeted costs will be meaningful.

For example, assume that the Forming Department actually worked 2,350 direct labor hours during January 19X2 and that the total utilities cost for the department was $1,104. How well has the supervisor controlled this cost element? Let us compare the actual cost with the amount that the flexible budget (Schedule F) shows should be the maximum utilities cost for the month.

Budgeted Cost for Month Based on 2,350 Hours
    Fixed Cost for Month (yearly cost, $1,200 ÷ 12 months) $ 100
    Variable Costs (2,350 hours × $.40 per hour)   940
    Total Budgeted Utilities Cost Based on 2,350 Hours $1,040
    Actual Costs Incurred During Month   1,104
       Unfavorable Budget Variance (overspent budget) $ 64

The computation shows that the department spent $64 more on utilities than the budget allowance for the month. This amount may be large enough to require further analysis, or it may be that the amount is considered unimportant. At any rate, the difference between goals and performance is clearly shown. This concept of pointing out the things that are not according to plan is part of the general philosophy of "management by exception." (Note, however, that this computation does not show how much the cost should have been for the number of trays produced, as opposed to the number of hours worked. In order to have this type of information, it is necessary to set manufacturing overhead standards, which are discussed in Chapter 23.)

Periodic Performance Report

Variations between budget allowances and actual results should be pinpointed as quickly as possible so that corrective action can be taken right away. Monthly (or even weekly or daily) reports of performance comparing actual and budgeted amounts are prepared. At the end of January 19X2, the Industrial Tray Company's cost accountant prepares a monthly overhead performance report (Exhibit 2), as shown on page 429.

The report shows that 4,700 trays were produced and 2,350 direct labor hours were spent in the work of manufacturing these trays. The fixed costs and the variable costs per hour shown in the flexible budget are used to compute the allowed costs for this level of production. Each actual cost is then compared with the budget allowance. The difference is shown in the Over or (Under) Budget column. This column is the heart of the report, and any expenditures that exceed the budget receive immediate attention if they are important. Although the $104 and $64 over-budget costs are small in dollar amounts, they may require investigation because they represent deviations of 5 or 6 percent ($104 ÷ $1,984 and $64 ÷ $1,104).

One column of the report is for explanatory comments. For instance, the notation Press No. 1 shows that the unusually high repair and maintenance cost of $896 was due to a breakdown in that press.

The report may be supplied to the department head in duplicate. He or she may then be asked to supply explanations, retain a copy, and forward the original to a superior for review. If very serious variances come to light, management might request weekly reports until the condition has been corrected.

INDUSTRIAL TRAY COMPANY
Monthly Overhead Performance Report

Exhibit 2

Department: Forming
Volume for Month: 4,700 units

Month: January, 19X2
Direct Labor Hours: 2,350

COST	VARIABLE RATE PER HOUR	Total Budget* for Actual Volume VARIABLE	FIXED	TOTAL	ACTUAL*	OVER OR (UNDER) BUDGET	COMMENTS
Controllable							
Indirect Materials	$ .80	$ 1,880		$ 1,880	$ 1,984	$104	
Indirect Labor	1.60	3,760	$3,000	6,760	6,588	(172)	
Payroll Taxes and Fringe Benefits	1.36	3,196	300	3,496	3,496	-0-	
Utilities	.40	940	100	1,040	1,104	64	
Repairs and Maintenance	.12	282	300	582	896	314	Press No. 1
Total		$10,058	$3,700	$13,758	$14,068	$310	
Noncontrollable							
Depreciation—Machinery and Equipment		-0-	$3,000	$ 3,000	$ 3,000	$-0-	
Depreciation—Buildings		-0-	-0-	-0-	-0-	-0-	
Property Taxes		-0-	400	400	400	-0-	
Property Insurance		-0-	40	40	40	-0-	
Total		$ -0-	$3,440	$ 3,440	$3,440	$-0-	
Total Departmental Overhead		$10,058	$7,140	$17,198	$17,508	$310	

*Figures rounded to nearest whole dollar.

Other Budgetary Considerations

The departmental budgets in this chapter have included only direct departmental overhead costs—those that can be assigned directly to the individual department. Service costs have not been allocated. The concern in this chapter has been with planning and cost control. The service department has a separate budget for control purposes. However, if the cost of a service is directly tied to the activities of a producing department on a measurable basis, the producing department may be charged with standard rates per unit of service. For example, if a factory has its own generating plant for electricity, it is customary to charge the producing departments a standard rate per kilowatt-hour of electricity used. The head of each producing department is thus made responsible for the electricity used.

Spreadsheet Programs and Budgeting

Elbow Grease, Inc., a manufacturer of household cleaning products, is in the midst of a struggle for market share. According to market surveys, Elbow Grease currently has 23 percent of the household products market, which puts it second, behind another large company with 27 percent. To evaluate its position in the market and to predict for the future, the cost accountant prepares a comprehensive budget each month for the following twelve months. No sooner is the cost accountant finished with one budget than it is time to prepare the next.

Until recently the computer system for budgeting was considered adequate. However, six months ago, the new vice president of finance asked the cost accountant to develop a budget for many possible sales levels. He began asking questions like, "What will our profit be if we sell only 95,000 bottles of Minus Mildew instead of the predicted 107,000?" Or, "How much cash will we need in January to pay the bills?"

Answering these questions took a substantial amount of time away from the continuous budgeting process. Luckily, the head of the data processing department found a program that both the vice president and the cost accountant could use to get fast answers. The program is a *spreadsheet* program. This type of software can be used for budgeting or any other type of repetitive process where one part of the process depends on the results of a previous part. In order to use a spreadsheet program, the formulas for each part of the budget must be entered into the software. For instance, if inventory must be kept at two times the next month's sales, the program must have this formula to correctly update inventory amounts. The cost accountant will work with the programmer to be sure all the formulas are correct.

Once this is done, the spreadsheet program can be used to speed up the generation of financial data. For example, if a sales figure changes, the program will change every aspect of the budget that is derived from sales; therefore, inventories, purchases, production, and cash flows will all be changed as a result of the shift in sales. Once the projected sales figure is keyed into the terminal, the spreadsheet program will rework the rest of the budget ("spread" it out) based on the sales figure. Then a spreadsheet will be quickly displayed on the video screen or it can be printed out as shown. The first spreadsheet shows amounts needed for June production of 800,000 units. The second report shows the impact when 1,000,000 units are planned. The cost accountant may also use this program to speed up the regular budgeting process. ∎

```
                MINUS MILDEW
     QUARTERLY PRODUCTION BUDGET (IN THOUSANDS)
                     APRIL    MAY    JUNE
SALES                  900     875     800
REQUIRED ENDING INVENTORY  1050     960    1020
TOTAL REQUIRED        1950    1835    1820
BEGINNING INVENTORY   1080    1050     960
REQUIRED PRODUCTION    870     785     860
     QUARTERLY PURCHASES BUDGET (IN THOUSANDS)
POUNDS XANTHUM PER UNIT   .50     .50     .50
POUNDS NEEDED FOR PROD.  435.00  392.50  430.00
REQUIRED ENDING INVENTORY 431.75  473.00  451.55
TOTAL POUNDS NEEDED     866.75  865.50  881.55
BEGINNING INVENTORY     478.50  431.75  473.00
REQUIRED PURCHASE       388.25  433.75  408.55
COST PER POUND            3.00    3.00    3.00
DOLLAR PURCHASE        1164.75 1301.25 1225.65
POUNDS RYTHEON PER UNIT   .24     .24     .24
POUNDS NEEDED FOR PROD.  208.80  188.40  206.40
REQUIRED ENDING INVENTORY 207.24  227.04  216.74
TOTAL POUNDS NEEDED     416.04  415.44  423.14
```

```
                MINUS MILDEW
     QUARTERLY PRODUCTION BUDGET (IN THOUSANDS)
                     APRIL    MAY    JUNE
SALES                  900     875    1000
REQUIRED ENDING INVENTORY  1050    1200    1020
TOTAL REQUIRED        1950    2075    2020
BEGINNING INVENTORY   1080    1050    1200
REQUIRED PRODUCTION    870    1025     820
     QUARTERLY PURCHASES BUDGET (IN THOUSANDS)
POUNDS XANTHUM PER UNIT   .50     .50     .50
POUNDS NEEDED FOR PROD.  435.00  512.50  410.00
REQUIRED ENDING INVENTORY 563.75  451.00  451.55
TOTAL POUNDS NEEDED     998.75  963.50  861.55
BEGINNING INVENTORY     478.50  563.75  451.00
REQUIRED PURCHASE       520.25  399.75  410.55
COST PER POUND            3.00    3.00    3.00
DOLLAR PURCHASE        1560.75 1199.25 1231.65
POUNDS RYTHEON PER UNIT   .24     .24     .24
POUNDS NEEDED FOR PROD.  208.80  246.00  196.80
REQUIRED ENDING INVENTORY 270.60  216.48  216.74
TOTAL POUNDS NEEDED     479.40  462.48  413.54
```

Principles and Procedures Summary

The master or operating budget is an effective management tool. Budgeting is essential in the planning, coordination, and control of business activities. A budget provides the means for defining the goals of the business and establishing steps for attaining these goals. Control is achieved by measuring actual results and by comparing these with budget figures that have been adjusted to the activity level achieved. Variations between the plan and the actual results can be pinpointed, and appropriate steps can be taken to correct them.

Review Questions

1. What is a budget?
2. What is the purpose of budgeting?
3. What is the master budget?
4. Explain the role of the budget director in the budgeting process.
5. What does planning involve in terms of budgeting?
6. Explain the importance of the sales budget in the overall budgeting process.
7. Why are economic forecasts important in budgeting?
8. What is the production budget? How is it prepared?
9. What data are used in computing the number of units to be manufactured?
10. What is a flexible budget? What is the advantage of a flexible budget?
11. What costs are summarized in the manufacturing costs budget?
12. How would a firm estimate the budgeted amount of direct labor?
13. What is included in a performance report?
14. How often should a performance report be prepared? Explain.
15. List the major budget schedules that become part of the master budget.

Managerial Discussion Questions

1. The management of the Olson Company is considering the establishment of a formal budgeting system. The president of the company wants to know how budgeting can help the company's planning. Respond.
2. Explain how a flexible budget can be used by management to help control costs.
3. The management of the Fleetwood Company has asked you, as a consultant, to explain briefly the steps in preparing a master budget. Respond to the request.
4. A company is setting up a budgetary system. A question has been raised as to whether the managers of the factory's operating departments should have a role in developing their own budgets. Express your opinion, giving reasons for your conclusion.
5. What types of economic reports or forecasts would be of special interest in preparing budgets for each of the following?
   a. A home builder
   b. A private business college
   c. A manufacturer of chain-link fences
6. The actual indirect labor costs for a department in May 19X1 were $87,200. The flexible budget for the level of activity achieved called for indirect labor costs of $82,300. With which personnel would management want to discuss this type of overrun?

7. A management consultant has suggested setting up a budgetary control system that will establish the *management by exception* principle in your company. What is meant by this term?

Exercises

1. **Preparing a sales budget.** In 19X1 the sales of Algon, a product of Wallace Manufacturers, were 1,024,000 units sold at an average price of $2.96 per unit. It is anticipated that the number of units sold in 19X2 will increase 6 percent and the average selling price per unit will increase by 12 percent. What are the company's budgeted sales of Algon for 19X2?

2. **Preparing a production budget.** The December 31, 19X1, inventory of Algon (from Exercise 1 above) is 82,000 units. The company wants to have an ending inventory on December 31, 19X2, equal to 8 percent of the sales in 19X2. What will be the budgeted production for 19X2?

3. **Computing the materials cost per unit.** Use the following information about the materials in Algon to prepare a schedule of materials cost per unit:

   Compound X: 8 ounces for each pound of Algon; cost per pound, $1.54.
   Filler: 4 ounces for each pound of Algon; cost per pound, $.40.
   Compound Y: 4 ounces for each pound of Algon; cost per pound, $.80.
   Packaging: 1 package per pound of Algon; cost per package, $.06.

4. **Preparing a materials budget.** Refer to the data on Algon given in Exercises 1, 2, and 3. Prepare a materials purchases budget for Algon, assuming that the beginning inventory consists of 40,000 pounds of Compound X; 20,000 pounds of filler; 20,000 pounds of Compound Y; and 80,000 packages. The firm wants to increase the quantity of each type of raw material in the ending inventory by 6 percent above the beginning inventory. Round to the nearest dollar.

5. **Preparing a direct labor budget.** The production budget for the Palmer Company, Inc., calls for manufacturing 90,200 units of a product during 19X5. Each unit is expected to require $2\frac{1}{4}$ hours of labor in the Forming Department at a rate of $10.20 per hour and $1\frac{1}{4}$ hours of labor in the Finishing Department at a rate of $7.50 per hour. Prepare the direct labor budget for the company for 19X5.

6. **Preparing a flexible overhead budget.** For 19X2, the overhead budget of the Extrusion Department of the Simon Company includes the following elements:

   Controllable Costs
   Indirect materials: $.25 per direct labor hour for variable costs plus $22,000 for fixed costs.

   Payroll taxes and fringe benefits: $2.20 per direct labor hour of variable costs plus $20,000 for fixed costs.

   Assume that the normal capacity is 62,000 direct labor hours. Determine the department's budget for these two items at 80, 90, 100, 110, and 120 percent of normal capacity.

7. **Preparing a monthly overhead performance report.** A portion of the flexible overhead budget of the Assembly Department of the Vista Company for 19X3 is shown.

Item	Variable Cost Element per Hour	Fixed Cost Element	Total Budgeted Cost at		
			90% of Capacity	100% of Capacity	110% of Capacity
Indirect					
Materials	$.80	$36,000	$108,000	$116,000	$124,000
Utilities	.40	1,200	37,200	41,200	45,200

Capacity is 100,000 direct labor hours. Production is expected to be equal during each month of the year. In April, a total of 8,400 hours were worked. The cost of indirect materials was $11,200 and the cost of utilities was $3,700.

Compute the budgeted amounts for these two cost elements based on the actual volume achieved in the month, and compute the amounts by which the actual costs were over (or under) these budgeted accounts.

8. **Computing an indirect labor variance and expected costs at different levels of activity.** The monthly fixed cost element of indirect labor in the Grinding Department of the Jefferson Gear Company is $6,000 and the variable cost element is $1.10 per direct labor hour. During March 19X2, production was 4,200 direct labor hours. Indirect labor costs were $10,300.

   a. Compute the amount of budget variance for indirect labor for the month.
   b. What would be the expected indirect labor cost at (1) 3,600 direct labor hours and at (2) 7,180 direct labor hours?

9. **Preparing a manufacturing overhead budget.** The monthly overhead costs of the Cleaning Department of the Midvale Corporation have been analyzed as follows:

	Variable (per direct labor hour)	Fixed (per month)
Supervision	—	$4,600
Other indirect labor	$ .80	2,400
Utilities	.30	800
Depreciation	—	2,000
Payroll taxes	1.07	630
Other taxes	—	300
Fringe benefits	.88	1,400
Supplies	.58	200

Assume that the department works 6,000 hours during June 19X3. Prepare an overhead budget for the month, showing the expected total for each cost element and the total for the department.

10. **Preparing a sales budget.** The Lambert Company has projected its cost of goods sold for 19X6 at $4,000,000, including fixed costs of $600,000. Variable costs are expected to be 80 percent of net sales. Compute the company's budgeted net sales for the period.

Problems

PROBLEM 21-1. Preparing a sales budget. The regional sales of the Weymouth Company for the year 19X1 have been forecast as follows:

Region	Sales
Boston	$12,000,000
Dallas	6,000,000
San Diego	4,500,000

The company sells three products. An analysis of past sales records shows the following normal regional distribution of sales by product:

Region	Motors	Generators	Coils
Boston	40%	40%	20%
Dallas	50%	20%	30%
San Diego	40%	30%	30%

Additional analysis shows the following distribution of sales by months for the first quarter and by quarters thereafter:

Region	First Quarter Jan.	First Quarter Feb.	First Quarter Mar.	Second Quarter	Third Quarter	Fourth Quarter
Boston	6%	6%	10%	30%	25%	23%
Dallas	8%	10%	12%	28%	22%	20%
San Diego	6%	8%	12%	30%	24%	20%

Instructions

Prepare a total sales budget in thousands (Schedule A) for the year 19X1. Show details by region and by product for each quarter and for each month of the first quarter.

PROBLEM 21-2. Preparing production and materials budgets. The Goodman Manufacturing Company makes a single product. Each unit requires the following raw materials:

Item	Quantity	Unit Cost	Total
Material A	2	$3.40	$6.80
Material X	3	.80	2.40
Material T	1	6.00	6.00

The beginning inventories on January 1, 19X2, are expected to be as follows:

Raw Materials
    Material A, 7,000 at $3.40 each
    Material X, 10,500 at $.80 each
    Material T, 3,500 at $6.00 each
Finished Goods, 4,000 units
Work in Process, 2,000 units (all materials added)

The sales forecast for the month of January 19X2 is 4,000 units; for February, 3,500 units; and for March, 3,000 units. Enough units should be on hand in the finished goods inventory to meet expected sales for the following month. The raw materials on hand should be equal to the following month's production requirements. The work in process inventory remains almost constant.

Instructions

1. Prepare a production budget (Schedule B) for the month of January 19X2.
2. Prepare a materials budget (Schedule D) for January.

PROBLEM 21-3. Preparing a monthly overhead performance report. The monthly flexible manufacturing overhead budget for the Assembly Department of the Callas Corporation is given below.

	Variable Cost Element per Hour	Fixed Cost Element	Direct Labor Hours				
			9,000	9,500	10,000	10,500	11,000
Indirect Labor	$ .30	$2,000	$ 4,700	$ 4,850	$ 5,000	$ 5,150	$ 5,300
Payroll Taxes and Fringe Benefits	1.20	1,000	11,800	12,400	13,000	13,600	14,200
Indirect Materials	.10	100	1,000	1,050	1,100	1,150	1,200
Power and Water	.20	30	1,830	1,930	2,030	2,130	2,230
Depreciation	—	600	600	600	600	600	600
Taxes and Insurance	—	400	400	400	400	400	400
Repairs	.04	115	475	495	515	535	555

During the month 19X1, the departmental volume was 9,100 direct labor hours. Actual costs for the month were as follows:

Indirect Labor	$ 4,820
Payroll Taxes and Fringe Benefits	12,470
Indirect Materials	1,040
Power and Water	1,812
Depreciation	600
Taxes and Insurance	400
Repairs	530

Instructions

1. Complete the monthly departmental overhead performance report (Exhibit 2). The costs for depreciation and for taxes and insurance are noncontrollable. Compare the budgeted costs for the actual volume attained with the actual costs for the month.
2. Which of the costs appear to be well controlled?
3. Which of the costs appear to be out of line?
4. Give some possible explanations for the lack of control over the items that appear to be significantly out of line.

PROBLEM 21-4. Preparing a direct labor budget and a flexible overhead budget. The James Corporation manufactures a single product requiring 2 hours of labor for each unit of product. Direct labor costs are budgeted at $8 per hour. The budgeted output (normal capacity) for 19X1 is 20,000 units. Overhead cost data are shown on page 436.

	Variable Cost Element per Direct Hour	Fixed Cost Element per Year
Indirect Labor	$1.10	$48,000
Payroll Taxes and Fringe Benefits	1.82	9,600
Indirect Materials	.20	1,000
Power	.10	3,000
Depreciation	—	12,000
Taxes and Insurance	—	6,420
Repairs	.06	3,850

Instructions

1. Prepare the direct labor budget (Schedule E) for the year.
2. Prepare a yearly flexible overhead budget (Schedule F) at 90, 100, and 110 percent of capacity. The costs for depreciation and for taxes and insurance are noncontrollable.

Alternate Problems

PROBLEM 21-1A. Preparing a sales budget. The district sales of the Dennison Company for the year 19X2 have been forecast as follows:

District	Sales
Seattle	$9,000,000
Chicago	6,000,000
Atlanta	3,000,000

The company sells three products. An analysis of past sales records shows the following normal district distribution of sales by product:

District	Siding	Roofing	Wallboard
Seattle	20%	50%	30%
Chicago	25%	45%	30%
Atlanta	30%	50%	20%

Additional analysis shows the following distribution of sales by months for the first quarter and by quarters thereafter:

District	First Quarter Jan.	Feb.	Mar.	Second Quarter	Third Quarter	Fourth Quarter
Seattle	4%	6%	10%	30%	30%	20%
Chicago	4%	7%	10%	30%	30%	19%
Atlanta	5%	8%	10%	25%	28%	24%

Instructions

Prepare a total sales budget in thousands (Schedule A) for the year 19X2. Show details by district and by product for each quarter and for each month of the first quarter.

PROBLEM 21-2A. Preparing production and materials budgets. The Hirito Company manufactures a single product. Each unit requires the following raw materials:

Item	Quantity	Unit Cost	Total
Frames	1	$12.00	$12.00
Panels	4	3.40	13.60
Assembly Units	1	2.85	2.85

The beginning inventories on January 1, 19X2, are expected to be as given below.

Raw Materials
　Frames, 2,200 at $12.00 each
　Panels, 8,800 at $3.40 each
　Assembly Units, 2,200 at $2.85 each
Finished Goods, 3,000 units
Work in Process, 2,000 units (all materials added)

The sales forecast for the month of January 19X2 is 3,000 units; for February, 2,200 units; and for March, 1,600 units. Enough units should be on hand in the finished goods inventory to meet expected sales for the following month. The raw materials on hand should be equal to the following month's production requirements. The work in process inventory remains almost constant.

Instructions

1. Prepare a production budget (Schedule B) for the month of January 19X2.
2. Prepare a materials budget (Schedule D) for January.

PROBLEM 21-3A. Preparing a monthly overhead performance report. The monthly flexible manufacturing overhead budget for the Assembly Department of the Cornwall Products Company is given below.

	Variable Cost Element per Hour	Fixed Cost Element	Direct Labor Hours				
			9,000	9,500	10,000	10,500	11,000
Indirect Labor	$.40	$1,000	$4,600	$4,800	$5,000	$5,200	$5,400
Payroll Taxes	.82	160	7,540	7,950	8,360	8,770	9,180
Indirect Materials	.08	100	820	860	900	940	980
Power and Water	.04	110	470	490	510	530	550
Depreciation	—	920	920	920	920	920	920
Taxes and Insurance	—	185	185	185	185	185	185
Repairs	.03	50	320	335	350	365	380

During the month of August 19X1 the departmental volume was 10,650 direct labor hours. Actual costs for the month were as follows:

Indirect Labor	$5,405
Payroll Taxes	8,970
Indirect Materials	942
Power and Water	548
Depreciation	920
Taxes and Insurance	185
Repairs	373

Instructions

1. Complete the monthly departmental overhead performance report (Exhibit 2). The costs for depreciation and for taxes and insurance are noncontrollable. Compare the budgeted costs for the actual volume attained with the actual costs for the month.
2. Which of the costs appear to be well controlled?
3. Which of the costs appear to be out of line?

4. Give some possible explanations for the lack of control over the items that appear to be significantly out of line.

PROBLEM 21-4A. Preparing a direct labor budget and a flexible overhead budget. The Princeton Company manufactures a single product requiring $\frac{1}{2}$ hour of labor for each unit of product. Direct labor costs are budgeted at $10 per hour. The budgeted output (normal capacity) for 19X4 is 60,000 units. Overhead cost data are as follows:

	Variable Cost Element per Direct Hour	Fixed Cost Element per Year
Indirect Labor	$.80	$36,000
Payroll Taxes and Fringe Benefits	1.16	7,500
Indirect Materials	.08	1,600
Power	.16	3,600
Depreciation	—	10,000
Taxes and Insurance	—	3,500
Repairs	.08	2,000

Instructions
1. Prepare the direct labor budget (Schedule E) for the year.
2. Prepare a yearly flexible overhead budget (Schedule F) at 90, 100, and 110 percent of capacity. The costs for depreciation and for taxes and insurance are noncontrollable.

Managerial Decisions

CASE 21-1. Based on an optimistic sales forecast, the management of the Usell Corporation has estimated production of 6,000 units of its product in 19X2. Management now wants to develop a budget for production costs based on the assumption that 6,000 units will be produced. However, certain members of management are less optimistic and believe that only 5,600 units can be sold. You have been asked to prepare a budget for production costs based on 6,000 units and one based on 5,600 units. The company has not previously had a budget. You analyze last year's production costs, when 5,000 units were produced, and learn the following facts:

1. To produce 5,000 units, 20,000 pounds of raw materials were required at an average cost of $8 per pound. However, at the end of 19X1, materials cost $8.20 per pound, and it is anticipated that materials will increase by an average of an additional 10 percent during 19X2. The beginning and ending inventories of materials on hand in 19X1 were so small that they were insignificant.
2. Each unit of product required 6.5 hours of direct labor. During 19X1, labor costs were $9 per hour. During the first half of 19X2, labor costs should remain at $9 per hour, but the firm's contract with its union calls for an increase to $9.75 per hour at the midpoint of 19X2. Production is spread evenly throughout the year. The installation of new equipment at the beginning of 19X2 is expected to reduce the average labor time to 5.9 hours per unit.
3. Overhead costs in 19X1 have been analyzed into fixed and variable parts, as follows:

	Fixed	Variable, per Labor Hour
Indirect Labor	$108,000	$2.00
Indirect Materials	1,000	.20

	Fixed	Variable, per Labor Hour
Payroll Taxes and Fringe Benefits	16,200	1.65
Depreciation	28,000	
Other Taxes and Insurance	6,000	
Power, Lighting, and Heating	12,000	1.00
Other Overhead Costs	16,000	1.80

It is anticipated that all indirect labor cost rates will increase by 12 percent and that payroll taxes and fringe benefits will be 16 percent of labor costs. The costs for indirect materials; for heating, lighting, and power; and for other overhead are expected to increase by 5 percent. Because of the new labor-saving equipment, depreciation will increase by $14,000 per year. Other taxes and insurance will increase by $4,000 per year.

Prepare the budget requested at production levels of 5,600 units and 6,000 units. Carry all unit costs to four decimal places. Round all budgeted costs to the nearest dollar.

CASE 21-2. The McKenzie Company installed a new budgeting system in 19X1. The budget was based on carefully prepared sales forecasts and production schedules. It was anticipated that during the year 120,000 units of its product would be manufactured, spread equally over each month and requiring 960,000 direct labor hours. The overhead budget was based on a careful analysis of fixed and variable costs.

In June 19X1, the president, your client, asked you for advice since you are an accountant. He was disturbed because the actual costs for May were over the budgeted amounts. The controller's report showed the yearly and monthly budgeted amounts and the actual results for May as follows:

Cost Item	Yearly Variable	Yearly Fixed	Yearly Total	Monthly Budget	Actual for May
Indirect Materials	$ 960,000	$ 40,000	$1,000,000	$ 83,333	$ 96,200
Indirect Labor	290,000	160,000	450,000	37,500	29,200
Payroll Taxes	1,658,000	32,000	1,690,000	140,833	141,200
Utilities	96,000	60,000	156,000	13,000	13,800
Repairs and Maintenance	96,000	30,000	126,000	10,500	14,700
Miscellaneous	48,000	50,000	98,000	8,167	8,666
Depreciation		72,000	72,000	6,000	7,000
Property Taxes and Insurance		80,000	80,000	6,667	7,200
	$3,148,000	$524,000	$3,672,000	$306,000	$317,966

You ask several questions and find, among other things, that production during the month was 11,250 units requiring 90,000 direct labor hours.

1. Explain to your client how a flexible budget would be a better tool for evaluating the performance of the production manager.
2. Prepare a monthly overhead performance report. Analyze each item in this report in order to evaluate how well the production manager has controlled costs.

CHAPTER

22

Standard Costs: Materials and Labor

■ ■ ■

A budget is a projection of future costs and revenues that is used for both planning and control purposes. Budget cost estimates are developed in various ways. One very important way in which budgeting techniques are used in manufacturing operations is in developing standard costs. Most well-managed manufacturing companies use standard costs.

Standard Costs

In a standard cost system, the emphasis is on what costs should be. *Standard manufacturing costs* are predetermined measures of the cost of each manufacturing element (materials, labor, and overhead) under specified, efficient operating conditions. These costs are expressed in terms of standard quantity and standard price (cost) per unit.

In Chapter 21, standard materials and labor costs were used in preparing budgets for the Industrial Tray Company. These standards are typically presented on a standard cost sheet such as Exhibit 1, on page 441.

In this chapter, the development and use of standard costs for materials and labor are presented. In Chapter 23, standard costs for manufacturing overhead will be discussed.

Uses of Standard Costs

Standard cost data can be used in numerous ways in addition to budgeting. The following are some uses of standard costs:

1. Reducing recordkeeping expenses by keeping records in terms of predetermined standard costs rather than varying historical costs that would require time-consuming computations.
2. Measuring inventory and cost of goods sold in preparing financial statements. (The use of standard costs eliminates complex calculations for inventories and cost of goods sold.)
3. Evaluating various operations by comparing actual and standard costs.
4. Aiding in decision making; for example, in setting prices and evaluating alternatives.

```
                     INDUSTRIAL TRAY COMPANY              Exhibit 1
                         Standard Cost Sheet
                         Chemical Tray KL-31

                                                        TOTAL COST
  Materials                   QUANTITY   UNIT COST        PER TRAY

    SM-2                        6 ft    $ 2.00 per ft     $12.000
    LF-6                        4 sets     .40 per set      1.600
    MS-1                       12 sets     .10 per set      1.200
    PV-2                      1/25 gal   16.00 per gal       .640
         Total Materials Cost per Tray                    $15.440

  Labor

    Forming Department          .5 hr   $12.00 per hr     $ 6.000
    Finishing Department        .7 hr    14.00 per hr       9.800
         Total Labor Cost per Tray                        $15.800

  Overhead

    Forming Department
      Variable Costs            .5 hr   $ 6.040 per hr    $ 3.020
      Fixed Costs               .5 hr     4.376 per hr      2.188
        Total for Forming
          Department                    $10.416           $ 5.208
    Finishing Department
      Variable Costs            .7 hr   $ 6.000 per hr    $ 4.200
      Fixed Costs               .7 hr     3.231 per hr      2.262
        Total for Finishing
          Department                    $ 9.231           $ 6.462
         Total Overhead Cost per Tray                     $11.670
  Total Standard Cost per Tray                            $42.910
```

Standard costs are often the best estimate of differential costs and incremental costs used in decision cost analysis. (Decision cost analysis will be discussed in Chapter 25.)

Setting Standards

The usefulness of standard costs depends on how realistic they are. Some companies rely almost entirely on past average costs in setting their standards. Other companies start with historical costs and adjust them for anticipated changes such as price increases or decreases for materials and rate changes for labor. A proper approach would be to use both historical costs and anticipated changes in prices and to obtain input from people within the company who can provide relevant information, such as the cost accountant, the industrial engineer, the purchasing manager, the personnel manager, and the production manager.

One procedure for determining standards involves analyzing engineering specifications in the light of past experience, projections of future events, and company policy. For example, engineering specifications may indicate that 8 pounds of raw material are required for each completed unit. Yet past experience shows that an average of 9 pounds per unit is used. Management may feel that if spoilage and inefficiencies are kept to an acceptable level, $8\frac{1}{2}$ pounds would be a realistic standard quantity per unit.

In setting standards, management must choose a level of operating efficiency with which to work. *Theoretical* or *ideal standards* are based on achieving perfection. *Normal* or *attainable standards* are based on a more realistic, though demanding, view of efficiency.

Theoretical Standards. Theoretical standards represent goals that could be attained only under perfect operating conditions. They make no provision for lost or idle time, breakdowns, and other factors that reduce efficiency. Since they can seldom be met, theoretical standards have a psychological disadvantage. Responsible supervisors often develop the attitude: Why try when we aren't expected to meet these goals anyway? As a result theoretical standards are seldom used.

Normal Standards. Normal standards represent goals that can be met under reasonably efficient operating conditions because they provide for idle time, breakdowns, and common operating problems. In using normal standards, management must succeed in encouraging top efficiency while keeping goals reasonable enough to be met. Most standard cost systems are based on normal standards.

Implementing a Standard Cost System

To develop and use a standard cost system, the accountant must do the following:

1. Establish standards for each cost element (materials, labor, and overhead).
2. Record actual costs incurred during the period.
3. Determine the standard costs for the number of units produced during the period.
4. Compute variances by comparing the actual costs of the units produced and the standard costs of those units.
5. Break down the variance for each element into its component parts in order to determine the cause of the variance.
6. Record production costs and variances.

The Industrial Tray Company decides to use a standard cost accounting system. Management has approved the standards shown on the standard cost sheet (Exhibit 1) on page 441. The cost accountant will follow the procedures listed above in accounting for the costs of materials and labor for January 19X2.

Materials Costs

Under the Industrial Tray Company's standard cost system, materials standards are set and the materials are accounted for as follows.

Establishing Standards

Quantity and price standards are set for each type of material used and are recorded on the standard cost sheet shown in Exhibit 1 on page 441.

Materials Quantity Standards. The engineers who design a product are responsible for determining how much material is needed for each unit. Detailed specifications, engineering studies, blueprints, and similar technical data show exactly what is needed. Sometimes test runs or analyses of past experience are used in developing quantity standards. Materials spoilage or waste that is a necessary part of the manufacturing process must be considered in setting the quantity standards. Then a quantity variance will show only excessive spoilage. Production managers should help set the materials quantity standards, since they must get the work done within these standards.

Materials Price Standards. Price standards are based on the prices that the firm expects to pay for materials during the coming period. If there is no reliable data on possible price changes, the prices at the time standards are set may be used. The purchasing agent is responsible for finding suppliers and taking advantage of competitive bidding. It is also the purchasing agent's job to buy in economical quantities and to make sure that cost and quality needs are both met. Purchasing agents should help to set price standards since they must explain price variances. During periods of inflation, it is customary to assume a price increase based on the company's recent history.

Recording Actual Costs

Actual costs incurred during the period are recorded in the Raw Materials account directly from the voucher register. A summary recording is made at the end of the month, as shown in the general journal entry below.

19X2				
Jan. 31	Raw Materials	121	XXX.XX	
	Vouchers Payable	201		XXX.XX
	Recorded purchases of raw materials during the month.			

Determining Standard Costs for Period

The standard cost of production for the period is computed by multiplying the total standard quantity for each type of material used by the standard cost per unit. These data are presented in a summary of materials costs (Exhibit 2), on page 444. The total standard quantity required for each material is the number of units produced during the period multiplied by the standard quantity of the material per unit. In Exhibit 2, the total standard quantity of Material SM-2 is 27,000 feet (4,500 trays × 6 feet per tray). The standard cost of Material SM-2 for January is $54,000 (27,000 feet × $2 per foot). The total standard materials cost for the month is $66,240.

Computing Variances

The total materials variance for each type of material is the difference between the standard cost of the number of units produced during the period and the actual cost. The actual costs and the variances are shown in the summary of materials costs (Exhibit 2). The total actual materials cost of $70,976 exceeds the total standard cost

Exhibit 2

INDUSTRIAL TRAY COMPANY
Summary of Materials Costs
Month Ended January 31, 19X2

Production: 4,500 Trays

MATERIAL	QUANTITY PER TRAY	TOTAL QUANTITY REQUIRED	UNIT COST	TOTAL COST	TOTAL QUANTITY USED	UNIT COST	TOTAL COST	TOTAL VARIANCE
		STANDARD			ACTUAL			
SM-2	6 ft	27,000	$ 2.00	$54,000	20,000	$ 2.00	$40,000	$1,504U
					7,600	2.04	15,504	
LF-6	4 sets	18,000	.40	7,200	16,000	.40	6,400	8F
					2,200	.36	792	
MS-1	12 sets	54,000	.10	5,400	54,000	.10	5,400	-0-
PV-2	$\frac{1}{25}$ gal	180	16.00	2,880	180	16.00	2,880	-0-
Total				$69,480			$70,976	$1,496U

of $69,480. This means that there is an *unfavorable* materials variance of $1,496 ($70,976 − $69,480). Notice that the unfavorable variance relates to Material SM-2. This variance amount is marked U to show that it is unfavorable.

Two factors could account for the total materials variance.

1. There may be a difference between the standard quantity called for and the actual quantity of materials used (a materials quantity or usage variance).
2. There may be a difference between the standard cost per unit and the actual cost per unit of materials used (a materials price or cost variance).

Materials Quantity Variance. The amount of materials quantity or usage variance is computed by comparing the cost of the standard quantity of materials at the standard price per unit with the cost of the actual quantity of materials at the standard price per unit. If the actual quantity used exceeds the standard quantity, there is an *unfavorable* materials quantity variance. Exhibit 2 shows both unfavorable and favorable balances. The variances are computed as follows:

Materials Quantity Variance = (Standard Quantity × Standard Price) − (Actual Quantity × Standard Price)

For Material SM-2, the quantity variance is unfavorable.

27,000 standard units × $2.00 standard price per unit	$54,000
27,600 actual units × $2.00 standard price per unit	55,200
Materials Quantity Variance (600 × $2)	$ 1,200U

For Material LF-6, the quantity variance is unfavorable.

18,000 standard units × $.40 standard price per unit	$7,200
18,200 actual units × $.40 standard price per unit	7,280
Materials Quantity Variance (200 × $.40)	$ 80U

Materials Price Variance. A materials price variance results when the actual price per unit differs from the standard price per unit. It is computed by taking the difference between the cost of the actual quantity used at the standard unit price and the cost of the actual quantity of materials used at the actual unit price. If the actual price per unit exceeds the standard price per unit, there is an unfavorable (U) variance. The variance is computed as follows:

Materials Price Variance = (Actual Quantity × Standard Price) − (Actual Quantity × Actual Price)

For Material SM-2, the price variance is unfavorable (U).

27,600 actual units × $2.00 standard price per unit		$55,200
20,000 actual units × $2.00 actual price per unit	$40,000	
7,600 actual units × $2.04 actual price per unit	15,504	55,504
Materials Price Variance		$ 304U

For material LF-6, the price variance is favorable (F).

18,200 actual units × $.40 standard price per unit		$7,280
16,000 actual units × $.40 actual price per unit	$6,400	
2,200 actual units × $.36 actual price per unit	792	7,192
Materials Price Variance		$ 88F

Note that there are no variances for Materials MS-1 and PV-2. The standard quantity equals the actual quantity used for both. The standard price also equals the actual price for both types of materials. (See Exhibit 2.)

The results of the materials quantity and price variance computations are presented in the materials variances summary. (See Exhibit 3.) The materials quantity variance plus the materials price variance equals the total variance for each type of material and for the period.

INDUSTRIAL TRAY COMPANY   Exhibit 3

Materials Variances Summary
Month Ended January 31, 19X2

MATERIAL	QUANTITY VARIANCE	PRICE VARIANCE	TOTAL VARIANCE
SM-2	$1,200U	$304U	$1,504U
LF-6	80U	88F	8F
Total	$1,280U	$216U	$1,496U

Recording Production Costs and Variances

Using the data from the summary of materials costs (Exhibit 2) and the materials variances summary (Exhibit 3), the accountant journalizes the production costs and variances for the period. The Work in Process account is charged with the total standard cost for the period, $69,480. The Raw Materials account is credited for the actual cost of materials used, $70,976. These two amounts are obtained from Exhibit 2. Any difference is accounted for by materials variances from Exhibit 3. Unfavorable variances are recorded as debits. Favorable variances are recorded as credits. Since both the materials quantity variance, $1,280, and the materials price variance, $216, were unfavorable, they are shown as debits. The complete entry is given below in general journal form.

19X2				
Jan. 31	Work in Process (Standard Cost)	122	69,480	
	Materials Quantity Variance	508	1,280	
	Materials Price Variance	509	216	
	Raw Materials (Actual Cost)	121		70,976
	Charged Work in Process with standard cost of materials, recorded actual cost of materials removed from inventory, and recorded materials variances.			

Recording Materials Variances As They Occur. The preceding variances were recorded only when the manufacturing costs were changed to work in process at the end of the month. However, many accountants feel that any variance in the price of materials should be recorded at the time the materials are purchased. This way, maximum control can be exercised at the time a variance occurs. This practice also allows the raw materials inventories to be carried at standard cost, with only quantities shown in the materials ledger. When materials are placed in production, their standard cost is debited to the Work in Process account and credited to the Raw Materials account.

Labor Costs

The procedure used in accounting for labor costs in a standard cost system is similar to that used for materials.

Establishing Standards

Both quantity (time) and price (rate) standards are established for direct labor and entered on the standard cost sheet (Exhibit 1), on page 441.

Labor Quantity Standards. Standards for direct labor quantity are based on human behavior, performance, and judgement. They are a good deal less exact than materials standards. Time and motion studies analyzing each step in the production process may be used in setting time standards. Production and time records that reflect past operating results are also useful. An analysis of the experience and skills of the available work force is essential.

Labor Rate Standards. Labor rate information is obtained from the personnel department and from labor union contracts. Standard labor rates are usually based on current rates being paid or scheduled to be paid. Often there will be no labor rate variances. However, labor rates may change during the period. Also, personnel doing the same job may be paid at different rates, or personnel earning different rates may be shifted from job to job or from department to department. Similarly, personnel with seniority may retire and new personnel earning a lower (or a higher) rate may be employed. In all these cases, labor rate variances may occur.

As shown in Exhibit 1 (page 441), the Forming Department has a quantity or time standard of .5 hour per tray and a price or rate standard of $12 per direct labor hour. The standard labor cost per tray in the Forming Department is $6 ($12 × .5).

Exhibit 1 shows only one direct labor rate for each department. Separate standards are often set for each labor operation within a department if different personnel are used. For instance, trainees may have a lower standard rate than experienced workers have.

Recording Actual Costs

Actual labor costs incurred during the period are charged to Factory Payroll Clearing at the end of the period, as shown in the summary entry that follows:

19X2				
Jan. 31	Factory Payroll Clearing	500	72,680	
	Salaries and Wages Payable (and other			
	liability accounts)	XXX		72,680
	Recorded actual direct labor costs during			
	the month.			

Determining Standard Costs for Period

The standard labor costs for the period are calculated using the actual production figure and data from the standard cost sheet (Exhibit 1). The summary of labor costs (Exhibit 4) is prepared. On this summary, the total standard labor hours in the Forming Department are 2,250 (4,500 trays at .5 hour per tray). The standard cost of labor in the Forming Department during January is $27,000 (2,250 hours at $12 per hour). The total standard labor cost for the month is $71,100 (4,500 trays at $15.80 per tray).

	INDUSTRIAL TRAY COMPANY							EXHIBIT 4
	Summary of Labor Costs							
	Month Ended January 31, 19X2							
	Production: 4,500 Trays							

	STANDARD				ACTUAL			
DEPARTMENT	HOURS PER TRAY	TOTAL HOURS	RATE PER HOUR	TOTAL COST	HOURS	RATE PER HOUR	TOTAL COST	TOTAL VARIANCE
Forming	.5	2,250	$12.00	$27,000	2,350	$12.40	$29,140	$2,140U
Finishing	.7	3,150	14.00	44,100	3,110	14.00	43,540	560F
Total				$71,100			$72,680	$1,580U

Computing Variances

The total labor variance for each department is the difference between the total standard cost of production for the period and the total actual labor cost incurred. The actual costs are shown in the summary of labor costs (Exhibit 4). Since the actual labor costs, $72,680, exceed the standard labor costs, $71,100, there is a total unfavorable labor variance of $1,580 for January.

The total variance shown on the summary is analyzed by type and by department. As with materials, two types of labor variances are computed for each department. The labor efficiency variance is comparable to the materials quantity variance. The labor rate variance is similar to the materials price variance.

Labor Efficiency Variance. The *labor efficiency variance,* also called the *labor time,* the *labor usage,* or the *labor quantity variance,* measures the effectiveness of labor. The production manager is usually responsible for this variance. The labor efficiency variance compares the cost of actual hours worked (based on the standard rate per hour) with the cost of standard hours allowed for the number of units produced. If the actual hours amount exceeds the standard hours amount, there is an unfavorable labor efficiency variance. The variance is computed as follows:

Labor Efficiency Variance = (Standard Quantity × Standard Rate) − (Actual Quantity × Standard Rate)

For the Forming Department, the labor efficiency variance is unfavorable.

2,250 standard hours × $12.00 standard rate per hour	$27,000
2,350 actual hours × $12.00 standard rate per hour	28,200
Labor Efficiency Variance (100 hours × 12.00 per hour)	$ 1,200U

For the Finishing Department, the labor efficiency variance is favorable.

3,150 standard hours × $14.00 standard rate per hour	$44,100
3,110 actual hours × $14.00 standard rate per hour	43,540
Labor Efficiency Variance (40 hours × $14.00 per hour)	$ 560F

Labor Rate Variance. The labor rate variance occurs when the actual labor rate differs from the standard labor rate. The variance is unfavorable if the actual rate exceeds the standard rate. Labor rates usually are set by a contract with a labor union or by the personnel department. In this sense, the labor rate variance is outside the control of the production manager. However, the choice of personnel within the department may affect the labor rate. The labor rate variance is computed as follows:

Labor Rate Variance = (Actual Quantity × Standard Rate) − (Actual Quantity × Actual Rate)

No labor rate variance occurred in the Finishing Department since the actual rate was the same as the standard rate (Exhibit 4).

For the Forming Department, the labor rate variance is unfavorable.

2,350 actual hours × $12.00 standard rate per hour	$28,200	
2,350 actual hours × $12.40 actual rate per hour	29,140	
Labor Rate Variance (2,350 hours × $.40 per hour)	$ 940U	

The labor efficiency and rate variances are summarized in Exhibit 5. The sum of the labor efficiency variance and the labor rate variance equals the total variance for each department and for the period.

INDUSTRIAL TRAY COMPANY			Exhibit 5
Labor Variances Summary			
Month Ended January 31, 19X2			
DEPARTMENT	LABOR EFFICIENCY VARIANCE	LABOR RATE VARIANCE	TOTAL VARIANCE
Forming	$1,200U	$940U	$2,140U
Finishing	560F	-0-	560F
Total	$ 640U	$940U	$1,580U

Recording Production Costs and Variances

The data from the summary of labor costs (Exhibit 4) and the labor variances summary (Exhibit 5) are used to journalize labor costs for the period. Work in Process is debited for the total standard labor cost of $71,100. Factory Payroll Clearing is credited for the actual costs of $72,680. Any difference is accounted for by the labor variances shown in the labor variances summary (Exhibit 5). Unfavorable variances are recorded as debits. Favorable variances are recorded as credits. Since both labor variances are unfavorable, they are shown as debits. The complete entry is shown below in general journal form.

19X2				
Jan. 31	Work in Process (Standard Cost)	122	71,100	
	Labor Efficiency Variance	510	640	
	Labor Rate Variance	511	940	
	Factory Payroll Clearing (Actual Cost)	500		72,680
	Charged Work in Process with standard			
	cost of direct labor, removed actual			
	labor cost from Factory Payroll Clear-			
	ing, and recorded labor variances.			

Systems Analysis

Prestige Paper Products, Inc., is a major manufacturer of household paper products with seven plants and 4,000 employees throughout the country. The data processing division, which is located in the main office in Chicago, has a staff of 30 systems analysts. A *systems analyst* is a "go between" who works with the users of data processing services within the company—for example, the payroll department—and the data processing division itself. When a department expresses a need for data processing services, the systems analyst studies the situation and makes recommendations to a management budget committee as to the type of computer equipment and programs that will meet the needs of the department. If the committee believes the department's needs can be handled economically and efficiently by the data processing division, it provides a budget for the project and gives its approval. The systems analyst then becomes the overseer of the project until it is completed.

William Dailey, the manager of PPP's Kentucky plant, was concerned about losing many purchase discounts because payments for supplies and materials were not being made during the discount period. He also felt that with up-to-the-minute information about the purchase of materials, the purchasing agents would be able to negotiate better deals. Dailey believed that if the accounts payable section had a computer, it would speed up the recording of invoices and the issuing of payments, and daily reports on purchases would be available.

PPP sent Susan Cantrell, a systems analyst from the home office, to the Kentucky plant to do a preliminary study. A preliminary study is a relatively brief investigation to prepare a report on the feasibility of budgeting an in-depth study of the problem. Within a week, Cantrell had interviewed Dailey and the accounts payable section chief and observed the section at work. She reported to the management committee that the situation could be handled at a reasonable cost. The committee gave her permission to do an in-depth study and make recommendations.

For the next two months, Cantrell interviewed all the accountants and clerks in the accounts payable department, made an organization chart with job descriptions, and constructed flow-charts and data-flow diagrams in order to chart the accounts payable process as it was being accomplished manually. As she did the on-site study, Cantrell noticed bottlenecks in the flow of paperwork that could be opened up by using a computer.

Cantrell reported her findings to the chief systems analyst, who made recommendations on specific computers and programs that would accomplish the task. She contacted the Kentucky plant's personnel officer to request time and space for training the accountants and clerks for the automated processing, and then met with Dailey for his approval of her final recommendations. Dailey felt that the plan would answer his needs, and gave his approval.

Final approval of the plan was given by the management committee based on the cost effectiveness projected in Cantrell's study. She is now in charge of installation of the computer and providing training in the use of the programs. ■

Principles and Procedures Summary

Standard costs are predetermined measures of what costs should be under efficient operating conditions. Standard cost data is used in budgeting, preparing financial statements, and making decisions.

Six steps are followed in a standard cost system.

1. Establish standards for each cost element.
2. Record actual costs incurred during the period.
3. Determine the standard costs for output during the period.
4. Compute variances by comparing actual and standard costs.
5. Break down the variances into their component parts in order to analyze them.
6. Record production costs and variances.

Review Questions

1. What are standard manufacturing costs?
2. What are theoretical standards?
3. What are normal standards?
4. Should theoretical standards or normal standards be used to set goals? Explain your answer.
5. What is a materials quantity standard?
6. What is a materials price standard?
7. Explain how materials quantity standards are set.
8. Explain how materials price standards are set.
9. Define the *standard materials cost* for a period.
10. What two variances account for the difference between actual materials cost and standard materials cost for a period?
11. Explain how to calculate the materials price variance.
12. Explain how to calculate the materials quantity variance.
13. How are labor quantity standards set?
14. Explain how the labor efficiency variance is computed.
15. Explain how the labor rate variance is computed.
16. Explain how materials price variances might be recorded at the time materials are purchased. What are the advantages of this procedure?

Managerial Discussion Questions

1. What are some advantages to management of a standard cost system?
2. The management of the McGill Corporation is developing standard costs. The vice president of production has heard of theoretical standards and thinks they should be used. Do you agree or disagree? Why?
3. Assume that you are a cost accountant at the Wagner Company. Briefly explain to management the reasons that variances between actual and standard costs of materials may exist.
4. Which level of management is usually responsible for labor rate variances?
5. As a production manager, would you be likely to have more control over materials price variances or materials usage variances? Explain.
6. The accountant for the McGill Corporation has noticed that historically when there have been favorable labor rate variances, there have been unfavorable labor efficiency variances. What factors may explain this situation?

1. **Computing materials quantity and price variances.** The Chapman Company manufactures a product using a special type of lumber. Each unit of product should require 2½ board feet. The standard cost of the lumber is $1.75 per board foot. During January 19X5, 28,260 units of product were manufactured, requiring 71,310 board feet of lumber at a total cost of $122,653.20. Compute the materials quantity variance and the materials price variance for the month. Show whether the variances are favorable or unfavorable.

2. **Computing materials quantity and price variances.** The standard materials cost of producing 1 pound of Wood Shine is as follows:

8½ ounces of Deepglo at 12 cents per ounce	$1.02
8½ ounces of Preservo at 30 cents per ounce	2.55
Total	$3.57

   During March 19X1, 4,000 pounds of Wood Shine were produced. The actual materials costs were as follows:

32,480 ounces of Deepglo at 12½ cents per ounce	$ 4,060.00
32,160 ounces of Preservo at 30½ cents per ounce	9,808.80
Total	$13,868.80

   Compute the materials price variances and the materials quantity variances for March 19X1. Show whether the variances are favorable or unfavorable.

3. **Making journal entries to record materials costs and variances.** Give the entries in general journal form to record the materials placed in process and the related variances from Exercise 2.

4. **Computing labor efficiency and rate variances.** The standard cost sheet calls for 1 hour, 45 minutes of labor in the Assembly Department for each desk manufactured by the New Hampshire Desk Company. The standard labor cost is $7.20 per hour. During December 19X7, a total of 220 desks were assembled, requiring 382 hours at a cost of $2,807.70. Compute the labor efficiency variance and the labor rate variance for the month. Show whether the variances are favorable or unfavorable.

5. **Making journal entries to record labor costs and variances.** Give entries in general journal form to charge the standard labor cost to Work in Process and to record the labor variances for the month from Exercise 4.

6. **Computing labor rate and efficiency variances.** In the Finishing Department of the Lucas Furniture Company, each bookcase manufactured requires 30 minutes of sanding labor and 45 minutes of painting labor. The standard wage rate for sanding personnel is $8 per hour, and the standard wage rate for painting personnel is $12 per hour. During October 19X1, 320 bookcases were manufactured. The sanding labor required was 158 hours at a total cost of $1,264, and the painting labor required was 246 hours at a total cost of $2,007.36. Compute the labor rate variances and the labor efficiency variances for the month. Show whether the variances are favorable or unfavorable.

7. **Making a journal entry to record labor costs and variances.** Give the entry in general journal form to charge the standard labor cost to Work in Process and to record the labor variances from Exercise 6.

8. **Computing labor rate and efficiency variances.** The standard labor cost for a unit of product is 3 hours of labor at $7.20 per hour. Compute the labor rate variance and the labor efficiency variance for the month of April 19X2, when 2,000 units were produced in each of the following assumed cases. Show whether the variances are favorable or unfavorable.
   a. 5,800 hours of labor were required at a total cost of $42,050.
   b. 5,800 hours of labor were required at a total cost of $41,644.
   c. 6,108 hours of labor were required at a total cost of $43,977.60.
   d. 6,108 hours of labor were required at a total cost of $44,771.64.

Problems

PROBLEM 22-1. Summarizing materials costs, quantity and price variances, and materials variances. The Channing Plastics Company manufactures a product called Myrtilex, which requires three raw materials. Production is in batches of 2,000 pounds of materials. Waste (which is thrown away) sometimes occurs. Standard costs are used as a control device. The standard materials costs for each batch of Myrtilex have been established as given below.

Material	Quantity	Standard Cost per Pound	Standard Cost per Batch
Plastic base	1,800 lb	$.15	$270
Tint	100 lb	.20	20
Hardener	100 lb	.25	25
Total	2,000 lb		$315

The output is packaged in containers of 25 pounds each. During the month of February 19X1, 2,400 containers of Myrtilex were produced. There was no beginning or ending work in process inventory. The materials actually used during February were as follows:

	Quantity	Total Cost
Plastic base	55,296 lb	$8,441
Tint	3,072 lb	592
Hardener	3,012 lb	781

Instructions
1. Prepare a summary of materials costs for the month of February (Exhibit 2). Carry the unit costs to five decimal places and round to four places. Show whether the variances are favorable (F) or unfavorable (U).
2. Compute the quantity and price variances for each of the materials.
3. Prepare a materials variances summary for the month (Exhibit 3).
4. Give the general journal entry on February 28, 19X1, to charge the standard materials costs to production and to record the price and quantity variances.

PROBLEM 22-2. Summarizing labor costs, efficiency and rate variances, and labor variances. In the Forming Department of the Mason Products Company, two classes of direct labor are used in the manufacturing process. Standard labor costs have been established for each unit of the product as follows:

Labor Class	Standard Hours	Standard Rate per Hour
Class DL-1	½ hr	$11.20
Class DL-2	1 hr	12.00

During the month of June 19X1, a total of 4,040 units were produced. The actual labor costs, by class, were as follows:

Labor Class	Hours	Cost
Class DL-1	2,106	$23,587.20
Class DL-2	4,010	49,724.00

Instructions

1. Prepare a summary of labor costs for the month of June (Exhibit 4). Show whether the variances are favorable (F) or unfavorable (U).
2. Compute the efficiency and rate variances for each class of labor.
3. Prepare a labor variances summary for the month (Exhibit 5).
4. Give the general journal entry on June 30 19X1, to charge the standard labor cost to production, to remove the actual cost of the labor used from the Factory Payroll Clearing account, and to record the labor efficiency and labor rate variances. Use Work in Process—Forming Department, 123.

PROBLEM 22-3. Summarizing materials quantity and price variances, labor efficiency and rate variances, and materials and labor variances. The Concord Company manufactures a product that is processed through two departments, Cutting and Fitting. All materials are added in the Cutting Department (the first department). Some data on standard costs that have been established for materials and labor are shown below.

Raw Materials
Panel units: 4 units at $2.10 each	$8.40
Assembly sets: 4 sets at 6 cents each	.24
Standard Materials Cost per Unit	$8.64

Direct Labor
Cutting Dept.: ⅙ hr at $9.60 per hr	$1.60
Fitting Dept.: ¼ hr at $8.00 per hr	2.00
Standard Direct Labor Costs per Unit	$3.60

During the month of May 19X1, 4,500 units of the product were manufactured. The actual costs of materials and labor were as follows:

Raw Materials
Panel units: 18,100 at $2.12 each	$38,372.00
Assembly sets: 18,050 at 5.5 cents each	992.75
Total Actual Materials Costs	$39,364.75

Direct Labor
Cutting Dept.: 752 hr at $9.60 per hr	$ 7,219.20
Fitting Dept.: 1,100 hr at $7.80 per hr	$8,580.00
Total Actual Direct Labor Costs	$15,799.20

Instructions

1. Compute the quantity and price variances for each of the two raw materials.
2. Prepare a materials variances summary (Exhibit 3).
3. Compute the labor efficiency and rate variances for each department.
4. Prepare a labor variances summary (Exhibit 5).
5. Give the general journal entries on May 31, 19X1, to do the following:
   a. Charge the standard costs of materials to production, record the actual costs of the raw materials used, and record the materials variances using separate accounts for materials quantity variances and materials price variances. Use Work in Process—Cutting Department 123.
   b. Charge the standard costs of direct labor to production, remove the actual labor costs from Factory Payroll Clearing, and record the labor variances using separate accounts for labor efficiency and labor rate variances. Use Work in Process—Fitting Department 124.

Alternate Problems

PROBLEM 22-1A. Summarizing materials costs, quantity and price variances, and materials variances. The Wellington Company manufactures a chemical product called Kalene, which requires three raw materials. Production is in batches of 1,040 gallons of raw materials that yield only 1,000 gallons of finished product. (Some evaporation of the inert base occurs, but the amount of evaporation varies slightly from batch to batch.) Standard costs are used as a control device. The standard materials costs for each batch of Kalene are as follows:

Material	Quantity	Standard Cost per Gallon	Standard Cost per Batch
Inert base	840 gal	$ .40	$ 336.00
Acid	160 gal	1.20	192.00
Activator	40 gal	20.50	820.00
Total	1,040 gal		$1,348.00

The output is packaged in 50-gallon drums. During the month of July 19X1, 300 drums of Kalene were produced. There was no beginning or ending work in process inventory. The materials actually used during July were as follows:

	Quantity	Cost per Gallon
Inert base	12,840 gal	$ .42
Acid	2,390 gal	1.12
Activator	612 gal	20.20

Instructions

1. Prepare a summary of materials costs for the month of July (Exhibit 2). Show whether the variances are favorable (F) or unfavorable (U).
2. Compute the quantity and price variances for each of the materials.
3. Prepare a material variances summary for the month (Exhibit 3).
4. Give the general journal entry on July 31, 19X1, to charge the standard materials costs to production and to record the price and quantity variances.

PROBLEM 22-2A. Summarizing labor costs, efficiency and rate variances, and labor variances. In the Finishing Department of the Paxton Tank Corporation, two classes of direct labor are used in the manufacturing process. Standard labor costs have been established for each unit of the product as follows:

Labor Class	Standard Hours	Standard Rate per Hour
Class FL-3	$\frac{1}{4}$ hr	$10.40
Class FL-4	2 hr	9.60

During the month of May 19X1, a total of 2,836 units were produced. The actual labor costs, by class, were as follows:

Labor Class	Hours	Cost
Class FL-3	716	$ 7,876.00
Class FL-4	5,512	52,915.20

Instructions

1. Prepare a summary of labor costs for the month of May (Exhibit 4). Show whether the variances are favorable (F) or unfavorable (U).
2. Compute the efficiency and rate variances for each class of labor.
3. Prepare a labor variances summary for the month (Exhibit 5).
4. Give the general journal entry on May 31, 19X1, to charge the standard labor cost to Work in Process, to remove the actual cost of labor used from the Factory Payroll Clearing account, and to record the labor efficiency and labor rate variances. Use Work in Process—Finishing Department 123.

PROBLEM 22-3A. Summarizing materials quantity and price variances, labor efficiency and rate variances, and materials and labor variances. The Walker Siding Company manufactures a building product that is processed through two departments, Pressing and Curing. All materials are added in the Pressing Department (the first department). Certain data concerning standard costs that have been established for materials and labor are given below:

Raw Materials
Magic Board: 20 sq ft at 20 cents per sq ft		$4.00
Filler: 14 lb at 12 cents per lb		1.68
Standard Materials Costs per Unit (10 sq ft)		$5.68

Direct Labor
Pressing Dept.: $\frac{1}{4}$ hr at $9.60 per hr		$2.40
Curing Dept.: $\frac{1}{10}$ hr at $8.00 per hr		.80
Standard Direct Labor Costs per Unit		$3.20

During the month of May 19X1, 10,000 units (100,000 square feet) of the product were manufactured. Actual costs of materials and labor were as shown below.

Raw Materials
Magic Board: 201,000 sq ft at 19.6 cents per sq ft		$39,396.00
Filler: 138,970 lb at 12.2 cents per lb		16,954.34
Total Actual Materials Costs		$56,350.34

Direct Labor
Pressing Dept.: 2,580 hr at $9.80 per hr $25,284.00
Curing Dept.: 987 hr at $8.20 per hr   8,093.40
   Total Actual Direct Labor Costs $33,377.40

Instructions

1. Compute the quantity and price variances for each of the two raw materials.
2. Prepare a materials variances summary (Exhibit 3).
3. Compute the labor efficiency and rate variances for each department.
4. Prepare a labor variances summary (Exhibit 5).
5. Give the entries in general journal form on May 31, 19X1, to do the following:
   a. Charge the standard costs of materials to production, record the actual costs of the raw materials used, and record the materials variances using separate accounts for materials quantity variances and materials price variances. Use Work in Process—Pressing Department 123.
   b. Charge the standard costs of direct labor to production, remove the actual labor costs from Factory Payroll Clearing, and record the labor variances using separate accounts for labor efficiency and labor rate variances. Use Work in Process—Curing Department 124.

CHAPTER

23

■ ■ ■

Standard Costs: Manufacturing Overhead

Manufacturing overhead costs are harder to control than labor and materials. Manufacturing overhead consists of numerous costs, few of which are directly related to an individual unit of product. The standard for manufacturing overhead per completed unit of product is not an engineered standard (one based on engineering and time and motion studies). Instead, it is the result of an allocation process that attempts to determine what costs should be and then allocates the costs to the units produced.

Overhead Costs

Before the period begins, overhead application rates are computed. These rates are based on estimated or budgeted manufacturing overhead for the period and some application basis, such as estimated or budgeted direct labor hours. Costs are applied to work in process during the period. The applied costs are determined by multiplying the standard overhead rate per hour by the standard hours allowed for the number of units produced. Actual costs incurred during the period are recorded in the Manufacturing Overhead Control account. Then, at the end of the period, costs are evaluated by comparing standard costs that were applied with the actual costs incurred. If any differences occur, they are analyzed through variance analysis.

Standard Cost System

Setting up and using a standard cost system for manufacturing overhead is done in the same way it is done for materials and labor. The specific steps follow:

1. Establishing standard costs per unit for overhead costs.
2. Recording the actual costs incurred during the period.
3. Determining the standard costs for the units produced during the period.
4. Computing variances by comparing the actual costs incurred during the period with the standard costs of the units produced during the period.
5. Breaking down the total variance into its component parts.
6. Recording the standard costs of the units produced and the variances from the standard costs.

The steps above were followed by the Industrial Tray Company in accounting for manufacturing overhead costs during January 19X2.

Establishing Standards

Manufacturing overhead standards are established by using estimated costs and a selected basis for application. The basis selected for applying overhead is usually direct labor hours. A rate per hour is found by dividing the estimated overhead by the estimated direct labor hours. The rate per completed unit is the standard overhead rate per hour multiplied by the standard direct labor hours per unit. Both variable and fixed rates per unit are computed in each department as shown in Exhibit 1.

INDUSTRIAL TRAY COMPANY   **Exhibit 1**
Standard Cost Sheet
Chemical Tray KL-31

MATERIALS	QUANTITY	UNIT COST	TOTAL COST PER TRAY
SM-2	6 ft	$ 2.00 per ft	$12.000
LF-6	4 sets	.40 per set	1.600
MS-1	12 sets	.10 per set	1.200
PV-2	$\frac{1}{25}$ gal	16.00 per gal	.640
Total Materials Cost per Tray			$15.440
Labor			
Forming Department	.5 hr	$12.00 per hr	$ 6.000
Finishing Department	.7 hr	14.00 per hr	9.800
Total Labor Cost per Tray			$15.800
Overhead			
Forming Department			
Variable Costs	.5 hr	$ 6.040 per hr	$ 3.020
Fixed Costs	.5 hr	4.376 per hr	2.188
Total for Forming Department		$10.416 per hr	$ 5.208
Finishing Department			
Variable Costs	.7 hr	$ 6.000 per hr	$ 4.200
Fixed Costs	.7 hr	3.231 per hr	2.262
Total for Finishing Department		$ 9.231 per hr	$ 6.462
Total Overhead Cost per Tray			$11.670
Total Standard Cost per Tray			$42.910

These overhead rates were determined as follows. For the Industrial Tray Company, the estimated overhead costs used in setting standard overhead rates are those budgeted at normal volume. In Chapter 21 a manufacturing overhead budget was developed for each producing and service department (page 425). This budget is summarized below for the year 19X2.

	Forming Department	Finishing Department	Factory Services Department	Total Cost
Variable Costs	$128,400	$178,080	$126,720	$433,200
Fixed Costs	85,680	44,520	136,800	267,000
Total	$214,080	$222,600	$263,520	$700,200

Overhead costs are applied in producing departments only. Service department costs must be allocated to these producing departments by the technique presented in Chapter 8. When standard costs are used, service department fixed costs and variable costs are usually allocated on different bases. For example, the variable costs of the Factory Services Department of the Industrial Tray Company are allocated on the basis of direct labor hours. The fixed costs are allocated on the basis of floor space occupied. These allocations are shown below.

	Basis	Forming Department	Finishing Department	Total Cost
Variable Costs	Direct Labor Hours	$52,800*	$ 73,920*	$126,720
Fixed Costs	Floor Space Occupied	45,600†	91,200†	136,800
Total		$98,400	$165,120	$263,520

*Based on 30,000 hours for Forming Department and 42,000 hours for Finishing Department.
†Based on 3,000 square feet for Forming Department and 6,000 square feet for Finishing Department.

The allocated variable and fixed costs of the service department are added to the variable and fixed costs of the individual producing departments as shown in the calculation below.

	Forming Department	Finishing Department
Variable Costs		
Departmental Variable Costs	$128,400	$178,080
Allocated Service Department Costs	52,800	73,920
Total Variable Costs	$181,200	$252,000
Fixed Costs		
Departmental Fixed Costs	$ 85,680	$ 44,520
Allocated Service Department Costs	45,600	91,200
Total Fixed Costs	$131,280	$135,720
Total Costs	$312,480	$387,720

The total estimated overhead cost after allocation of service department costs is divided by the budgeted labor hours in each producing department. This gives the standard overhead rates per hour, as shown on page 461. Note that separate variable and fixed rates are calculated.

	Total Cost		Total Hours		Standard Rates per Hour
Forming Department					
Variable Costs	$181,200	÷	30,000	=	$ 6.040
Fixed Costs	131,280	÷	30,000	=	4.376
Total					$10.416
Finishing Department					
Variable Costs	$252,000	÷	42,000	=	$ 6.000
Fixed Costs	135,720	÷	42,000	=	3.231
Total					$ 9.231

The standard overhead rate per unit is computed by multiplying the standard rate per hour by the standard hours per unit, as shown below. These rates are then entered on the standard cost sheet. The standard cost sheet (Exhibit 1) for the Industrial Tray Company is shown on page 459.

	Standard Overhead per Tray	
	Variable	Fixed
Forming Department		
Variable Costs (.5 hr × $6.04 per hr)	$3.020	
Fixed Costs (.5 hr × $4.376 per hr)		$2.188
Finishing Department		
Variable Costs (.7 hr × $6 per hr)	4.200	
Fixed Costs (.7 hr × $3.231 per hr)		2.262
Total	$7.220	$4.450

Summary

Variable	$ 7.220
Fixed	4.450
Total	$11.670

Recording Actual Costs

Actual manufacturing overhead costs are accounted for in two steps. The first step is to record the actual costs incurred. The second step is to allocate the service department costs to the producing departments. Then it is easier to compare the actual costs with the standard costs charged to production.

Actual overhead costs incurred are recorded in the same manner as presented in Chapter 8. A summary entry for January is shown here.

19X2				
Jan. 31	Manufacturing Overhead Control	501	55,230.40	
	Various Payables (Prepaid Expenses, etc.)	XXX		55,230.40
	Recorded actual overhead costs during the month.			

The schedule of actual overhead costs (Exhibit 2) shows these costs classified by the department in which they were incurred.

INDUSTRIAL TRAY COMPANY			Exhibit 2
Schedule of Actual Overhead Costs			
Month Ended January 31, 19X2			
	FORMING DEPARTMENT (2,350 HR)	**FINISHING DEPARTMENT (3,110 HR)**	**FACTORY SERVICES DEPARTMENT**	**TOTAL**
Variable Costs	$10,060.00	$13,310.80	$ 9,609.60	$32,980.40
Fixed Costs	7,140.00	3,710.00	11,400.00	22,250.00
Total	$17,200.00	$17,020.80	$21,009.60	$55,230.40

The service department costs for January, $21,009.60, must be allocated to the producing departments. The allocation is made using the following schedule, Exhibit 3. (Allocated costs are usually rounded to the nearest whole dollar.) As with budgeted overhead, variable costs are allocated on the basis of direct labor hours, and fixed costs are allocated on the basis of floor space occupied. The allocated costs are entered in the summary of manufacturing overhead costs. (See Exhibit 4 on page 463.)

INDUSTRIAL TRAY COMPANY			Exhibit 3
Schedule of Allocation of Service Department Costs			
Month Ended January 31, 19X2			
	FORMING DEPARTMENT	**FINISHING DEPARTMENT**	**TOTAL COST**
Variable Costs			
Departmental Variable Costs	$10,060.00	$13,310.80	$23,370.80
Allocation of Service Dept.			
Costs*	4,136.00	5,473.60	9,609.60
Total Variable Costs	$14,196.00	$18,784.40	$32,980.40
Fixed Costs			
Departmental Fixed Costs	$ 7,140.00	$ 3,710.00	$10,850.00
Allocation of Service Dept.			
Costs†	3,800.00	7,600.00	11,400.00
Total Fixed Costs	$10,940.00	$11,310.00	$22,250.00
Total Costs	$25,136.00	$30,094.40	$55,230.40

*Based on 2,350 hours for Forming Department and 3,110 for Finishing Department.
†Based on 3,000 square feet for Forming Department and 6,000 square feet for Finishing Department.

Determining Standard Costs for Period

Direct labor hours are used to apply manufacturing overhead to production. Thus the standard cost applied during the period is the standard hours allowed multiplied by the standard overhead rate per hour. The standard hours allowed is the product of the standard hours per completed unit and the number of units produced during the period. The standard hours in the Forming Department totaled 2,250 (4,500 trays × .5 hour per tray). The standard cost of manufacturing overhead in this department is $23,436 (2,250 hours × $10.416 per hour). Similarly, the standard overhead in the Finishing Department for the month is $29,077.65 (3,150 standard hours × $9.231 per hour). The total standard overhead cost for the month is thus $52,513.65. This figure is $1.35 less than the total standard cost of $52,515.00 obtained by multiplying the standard cost of $11.670 per tray, shown on the standard cost sheet on page 459, by the 4,500 trays produced during the month. This difference is due to rounding and can be ignored.

The standard manufacturing overhead costs for January are presented in Exhibit 4, along with the actual costs for the month.

INDUSTRIAL TRAY COMPANY   Exhibit 4
Summary of Manufacturing Overhead Costs
Month Ended January 31, 19X2

Actual Production 4,500 Trays

| | | STANDARD | | | ACTUAL | | |
DEPARTMENT	HOURS PER TRAY	TOTAL HOURS	RATE PER HOUR	TOTAL COST	TOTAL HOURS	TOTAL COST	TOTAL VARIANCE
Forming	.5	2,250	$10.416	$23,436.00	2,350	$25,136.00	$1,700.00U
Finishing	.7	3,150	9.231	29,077.65	3,110	30,094.40	1,016.75U
Total				$52,513.65		$55,230.40	$2,716.75U

Computing Variances

The total manufacturing overhead variance in each department is the difference between the standard costs of production (the standard hours allowed for the units produced multiplied by the standard overhead rate per hour) and the actual costs incurred. In January, the total variance is $1,700.00 in the Forming Department and $1,016.75 in the Finishing Department (see Exhibit 4).

It is very important to management in its efforts to control costs to know why the actual costs incurred during the period differed from the standard costs for the work. To provide this information, the accountant analyzes the total variance in each department and divides it into its component parts. This analysis may be done by using either a two-variance method or a three-variance method.

The Two-Variance Method

In the two-variance method, the total variance for a department is separated into the budget variance and the volume variance.

1. The *budget variance* (or *controllable variance*) in each department is the difference between (a) the actual costs incurred and (b) the overhead in the flexible budget for the standard hours allowed for the units produced.
2. The *volume variance* (or *capacity variance*) results from the fact that the number of direct labor hours for which overhead was charged to production differs from the number of hours on which the original budget used to compute the standard overhead rate was based.

An analysis of the $1,700 unfavorable overhead variance in the Forming Department, using the two-variance method, shows an unfavorable budget variance of $606 and an unfavorable volume variance of $1,094. For the Finishing Department, an analysis of the $1,016.75 unfavorable overhead variance shows a favorable budget variance of $115.60 and an unfavorable volume variance of $1,132.35. The analysis procedure is described below.

Budget Variance. As previously pointed out, the overhead budget variance is computed by comparing (1) the actual costs incurred and (2) the overhead in the flexible budget for the standard hours allowed for the number of units produced. The budgeted overhead for the number of units produced consists of two parts.

1. *Variable costs.* The total variable cost allowed for the number of units produced is computed by multiplying (a) the standard direct labor hours allowed for the number of units produced by (b) the standard overhead rate per hour for variable costs. The variable costs allowed for the Industrial Tray Company's actual production in the Forming Department for January would be $13,590 (2,250 standard hours × $6.04 per hour).
2. *Fixed costs.* The fixed costs budgeted for the period are usually known or can easily be determined. For the Forming Department, the budgeted annual fixed costs are $131,280, as shown in the table on page 460. Thus, the fixed costs for one month are $10,940 (one-twelfth of the annual budgeted costs).

Forming Department. The total flexible budget in the Forming Department for 4,500 units is $24,530, which is computed as follows:

Variable costs	
(2,250 standard hours × $6.04 per hour)	$13,590.00
Fixed costs	
($\frac{1}{12}$ × annual fixed costs of $131,280)	10,940.00
Total	$24,530.00

The manufacturing overhead budget variance in the Forming Department is thus an unfavorable variance of $606.

Actual costs (from Exhibit 4 on page 463)	$25,136.00
Budgeted costs for standard hours (computed above)	24,530.00
Manufacturing overhead budget variance	$ 606.00U

If the budgeted fixed manufacturing overhead and the actual fixed overhead are equal, the budget variance results from a difference between the variable costs budgeted and the variable costs incurred. Since most variable costs are controllable at the departmental level, the manufacturing overhead variance is often called the *controllable variance*. However, if fixed costs incurred are different from those budgeted, that difference will also be reflected in the budget variance. (As discussed later under the three-variance method, the budget variance can be further analyzed into a *spending* variance and an *efficiency* variance.)

Finishing Department. In the Finishing Department, the fixed costs are $11,310 per month, which is one-twelfth of the budgeted annual costs of $135,720. The total of the budgeted costs is $30,210, which is computed as follows:

Variable costs	
(3,150 standard hours × $6.00 per hour)	$18,900.00
Fixed costs	
($\frac{1}{12}$ × annual fixed costs of $135,720)	11,310.00
Total	$30,210.00

The manufacturing overhead budget variance in the Finishing Department is thus a favorable variance of $115.60, as shown here.

Actual costs (from Exhibit 4 on page 463)	$30,094.40
Budgeted costs for standard hours (computed above)	30,210.00
Manufacturing overhead budget variance	$ 115.60F

Volume Variance. In almost every case, the standard hours allowed for units actually produced during the current period will differ from the number of hours originally budgeted in setting the standard overhead rates. As a result, the fixed overhead charged to production will rarely be the same amount as that allowed in the budget for the output of the period. The resulting difference is called the *volume variance*.

Forming Department. For the Forming Department, the volume variance is unfavorable, as shown here.

Standard costs charged to production		
(2,250 standard hours × $10,416 per hour)		$23,436.00
Budgeted costs for production attained		
Variable Costs (2,250 hours × $6.04 per hour)	$13,590.00	
Fixed Costs ($\frac{1}{12}$ × $131,280)	10,940.00	24,530.00
Manufacturing overhead volume variance		$ 1,094.00U

The unfavorable volume variance in the Forming Department arises because the fixed overhead rate of $4.376 included in the total overhead rate of $10.416 (page 459) was based on the assumption that 2,500 hours would be worked during the month, while only the 2,250 hours allowed for the 4,500 units produced were actually charged to production. Thus $1,094 (250 hours × $4.376) of fixed costs were underapplied.

Finishing Department. For the Finishing Department, the volume variance is also unfavorable.

Standard costs charged to production
    (3,150 standard hours × $9.231 per hour) $29,077.65
Budgeted costs for production attained
    Variable costs (3,150 hours × $6.00 per hour) $18,900.00
    Fixed costs ($\frac{1}{12}$ × $135,720)   11,310.00   30,210.00
        Manufacturing overhead volume variance $ 1,132.35U

Summarizing the Budget and Volume Variances.

A review of the variance analysis in the Forming Department shows the following:

Actual costs $25,136.00 ⎫
Budget allowance based on standard hours for   ⎬ $606.00U
    units produced   24,530.00 ⎰ Budget Variance
                                                                    $1,094U
Standard costs   23,436.00 ⎰ Volume Variance

The variance analysis for the Finishing Department can be summarized as shown below.

Actual costs $30,094.40 ⎫
Budget allowance based on standard hours for   ⎬ $115.60F
    units produced   30,210.00 ⎰ Budget Variance
                                                                    $1,132.35U
Standard costs   29,077.65 ⎰ Volume Variance

The Three-Variance Method

Although the budget variance computed above is a measure of cost control in that it shows the variance between actual costs and what costs should have been for the volume of production for the period, many companies want a more detailed explanation of why this difference exists. The budget variance can be divided into the *spending variance* and the *efficiency variance*. The spending variance compares what should have been spent for the *actual* hours worked with the actual costs for those hours. The efficiency variance compares the budgeted costs for the *standard* hours worked with the budgeted costs for the actual hours worked. Thus a three-variance method of analysis results in a volume variance (computed in the same way as under the two-variance method), a spending variance, and an efficiency variance.

The $1,700 unfavorable variance in the Forming Department was determined under the two-variance method to consist of a $606 unfavorable budget variance and a $1,094 unfavorable volume variance. Under the three-variance method of analysis, the volume variance will continue to be an unfavorable variance of $1,094. An analysis of the budget variance of $606 shows that it is made up of a $2 unfavorable spending variance and a $604 unfavorable efficiency variance.

In the two-variance method, discussed on pages 463 to 464, the $1,016.75 unfavorable overhead variance in the Finishing Department was shown to consist of a $115.60 favorable budget variance and a $1,132.35 unfavorable volume variance. A further analysis of the $115.60 budget variance shows that it consists of a $124.40 unfavorable spending variance and a $240.00 favorable efficiency variance.

Spending Variance. As noted on page 466, the spending variance compares what should have been spent for the *actual hours worked* with the actual costs for those hours.

Forming Department. For the Forming Department, the spending variance of $2 is computed as follows:

Budget for actual hours worked

Variable costs (2,350 actual hours × $6.04 per hour)	$14,194.00	
Fixed costs ($\frac{1}{12}$ × annual costs of $131,280)	10,940.00	
Total budget for actual hours		$25,134.00
Actual costs (from Exhibit 4, page 463)		25,136.00
Manufacturing overhead spending variance		$ 2.00U

Finishing Department. For the Finishing Department, an analysis shows an unfavorable spending variance of $124.40.

Budget for actual hours worked

Variable costs (3,110 actual hours × $6 per hour)	$18,660.00	
Fixed costs ($\frac{1}{12}$ × annual costs of $135,720)	11,310.00	
Total budget for actual hours		$29,970.00
Actual costs (from Exhibit 4, page 463)		30,094.40
Manufacturing overhead spending variance		$ 124.40U

Efficiency Variance. The efficiency variance compares the budgeted amount for the *standard hours allowed* for the current production with the budgeted cost for the *actual hours worked*. Since the fixed costs budgeted for the hours allowed for the current production are the same as those budgeted for the actual hours worked, only the variable costs need to be considered in computing the efficiency variance.

Forming Department. For the Forming Department, the efficiency variance is $604.

Budget based on standard hours

Variable costs (2,250 standard hours × $6.04 per hour)	$13,590.00	
Fixed costs ($\frac{1}{12}$ × annual costs of $131,280)	10,940.00	
Total budget for standard hours		$24,530.00
Budget based on actual hours (from above)		25,134.00
Manufacturing overhead efficiency variance		$ 604.00U

Finishing Department. The efficiency variance in the Finishing Department may be computed as follows:

Budgeted variable overhead for standard hours (3,150 hours × $6.00 per hour)	$18,900.00
Budgeted variable overhead for actual hours (3,110 hours × $6.00 per hour)	18,660.00
Manufacturing overhead efficiency variance	$ 240.00F

Summarizing the Volume, Spending, and Efficiency Variances. Under the three-variance method, the total unfavorable overhead variance of $1,700 in the Forming Department can be summarized as follows:

Standard costs	$23,436.00	$1,094.00U Volume Variance
Budget for standard hours	24,530.00	$604.00U Efficiency Variance
Budget for actual hours	25,134.00	
Actual costs	25,136.00	$2.00U Spending Variance

The figures for the Finishing Department are as shown.

Standard costs	$29,077.65	$1,132.35U Volume Variance
Budget for standard hours	30,210.00	$240.00F Efficiency Variance
Budget for actual hours	29,970.00	
Actual costs	30,094.40	$124.40U Spending Variance

The manufacturing overhead variances for the month of January that were determined by the three-variance analysis are summarized in Exhibit 5. As you have seen, the spending variance plus the efficiency variance equals the budget variance. The total variance equals the budget variance plus the volume variance.

INDUSTRIAL TRAY COMPANY   Exhibit 5
Manufacturing Overhead Variances Summary
Month Ended January 31, 19X2

DEPARTMENT	SPENDING VARIANCE	EFFICIENCY VARIANCE	BUDGET VARIANCE	VOLUME VARIANCE	TOTAL VARIANCE
Forming	$ 2.00U	$604.00U	$606.00U	$1,094.00U	$1,700.00U
Finishing	124.40U	240.00F	115.60F	1,132.35U	1,016.75U
Total	$126.40U	$364.00U	$490.40U	$2,226.35U	$2,716.75U

Recording Product Costs and Variances

The production costs for the period are journalized. The data used are from the summary of manufacturing overhead costs (Exhibit 4) and the manufacturing overhead variances summary (Exhibit 5). The Work in Process account is charged for the total standard costs of $52,513.65 for the period. The Manufacturing Overhead Control account is credited for the actual overhead costs incurred, which totaled $55,230.40. Any difference is accounted for by the manufacturing overhead variances from Exhibit 5. If a two-variance system is used, the entry is as shown on page 469.

19X2					
Jan. 31	Work in Process (Standard Cost)	122	52,513.65		
	Manufacturing Overhead Budget Variance	507	490.40		
	Manufacturing Overhead Volume Variance	508	2,226.35		
	Manufacturing Overhead Control				
	(Actual Cost)	501		55,230.40	
	Charged Work in Process with standard				
	costs, cleared actual overhead costs				
	from the control account, and recorded				
	the variances.				

If a three-variance system were used, Manufacturing Overhead Spending Variance would be debited for $126.40 and Manufacturing Overhead Efficiency Variance would be debited for $364.00. These two accounts would replace Manufacturing Overhead Budget Variance. All other accounts would be debited and/or credited in the same way as in a two-variance system.

Disposition of Standard Cost Variances

There is no unanimous agreement on the proper handling of standard cost variances. Some of the procedures currently used for disposing of the variance accounts are outlined below.

- The variances are prorated each month among Cost of Goods Sold, Finished Goods, and Work in Process. This restores the accounts to actual cost.
- The variances are allowed to accumulate each month until the end of the year when the variance accounts are either prorated or closed into Cost of Goods Sold.
- The variance accounts are closed into Cost of Goods Sold at the end of each month. The variances are shown as a part of the Cost of Goods Sold on the income statement. (See the income statement at the top of page 470.)
- The variances are closed into the Income and Expense Summary account at the end of each month and are shown as other income or other expense on the income statement.

For amounts that are immaterial, probably the most common practice is to accumulate variances during the year and then close them into Cost of Goods Sold at the end of the year. If the amounts are large, they should be allocated among Cost of Goods Sold, Finished Goods, and Work in Process.

Transfer of Finished Goods

Under a standard cost system, units of production completed during the period are valued at their standard cost when transferred from Work in Process to Finished Goods. Thus the 4,500 trays completed in January at a standard cost of $42.910 apiece are transferred by means of the following general journal entry:

```
                        INDUSTRIAL TRAY COMPANY
                         Partial Income Statement
                       Month Ended January 31, 19X2

Sales                                                      $307,200.00

Cost of Goods Sold (at
    Standard Cost)                              $205,968.00
    Add Materials Quantity Variance   $1,280.00
        Materials Price Variance         216.00
        Labor Efficiency Variance        640.00
        Labor Rate Variance              940.00
        Mfg. Overhead Volume
            Variance                   2,226.35
        Mfg. Overhead Budget
            Variance                     490.40    5,792.75
    Cost of Goods Sold—Adjusted                              211,760.75
Gross Profit on Sales                                      $ 95,439.25
Operating Expenses                                           72,776.00
Net Income Before Income Taxes                             $ 22,663.25

Provision for Income Taxes                                    3,400.00
Net Income After Income Taxes                              $19,263.25
```

19X2				
Jan. 31	Finished Goods (Standard Cost)	126	193,095.00	
	Work in Process (Standard Cost)	122		193,095.00
	Removed standard cost of 4,500 trays at $42.910 each from Work in Process and transferred cost to Finished Goods.			

Finally, when products are sold, the transfer from Finished Goods to Cost of Goods Sold is also priced at standard cost. If 4,800 trays were sold during the month, the transfer would be recorded as follows:

19X2				
Jan. 31	Cost of Goods Sold (Standard Cost)	415	205,968.00	
	Finished Goods (Standard Cost)	126		205,968.00
	Recorded cost of sales of 4,800 trays with standard cost of $42.910 each.			

Principles and Procedures Summary

Setting up and using a standard cost system for manufacturing overhead is much the same as for materials and labor. However, service department overhead costs must be allocated, and the overhead costs must be separated into fixed and variable costs.

A two-variance or three-variance system may be used to analyze differences between standard and actual overhead costs. The most widely used system is a two-variance system. In this system, a budget or controllable variance and a volume variance are computed. The budget variance is for variable costs. The volume variance is for fixed costs. In a three-variance system, the budget variance is divided into two parts: a spending variance and an efficiency variance.

Review Questions

1. Why are overhead costs harder to control than materials and labor costs?
2. How is the standard overhead rate per hour computed? What is the relationship between the standard overhead rate per direct labor hour and the standard overhead rate per unit of product?
3. When standard costs are used, how are service department costs allocated?
4. How is the total manufacturing overhead variance in a department computed?
5. How is the overhead budget variance computed? Is the budget variance related mainly to variable costs or to fixed costs?
6. Is the manufacturing overhead variance a controllable variance? Explain.
7. Explain how the manufacturing overhead efficiency variance is computed.
8. What is the manufacturing overhead spending variance?
9. Is an unfavorable variance recorded by a debit or by a credit?
10. What is the most common way to dispose of variances?
11. Describe the journal entry to charge overhead to Work in Process under a standard cost system.
12. What entry is made to transfer the cost of completed products from Work in Process to Finished Goods when a standard cost accounting system is used?

Managerial Discussion Questions

1. Is management likely to be more interested in the total overhead variance or the individual components of the variance? Why?
2. Cost analysis at a company shows management that during the month of April the budgeted overhead for the level of production actually exceeded the actual costs incurred. Is this situation favorable or unfavorable? What reasons might exist for this situation?
3. During March 19X4, the Gold Star Company had a substantial unfavorable manufacturing overhead volume variance. As a result, the company's top management asked the production manager to explain the variance. What factors are likely to be included in the production manager's explanation?
4. The controller of the Allen Products Corporation closes all overhead variances into Cost of Goods Sold at the end of each year. Management has questioned a rather large amount that was charged off because of underapplied overhead at the end of the year just past. What arguments might the controller use to support this action?

5. The Chang Corporation has been using a two-variance approach to analyze overhead variances. Management has learned that some companies use a three-variance method and wants to know why and how this method differs from the one now being used. Explain.

Exercises

DATA FOR EXERCISES 1–9

The standard manufacturing overhead cost of one unit of product in a department is $17.50 for 19X1, computed as follows:

Number of units produced at normal volume	10,000 units
Number of direct labor hours at normal volume	25,000 hours
Fixed overhead budgeted	$100,000
Variable overhead budgeted (25,000 hours at $3 per hour)	75,000
Total budgeted costs at normal capacity	175,000
Standard overhead per unit ($175,000 ÷ 10,000 units)	17.50

During May, 1,200 units were produced requiring 3,010 hours of labor. The total costs were

Fixed	$ 8,333
Variable	8,729
Total	$17,062

1. **Computing budgeted fixed overhead costs.** Assuming that all fixed costs are incurred evenly throughout the year, determine the total budgeted fixed overhead costs for May.
2. **Computing budgeted variable overhead costs.** Determine the total budgeted variable overhead costs for the 1,200 units produced in May.
3. **Computing total budgeted overhead costs.** Determine the total budgeted overhead costs for the 1,200 units produced.
4. **Computing standard overhead costs.** Determine the standard overhead costs of the 1,200 units produced.
5. **Computing a total overhead variance.** Determine the total overhead variance for the month. Is it favorable or unfavorable?
6. **Computing an overhead efficiency variance.** Determine the overhead efficiency variance for the month. Is it favorable or unfavorable?
7. **Computing an overhead spending variance.** Determine the overhead spending variance for the month. Is it favorable or unfavorable?
8. **Computing an overhead volume variance.** Determine the overhead volume variance for the month. Is it favorable or unfavorable?
9. **Making a journal entry to record overhead costs and variances.** Give the entry in general journal form to charge the manufacturing overhead costs to production and to record the overhead variances computed in the preceding exercises.

Problems

PROBLEM 23-1. Computing a total overhead variance, a budget variance, and a volume variance. The Grossinger Manufacturing Company uses a standard cost system. The manufacturing overhead standard rate of $2.50 per unit is based on a normal yearly volume of 80,000 units, requiring 40,000 direct labor hours, and on normal budgeted costs at that volume as shown.

Fixed Costs	$120,000
Variable Costs	80,000
Total	$200,000

During the month of April 19X1, the company produced 6,800 units of its product, requiring 3,290 direct labor hours. Actual manufacturing overhead costs for the month included fixed costs of $10,000 and variable costs of $6,720.

Instructions

1. Compute the total variance between the actual and standard overhead costs for the month of April. Show whether the variances are favorable (F) or unfavorable (U).
2. Divide the variance into its component parts—a budget variance and a volume variance.

PROBLEM 23-2. Computing materials, labor, and overhead variances. The Burnett Corporation manufactures one product. Its standard costs under efficient operating conditions are as follows:

Material, 12 gal at $.40 per gal	$ 4.80
Direct Labor, 1 hr at $6 per hr	6.00
Manufacturing Overhead, 1 hr at $4 per hr	4.00
Total Standard Costs per Unit	$14.80

The manufacturing overhead rate is based on a normal yearly volume of 200,000 direct labor hours. The fixed overhead costs total $240,000 per year. Production and cost figures for the month of May 19X1 are as follows:

Units of Product Manufactured	15,000 units
Raw Materials Used	182,300 gal
Direct Labor Hours Worked	15,400 hr
Cost per Gallon of Raw Materials	$.38
Labor Rate per Hour	$6.20
Manufacturing Overhead Costs Incurred	$66,200.00

Instructions

1. Compute the total materials variance from the standard. Divide this variance into its two component parts, showing whether each is favorable or unfavorable.
2. Compute the total labor variance from the standard. Divide this variance into its two component parts, showing whether each is favorable or unfavorable.
3. Compute the total manufacturing overhead variance from the standard. Divide this variance into the budget variance and the volume variance. Then divide the budget variance into its two component parts.
4. Which person in the company is most likely to be responsible for each of the variance factors that you determined above?

PROBLEM 23-3. Making journal entries to charge costs to production, to record variances, and to transfer costs to finished goods. The actual costs, standard costs, and variances applicable to work performed in the Production Department of the Akito Company during August 19X5 are given below.

	Actual Costs	Standard Costs	Variances
Materials	$147,300	$146,900	Price: $910 favorable Quantity: $1,310 unfavorable
Labor	81,000	81,150	Rate: $250 unfavorable Efficiency: $400 favorable
Manufacturing Overhead	46,625	46,300	Volume: $450 unfavorable Efficiency: $355 favorable Spending: $230 unfavorable

During the month, a total of 455 units with a standard cost of $274.35 each were completed and transferred to finished goods.

Instructions
1. Give the entries in general journal form to record each of the following. (Date the entries August 31, 19X5.)
   a. Charge the raw materials to production and record the materials variances.
   b. Charge the labor to production and record the labor variances.
   c. Charge the manufacturing overhead to production and record the variances.
   d. Transfer the completed units to finished goods.
2. Explain briefly how the variances might be handled on the financial statements.

PROBLEM 23-4. Computing standard overhead cost, a total overhead variance, a budget variance, and spending and efficiency variances. The Denmead Company's standard overhead rate is $10 per direct labor hour, based on expected production of 50,000 units of its product during the year. The overhead rate is based on budgeted fixed costs of $800,000 and budgeted variable costs of $200,000. Each unit requires 2 direct labor hours to complete.

During the year 19X7, 60,000 units were produced, requiring 122,000 hours of direct labor. The actual total overhead was $1,087,000.

Instructions
1. Compute the standard overhead cost per unit of product.
2. Compute the standard overhead cost charged to Work in Process during the year.
3. Compute the total overhead variance for the year and show whether it is favorable or unfavorable.
4. Compute the budget variance and the volume variance and show whether each is favorable or unfavorable.
5. Divide the budget variance into the spending variance and the efficiency variance and show whether each is favorable or unfavorable.

Alternate Problems

PROBLEM 23-1A. Computing a total overhead variance, a budget variance, and a volume variance. Wilkinson, Inc., uses a standard cost system. The manufacturing overhead standard rate of $6 per unit of its product is based on a normal yearly volume of 100,000 units, requiring 20,000 direct labor hours, and on normal budgeted costs at that volume as shown.

Fixed Costs	$200,000
Variable Costs	400,000
Total	$600,000

During the month of May 19X1, the company produced 8,200 units of its product, requiring 1,700 direct labor hours. Actual manufacturing overhead costs for the month included fixed costs of $16,667 and variable costs of $33,260.

Instructions

1. Compute the total variance between the actual and standard overhead costs for the month of May. Round off amounts to the nearest dollar. Show whether the variances are favorable (F) or unfavorable (U).
2. Divide the variance into its parts—a budget variance and a volume variance.

PROBLEM 23-2A. Computing materials, labor, and overhead variances. The Tallahassee Company manufactures one product. Its standard costs under efficient operating conditions are as follows:

Material, 5 lb at $4 per lb	$20.00
Direct Labor, 3 hr at $6 per hr	18.00
Manufacturing Overhead, 3 hr at $3 per hr	9.00
Total Standard Costs per Unit	$47.00

The manufacturing overhead rate is based on a normal yearly volume of 360,000 direct labor hours. The fixed overhead totals $360,000 per year. Production and cost figures for the month of April 19X1 are as follows:

Units of Product Manufactured	10,500 units
Raw Materials Used	53,000 lb
Direct Labor Hours Worked	31,320 hr
Cost per Pound of Raw Materials	$4.04
Direct Labor Rate per Hour	$6.08
Manufacturing Overhead Costs Incurred	$92,200.00

Instructions

1. Compute the total materials variance from the standard. Divide this variance into its two component parts, showing whether each is favorable or unfavorable.
2. Compute the total direct labor variance from the standard. Divide this variance into its two component parts, showing whether each is favorable or unfavorable.
3. Compute the total manufacturing overhead variance from the standard. Divide this variance into the budget variance and the volume variance. Then divide the budget variance into its two component parts.
4. Which person in the company is most likely to be responsible for each of the variance factors that you determined above?

PROBLEM 23-3A. Making journal entries to charge costs to production, to record variances, and to transfer costs to finished goods. The actual costs, standard costs, and variances applicable to work performed in the Production Department of the Reardon Company during July 19X1 are given on page 476.

	Actual Costs	Standard Costs	Variances
Materials	$294,600	$293,800	Price: $1,820 favorable
			Quantity: $2,620 unfavorable
Labor	162,000	162,300	Rate: $500 unfavorable
			Efficiency: $800 favorable
Manufacturing Overhead	93,250	92,600	Volume: $900 unfavorable
			Efficiency: $710 favorable
			Spending: $460 unfavorable

During the month, a total of 910 units with a standard cost of $548.70 each were completed and transferred to finished goods.

Instructions

1. Give general journal entries dated July 31, 19X1, to record the following:
   a. Charge the raw materials to production and record the materials variances.
   b. Charge the labor to production and record the labor variances.
   c. Charge the manufacturing overhead to production and record the variances.
   d. Transfer the completed units to finished goods.
2. Explain briefly how the variances might be handled on the financial statements.

PROBLEM 23-4A. Computing standard overhead cost, a total overhead variance, a budget variance, and spending and efficiency variances. The Gregory Corporation's standard overhead rate is $24 per direct labor hour. The overhead rate is based on budgeted fixed costs of $400,000 and budgeted variable costs of $200,000. Each unit requires 15 minutes of direct labor.

During the year, 27,000 units were produced, requiring 32,000 direct labor hours, at an actual total overhead cost of $672,000.

Instructions

1. Compute the standard overhead cost per unit of product.
2. Compute the standard overhead cost charged to Work in Process during the year.
3. Compute the total overhead variance for the year and show whether it is favorable or unfavorable.
4. Compute the budget variance and the volume variance and show whether each is favorable or unfavorable.
5. Divide the budget variance into the spending variance and the efficiency variance and show whether each is favorable or unfavorable.

3

Budgets and Standard Costs

In this project you will apply the techniques and principles of budgeting and standard costs to the operations of Fast Truck, Inc. You will prepare budgets for the year ended December 31, 19X6, and you will compute variances for the month of January 19X6.

Budgets and Standards

Fast Truck, Inc., is a manufacturer of a battery-powered plastic toy truck that is sold in toy stores across the country. In the firm's manufacturing process, specially trained employees operate injection molding machines that form semiliquid plastic into the body of the truck. Assemblers insert a battery-driven motor assembly, which the firm purchases from a subcontractor, into the molded truck body. Then the assemblers add wheels and axles (also purchased from a subcontractor) and decorative trim to complete the toy.

Sales Budget

In order to prepare a sales budget for 19X6, the sales manager for Fast Truck, Inc., studied the following: sales data relating to the toy truck; demographic data about the number of children ages 3 to 6 in the population; and predictions of future economic conditions. Using this data, a sales budget of 122,000 trucks was set for 19X6.

Production Budget

Fast Truck, Inc., expects to begin 19X6 with an inventory of 14,000 completed toy trucks. The company would like to reduce its finished goods inventory of toy trucks at the end of 19X6 by 2,000 trucks, to 12,000.

Standards

With the aid of the engineering staff, the purchasing department, the factory supervisors, and the personnel department, Fast Truck, Inc., has established the following standards for direct materials and direct labor, which should be attainable under normal circumstances. Data related to direct materials follow:

Material	Quantity	Cost per Unit	Cost per Truck
Plastic	1.5 lb per truck	$1.70 per lb	$2.55
Motor assembly	1 motor per truck	3.25 per motor	3.25
Wheels and axles	1 set per truck	.20 per set	.20
			$6.00

NOTE: Paint and stickers for decorative trim are considered part of indirect materials.

Data related to direct labor follow:

Job Title	Hours per Truck	Rate per Hour	Cost per Truck
Molders	.2	$7.50	$1.50
Assemblers	.3	9.00	2.70
	.5		$4.20

Materials Budget

Beginning inventories of raw materials on January 1, 19X6, are expected to be as follows:

Material	Amount
Plastic	11,000 lb
Motors	8,000 motors
Wheels and axles	5,000 sets

Fast Truck, Inc., would like to have enough raw materials on hand at the end of the year to equal the following percentages of the 19X6 budgeted requirements:

Material	Percentage of 19X6 Budget
Plastic	5%
Motors	10%
Wheels and axles	1%

Manufacturing Overhead Budget

The company has prepared the manufacturing overhead budget for the year 19X6, as shown on page 479.

Budgeting Procedures to Be Completed

As part of the budgeting process of Fast Truck, Inc., you are to prepare the following budgets for the year ended December 31, 19X6. Remember that the sales budget has already been prepared. (See text page 477.) (All the forms required to complete the budgeting procedures are found in the *Study Guide and Working Papers.* If you are not using the *Study Guide and Working Papers,* you may prepare your answers on analysis paper or on lined paper.)

A-1. Prepare a production budget.
A-2. Prepare a materials budget.
A-3. Prepare a direct labor budget.
A-4. Prepare a manufacturing costs budget. (Include costs per truck.)
A-5. Prepare a monthly flexible overhead budget at 90, 100, and 110 percent of capacity.

```
                          FAST TRUCK, INC.
                     Manufacturing Overhead Budget
                     Year Ended December 31, 19X6
             (Based on 60,000 direct labor hours and 120,000 trucks)
```

	VARIABLE OVERHEAD	FIXED OVERHEAD	TOTAL OVERHEAD
Controllable Costs			
Indirect Materials	$ 1,200	—	$ 1,200
Indirect Labor	60,000	$ 60,000	120,000
Payroll Taxes and Fringe Benefits	84,000	9,000	93,000
Utilities	9,600	12,000	21,600
Repairs and Miscellaneous	10,200	9,600	19,800
Noncontrollable Costs			
Depreciation	—	42,000	42,000
Insurance	—	12,000	12,000
Total Manufacturing Overhead	$165,000	$144,600	$309,600

Standard Cost Accounting Procedures to Be Completed

During January 19X6, Fast Truck, Inc., manufactured 9,600 toy trucks. The actual costs of materials, labor, and overhead were as follows:

Material	Amount
Plastic	14,100 lb at $1.80 per lb
Motors	9,950 motors at $3.12 per motor
Wheels and axles	9,775 sets at $.24 per set

Direct Labor	Hours	Rate
Molders	1,860 hr	$7.60 per hr
Assemblers	3,020 hr	9.20 per hr

Overhead	Amount
Variable	$13,120
Fixed	12,050

As part of the standard cost system at Fast Truck, Inc., you are to prepare the following for the month of January 19X6. For all variances computed, show whether they are favorable or unfavorable. (If you are not using the *Study Guide and Working Papers,* you may prepare your answers on analysis paper or on lined paper.)

B-1. Prepare a summary of materials costs.
B-2. Prepare a summary of labor costs.
B-3. Compute the quantity and price variances for each material.
B-4. Compute the efficiency and rate variances for each type of labor.
B-5. Compute the total manufacturing overhead variance, and divide it into the budget variance and the volume variance.
B-6. Prepare entries in general journal form to record each of the following. (Omit explanations.)

a. Charge the raw materials to production and record the materials variances.

b. Charge the labor to production and record the labor variances.

c. Charge the manufacturing overhead to production and record the overhead variances.

d. Transfer the completed units to finished goods.

Managerial Decisions

From the data given on pages 477 to 479 and the work you have done, answer the following questions about the operations of Fast Truck, Inc. (Write your answers to these questions on the ruled paper provided in the *Study Guide and Working Papers* or on separate sheets.)

1. What factors might cause Fast Truck, Inc., to revise its sales budget for the year?
2. What factors might have influenced the management of Fast Truck, Inc., to set the level of the ending inventory for plastic, motors, and wheels and axles at 5, 10, and 1 percent of budgeted requirements for the year?
3. a. Assume that production in February was 11,000 trucks.
   (1) What would be the total budgeted variable overhead cost?
   (2) What would be the total budgeted fixed overhead cost?
   (3) What would be the total budgeted overhead cost?
   b. Assume that production in March was 10,500 trucks.
   (1) What would be the total budgeted cost for indirect materials?
   (2) What would be the total budgeted cost for utilities?
   (3) What would be the total budgeted cost for insurance?
4. If Fast Truck, Inc., wanted to make a gross profit of 40 percent for the year, what selling price would it use?
5. The president of Fast Truck, Inc., thinks that the standard costs should be based on theoretical standards instead of normal standards as a way to motivate employees to reach a higher level of performance. What do you think about this plan?
6. Explain how the variances that you have computed for Fast Truck, Inc., might be handled on the financial statements.
7. Answer the following questions about the materials variances:
   a. Give some possible causes for each materials variance that you computed.
   b. Which person in the company is probably responsible for each of these variances?
8. Answer the following questions about the labor variances:
   a. Give some possible causes for each labor variance that you computed.
   b. Which person in the company is probably responsible for each of these variances?
9. Answer the following questions about the manufacturing overhead variances:
   a. Give some possible causes for each overhead variance that you computed.
   b. Which person in the company is probably responsible for each of these variances?

CHAPTER 24

Direct Costing: Cost-Volume-Profit Analysis (Break-Even Analysis)

■ ■ ■

The systems you have studied up to this point have used a concept known as absorption costing in assigning costs to products. This chapter will cover a new concept—direct costing. In addition, the concept of cost-volume-profit analysis will be introduced.

Absorption Costing

Absorption or *full costing* is based on the idea that all manufacturing costs, both direct and indirect, should be assigned to the cost of goods manufactured. These costs are then offset against the revenue for the period in which the goods are sold. Materials and labor costs are identified directly with units manufactured. Manufacturing overhead costs are assigned to production using some method of allocation. The validity and usefulness of product costs determined with absorption costing depend on the ability to allocate indirect costs in a reasonably correct manner.

Direct Costing

Direct or *variable costing* is based on the idea that not all factory costs are directly related to the product manufactured. Only those costs that are so closely associated with the product that they vary proportionately with the volume of production are assigned as product costs under direct costing.

Fixed costs are considered period costs. *Period costs* are costs that are identified with measured time intervals rather than with goods or services. They are charged directly to expense in the period in which they are incurred. These are generally the costs of providing the conditions for production rather than the actual costs of production. For example, depreciation, property taxes, property insurance, factory supervision, and a part of utilities are typical fixed costs necessary to carry on production. Such costs should be charged against revenue in the period incurred. In direct costing the only costs charged to the product are those costs which, because they have been incurred during the period, will not have to be incurred in some future period. Materials, direct labor, and variable manufacturing overhead are examples of such costs. These costs are deferred or inventoried until the product is sold. On the other hand, fixed costs must be incurred during each period regardless of whether products are sold or are kept in inventory.

Comparing Absorption Costing and Direct Costing

A comparison of absorption costing and direct costing makes it easier to evaluate and understand the two concepts. The Jarco Company manufactures one style of factory strength shelving and uses standard costing. Based on its normal production volume of 5,000 units, a standard cost sheet was prepared (Exhibit 1), as shown below.

The product has a sales price per unit of $100. Fixed selling and administrative expenses are estimated at $50,000. Variable selling and administrative expenses are estimated at $8 per unit sold.

JARCO COMPANY Standard Cost Sheet		Exhibit 1
Materials		$20.00
Labor		15.00
Manufacturing Overhead		
Variable Costs	$ 5.00	
Fixed Costs ($150,000 ÷ 5,000 units)	30.00	35.00
Standard Manufacturing Cost per Unit		$70.00

The budgeted income statement (Exhibit 2) for the year 19X1 appears on page 483.

During the year 19X1, there were 5,000 units produced but only 3,000 units were sold, and the following actual costs were incurred:

Materials	$100,000	
Labor	75,000	
Manufacturing Overhead		
Fixed	150,000	
Variable	25,000	
Selling and Administrative		
Fixed	50,000	
Variable	24,000	

The company had no beginning inventory of finished goods on January 1, 19X1.

Absorption Costing Approach

Based on the data for 19X1 above, an income statement using absorption costing is prepared, as shown in Exhibit 3, on page 483. Note that with absorption costing, a net income of $16,000 is calculated. Fixed manufacturing costs are $30 per unit

```
                JARCO COMPANY                          Exhibit 2
            Budgeted Income Statement
            Year Ending December 31, 19X1

Sales (5,000 units at $100 each)                       $500,000.00

Cost of Sales

  Materials (5,000 units at $20
    each)                                 $100,000.00
  Labor (5,000 units at $15 each)           75,000.00
  Manufacturing Overhead
    Fixed               $150,000.00
    Variable (5,000 units at $5
      each)               25,000.00        175,000.00   350,000.00
Gross Margin on Sales                                  $150,000.00

Selling and Administrative

  Expenses

  Fixed                                   $ 50,000.00
  Variable (5,000 units at $8 each)         40,000.00    90,000.00
Estimated Net Income                                   $ 60,000.00
```

(Exhibit 1). The ending inventory shown on the income statement (Exhibit 3) includes $60,000 in fixed costs (2,000 units × $30). This amount is carried forward as part of the beginning inventory on January 1, 19X2.

```
                JARCO COMPANY                          Exhibit 3
                Income Statement
               (Absorption Costing)
            Year Ended December 31, 19X1

Sales (3,000 units at $100 each)                       $300,000

Cost of Sales

  Materials (5,000 units at $20 each)     $100,000
  Labor (5,000 units at $15 each)           75,000
  Manufacturing Overhead (5,000 units
    at $35 each)                           175,000
    Total Cost of Goods Manufactured      $350,000
  Less Ending Inventory, December 31
    (2,000 units at $70 each)              140,000       210,000
Gross Margin on Sales                                   $ 90,000
Selling and Administrative Expenses

  Fixed                                   $ 50,000
  Variable (3,000 units at $8 each)         24,000        74,000
Net Income                                             $ 16,000
```

During the year 19X2, production was cut to 3,250 units but sales rose to 4,750 units. Actual costs for 19X2 follow:

Materials	$ 65,000
Labor	48,750
Manufacturing Overhead	
Fixed	150,000
Variable	16,250
Selling and Administrative	
Fixed	50,000
Variable	38,000

There is an unfavorable manufacturing overhead volume variance of $52,500 since not all fixed costs were applied.

Actual fixed manufacturing costs	$150,000
Applied fixed costs (3,250 units at $30 per unit)	97,500
Unfavorable variance (underapplied overhead)	$ 52,500

The income statement for 19X2, based on absorption costing, is shown in Exhibit 4 on page 485. One of the problems of using absorption costing is clearly shown in Exhibit 4. Sales rose from 3,000 to 4,750 units in 19X2. Yet net income declined from $16,000 to $2,000. Certainly, the cost accountant must be prepared to explain such seemingly contradictory results. However, the impact of changes in sales and production volume under absorption costing are difficult to explain to management.

Direct Costing Approach

Direct costing is rarely used for outside financial reporting because it does not conform to generally accepted accounting principles. However, many accountants think direct costing is better than absorption costing for use within a company. Under direct costing, the net income or net loss is directly related to sales revenue. The net income or net loss is not affected by variations in inventory levels or by production changes. Furthermore, direct costing emphasizes the full impact of fixed costs on net income since these costs are not deferred but are charged to expense when they are incurred. For the same reason, no arbitrary allocations of fixed overhead are required.

Management requires a knowledge of cost behavior under various operating conditions and at different levels of output. Also, costs must be classified into their fixed and variable components in most analyses performed for planning and control purposes. Under direct costing, the data are available in this form in the accounting records. This is a basic advantage of direct costing for management. Thus, management is willing to incur extra costs to accumulate direct cost data.

Direct costing is particularly valuable since it concentrates attention on the *contribution margin,* the excess of revenue over variable costs. The contribution margin is the amount available to cover fixed costs and produce a profit.

Using the data from the Jarco Company, income statements for 19X1 (Exhibit 5, page 486) and 19X2 (Exhibit 6, page 487) are prepared using direct costing.

In 19X1, a difference of $60,000 exists between the net income of $16,000 reported under absorption costing and the net loss of $44,000 reported under direct

Exhibit 4

JARCO COMPANY
Income Statement
(Absorption Costing)
Year Ended December 31, 19X2

Sales (4,750 at $100 each)		$475,000
Cost of Sales		
Beginning Inventory, January 1	$140,000	
Materials (3,250 at $20 each)	$ 65,000	
Labor (3,250 at $15 each)	48,750	
Manufacturing Overhead (3,250 at $35 each)	113,750 227,500	
Total Cost of Goods Manufactured	$367,500	
Less Ending Inventory, December 31 (500 at		
$70 each)	35,000	
Cost of Sales at Standard	$332,500	
Add Unfavorable Overhead Volume Variance	52,500 385,000	
Gross Margin on Sales		$ 90,000
Selling and Administrative Expenses		
Fixed	$ 50,000	
Variable	38,000 88,000	
Net Income		$ 2,000

costing. The $60,000 reflects the fixed costs associated with the 2,000 unsold units (2,000 × $30), which, under absorption costing, are carried forward as an asset to be charged against revenue only in a later period when the units are sold. Under direct costing, the fixed costs are considered to be period costs and are matched against revenue in the year the costs are incurred. No part of fixed costs is included in the finished goods inventory or the work in process inventory under direct costing.

In 19X2, a net income of $47,000 is reported under direct costing, compared with a net income of $2,000 under absorption costing. The difference, $45,000, reflects fixed costs from prior years that were charged against the current year's (19X2) revenue under absorption costing (1,500 × $30). The 1,500 units represent reduction in inventory from 2,000 to 500 units, as shown in Exhibit 7 on page 487.

One major advantage of direct costing is that it more clearly reflects the impact of volume on costs and profits. When the Jarco Company's sales increased by 58 percent in 19X2, its net income under direct costing reflected the increase. The Jarco Company went from a net loss of $44,000 in 19X1 to a net income of $47,000 in 19X2. However, when sales increased, the net income under absorption costing dropped from $16,000 to $2,000.

Sometimes production and sales are equal. This means that there is no change in inventories. When this happens, both direct costing and absorption costing report the same net income. If production is greater than sales, and inventories increase, the net income under absorption costing will be greater than under direct costing. This is because under absorption costing some of the fixed costs incurred during the year will be deferred as part of the cost of the increase in the finished goods inventory. However, under direct costing, all the fixed costs are charged to expense in the year they are incurred. Therefore, a decrease in inventory results in a lower net income under absorption costing than under direct costing. Under direct costing, the only fixed costs charged to expense are those incurred in the current period. Under absorption costing, the fixed costs (included in the units represented by the reduction in the beginning inventory) are also charged against revenues in any period that the number of units sold exceeds the number of units produced.

The use of direct costing increases the meaningfulness of overall financial reporting. Many accountants, however, feel that the prime benefit of direct costing is the use of the data in profitability, break-even, and decision cost analyses. Direct costing has not yet been approved by groups that set external reporting requirements.

JARCO COMPANY Income Statement (Direct Costing) Year Ended December 31, 19X1		Exhibit 5
Sales (3,000 units at $100 each)		$300,000
Variable Costs		
Manufacturing Costs		
Materials (5,000 units at $20 each)	$100,000	
Labor (5,000 units at $15 each)	75,000	
Manufacturing Overhead (5,000 units at $5 each)	25,000	
Total Variable Manufacturing Costs	$200,000	
Less Ending Inventory, December 31 (2,000 units at $40 each)	80,000	
Net Variable Manufacturing Costs	$120,000	
Selling and Administrative Expenses (3,000 units at $8 each)	24,000	144,000
Contribution Margin		$156,000
Fixed Costs		
Manufacturing Costs	$150,000	
Selling and Administrative Expenses	50,000	200,000
Net Loss		$(44,000)

Cost-Volume-Profit Relationships

The importance of the relationship between the volume of activity and the costs incurred has been stressed throughout this book. Direct costing, which was discussed earlier in this chapter, emphasizes the relationship between costs, volume, and profits. Management's use of cost-volume-profit (C-V-P) relationships goes far beyond direct costing, however. The analysis of C-V-P data helps to provide the answers to such questions as the ones on pages 487 and 488.

```
                        JARCO COMPANY                          Exhibit 6
                        Income Statement
                        (Direct Costing)
                   Year Ended December 31, 19X2

Sales (4,750 units at $100 each)                                $475,000

Variable Costs

   Manufacturing Costs
      Beginning Inventory, January 1              $ 80,000
      Materials (3,250 units
         at $20 each)                  $65,000
      Labor (3,250 units
         at $15 each)                   48,750
      Manufacturing Overhead (3,250 units
         at $5 each)                    16,250    130,000
         Total Variable Manufacturing Costs      $210,000
      Less Ending Inventory, December 31
         (500 units at $40 each)                   20,000
         Net Variable Manufacturing Costs        $190,000
   Selling and Administrative Expenses
      (4,750 units at $8 each)                      38,000    228,000
Contribution Margin                                          $247,000

Fixed Costs

   Manufacturing Costs                           $150,000
   Selling and Administrative Expenses             50,000    200,000
Net Income                                                   $  47,000
```

```
                        JARCO COMPANY                          Exhibit 7
                     Reconciliation of Net Income
                 Direct Costing and Absorption Costing
                   Year Ended December 31, 19X2

Net Income—Direct Costing                                      $47,000
Less Net Income—Absorption Costing Difference                    2,000
                                                               $45,000

Beginning Finished Goods Inventory in Units      2,000
Less Ending Finished Goods Inventory in Units      500
   Inventory Change Extended at Fixed Rate       1,500 at $30  $45,000
```

1. What sales volume is required in order for the business to "break even" (to have neither a profit nor a loss)?
2. What sales volume would be necessary to produce a given amount of profit for the period?

3. What would be the impact of a specific change in gross profit per unit or of a specific change in the gross profit percentage?

Examples of the use of C-V-P analysis in answering such questions are given in the following pages.

Computing the Break-Even Point

In cost-volume-profit analysis, all costs—manufacturing, selling, and administrative—are separated into their fixed and variable components. The contribution margin is then computed by subtracting variable costs from sales. The contribution margin shows the amount that is available to pay fixed costs and to earn a profit. The use of this technique in computing the break-even point can best be explained with a simple example.

Susan Bell, a laundromat owner, has an opportunity to install a vending machine that will sell snack food. The machine has a fixed rental of $75 per month. She can purchase the packaged snack food in large quantities at 50 cents per package, including all taxes. She plans to sell them in the machine at 75 cents per package. Before deciding on whether to rent the machine, she must know how many packages of snack food she must sell each month to break even.

Several approaches can be used in computing the break-even sales volume. The contribution margin approach is based on the fact that from each package of snack food sold, 25 cents (selling price of 75 cents less variable costs of 50 cents) will be available for paying fixed costs and earning a profit. The number of packages of snack food that must be sold to break even is the number required at the contribution margin of 25 cents per package to pay the fixed costs of $75 per month. This number is calculated as follows:

$$\text{Break-Even Sales in Units per Period} = \frac{\text{Fixed Costs per Period}}{\text{Contribution Margin per Unit}}$$

$$= \frac{\$75 \text{ per month}}{25\cent \text{ per package}}$$

$$= 300 \text{ packages of snack food per month}$$

The break-even point may be computed by expressing the variable costs and contribution margin as percentages of the sales price. In this example, the variable costs are $66\frac{2}{3}$ percent of sales, and the contribution margin is $33\frac{1}{3}$ percent.

$$\text{Variable Cost Ratio} = \frac{\text{Variable Costs per Unit}}{\text{Sales Price per Unit}}$$

$$= \frac{50\cent \text{ per package}}{75\cent \text{ per package}} = 66\frac{2}{3} \text{ percent}$$

$$\text{Contribution Margin Ratio} = \frac{\text{Contribution Margin per Unit}}{\text{Sales Price per Unit}}$$

$$= \frac{25\cent \text{ per package}}{75\cent \text{ per package}} = 33\frac{1}{3} \text{ percent}$$

These ratios show that $33\frac{1}{3}$ percent of every sales dollar is available for paying fixed costs and earning a profit. Since there is no profit at the break-even point, the contribution margin at that point equals the fixed costs.

$$\text{Break-Even Sales in Dollars} = \frac{\text{Fixed Costs per Period}}{\text{Contribution Margin Ratio}}$$

$$= \frac{\$75 \text{ per month}}{.33\frac{1}{3}} = \$225 \text{ per month}$$

Estimating Profits at Different Sales Volumes

One way in which management commonly uses C-V-P analysis is to estimate what profits would be earned at different sales volumes, assuming that no change in selling price, variable costs per unit, or total fixed costs will occur. Once the contribution margin has been determined, it is an easy matter to estimate profit (or loss) at any level of sales.

For example, suppose that Susan Bell, for whose business the break-even point was computed above to be 300 packages of snack food a month, estimates that she will sell an average of 1,000 packages each month. The estimated profit will be $175 per month, computed by multiplying the contribution margin per unit by the projected sales and subtracting the fixed costs.

$$\text{Profit} = (\text{Unit Sales} \times \text{Contribution Margin per Unit}) - \text{Fixed Costs per Period}$$

$$= (1,000 \text{ packages} \times 25\text{¢ per package}) - \$75 \text{ per month}$$

$$= \$250 - \$75 = \$175 \text{ per month}$$

Estimating the Sales Necessary to Earn a Desired Profit

The break-even approach is also used to estimate sales required to make a specific profit. For example, what sales are needed for Susan Bell to make a profit of $50 a month?

$$\text{Sales in Dollars for Specific Profit} = \frac{\text{Fixed Costs per Period} + \text{Profit per Period}}{\text{Contribution Margin Ratio}}$$

$$= \frac{\$75 \text{ per month} + \$50 \text{ per month}}{.33\frac{1}{3}}$$

$$= \$375 \text{ per month}$$

The sales in units required for a specific profit level are as follows:

$$\text{Sales in Units for Specific Profit} = \frac{\text{Fixed Costs per Period} + \text{Profit per Period}}{\text{Contribution Margin per Unit}}$$

Thus, 500 packages a month must be sold to earn $50:

$$\text{Sales in Units} = \frac{\$75 \text{ per month} + \$50 \text{ per month}}{25\text{¢ per package}}$$

$$= 500 \text{ packages per month}$$

Break-Even Chart

A *break-even chart* may be prepared by the cost accountant to show the expected profit at any sales volume (either quantity or dollar volume). The illustration below shows the relation between volume, costs, and profits when volume is expressed in packages of snack food.

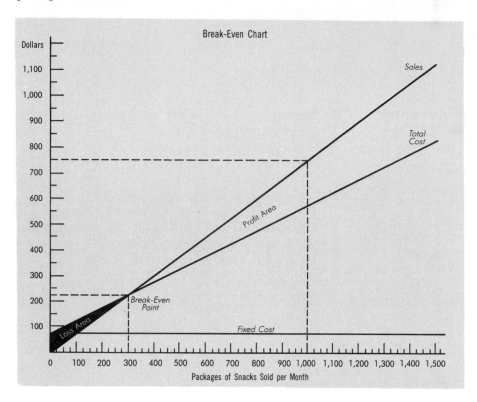

The vertical scale of the break-even chart above shows both the revenue from the sales of snack food and the total costs. The number of packages of snack food sold per month is given on the horizontal scale. The chart shows that the total revenue (sales) line and the total cost line cross at the break-even point of 300 packages per month. The estimated profit that would be earned at any volume of sales can be easily determined. For example, the chart shows that if the monthly sales are 1,000 packages, the total sales revenue will be $750 and the total costs will be $575, resulting in a profit of $175.

A break-even chart for a more complex business is shown on page 492. Sales, expressed in terms of total sales revenue instead of in terms of units sold, are shown on the horizontal axis. When a business sells more than one type of product, it is not practical to express sales in the number of units sold. The construction of this chart is discussed below.

Break-Even Analysis Based on Sales

The break-even analysis technique can be applied to a much more complex business than the one that has been illustrated—Susan Bell's proposed vending machine for snack food. All that is required is that the accountant be able to separate all costs into their variable and fixed components. For example, the accountant of the Marshall Manufacturing Company, which makes a variety of products, has analyzed and classified the costs of both manufacturing and nonmanufacturing operations and has prepared a budget based on the company's expected sales of $3,968,000 for 19X2.

MARSHALL MANUFACTURING COMPANY — Exhibit 8
Budget Showing Variable and Fixed Costs
Year Ending December 31, 19X2

Sales			$3,968,000
Costs			
Variable Costs			
Manufacturing Costs	$2,384,520		
Nonmanufacturing Costs	620,000		
Total Variable Costs		$3,004,520	
Fixed Costs			
Manufacturing Costs	$ 267,000		
Nonmanufacturing Costs	328,000		
Total Fixed Costs		595,000	
Total Variable and Fixed Costs			3,599,520
Budgeted Profit			$ 368,480

The contribution margin ratio can now be computed. First, the contribution margin—the excess of sales volume over total variable costs—is computed. This shows that at the budgeted sales level, $963,480 ($3,968,000 − $3,004,520), will be available to cover fixed costs and earn a profit. The contribution margin ratio is therefore 24.3 percent (rounded to the nearest one-tenth of a percent).

$$\text{Contribution Margin Ratio} = \frac{\text{Contribution Margin}}{\text{Sales}}$$

$$= \frac{\$963,480}{\$3,968,00} = 24.3 \text{ percent}$$

Since at the break-even point the contribution margin will equal fixed costs and since the contribution margin is 24.3 percent of sales, the break-even sales can be computed as $2,449,000 (rounded to the nearest thousand dollars).

$$\text{Sales at Break-Even Point} = \frac{\text{Fixed Costs per Period}}{\text{Contribution Margin Ratio}}$$

$$= \frac{\$595,000}{.243} = \$2,449,000$$

The break-even chart on page 492 is for the Marshall Manufacturing Company. Sales, expressed in millions of dollars, are shown on the horizontal axis, while sales and total costs, both expressed in millions of dollars, are shown on the vertical axis. The dashed lines show the break-even point is $2,499,000. No profit will be produced until the break-even point is passed, as shown in the profit area on the chart. Notice the great increase in dollar profits as volume increases past the break-even point.

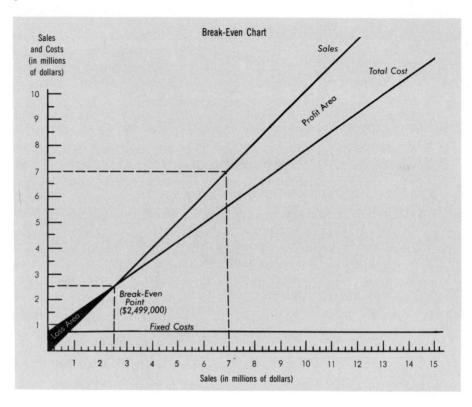

Break-Even Chart

Analyzing the Effects of Changes in C-V-P Factors

Cost-volume-profit analysis and break-even analysis are often used by management in estimating the effects on profits that would result from changes in economic conditions, operating conditions, or marketing strategies. For example, suppose that the marketing manager of the Marshall Manufacturing Company, whose budget and break-even chart were discussed above, proposes entering into a contract with an advertising agency that will cost an additional $32,000 per year for a period of three years. The management of the Marshall Manufacturing Company asks the accountant to estimate the annual increase in sales that would be necessary to justify this increase in advertising costs.

The accountant would probably consider this contract to represent an increase in fixed costs of $32,000 per year. Assuming no change in prices and no increase in other fixed costs resulting from an increase in sales volume, the accountant can make the estimate quickly. She has already estimated that 24.3 percent of each sales dollar is available for paying fixed costs and earning a profit. Thus, if the increase of $32,000 in fixed costs is to be recovered, sales volume must increase by about $131,700 ($32,000 ÷ .243). If management feels that sales cannot be increased by at least that amount, the contract should not be entered into.

It is obvious that in making management decisions, many factors must be considered. For example, in the above case, such factors as whether additional fixed costs will be necessary to maintain the required sales growth is an important consideration. In addition, even though the contract is for only a three-year period, it is likely that at least part of the higher level of sales obtained by the advertising may be kept even after the advertising is ended because of the goodwill and loyalty of the new customers who were attracted by the advertising campaign. Although consideration of such factors may change the decision, the ability to use C-V-P analysis greatly simplifies the task of arriving at a decision.

Computerized Accounting and Marketing Strategies

Long Haul, Inc., is a motor carrier that ships goods all over the United States. The marketplace in which Long Haul operates has changed since the Motor Carrier Act of 1980, which deregulated the trucking industry. New markets that were previously barred have become available. Truckers can bargain and compete in the areas of rates and services. Management of Long Haul, Inc., has decided that their information system should change and grow with the industry. In order for the company to survive in the marketplace, the system should provide easy access to current information on market forecasts, market size, and trends. They also needed data on Long Haul, Inc.'s, freight system, including coordination and feedback information. To keep current, representatives from the marketing, accounting, operations, personnel, and traffic departments meet monthly with the president and chairman of the board to plan.

B. I. Grigg, the cost accountant for Long Haul, uses the company's microcomputer to develop accounting information that will aid in the planning process. Mr. Grigg determines the profitability of the traffic system using standard costs and budgets in conjunction with contribution and profit margin ratios. Using the computer, profitability can be determined for the entire traffic system or for individual truck terminals, counties, states, or regions. Also, in order to predict the activities of shippers who may contract with Long Haul, Inc., Mr. Grigg maintains a computerized shipper file with the following for each shipper.

1. Past volumes shipped
2. Past contributions to profit
3. Location
4. Profitability of the shippers

At every monthly meeting, the information provided by Mr. Grigg is combined with other data (such as geographical statistics) to determine market strategies. ■

Principles and Procedures Summary

In direct costing, only variable manufacturing costs are considered product costs and used to price inventories. Fixed costs are classified as period costs and are charged against revenue in the period in which they are incurred. The direct costing method clearly reflects the impact of volume on costs and profits.

Direct costing is only one example of how the relationship between cost, volume, and profit can be shown. There are many other ways in which the accountant can make use of this relationship. By computing the contribution margin (the excess of sales over variable costs), the accountant determines the amount that is available for paying fixed costs and earning a profit. Through the use of the contribution margin, the accountant can compute the break-even point or can quickly estimate the profit that would result at any level of sales. C-V-P analysis also serves as a valuable tool for evaluating various operating plans.

Review Questions

1. How does absorption costing differ from direct costing as far as the costs considered when using the two methods?
2. Does direct costing assume that all factory costs are directly related to the product? Explain.
3. Under direct costing, how are fixed manufacturing overhead costs accounted for?
4. Is direct costing widely used in published financial reports?
5. Which method, direct costing or absorption costing, more clearly measures the impact of volume on costs and profits? Explain.
6. Assuming that more units are produced than are sold, would reported net income be larger under absorption costing or under direct costing? Why?
7. Under direct costing, how is profit affected by variations in the inventory of finished goods?
8. Under direct costing, what costs enter into the cost of finished goods?
9. What is meant by the term *contribution margin*?
10. What is meant by the term *break-even point*?
11. What is a break-even chart?
12. What is a C-V-P analysis?
13. Explain why profits will generally increase as volume increases.
14. Why is it sometimes not feasible to have the horizontal axis in a break-even chart expressed in units of product sold?
15. Explain why the cost line in a break-even chart does not start at zero cost.

Managerial Discussion Questions

1. What are the advantages to management of using a direct costing approach instead of an absorption costing approach?
2. You have told management that one of the advantages of direct costing is that it concentrates attention on the contribution margin. Management asks how contribution margin can be used in management control and decision making. Explain how.
3. Of what benefit to management is a break-even chart?
4. Explain how management can use the break-even approach to estimate quickly the sales volume needed to make a specific desired profit.
5. A company has computed its break-even point. A proposal has been made to increase fixed costs by $40,000 per year. This would result in a decrease in variable costs of $1.70 per unit. Explain how the accountant would go about determining the impact of this proposal on the break-even point.

Exercises

DATA FOR EXERCISES 1–4

The Harris Company has the following standard costs per unit for its one product:

Materials		$10
Labor		4
Manufacturing Overhead		
Variable	$4	
Fixed	8	12
Total		$26

The fixed cost of $8 per unit is based on producing 10,000 units and fixed overhead of $80,000. The sales price is $40 per unit. Selling and administrative expenses are as follows: variable, $2 per unit; fixed, $50,000 per year. During 19X1, 10,000 units were produced and sold.

1. **Computing a contribution margin.** Compute the Harris Company's contribution margin per unit for 19X1. Compute the total fixed costs for 19X1.
2. **Preparing an income statement on the basis of direct costing.** Prepare an income statement for the Harris Company for 19X1 based on direct costing.
3. **Computing a break-even point.** Compute the Harris Company's break-even point in units.
4. **Preparing an income statement on the basis of absorption costing.** Prepare an income statement for the Harris Company for 19X1 based on absorption costing.

DATA FOR EXERCISES 5 AND 6

Use the same information as given above for the Harris Company except that in 19X1, 10,800 units were produced and 10,000 units were sold.

5. **Preparing an income statement on the basis of direct costing.** Prepare an income statement for 19X1 based on direct costing.
6. **Preparing an income statement on the basis of absorption costing.** Prepare an income statement for 19X1 based on absorption costing.

7. **Computing a break-even point.** The Lewiston Company manufactures a product that sells for $124 per unit. The variable manufacturing costs are $60 per unit; the variable selling and administrative expenses are $20 per unit. The fixed manufacturing costs are $192,000 per year; the fixed selling and administrative expenses are $308,000 per year. Compute the number of units that must be sold each year for the company to break even.
8. **Determining sales volume.** A company's contribution margin ratio is 40 percent. Its fixed costs total $300,000 per year. What sales volume must be attained in order for the company to earn $150,000 per year?   /125000
9. **Determining sales volume.** A company's contribution margin is 48 percent. A proposal has been made to install certain equipment that would result in an increase of $50,000 per year in fixed costs, but would increase the contribution margin (through a decrease in variable costs) to 54 percent. Existing fixed costs are $260,000 per year. What increase in sales volume would be necessary in order to justify purchasing the equipment?

304o7

DATA FOR EXERCISES 10–13

An accounting student at Centerville College has taken a part-time job selling pack-aged cookies. Each box of cookies costs him $1.00 and has a selling price of $1.75. He estimates that operating costs will include fixed costs of $300 per month. His variable costs will be $.20 per box in addition to the cost of the cookies.

10. **Computing a break-even point.** Compute the contribution margin per unit. Compute the break-even point of the cookie business in units.
11. **Forecasting profit based on break-even analysis.** If sales total 500 boxes of cookies a month, what will be his net income or net loss?
12. **Forecasting profit based on break-even analysis.** If sales total 1,220 boxes of cookies a month, what will be his net income or net loss?
13. **Computing a contribution margin.** If sales total 800 boxes of cookies a month, what will be the total contribution margin of the cookie business?

Problems

PROBLEM 24-1 Preparing an income statement using absorption and direct costing. The Ellsworth Manufacturing Company makes one product. The company uses standard costing. During the year 19X5, the normal volume of 4,000 units was produced, and 3,000 units were sold for $200 each. Assume that there was no beginning inventory on January 1, 19X5. The following data are provided for the year 19X5:

	Costs Budgeted		Costs Incurred	
Materials ($40 per unit)		$160,000		$160,000
Labor ($50 per unit)		200,000		200,000
Manufacturing Overhead				
Fixed	$200,000		$200,000	
Variable ($10 per unit)	40,000	240,000	40,000	240,000
Rate per unit				
$240,000 ÷ 4,000 units		60		
Selling and Administrative				
Expenses				
Fixed	$ 80,000		$ 80,000	
Variable ($12 per unit sold)	48,000	128,000	36,000	116,000

Instructions

1. Prepare an income statement for the year 19X5 using absorption costing.
2. Prepare an income statement for the year 19X5 using direct costing.
3. Prepare a reconciliation of the net income under direct costing and absorption costing.

PROBLEM 24-2. Preparing an income statement using absorption and direct costing. During the year 19X6, the Dumont Manufacturing Company produced 5,400 units and sold 6,000 units at $200 each. The costs incurred were as follows:

Materials (5,400 units at $40 per unit)		$216,000
Labor (5,400 units at $50 per unit)		270,000
Manufacturing Overhead		
Fixed	$200,000	
Variable (5,400 units at $10 per unit)	54,000	254,000

Selling and Administrative Expenses
Fixed $ 80,000
Variable (6,000 units at $12 per unit)   72,000   152,000

Instructions

1. Prepare an income statement for the year 19X6 using absorption costing. The beginning inventory was $150,000.
2. Prepare an income statement for the year 19X6 using direct costing. The beginning inventory was $100,000.
3. Prepare a reconciliation of the net income under direct costing and absorption costing.

PROBLEM 24-3. Preparing a break-even analysis; forecasting net income. The Fieldstone Manufacturing Company produces one product, which is sold at a fixed price of $60 per unit. The yearly fixed costs of the company total $240,000. During the year 19X2, the company sold 12,000 units and reported a net income of $48,000.

Instructions

1. Compute the company's break-even sales in units and in dollars.
2. Prepare a simple break-even chart.
3. Compute the sales in units needed for the company to earn a net income of $80,000.

PROBLEM 24-4. Preparing a break-even analysis; forecasting net income or net loss. The Burke Corporation produces one product, which is sold at a fixed price of $10 per unit. For the year 19X1, the company operated at full capacity and a total of 100,000 units were sold. The company's fixed costs totaled $300,000 and the variable costs for the year were $500,000.

Instructions

1. Compute the company's break-even sales in units and in dollars.
2. Prepare a simple break-even chart.
3. How many units must be sold to make a net income of $120,000?
4. Assume that the company has forecast a net loss of $20,000 in 19X2. If all the other data given are correct, how many units are forecast to be sold in 19X2?

PROBLEM 24-5. Preparing a break-even analysis. Certain data related to the operations of the Nordon Corporation are given below.

Per Unit

Selling price	$10.00
Variable manufacturing costs	2.00
Variable selling and administrative expenses	4.00
Fixed manufacturing costs (based on 100,000 units)	.50
Fixed selling and administrative expenses (based on 100,000 units)	1.30

Instructions

1. Compute the projected annual break-even sales in units.
2. Assume that the selling price increases by 20 percent, variable manufacturing costs increase by 10 percent, variable selling and administrative expenses remain

the same, and total fixed costs increase to $208,000. How many units must be sold to produce a profit equal to 5 percent of sales?

PROBLEM 24-1A. Preparing an income statement using absorption and direct costing. The McKay Company manufactures one product. The company uses standard costing. During the year 19X2, the normal volume of 10,000 units was produced, and 7,500 units were sold for $198 each. Assume that there was no beginning inventory on January 1, 19X2. The following data are provided for the year 19X2:

	Costs Budgeted		Costs Incurred	
Materials ($39 per unit)		$390,000		$390,000
Labor ($49 per unit)		490,000		490,000
Manufacturing Overhead				
Fixed	$500,000		$500,000	
Variable ($9 per unit)	90,000	590,000	90,000	590,000
Rate per unit ($590,000 ÷				
10,000 units)		59		
Selling and Administrative				
Expenses				
Fixed	$198,000		$198,000	
Variable ($12.50 per unit sold)	125,000	323,000	93,750	291,750

Instructions

1. Prepare an income statement for the year 19X2 using absorption costing.
2. Prepare an income statement for the year 19X2 using direct costing.
3. Prepare a reconciliation of the net income under direct costing and absorption costing.

PROBLEM 24-2A. Preparing an income statement using absorption and direct costing. During the year 19X3 the Chin Company produced 13,500 units and sold 15,000 units at $198 each. The costs incurred were as follows:

Materials (13,500 units at $39 per unit)		$526,500
Labor (13,500 units at $49 per unit)		661,500
Manufacturing Overhead		
Fixed	$500,000	
Variable (13,500 units at $9 per unit)	121,500	621,500
Selling and Administrative Expenses		
Fixed	$198,000	
Variable (15,000 units at $12.50 per unit)	187,500	385,500

Instructions

1. Prepare an income statement for the year 19X3 using absorption costing. The beginning inventory was $367,500.
2. Prepare an income statement for the year 19X3 using direct costing. The beginning inventory was $242,500.
3. Prepare a reconciliation of the net income under direct costing and absorption costing.

PROBLEM 24-3A. **Preparing a break-even analysis; forecasting net income.**
The Bancroft Manufacturing Company produces one product, which is sold at a fixed price of $8 per unit. The yearly fixed costs of the company total $640,000. During the year 19X1, the company sold 500,000 units and reported a net income of $160,000.

Instructions
1. Compute the company's break-even sales in units and in dollars.
2. Prepare a simple break-even chart.
3. Compute the sales in units needed for the company to earn a net income of $300,000.

PROBLEM 24-4A. **Preparing a break-even analysis; forecasting net income or net loss.** The Stanley Manufacturing Company produces one product, which is sold at a fixed price of $30 per unit. For the year 19X1, the company operated at full capacity and a total of 40,000 units were sold. The company's fixed costs totaled $40,000, and the variable costs for the year were $960,000.

Instructions
1. Compute the company's break-even sales in units and in dollars.
2. Prepare a simple break-even chart.
3. How many units must be sold to make a net income of $80,000?
4. Assume that the company has forecast a net loss of $24,000 in 19X2. If all the other data given are correct, how many units are forecast to be sold in 19X2?

PROBLEM 24-5A. **Preparing a break-even analysis.** Certain data related to the operations of the Myers Corporation are given below.

	Per Unit
Selling price	$30.00
Variable manufacturing costs	10.00
Variable selling and administrative expenses	9.00
Fixed manufacturing costs (based on 150,000 units)	4.00
Fixed selling and administrative expenses (based on 150,000 units)	4.00

Instructions
1. Compute the projected annual break-even sales in units.
2. Assume that the selling price increases by 15 percent, variable manufacturing costs decrease by 1 percent, variable selling and administrative expenses increase by 5 percent, and total fixed costs increase to $1,500,000. How many units must be sold to produce a profit equal to 12 percent of sales?

Managerial Decisions

CASE 24-1. A manufacturer of high-quality hand-crafted luggage sells 10,000 units per year at a selling price of $180 per unit. At the end of the current year, a new labor contract is being negotiated. The proposed contract calls for an increase of 12 percent in direct labor rates and would result in an increase of $10,000 per year in fixed costs. Data about current operations are shown below.

	Per Unit
Sales price	$180
Variable costs	
Materials	30
Labor (including taxes and fringe benefits)	60
Factory overhead, selling expenses, and administrative expenses	40
Fixed costs (based on a volume of 10,000 units per year)	30

Management has asked you, the accountant, for assistance in estimating the results of several strategies that are being considered to offset the effects of the wage increase. You are to provide this assistance by answering the following questions:

1. If prices are unchanged, what volume of sales will be necessary to break even?
2. What sales price per unit will be necessary to keep profits at the present level if the number of units sold remains at 10,000 per year and the proposed labor contract takes effect?
3. If the selling price is increased by $10 per unit and there is a resulting decline of 2 percent in the number of units sold, what amount of profit should be anticipated, considering the proposed labor agreement?
4. What factors should management consider in deciding on a course of action?

CASE 24-2. Royal Suppliers distributes beauty and barber supplies to retail stores, beauty salons, and barber shops. Early in 19X1, the company decided to develop and market its own line of shampoos and hair conditioners. It contracted with another firm to manufacture and package the products. After several months, the management of Royal Suppliers became quite concerned over the profitability of the new line. An analysis of operations is shown below.

	Fixed Costs per Month	Percent of Selling Price per Bottle
Average cost of products		30
Average cost of containers and packaging		10
Average freight in		2
Average delivery costs (all variable)		6
Sales commissions		10
Advertising		
Variable		5
Fixed	$400	
Warehousing		
Variable		3
Fixed	400	
Other		
Variable		2
Fixed	600	

Last month, sales were only $2,000. Several managers have suggested that this line of products should be discontinued.

1. What sales volume would be necessary for the company to break even on this line of products, assuming that the expense data given are reliable?
2. List the most important questions that should be asked by management to arrive at a decision about whether or not to discontinue this line of products.

CHAPTER
25

■ ■ ■

Analysis of Manufacturing Costs for Decision Making

One of the basic functions of management is decision making. Often decision making means selecting a course of action from among a set of alternatives. There are always at least two alternatives.

Decision Making

In the decision process, management requires as much measurable data, properly analyzed, as is possible to handle. It is the accountant's job to gather the data and present it to management. The accountant analyzes the data in a manner that will make effective and efficient decision making easier.

The decision process may be summarized as follows:

1. Defining the problem
2. Identifying workable alternatives
3. Determining the relevant cost and revenue data
4. Evaluating the data
5. Considering any other nonmeasurable data
6. Making a decision

Defining the Problem and Identifying Alternatives

In many situations that involve decision making based on an analysis of manufacturing costs, the problem can easily be identified and often results in a yes or no decision. Sometimes, however, when management is attempting to analyze a situation to determine the problem, facts may be uncovered that disclose other problems or several alternative solutions to the problem.

For example, cost data may show that the cost of manufacturing a specific part of a finished product has been increasing and that some corrective action must be taken. An analysis may suggest that a machine used in manufacturing the part has become so old that repair and maintenance costs are high and that production is often halted so that repairs can be made. In analyzing the apparent problem of aged machinery, other problem areas may be revealed—manufacturing specifications may be beyond the capabilities of the machine; defective raw materials may have been used, resulting in damage to the equipment; personnel may not have been properly trained; or many other inefficiencies or unsatisfactory manufacturing conditions may exist.

The alternatives seem to be either to repair the existing machine or to replace it with a new one. However, there may be other solutions. For example, it may be desirable to purchase the part made by that machine from an outside supplier or subcontractor, rather than to continue to manufacture the part within the factory. Or, it might be possible to replace this part with a different part, either manufactured by the company or purchased from an outsider. It is obvious that the analysis of manufacturing costs is only one element in arriving at a solution to the problem.

Determining Relevant Cost and Revenue Data

The most basic requirement of costs for decision-making purposes is relevancy. Not all costs are relevant to the decision at hand. For planning purposes, the relevant costs are future or expected costs. Historical costs are irrelevant except to the extent they serve as a basis for estimating future outlays. Further, only those costs that will change as a result of a decision are relevant. For control purposes, relevant costs are those pertinent to the operation being evaluated.

If a decision must be made to replace a machine, the book value of the existing machine is a historical cost and therefore is irrelevant. The cost of the new machine, however, is relevant. If a decision must be made to close a warehouse, the salaries of the warehouse personnel are relevant if these workers will be terminated when the warehouse closes. The nonrefundable prepaid rent on the warehouse for the remainder of the year is irrelevant since it has been paid and cannot be recovered.

A historical cost that has been incurred and thus is irrelevant for decision-making purposes is called a *sunk cost*. The prepaid rent and the cost of the existing machine discussed above are both sunk costs.

Controllability of Costs

Another concept involved in the analysis of cost data is controllability. Costs may be classified as controllable or noncontrollable. In reality, all costs are controllable at one level or another within a company. The classification pinpoints controllability at a particular level of management. *Controllable costs* at a specific level are those costs that can be authorized at that level. *Noncontrollable costs* at a particular level are costs that were authorized at some other level. For example, a department manager probably has control over the supplies used in the department but has no control over the plant depreciation allocated to the department.

Opportunity Costs

Not all costs used in decision making appear in the accounting records. *Opportunity costs* are earnings or potential benefits foregone because a certain course of action is taken. For example, assume a decision is to be made between purchasing additional equipment and investing in top grade bonds or stocks. The opportunity cost of a decision to purchase the equipment equals the estimated interest or dividends lost on the bonds or stocks when the funds are used for the purchase of equipment.

Differential Costs and Incremental Costs

In decision making, management always compares two or more alternatives. Even in deciding on the purchase of a machine where only one bid has been received from possible suppliers, management has two alternatives: to accept or to reject the bid. A *differential cost* is the difference in cost between one alternative and another. For example, the difference in cost between using a hand-operated process and an automated press would be a differential cost. While the term *incremental cost* is often used interchangeably with differential cost, incremental cost actually means only an increase in cost from one alternative to another. For example, if it costs $2,000 to produce 20 units and $2,800 to produce 30 units, the incremental cost of producing the additional 10 units is $800.

Differential Revenues

Many decisions based on the analysis of financial data involve not only differential costs but also differential revenues. *Differential revenues* is the term used to describe the difference in revenues that will result from choosing one course of action over another. Most changes in pricing and most decisions to discontinue a product or a department or to add a new product involve analyzing not only the effects on costs resulting from the proposed action, but also the effects on revenues. If both of these factors can be estimated, the effects on profit can also be estimated.

Evaluating Data and Considering Nonmeasurable Data

The analysis of manufacturing costs, if properly planned and carried out, will generally provide a sound basis on which to arrive at a decision. The analysis typically produces a quantitative guide for making a decision. If the facts on which the analysis is based are incorrect or irrelevant, the analysis may be useless. Thus, it is essential that correct and relevant data be used and that management know how to evaluate the results of the analysis.

Since the analysis of financial data is essentially numerical analysis, it cannot be the sole factor considered in arriving at business decisions. Factors such as customer relations, employee morale, supplier relations, and other areas of the business's activities must also be considered. The impact of these factors is hard to quantify and is often subjective. Nevertheless, while the analysis of financial data provides a sound basis for making decisions, nonmeasurable data must be considered as well.

Making a Decision

Once financial data have been analyzed and the nonmeasurable factors have been considered, a rational decision can be reached. In a well-run business, procedures will be established to later evaluate whether the correct decision was made. That, too, involves analysis of financial data.

Common Decisions in a Cost Accounting Environment

When data are evaluated, the concepts of relevant costs and differential costs, presented above, and the contribution approach (discussed in Chapter 24) are used. Management must evaluate the potential profitability of each alternative and the difference in profitability between two or more alternatives. There are many decisions that must be made by management, all using financial data. Five typical situations have been chosen for illustration in this chapter.

1. Buying machinery
2. Adding or dropping a product
3. Making or buying a part
4. Specially pricing a product
5. Replacing equipment

Buying Machinery

The management of Ortiz Manufacturers is considering whether to buy a machine that will improve labor productivity. The machine has a 10-year useful life with no anticipated salvage value. A decision is reached by following the decision process outlined previously.

Defining the Problem. The problem is whether or not to buy the machine.

Identifying Workable Alternatives. One alternative is to buy the machine. The other alternative is not to buy it.

Determining Relevant Cost and Revenue Data. The following cost and revenue data are provided for the two alternatives:

	If Machine Is Not Bought	If Machine Is Bought
Annual sales	8,000 units	8,000 units
Sales price per unit	$ 20.00	$ 20.00
Cost of machine		15,000.00
Cost data		
Materials cost per unit	8.00	8.00
Labor cost per unit	6.00	5.50
Variable overhead cost per unit	2.00	2.00
Fixed overhead cost per year	12,000.00	13,500.00*

*Includes yearly depreciation of $1,500 on the machine.

Evaluating the Data. The data may be evaluated by computing the net income under each alternative and comparing the difference. Or, management may look only at the differential cost and revenue data. Using a contribution approach, the net income under each alternative is computed, as shown in Exhibit 1, on page 505.

The analysis show that there is an annual savings of $2,500 each year if the machine is bought. Note that sales revenue, materials cost, and variable overhead costs remain the same for both alternatives.

Considering Nonmeasurable Data and Making a Decision. At this point, other factors affecting the decision, such as employee morale and the quality of the

	ORTIZ MANUFACTURERS		Exhibit 1
	Analysis of Proposed Purchase of Machine		

	IF MACHINE IS NOT BOUGHT	DIFFERENCE	IF MACHINE IS BOUGHT
Sales (Annual)	$160,000		$160,000
Variable Costs			
Materials	$ 64,000		$ 64,000
Labor	48,000	$4,000	44,000
Manufacturing Overhead	16,000		16,000
Total Variable Costs	$128,000		$124,000
Contribution Margin	$ 32,000		$ 36,000
Fixed Costs	12,000	(1,500)	13,500
Net Income	$ 20,000	$2,500	$ 22,500

product, are considered before making a final decision. The management of Ortiz Manufacturers feels that employee morale will improve and expects no change in product quality. Management decides to buy the machine.

Adding or Dropping a Product

Ortiz Manufacturers makes three products. Management is thinking about discontinuing Product C after reviewing the income statement for the past year shown in Exhibit 2.

	ORTIZ MANUFACTURERS			Exhibit 2
	Income Statement			
	(Absorption Costing)			
	Year Ended December 31, 19X1			

	PRODUCT A	PRODUCT B	PRODUCT C	TOTAL
Sales	$10,000	$18,000	$22,000	$50,000
Cost of Goods Sold	4,750	6,600	22,500	33,850
Gross Margin	$ 5,250	$11,400	$ (500)	$16,150
Operating Expenses	2,000	2,700	4,200	8,900
Net Income or (Loss)	$ 3,250	$ 8,700	$(4,700)	$ 7,250
Related Data:				
Units Sold	1,000	1,200	2,000	
Sales Price per Unit	$ 10.00	$ 15.00	$ 11.00	
Variable Manufacturing				
Cost per Unit	2.50	3.00	8.00	
Variable Operating				
Expenses per Unit	1.50	1.00	1.20	
Fixed Manufacturing Costs	2,250.00	3,000.00	6,500.00	
Fixed Operating Expenses	500.00	1,500.00	1,800.00	

The steps in the decision process are as follows.

Defining the Problem. The problem is to decide whether Product C should be dropped. A net loss of $4,700 was computed for that product during the year.

Identifying Workable Alternatives. The two alternatives being considered are to continue manufacturing Product C or to drop the product.

Determining Relevant Cost and Revenue Data. Relevant data can be found by use of the contribution approach. Exhibit 3 presents the income statement prepared under the direct costing approach. This income statement shows that Product C has a contribution margin of $3,600.

	PRODUCT A	PRODUCT B	PRODUCT C	TOTAL
	ORTIZ MANUFACTURERS			**Exhibit 3**
	Income Statement			
	(Direct Costing)			
	Year Ended December 31, 19X1			
Sales	$10,000	$18,000	$22,000	$50,000
Variable Costs				
Manufacturing	$ 2,500	$ 3,600	$16,000	$22,100
Operating	1,500	1,200	2,400	5,100
Total Variable Costs	$ 4,000	$ 4,800	$18,400	$27,200
Contribution Margin	$ 6,000	$13,200	$ 3,600	$22,800
Fixed Costs				
Manufacturing	$ 2,250	$ 3,000	$ 6,500	$11,750
Operating	500	1,500	1,800	3,800
Total Fixed Costs	$ 2,750	$ 4,500	$ 8,300	$15,550
Net Income or (Loss)	$ 3,250	$ 8,700	$(4,700)	$ 7,250

Evaluating the Data. Since Product C contributes $3,600 toward covering fixed costs and making a profit, dropping Product C will reduce the company's net income by $3,600 if all fixed costs that have been allocated to Product C continue. Exhibit 4, on page 507, shows the effects that the elimination of Product C would have on the income statement. Note that the company's total net income is reduced to $3,650. When Product C was included, the total net income was $7,250 (see Exhibit 3). The smaller net income of $3,650 results from the absence of Product C's contribution margin ($7,250 − $3,600).

Considering Nonmeasurable Data and Making a Decision. While other relevant factors should be considered, the quantitative (measurable) analysis shows that Product C should not be dropped.

```
┌──────────────────────────────────────────────────────────────────────┐
│                    ORTIZ MANUFACTURERS                    Exhibit 4    │
│                       Income Statement                                 │
│                      (Direct Costing)                                  │
│                  Year Ended December 31, 19X1                          │
│                    (Eliminating Product C)                             │
│                                                                        │
│                           PRODUCT A      PRODUCT B       TOTAL         │
│   Sales                    $10,000        $18,000       $28,000        │
│   Variable Costs                                                       │
│      Manufacturing         $ 2,500        $ 3,600       $ 6,100        │
│      Operating               1,500          1,200         2,700        │
│         Total Variable Costs $ 4,000       $ 4,800       $ 8,800       │
│   Contribution Margin      $ 6,000        $13,200       $19,200        │
│   Fixed Costs*                                                         │
│      Manufacturing         $ 5,036        $ 6,714       $11,750        │
│      Operating                 950          2,850         3,800        │
│         Total Fixed Costs  $ 5,986        $ 9,564       $15,550        │
│   Net Income               $    14        $ 3,636       $ 3,650        │
│                                                                        │
│   *Allocated on the basis of original departmental fixed costs.       │
└──────────────────────────────────────────────────────────────────────┘
```

Making or Buying a Part

The Keller Company now buys a certain part for $10 per unit. Each year 12,000 parts are purchased. This part could be manufactured in the company's Machining Department.

Defining the Problem. The problem is to decide whether the company should continue to buy the part or whether it should manufacture the part.

Identifying Workable Alternatives. The alternatives are to buy the part or to manufacture it.

Determining Relevant Cost and Revenue Data. The purchase price of the product is $10 per unit. The Machining Department has a capacity of 20,000 direct labor hours per year. This department has been operating at a level of 15,000 hours for several years. Labor costs are $8 per hour in the Machining Department. Variable manufacturing overhead is $4 per hour. Annual fixed costs total $60,000. The estimated unit cost of the materials needed to manufacture the part is $4.40. Four parts can be produced per hour.

Evaluating the Data. The data can be analyzed on a per unit or annual cost basis. If a per unit approach is used, as shown in Exhibit 5, on page 508, there is a savings of $2.60 per part if the part is manufactured. The unit savings total $31,200 per year (12,000 parts × $2.60).

Note that the fixed manufacturing overhead costs are not considered since these costs remain the same whether the part is purchased or manufactured.

```
                    KELLER COMPANY                        Exhibit 5
                  Make or Buy Analysis
Cost to Purchase Part                                        $10.00
Cost to Manufacture Part
   Variable Costs Only
      Materials                                $4.40
      Labor (¼ hr at $8.00 per hr)              2.00
      Manufacturing Overhead (¼ hr at $4.00 per hr)  1.00    7.40
Differential Cost (savings per part if manufactured)       $ 2.60
```

Considering Nonmeasurable Data and Making a Decision. The Keller Company decides to make the part as long as the Machining Department is not working up to its capacity. Management should reconsider this decision if the volume of the department's production increases.

Specially Pricing a Product

The concepts used in evaluating make or buy alternatives also apply to special pricing decisions. Assume that the Keller Company is operating at a volume below full capacity and has an opportunity for a one-time sale of additional products. This sale will increase the firm's profits if the price is greater than the variable costs per unit.

Management must be careful to ensure that a special sale will not hurt its existing sales. Special product pricing is not satisfactory as a long-range pricing strategy since all costs, including fixed costs, must eventually be covered if a profit is to be made.

Every year the Keller Company manufactures 32,000 bicycle accessories called Wingos in the Machining Department. The total standard cost per unit is $12.50, as shown in Exhibit 6, and Wingos regularly sell for $20 each. An Australian company offers to buy 4,000 Wingos at $10 per unit and pay all freight charges from the factory. Management at first rejects the offer, but the company's cost accountant advises them to reconsider on the basis of the analysis shown in Exhibit 7, on page 509.

```
                    KELLER COMPANY                        Exhibit 6
                  Standard Cost Sheet

Materials                                                  $ 3.50
Labor (½ hr at $8.00 per hr)                                 4.00
Manufacturing Overhead
   Variable (½ hr at $4.00 per hr)             $2.00
   Fixed ($60,000 ÷ 20,000 hr)                  3.00         5.00
Total Standard Cost per Unit                               $12.50
```

Defining the Problem. Should the company accept an offer of $10 per unit for a product that has a total standard cost per unit of $12.50?

Identifying Workable Alternatives. The two alternatives are to accept or to reject the offer.

Determining Relevant Cost and Revenue Data. The relevant revenue is $10 per unit, while the relevant cost is $9.50 per unit. The relevant cost here is the total of the variable costs per unit ($3.50 + $4.00 + $2.00 = $9.50), as shown in Exhibit 6.

Evaluating the Data. As in make or buy decisions, either a per unit or a total annual impact basis can be used. Exhibit 7 shows that on a per unit basis, a $.50 margin results from the sale.

KELLER COMPANY		Exhibit 7
Special Product Pricing Analysis		
(By Unit)		
Differential Revenue per Unit		$10.00
Differential Cost per Unit		
Materials	$3.50	
Labor	4.00	
Variable Manufacturing Overhead	2.00	9.50
Differential Contribution Margin per Unit		$ .50

The differential contribution margin of $.50 per unit increases the firm's net income for the period by $2,000 (4,000 units × $.50). The results on an annual basis are presented in Exhibit 8, on page 510.

Considering Nonmeasurable Data and Making a Decision. If the Keller Company's other sales will not suffer, the firm should probably sell the product at the special price.

Replacing Equipment

The decision process for replacing existing equipment is much like that for buying new machinery. It is important to understand, however, that when a decision is made about whether to replace existing equipment, the original cost of the equipment and its book value are not considered because both are sunk costs. (The book value equals the original cost less the accumulated depreciation. The sunk costs are costs that have already been incurred and therefore have no impact on future decisions.) Whether the existing equipment is replaced or not, its book value is charged off against revenue. The only difference is whether the book value is charged off immediately or over a period of years. If the equipment is not replaced, the book value is charged off over future periods as depreciation. If the equipment is replaced, the book value is charged off immediately.

Assume that Ortiz Manufacturers bought the machinery as the result of the earlier evaluation (pages 504–505). Five years later an equipment supplier tells the company that a new development has made the machine obsolete (out of date). A new

| KELLER COMPANY | | Exhibit 8 |
| Special Product Pricing Analysis | | |
	SPECIAL ORDER REJECTED	DIFFERENCE	SPECIAL ORDER ACCEPTED
Sales (Annual)			
Regular Sources (32,000 at $20 each)	$640,000		$640,000
Special Order (4,000 at $10 each)	—	$40,000	40,000
Total Sales	$640,000		$680,000
Variable Costs			
Materials (at $3.50 per unit)	$112,000	(14,000)	$126,000
Labor (at $4.00 per unit)	128,000	(16,000)	144,000
Manufacturing Overhead (at $2.00 per unit)	64,000	(8,000)	72,000
Total Variable Costs	$304,000		$342,000
Contribution Margin	$336,000		$338,000
Less Fixed Costs	60,000		60,000
Net Income	$276,000	$ 2,000	$278,000

model is available. This model, which has a list price of $12,500, has a five-year estimated useful life with no salvage value. The new machine is more efficient. It should reduce labor costs per unit from $5.50 to $4.75. It should also reduce variable manufacturing overhead from $2 to $1.75 per unit. No trade-in allowance is provided for the old equipment, and the old equipment has no resale value.

Defining the Problem. Should the company replace the existing machine?

Identifying Workable Alternatives. The alternatives are to retain the old machine or to buy a new one.

Determining Relevant Cost and Revenue Data. The relevant cost data consists of the cost of the new machine and the savings (cost reductions) per unit that the firm would obtain from using the new machine.

Evaluating the Data. A good evaluation can be made by comparing the results of the two alternatives over the next five years. This period represents the remaining useful life of the existing equipment. It also represents the estimated useful life of the new equipment. Exhibit 9, on page 511, shows net income of $112,500 if the equipment is retained, compared with net income of $140,000 if the equipment is replaced.

The equipment replacement analysis shows a savings of $27,500 over the five-year period ($5,500 per year) as a result of replacing the equipment. The net annual

	ORTIZ MANUFACTURERS		Exhibit 9
	Equipment Replacement Analysis		
	(5-Year Income)		
	RETAINING EXISTING EQUIPMENT	DIFFERENCE	REPLACING EQUIPMENT
Sales	$800,000		$800,000
Variable Costs			
Materials	$320,000		$320,000
Labor	220,000	$30,000	190,000
Manufacturing Overhead	80,000	10,000	70,000
Total Variable Costs	$620,000		$580,000
Contribution Margin	$180,000		$220,000
Less: Fixed Costs	$ 67,500	(5,000)	$ 72,500
Loss on Disposal of			
Existing Equipment		(7,500)	7,500
Total	$ 67,500		$ 80,000
Net Income	$112,500	$27,500	$140,000

savings may also be calculated by subtracting the depreciation on the new equipment from the annual variable cost reductions in labor and overhead, as shown in Exhibit 10.

ORTIZ MANUFACTURERS	Exhibit 10
Equipment Replacement Analysis	
(Annual Savings)	
Variable Cost Reductions	
Labor ($5.50 − $4.75)	$ .75 per unit
Manufacturing Overhead ($2.00 − $1.75)	.25 per unit
Total per Unit	$ 1.00 per unit
Total Units	8,000 units
Total Variable Cost Reduction	$8,000
Less Depreciation on New Equipment ($12,500 ÷ 5)	2,500
Net Annual Savings From Replacement	$5,500

In addition to calculating the savings, an analysis of the return on investment can be made. This analysis is presented in Chapter 27.

Considering Nonmeasurable Data and Making a Decision. If there are no employee morale or union problems as a result of the reduction in labor, Ortiz should replace the equipment.

Product Codes and Inventory Control

The Replicars Company is a manufacturer of automobiles designed to resemble classic cars of the past but with modern components under the hood. Replicars buys engines, transmissions, and other mechanical parts from the three major U.S. automotive companies.

Replicars is following the lead of the major automotive manufacturers by insisting that its suppliers attach bar-code labels to the components shipped to the Replicars factory. The vice president of production believes that bar codes—the thick and thin, black and white lines found on grocery items and other consumer products—will be useful for inventory control because taking inventory will be faster and more accurate if it is done with bar-code readers. The readers are pens that catch and record the symbols of the bar code when the wandlike devices are passed over labels. Use of these bar-code readers is more efficient than taking inventory manually because it eliminates the errors that are often made in writing the counts on inventory sheets. Also, one employee can take a physical inventory in less time than it previously took two employees to accomplish this work.

Replicars' plant manager has already noticed other benefits of bar codes. They allow better tracking of materials moving through the assembly process, making valuation of the work in process inventory faster and more precise. The bar codes also allow factory personnel to quickly trace and remove from operations any materials belonging to a batch that has an abnormally high rate of defects. The materials can then be returned to the supplier. ■

Principles and Procedures Summary

A major function of management is decision making. The cost accountant plays a vital role in gathering and analyzing data to assist management in this process.

The decision process involves six basic steps.

1. Defining the problem
2. Identifying workable alternatives
3. Determining the relevant cost and revenue data
4. Evaluating the data
5. Considering any other nonmeasurable data
6. Making a decision

The use of relevant costs and differential costs together with the contribution approach makes evaluating data easier and more accurate.

Typical decisions requiring analysis of financial data that must be made by management are buying machinery, adding or dropping products, making or buying parts, special pricing of products, and replacing equipment.

Review Questions

1. Define relevant costs.
2. What is a sunk cost? Give an example.

3. What are opportunity costs? Give an example.
4. Distinguish between differential costs and incremental costs.
5. What is meant by differential revenues?
6. When management is making a business decision, are sunk costs more important than incremental costs? Explain.
7. Why must nonmeasurable factors be considered in decision making?
8. Explain this statement: "There are always at least two alternatives."
9. What role does the accountant play in the decision-making process?
10. In deciding whether a new labor-saving machine should be purchased, what type of cost data is relevant?
11. What types of nonmeasurable data might be considered in deciding whether to purchase a new labor-saving machine?
12. In deciding whether to manufacture a special order of a product at a lower-than-normal price, what is the major nonmeasurable consideration?
13. Is the book value of existing equipment considered in deciding whether or not to purchase new equipment? Why?
14. Is the trade-in value or the resale value of existing equipment a relevant cost in a decision about whether or not to replace the existing equipment with new equipment? Why?
15. Is absorption costing or direct costing more useful in making managerial decisions? Why?
16. When using absorption costing, why may it be profitable to continue to manufacture a product line that is being sold at a loss?
17. If a manufacturing plant is not operating at full capacity, why might a company decide to manufacture a part that is currently being purchased from an outside supplier?

Managerial Discussion Questions

1. Assume that the management of a firm where you are employed as an accountant has asked you to list the steps that they should use in making decisions from a set of alternatives. Prepare a list.
2. What data should management look at in making a decision about whether to replace old equipment with more modern machinery?
3. What type of information does management need in making a decision about whether to add or drop a product line?
4. The Stratford Company has substantial capacity that is not being used in current manufacturing operations. The management is considering making bids on government supply contracts. What type of information would be useful in setting bid prices for these special jobs or products?
5. The Kent Company is considering the purchase of a new, more efficient machine to replace an existing machine that has a book value of $25,000. The president of the Kent Company is concerned about how to handle this book value in deciding whether to purchase the new machine. Explain how the book value should be treated in this situation.

Exercises

1. **Evaluating a decision to add or drop a product.** The Dallas Company manufactures three products. An income statement for 19X1 that is based on absorption costing shows the following information for one product, Super-Widgets:

Sales (6,000 units at $40 each)	$240,000
Cost of goods sold	225,000
Gross margin on sales	$ 15,000
Operating expenses	45,000
Net loss on Super-Widgets	$(30,000)

What additional information is necessary in making a decision about whether to discontinue Super-Widgets?

2. **Making a decision to add or drop a product.** In addition to the information given in Exercise 1, refer to the following information relating to the income statement for Super-Widgets:
   a. Variable manufacturing costs, $30 per unit.
   b. Fixed manufacturing costs, $45,000.
   c. Of the fixed costs, $20,000 is directly related to the production of Super-Widgets and would be eliminated if Super-Widgets were discontinued.
   d. Variable operating expenses per unit, $5.
   e. Fixed operating expenses, $15,000. (None of the fixed operating expenses would be eliminated by discontinuing Super-Widgets.)

   Based on measurable data, should Super-Widgets be discontinued?

3. **Making a decision to add or drop a product.** Assume the same data as given in Exercises 1 and 2, except that $40,000 (instead of $20,000) of the fixed manufacturing costs would be eliminated if Super-Widgets were discontinued. Should the company discontinue Super-Widgets?

4. **Making a decision to manufacture or buy.** The Schultz Company is manufacturing a part that it uses in its finished product. Costs of the part, according to the standard cost sheet, are as follows:

Costs per Unit	
Materials	$3.00
Labor	1.00
Overhead:	
Variable	1.20
Fixed	2.50

One department of the company makes 80,000 units of the part each year. The fixed overhead rate is based on $200,000 of fixed overhead costs allocated to this department. About $80,000 of the fixed overhead would be eliminated if the part were not manufactured. The company has an opportunity to purchase the part from an outside supplier for $6 per unit. Should the company continue to manufacture the part or should it accept the outside offer?

5. **Making a decision to manufacture or buy.** Assume the same facts as in Exercise 4, except that the part can be purchased from an outside supplier for $5.15 per unit. Should the company continue to manufacture the part or should it accept the outside offer?

6. **Making a decision to manufacture or buy.** Assume the same facts as in Exercise 4, except that the part can be purchased from an outside supplier for $6.25. Should the company continue to manufacture the part or should it accept the outside offer?

7. **Making a decision about special pricing.** A company's standard cost sheet for its single product shows the following:

Materials		$10.00
Labor (1 hr at $6 per hr)		6.00
Manufacturing Overhead		
Variable (1 hr at $4 per hr)	$4.00	
Fixed ($30,000 ÷ 5,000 hr)	6.00	10.00
Total		$26.00

The normal selling price of the product is $30. The company is operating at only about 60 percent capacity. It has received an offer to sell 2,000 units to a foreign government at a price of $18.50 per unit. Additional selling and administrative expenses applicable to the special order would be $.50 per unit. Should the order be accepted? Show all calculations.

8. **Making a decision about special pricing.** Assume the same facts as in Exercise 7, except that the foreign government's order would be at a price of $22.50 per unit. Should the order be accepted? Show all calculations.

9. **Making a decision about special pricing.** Assume the same facts as in Exercise 7 except that the foreign government's order would be at a price of $23.50 per unit, and additional selling and administrative expenses would be $1 per unit. Should the order be accepted? Show all calculations.

Problems

PROBLEM 25-1. Making a decision to manufacture or buy. The Cornell Products Company is currently manufacturing a part. An outside supplier has offered to provide the part for $22 per unit. Cost data relating to production of the part for the past year, when 6,000 units were manufactured, follow. Fixed costs are allocated on the basis of direct labor hours.

Materials	$63,600
Direct Labor	67,200
Indirect Labor	800
Variable Overhead	2,400
Fixed Overhead	6,000

If the part is purchased outside, the equipment can be used in producing other items that are in demand. A shipping cost of $.50 per unit is incurred if the part is purchased.

Instructions
1. Prepare a make or buy analysis comparing the unit costs of manufacturing the part with the unit costs of purchasing it. Round off to the nearest cent.
2. Recommend a course of action to management.

PROBLEM 25-2. Making a decision about special pricing. The Fisher Company produces a compressor used in automobile air conditioning units. Annual production totals 100,000 units, each of which regularly sells for $40. The standard cost sheet data is shown on page 516. Nonmanufacturing costs are $4 per unit for variable costs and $5 per unit for fixed costs.

Materials		$ 8.00
Labor (2 hr × $3.50 per hr)		7.00
Manufacturing Overhead		
Variable (1 hr × $3 per hr)	$3.00	
Fixed (1 hr × $6.40 per hr)	6.40	9.40
Total Standard Cost per Unit		$24.40

A foreign manufacturer needs 10,000 units and offers $24 per unit plus shipping costs. The sales manager is opposed to accepting the $24 price. He says: "I know the product will not be sold in the United States where it would compete with our regularly priced goods, but we will lose $.40 on every unit. We will be using some of our idle capacity, but taking a loss like this doesn't make sense." The cost accountant replies that it is a good deal and the company should accept the offer.

Instructions

1. Prepare the two special product pricing analyses used by the cost accountant. On the second analysis, round off the figures to thousands of dollars. NOTE: Although the variable manufacturing costs applicable to the units in the special order may be higher or lower than such costs for the standard units, assume that these costs will be the same for all units.

2. Explain whether the special order should be accepted or rejected and why.

PROBLEM 25-3. Making a decision to add or drop a product. The income statement for the McCartney Manufacturing Company is shown below. Management is concerned over the loss on Product Z.

McCARTNEY MANUFACTURING COMPANY
Income Statement
(Absorption Costing)
Year Ended December 31, 19X2

	PRODUCT X	PRODUCT Y	PRODUCT Z	TOTAL
Sales	$25,000	$90,000	$15,000	$130,000
Cost of Goods Sold				
Materials	$ 3,000	$15,000	$ 2,000	$ 20,000
Labor	5,000	20,000	4,000	29,000
Manufacturing Overhead	2,500	10,000	2,000	14,500
Total	$10,500	$45,000	$ 8,000	$ 63,500
Gross Margin on Sales	$14,500	$45,000	$ 7,000	$ 66,500
Operating Expenses	10,000	25,000	9,000	44,000
Net Income or (Loss)	$ 4,500	$20,000	$(2,000)	$ 22,500

Materials and labor are variable costs. Manufacturing overhead is applied at 50 percent of the direct labor cost. Variable overhead is 10 percent of the direct labor cost. Fixed overhead totals $11,600 per year. Variable operating expenses are 20 percent of the sales dollars. Fixed operating expenses total $18,000. The fixed overhead costs and operating expenses are expected to continue if Product Z is dropped.

Instructions

1. Prepare an income statement using direct costing to show the effects of retaining Product Z. You must first compute the variable manufacturing costs by product.
2. Prepare an income statement using direct costing to show the effects of dropping Product Z.
3. Explain what decision should be made and why.

PROBLEM 25-4. Evaluating a decision to purchase equipment. The Engineering Department of the Elias Manufacturing Company has recommended a change in production methods. The change involves the purchase of a machine for $270,000. A study of operating costs under the existing and proposed methods was made. The estimated annual operating costs that differ under the two methods are as follows. The new equipment has a 10-year useful life with no scrap value.

	Current Method	Proposed Method
Labor	$193,000	$137,000
Supervision	15,000	15,000
Power	197,000	184,000
Maintenance	19,000	10,000

Instructions

1. Compute the difference in annual net income if the proposed change in production methods is made. Assume that sales will not change and that the only additional fixed cost will be the depreciation on the new machine.
2. List other factors that should be considered in making the decision.

Alternate Problems

PROBLEMS 25-1A. Making a decision to manufacture or buy. The Gonzalez Company is currently manufacturing a part. An outside supplier has offered to provide the part for $55 per unit. Cost data relating to production of the part for the past year, when 3,000 units were manufactured, are given here. Fixed costs are allocated on the basis of direct labor hours.

Materials	$79,500
Direct Labor	84,000
Indirect Labor	1,000
Other Variable Costs	3,000
Miscellaneous Fixed Costs	7,500

If the part is purchased outside, the equipment can be used in producing other items that are in demand. A shipping cost of $1.24 per unit will be incurred if the part is purchased.

Instructions

1. Prepare a make or buy analysis comparing the unit costs of manufacturing the part with the unit costs of purchasing it. Round off to the nearest cent.
2. Recommend a course of action to management.

PROBLEM 25-2A. Making a decision about special pricing. The Brenner Company produces a part used in automobiles. Annual production is 200,000 units, each of which regularly sells for $100. The standard cost sheet data is shown below. Nonmanufacturing costs are $10 per unit for variable costs and $12.50 per unit for fixed costs.

Materials		$20.00
Labor (2 hr × $8.75 per hr)		17.50
Manufacturing Overhead		
Variable (1 hr × $7.50 per hr)	$ 7.50	
Fixed (1 hr × $16 per hr)	16.00	23.50
Total Standard Cost per Unit		$61.00

A foreign manufacturer needs 20,000 units and offers $60 per unit plus shipping costs. None of these units would be sold in the Brenner Company's normal market. The company's president is opposed to accepting the order. He does not want to lose $1 on each unit. The cost accountant thinks that the company should accept the offer.

Instructions

1. Prepare the two special product pricing analyses used by the cost accountant. On the second analysis, round off the figures to thousands of dollars. NOTE: Although the variable manufacturing costs applicable to the units in the special order may be higher or lower than such costs for the standard units, assume that these costs will be the same for all units.
2. Explain whether the special order should be accepted or rejected and why.

PROBLEM 25-3A. Making a decision to add or drop a product. The income statement for the Caldwell Manufacturing Company appears below. Management is concerned over the loss on Product C.

CALDWELL MANUFACTURING COMPANY
Income Statement
(Absorption Costing)
Year Ended December 31, 19X1

	PRODUCT A	PRODUCT B	PRODUCT C	TOTAL
Sales	$62,500	$225,000	$37,500	$325,000
Cost of Goods Sold				
Materials	$ 7,500	$ 37,500	$ 5,000	$ 50,000
Labor	12,500	50,000	10,000	72,500
Manufacturing Overhead	6,250	25,000	5,000	36,250
Total	$26,250	$112,500	$20,000	$158,750
Gross Margin	$36,250	$112,500	$17,500	$166,250
Operating Expenses	25,000	62,500	22,500	110,000
Net Income or (Loss)	$11,250	$ 50,000	$(5,000)	$ 56,250

Materials and labor are variable costs. Manufacturing overhead is applied at the rate of 50 percent of the direct labor cost. Variable overhead is 10 percent of the direct labor cost. Fixed overhead totals $29,000 per month. Variable operating expenses are 20 percent of the sales dollars. Fixed operating expenses total $45,000. The fixed overhead costs and operating expenses are expected to continue if Product C is dropped.

Instructions
1. Prepare an income statement using direct costing to show the effects of retaining Product C. You must first compute the variable manufacturing costs by product.
2. Prepare an income statement using direct costing to show the effects of dropping Product C.
3. Explain what decision should be made and why.

PROBLEM 25-4A. Evaluating a decision to purchase equipment. The Engineering Department of the Ettinger Company has recommended a change in production methods. The change involves the purchase of a machine for $135,000. A study of operating costs under the existing and proposed methods was made. The estimated annual operating costs that differ under the two methods are as follows. The new equipment has an 8-year useful life with no scrap value.

	Current Method	Proposed Method
Labor	$96,500	$68,500
Supervision	7,500	7,500
Power	98,500	92,000
Maintenance	9,500	5,000

Instructions
1. Compute the difference in annual net income if the proposed change in production methods is made. Assume that sales will not change and that the only additional fixed cost will be depreciation on the new machine.
2. List other factors that should be considered in making the decision.

Managerial Decisions

CASE 25-1. The cost accountant at the Glass Company has prepared an analysis of the profitability of each of the firm's four products. That analysis is presented below. All fixed costs are allocated costs.

	Totals	Product P	Product Q	Product R	Product S
Sales	$62,600	$10,000	$18,000	12,600	$22,000
Cost of Goods Sold	44,274	4,750	7,056	13,968	18,500
Gross Profit on Sales	$18,326	$ 5,250	$10,944	$(1,368)	$ 3,500
Operating Expenses	12,012	1,990	2,976	2,826	4,220
Net Income	$ 6,314	$ 3,260	$ 7,968	$(4,194)	$ (720)
Units Sold		1,000	1,200	1,800	2,000
Sales Price per Unit		$10.00	$15.00	$ 7.00	$11.00
Variable Cost of Goods Sold per Unit		$ 2.50	$ 3.00	$ 6.50	$ 6.00
Variable Operating Expenses per Unit		$ 1.17	$ 1.25	$ 1.00	$ 1.20

Several suggestions have been made about changing the product mix in order to reduce or eliminate the loss on Products R and S. The company's management has asked you to prepare an analysis of the effects on the company's net income before taxes of each of the following proposals. (In each case, consider only the product changes stated in the proposal. The activity of other products remains unchanged.)

Proposal 1.   Discontinue Product R.

Proposal 2.   Increase the sales price of Product R to $8. This will probably result in a decrease in the number of units sold to 1,500.

Proposal 3.   Use that part of the plant in which Product R is made to produce a new product, Z. The total variable costs and expenses per unit of Product Z are estimated at $8.05, and it is estimated that 1,600 units can be produced and sold at $9.50 each.

Proposal 4.   Use that part of the plant in which Product P is made to produce Product S. Reduce the production of Product P to 500 units, to be sold at $12 each. Increase the production of Product S to 2,500 units, to be sold at $10.50 each.

CASE 25-2. In manufacturing its main product, the Bernard Corporation uses a process that requires two employees to manually control certain equipment. For several years, a sales representative of an equipment manufacturer has urged the vice president of production at the Bernard Corporation to purchase automated control equipment that would replace the two employees. The vice president has resisted this, although the firm's controller has urged that the equipment be purchased. This equipment is actually a computer system that will monitor the sensitive machines needed to manufacture the Bernard Corporation's cutting tools. The computer will also indicate defects in the product that are too small for a human operator to notice. Early in 19X1, one of the employees involved announced that he planned to retire in July and the production manager wishes to move the second employee to another job. The controller thinks this is a good time to buy the automated control equipment. The data given here have been accumulated by the controller to support his argument.

	Amount per Year
Present wages of two employees	$30,000
Payroll taxes	2,800
Fringe benefits	4,800
Additional costs when employees are absent from work for vacation, illness, etc. (average)	3,600
Variable costs related to timekeeping, payroll, etc.	600

The automated control equipment would cost $200,000. Other estimated costs related to the equipment follow:

	Amount per Year
Property taxes	$ 2,400
Interest on money to be borrowed to purchase equipment (average)	18,000
Insurance on equipment	500
Repairs and maintenance	1,000
Power	600

The equipment would have an estimated life of 10 years. The expected volume and sales price per unit of output would be unchanged.

1. Based solely on the measurable data given, should the company purchase the automated control equipment? Show all calculations.
2. What other factors seem to be the most important in the decision? List some that might cause you to reverse your decision and discuss why this might happen.

26

Analysis of Nonmanufacturing Costs for Decision Making

■ ■ ■

In the previous chapters, emphasis has been placed on manufacturing costs. In direct costing and in specific decision cases, total nonmanufacturing costs, sometimes classified as fixed and variable costs, have also been included in various analyses. But attention has not been directed to specific nonmanufacturing cost elements. In this chapter, special emphasis will be given to the analysis and control of costs related to nonmanufacturing activities, such as distribution functions and the operation of service businesses.

Cost Accounting and Nonmanufacturing Activities

The application of cost accounting concepts and procedures to nonmanufacturing activities offers new challenges to accountants. Historically, cost accounting has focused on manufacturing operations. Cost accounting systems—such as job order costing, process costing, and standard costing—and budgeting and control techniques have been developed that superbly meet the needs of manufacturing businesses. In recent years, however, manufacturing has declined, and service activities and distribution functions have gained increased importance in the American economy. As a result, cost accountants have been called on to use their skills in developing cost accounting and control techniques for service businesses and distribution operations. In this chapter, we will examine some of the common approaches to applying cost accounting analysis and controls in nonmanufacturing activities.

Distribution Cost Analysis and Control

It is very difficult to standardize, measure, predict, and control nonmanufacturing costs such as selling, delivery, and administration. These are commonly referred to as *distribution costs* since they are not involved in the production of products but rather in the process of getting the products to the marketplace. Often, it is almost impossible to determine directly the relationship between the costs incurred and the benefits resulting from those costs. Some costs incurred in distribution activities are expected to provide benefits in future periods; however, both the benefits and the periods affected may be indefinite and difficult to measure. A good example is the cost of an advertising campaign to promote a new product. It may be years before the outcome will be clear and, even then, the results of these expenditures can never be measured with precision.

Additionally, nonmanufacturing activities, especially selling activities, are difficult to standardize. Each salesperson has his or her own approach to selling. Similarly, each customer may require different sales efforts. Also, certain products may have to be sold differently from others. As a result, in most distribution activities, emphasis is placed on increasing sales volume, with not much attention given to planning and control of costs. However, if a firm's producing departments operate profitably but selling and warehousing activities are inefficient and costly, potential profits for the business will be substantially reduced. This makes it even more important for the accountant to recognize the need to analyze, plan, and control nonmanufacturing costs.

There is, however, no standard approach to planning and controlling distribution activities. Since the operating functions and techniques vary from company to company, and even within a company, the accountant must be alert to opportunities for planning and control and must be able to develop analytical techniques appropriate to the circumstances. In this chapter, some common techniques are explained and illustrated. However, the ideas discussed here are merely examples of the types of techniques that might be used.

Adequate planning and control of distribution costs depends on the accountant's ability to select the proper analytical techniques, apply them, and skillfully interpret the results. In this chapter, basic principles of budgeting distribution costs and various techniques for analyzing and controlling costs are examined.

Budgeting Distribution Costs

In manufacturing operations, variable costs depend on the production level. Fixed costs exist because of managerial decisions. For example, direct labor, direct materials, and variable overhead costs all change directly with the volume of output. Fixed costs such as depreciation, taxes, and insurance exist because of managerial decisions to purchase facilities, and, thus, commit the business to pay these costs in the future. In comparison, many nonmanufacturing expenses bear no relation to existing facilities or to volume. Instead, these costs are *discretionary;* that is, they depend entirely on managerial decisions. For example, in most companies, advertising expenses do not vary directly with production and are not fixed in amount. In fact, advertising expenses may vary in inverse relation to production or sales; as sales fall, advertising is likely to be increased to boost sales. The amount spent will depend on the decisions made by management. Those responsible for the decisions estimate the need for advertising and make plans for obtaining the desired coverage.

Even these discretionary costs can be budgeted by using the same approaches and techniques used in budgeting the costs of manufacturing operations. For instance, the fixed portion of management salaries and sales salaries can be forecast using past experience, known salary rates, and expected personnel requirements. Sales representatives' commissions can be budgeted from the knowledge of commission rates and volume factors. Sales representatives' travel costs can be based on past experience, known rates for travel and living expenses, and expected volume.

Distribution costs for standardized activities can also be budgeted with the techniques used in planning cost of manufacturing operations. One such cost is the expense of handling goods in the warehouse, which may be estimated by using the same procedures as are used in estimating indirect labor costs in the factory. Delivery costs, packing costs, billing expenses, and many other costs can be subjected to the same kind of fixed-variable cost analysis. Also, forecasts based on expected cost-volume relationships can be made.

Controlling Distribution Costs

Control of nonmanufacturing costs is subject to the same limitations and special considerations that make it difficult to budget such costs. Since some costs do not relate to a measurable activity and some activities are difficult to standardize, the development of good techniques for controlling nonmanufacturing costs is difficult. In sales and distribution, three major procedures are used for controlling and measuring performance. These procedures are the percentage-of-sales analysis, the flexible budget, and the comparison of sales or costs with other measurable factors.

Percentage-of-Sales Analysis

One way to measure the efficiency of distribution activities is to express each distribution expense as a percentage of sales. For example, it is customary in analyzing financial statements to express sales salaries as a percentage of net sales. One company's income statement may show that sales salaries are 8 percent of net sales, whereas a similar company's report may show that sales salaries are 10 percent of net sales. The lower percentage could mean that the first company has better control of sales salaries. However, further investigation will be necessary to determine if this is so. It may be that different services are provided, that gross profit percentages are different, or that other factors differ.

Percentage-of-sales analysis is used primarily for comparisons of different companies or of segments of a company. In addition, comparisons of the results for different fiscal periods are nearly always made for planning and control purposes. For example, if advertising was 6 percent of sales last year and 4 percent this year, it might show that advertising money and media are being used more efficiently this year. On the other hand, it may suggest that too little is being spent on advertising this year.

It is extremely helpful to make percentage-of-sales analyses of operations by segments of a distribution business. The variety of segments for which costs can be classified and analyzed is almost endless. Almost any organizational segment, activity, function, or other identifiable factor may be selected as the focal point of analysis. It is possible to determine the contribution to profit of each region, territory, area, district, individual branch, or store, or even of each salesperson, product, or customer. These analyses help to pinpoint costs that may be out of line in one or more segments of the business and to measure the profitability of each segment. Also, such analyses may instill a spirit of competition that will cause employees in different segments of the business to work harder to improve profitability.

The following example illustrates the typical use of percentage-of-sales analysis for segments of a business. Looking Good Suppliers, a distributor of cosmetics and other personal care products, operates 78 stores throughout the western portion of the United States. The company's home office is in Dallas, and it has three districts—Rocky Mountain, Great Plains, and West Coast—each with a district manager. The stores sell a line of "professional products" to beauty salons and barber shops and other product lines to individual customers for use in the home. The products are grouped into five categories: cosmetics; hair products; skin-care products; appliances such as hair dryers; and equipment such as combs, brushes, and scissors. Beauty salons and barber shops pay a lower price than retail customers.

In order to plan and control the operations of the 78 stores, the company analyzes profitability in many ways. The smaller the unit or activity chosen for measurement, the more difficult it becomes to measure profit with precision and the less reliable the results become. Thus net profit is measured for the larger segments such as each district and each retail store, while gross profit is used for individual product lines and for each type of customer. Every item on each district's income statement is expressed as a percentage of that district's net sales. The same procedure is used for each item on each store's income statement.

Analysis by District

For Looking Good Suppliers, the profitability of each district is relatively easy to measure because most expenses (except interest, warehousing, and general and administrative overhead of the corporate offices) can be identified directly with a specific district. The income statements of the three districts for 19X8 are given on page 526.

The accountant and management will carefully examine the percentage of sales for each item on the income statements by district. The percentage figures will be compared with the corresponding figures for the previous period. In addition, percentage figures for each district will be compared with the corresponding figures for other districts. Variations will be analyzed to determine the reasons behind them. This type of analysis will be useful in controlling costs as well as in evaluating operations.

On the income statements of the districts, all expenses are classified as direct operating expenses or indirect expenses. Since the direct operating expenses (which include all expenses except those related to financing, the central warehouse, and the corporate offices) are considered to be controllable by the district managers, no classification of controllable versus noncontrollable expenses appears on the district income statements.

Analysis by Store

Obviously the management of Looking Good Suppliers is interested in the profitability of each store and in analyzing the differences in profit between the stores. To illustrate the statements prepared for each store's operations, the income statements of two stores, Store 18 and Store 26, are shown on page 528. Note that these statements contain only the costs directly identified with each store. They do not include the allocated costs of the home office or the district manager's office. The expenses of the stores are classified as controllable (those over which the store manager has a high degree of control) or as noncontrollable (those over which the store manager has little control).

LOOKING GOOD SUPPLIERS
Income Statements by District
Year Ended December 31,19X8

ITEM	DISTRICT 1 AMOUNT	%	DISTRICT 2 AMOUNT	%	DISTRICT 3 AMOUNT	%
Sales	$5,018,000	100.20	$7,527,000	100.20	$7,025,000	100.18
Less Sales Returns and Allowances	10,100	.20	15,300	.20	12,600	.18
Net Sales	$5,007,900	100.00	$7,511,700	100.00	$7,012,400	100.00
Cost of Goods Sold	2,616,000	52.24	3,900,000	51.92	3,640,000	51.91
Gross Profit on Sales	$2,391,900	47.76	$3,611,700	48.08	$3,372,400	48.09
Direct Operating Expenses:						
Store Salaries	$ 734,000	14.66	$ 849,000	11.30	$ 918,400	13.10
Administrative Salaries	80,000	1.60	90,000	1.20	91,000	1.30
Payroll Benefits and Taxes	193,400	3.86	229,400	3.05	245,600	3.50
Rent	315,000	6.29	402,000	5.35	420,000	5.99
Utilities	77,800	1.55	127,000	1.69	112,000	1.60
Telephone	35,000	.70	42,500	.57	47,300	.67
Maintenance and Repairs	26,200	.52	31,600	.42	39,800	.57
Advertising	60,000	1.20	66,000	.88	86,800	1.24
Supplies	18,000	.36	26,500	.35	23,000	.33
Credit Card Fees	5,200	.10	8,400	.11	7,900	.11
Postage	4,100	.08	6,700	.09	5,400	.08
Travel and Entertainment	3,000	.06	3,600	.05	3,700	.05
Taxes and Insurance	20,400	.41	34,000	.45	20,700	.30
Depreciation	49,600	.99	75,300	1.00	70,500	1.01
Miscellaneous	5,100	.10	7,800	.10	9,000	.13
Total Direct Expenses	$1,626,800	32.48	$1,999,800	26.62*	$2,101,100	29.96*
Net Income Before Indirect Expenses	$ 765,100	15.28	$1,611,900	21.46	$1,271,300	18.13
Indirect Expenses:						
Interest	$ 40,000	.80	$ 60,000	.80	$ 56,000	.80
Warehouse	78,500	1.57	117,000	1.56	109,200	1.56
General and Administrative	50,200	1.00	75,300	1.00	70,300	1.00
Total Indirect Expenses	$ 168,700	3.37	$ 252,300	3.36	$ 235,500	3.36
Net Income Before Income Taxes	$ 596,400	11.91	$1,359,600	18.10	$1,035,800	14.77
Allocated Income Taxes	239,000	4.77	543,800	7.24	414,000	5.90
Net Income After Income Taxes	$ 357,400	7.14	$ 815,800	10.86	$ 621,800	8.87

*Adjusted for rounding.

The management of Looking Good Suppliers prefers to compare the operations of the stores on the basis of each store's contribution after direct costs only. This is because indirect costs cannot be identified specifically with an individual store. The contributions of all the stores make up a fund available for paying indirect expenses and taxes and for producing a profit. The management of Looking Good Suppliers thinks that this contribution is the best measure of the performance of a store. In some businesses, however, a part of (or even all) the indirect expenses may be allocated to individual stores, and operating performance is measured by the profit that remains after indirect cost allocations. This procedure, which requires the allocation (sometimes the rather arbitrary allocation) of indirect costs, may be followed on the theory that every segment should be responsible for a part of the general expenses and that a segment does not truly produce a profit until its share of the indirect costs are covered.

Using the Flexible Budget to Control Distribution Costs

Flexible budgets may be used to control the costs of distribution in much the same way as they are used to control manufacturing costs, especially when distribution activities can be reduced to repetitive operations measurable in terms of some base. The following list illustrates some of the quantifiable bases that can be used in determining the variability of costs:

- Sales representatives' salaries: number of calls made, number of miles traveled, or sales volume
- Sales representatives travel expenses: miles traveled or number of calls
- Delivery expense: number of items delivered, number of miles traveled by truck, or weight delivered
- Warehouse expense: weight or number of units handled
- Billing costs: number of invoice lines or number of units handled

It is common in retail stores to express cost variability on the basis of sales volume. For example, Looking Good Suppliers requires monthly, quarterly, and yearly flexible budgets for each store. The flexible budget for Store 18 for 19X8 is shown on page 529.

In distribution activities, as in manufacturing, a key step in using the flexible budget as a cost control tool is to promptly and regularly compare costs with the budget allowance for the volume attained. For example, Store 18 had sales of $252,000 in 19X8. A comparison of actual results with the flexible budget based on sales of $252,000 is shown on page 530.

The comparison of actual costs with the flexible budget illustrated on page 529 is for the entire year 19X8. However, making this comparison only on an annual basis would be ineffective in controlling costs because action could not be taken promptly to correct problems. Instead, monthly comparisons must be made so that important variances can be investigated at the earliest possible moment. The management of Looking Good Suppliers would have taken steps to investigate and correct certain deviations that appear in the comparison shown above. For example, the gross profit on sales is substantially below the amount shown in the flexible budget for sales at this level. There may be logical reasons for this. For instance, the portion of sales made to beauty salons (which has a lower gross profit than the sales made to retail customers) may be greater than expected when the flexible budget was set up. In any event, a thorough investigation of this variance would be in order. Similarly, the reasons for the variance in store salaries, although favorable, should be determined.

LOOKING GOOD SUPPLIERS
Income Statements—Stores 18 and 26
Year Ended December 31, 19X8

ITEM	STORE 18 AMOUNT	STORE 18 PERCENT	STORE 26 AMOUNT	STORE 26 PERCENT
Sales	$252,345	100.14	$299,955	100.27
Sales Returns and Allowances	345	.14	800	.27
Net Sales	$252,000	100.00	$299,155	100.00
Cost of Goods Sold	131,084	52.02	147,155	49.19
Gross Profit on Sales	$120,916	47.98	$152,000	50.81
Operating Expenses				
Controllable Expenses:				
Store Salaries	$ 30,723	12.19	$ 25,413	8.49
Payroll Taxes	2,542	1.01	1,715	.57
Employee Insurance	1,329	.53	1,173	.39
Workers' Compensation Insurance	396	.16	280	.09
Pension and Retirement	3,072	1.22	2,541	.85
Utilities	3,639	1.44	1,798	.60
Telephone	1,567	.62	859	.29
Maintenance and Repairs	1,168	.46	1,403	.47
Advertising	2,700	1.07	2,300	.77
Supplies	681	.27	533	.18
Credit Card Fees	357	.14	277	.09
Postage	204	.08	131	.04
Travel and Entertainment	282	.11	420	.14
Bad Debts	258	.10	60	.02
Cash Short or (Over)	(456)	(.18)	127	.04
Miscellaneous	967	.38	800	.27
Total Controllable Expenses	$ 49,429	19.61*	$ 39,830	13.31*
Noncontrollable Expenses:				
Rent	$ 14,923	5.92	$ 11,573	3.87
Depreciation	2,334	.93	651	.22
Casualty Insurance	610	.24	720	.24
Property Taxes	912	.36	361	.12
Total Noncontrollable Expenses	$ 18,779	7.45	$ 13,305	4.45
Total Operating Expenses	$ 68,208	27.06	$ 53,135	17.76
Contribution of Store	$ 52,708	20.92	$ 98,865	33.05

*Adjusted for rounding.

LOOKING GOOD SUPPLIERS
Flexible Budget—Store 18
Year Ending December 31, 19X8

ITEM	COST FORMULA FIXED PORTION	COST FORMULA VARIABLE PORTION (% OF SALES)	SALES VOLUME			
Sales			$200,000	$225,000	$250,000	$275,000
Cost of Goods Sold		50.00	$100,000	$112,500	$125,000	$137,500
Gross Profit on Sales		50.00	$100,000	$112,500	$125,000	$137,500
Operating Expenses						
Controllable Expenses:						
Store Salaries	$20,000	5.00	$ 30,000	$ 31,250	$ 32,500	$ 33,750
Payroll Taxes	1,600	.40	2,400	2,500	2,600	2,700
Employee Insurance	1,200	.10	1,400	1,425	1,450	1,475
Workers' Compensation						
Insurance	220	.08	380	400	420	440
Pension and Retirement	2,000	.50	3,000	3,125	3,250	3,375
Utilities	3,600		3,600	3,600	3,600	3,600
Telephone	1,500		1,500	1,500	1,500	1,500
Maintenance and Repairs	600	.20	1,000	1,050	1,100	1,150
Advertising	2,700		2,700	2,700	2,700	2,700
Supplies	200	.20	600	650	700	750
Credit Card Fees		.20	400	450	500	550
Postage	240		240	240	240	240
Travel and Entertainment	100	.10	300	325	350	375
Bad Debts		.10	200	225	250	275
Miscellaneous		.30	600	675	750	825
Total Controllable Expenses	$33,960	7.18	$ 48,320	$ 50,115	$ 51,910	$ 53,705
Noncontrollable Expenses:						
Rent	$14,923		$ 14,923	$ 14,923	$ 14,923	$ 14,923
Depreciation	2,334		2,334	2,334	2,334	2,334
Casualty Insurance	600		600	600	600	600
Property Taxes	900		900	900	900	900
Total Noncontrollable Expenses	$18,757		$ 18,757	$ 18,757	$ 18,757	$ 18,757
Total Operating Expenses	$52,717	7.18	$ 67,077	$ 68,872	$ 70,667	$ 72,462
Contribution of Store			$ 32,923	$ 43,628	$ 54,333	$ 65,038

In this case, there may be evidence that the budgeted allowance for sales salaries is too high. Of major concern would be the large amount of cash over, which suggests either shortcomings in the procedures for handling cash or in the accounting records.

LOOKING GOOD SUPPLIERS
Comparisons of Actual Results With Flexible Budget—Store 18
Year Ending December 31, 19X8

	FLEXIBLE BUDGET FOR SALES OF $252,000	ACTUAL	VARIANCE OVER (UNDER)
Sales	$252,000	$252,000	
Cost of Goods Sold	126,000	131,084	$ 5,084
Gross Profit on Sales	$126,000	$120,916	$(5,084)
Operation Expenses			
Controllable Expenses:			
Store Salaries	$ 32,600	$ 30,723	$(1,877)
Payroll Taxes	2,608	2,542	(66)
Employee Insurance	1,452	1,329	(123)
Workers' Compensation			
Insurance	422	396	(26)
Pension and Retirement	3,260	3,072	(188)
Utilities	3,600	3,639	39
Telephone	1,500	1,567	67
Maintenance and Repairs	1,104	1,168	64
Advertising	2,700	2,700	0
Supplies	704	681	(23)
Credit Card Fees	504	357	(147)
Postage	240	204	(36)
Travel and Entertainment	352	282	(70)
Bad Debts	252	258	6
Cash Short or (Over)	-0-	(456)	(456)
Miscellaneous	756	967	211
Total Controllable Expenses	$ 52,054	$ 49,429	$(2,625)
Noncontrollable Expenses:			
Rent	$ 14,923	$ 14,923	-0-
Depreciation	2,334	2,334	-0-
Casualty Insurance	600	610	$ 10
Property Taxes	900	912	12
Total Noncontrollable Expenses	$ 18,757	$ 18,779	$ 22
Total Operating Expenses	$ 70,811	$ 68,208	$(2,603)
Contribution of Store	$ 55,189	$ 52,708	$(2,481)

Break-Even Analysis

Break-even analysis is a familiar tool that is of great value in analyzing distribution activities, especially in making decisions about the operations of sales divisions or segments. For example, if the management of Looking Good Suppliers prepared a break-even chart for Store 18 at the same time that it prepared the flexible budget given on page 529, the chart would appear as shown on page 531.

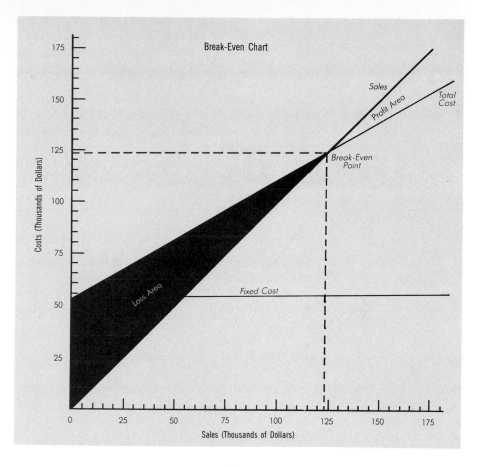

The break-even point for Store 18 can be determined in this manner. First, find the contribution margin on sales by deducting the percent of sales for cost of goods sold (50 percent) and for variable operating expenses (7.18 percent) from 100 per cent. For this store, the contribution margin on sales is 42.82 percent (50 percent + 7.18 percent = 57.18 percent; 100 percent − 57.18 percent = 42.82 percent). At the break-even point, the 42.82 percent contribution margin in dollars would equal the budgeted fixed costs of $52,717 for the year. The break-even point in dollars for Store 18, rounded to the nearest dollar, is $123,113.

42.82 percent of sales = $52,717

Sales = $52,717 ÷ 42.82 percent = $123,113

Operating Analyses

Earlier in this chapter it was suggested that the accountant must be alert to the development and use of analytical procedures that will help in controlling distribution costs and increasing profits. The flexible budget is only one tool. Another useful technique is analyzing the activities that underlie the items on the income statement. Many types of analysis may be made for almost every revenue and expense item. A few illustrations will suggest the types of analysis that might prove useful.

Analysis of Sales

Obviously the amount of sales is of crucial importance to a business. Studies of the characteristics of a company's sales, its customers, its products, and its sales procedures provide the accountant with information that helps management to increase profits. Typical analyses are discussed below.

Sales per Square Foot of Floor Space Occupied. Computing the sales per square foot of the floor space used for selling activities (sales for the period divided by the square feet of floor space) may help to answer such questions as whether there is too much floor space for the existing sales volume and for potential sales volume. A comparison of the sales per square foot of the floor space occupied by each business segment, such as each retail store run by Looking Good Suppliers, might reveal that some stores are operating more efficiently than others. The operations of all stores can be studied to determine how stores that use space poorly can increase their sales per square foot.

Average Sales per Order or Average Sales per Invoice. Small orders are costly. Sales efforts, handling costs, billing costs, and other costs may be almost as great for a small order as for a large one. Clearly, large orders would be desirable. Special efforts should be made to increase the size of each order of customers with low average sales per invoice.

Analysis of Total Sales Made to Each Customer During the Period. A business may classify its customers on the basis of the total sales made to each during a period. For example, Looking Good Suppliers uses the following schedule to classify its trade customers—beauty salons and barber shops.

Sales for Past Year
$10,000 or over
  5,000 to $9,999
  4,000 to 4,999
  2,000 to 3,999
   500 to 1,999
Less than   500

This analysis may lead to further examination of the cost of serving customers who make small annual purchases. Such questions as the following will lead to further analysis of operations:

- Is the gross profit on small sales adequate to cover the costs of servicing these customers?
- Should some small accounts be dropped?
- What can be done to increase the purchases of each customer?
- Should price differentials between large and small customers be increased?
- Does each customer who makes small purchases represent growth potential?
- Should sales representatives continue to call on small customers in remote areas?

Analysis of Sales by Product Classes. Some products show lower gross profit rates than others or require greater selling efforts or higher delivery costs. Some product lines may have the potential for future growth, while other product lines may be "dying." Typical questions to ask in such analyses include the following:

- Should certain product lines with a low gross profit be dropped?
- What are the unusual costs related to each product line?
- Which product lines have high turnover and which product lines have low turnover?
- What are the space requirements for storing each product line?

Obviously, answering questions such as those listed above will require a detailed analysis of sales records, inventory records, warehouse reports, and many other types of records that cover a wide range of operations.

The analyses discussed in this section are merely examples of the methods that can be used to examine distribution activities and measure their efficiency. Remember that the accountant must constantly be alert to the operations of the business where he or she is employed in order to develop effective cost control procedures.

Analysis of Expenses

Many of the analyses of sales described above lead directly into an investigation of expenses and cost behavior. Every expense item on the income statement represents a potential area of research and analysis. Some expense items are normally larger than others, and some may be easier to control than others. Thus, the accountant must carefully study the cost structure of the business in order to determine where the effort to analyze expenses can achieve the greatest benefits. Sales salaries and commissions almost always form a large part of distribution expenses; therefore, it would be worthwhile to analyze this item. Some analyses that can be made of this item follow:

- Percentage of total sales salaries to total net sales
- Percentage of sales salaries to the net sales of each salesperson
- Average sales per day, per week, per month, or per year for each salesperson
- Sales returns and allowances of each salesperson as a percent of that person's net sales
- Average number of customer calls as compared to the number of sales made by each salesperson for the period

The analysis of sales salaries and commissions is closely related to the analyses of other aspects of sales. As a matter of fact, many of the revenue and expense classifications on the income statement closely reflect related distribution activities of the business.

Cost Accounting for Service Businesses

The service sector of the economy has grown dramatically in the past 20 years. This growth is a result of technological changes as well as of the increasing affluence and leisure time of society. Technology has increased the output per labor hour in manufacturing and agriculture, so that a much smaller portion of the labor force is required for those activities. Technology has also led to new products and services. The computer industry and the telecommunications industry are but two areas that have resulted from the technological revolution and have quickly become essential elements of the world's economy.

Technology and increased affluence have also led to rapid growth in other purely service-oriented businesses. For example, the number of firms providing a wide variety of financial services, such as commercial banks, investment banking firms, brokerage firms, financial management companies, credit card companies, and insurance companies, has greatly expanded. Health care facilities, educational institutions, governmental agencies, legal and accounting firms, transportation companies, travel agencies, and even restaurants are other examples of rapidly growing operations that provide services rather than manufacture products.

Accounting fills an important need in service businesses. The requirements of management and other interested parties such as creditors and stockholders for general financial information are met by the basic financial reports such as the income statement, the balance sheet, and the funds flow statement. However, when management needs to make business decisions, such as setting prices, planning and directing activities, and controlling costs, the general financial statements are inadequate. Cost accounting techniques can be used to provide information that helps in the decision-making process. The concepts and practices of cost accounting for manufacturing businesses, which were discussed in previous chapters of this book, may be applied to service firms as well.

Historically, cost accounting has been much more widely used in manufacturing operations than in service activities. This is because costs are more easily identified with the physical units of goods manufactured than they are with services provided. Also, in manufacturing operations, one of the chief purposes of cost accounting has been to determine the cost of inventories. In service businesses, there are no inventories. Finally, in service businesses, it is often difficult to relate costs to specific activities. As a result of these factors, cost accounting for companies that provide services has been neglected.

In the remainder of this chapter, we will examine how cost accounting techniques can be used in service businesses. It should be kept in mind that there are great differences between the activities and organizational structures of various types of service operations. For example, a hospital and a law firm are run very differently, but both are service operations. Thus, the application of cost accounting techniques to service activities in a specific situation may be unique.

Accumulating Costs

In manufacturing activities, costs are accumulated by jobs or by departments and are then assigned to individual units of product. In service businesses, the center for cost measurement and cost control—and thus for cost accumulation—is also usually the department. Departments are established and organized to provide specific services or perform specific functions. The department manager is responsible for the efficient operations of the department. Thus, if efficiency and effectiveness are to be measured, costs must be accumulated on a departmental basis. In addition, appropriate accumulation of costs is necessary so that prices of services may be determined on a logical and timely basis.

Some departments are set up solely to provide services to other departments in the firm. These service departments do not earn income directly. Instead, they incur costs as they provide services to other departments in the firm that do earn income. Thus, they are often referred to as *cost centers*. For example, in a commercial bank the building services department provides space, lighting, heat, air conditioning, power, cleaning, and similar services for all the other departments in the bank. The data processing department, the accounting department, the security department, and the mailroom also provide services for the entire bank.

Service departments are designed to provide efficient services at the lowest possible cost. The type of service departments required by a firm depends on the nature of the firm's activities and on its organizational structure.

In every service business, there are departments or other organizational units that provide services directly to customers or clients and earn income. These departments may be referred to as sales departments. Since they deal directly with customers and earn income, they are called *profit centers*. In a commercial bank, the commercial loan department, consumer loan department, trust department, depositor services department, and credit card department are examples of profit centers. In a public accounting firm, the profit centers might be the tax department, the auditing department, the management services department, and the writeup department (a department that maintains accounting records for clients). In most service businesses, there is a need to determine the profitability of each profit center.

If cost accounting techniques are to be used by a service business, procedures must be developed for properly accumulating and classifying costs and revenues. In addition, procedures must be developed for measuring, recording, and reporting the level of activity. Since there are no physical products being manufactured, the service business must find other reasonable measures of effort and accomplishment. For example, within one department, the number of personal visits from customers, the number of telephone calls received from customers, the number of hours worked by employees, and the number of forms completed may be important in measuring activity and in computing and controlling costs.

Analyzing Costs

In order to prepare budgets, control costs, and evaluate performance, costs must be divided into their fixed and variable components. The process for analyzing cost behavior in a service business is almost identical to that described in Chapter 20 for a manufacturing business, except that the level of activity is not expressed in terms of direct labor hours. Instead, it is expressed in terms of the unit of activity appropriate for the department. For example, in a bank's new deposits department, the activity measured would be the number of accounts opened during the period. Similarly, in a hospital, the activity for a nursing floor might be the number of days that patients occupy rooms on the floor. The activity measured in an academic department of a college might be the number of credit hours taught in the department.

Preparing Operating and Flexible Budgets

The operating budget and flexible budgets for a service business are prepared in the same way as for a manufacturing company. A detailed budgeted income statement is prepared for each profit center, and a detailed expense budget is prepared for each cost center. The departmental budgets are combined into the firm's operating budget. The operating budget, which becomes part of the master budget, reflects the activity level and the resulting revenue and cost levels expected for the budget period.

For example, suppose that a large accounting firm has three profit centers: its auditing, tax, and management consulting departments. The revenue budget for the period is based on an analysis of the revenues from services provided during the pervious period and on an estimate of the growth or decline in revenues that will be earned from services in the future. An analysis of the number of clients, types of clients, types of services used by each client and number of professional staff hours required for each client in the past period is the starting point. Adjustments for changes in the rates charged, new services to be provided to existing clients, the addition of new clients, and similar factors are used to modify the figures for the prior year's operations to arrive at the revenue budget for the new period. Based on an analysis of cost behavior in the previous period, and on adjustments for changes in salaries and benefits, for changes in economic conditions such as more inflation, and for other anticipated changes, the expense budget can be prepared. The procedures for estimating total fixed costs and total variable costs are identical to those described in Chapter 20 for manufacturing operations.

Although the operating budget offers a basis for planning operations, it does not provide a satisfactory tool for controlling costs. Instead, a service business needs a flexible budget similar to the flexible budget for a manufacturing business, which was explained in Chapter 21. Variable costs that will be incurred during the period depend on the level of activity. If the actual level differs from the activity level used in preparing the operating budget, costs (and profits) will differ from those projected in the operating budget. For example, if the tax department of a public accounting firm prepares an operating budget based on the assumption that it will use 20,000 hours of professional labor during the year, the budget is valid only if that number of hours is actually used. If 22,000 hours are required, management will want to know the budget allowance for each cost element at a level of 22,000 hours.

In order to be able to measure what costs should be at the actual level of activity, a flexible budget is prepared. The variable costs in the flexible budget are found by multiplying the variable cost per unit of activity for each cost element by the number of units of activity assumed. Again, the procedure followed is almost identical to that used in a manufacturing business.

Using Standard Costs

In many service businesses, standard costs are developed for use in controlling costs and in making such decisions as what prices to charge for the various types of services. The procedures for developing and applying standard costs are similar to those used in manufacturing businesses. Fixed costs and variable costs (based on a high, but attainable, level of efficiency) are estimated for the expected or normal activity level. The standard cost per unit of activity is found by dividing the budgeted costs by the number of activity units budgeted. At the end of the period, the total standard cost (the number of units of activity multiplied by the standard cost per unit of activity) is compared with the total actual cost, and the variance is computed. If there is some reliable measure of output activity, the variance between actual costs and standard costs often can be broken into a pricing variance and an efficiency variance in much the same way that labor cost variances are analyzed in manufacturing operations.

For example, suppose that in a dry cleaning firm, a standard time of 8 minutes has been developed for pressing men's trousers and the standard labor rate is $9 per hour for pressers. Thus, the standard labor cost of pressing a pair of trousers is $1.20 (8 ÷ 60 × $9). During the month of September 19X1, a total of 3,624 pairs of trousers were pressed, requiring 516 hours of pressing labor at a total cost of $4,944 ($9.5814 per hour). The standard labor cost for the 3,624 pairs of trousers is $4,348.80 (3,624 × $1.20). Since the actual cost of $4,944 exceeded the standard cost of $4,348.80 by $595.20, management wishes to know why the variance exists. Using the variance analysis techniques discussed in Chapter 22, an unfavorable labor efficiency variance of $295.20 and an unfavorable labor rate variance of $300 can be computed as follows:

Labor Efficiency Variance

The standard hours allowed for the 3,624 pairs of trousers is 483.2 hours (3,624 pairs ÷ 7.5 pairs per hour), while the actual time required was 516 hours.

Actual Hours (516) × Standard Rate ($9)	$4,644.00
Standard Hours (483.2) × Standard Rate ($9)	4,348.80
Efficiency Variance	$ 295.20U

Labor Rate Variance

Actual Hours (516) × Standard Rate ($9)	$4,644.00
Actual Hours (516) × Actual Rate ($9.5814)	4,944.00
Rate Variance	$ 300.00U
Total Variance	$ 595.20U

In many service businesses, it is not possible to quantify output and establish standard costs for each unit. Nevertheless, even in such instances, standard costs will be useful in setting prices and making other decisions.

Principles and Procedures Summary

Nonmanufacturing costs have received far less attention in cost accounting than have manufacturing costs. Nevertheless, many of the techniques used in accounting for manufacturing are applicable to distribution activities. The basic concepts of planning, including budgeting, are easily applied. Similarly, such cost control tools as the flexible budget may be used. It is very common in distribution activities to prepare income statements for various segments of the business and to prepare vertical analyses, expressing each item as a percent of net sales.

The accountant also has an opportunity to make special analyses of the activities that give rise to each item on the income statement. Analyses of sales activities are especially important because they lead to decisions that could increase the company's profitability.

Historically, cost accounting procedures have generally been applied to manufacturing businesses. However, the recent growth in the service sector of the economy has led an increasing number of service businesses to use cost accounting techniques to measure operations and to provide data for decision-making purposes. The procedures used must be adapted to the operations of each service business.

Review Questions

1. What are distribution costs?
2. What are controllable fixed costs?
3. What is meant by the term *contribution margin*?
4. Why is it more difficult to control distribution costs than it is to control manufacturing costs?
5. What is a percentage-of-sales analysis?
6. Would percentage-of-sales analysis be more useful and reliable when applied to a large segment of a business (for example, a district) or to a smaller segment (for example, the Menswear Department in a department store)? Why?
7. What is the difference between controllable distribution expenses and noncontrollable distribution expenses?
8. List some possible bases for determining cost variability for each of the following:
   a. Warehouse activities
   b. Billing
   c. Deliveries by truck
9. Why is the flexible budget for a retail store normally based on levels of sales volume?
10. In some companies, advertising is a variable expense for a given year, while in other companies, advertising is considered a fixed expense for a given year. Explain why this is possible.
11. Name some cost accounting techniques used in manufacturing businesses that may be applied in the analysis and control of distribution costs.
12. Explain how each of the following calculations is made and how each might be useful in analyzing and controlling distribution costs:
    a. Sales per square foot of floor space
    b. Average sales per salesperson's call
    c. Average number of sales calls per day
    d. Average amount of sales per order
13. What would be the major problem in attempting to measure profit for each group of customers?
14. What are discretionary costs? Give two examples.
15. How often should comparison of actual results with the flexible budget be made? Why?
16. Why has cost accounting been more widely used in manufacturing businesses than in service businesses?
17. How does a cost center differ from a profit center?
18. Explain the two types of departments that are found in service businesses.
19. Why is it necessary to develop procedures for measuring, recording, and reporting the level of activity in order to apply cost accounting techniques in a service business?

Managerial Discussion Questions

1. How does a contribution margin approach help management evaluate the performance of one segment of a business?

2. If a segment has no positive contribution margin, what options should management examine?

3. Top Value Electronic Products has made a percentage-of-sales analysis for each of its nine stores. For eight stores, the rent expense is 5.2 percent of net sales, while in one store the rent expense is 9.7 percent of net sales. As controller of the company, you want to know why the rent expense is so high for the one store. What are some possible reasons?

4. The Carlton Company has analyzed its customers by volume of annual sales. The company has found that the average annual sales to a customer are $22,820. However, annual sales to 3 percent of the customers are under $500 each. What steps should the Carlton Company take with these customers?

5. The Beck Company, a wholesale distributor, has recorded an operating loss for each of the past three years. A percentage-of-sales analysis shows that its gross profit is 21.6 percent. The average gross profit rate for the industry is 24.8 percent. What questions should be asked by management about the firm's gross profit rate?

6. The Akron Company operates over 100 retail stores. Net income after income taxes is computed for each store. Included in the computation are allocated home office expenses, allocated interest expense, and allocated federal income taxes. Since the store managers are paid a bonus based on the amount of net income, some managers have protested the inclusion of allocated expenses in the calculation. Comment on this objection.

7. The Murray Corporation employs eight outside sales representatives. In preparing a flexible budget, the accountant based the sales representatives' travel costs on sales volume. Comment on this basis for budgeting travel costs.

8. The president of the Columbia Corporation has suggested that all district managers be paid a commission based on the profit after controllable expenses. The vice president of sales argues that the commission for district managers should be based on net sales. What is your suggestion? Why?

9. The H & J Company handles over 2,000 products. The firm is considering whether to drop certain product lines. An analysis of the inventory records shows that 200 products make up less than 1 percent of the total inventory. What other information would be needed to reach a decision on which, if any, products should be discontinued?

10. What use is made of a flexible budget in a service business?

11. Under what circumstances can standard costs be used by the management of a service business to measure efficiency?

Exercises

1. **Preparing an analysis of sales.** Selected information about two stores owned by the Springfield Company is given on page 540. This information concerns the month of May 19X2.

	Store 1	Store 2
Net sales	$32,000	$24,000
Number of sales transactions	1,682	1,290
Square feet of floor space	1,800	1,200
Number of salespersons	4	3

For each store, compute the following:
a. Sales volume per square foot of floor space
b. Average sales amount per sales transaction
c. Average monthly sales per salesperson
d. Average number of sales transactions per month per salesperson

2. **Preparing a break-even analysis.** The Santos Company's gross profit rate is 40 percent of net sales, its variable expenses are 31 percent of net sales, and its monthly fixed costs are $12,000.

a. Compute the company's monthly break-even sales volume.
b. What will the estimated profit or loss be if the sales volume is $68,000?

3. **Preparing an analysis of sales.** The Nash Company has analyzed the records of its field sales representatives. Data for two of these employees for the month of September 19X6 are given below.

	Martin	Russo
Number of sales calls made	88	78
Net sales	$120,000	$104,000
Number of sales invoices	240	260
Number of customers in area	120	120

Compute the following for each salesperson:
a. Average sales per sales invoice
b. Number of invoices per sales call
c. Average sales per sales call made
d. Percent of potential customers called on during month
e. Average sale per potential customer for month

4. **Preparing a flexible budget for delivery expense.** The Sullivan Company has average sales per delivery of $200. The Delivery Department's monthly fixed costs are $4,000, and its variable costs are $25 per delivery. Compute the company's budget for delivery expenses at the following sales volumes:
a. $100,000
b. $160,000

5. **Deciding on an activity basis for setting standards.** The accountant for the Goldberg Company is seeking to develop standard costs for as many of its distribution activities as possible. What activity basis might be used for setting standards for each of the following costs for the company?
a. Deliveries by truck
b. Travel of sales representatives
c. Shipping of goods to customers

6. **Preparing a flexible budget for rent expense.** The Richards Company has several stores, all in rented buildings. In preparing the flexible budgets for the stores, the accountant finds that most lease contracts for the stores are similar to

the one for Store 84. For Store 84, the monthly rental is 6 percent of net sales for the month, but in no case is the monthly rental to be less than $1,500 per month. What amount of rent would be provided at the following sales levels?

a. $18,000

b. $24,000

c. $31,000

7. **Preparing a flexible budget for general expenses.** The Marietta Company has four sales divisions. It allocates all general office expenses to these divisions. Fixed expenses of $24,000 per month are allocated equally to the divisions. All other expenses are allocated on the basis of sales.

For the month of December 19X5, the sales were: $800,000 for Division A; $1,000,000 for Division B; $1,200,000 for Division C; and $900,000 for Division D. The total general office expenses for the month were $38,000. How much of the general office expenses would be allocated to each division for the month?

8. **Preparing an analysis of sales orders.** The Douglas Company has analyzed the sales of each of its salespeople. Data relating to the customers of Sandra Larson are shown below.

Monthly Sales	Number of Customers	Gross Profit Rate (%)
$1,000 to $1,444	3	26
700 to 999	22	27
500 to 699	20	28
300 to 499	18	29
200 to 299	15	30
Under $200 (average, $120)	12	30

Costs for a salesperson to call on a customer are estimated to be $10 per call plus 2 percent of the sales volume of the order received. Costs for handling an order are estimated to be $3, plus 2 percent of sales.

a. Compute the estimated average contribution or average loss on each order that is under $200.

b. Compute the estimated average contribution or average loss on each order that is between $700 and $999, assuming that the average of such orders is $800.

9. **Making a decision to close or continue to operate a store.** A new accountant at the Faulkner Company has made an analysis of the profitability of each of the company's 20 stores. The following data relate to Store 6:

Sales for year	$1,200,000
Cost of goods sold	840,000
Gross profit on sales	$ 360,000
Direct expenses incurred in store	338,000
Contribution of store	$ 22,000
Indirect expenses:	
General and administrative	$ 30,000
Interest	8,000
Total indirect expenses	$ 38,000
Net loss for year	$ (16,000)

The accountant suggests that the store should be closed.

a. Do you agree or disagree?

b. What additional information would be helpful in making this decision?

Problems

PROBLEM 26-1. Preparing a profitability analysis by departments. The Safeguard Products Company sells security systems through its Security Department, citizen band radios through its CB Department, AM and FM radios through its Commercial Department, and police radios through its Police Products Department. The following data are for the year 19X1. All figures have been rounded to the nearest $100, and physical quantities have been omitted.

	Security Department	CB Department	Commercial Department	Police Products Department
Selling and Administrative Expenses				
Controllable—Variable	$ 38,400	$ 21,900	$ 16,200	$ 35,600
Controllable—Fixed	17,500	9,300	7,100	9,300
Noncontrollable*	38,700	22,000	16,400	10,100
Manufacturing Overhead				
Variable	234,900	125,200	95,900	101,300
Fixed	124,900	79,600	55,800	59,300
Sales	469,800	250,300	191,800	202,600

*Allocated on the basis of the square footage in each department.

Instructions

Prepare a profitability analysis by departments for the year 19X1.

PROBLEM 26-2. Preparing a percentage-of-sales analysis. Economy Auto Parts, Inc., operates two retail auto parts stores. A monthly income statement is prepared for each store. This statement reflects both the direct operating expenses of the stores and the allocated indirect expenses. The combined statements for October 19X8 are shown below.

	Store 1	Store 2
Net Sales	$40,000	$65,000
Cost of Goods Sold	25,000	41,200
Gross Profit on Sales	$15,000	$23,800
Direct Expenses:		
Salaries and Commissions	$ 4,000	$ 4,800
Payroll Benefits	600	725
Delivery Fees	1,000	800
Advertising	300	290
Credit Card Fees	280	310
Supplies	350	450
Rent	1,800	2,100

	Store 1	Store 2
Utilities	350	480
Repairs and Maintenance	220	90
Property Taxes	200	210
Depreciation	600	750
Auto and Truck	500	800
Miscellaneous	800	1,000
Total Direct Expenses	$11,000	$12,805
Contribution After Direct Expenses	$ 4,000	$10,995
Indirect Expenses:		
Purchasing	$ 600	$ 800
General and Administrative	2,400	2,600
Interest	800	1,000
Total Indirect Expenses	$ 3,800	$ 4,400
Net Income for Month	$ 200	$ 6,595

Instructions

1. For each store, prepare an analysis expressing each item on the income statement as a percent of net sales. Round the percents to one decimal place.
2. Compare the percentages for the two stores. Note the differences.
3. What types of questions would management ask about each of the differences listed in Instruction 2?

PROBLEM 26-3. Preparing a monthly flexible budget. Nilson Distributors has a gross profit of 30 percent of net sales. After analyzing its operating expenses, the firm determined that its fixed expenses and its variable expenses (expressed as a percent of net sales) are as shown below.

	Fixed Expenses (Monthly)	Variable Expenses (Percent of Net Sales)
Sales Salaries	$12,000	1.5
Delivery Salaries	5,200	2.0
Other Salaries	4,800	-0-
Payroll Taxes	6,000	.4
Advertising	1,200	-0-
Supplies	300	.1
Rent	3,600	-0-
Utilities	700	-0-
Repairs	200	-0-
Property Taxes	300	-0-
Auto and Truck	600	.5
Miscellaneous	820	1.2

Instructions

Prepare a monthly flexible budget for the company at sales levels of $120,000, $150,000, and $180,000.

PROBLEM 26-4. Preparing a break-even analysis. Refer to the data for Nilson Distributors in Problem 26-3 to complete the following:

Instructions

1. Compute the monthly sales volume at the break-even point for Nilson.
2. Prepare a monthly break-even chart. NOTE: Both the horizontal axis and the vertical axis should represent dollars.
3. What sales volume would be required to earn a net income of $10,000 for the month?
4. The sales manager of Nilson Distributors estimates that if the average sales price of merchandise were to be decreased by 2 percent, the number of units sold could be increased by 8 percent.
   a. What effect would this have on the break-even point?
   b. What would be the new break-even point?

PROBLEM 26-5. Comparing budgeted and actual amounts. Krause and LeMay is a public accounting firm. Its auditing department earned a departmental net income (contribution) of $603,000 during 19X1. This amount was less than the net income projected in the firm's operating budget (shown below) even though the number of billable hours for the year exceeded the budgeted number. (*Billable hours* are the hours for which clients are charged. Some hours worked by the firm's staff are not billable because the staff members are not involved in an audit job for a client.) The department's managing partner has asked you to prepare a comparison of the actual results and the results that would have been anticipated in a flexible budget based on 48,000 billable hours, the actual number of billable hours for the year.

	Income Statement (Actual)	Operating Budget
Billable Hours	48,000	42,000
Revenues From Charges to Clients	$3,000,000	$2,730,000
Fixed Professional Salaries	$ 520,000	$ 500,000
Variable Professional Salaries	1,070,000	900,000
Other Fixed Expenses	420,000	420,000
Other Variable Expenses	387,000	273,000
Total Departmental Expenses	$2,397,000	$2,093,000
Departmental Contribution	$ 603,000	$ 637,000

Instructions

Prepare a three-column statement showing the actual income statement figures, the flexible budget based on actual billable hours, and the variance between each item.

Alternate Problems

PROBLEM 26-1A. Preparing a profitability analysis by departments. The Evergreen Products Company sells lawn and garden supplies to home owners through its Retail Department, gardening tools to garden centers through its Equipment Department, plastic containers to nurseries through its Plastic Products Department, and lawn furniture to garden centers through its Furniture Department. The following data are for the year 19X1. All figures have been rounded to the nearest $100, and physical quantities have been omitted.

	Retail Department	Equipment Department	Plastic Products Department	Furniture Department
Selling and Administrative Expenses				
Controllable—Variable	$ 96,000	$ 54,700	$ 39,900	$ 83,000
Controllable—Fixed	42,700	31,100	16,700	21,100
Noncontrollable*	96,700	55,000	41,000	25,300
Manufacturing Overhead				
Variable	594,800	377,800	240,000	253,300
Fixed	312,300	199,200	139,500	148,300
Sales	1,174,500	625,800	479,500	506,500

*Allocated on basis of square footage in each department.

Instructions

Prepare a profitability analysis by departments for the year 19X1.

PROBLEM 26-2A. Preparing a percentage-of-sales analysis. Discount Furniture, Inc., operates three retail furniture stores. A monthly income statement is prepared for each store. This statement shows both the direct operating expenses of the stores and the allocated indirect expenses. The combined statements for March 19X7 are shown below.

	Store 1	Store 2	Store 3
Net Sales	$120,000	$160,000	$88,000
Cost of Goods Sold	62,000	91,000	45,000
Gross Profit on Sales	$ 58,000	$ 69,000	$43,000
Direct Expenses:			
Salaries and Commissions	$ 12,000	$ 14,200	$12,200
Payroll Benefits	3,000	3,500	2,550
Delivery Fees	1,300	1,480	1,200
Advertising	2,240	2,360	2,240
Credit Card Fees	1,660	2,200	1,140
Supplies	1,240	1,320	1,160
Rent	2,100	2,200	1,600
Utilities	560	950	625
Repairs and Maintenance	300	160	325
Property Taxes	250	320	250
Depreciation	2,000	2,000	1,140
Miscellaneous	1,400	1,600	1,130
Total Direct Expenses	$ 28,050	$ 32,290	$25,560
Contribution After Direct Expenses	$ 29,950	$ 36,710	$17,440

Indirect Expenses:

Purchasing	$ 2,400	$ 3,200	$ 1,780
General and Administrative	4,800	6,400	3,920
Interest	800	1,000	800
Total Indirect Expenses	$ 8,000	$ 10,600	$ 6,500
Net Income for Month	$ 21,950	$ 26,110	$10,940

Instructions

1. For each store, prepare an analysis expressing each item on the income statement as a percent of net sales. Round the percents to one decimal place.
2. Compare the percentages for the three stores. Note the differences.
3. What types of questions would management ask about each of the differences listed in Instruction 2?

PROBLEM 26-3A. Preparing a monthly flexible budget. The Van Doren Company has a gross profit of 45 percent of net sales. After analyzing its operating expenses, the firm determined that its fixed monthly expenses and its variable expenses (expressed as a percent of net sales) are as shown below.

	Fixed Expenses (Monthly)	Variable Expenses (Percent of Net Sales)
Sales Salaries	$3,000	2.0
Warehouse Salaries	1,200	-0-
Office Salaries	2,600	-0-
Payroll Taxes	1,380	0.4
Advertising	600	-0-
Delivery	1,200	1.0
Supplies	100	0.5
Rent	3,000	-0-
Utilities	450	-0-
Repairs	100	-0-
Property Taxes	150	-0-
Miscellaneous	300	1.0

Instructions

Prepare a monthly flexible budget for the company at sales levels of $30,000, $40,000, and $50,000.

PROBLEM 26-4A. Preparing a break-even analysis. Refer to the data for the Van Doren Company in Problem 26-3A to complete the following:

Instructions

1. Compute the monthly sales volume at the break-even point for the Van Doren Company.
2. Prepare a monthly break-even chart. NOTE: Both the horizontal axis and the vertical axis should represent dollars.
3. What sales volume would be required to earn a net income of $10,000 for the month?
4. The sales manager of the Van Doren Company estimates that if the average sales price of merchandise were to be decreased by 4 percent, the number of units sold could be increased by 10 percent.

a. What effect would this have on the break-even point?

b. What would be the new break-even point?

PROBLEM 26-5A. Comparing budgeted and actual amounts. Excel Consultants, Inc., is a business consulting firm. During the year 19X1 the firm earned a net income of $136,000. This amount was more than the net income projected in the firm's operating budget. Management thinks this is largely due to the fact that 6,200 billable hours were worked, while the budget was for 6,000 billable hours. (*Billable hours* are the hours for which clients are charged. Some hours worked by the firm's staff are not billable because the staff members are not involved in a consulting job for a client.) The firm's managing partner has asked you to prepare a comparison of the actual results and the results that would have been anticipated in a flexible budget based on 6,200 billable hours, the actual number of billable hours for the year.

	Income Statement (Actual)	Operating Budget
Billable Hours	6,200	6,000
Revenues From Charges to Clients	$705,000	$660,000
Fixed Professional Salaries	$210,000	$200,000
Variable Professional Salaries	108,000	120,000
Other Fixed Expenses	100,000	100,000
Other Variable Expenses	151,000	134,000
Total Expenses	$569,000	$554,000
Net Income for Year	$136,000	$106,000

Instructions

Prepare a three-column statement showing the actual income statement figures, the flexible budget based on actual billable hours, and the variance between each item.

Managerial Decisions

CASE 26-1. The Shop at Home Company is a mail-order house. During the year it sends catalogs to several hundred thousand customers who order the company's specialty products by mail. The Shop at Home Company pays postage or freight on all products sold. Customers may either send a cash payment (by personal check) with their orders (in which case they are entitled to take a discount of 4 percent on the sales price), or they may purchase on open account. Approximately 50 percent of all orders are accompanied by a cash payment.

The company's profits have declined in recent years. The controller argues that one reason for the decrease in profits is that there has been a large growth in the number of customers ordering small quantities of merchandise. Over 20,000 orders of less than $10 each have been received in each of the past two years. These small orders represent about 20 percent of the total number of invoices for the year and about 8 percent of the total dollar volume of sales. The controller has suggested that one of three steps be taken.

a. Accept no order for less than $10.

b. Add a handling charge of $1 to all orders for less than $10.

c. Require a cash payment on all orders and eliminate the discount for cash payments.

The controller also submitted the following information, on which he based his recommendations:

Cost of order and invoice forms for each shipment	$ .20
Labor costs to process orders and invoices (15 min)	1.50
Accounts receivable processing (6 min)	.60
Postage for billing	.20
Other billing costs	.30
Minimum cost to remove merchandise from shelves, package items, and prepare them for shipment	1.00
Supplies for shipment	.30
Minimum postage for shipment	.55
Gross profit rate	50 percent

1. Assuming that 20,000 small orders are involved and that the average of each order is $8, estimate the effect on the firm's profit of each of the controller's suggested courses of action. (Make your estimates as accurate as you can from the available information.)
2. What other factors must be considered in making a decision?
3. What is your recommended course of action? Why?

CASE 26-2. The Oakville Medical Center operates a general hospital but rents space and beds to separate entities for specialized areas such as pediatrics, maternity, and psychiatry. The medical center charges each separate entity for common services to its patients such as meals and laundry and for administrative services such as billing and collections. All uncollectible accounts are charged directly to the entity. Space and bed rentals are fixed for the year.

During the entire year ended June 30, 19X1, the Pediatrics Department at the Oakville Medical Center charged each patient an average of $240 per day, had a capacity of 60 beds, operated 24 hours per day for 365 days, and had revenue of $4,552,000.

Expenses charged by the medical center to the Pediatrics Department for the year ended June 30, 19X1, were as follows:

	Amount Allocated on Basis of:	
	Patient Days	Bed Capacity
Dietary	$ 171,808	
Janitorial		$ 51,200
Laundry	112,000	
Laboratory, other than direct charges to patients	191,200	
Pharmacy	135,200	
Repairs and maintenance	20,800	28,560
General administrative services		527,040
Rent		1,101,280
Billing and collections	160,000	
Uncollectible accounts expense	188,000	
Other	72,192	103,920
	$1,051,200	$1,812,000

The only personnel directly employed by the Pediatrics Department are supervising nurses, nurses, and aides. The medical center has minimum personnel requirements based on total annual patient days. These requirements, beginning at the minimum expected level of operation follow:

Annual Patient Days	Aides	Nurses	Supervising Nurses
10,000–14,000	21	11	4
14,001–17,000	22	12	4
17,001–23,725	22	13	4
23,726–25,550	25	14	5
25,551–27,375	26	14	5
27,376–29,200	29	16	6

The staffing levels above represent full-time equivalents, and it should be assumed that the Pediatrics Department always employs only the minimum number of required full-time equivalent personnel.

Annual salaries (including payroll taxes and fringe benefits) for each class of employee follow: supervising nurses, $72,000; nurses, $52,000; and aides, $20,000. Salary expense for the year ended June 30, 19X1, for supervising nurses, nurses, and aides was $288,000, $676,000, and $440,000, respectively.

The Pediatrics Department operated at 100 percent capacity during 111 days for the past year. It is estimated that during 90 of these capacity days, the demand averaged 17 patients more than capacity and even went as high as 20 patients more on some days. The medical center has an additional 20 beds available for rent for the year ending June 30, 19X2.

Instructions

1. Calculate the *minimum* number of patient days required for the Pediatrics Department to break even for the year ending June 30, 19X2, if the additional 20 beds are not rented. Patient demand is unknown, but assume that revenue per patient day, cost per patient day, cost per bed, and employee salary rates will remain the same as for the year ended June 30, 19X1.

2. Assuming that patient demand, revenue per patient day, cost per patient day, cost per bed, and employee salary rates for the year ending June 30, 19X2, remain the same as for the year ended June 30, 19X1, should the Pediatrics Department rent the additional 20 beds? Show the annual gain or loss from the additional beds.

CHAPTER

27

Capital Planning

■ ■ ■

The analysis of proposed capital expenditures is an extension of the decision-making process discussed in the previous chapter. It also relates to the budgeting activities of a company because the capital expenditures budget is a necessary part of the company's master budget.

The Nature of Capital Expenditures

Capital expenditures for land, buildings, machinery, and equipment involve long-range commitments of funds to produce future benefits. These expenditures normally involve large cash outlays. The outlays must be financed from working capital or through funds obtained by issuing capital stock or by taking on long-term obligations such as mortgages and other loans. These are considered long-term commitments because working capital is only gradually restored as the use of the acquired asset creates revenue or results in cost reductions.

Because capital expenditures are a long-term commitment, it is difficult to reverse the decision once the outlay has been authorized. The outlay becomes a sunk cost that can be recovered only over a long period of time through use of the asset. Extreme care must therefore be taken to avoid incorrect decisions in this area.

Profitability is a major consideration. In estimating the profit to be obtained from a capital expenditure, predictions must be made for several years in advance. Revenue that may be produced and costs that may be incurred as the result of the capital expenditure must be considered in long-range terms.

Capital Expenditure Analysis

Management usually sets guidelines for developing and evaluating proposed capital expenditures. One guideline is the classification of proposed outlays by the nature of the project. Management's goals as to maximum time for recovery of invested funds and minimum profitability of the project provide further guidelines. The availability of funds for capital outlays is always an important factor in analyzing proposed expenditures.

Classification of Capital Expenditures

To evaluate proposed outlays more effectively, management requires that proposals be classified according to their nature. One such classification system follows:

Type 1: Projects to meet legal or safety requirements. These have top priority because they are unavoidable if the company is to stay in business.

Type 2: Projects to replace equipment.

Type 3: Projects to expand facilities.

Type 4: Projects to improve existing products or to add new products.

These categories are not mutually exclusive. This means that some projects may belong in more than one group. For example, local or state laws requiring pollution controls may make it necessary to replace old equipment that emits fumes. The replacement of this equipment is both a Type 1 and a Type 2 project. Similarly, the replacement of a machine with one of higher capacity would be both a Type 2 and a Type 3 project. The classification system, however, provides a basis for setting other guidelines.

Recovery Guidelines

Management may specify the maximum period of time it expects for recovery of an investment. This period of time may vary with the type of investment. For example, the period of time allowed to recover funds from a major plant expansion project would be longer than the period acceptable for funds invested in adding a specialty product that is known to be a fad with a relatively short market life.

Profitability Guidelines

Minimum profitability guidelines also vary with the type of project. In the case of proposals to meet legal or safety requirements, profitability may not be a consideration. In such cases, comparisons of alternative means of meeting specified requirements concentrate on minimizing costs. The more speculative the nature of the project, the higher the minimum acceptable return will be to allow for the risk involved.

Other facts also affect the minimum return expected on a project. If funds required to finance the outlay must be borrowed, the return must be greater than the interest rate. If available funds are to be used, the opportunity cost concept presented in Chapter 25 is used. In this case, the opportunity cost would be the alternative use of the funds. As a minimum, the return on the proposed expenditure should be greater than the interest that could be earned by investing the funds in risk-free government securities.

Availability of Funds

Proposed capital outlays are normally presented and evaluated at the time the annual budget is being prepared. However, emergencies, such as equipment breakdowns and fire losses, may result in capital expenditure proposals at other times during the year.

As part of the annual budget process, management may identify a specific sum of money available for capital outlays during the coming year. A ranking of proposals is made from which management selects the projects to be funded. When management decides to authorize proposals in excess of currently available funds or when unforeseen events result in proposals during the year, the method of financing these expenditures must be carefully decided. The effects of the method on the short-term and long-term financial condition of the business must be considered.

Evaluation Techniques

Various techniques are used in the evaluation process either separately or together. Each technique provides a measure of some aspect of the proposal. This measure may be compared with previously established guidelines as well as with alternative proposals. Among the more widely used methods are the payback period, the return on investment, and the time-adjusted rate of return. While a detailed study of the time-adjusted rate of return is beyond the scope of this book, the payback reciprocal is presented as a reasonably accurate yet easily calculated approximation of the time-adjusted rate of return.

Payback Period

A widely used guideline for evaluating proposed capital expenditures is the number of years required to recover the investment. The *payback period* is the length of time it should take for the cash earnings or savings from the project to return the amount of the initial outlay. This period is computed by dividing the initial outlay by the annual cash earnings or savings.

$$\text{Payback Period} = \frac{\text{Investment}}{\text{Annual Cash Earnings or Savings}}$$

Obviously, a short payback period, which means rapid recovery of an investment, is better than a longer payback period.

The payback period method has several advantages. It is easy to calculate. It serves as a screening device to eliminate proposals requiring long recovery periods. Also, it provides some indication of profitability. This method is widely used. Most commonly, it is applied along with other techniques.

A major limitation of this method is that it ignores the economic life of the project. Thus it does not provide a clear indication of profitability. Sole reliance on the payback method could be disastrous. For example, assume that the payback period for Project A is 7 years and the payback period for Project B is 10 years. If Project A had an economic life of 5 years and Project B had an economic life of 15 years, the initial investment in Project A would never be recovered. Even though the payback period of Project B is longer, it is a far more desirable investment than is Project A.

The failure to consider the time value of money and the lack of standards for specifying maximum payback periods are additional shortcomings of the payback period method.

Two cases from Chapter 25 can be used to illustrate the use of the payback period method. Ortiz Manufacturers was considering the purchase of a machine for $15,000 (pages 504 and 505). The annual cash savings (reduced labor costs) were $4,000. The payback period is 3.75 years.

$$\text{Payback Period} = \frac{\text{Investment}}{\text{Annual Cash Earnings or Savings}}$$

$$= \frac{\$15,000}{\$4,000} = 3.75 \text{ years}$$

Five years later, Ortiz Manufacturers was considering the replacement of existing equipment with new equipment at a cost of $12,500 (pages 509 to 511). The cash savings were $8,000 (8,000 units × $1 per unit). Thus a payback period of 1.56 years is anticipated.

$$\text{Payback Period} = \frac{\text{Investment}}{\text{Annual Cash Earnings or Savings}}$$

$$= \frac{\$12,500}{\$8,000} = 1.56 \text{ years}$$

In these two cases, the payback period is compared with guidelines established by management. If these guidelines are met, the payback periods can be compared with the payback periods of other proposals. Additional methods of evaluation, such as the rate of return on investment, are normally used along with the payback period in making a decision.

Return on Investment

As just noted, the payback period is rarely used alone in evaluating projects. Management generally wants to use some index of profitability as well. One such index is the *rate of return on investment*. This is also called the *accounting method* or the *financial statement method* since financial statement data are used in the calculation.

The rate of return is the average rate (percentage) of profit on the investment. Management always seeks the highest rate of return on funds to be invested. This rate may be computed in one of two ways. The additional net income produced by the capital outlay may be divided either by the original investment or by the average investment over the life of the asset. While the total amount of the original investment is used more often, some accountants prefer to use the average investment. Their reasoning is that the original outlay is recovered during the life of the project. This means that not all the original cost is invested during the life of the project. As a result, using the original outlay results in an understatement of the effective rate of return.

The average investment would theoretically be computed by adding the initial outlay and the book value (undepreciated cost) at the end of each year and dividing this total by the number of figures used in the addition. For example, if an asset with a depreciable life of 4 years and no salvage value was purchased for $100,000, the average investment would be computed as follows, assuming the straight-line method is used in computing depreciation:

Initial investment	$100,000
Book value—end of Year 1	75,000
Book value—end of Year 2	50,000
Book value—end of Year 3	25,000
Book value—end of Year 4	-0-
Total	$250,000

$$\text{Average Investment} = \frac{\$250,000}{5} = \$50,000$$

If the asset in the above example had an estimated salvage value of $20,000 at the end of 4 years, the annual straight-line depreciation would be $20,000 and the average investment would be $60,000, computed as follows:

Initial investment	$100,000
Book value—end of Year 1	80,000
Book value—end of Year 2	60,000
Book value—end of Year 3	40,000
Book value—end of Year 4	20,000
Total	$300,000

$$\text{Average Investment} = \frac{\$300,000}{5} = \$60,000$$

When straight-line depreciation is used, the average investment can be computed much more simply by using only two figures, the initial investment and the book value at the end of the asset's useful life (the anticipated salvage value). In the above illustration, the average investment could be computed as follows:

$$\text{Average Investment} = \frac{\text{Initial Investment} + \text{Estimated Salvage}}{2}$$

$$= \frac{\$100,000 + \$20,000}{2} = \frac{\$120,000}{2} = \$60,000$$

However, if another depreciation method is used, the calculation of average investment will require the use of year-end book values, as previously illustrated.

The rate of return is computed according to the following formula:

$$\text{Rate of Return on Investment} = \frac{\text{Additional Annual Net Income}}{\text{Investment}}$$

Note that the additional annual net income may be computed by subtracting the annual depreciation from the annual cash earnings or savings used in computing the payback period.

Additional Annual Net Income = Annual Cash Earnings or Savings − Depreciation

Using the data from Chapter 25, the proposed purchase of machinery by Ortiz Manufacturers can be evaluated by the rate of return method. The additional annual net income of $2,500 (Exhibit 1 in Chapter 25) is divided by the initial investment of $15,000. The result is an annual rate of return of 17 percent on the initial investment.

$$\text{Rate of Return on Initial Investment} = \frac{\text{Additional Annual Net Income}}{\text{Investment}}$$

$$= \frac{\$2,500}{\$15,000} = 17 \text{ percent}$$

The same rate is calculated using the annual cash earnings or savings adjusted for depreciation. The $4,000 represents the increase in the contribution margin from $32,000 to $36,000 (Exhibit 1, Chapter 25).

$$\text{Rate of Return on Initial Investment} = \frac{\text{Annual Cash Earnings or Savings} - \text{Depreciation}}{\text{Investment}}$$

$$= \frac{\$4,000 - \$1,500}{\$15,000} = 17 \text{ percent}$$

If the rate is based on the average investment, note that it is 33 percent. The average investment is $7,500 ($15,000 ÷ 2) since straight-line depreciation is used and there is no salvage value.

$$\text{Rate of Return on Average Investment} = \frac{\text{Additional Annual Net Income}}{\text{Average Investment}}$$

$$= \frac{\$2,500}{\$7,500} = 33 \text{ percent}$$

Thus the annual profit resulting from the project is 33 percent of the average unrecovered investment in the asset.

In analyzing the data for the decision about replacing the equipment, the additional annual net income of $5,500 ($27,500 ÷ 5) shown in Exhibit 9 of Chapter 25 is divided by the investment of $12,500. In this case, a return of 44 percent on the initial investment is projected.

$$\text{Rate of Return on Initial Investment} = \frac{\text{Additional Annual Net Income}}{\text{Investment}}$$

$$= \frac{\$5,500}{\$12,500} = 44 \text{ percent}$$

The rate of return method provides management with more information than the payback method since it takes into consideration the economic life of the project and its projected profitability. However, it does not consider the time value of money. Thus, it is often referred to as the *simple* rate of return method.

Time-Adjusted Rate of Return

The major drawback of the return on investment method is that it fails to consider the time value of money. A dollar received today certainly is more valuable than a dollar to be received a year from now. For example, if you invest $100 today at 10 percent, you receive $110 at the end of the year. Thus $110 to be received a year from now would justify an investment of only $100 ($10 less than $110 today) if 10 percent investment opportunities are available.

To find the time-adjusted rate of return on investment, the payback period and an annuity table (shown on page 556) are used. The line representing the economic life of the project (found in the first column) is read across until a number approximating the payback period is reached. The heading of the column in which that number appears shows the approximate time-adjusted or discounted rate of return.

In the case of the proposed purchase of a machine by Ortiz Manufacturers, the payback period is 3.75 and the economic life of the machine is 10 years. Thus the time-adjusted rate of return is between 22 percent (where the factor is 3.923) and 24 percent (where the factor is 3.682) since 3.75 is between these two factors.

*Annuity Table: Present Value of $1 Received or Paid Annually**

Years	2%	6%	10%	14%	16%	18%	20%	22%	24%	25%	30%	40%	50%
1	.980	.943	.909	.877	.862	.847	.833	.820	.806	.800	.769	.714	.667
2	1.942	1.833	1.736	1.647	1.605	1.566	1.528	1.492	1.457	1.440	1.361	1.224	1.111
3	2.884	2.673	2.487	2.322	2.246	2.174	2.106	2.042	1.981	1.952	1.816	1.589	1.407
4	3.808	3.465	3.170	2.914	2.798	2.690	2.589	2.494	2.404	2.362	2.166	1.849	1.605
5	4.713	4.212	3.791	3.433	3.274	3.127	2.991	2.864	2.745	2.689	2.436	2.035	1.737
6	5.601	4.917	4.355	3.889	3.685	3.498	3.326	3.167	3.020	2.951	2.643	2.168	1.824
7	6.472	5.582	4.868	4.288	4.039	3.812	3.605	3.416	3.242	3.161	2.802	2.263	1.883
8	7.325	6.210	5.335	4.639	4.344	4.078	3.837	3.619	3.421	3.329	2.925	2.331	1.992
9	8.163	6.802	5.759	4.946	4.607	4.303	4.031	3.786	3.566	3.463	3.019	2.379	1.948
10	8.983	7.360	6.145	5.216	4.833	4.494	4.192	3.923	3.682	3.571	3.092	2.414	1.965
11	9.787	7.887	6.495	5.453	5.029	4.656	4.327	4.035	3.776	3.656	3.147	2.438	1.977
12	10.575	8.384	6.814	5.660	5.197	4.793	4.439	4.127	3.851	3.725	3.190	2.456	1.985
13	11.348	8.853	7.103	5.842	5.342	4.910	4.533	4.203	3.912	3.780	3.223	2.468	1.990
14	12.106	9.295	7.367	6.002	5.468	5.008	4.611	4.265	3.962	3.824	3.249	2.477	1.993
15	12.849	9.712	7.606	6.142	5.575	5.092	4.675	4.315	4.001	3.859	3.268	2.484	1.995
16	13.578	10.106	7.824	6.265	5.669	5.162	4.730	4.357	4.033	3.887	3.283	2.489	1.997
17	14.292	10.477	8.022	6.373	5.749	5.222	4.775	4.391	4.059	3.910	3.295	2.492	1.998
18	14.992	10.828	8.201	6.467	5.818	5.273	4.812	4.419	4.080	3.928	3.304	2.494	1.999
19	15.678	11.158	8.365	6.550	5.877	5.316	4.844	4.442	4.097	3.942	3.311	2.496	1.999
20	16.351	11.470	8.514	6.623	5.929	5.353	4.870	4.460	4.110	3.954	3.316	2.497	1.999
21	17.011	11.764	8.649	6.687	5.973	5.384	4.891	4.476	4.121	3.963	3.320	2.498	2.000
22	17.658	12.042	8.772	6.743	6.011	5.410	4.909	4.488	4.130	3.970	3.323	2.498	2.000
23	18.292	12.303	8.883	6.792	6.044	5.432	4.925	4.499	4.137	3.976	3.325	2.499	2.000
24	18.914	12.550	8.985	6.835	6.073	5.451	4.937	4.507	4.143	3.981	3.327	2.499	2.000
25	19.523	12.783	9.077	6.873	6.097	5.467	4.948	4.514	4.147	3.985	3.329	2.499	2.000

*Partial table

Payback Reciprocal Method. A rough approximation of the time-adjusted rate can be found quickly by computing the payback reciprocal. Two conditions must be met for this to be a close approximation. First, there must be an even flow of annual cash earnings or savings. Second, the economic life of the project must be at least twice the payback period. The payback reciprocal is computed as follows:

$$\text{Payback Reciprocal} = \frac{1}{\text{Payback Period}}$$

In the example of the proposed purchase of a machine by Ortiz Manufacturers, the approximate time-adjusted rate of return of 27 percent is computed by the payback reciprocal approach. Note that the economic life of 10 years is more than twice the payback period, 3.75 years.

$$\text{Payback Reciprocal} = \frac{1}{\text{Payback Period}}$$

$$= \frac{1}{3.75} = 27 \text{ percent}$$

The time-adjusted rate of 27 percent computed using the payback reciprocal roughly approximates the 22 to 24 percent rate computed from the annuity table.

It is important to note that four different rates of return have been found in the case of the proposed machine purchase.

Rate of Return on Initial Investment	17 percent
Rate of Return on Average Investment	33 percent
Time-Adjusted Rate of Return (Using Annuity Table)	23 percent
Payback Reciprocal	27 percent

While each method has its advantages and limitations, management must have a particular method in mind when guidelines for evaluation are set. Further, when comparing two or more alternative proposals, the same method of computing the rate of return must be used in each case in order to ensure a logical and fair comparison.

In evaluating capital expenditure proposals, other factors besides the payback period and the return on investment must be taken into account. Factors such as income taxes, the effects on labor relations, the rapidity of changes in technology, future interest rates, the potential for higher quality products, and the potential for better customer service should also be considered. Some of these factors are difficult to quantify but are of great importance. Management must use judgment as well as numbers in making decisions about capital expenditures.

Cost Accounting for a High-Technology Investment

Midwest Metal Products, a large manufacturer, bought a robot three years ago. The robot is an automated spot-welding system that can be programmed to perform various welding functions on the assembly line.

Before the robot was purchased, the senior executives at Midwest Metal Products were divided as to the cost effectiveness of this major investment. The plant manager and senior engineer wanted to purchase the robot, but the cost accountant and the controller believed it would not provide an adequate return on investment (ROI). The cost accountant had prepared a statement showing that whether the ROI method or the discounted cash flow method was used, purchase of the machine would not be a wise investment.

The plant manager said that the accountant's figures for savings from the use of the robot were based on direct labor in the factory and therefore evaluated the robot solely in terms of how many workers it would replace. The senior engineer stated that the accountant was overlooking factors such as improved quality and greater flexibility in the manufacturing process and was relying only on the ROI and discounted cash flow calculations.

The president of the company was committed to improving the manufacturing process, so she decided to take a chance and purchase the robot.

Today the robot's ability in welding has improved the quality of the finished goods, greatly reduced waste, and provided shorter lead times for making new products. This high-technology purchase has paid off. In just three years, it has returned its cost. The company's president has called in a consultant to work with the cost accountant and the plant manager to come up with new ROI standards that will reflect investment intangibles such as higher-quality goods, greater flexibility, and lower inventory costs. ■

Principles and Procedures Summary

Capital expenditures usually involve large amounts of money and long-range commitment. Special care must be taken in evaluating proposed capital outlays. Management usually sets guidelines for classification of expenditures, periods for recovery of outlay, and goals for profitability.

Among the most widely used techniques for evaluating capital expenditure proposals are the payback period, the return on investment, and the time-adjusted rate of return. In the case of the time-adjusted rate of return, an approximate rate can be found by using the payback reciprocal method.

Review Questions

1. What is meant by the term *capital expenditures?*
2. Capital expenditures become sunk costs. Explain.
3. List various classifications of capital expenditures that might permit easier evaluation by management.
4. What is meant by payback period? How is the payback period computed?
5. In general, would management prefer a project with a short payback period or a long one? Why?
6. How is the rate of return on an investment computed?
7. What is the major shortcoming of the payback period method?
8. What is meant by time-adjusted rate of return? Why is it useful for evaluating investment opportunities?
9. What is the payback reciprocal? How is it used in evaluating investment opportunities?
10. Should management use only one method of evaluating capital projects? Explain.

Managerial Discussion Questions

1. What type of guidelines might management set in analyzing and evaluating proposed capital outlays?
2. What impact does the availability of funds have on management's evaluation of capital investment opportunities?
3. How would you explain to management the strengths and weaknesses of the payback period method as a means for evaluating capital outlays?
4. The Dayton Company has traditionally used an unadjusted rate of return method for evaluating capital projects. A young accountant recently hired by the com-

pany suggests that it should use a time-adjusted rate of return. Explain what is meant by this, and give reasons to support the recommendation.

5. Assume that you work as an accountant at the Hadley Corporation. Management has asked you to recommend the capital outlay evaluation method that you think is most useful. Indicate the one that you recommend, giving reasons to support your answer.

Exercises

1. **Computing the payback period.** The Stanford Company is considering an investment of $100,000 in only one of two proposed projects. The first project, which has an estimated useful life of 5 years, will produce a net increase in cash earnings of $30,000 per year. The second project has an estimated useful life of 10 years and will produce a net increase in cash earnings of $24,000 per year. Compute the payback period for each of the proposals. Would you suggest that the project with the shortest payback period be the one chosen? Explain.

2. **Computing the rate of return on initial and average investment.** An asset costing $100,000 will have an estimated net salvage value of $10,000 at the end of its 10-year life. It is expected to produce a net cash inflow of $16,000 per year. Straight-line depreciation will be used.
   a. Compute the simple rate of return on the beginning investment.
   b. Compute the simple rate of return on the average investment.

DATA FOR EXERCISES 3–7

The Harley Corporation is considering the purchase of a machine at a cost of $64,000. The machine has an estimated useful life of 10 years and no salvage value. It is anticipated that the machine will result in annual cash savings of $16,000.

3. **Computing the payback period.** What is the payback period?

4. **Computing the rate of return on initial investment.** The Harley Corporation uses the straight-line method for computing depreciation. What is the anticipated rate of return on the initial investment in the machine?

5. **Computing the rate of return on average investment.** What is the anticipated rate of return on the average investment in the machine?

6. **Computing the time-adjusted rate of return.** What is the approximate time-adjusted rate of return on the machine?

7. **Computing the payback reciprocal.** What is the payback reciprocal for the machine?

DATA FOR EXERCISES 8–12

The Century Metals Company is considering the purchase of a machine that will cost $120,000. It has an expected useful life of 8 years and will have no salvage value. It is estimated that the machine will result in annual cash savings of $20,000.

8. **Computing the payback period.** What is the payback period?

9. **Computing the rate of return on initial investment.** The Century Metals Company uses the straight-line method in computing depreciation. What is the anticipated rate of return on the initial investment in the machine?

10. **Computing the rate of return on average investment.** What is the anticipated rate of return on the average investment in the machine?

11. **Computing the time-adjusted rate of return.** What is the approximate time-adjusted rate of return on the machine?
12. **Computing the payback reciprocal.** What is the payback reciprocal for the machine?

Problems

PROBLEM 27-1. **Evaluating a project by the payback period, rate of return on initial and average investment, and payback reciprocal.** The Ryan Furniture Company is thinking of buying a special-purpose machine. The company estimates that it can save $20,000 per year in cash operating costs for the next 8 years if it purchases the machine for $72,000. There is no expected salvage value at the end of the 8-year useful life of the machine.

Instructions

1. Compute the payback period.
2. Compute the rate of return on investment based on the initial investment and based on the average investment. Round off to the nearest tenth of a percent.
3. Compute the payback reciprocal. Round off to the nearest tenth of a percent.

PROBLEM 27-2. **Evaluating a project by the payback period, rate of return on initial and average investment, and payback reciprocal.** A proposal has been made by the Cutting Department at Tyler Wood Products, Inc., to replace a machine that has 8 years of useful life remaining with a more efficient model. Relevant annual operating costs are shown below.

	Old Machine	New Machine
Labor	$29,000	$15,000
Maintenance	7,000	5,000
Power	4,000	5,500
Depreciation	2,500	5,000

The old machine cost $50,000 and has a book value of $20,000. The new machine costs $30,000 and has an estimated useful life of 6 years with no salvage value. The current salvage value of the old equipment is equal to the cost of its removal.

Instructions

1. Determine the annual cash savings, and compute the payback period. Round off your answer to two decimal places.
2. Compute the rate of return on investment based on the initial investment and based on the average investment. Round off to the nearest hundredth of a percent.
3. Compute the payback reciprocal. Round off to the nearest tenth of a percent.

PROBLEM 27-3. **Evaluating projects by the payback period and the rate of return on investment.** Four capital expenditure proposals received by the Sutherland Company are described below.

	Proposal A	Proposal B	Proposal C	Proposal D
Investment Required	$250,000	$779,000	$785,000	$219,000
Annual Cash Earnings	$ 48,000	$160,000	$200,000	$ 32,000
Depreciable Life in Years	10	25	10	20

The treasurer of the company recommends that the projects be ranked according to payback period. Management can select those projects from which the investment will be recovered most rapidly. The controller recommends ranking the projects by rate of return on investment.

Instructions
1. Calculate the payback period for each proposal. Round off your answer to one decimal place. Rank the proposals in order by payback period.
2. Calculate the rate of return on investment for each proposal, using the initial investment as the base. Round off to the nearest tenth of a percent. Rank the proposals in order by rate of return on investment.
3. Which ranking would you prefer? Why?

PROBLEM 27-4. Evaluating projects by the time-adjusted rate of return and the payback reciprocal. Refer to the data given in Problem 27-3, and carry out the following instructions.

Instructions
1. Using the payback period and the annuity table on page 556, determine the approximate time-adjusted rate of return for each of the four proposals.
2. Using the payback period reciprocal, determine the approximate time-adjusted rate of return for each of the four proposals.

PROBLEM 27-5. Evaluating a project by the payback period, payback reciprocal, time-adjusted rate of return, and rate of return on initial investment. The Levy Corporation has an opportunity to expand its production by buying a new machine at a cost of $400,000. The machine has an estimated useful life of 4 years, would be depreciated under the straight-line method, and is expected to have no salvage value. The machine would add $160,000 per year in net cash flow after taxes.

Instructions
1. Compute the payback period.
2. Compute the payback reciprocal.
3. Compute the time-adjusted rate of return (to the nearest whole percent). (Use the table on page 556.)
4. Compute the rate of return on the initial investment (to the nearest tenth of a percent).

Alternate Problems

PROBLEM 27-1A. Evaluating a project by the payback period, rate of return on initial and average investment, and payback reciprocal. The management of the Webb Plastics Company has requested information about a proposal to invest $2,000,000 in a new plant. A study shows that the plant can produce an annual net income of $300,000 before depreciation. The plant has an estimated useful life of 20 years with no salvage value. Straight-line depreciation will be used.

Instructions
1. Compute the payback period. Round off your answer to one decimal place.
2. Compute the rate of return on investment based on the initial investment and based on the average investment.

3. Compute the payback reciprocal. Round off to the nearest tenth of a percent.

PROBLEM 27-2A. Evaluating a project by the payback period, rate of return on initial and average investment, and payback reciprocal. A proposal has been made by the Domingo Food Products Department at Packaging, Inc., to replace a machine that has 6 years of useful life remaining with a more efficient model. Relevant annual operating costs are shown below.

	Old Machine	New Machine
Labor	$72,500	$37,500
Maintenance	17,500	12,500
Power	10,000	13,750
Depreciation	6,250	13,750

The old machine cost $90,000 and has a book value of $37,500. The new machine costs $82,500 and has an estimated useful life of 6 years with no salvage value. The current salvage value of the old equipment is equal to the cost of its removal.

Instructions

1. Determine the annual cash savings, and compute the payback period. Round off your answer to two decimal places.
2. Compute the rate of return on investment based on the initial investment and based on the average investment. Round off to the nearest tenth of a percent.
3. Compute the payback reciprocal. Round off to the nearest tenth of a percent.

PROBLEM 27-3A. Evaluating projects by the payback period and the rate of return on investment. Four capital expenditure proposals received by the Duffy Corporation are described below.

	Proposal A	Proposal B	Proposal C	Proposal D
Investment Required	$280,000	$1,600,000	$1,600,000	$500,000
Annual Cash Earnings	$ 50,000	$ 300,000	$ 385,000	$ 70,000
Depreciable Life in Years	12	25	10	22

The treasurer of the company recommends that the projects be ranked according to payback period. Management can select those projects from which the investment will be recovered most rapidly. The controller recommends ranking the projects by rate of return on investment.

Instructions

1. Calculate the payback period for each proposal. Round off your answer to one decimal place. Rank the proposals in order by payback period.
2. Calculate the rate of return on investment for each proposal, using the initial investment as the base. Round off to the nearest hundredth of a percent. Rank the proposals in order by return on investment.
3. Which ranking would you prefer? Why?

PROBLEM 27-4A. Evaluating projects by the time-adjusted rate of return and the payback reciprocal. Refer to the data given in Problem 27-3A, and carry out the following instructions.

Instructions

1. Using the payback period and the annuity table on page 556, determine the approximate time-adjusted rate of return for each of the four proposals.
2. Using the payback period reciprocal, determine the approximate time-adjusted rate of return for each of the four proposals.

PROBLEM 27-5A. **Evaluating a project by the payback period, payback reciprocal, time-adjusted rate of return, and rate of return on initial investment.** The DeSilva Company has an opportunity to expand its production by buying new equipment at a cost of $140,000. The equipment has an estimated useful life of 5 years, would be depreciated under the straight-line method, and is expected to have no salvage value. The equipment would add $50,000 per year in net cash flow after taxes.

Instructions

1. Compute the payback period.
2. Compute the payback reciprocal.
3. Compute the time-adjusted rate of return (to the nearest whole percent). (Use the table on page 556.)
4. Compute the rate of return on the initial investment (to the nearest tenth of a percent).

Managerial Decisions

CASE 27-1. The Rinaldi Company is considering the purchase of a machine at a cost of $800,000 to manufacture a new product. The machine has an estimated useful life of 8 years and no salvage value. It is expected that the machine will produce from 80,000 to 100,000 units of the product per year and that all units will be sold at $10 each. Costs other than those related to the machine are as follows:

Materials	$5 per unit
Labor	1 per unit
Variable overhead	1 per unit

The machine would occupy space now standing empty and with no intended use. Fixed costs allocated to the space are $12,000 per year. The following costs are related to the machine. (The company uses straight-line depreciation.)

Taxes	$ 8,000 per year
Insurance	8,000 per year
Repairs and maintenance	4,000 per year
Power	20 cents per unit produced
Miscellaneous	$ 4,000 per year
Interest (average) on the investment	60,000 per year

Write a memorandum to management stating whether the company should purchase the machine and produce the new product. In reaching your decision, use each of the analytical methods presented in this chapter. Show all calculations.

Index